CHILTON BOOK COMPANY

REPAIR & TUNE-UP GUIDE

FORD BRONCO 1966-86

All U.S. and Canadian models of full-size Bronco

SO-AAM-191

President, Chilton Enterprises	David S. Loewith
Senior Vice President	Ronald A. Hoxter
Publisher and Editor-In-Chief	Kerry A. Freeman, S.A.E.
Managing Editors	Peter M. Conti, Jr. □ W. Calvin Settle, Jr., S.A.E.
Assistant Managing Editor	Nick D'Andrea
Senior Editors	Debra Gaffney □ Ken Grabowski, A.S.E., S.A.E.
	Michael L. Grady □ Richard J. Rivele, S.A.E.
	Richard T. Smith □ Jim Taylor
	Ron Webb
Director of Manufacturing	Mike D'Imperio
Editor	Michael A. Newsome

CHILTON BOOK COMPANY
Radnor, Pennsylvania
19089

SAFETY NOTICE

Proper service and repair procedures are vital to the safe, reliable operation of all motor vehicles, as well as the personal safety of those performing repairs. This book outlines procedures for servicing and repairing vehicles using safe, effective methods. The procedures contain many NOTES, CAUTIONS and WARNINGS which should be followed along with standard safety procedures to eliminate the possibility of personal injury or improper service which could damage the vehicle or compromise its safety.

It is important to note that repair procedures and techniques, tools and parts for servicing motor vehicles, as well as the skill and experience of the individual performing the work vary widely. It is not possible to anticipate all of the conceivable ways or conditions under which vehicles may be serviced, or to provide cautions as to all of the possible hazards that may result. Standard and accepted safety precautions and equipment should be used during cutting, grinding, chiseling, prying, or any other process that can cause material removal or projectiles.

Some procedures require the use of tools specially designed for a specific purpose. Before substituting another tool or procedure, you must be completely satisfied that neither your personal safety, nor the performance of the vehicle will be endangered.

Although the information in this guide is based on industry sources and is as complete as possible at the time of publication, the possibility exists that the manufacturer made later changes which could not be included here. While striving for total accuracy, Chilton Book Company cannot assume responsibility for any errors, changes, or omissions that may occur in the compilation of this data.

PART NUMBERS

Part numbers listed in this reference are not recommendations by Chilton for any product by brand name. They are references that can be used with interchange manuals and aftermarket supplier catalogs to locate each brand supplier's discrete part number.

SPECIAL TOOLS

Special tools are recommended by the vehicle manufacturer to perform their specific job. Use has been kept to a minimum, but where absolutely necessary, they are referred to in the text by the part number of the tool manufacturer. These tools can be purchased, under the appropriate part number, from Owatonna Tool Company, Owatonna, MN 55060 or an equivalent tool can be purchased locally from a tool supplier or parts outlet. Before substituting any tool for the one recommended, read the SAFETY NOTICE at the top of this page.

ACKNOWLEDGMENTS

The Chilton Book Company expresses its appreciation to the Ford Motor Company, Dearborn, Michigan, for their generous assistance.

Copyright © 1987 by Chilton Book Company
All Rights Reserved
Published in Radnor, Pennsylvania 19089 by Chilton Book Company

Manufactured in the United States of America
Tenth Printing, August 1993

Chilton's Repair & Tune-Up Guide: Ford Bronco 1966–86
ISBN 0-8019-7755-X pbk.
Library of Congress Catalog Card No. 86-4777

CONTENTS

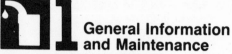

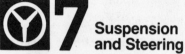

Quick Reference
Specifications For Your Vehicle

Fill in this chart with the most commonly used specifications for your vehicle. Specifications can be found in Chapters 1 through 3 or on the tune-up decal under the hood of the vehicle.

 Tune-Up

Firing Order_____

Spark Plugs:

    Type_____

    Gap (in.)_____

Torque (ft. lbs.)_____

Idle Speed (rpm)_____

Ignition Timing (°)_____

    Vacuum or Electronic Advance (Connected/Disconnected)_____

Valve Clearance (in.)

    Intake_____   Exhaust_____

 Capacities

Engine Oil Type (API Rating)_____

    With Filter Change (qts)_____

    Without Filter Change (qts)_____

Cooling System (qts)_____

Manual Transmission (pts)_____

    Type_____

Automatic Transmission (pts)_____

    Type_____

Front Differential (pts)_____

    Type_____

Rear Differential (pts)_____

    Type_____

Transfer Case (pts)_____

    Type_____

FREQUENTLY REPLACED PARTS
Use these spaces to record the part numbers of frequently replaced parts.

PCV VALVE	OIL FILTER	AIR FILTER	FUEL FILTER
Type_____	Type_____	Type_____	Type_____
Part No._____	Part No._____	Part No._____	Part No._____

General Information and Maintenance

HOW TO USE THIS BOOK

Chilton's Repair & Tune-Up Guide for the Ford Bronco is intended to teach you more about the inner workings of your Bronco and save you money on its upkeep. The first two chapters will be used the most, since they contain maintenance and tune-up information and procedures. The following chapters concern themselves with the more complex systems of your Bronco. Operating systems from engine through brakes are covered to the extent that we feel the average do-it-yourselfer should get involved. This book will not explain such things as rebuilding the differential for the simple reason that the expertise required and the investment in special tools make this task uneconomical. We will tell you how to change your own brake pads and shoes, replace points and plugs, and many more jobs that will save you money, give you personal satisfaction, and help you avoid problems.

A secondary purpose of this book is a reference for owners who want to understand their Bronco and/or their mechanics better. In this case, no tools at all are required.

The sections begin with a brief discussion of the system and what it involves, followed by adjustments, maintenance, removal and installation procedures, and repair or overhaul procedures. When repair is not considered feasible, we tell you how to remove the part and then how to install the new or rebuilt replacement. In this way, you at least save the labor costs. Backyard repair of such components as the alternator is just not practical.

Two basic mechanic's rules should be mentioned here. One, whenever the left side of the Bronco or engine is referred to, it is meant to specify the driver's side of the Bronco. Conversely, the right side of the Bronco means the passenger's side. Secondly, most screws and bolts are removed by turning counterclockwise, and tightened by turning clockwise.

Safety is always the most important rule. Constantly be aware of the dangers involved in working on an automobile and take the proper precautions. Use jackstands when working under a raised vehicle. Don't smoke or allow an exposed flame t come near the battery or any part of the fuel system. Always use the proper tool and use it correctly; bruised knuckles and skinned fingers aren't a mechanic's standard equipment. Always take your time and have patience. Once you have some experience, working on your Bronco will become an enjoyable hobby.

TOOLS AND EQUIPMENT

It would be impossible to catalog each and every tool that you may need to perform all the operations included in this book. It would also not be wise for the amateur to rush out and buy an expensive set of tools on the theory that he may need one of them at some time. The best approach is to proceed slowly, gather together a good quality set of those tools that are used most frequently. Don't be misled by the low cost of bargain tools. It is far better to spend a little more for quality, name brand tools. Forged wrenches, 10 or 12 point sockets and fine tooth ratchets are by far preferable to their less expensive counterparts. As any good mechanic can tell you, there are few worse experiences than trying to work on a truck with bad tools. Your monetary savings will be far outweighed by frustration and mangled knuckles.

Begin accumulating those tools that are used most frequently; those associated with routine maintenance and tune-up. In addition to the normal assortment of screwdrivers and pliers, you should have the following tools for routine maintenance jobs:

1. SAE wrenches, sockets and combination open end/box end wrenches;

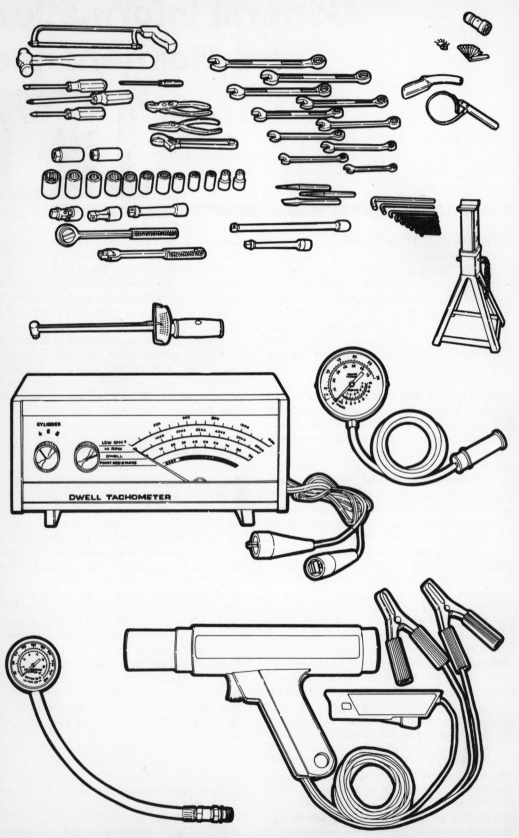

This basic collection of hand tools will handle most of your automotive needs

2. Jackstands, for support;
3. Oil filter wrench;
4. Oil filler spout or funnel;
5. Grease gun, for chassis lubrication;
6. Hydrometer, for checking the battery;
7. A low flat pan for draining oil.
8. Lots of rags for wiping up the inevitable mess.

In addition to the above items, there are several others that are not absolutely necessary, but are handy to have around. These include oil drying compound, a transmission funnel, and the usual supply of lubricants, antifreeze and fluids, although these can be purchased as needed. This is a basic list for routine maintenance, but only your personal needs an accurately determine your list of tools.

The second list of tools is for tune-ups. While the tools involved here are slightly more sophisticated, they need not be outrageously expensive. There are several inexpensive tach/dwell meters on the market that are every bit as good for the average mechanic as a $100.00 professional model. Just be sure that it goes to at lest 1,200–1,500 rpm on the tach scale, and that it works on 4, 6 and 8 cylinder engines. A basic list of tune-up equipment could include:

1. Tach/dwell meter;
2. Spark plug wrench;
3. Timing light (preferably a DC light that works from the Bronco's battery);
4. A set of flat feeler gauges;
5. A set of round wire spark plug gauges.

In addition to these basic tools, there are several other tools and gauges you may find useful. These include:

1. A compression gauge. The screw-in type is slower to use, but eliminates the possibility of a faulty reading due to escaping pressure;
2. A manifold vacuum gauge;
3. A test light;
4. An induction meter. This is used for determining whether or not there is current in a wire. These are handy for use if a wire is broken somewhere in a wiring harness. As a final note, you will probably find a torque wrench necessary for all but the most basic work. The beam type models are perfectly adequate, although the newer click type are more precise.

Special Tools

Normally, the use of special factory tools is avoided for repair procedures, since these are not readily available for the do-it-yourself mechanic. When it is possible to perform the job with more commonly available tools, it will be pointed out, but occasionally, a special tool was designed to perform a specific function and should be used. Before substituting another

tool, you should be convinced that neither your safety nor the performance of the vehicle will be compromised.

Some special tools are available commercially from major tool manufacturers. Others for your Ford Bronco can be purchased from your dealer or from Owatonna Tool CO., Owatonna, Minnesota 55060.

SERVICING YOUR BRONCO SAFELY

It is virtually impossible to anticipate all of the hazards involved with automotive maintenance and service but common sense will prevent most accidents.

The rules of safety for mechanics range from "don't smoke around gasoline," to "use the proper tool for the job." The trick to avoid injuries is to develop safe work habits and take every possible precaution.

Do's

• Do keep a fire extinguisher and first aid kit within easy reach.
• Do wear safety glasses or goggles when cutting, drilling, grinding or prying. If you wear glasses for the sake of vision, then they should be made of hardened glass that can serve also as safety glasses, or wear safety goggles over your regular glasses.
• Do shield your eyes whenever you work around the battery. Batteries contain sulphuric acid; in case of contact with eyes or skin, flush the area with water or a mixture of water and baking soda and get medical attention immediately.
• Do use safety stands for any under-truck service. Jacks are for raising vehicles; safety stands are for making sure the vehicle stays raised until you want it to come down. Whenever the vehicle is raised, block the wheels remaining on the ground and set the parking brake.
• Do use adequate ventilation when working with any chemicals. Asbestos dust resulting from brake lining wear can cause cancer.
• Do disconnect the negative battery cable when working on the electrical system. The primary ignition system can contain up to 40,000 volts.
• Do follow manufacturer's directions whenever working with potentially hazardous materials. Both brake fluid and antifreeze are poisonous if taken internally.
• Do properly maintain your tools. Loose hammerheads, mushroomed punches and chisels, frayed or poorly grounded electrical cords, excessively worn screwdrivers, spread wrenches (open end), cracked sockets, slipping

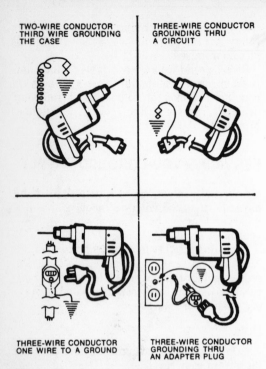

TWO-WIRE CONDUCTOR THIRD WIRE GROUNDING THE CASE

THREE-WIRE CONDUCTOR GROUNDING THRU A CIRCUIT

THREE-WIRE CONDUCTOR ONE WIRE TO A GROUND

THREE-WIRE CONDUCTOR GROUNDING THRU AN ADAPTER PLUG

When using electric tools make sure they are properly grounded

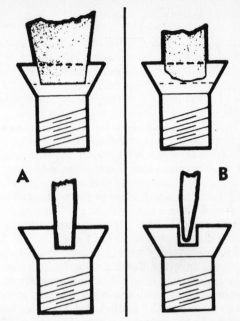

Keep screwdriver tips in good shape. They should fit the slot as shown in "A". If they look like those in "B", they need grinding or replacing

ratchets, or faulty droplight sockets can cause accidents.

• Do use the proper size and type of tool for the job being done.

• Do when possible, pull on a wrench handle rather than push on it, and adjust your stance to prevent a fall.

• Do be sure that adjustable wrenches are tightly adjusted on the nut or bolt and pulled so that the face is on the side of the fixed jaw.

• Do select a wrench or socket that fits the nut or bolt. The wrench or socket should sit straight, not cocked.

• Do strike squarely with a hammer to avoid glancing blows.

• Do set the parking brake and block the

drive wheels if the work requires that the engine be running.

Don'ts

• Don't run an engine in a garage or anywhere else without proper ventilation-EVER! carbon monoxide is poisonous; it is absorbed by the body 400 times faster than oxygen; it takes a long time to leave the human body and you can build up a deadly supply of it in your system by simply breathing in a little every day. You may not realize you are slowly poisoning yourself. Always use power vents, windows, fans or open the garage doors.

• Don't work around moving parts while

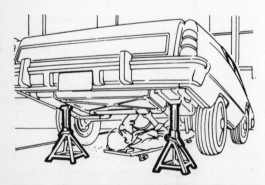

Always use jackstands when working under the truck

When you're using an open end wrench, use the correct size and position it properly on the flats of the nut or bolt

wearing a necktie or other loose clothing. Short sleeves are much safer than long, loose sleeves. Hard-toed shoes with neoprene soles protect your toes and give a better grip on slippery surfaces. Jewelry such as watches, fancy belt buckles, beads or body adornment of any kind is not safe working around a truck. Long hair should be hidden under a hat or cap.

• Don't use pockets for toolboxes. A fall or bump can drive a screwdriver deep into your body. Even a wiping cloth hanging from the back pocket can wrap around a spinning shaft of fan.

• Don't smoke when working around gasoline, cleaning solvent or other flammable material.

• Don't smoke when working around the battery. When the battery is being charged, it gives off explosive hydrogen gas.

• Don't use gasoline to wash your hands; there are excellent soaps available. Gasoline may contain lead, and lead can enter the body through a cut, accumulating in the body until you are very ill. Gasoline also removes all the natural oils from the skin so that bone dry hands will suck up oil and grease.

• Don't service the air conditioning system unless you are equipped with the necessary tools and training. The refrigerant, R-12 is extremely cold and when exposed to the air, will instantly freeze any surface it comes in contact with, including your eyes. Although the refrigerant is normally non-toxic, R-12 becomes a deadly poisonous gas in the presence of an open flames. One good whiff of the vapors from the burning refrigerant can be fatal.

HISTORY

For the years 1966–77 Bronco remained basically unchanged. Some of the noteworthy changes were, the introduction of electric wipers in 1968, replacing the vacuum units; the introduction in 1973 of automatic transmission and power steering, and, in 1975, front disc brakes, with power assist optional.

Beginning with the 1978 model year, Bronco was completely redesigned. Bearing no relationship with the earlier models, the 1978–86 Bronco is build on an F-150 pick-up chassis. With the exception of the sheet metal, the truck is almost identical to the F-150 4x4. The 1978–79 models are identical insofar as equipment goes. Engine availability was limited to a base 351M V8 with an optional 400 V8. IN 1980 the Bronco line was slightly downsized as were all Ford trucks. In a move toward economy the base engine was the 300 cid inline 6, with a 302 V8 as the optional big 8. The high-

light of the 1980 model year was the introduction of a first in production American made trucks; independent front drive axle. This unit, the Dana 44-IFS, will be described in the drive axle section.

IDENTIFICATION

Serial Number

The vehicle identification number is found on the rating plate located on the inside of the glove compartment door. It is also stamped on the Safety Certification Label attached to the driver's side door rear pillar.

Vehicle Identification Number

The VIN is found on a stamped plate located on the upper left corner of the instrument panel, visible through the windshield.

Engine

The engine identification tag identified the cubic inch displacement of the engine, the model year, the year and month in which the engine was built, where it was built and the change level number. The change level is usually the number one (1), unless there are parts on the engine that will not be completely interchangeable and will require minor modification.

The engine identification tag is located under the ignition coil attaching bolt.

Transmission

The transmission identification number is located on a metal tag or plate attached to the case or is stamped directly on the transmission case.

Drive Axle

Axle identification and ratio can be determined from the I.D. tag located under one of the bolts on the differential carrier housing.

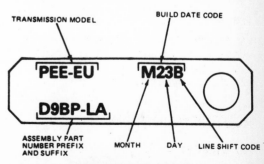

C-4 automatic transmission I.D. tag

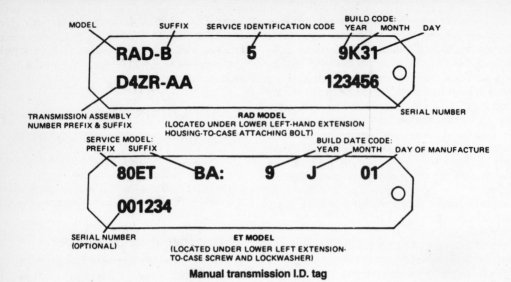

Manual transmission I.D. tag

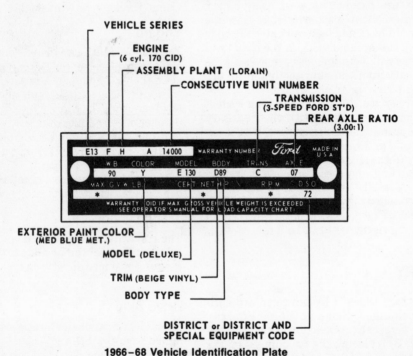

1966–68 Vehicle Identification Plate

Transfer Case

The transfer case identification number is located on a metal tag or plate attached to the front of the case or stamped directly into the face of the transfer case.

ROUTINE MAINTENANCE

Air Cleaner

Two types of air cleaners have been used: a replaceable paper type and an oil bath unit.

The procedure for cleaning an oil bath air cleaner and refilling the reservoir is as follows:

1. Unlock and open the engine compartment.

2. Remove the carburetor-to-air cleaner retaining wing nut. On a closed crankcase ventilation equipped engine, loosen the hose clamp at the air cleaner body and disconnect the hose. On the 300 six engine, remove the bolts securing the air cleaner body to the support brackets.

3. Remove the air cleaner assembly from the engine. Be careful not to spill the oil out of the air cleaner.

4. Remove the cover and drain the oil from

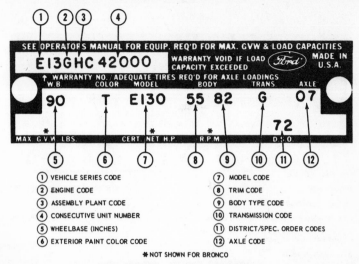

① VEHICLE SERIES CODE
② ENGINE CODE
③ ASSEMBLY PLANT CODE
④ CONSECUTIVE UNIT NUMBER
⑤ WHEELBASE (INCHES)
⑥ EXTERIOR PAINT COLOR CODE

⑦ MODEL CODE
⑧ TRIM CODE
⑨ BODY TYPE CODE
⑩ TRANSMISSION CODE
⑪ DISTRICT/SPEC. ORDER CODES
⑫ AXLE CODE

✱ NOT SHOWN FOR BRONCO

1969 Vehicle Identification Plate

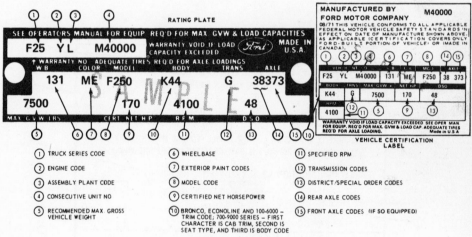

① TRUCK SERIES CODE
② ENGINE CODE
③ ASSEMBLY PLANT CODE
④ CONSECUTIVE UNIT NO
⑤ RECOMMENDED MAX. GROSS VEHICLE WEIGHT

⑥ WHEELBASE
⑦ EXTERIOR PAINT CODES
⑧ MODEL CODE
⑨ CERTIFIED NET HORSEPOWER
⑩ BRONCO, ECONOLINE AND 100-6000 – TRIM CODE; 700-9000 SERIES – FIRST CHARACTER IS CAB TRIM, SECOND IS SEAT TYPE, AND THIRD IS BODY CODE

⑪ SPECIFIED RPM
⑫ TRANSMISSION CODES
⑬ DISTRICT/SPECIAL ORDER CODES
⑭ REAR AXLE CODES
⑮ FRONT AXLE CODES (IF SO EQUIPPED)

1970–72 Vehicle Identification Plate

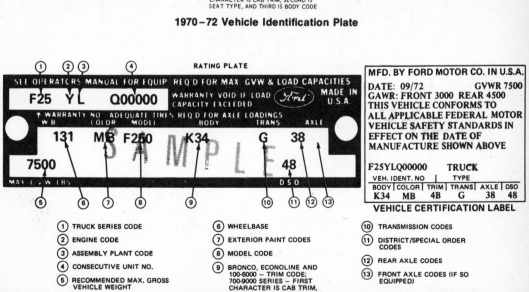

① TRUCK SERIES CODE
② ENGINE CODE
③ ASSEMBLY PLANT CODE
④ CONSECUTIVE UNIT NO.
⑤ RECOMMENDED MAX. GROSS VEHICLE WEIGHT

⑥ WHEELBASE
⑦ EXTERIOR PAINT CODES
⑧ MODEL CODE
⑨ BRONCO, ECONOLINE AND 100-6000 – TRIM CODE; 700-9000 SERIES – FIRST CHARACTER IS CAB TRIM, SECOND IS SEAT TYPE, AND THIRD IS BODY CODE

⑩ TRANSMISSION CODES
⑪ DISTRICT/SPECIAL ORDER CODES
⑫ REAR AXLE CODES
⑬ FRONT AXLE CODES (IF SO EQUIPPED)

1973–77 Vehicle Identification Plate

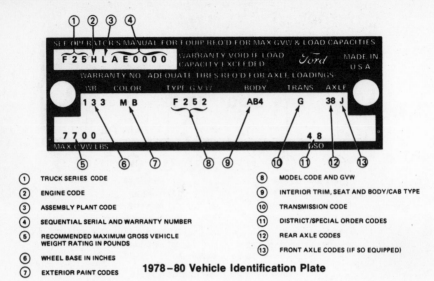

1. TRUCK SERIES CODE
2. ENGINE CODE
3. ASSEMBLY PLANT CODE
4. SEQUENTIAL SERIAL AND WARRANTY NUMBER
5. RECOMMENDED MAXIMUM GROSS VEHICLE WEIGHT RATING IN POUNDS
6. WHEEL BASE IN INCHES
7. EXTERIOR PAINT CODES

8. MODEL CODE AND GVW
9. INTERIOR TRIM, SEAT AND BODY/CAB TYPE
10. TRANSMISSION CODE
11. DISTRICT/SPECIAL ORDER CODES
12. REAR AXLE CODES
13. FRONT AXLE CODES (IF SO EQUIPPED)

1978–80 Vehicle Identification Plate

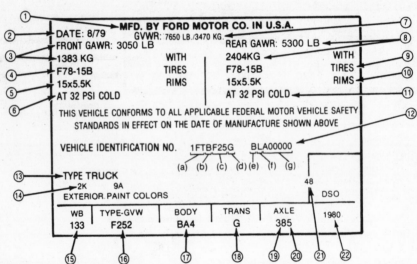

1. Name of Manufacturer
2. Date of Manufacture
3. Front Gross Axle Weight Ratings in Pounds (LB) and Kilograms (KG)
4. Front Tire Size
5. Rim Size
6. Front Tire Cold PSI
7. Gross Vehicle Weight Rating in Pounds (LB) and Kilograms (KG)

8. Rear Gross Axle Weight Rating in Pounds (LB) and Kilograms (KG)
9. Rear Tire Size
10. Rim Size
11. Rear Tire Cold PSI
12. Vehicle Identification Number
    (a) World Manufacturer Identifier
    (b) Brakes and GVWR
    (c) Line, Series and Body Type
    (d) Engine Code
    (e) Model Year
    (f) Assembly Plant Code
    (g) Sequential Serial and Model Year

13. Type Vehicle
14. Exterior Paint Codes (two sets of figures designates a two-tone)
15. Wheelbase in Inches
16. Model Code and GVW
17. Interior Trim, Seat and Body/Cab Type
18. Transmission Code
19. Rear Axle Code
20. Front Axle Code if so Equipped
21. District/Special Order Codes
22. Vehicle Model Year

1981 Truck Certification Label

Engine Codes

Engine	66	67	68	69	70	71	72	73	74	75	76	77	78	79	80	81	82	83	84–86
6-170	F	F	F	F	F	F	F												
6-200						S	S												
8-289	N	N	N																
6-300															E	E	E	E	Y
8-302				G	G	G	G	G	G	G	G	G			F	F	F	F	F
8-351W															G	G	G	G	G①
8-351M												H	H						
8-400												S	S						

① 1985–86:H

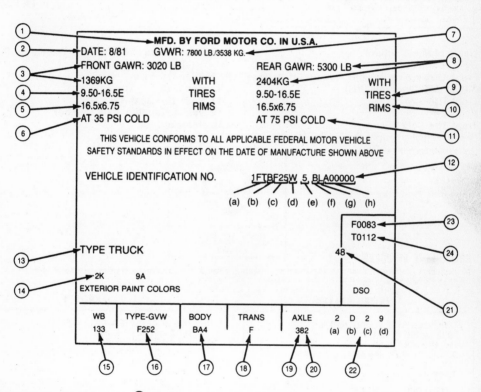

① Name and Location of Manufacturer
② Date of Manufacture
③ Front Gross Axle Weight Ratings in Pounds (LB) and Kilograms (KG)
④ Front Tire Size
⑤ Rim Size
⑥ Front Tire Cold PSI
⑦ Gross Vehicle Weight Rating in Pounds (LB) and Kilograms (KG)
⑧ Rear Gross Axle Weight Rating in Pounds (LB) and Kilograms (KG)
⑨ Rear Tire Size

⑩ Rim Size
⑪ Rear Tire Cold PSI
⑫ Vehicle Identification Number
  (a) World Manufacturer Identifier
  (b) Brake Type and Gross Vehicle Weight Rating (GVWR) Class
  (c) Model or Line, Series, Chassis and Cab Type
  (d) Engine Type
  (e) Check Digit
  (f) Model Year
  (g) Assembly Plant Code
  (h) Sequential Serial and Model Year
⑬ Type Vehicle
⑭ Exterior Paint Codes (two sets of figures designates a two-tone)
⑮ Wheelbase in Inches

⑯ Model Code and GVW
⑰ Interior Trim, Seat and Body/Cab Type
⑱ Transmission Code
⑲ Rear Axle Code
⑳ Front Axle Code if so Equipped
㉑ District/Special Order Codes
㉒ Suspension Identification Codes
  (a) Aux./Opt. Usage Code (Front)
  (b) Front Spring Code
  (c) Aux./Opt. Usage Code (Rear)
  (d) Rear Spring Code
㉓ Front Axle Accessory Reserve Capacity in Pounds
㉔ Total Accessory Reserve Capacity in Pounds

1982–86 Truck Certification Label

COMPLETE VEHICLES

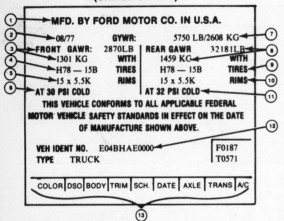

(UNITED STATES)

1 → MFD. BY FORD MOTOR CO. IN U.S.A.

2 → 08/77   GYWR: 5750 LB/2608 KG ← 7
3 → FRONT GAWR: 2870LB   REAR GAWR   32181LB ← 8
4 → 1301 KG   WITH   1459 KG   WITH ← 9
5 → H78 — 15B   TIRES   H78 — 15B   TIRES ← 9
   → 15 x 5.5K   RIMS   15 x 5.5K   RIMS ← 10
6 → AT 30 PSI COLD   AT 32 PSI COLD ← 11

THIS VEHICLE CONFORMS TO ALL APPLICABLE FEDERAL
MOTOR VEHICLE SAFETY STANDARDS IN EFFECT ON THE DATE
OF MANUFACTURE SHOWN ABOVE.

VEH IDENT NO.   E04BHAE0000 ← 12   F0187
TYPE   TRUCK   T0571

COLOR	DSO	BODY	TRIM	SCH.	DATE	AXLE	TRANS	A/C

13

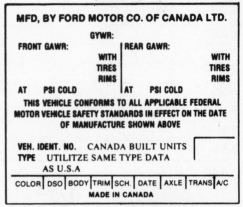

(CANADA)

MFD. BY FORD MOTOR CO. OF CANADA LTD.

GYWR:
FRONT GAWR: REAR GAWR:
    WITH   WITH
    TIRES   TIRES
    RIMS   RIMS
AT   PSI COLD   AT   PSI COLD

THIS VEHICLE CONFORMS TO ALL APPLICABLE FEDERAL
MOTOR VEHICLE SAFETY STANDARDS IN EFFECT ON THE DATE
OF MANUFACTURE SHOWN ABOVE

VEH. IDENT. NO.   CANADA BUILT UNITS
TYPE   UTILITZE SAME TYPE DATA
    AS U.S.A

COLOR	DSO	BODY	TRIM	SCH.	DATE	AXLE	TRANS	A/C

MADE IN CANADA

1 Name of Manufacturer
2 Date of Manufacture
3 Front Gross Axle Weight Ratings in Pounds (LB) and Kilograms (KG)
4 Front Tire Size
5 Rim Size
6 Front Tire Cold PSI
7 Gross Vehicle Weight Rating in Pounds (LB) and Kilograms (KG)

8 Rear Gross Axle Weight Rating in Pounds (LB) and Kilograms (KG)
9 Rear Tire Size
10 Rim Size
11 Rear Tire Cold PSI
12 Vehicle Identification Number
13 Vehicle Data

DECAL APPLIED TO
ALL CANADIAN BUILT
UNITS.

INCOMPLETE VEHICLES

THE INCOMPLETE VEHICLE LABEL IS ATTACHED TO A BOOKLET (INCOMPLETE VEHICLE MANUAL) AND SECURED TO A
SUITABLE INTERIOR LOCATION FOR INFORMATION USE AT DESTINATION.

(UNITED STATES)

THIS INCOMPLETE VEHICLE MFD. BY
FORD MOTOR COMPANY
THE AMERICAN ROAD
DEARBORN, MICHIGAN 48121 ON: 08/77
VEH. IDENT. NO. E37HHAE0002
GVWR 1000 LB/4335 KG

FRONT GAWR	REAR GAWR	REAR REAR GAWR
4000 LB	6700 LB	LB
1814 KG	3039 KG	KG

FRONT	REAR
8.00 — 16.5E	8.00 — 16.5E
16.5 x 6.0	16.5 x 6.0
60	55

TIRES
RIMS
PSI COLD

MAY BE
COMPLETED AS: TRUCK BUS (NOT SCHOOL BUS)

(EXPORT)

THIS INCOMPLETE VEHICLE MFD. BY
FORD MOTOR COMPANY
THE AMERICAN ROAD
DEARBORN, MICHIGAN 48121 ON: 08/77
VEH. IDENT. NO.
GVWR

FRONT GAWR	REAR GAWR	REAR REAR GAWR

FRONT	REAR

TIRES
RIMS
PSI COLD

MAY BE   THIS VEHICLE MFD FOR EXPORT
COMPLETED AS: ONLY ON DATE SHOWN ABOVE

NOTE — The same information is on all safety certification decal although the location of the information on the decal may be different.

1978–80 Vehicle Certification Plates

Rear Axle Codes and Ratios
Read Ratios Across

Codes	66	67/68	69	70	71	72	73	74	75	76	77	78	79	80	81	82	83	84–86
01	3.50	3.50																
02	4.00	4.00					3.00	3.00	3.00	3.00	3.00							
03							4.11											
04							4.57											
07	3.00	3.00																
11	3.50	3.50					3.50	3.50	4.11									
12	4.11	4.11					3.70	3.70	3.70									
13	4.56	4.56																4.11
A7	3.00	3.00																
B1	3.50	3.50																
B2	4.11	4.11																4.10
B3	4.57	4.57																3.54
08			3.50	3.50	3.50	3.50	3.50	3.50	3.50	3.50	3.50							
05			4.11	4.11	4.11	4.11	4.11	4.11	4.11	4.11	4.11							
17			3.25	3.25	3.25	3.25	3.25	3.25	3.25	3.25	3.25							2.47
09			3.70	3.70	3.70	3.70	3.70	3.70	3.70	3.70	3.70							
71			3.54	3.54	3.54	3.54	3.54	3.54	3.54	3.54	3.54							
72			3.73	3.73	3.73	3.73	3.73	3.73	3.73	3.73	3.73							4.10
73			4.10	4.10	4.10	4.10	4.10	4.10	4.10	4.10	4.10							3.54
G1			3.54	3.54	3.54	3.54	3.54	3.54										
G3			4.10	4.10	4.10	4.10	4.10	4.10										3.54
06				4.57														
31				3.54														3.07
33				3.73														3.54
35				4.10														
36				4.56														
C1				3.54														
C3				3.73														3.54
C5				4.10														
B4							4.10	4.10	4.10	4.10	4.10							3.73
C7							3.54											
C8							3.73	3.73	3.73	3.73	3.73	3.73						
D7							4.10	4.10	4.10	4.10	4.10	4.10	4.10	4.10	4.10			
10							3.25	3.25										
18							3.50										3.08	3.08
22							4.88											
14									3.00							3.00		3.00
15									3.25									
16									3.50							3.50		3.50

Rear Axle Codes and Ratios (cont.)

Read Ratios Across

										Years								
Codes	66	67/68	69	70	71	72	73	74	75	76	77	78	79	80	81	82	83	84–86
19																	3.55	3.55
23						3.31	3.31	3.31	3.31	3.31	3.31	3.31	3.31	3.31				3.54
24							4.10	4.10	4.10	4.10	4.10	4.10	4.10					3.73
25							3.31											
26							3.54	3.54										3.55
38									3.73	3.73	3.73	3.73						
B5							3.31	3.31										
D6							3.73	3.73	3.73	3.73	3.73							
H2							3.50	3.50	3.50	3.50	3.50	3.50	3.50	3.50	3.50			
H3							4.11	4.11	4.11	4.11	4.11							4.11
H4							3.25	3.25	3.25	3.25	3.25	3.25	3.25	3.25	3.25	3.00		3.00
H5									3.70	3.70	3.70							
H6																3.50		
H7													3.00	3.00	3.00			
H8																	3.08	3.08
H9												4.11	4.11	4.11	4.11		3.55	3.55

Transmission Code Chart

Code	Description
A (1965)	Ford-Manual-3 Speed
B (1965–78)	Warner T-85-3 Speed
C	Ford-Manual-3 Speed
D	Warner T-89-3 Speed
E	Warner T-87-3 Speed
F	Warner T-18-4 Speed
N (1965)	New Process 435-4 Speed
A (1966–86)	New Process 435-4 Speed
P	Warner T-19-4 Speed
B (1979–86)	Clark-4 Speed O.D.
G	Automatic C4
W	Automatic C5
P	Automatic C6 thru 1977
K	Automatic C6 1978–86
J	Automatic FMX
T	Automatic Overdrive

the reservoir. Wash all of the air cleaner parts in a suitable cleaning solvent. Dry all of the parts with compressed air or allow them to air dry.

5. Inspect the gasket between the oil reservoir chamber and the air cleaner body. Replace the gasket as necessary.

6. Saturate the filter element with clean engine oil.

7. Fill the oil reservoir to the full mark with engine oil. Use SAE 30 above 32°F (0°C) and SAE 20 for low temperatures.

8. Replace the air cleaner assembly on the carburetor and tighten the wing nut.

NOTE: *Check the air filter more often if the vehicle is operated under unusually dusty conditions and replace or clean it as necessary.*

The procedure for replacing the paper air cleaner element is as follows:

1. Unlock and open the engine compartment cover.

2. Remove the wing nut holding the air cleaner assembly to the top of the carburetor.

3. Disconnect the crankcase ventilation hose at the air cleaner and remove the entire air cleaner assembly from the carburetor.

4. Remove and discard the old filter element, and inspect the condition of the air cleaner mounting gasket. Replace the gasket as necessary.

5. Install the air cleaner body on the carburetor so that the word FRONT faces toward the front of the vehicle.

6. Place the new filter element in the air cleaner body and install the cover and tighten the wing nut. If the word TOP appears on the element, make sure that the side the word appears on is facing up when the element is in place.

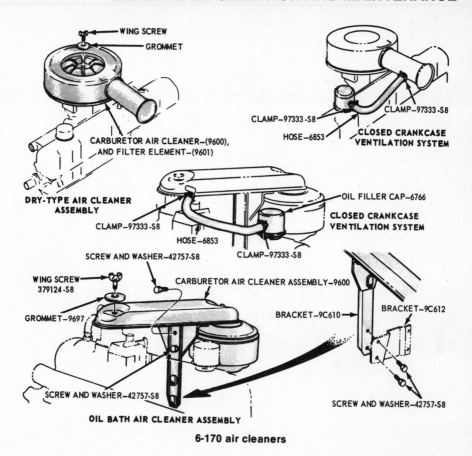

WING SCREW
GROMMET

CARBURETOR AIR CLEANER—(9600),
AND FILTER ELEMENT—(9601)

**DRY-TYPE AIR CLEANER
ASSEMBLY**

CLAMP—97333-S8
HOSE—6853
CLAMP—97333-S8

**CLOSED CRANKCASE
VENTILATION SYSTEM**

OIL FILLER CAP—6766

CLAMP—97333-S8
HOSE—6853
CLAMP—97333-S8

**CLOSED CRANKCASE
VENTILATION SYSTEM**

SCREW AND WASHER—42757-S8

WING SCREW
379124-S8

GROMMET—9697

CARBURETOR AIR CLEANER ASSEMBLY—9600

BRACKET—9C610

BRACKET—9C612

SCREW AND WASHER—42757-S8

SCREW AND WASHER—42757-S8

OIL BATH AIR CLEANER ASSEMBLY

6-170 air cleaners

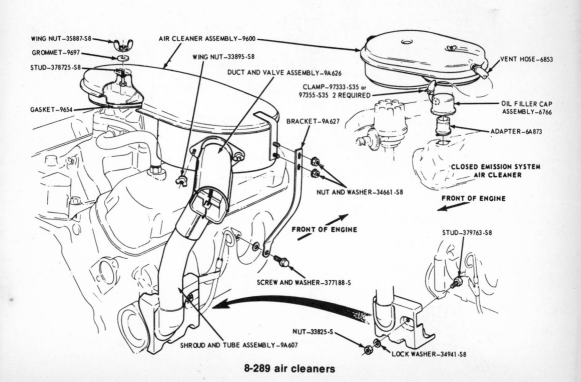

WING NUT—35887-S8
GROMMET—9697
STUD—378725-S8

AIR CLEANER ASSEMBLY—9600

WING NUT—33895-S8

DUCT AND VALVE ASSEMBLY—9A626

VENT HOSE—6853

CLAMP—97333-S35 or
97355-S35 2 REQUIRED

GASKET—9654

BRACKET—9A627

OIL FILLER CAP
ASSEMBLY—6766

ADAPTER—6A873

**CLOSED EMISSION SYSTEM
AIR CLEANER**

NUT AND WASHER—34661-S8

FRONT OF ENGINE

FRONT OF ENGINE

STUD—379763-S8

SCREW AND WASHER—377188-S

NUT—33825-S

SHROUD AND TUBE ASSEMBLY—9A607

LOCK WASHER—34941-S8

8-289 air cleaners

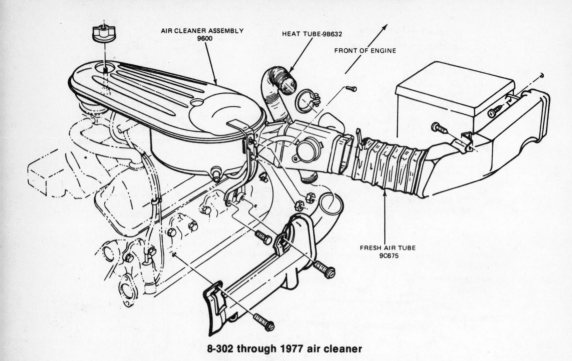

8-302 through 1977 air cleaner

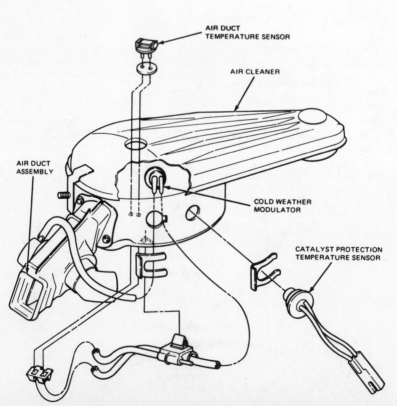

1975–77 catalyst protection temperature sensor

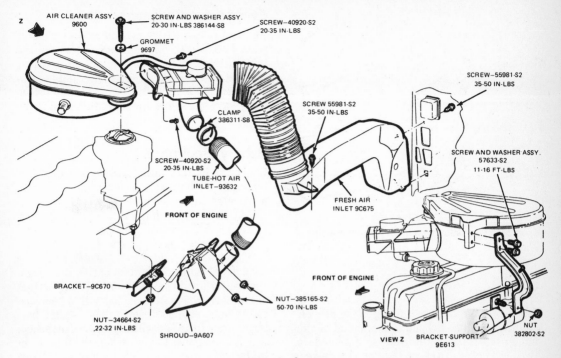

6-300 air cleaner

7. Connect the crankcase ventilation hose to the air cleaner.

Fuel Filter

It is recommended that the fuel filter be replaced periodically. The inline filter is of one piece construction and cannot be cleaned.

1. Remove the air cleaner.

2. Loosen the retaining clamp securing the fuel inlet hose to the fuel filter.

3. Unscrew the fuel filter from the hose and discard the retaining clamp.

4. Screw the new filter into the carburetor.

5. Attach the inlet hose to the filter, using a new clamp.

6. Replace the air cleaner.

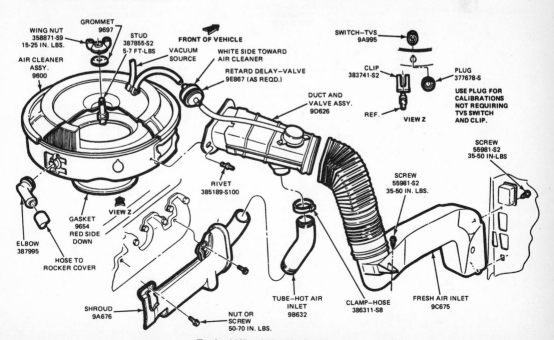

Typical V8, 1978–83 air cleaner

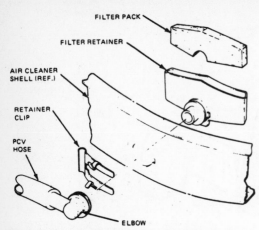

Crankcase ventilation filter in air cleaner housing

PCV Valve

Check the PCV valve according to the Preventive Maintenance Schedule at the end of this chapter to see if it is free and not gummed up, stuck or blocked. To check the valve, remove it from the engine and work the valve by sticking a screwdriver in the crankcase side of the valve. It should move. It is possible to clean the PCV valve by soaking it in a solvent and blowing it out with compressed air. This can restore the valve to some level of operating order.

This should be used in emergency situations. Otherwise, the valve should be replaced.

Evaporative Canister

The fuel evaporative emission control canister should be inspected for damage or leaks at the hose fittings. Repair or replace any old or cracked hoses. Replace the canister if it is damaged in any way. The canister is located on the right side (passenger) fender wall, under the hood.

Battery Electrolyte

Check the battery fluid level (except in Maintenance Free batteries) at least once a month; more often in hot weather.

CAUTION: *Keep flame or sparks away from the battery; it gives off explosive hydrogen gas, while it is being charged.*

Water may be added to a battery when the level drops below the bottom of the filler neck. Add water until the level contacts the bottom of the neck. the water surface will appear distorted upon contact with the neck. Some batteries use a filler cap with a glass rod attached, which will appear to glow when the fluid level in the cell is low. Another band has a small eye in the top of the case, which glows when the electrolyte is low.

The battery should be kept clean and free from corrosion. Corrosion may be removed with a solution of baking soda and water and a stiff wire brush. After assembly, coat the terminals and cable ends with grease. This will prevent a corrosion build up.

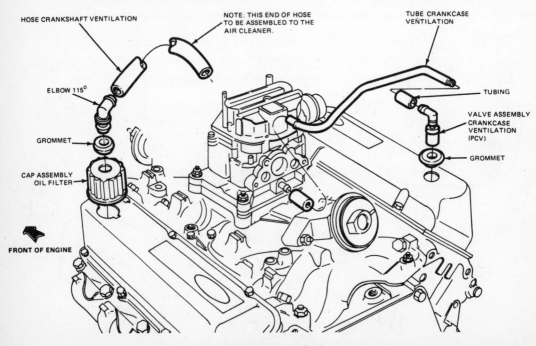

PCV system, typical

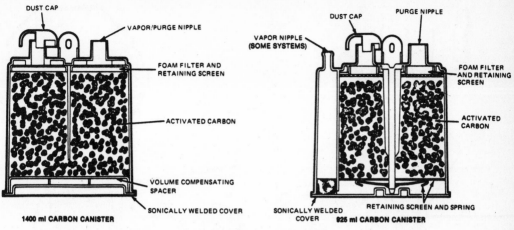

Carbon canister cross-sections

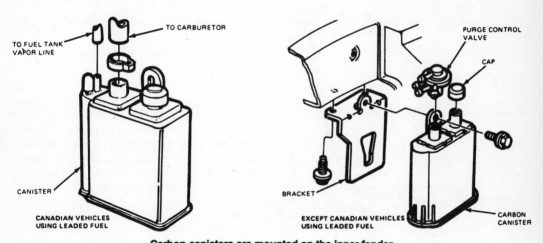

Carbon canisters are mounted on the inner fender

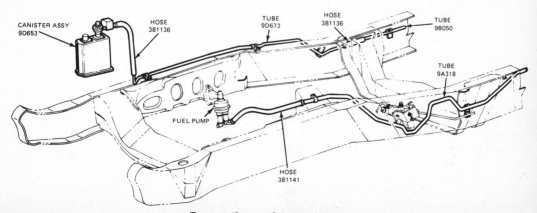

Evaporative canister and lines

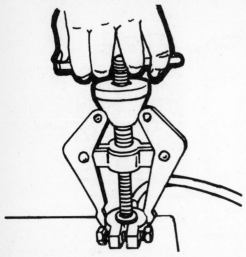

Top terminal battery cable can be removed with this inexpensive tool

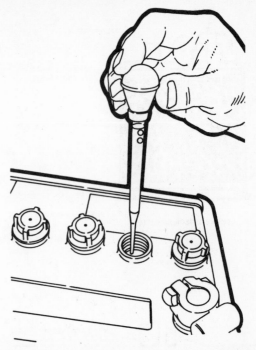

An inexpensive hydrometer will quickly test the battery's state of charge

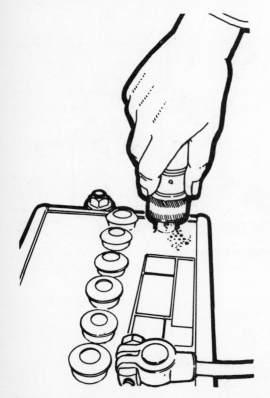

Clean the battery posts with a wire terminal cleaner

It is a good idea to have a reliable, inexpensive hydrometer on hand to check the battery condition. A fully charged battery will read around 1250, or in the green area, depending on the type of hydrometer used. A battery's efficiency is reduced in cold weather, so it should be checked more frequently and recharged when necessary.

At least once a year, check the specific gravity of the battery. It should be between 1.20–1.26. Clean and tighten the clamps and apply a thin coat of petroleum jelly to the terminals. This will help to retard corrosion. The terminals can be cleaned with a staff wire brush or with an inexpensive terminal cleaner designed for this purpose.

If water is added during freezing weather, the truck should be driven several miles to allow the electrolyte and water to mix. Otherwise the battery could freeze.

If the battery becomes corroded, a solution of baking soda and water will neutralize the corrosion. This should be washed off after making sure that the caps are securely in place. Rinse the solution off with cold water.

Some batteries were equipped with a felt terminal washer. This should be saturated with engine oil approximately every 6,000 miles. This will also help to retard corrosion.

If a fast charger is used while the battery is in the truck, disconnect the battery before connecting the charger.

NOTE: *Keep flame or sparks away from the battery; it gives off explosive hydrogen gas.*

TESTING THE MAINTENANCE FREE BATTERY

All later model trucks are equipped with maintenance free batteries, which do not require normal attention as far as fluid level checks

SPECIFIC GRAVITY (@ 80°F.) AND CHARGE Specific Gravity Reading (use the minimum figure for testing)	
Minimum	**Battery Charge**
1.260	**100% Charged**
1.230	**75% Charged**
1.200	**50% Charged**
1.170	**25% Charged**
1.140	**Very Little Power Left**
1.110	**Completely Discharged**

Battery specific gravity. Some testers have colored balls which correspond to the numerical values in the left column

are concerned. However, the terminals require periodic cleaning, which should be performed at least once a year.

The sealed top battery cannot be checked for charge in the normal manner, since there is no provision for access to the electrolyte. To check the condition of the battery:

1. If the indicator eye on top of the battery is dark, the battery has enough fluid. If the eye is light, the electrolyte fluid is too low and the battery must be replaced.

2. If a green dot appears in the middle of the eye, the battery is sufficiently charged. Proceed to Step 4. If no green dot is visible, charge the battery as in Step 3.

3. Charge the battery at this rate:

Charging Rate Amps	Time
75	40 min
50	1 hr
25	2 hr
10	5 hr

CAUTION: *Do not charge the battery for more than 50 amp/hours. If the green dot appears, or if electrolyte squirts out of the vent hole, stop the charge and proceed to Step 4. It may be necessary to tip the battery from*

Clean the cable ends with a stiff wire cleaning tool

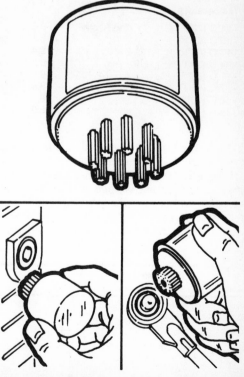

Side terminal batteries require a special wire brush for cleaning

side to side to get the green dot to appear after charging.

4. Connect a battery load tester and a voltmeter across the battery terminals (the battery cables should be disconnected from the battery). Apply a 300 amp load to the battery for 15 seconds to remove the surface charge. Remove the load.

5. Wait 15 seconds to allow the battery to recover. Apply the appropriate test load, as specified in the following chart:

Battery Capacity (Ampere-Hrs.)	Discharge Rate (Amperes)
36 Maintenance-Free	155
45 Maintenance-Free	190
48 Maintenance-Free	205
54 Maintenance-Free	225
63 Maintenance-Free	260
68 Maintenance-Free	235
83 Maintenance-Free	350
71 Maintenance-Free	235
77 Conventional Batt.	225
81 Conventional Batt.	175
(Cold Cranking Amps)	
1050	525
850	425

Voltage Readings at 15 seconds For Good Battery (Battery Capacity Test).

Approximate Battery Temperature	Minimum Voltage	
21°C (70°F)	And Above	9.6
15°C (59°F)		9.5
10°C (50°F)		9.4
4°C (39°F)		9.3
− 1°C (30°F)		9.1
− 7°C (19°F)		8.9
−12°C (10°F)		8.7
−18°C (0°F)		8.5

Apply the load for 15 seconds while reading the voltage. Disconnect the load.

6. Check the results against the following chart. If the battery voltage is at or above the specified voltage for the temperature listed, the battery is good. If the voltage falls below what's listed, the battery should be replaced.

Temperature (°F)	Minimum Voltage
70 or above	9.6
60	9.5
50	9.4
40	9.3
30	9.1
20	8.9
10	8.7
0	8.5

FILLING THE BATTERY

Batteries should be checked for proper electrolyte level at least once a month or more frequently. Keep a close eye on any cell or cells that are unusually low or seem to constantly need water. This may indicate a battery on its last legs, a leak, or a problem with the charging system.

Top up each cell to about ⅜" (9.5mm) above the tops of the plates. Always use distilled water (available in supermarkets or auto parts stores), because most tap water contains chemicals and minerals that may slowly damage the plates of your battery.

CABLES AND CLAMPS

Twice a year, the battery terminal posts and the cable clamps should be cleaned. Loosen the clamp bolts (you may have to brush off any corrosion with a baking soda and water solution if they are really messy) and remove the cables, negative cable first. On batteries with posts on top, the use of a battery clamp puller is recommended. It is easy to break off a battery terminal if a clamp gets stuck without the puller. These pullers are inexpensive and available in most auto parts stores or auto departments. Side terminal battery cables are secured with a bolt.

The best tool for battery clamp and terminal maintenance is a battery terminal brush. This inexpensive tool has a female ended wire brush for cleaning terminals, and a male ended wire brush inside for cleaning the insides of battery clamps. When using this tool, make sure you get both the terminal posts and the insides of the clamps nice and shiny. Any oxidation, corrosion or foreign material will prevent a sound electrical connection and inhibit either starting or charging. If your battery has side terminals, there is also a cleaning tool available for these.

Before installing the cables, remove the battery holddown clamp or strap and remove the battery. Inspect the battery casing for leaks or cracks (which unfortunately can only be fixed by buying a new battery). Check the battery tray, wash it off with warm soapy water, rinse and dry. Any rust on the tray should be sanded away, and the tray given at least two coats of a quality anti-rust paint. Replace the battery, and install the holddown clamp or strap, but do not overtighten.

Reinstall your clean battery cables, negative cable last. Tighten the cables on the terminal posts snugly; do not overtighten. Wipe a thin coat of petroleum jelly or grease all over the outsides of the clamps. This will help to inhibit corrosion.

Finally, check the battery cables themselves. If the insulation of the cables is cracked or broken, or if the ends are frayed, replace the cable with a new cable of the same length or gauge.

NOTE: *Batteries give off hydrogen gas, which is explosive. DO NOT SMOKE around the battery! The battery electrolyte contains sulfuric acid; if you should splash any into your eyes or skin, flush with plenty of clear water and get immediate medical help.*

BATTERY CHARGING AND REPLACEMENT

Charging a battery is best done by the slow charging method (often called trickle charging), with a low amperage charger. Quick charging a battery can actually "cook" the battery, damaging the plates inside and decreasing the life of the battery drastically. Any charging should be done in a well ventilated area away from the possibility of sparks or flame. The cell caps (not found on maintenance free batteries) should be unscrewed from their cells, but not removed.

If the battery must be quick charged, check the cell voltages and the color of the electrolyte a few minutes after the charge is started. If cell voltages are not uniform or if the electrolyte is discolored with brown sediment, stop the quick charging in favor of a trickle charge. A common indicator of an overcharged battery is the frequent need to add water to the battery.

Exhaust Manifold Heat Riser Valve

Check the thermostatic spring of the valve to make sure it is hooked up on the stop pin. The spring stop is at the top of the valve housing when the valve is properly installed.

Make sure the spring holds the valve closed. Actuate the counterweight by hand to make sure it moves freely through approximately 90° of rotation without binding.

The valve is closed when the engine is cold. However, a properly operating valve will open when very light finger pressure is applied to the counterweight. Rapidly accelerate the engine to make sure the valve momentarily opens. The valve is designed to open when the engine is at normal operating temperature and is operated at high rpm.

Lubricate and free the value with the non-flammable solvent if the valve is sluggish or stuck.

Belts

INSPECTION

At the interval specified in the Maintenance Intervals chart, check the water pump, alternator, power steering pump (if equipped), air

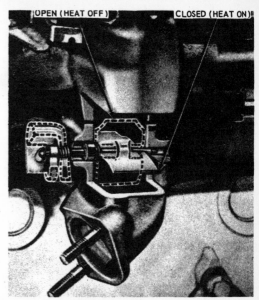

Six-cylinder exhaust control valve—typical

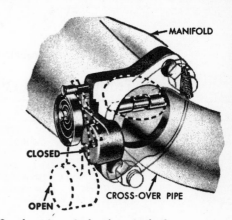

V8 exhaust control valve—typical

conditioning compressor (if equipped) and air pump (if equipped) drive belts for proper tension. Also look for signs of wear, fraying, separation, glazing, and so on, and replace the belts as required.

BELT TENSION

Belt tension should be checked with a gauge made for the purpose. If a tension gauge is not available, tension can be checked with moderate thumb pressure applied to the belt at its longest span midway between pulleys. If the belt has a free span less than 12″ (305mm), it should deflect approximately ⅛–¼″ (3–6mm). If the span is longer than 12″ (305mm), deflection can range between ⅛″ (3mm) and ⅜″ (9.5mm).

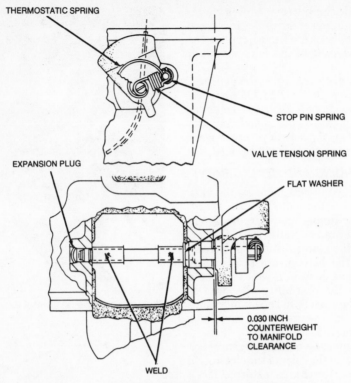

THERMOSTATIC SPRING

STOP PIN SPRING

VALVE TENSION SPRING

EXPANSION PLUG

FLAT WASHER

0.030 INCH COUNTERWEIGHT TO MANIFOLD CLEARANCE

WELD

Checking heat riser movement

Troubleshooting the Serpentine Drive Belt

Problem	Cause	Solution
Tension sheeting fabric failure (woven fabric on outside circumference of belt has cracked or separated from body of belt)	• Grooved or backside idler pulley diameters are less than minimum recommended	• Replace pulley(s) not conforming to specification
	• Tension sheeting contacting (rubbing) stationary object	• Correct rubbing condition
	• Excessive heat causing woven fabric to age	• Replace belt
	• Tension sheeting splice has fractured	• Replace belt
Noise (objectional squeal, squeak, or rumble is heard or felt while drive belt is in operation)	• Belt slippage	• Adjust belt
	• Bearing noise	• Locate and repair
	• Belt misalignment	• Align belt/pulley(s)
	• Belt-to-pulley mismatch	• Install correct belt
	• Driven component inducing vibration	• Locate defective driven component and repair
	• System resonant frequency inducing vibration	• Vary belt tension within specifications. Replace belt.
Rib chunking (one or more ribs has separated from belt body)	• Foreign objects imbedded in pulley grooves	• Remove foreign objects from pulley grooves
	• Installation damage	• Replace belt
	• Drive loads in excess of design specifications	• Adjust belt tension
	• Insufficient internal belt adhesion	• Replace belt
Rib or belt wear (belt ribs contact bottom of pulley grooves)	• Pulley(s) misaligned	• Align pulley(s)
	• Mismatch of belt and pulley groove widths	• Replace belt
	• Abrasive environment	• Replace belt
	• Rusted pulley(s)	• Clean rust from pulley(s)
	• Sharp or jagged pulley groove tips	• Replace pulley
	• Rubber deteriorated	• Replace belt

Troubleshooting the Serpentine Drive Belt (cont.)

Problem	Cause	Solution
Longitudinal belt cracking (cracks between two ribs)	• Belt has mistracked from pulley groove	• Replace belt
	• Pulley groove tip has worn away rubber-to-tensile member	• Replace belt
Belt slips	• Belt slipping because of insufficient tension	• Adjust tension
	• Belt or pulley subjected to substance (belt dressing, oil, ethylene glycol) that has reduced friction	• Replace belt and clean pulleys
	• Driven component bearing failure	• Replace faulty component bearing
	• Belt glazed and hardened from heat and excessive slippage	• Replace belt
"Groove jumping" (belt does not maintain correct position on pulley, or turns over and/or runs off pulleys)	• Insufficient belt tension	• Adjust belt tension
	• Pulley(s) not within design tolerance	• Replace pulley(s)
	• Foreign object(s) in grooves	• Remove foreign objects from grooves
	• Excessive belt speed	• Avoid excessive engine acceleration
	• Pulley misalignment	• Align pulley(s)
	• Belt-to-pulley profile mismatched	• Install correct belt
	• Belt cordline is distorted	• Replace belt
Belt broken (Note: identify and correct problem before replacement belt is installed)	• Excessive tension	• Replace belt and adjust tension to specification
	• Tensile members damaged during belt installation	• Replace belt
	• Belt turnover	• Replace belt
	• Severe pulley misalignment	• Align pulley(s)
	• Bracket, pulley, or bearing failure	• Replace defective component and belt
Cord edge failure (tensile member exposed at edges of belt or separated from belt body)	• Excessive tension	• Adjust belt tension
	• Drive pulley misalignment	• Align pulley
	• Belt contacting stationary object	• Correct as necessary
	• Pulley irregularities	• Replace pulley
	• Improper pulley construction	• Replace pulley
	• Insufficient adhesion between tensile member and rubber matrix	• Replace belt and adjust tension to specifications
Sporadic rib cracking (multiple cracks in belt ribs at random intervals)	• Ribbed pulley(s) diameter less than minimum specification	• Replace pulley(s)
	• Backside bend flat pulley(s) diameter less than minimum	• Replace pulley(s)
	• Excessive heat condition causing rubber to harden	• Correct heat condition as necessary
	• Excessive belt thickness	• Replace belt
	• Belt overcured	• Replace belt
	• Excessive tension	• Adjust belt tension

REMOVAL, INSTALLATION AND ADJUSTMENT

1. Loosen the driven accessory's pivot and mounting bolts.

2. Move the accessory toward or away from the engine until the tension is correct. You can use a wooden hammer handle, or broomstick, as a lever, but do not use anything metallic, such as a prybar.

3. Tighten the bolts and recheck the tension. If new belts have been installed, run the engine for a few minutes, then recheck and readjust as necessary.

It is better to have belts too loose than too tight, because overtight belts will lead to bearing failure, particularly in the water pump and alternator. However, loose belts place an extremely high impact load on the driven component due to the whipping action of the belt.

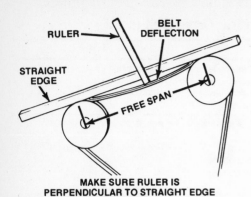

Measuring belt deflection

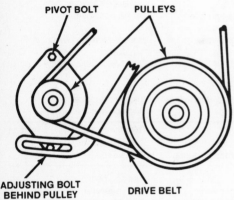

Some accessories can be moved only if the pivot bolt is loosened

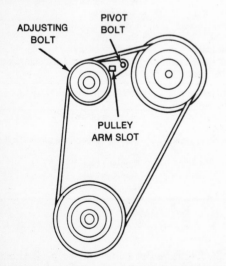

Some pulleys have a rectangular slot to aid in moving the accessory

Hoses

REMOVAL AND INSTALLATION

1. Drain the existing antifreeze and coolant. Open the radiator and engine drain petcocks, or disconnect the bottom radiator hose, at the radiator outlet.

NOTE: *Before opening the radiator petcock, spray it with some penetrating lubricant.*

2. Loosen the clamps on each end of the hose to be removed.

3. Slide the hose off the connections.

4. Position the clamps on each end of the hose to be removed.

5. Slide the hose onto the connections, then tighten the clamps. If the connections have a bead around the edges, make sure the clamps are located beyond the beads.

6. Refill the cooling system with coolant. Run the engine for several minutes, then check the hose connection for leaks.

Air Conditioning System

CAUTION: *Do not attempt to charge or discharge the refrigerant system unless you are thoroughly familiar with its operation and the hazards involved. The compressed refrigerant used in the air conditioning system expands and evaporates into the atmosphere at a temperature of –21.7°F (–30°C) or less. This will freeze any surface, including your eyes, that it contacts. In addition, the refrigerant decomposes into a poisonous gas in the presence of flame.*

SYSTEM INSPECTION

The air conditioning system should be checked periodically for worn hoses, loose connections, low refrigerant, leaks, dirt and bugs. If any of these conditions exist, they must be corrected or they will reduce the efficiency of your air conditioning system.

SAFETY PRECAUTIONS

There are two particular hazards associated with air conditioning systems and they both relate to the refrigerant gas.

First, the refrigerant gas is an extremely cold substance. When exposed to air, it will instantly freeze any surface it comes in contact with, including your eyes. The other hazards relates to fire. Although normally non-toxic, refrigerant gas becomes highly poisonous in the presence of an open flame. One good whiff of the vapor formed by burning refrigerant can be fatal. Keep all forms of fire (including cigarettes) well clear of the air conditioning system.

Any repair work to an air conditioning system should be left to a professional. Do not, under any circumstances, attempt to loosen or tighten any fittings or perform any work other than that outlined here.

HOW TO SPOT WORN V-BELTS

V-Belts are vital to efficient engine operation—they drive the fan, water pump and other accessories. They require little maintenance (occasional tightening) but they will not last forever. Slipping or failure of the V-belt will lead to overheating. If your V-belt looks like any of these, it should be replaced.

This belt has deep cracks, which cause it to flex. Too much flexing leads to heat build-up and premature failure. These cracks can be caused by using the belt on a pulley that is too small. Notched belts are available for small diameter pulleys.

Cracking or weathering

Oil and grease on a belt can cause the belt's rubber compounds to soften and separate from the reinforcing cords that hold the belt together. The belt will first slip, then finally fail altogether.

Softening (grease and oil)

Glazing is caused by a belt that is slipping. A slipping belt can cause a run-down battery, erratic power steering, overheating or poor accessory performance. The more the belt slips, the more glazing will be built up on the surface of the belt. The more the belt is glazed, the more it will slip. If the glazing is light, tighten the belt.

Glazing

The cover of this belt is worn off and is peeling away. The reinforcing cords will begin to wear and the belt will shortly break. When the belt cover wears in spots or has a rough jagged appearance, check the pulley grooves for roughness.

Worn cover

This belt is on the verge of breaking and leaving you stranded. The layers of the belt are separating and the reinforcing cords are exposed. It's just a matter of time before it breaks completely.

Separation

HOW TO SPOT BAD HOSES

Both the upper and lower radiator hoses are called upon to perform difficult jobs in an inhospitable environment. They are subject to nearly 18 psi at under hood temperatures often over 280°F., and must circulate nearly 7500 gallons of coolant an hour—3 good reasons to have good hoses.

A good test for any hose is to feel it for soft or spongy spots. Frequently these will appear as swollen areas of the hose. The most likely cause is oil soaking. This hose could burst at any time, when hot or under pressure.

Swollen hose

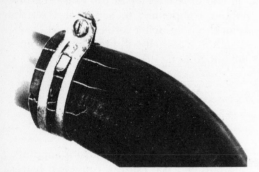

Cracked hoses can usually be seen but feel the hoses to be sure they have not hardened; a prime cause of cracking. This hose has cracked down to the reinforcing cords and could split at any of the cracks.

Cracked hose

Weakened clamps frequently are the cause of hose and cooling system failure. The connection between the pipe and hose has deteriorated enough to allow coolant to escape when the engine is hot.

Frayed hose end (due to weak clamp)

Debris, rust and scale in the cooling system can cause the inside of a hose to weaken. This can usually be felt on the outside of the hose as soft or thinner areas.

Debris in cooling system

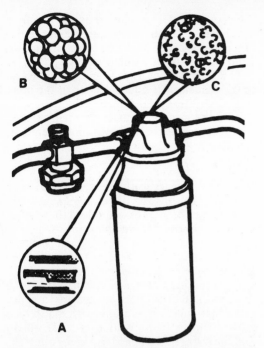

Oil streaks (A), constant bubbles (B) or foam (C) indicate there is not enough refrigerant in the system. Occasional bubbles during initial operation is normal. A clear sight glass indicates a proper charge of refrigerant or no refrigerant at all, which can be determined by the presence of cold air at the outlets in the car. If the glass is clouded with a milky white substance, have the receiver/drier checked professionally

CHECKING FOR OIL LEAKS

Refrigerant leaks show up as oily areas on the various components because the compressor oil is transported around the entire system along with the refrigerant. Look for oily spots on all the hoses add lines, especially on the hose and tubing connections. If there are oily deposits, the system may have a leak, and you should have it checked by a qualified repairman.

NOTE: *A small area of oil on the front of the compressor is normal and no cause for alarm.*

KEEP THE CONDENSER CLEAR

Periodically inspect the front of the condenser for bent fins or foreign material (dirt, bugs, leaves, etc.) If any cooling fins are bent, straighten them carefully with needlenosed pliers. You can remove any debris with a stiff bristle brush or hose.

OPERATE THE A/C SYSTEM PERIODICALLY

A lot of A/C problems can be avoided by simply running the air conditioner at least once a week, regardless of the season. Let the system run for at least 5 minutes a week (even in the winter), and you'll keep the internal parts lubricated as well as preventing the hoses from hardening.

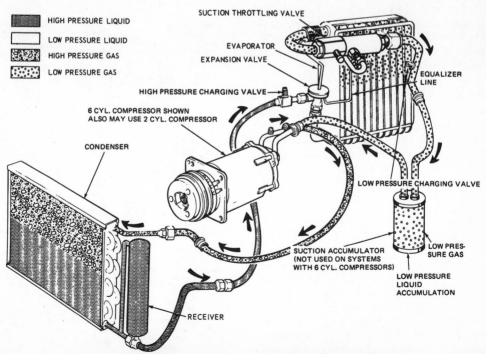

Typical air conditioning system, showing all working components

REFRIGERANT LEVEL CHECK

There are two ways to check refrigerant level, depending on how your model is equipped.

With Sight Glass

The first order of business when checking the sight glass is to find the sight glass. It will either be in the head of the receiver/drier, or in one of the metal lines leading from the top of the receiver/drier. Once you've found it, wipe it clean an proceed as follows:

1. With the engine and the air conditioning system running, look for the flow of refrigerant through the sight glass. If the air conditioner is working properly, you'll be able to see a continuous flow of clear refrigerant through the sight glass, with perhaps an occasional bubble at very high temperatures.

2. Cycle the air conditioner on and off to make sure what you are seeing is clear refrigerant. Since the refrigerant is clear, it is possible to mistake a completely discharged system for one that is fully charged. Turn the system off and watch the sight glass. If there is refrigerant in the system, you'll see bubbles when the system is running, and the air flow from the unit in the truck is delivering cold air, everything is OK.

3. If you observe bubbles in the sight glass while the system is operating, the system is low on refrigerant. Have it checked by a professional.

4. Oil streaks in the sight glass are an indication of trouble. Most of the time, if you see oil in the sight glass, it will appear as a series of streaks, although occasionally it may be a solid stream of oil. In either case, it means that part of the charge has been lost.

Without Sight Glass

On vehicles that are not equipped with sight glasses, it is necessary to feel the temperature difference in the inlet and outlet lines at the receiver/drier to gauge the refrigerant level. Use the following procedure.

1. Locate the receiver/drier. It will generally be up front near the condenser. It is shaped like a small fire extinguisher and will always have two lines connected to it. One line goes to the expansion valve and the other goes to the condenser.

2. With the engine and the air conditioner running, place one hand on the line between the receiver/drier and the expansion valve, and the other on the line from the compressor to the condenser. Gauge their relative temperatures. If they are both the same approximate temperature, the system is correctly charged.

3. If the line from the expansion valve to the receiver/drier is a lot colder than the line from the condenser to the compressor, then the system is overcharged. It should be noted that this is an extremely rare condition.

4. If the line that leads from the compressor to the condenser is a lot colder than the other line, the system is undercharged.

5. If the system is undercharged or overcharged, have it checked by a professional air conditioning mechanic.

GAUGE SETS

Most of the service work performed in air conditioning requires the use of two gauges, one for the high (head) pressure side of the system, the other for the low (suction).

The low side gauge records both pressure and vacuum. Vacuum readings are calibrated from 0 to no less than 60 psi.

The high side gauge measures pressure from 0 to at least 600 psi. Both gauges are threaded into a manifold that contains two hand shut off valves. Proper manipulation of these valves and the use of the attached test hoses allow the user to perform the following services:

1. Test high and low side pressures.

2. Remove air, moisture, and contaminated refrigerant.

3. Purge the system of refrigerant.

4. Charge the system with refrigerant.

The manifold valves are designed so they have no direct effect on gauge readings, but serve only to provide for, or cut off, flow of re-

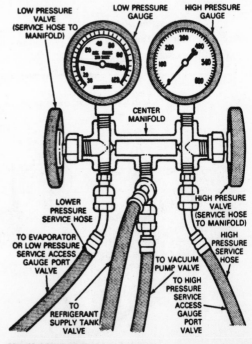

Manifold gauge set

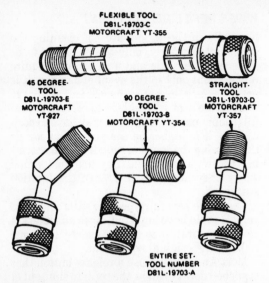

FLEXIBLE TOOL
D81L-19703-C
MOTORCRAFT YT-355

45 DEGREE-
TOOL
D81L-19703-E
MOTORCRAFT
YT-927

90 DEGREE-
TOOL
D81L-19703-B
MOTORCRAFT YT-354

STRAIGHT-
TOOL
D81L-19703-D
MOTORCRAFT
YT-357

ENTIRE SET-
TOOL NUMBER
D81L-19703-A

High pressure service valve and adapter

frigerant through the manifold. During all testing and hook-up operations, the valves are kept in a closed position to avoid disturbing the refrigeration system. The valves are opened only to purge the system of refrigerant or to charge it. When purging the system, the center hose is uncapped at the lower end, and both valves are cracked open slightly. This allows refrigerant pressure to force the entire contents of the system out through the center hose. During charging, the valve on the high side of the manifold is closed, and the valve on the low side is cracked open. Under these conditions, the low pressure in the evaporator will draw refrigerant from the relatively warm refrigerant storage container into the system.

DISCHARGING THE SYSTEM

CAUTION: *Perform in a well ventilated area. The compressed refrigerant used in the air conditioning system expands and evaporates into the atmosphere at a temperature of –21.7°F (–29.8°C) or less. This will freeze any surface (including your eyes) that it contacts. In addition, the refrigerant decomposes into a poisonous gas in the presence of flame.*

1. Operate the air conditioner for at least 10 minutes.
2. Attach the gauges, shut off the engine, and the air conditioner.
3. Place a container or rag at the outlet of the center charging hose on the gauge. The refrigerant will be discharged there and this precaution will control its uncontrolled exposure.
4. Open the low side hand valve on the gauge slightly.
5. Open the high side hand valve slightly.
NOTE: *Too rapid a purging process will be*

identified by the appearance of an oily foam. If this occurs, close the hand valves a little more until this condition stops.

6. Close both hand valves on the gauge set when the pressures read 0 and all the refrigerant has left the system.

NOTE: *The system should always be discharged before attempting to remove any hoses or component parts of the air conditioning system.*

CHARGING

CAUTION: *Never attempt to charge the system by opening the high pressure gauge control while the compressor is operating. The compressor accumulating pressure can burst the refrigerant container, causing severe personal injury.*

Systems With Sight Glass

In this procedure the refrigerant enters the suction side of the system as a vapor while the compressor is running. Before proceeding, the system should be in a partial vacuum after adequate evacuation. Both hand valves on the gauge manifold should be closed.

1. Attach both test hoses to their respective service valve ports. Mid-position manually operated service valves, if present.
2. Install the dispensing valve (closed position) on the refrigerant container. (Single and multiple refrigerant manifolds are available to accommodate one to four 15 oz. cans.)
3. Attach the center charging hose to the refrigerant container valve.
4. Open dispensing valve on the refrigerant valve.
5. Loosen the center charging hose coupler where it connect to the gauge manifold to allow the escaping refrigerant to purge the hose of contaminants.
6. Tighten the center charging hose connector.
7. Purge the low pressure test hose at the gauge manifold.
8. Start the truck engine, roll down the truck windows and adjust the air conditioner to maximum cooling. The truck engine should be at normal operating temperature before proceeding. The heated environment helps the liquid vaporize more efficiently.
9. Crack open the low side hand valve on the manifold. Manipulate the valve so that the refrigerant that enters the system does not cause the low side pressure to exceed 40 psi. Too sudden·a surge may permit the entrance of unwanted liquid to the compressor. Since liquids cannot be compressed, the compressor will suffer damage if compelled to attempt it. If the suction side of the system remains in a vacuum

the system is blocked. Locate and correct the condition before proceeding any further.

NOTE: *Placing the refrigerant can in a container of warm water (no hotter than +125°F [+51.6°C]) will speed the charging process. Slight agitation of the can is helpful too, but be careful not to turn the can upside down.*

Systems Without Sight Glass

When charging the system, attach only the low pressure line to the low pressure gauge port, located on the accumulator. Do not attach the high pressure line to any service port or allow it to remain attached to the pump after evacuation. Be sure both the high and the low pressure control valves are closed on the gauge set. To complete the charging of the system, follow the outline below:

1. Start the engine and allow it to run at idle, with the cooling system at normal operating temperature.

2. Attach the center gauge hose to a single or multican dispenser.

3. With the multican dispenser inverted, allow one pound of the contents of one or two 14 oz. cans to enter the system through the low pressure side by opening the gauge low pressure valve.

4. Close the low pressure gauge control valve and turn the A/C system on to engage the compressor. Place the blower motor in its high mode.

5. Open the low pressure gauge control valve and draw the remaining charge into the system.

6. Close the low pressure gauge control valve and the refrigerant source valve, on the multican dispenser. Remove the low pressure hose from the accumulator quickly to avoid loss of refrigerant through the Schraeder valve.

7. Install the protective cap on the gauge ports and check for leakage.

8. Test the system for proper operation.

NOTE: *This book contains testing and charging procedures for your Ford Bronco's air conditioning system. More comprehensive testing, diagnosis and service procedures may be found in CHILTON'S GUIDE TO AIR CONDITIONING AND REPAIR, book part number 7580, available at your local retailer.*

Windshield Wipers

Intense heat from the sun, snow and ice, road oils and the chemicals used in windshield washer solvents combine to deteriorate the rubber wiper refills. The refills should be replaced about twice a year or whenever the blades begin to streak or chatter.

WIPER REFILL REPLACEMENT

Normally, if the wipers are not cleaning the windshield properly, only the refill has to be replaced. The blade and arm usually require replacement only in the event of damage. It is not necessary (except on new Trico® refills) to remove the arm or the blade to replace the refill (rubber part), though you may have to position the arm higher on the glass. You can do this turning the ignition switch on and operating the wipers. When they are positioned where they are accessible, turn the ignition switch off.

There are several types of refills and your vehicle could have any kind, since aftermarket blades and arms may not use exactly the same refill as the original equipment.

Most Anco® styles use a release button that is pushed down to allow the refill to slide out of the yoke jaws. The new refills slide in and locks in place. Some Anco® refills are removed by locating where the metal backing strip or refill is wider. Insert a small screwdriver blade between the frame and the metal backing strip. Press down to release the refill from the retaining tab.

The Trico® style is unlocked at one end by squeezing 2 metal tabs, and the refill is slid out of the frame jaws. When the new refill is installed, the tabs will click into place, locking the refill.

The polycarbonate type is held in place by a locking lever that is pushed downward out of the groove in the arm to free the refill. When the new refill is installed, it will lock in place automatically.

The Tridon® refill has a plastic backing strip with a notch about an inch from the end. Hold the blade (frame) on a hard surface so that the frame is tightly bowed. Grip the tip of the backing strip and pull up while twisting counterclockwise. The backing strip will snap out of the retaining tab. Do this for the remaining tabs until the refill is free of the arm. The length of these refills is molded into the end and they should be replaced with identical types.

No matter which type of refill you use, be sure that all of the frame claws engage the refill. Before operating the wipers, be sure that no part of the metal frame is contacting the windshield.

Tires and Wheels

The tires should be rotated as specified in the Maintenance Intervals Chart. Refer to the accompanying illustrations for the recommended rotation patterns.

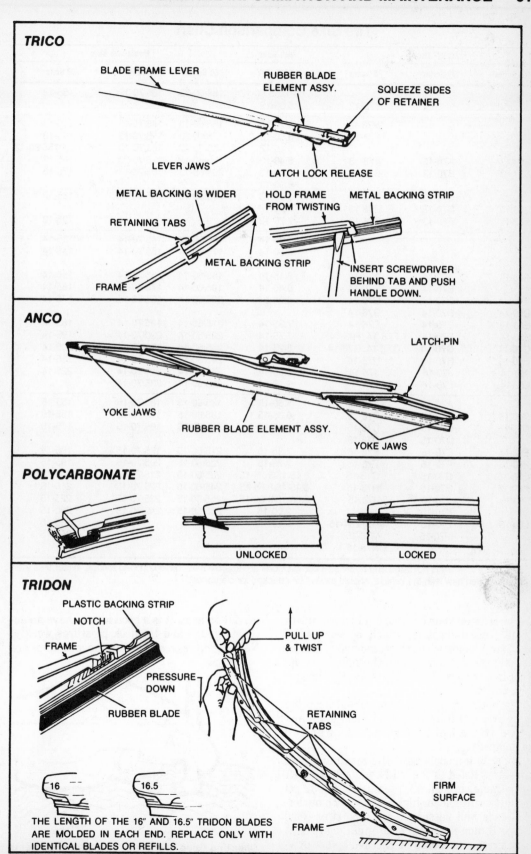

TRICO

BLADE FRAME LEVER

RUBBER BLADE ELEMENT ASSY.

SQUEEZE SIDES OF RETAINER

LEVER JAWS

LATCH LOCK RELEASE

METAL BACKING IS WIDER

RETAINING TABS

METAL BACKING STRIP

FRAME

HOLD FRAME FROM TWISTING

METAL BACKING STRIP

INSERT SCREWDRIVER BEHIND TAB AND PUSH HANDLE DOWN.

ANCO

LATCH-PIN

YOKE JAWS

RUBBER BLADE ELEMENT ASSY.

YOKE JAWS

POLYCARBONATE

UNLOCKED

LOCKED

TRIDON

PLASTIC BACKING STRIP

NOTCH

FRAME

PULL UP & TWIST

PRESSURE DOWN

RUBBER BLADE

RETAINING TABS

16

16.5

THE LENGTH OF THE 16" AND 16.5" TRIDON BLADES ARE MOLDED IN EACH END. REPLACE ONLY WITH IDENTICAL BLADES OR REFILLS.

FIRM SURFACE

FRAME

Popular styles of wiper refills

Tire Size Comparison Chart

"Letter" sizes			inch Sizes	Metric-inch Sizes		
"60 Series"	"70 Series"	"78 Series"	1965–77	"60 Series"	"70 Series"	"80 Series"
		Y78-12	5.50-12, 5.60-12 6.00-12	165/60-12	165/70-12	155-12
		W78-13	5.20-13	165/60-13	145/70-13	135-13
		Y78-13	5.60-13	175/60-13	155/70-13	145-13
			6.15-13	185/60-13	165/70-13	155-13, P155/80-13
A60-13	A70-13	A78-13	6.40-13	195/60-13	175/70-13	165-13
B60-13	B70-13	B78-13	6.70-13	205/60-13	185/70-13	175-13
			6.90-13			
C60-13	C70-13	C78-13	7.00-13	215/60-13	195/70-13	185-13
D60-13	D70-13	D78-13	7.25-13			
E60-13	E70-13	E78-13	7.75-13			195-13
			5.20-14	165/60-14	145/70-14	135-14
			5.60-14	175/60-14	155/70-14	145-14
			5.90-14			
A60-14	A70-14	A78-14	6.15-14	185/60-14	165/70-14	155-14
	B70-14	B78-14	6.45-14	195/60-14	175/70-14	165-14
	C70-14	C78-14	6.95-14	205/60-14	185/70-14	175-14
D60-14	D70-14	D78-14				
E60-14	E70-14	E78-14	7.35-14	215/60-14	195/70-14	185-14
F60-14	F70-14	F78-14, F83-14	7.75-14	225/60-14	200/70-14	195-14
G60-14	G70-14	G77-14, G78-14	8.25-14	235/60-14	205/70-14	205-14
H60-14	H70-14	H78-14	8.55-14	245/60-14	215/70-14	215-14
J60-14	J70-14	J78-14	8.85-14	255/60-14	225/70-14	225-14
L60-14	L70-14		9.15-14	265/60-14	235/70-14	
	A70-15	A78-15	5.60-15	185/60-15	165/70-15	155-15
B60-15	B70-15	B78-15	6.35-15	195/60-15	175/70-15	165-15
C60-15	C70-15	C78-15	6.85-15	205/60-15	185/70-15	175-15
	D70-15	D78-15				
E60-15	E70-15	E78-15	7.35-15	215/60-15	195/70-15	185-15
F60-15	F70-15	F78-15	7.75-15	225/60-15	205/70-15	195-15
G60-15	G70-15	G78-15	8.15-15/8.25-15	235/60-15	215/70-15	205-15
H60-15	H70-15	H78-15	8.45-15/8.55-15	245/60-15	225/70-15	215-15
J60-15	J70-15	J78-15	8.85-15/8.90-15	255/60-15	235/70-15	225-15
	K70-15		9.00-15	265/60-15	245/70-15	230-15
L60-15	L70-15	L78-15, L84-15	9.15-15			235-15
	M70-15	M78-15				255-15
		N78-15				

Note: Every size tire is not listed and many size comparisons are approximate, based on load ratings. Wider tires than those supplied new with the vehicle, should always be checked for clearance.

The tires on your truck should have built-in tread wear indicators, which appear as ½" (12.7mm) bands when the tread depth gets as low as ¹⁄₁₆" (1.6mm). When the indicators appear in 2 or more adjacent grooves, it's time for new tires.

For optimum tire life, you should keep the tires properly inflated, rotate them often and have the wheel alignment checked periodically.

Some late models have the maximum load pressures listed in the V.I.N. plate on the left door frame. In general, pressure of 28–32 psi would be suitable for highway use with moderate loads and passenger car type tires (load range B, non-flotation) of original equipment size. Pressures should be checked before driving, since pressure can increase as much as 6 psi due to heat. It is a good idea to have an accurate gauge and to check pressures weekly. Not all gauges on service station air pumps are

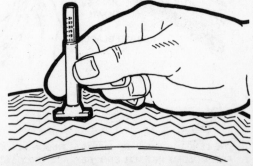

Checking tread depth with an inexpensive depth tester

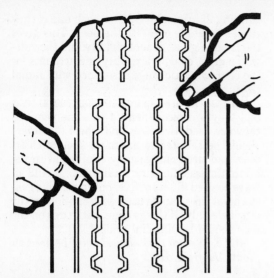

Since 1968, tread wear indicators have been built into tires

to be trusted. In general, truck type tires require higher pressures and flotation type tires, lower pressures.

TIRE ROTATION

It is recommended that you have the tires rotated every 6,000 miles. There is no way to give a tire rotation diagram for every combination of tires and vehicles, but the accompanying diagrams are a general rule to follow. Radial tires should not be cross-switched; they last longer if their direction of rotation is not changed. Truck tires sometimes have directional tread, indicated by arrows on the sidewalls; the arrow shows the direction of rotation. They will wear very rapidly if reversed.

Studded snow tires will lose their studs if their direction of rotation is reversed.

NOTE: *Mark the wheel position or direction of rotation on radial tires or studded snow tires before removing them.*

If your truck is equipped with tires having different load ratings on the front and the rear, the tires should not be rotated front to rear. Rotating these tires could affect tire life (the tires with the lower rating will wear faster, and could become overloaded), and upset the handling of the truck.

TIRE USAGE

The tires on your truck were selected to provide the best all around performance for normal operation when inflated as specified. Oversize tires (Load Range D) will not increase the maximum carrying capacity of the vehicle, although they will provide an extra margin of tread life. Be sure to check overall height before using larger size tires which may cause interference with suspension components or wheel wells. When replacing conventional tire sizes with other tire size designations, be sure to check the manufacturer's recommendations. Interchangeability is not always possible because of differences in load ratings, tire dimensions, wheel well clearances, and rim size. Also due to differences in handling characteristics, 70 Series and 60 Series tires should be used only in pairs on the same axle; radial tires should be used only in sets of four.

The wheels must be the correct width for the tire. Tire dealers have charts of tire and rim compatibility. A mismatch can cause sloppy handling and rapid tread wear. The old rule of thumb is that the tread width should match

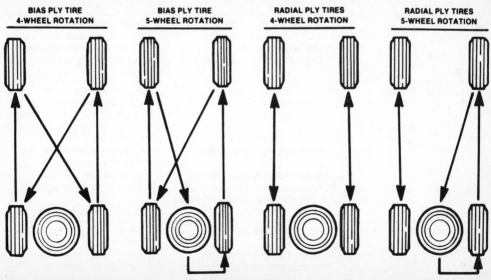

Tire rotation pattern

the rim width (inside bead to inside bead) within an inch. For radial tires, the rim width should be 80% or less of the tire (not tread) width.

The height (mounted diameter) of the new tires can greatly change speedometer accuracy, engine speed at a given road speed, fuel mileage, acceleration, and ground clearance. Tire manufacturers furnish full measurement specifications. Speedometer drive gears are available for correction.

NOTE: *Dimensions of tires marked the same size may vary significantly, even among tires from the same manufacturer.*

The spare tire should be usable, at least for low speed operation, with the new tires.

TIRE DESIGN

For maximum satisfaction, tires should be used in sets of five. Mixing or different types (radial, bias-belted, fiberglass belted) should be avoided. Conventional bias tires are constructed so that the cords run bead-to-bead at an angle. Alternate plies run at an opposite angle. This type of construction gives rigidity to both tread and sidewall. Bias-belted tires are similar in construction to conventional bias ply tires. Belts run at an angle and also at a 90° angle to the bead, as in the radial tire. Tread life is improved considerably over the conventional bias tire. The radial tire differs in construction, but instead of the carcass plies

running at an angle of 90° to each other, they run at an angle of 90° to the bead. This gives the tread a great deal of rigidity and the sidewall a great deal of flexibility and accounts for the characteristic bulge associated with radial tires.

Ford trucks are capable of using radial tires and they are recommended in some years. If they are used, tire sizes and wheel diameters should be selected to maintain ground clearance and tire load capacity equivalent to the minimum specified tire. Radial tires should always be used in sets of five, but in an emergency radial tires can be used with caution on the rear axle only. If this is done, both tires on the rear should be of radial design.

NOTE: *Radial tires should never be used on only the front axle.*

FLUIDS AND LUBRICATIONS

Fuel Recommendations

All Bronco engines through 1974 are designed to operate on regular grade gasoline. If the vehicle is being used for heavy duty service, do not use unleaded gas. If the Bronco is being used in light duty service, a tank of unleaded gas can be used without any problems. If your vehicle pings or knocks, use a high octane fuel or retard the ignition timing of the engine, but

Troubleshooting Basic Wheel Problems

Problem	Cause	Solution
The car's front end vibrates at high speed	• The wheels are out of balance • Wheels are out of alignment	• Have wheels balanced • Have wheel alignment checked/adjusted
Car pulls to either side	• Wheels are out of alignment • Unequal tire pressure • Different size tires or wheels	• Have wheel alignment checked/adjusted • Check/adjust tire pressure • Change tires or wheels to same size
The car's wheel(s) wobbles	• Loose wheel lug nuts • Wheels out of balance • Damaged wheel • Wheels are out of alignment • Worn or damaged ball joint • Excessive play in the steering linkage (usually due to worn parts) • Defective shock absorber	• Tighten wheel lug nuts • Have tires balanced • Raise car and spin the wheel. If the wheel is bent, it should be replaced • Have wheel alignment checked/adjusted • Check ball joints • Check steering linkage • Check shock absorbers
Tires wear unevenly or prematurely	• Incorrect wheel size • Wheels are out of balance • Wheels are out of alignment	• Check if wheel and tire size are compatible • Have wheels balanced • Have wheel alignment checked/adjusted

Troubleshooting Basic Tire Problems

Problem	Cause	Solution
The car's front end vibrates at high speeds and the steering wheel shakes	• Wheels out of balance • Front end needs aligning	• Have wheels balanced • Have front end alignment checked
The car pulls to one side while cruising	• Unequal tire pressure (car will usually pull to the low side) • Mismatched tires • Front end needs aligning	• Check/adjust tire pressure • Be sure tires are of the same type and size • Have front end alignment checked
Abnormal, excessive or uneven tire wear See "How to Read Tire Wear"	• Infrequent tire rotation • Improper tire pressure • Sudden stops/starts or high speed on curves	• Rotate tires more frequently to equalize wear • Check/adjust pressure • Correct driving habits
Tire squeals	• Improper tire pressure • Front end needs aligning	• Check/adjust tire pressure • Have front end alignment checked

not more than 3° from the setting required for normal operation. This is recommended only for an emergency situation until you can get some higher octane fuel. A little knocking at low speeds is acceptable, but continued knock at high speeds is damaging to the engine. All 1975 and later Bronco engines are to be operated on unleaded gasoline only!

Engine Oil Recommendations

Many factors help to determine the proper oil for your Bronco. The big question is what viscosity to use and when. The whole question of viscosity revolves around the lowest anticipated ambient temperature to be encountered before your next oil change. The recommended viscosities for sustained temperatures ranging from below 0°F (−18TC) to above 32°F (0°C) are listed below. Multiviscosity oils are recommended because of their wider range of acceptable temperatures and driving conditions.

NOTE: *Always us detergent oil. Detergent oil does not clean or loosen deposits, it merely prevents or inhibits the formation of deposits.*

Lowest Sustained Air Temperature Anticipated	Multiviscosity Engine Oil
Above 32°F	SAE 10W-30, 10W-40 20W-40, or 20W-50
Above 0°F	SAE 10W-30, or 10W-40
Below 0°F	SAE 5W-20, or 5W-30

OIL LEVEL CHECK

Check the engine oil level every time you fill the gas tank. The oil level should be above the ADD mark and not above the FULL mark on the dipstick. Make sure that the dipstick is inserted into the crankcase as far as possible and that the vehicle is resting on level ground.

NOTE: *The engine oil should be checked only when warm (operating temperature).*

CHANGING OIL AND FILTER

Change the oil and filter according t the Preventive Maintenance Schedule at the end of this chapter. Always use a good brand of the proper viscosity oil and a known brand of oil

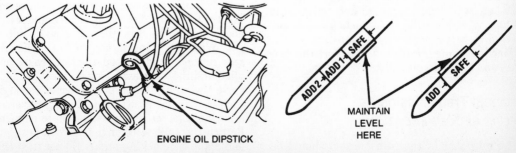

ENGINE OIL DIPSTICK

MAINTAIN LEVEL HERE

Checking engine oil level

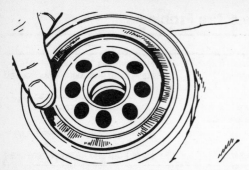

Lubricate the gasket on the new filter with clean engine oil. A dry gasket may not make a good seal and will allow the filter to leak

filter. If the vehicle is driven in severe climate or heavy dust conditions, a more frequent change schedule is advised. It is a good idea to change the filter every time the oil is changed. If the old filter is retained, a quart of dirty oil is left in the engine. Before draining the oil, make sure that the engine is at operating temperature. Hot oil will hold more impurities in suspension and will flow better, allowing the removal of more oil and dirt.

Drain the oil into a suitable receptacle. After the drain plug is loosened, unscrew the plug with your fingers, using a rag to shield your fingers from the heat. Push in on the plug as you unscrew it so you can feel when all of the screw threads are out of the hole. You can then remove the plug quickly with the minimum amount of oil running down your arm and you will also have the plug in your hand and not in the bottom of a pan of hot oil. Be careful of the oil. If it is at operating temperatures it is hot enough to burn you.

To change the filter, raise and support the vehicle on jackstands. Place a container under the filter to catch the oil. The use of a filter wrench is highly recommended. Place the wrench over the filter and loosen it. Remove the wrench and unscrew the filter by hand. If for some reason, the filter will not budge, even when using a filter wrench, drive a screwdriver through the filter near the top. Use this to turn the filter.

When installing a new filter, lubricate the gasket with clean engine oil and tighten the filter by hand until it contacts the engine. Turn it ½ turn past this contact point. Overtightening the filter will distort the gasket and cause an oil leak.

Manual Transmission
FLUID RECOMMENDATION

The lubricant in the transmission should be checked and changed periodically, except when the vehicle has been operated in deep water and water has entered the transmission. When this happens, change the lubricant in the transmission as soon as possible. Use SAE 80/90 gear oil only, in the manual transmission

LEVEL CHECK

Before checking the lubricant level in the transmission, make sure that the vehicle is on level ground. Remove the fill plug from the right side of the transmission. Remove the plug slowly when it starts to reach the end of the threads on the plug. Hold the plug up against the hole and move it away slowly. This is to minimize the loss of lubricant through the fill hole. The level of the lubricant should be up to the bottom of the fill hole. If lubricant is not present at the bottom of the fill hole, add SAE 90 or 80 transmission lube until it reaches the proper level. A squeeze bottle or siphon gun is used to fill a manual transmission with lubricant.

DRAIN AND REFILL

Drain and refill the transmission daily if the vehicle has been operating in water. All you have to do is remove the drain plug which is located at the bottom of the transmission. Allow all the lubricant to run out before replacing the plug. Replace the oil with the correct fluid. If you are experiencing hard shifting and the weather is very cold, use a lighter weight fluid in the transmission. If you don't have a pressure gun to install the oil, use a suction gun.

Automatic Transmission
FLUID RECOMMENDATIONS

Use only Type F transmission fluid for models 1966–77 and type CJ or Dexron®II for 1978–86 models.

LEVEL CHECK

The fluid level in an automatic transmission is checked when the transmission is at operating temperatures. If the vehicle has been sitting and is cold, drive it at highway speeds for at least 20 minutes to warm up the transmission. The transmission dipstick is located under the hood, against the firewall, on the right side.

1. With the transmission in Park, the engine running at idle speed, the foot brakes applied and the vehicle resting on level ground, move the transmission gear selector through each of the gear positions, including Reverse, allowing time for the transmission to engage. Return the shift selector to the Park position and apply the parking brake. Do not turn the engine off, but leave it running at idle speed.

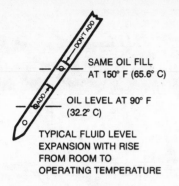

SAME OIL FILL
AT 150° F (65.6° C)

OIL LEVEL AT 90° F
(32.2° C)

TYPICAL FLUID LEVEL
EXPANSION WITH RISE
FROM ROOM TO
OPERATING TEMPERATURE

2. Clean all dirt from around the transmission dipstick cap and the end of the filler tube.

3. Pull the dipstick out of the tube, wipe it off with a clean cloth, and push it back into the tube all the way, making sure that it seats completely.

4. Pull the dipstick out of the tube again and read the level of the fluid on the stick. The level should be between the ADD and FULL marks. If fluid must be added, add enough fluid through the tube to raise the level up to between the ADD and FULL marks. Do not overfill the transmission because this will cause foaming and loss of fluid through the vent and malfunctioning of the transmission.

DRAIN AND REFILL

The transmission is filled at the factory with a high quality fluid that both transmits power and lubricates and will last a long time. In most cases, the need to change the fluid in the automatic transmission will never arise under normal use. But since this is a 4-WD vehicle and most likely will be subject to more severe operating conditions than a conventional vehicle, the fluid may have to be replaced. An in-

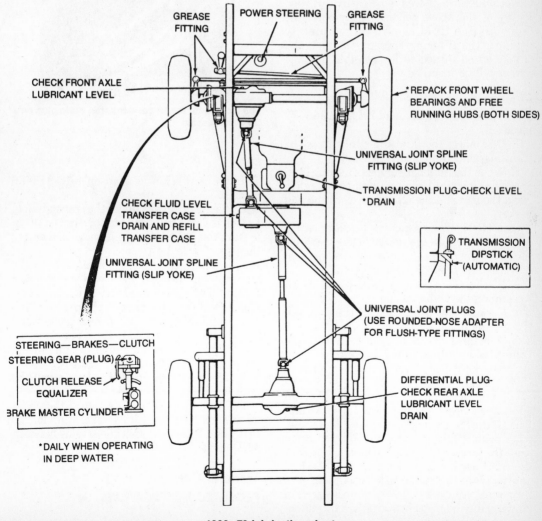

GREASE FITTING

POWER STEERING

GREASE FITTING

CHECK FRONT AXLE
LUBRICANT LEVEL

*REPACK FRONT WHEEL
BEARINGS AND FREE
RUNNING HUBS (BOTH SIDES)

UNIVERSAL JOINT SPLINE
FITTING (SLIP YOKE)

TRANSMISSION PLUG-CHECK LEVEL
*DRAIN

CHECK FLUID LEVEL
TRANSFER CASE
*DRAIN AND REFILL
TRANSFER CASE

TRANSMISSION
DIPSTICK
(AUTOMATIC)

UNIVERSAL JOINT SPLINE
FITTING (SLIP YOKE)

UNIVERSAL JOINT PLUGS
(USE ROUNDED-NOSE ADAPTER
FOR FLUSH-TYPE FITTINGS)

STEERING—BRAKES—CLUTCH
STEERING GEAR (PLUG)
CLUTCH RELEASE
EQUALIZER
BRAKE MASTER CYLINDER

DIFFERENTIAL PLUG-
CHECK REAR AXLE
LUBRICANT LEVEL
DRAIN

*DAILY WHEN OPERATING
IN DEEP WATER

1966–79 lubrication chart

ternal leak in the radiator could develop and contaminate the fluid, necessitating fluid replacement.

The extra load of operating the vehicle in deep sand, towing a heavy trailer, etc., causes the transmission to create more heat due to increased friction. This extra heat is transferred to the transmission fluid and, if the oil is allowed to become too hot, it will change its chemical composition or become scorched. When this occurs, valve bodies become clogged and the transmission doesn't operate as efficiently as it should. Serious damage to the transmission can result.

You can tell if the transmission fluid is scorched by noting a distinctive burned smell and discoloration. Scorched transmission fluid is dark brown or black as opposed to its normal bright, clear red color. Since transmission fluid "cooks" in stages, it may develop forms of sludge or varnish. Pull the dipstick out and place the end on a tissue or paper towel. Particles of sludge can be seen more easily this way. If any of the above conditions do exist, the transmission fluid should be completely drained, the filtering screens cleaned, the transmission inspected for possible damage and new fluid installed.

C4

This transmission is used on all 1966–77 models.

1. Disconnect the fluid filler tube from the transmission pan to drain the fluid.

2. When the fluid has stopped draining from the transmission, remove and thoroughly clean the pan and the screen. Discard the pan gasket.

CAUTION: *When removing the filter on C4 transmissions, be careful not to lose the throttle pressure limit valve and spring when separating the filter from the valve body.*

3. Place a new gasket on the pan and install the pan on the transmission.

4. Connect the filler tube to the pan and tighten the fitting securely.

5. Add three quarts of type F fluid to the transmission through the dipstick tube.

6. Check the fluid level. With the transmission at room temperatures (70–95°F [21–35°C]) and the engine idling, the level should be between the middle and top holes on the dipstick. If the fluid level is below the middle hole, add enough fluid through the filler tube to raise the level to between the middle hole and the ADD mark. Please not that this check is only for when the transmission is at room temperatures. See the Fluid Level Checks section for checking the transmission when it is at operating temperatures

7. Replace the dipstick.

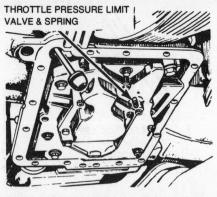

C4 throttle pressure limit valve and spring. They are held in place by the filter. The valve is installed with the large end toward the valve body; the spring fits over the valve stem

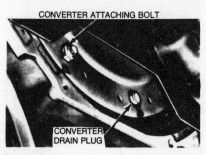

The location of the torque converter drain plug on a C4 transmission

C6

This transmission is used on all 1978–86 models.

1. Place a drain pan under the transmission. Loosen the pan bolts and pull one corner down to start the fluid draining. Remove and empty the pan.

2. When all the fluid has drained from the transmission, remove and clean the pan and screen. Make sure not to leave any solvent residue or lint from the rags in the pan.

3. Install the pan with a new gasket and tighten the bolts in a criss-cross pattern.

4. Add three quarts of fluid through the dipstick tube. Use type CJ (Ford Spec. ESP-M2C138-CJ) or Dexron®II. The level should be at or below the ADD mark.

5. Check the fluid level as soon as the transmission reaches operating temperature for the first time. Make sure that the level is between ADD and full.

Transfer Case
FLUID RECOMMENDATIONS

Use the recommended fluids listed below when refilling or adding fluid.

Transmission Fluid Indications

The appearance and odor of the transmission fluid can give valuable clues to the overall condition of the transmission. Always note the appearance of the fluid when you check the fluid level or change the fluid. Rub a small amount of fluid between your fingers to feel for grit and smell the fluid on the dipstick.

If the fluid appears:	It indicates:
Clear and red colored	• Normal operation
Discolored (extremely dark red or brownish) or smells burned	• Band or clutch pack failure, usually caused by an overheated transmission. Hauling very heavy loads with insufficient power or failure to change the fluid, often result in overheating. Do not confuse this appearance with newer fluids that have a darker red color and a strong odor (though not a burned odor).
Foamy or aerated (light in color and full of bubbles)	• The level is too high (gear train is churning oil) • An internal air leak (air is mixing with the fluid). Have the transmission checked professionally.
Solid residue in the fluid	• Defective bands, clutch pack or bearings. Bits of band material or metal abrasives are clinging to the dipstick. Have the transmission checked professionally.
Varnish coating on the dipstick	• The transmission fluid is overheating

- 1966–77 all models; SAE 50 above 10°F (–12°C); SAE 30 below 10°F (–12°C)
- 1978–79 New Process 205: SAE 90
  New Process 203: SAE 90
- 1980–86 all models: Dexron®II or Ford CJ

LEVEL CHECK

Position the vehicle on level ground. Remove the transfer case full plug located on the left side of the transfer case. The fluid level should be up on the fill hole. If lubricant doesn't run out when the plug is removed, add lubricant until it does run out and then replace the fill plug.

DRAIN AND REFILL

The transfer case is serviced at the same time and in the same manner as the transmission. Clean the area around the filler and drain

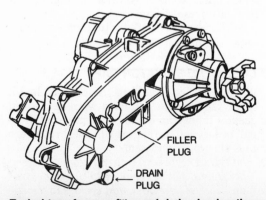

Typical transfer case filler and drain plug locations (New Process case shown)

plugs and remove the filler plug on the side of the transfer case. Remove the drain plug on the bottom of the transfer case and allow the lubricant to drain completely. Clean and install the drain plug. Add the proper lubricant

Front and Rear Axle

FLUID RECOMMENDATIONS

Use hypoid gear lubricant SAE 80 or 90.
  NOTE: *On models with the front locking differential, add 2 oz. of friction modifier Ford part #EST-M2C118-A. On models with the rear locking differential, use only locking differential fluid Ford part #ESW-M2C119-A or its equivalent.*

LEVEL CHECK

Clean the area around the fill plug, which is located in the housing cover, before removing the plug. The lubricant level should be maintained to the bottom of the fill hole with the axle in its normal running position. If lubricant does not appear at the hole when the plug is removed, additional lubricant should be added.

DRAIN AND REFILL

Drain and refill the front and rear axle housings according to the Preventive Maintenance Schedule at the end of this chapter. Remove the oil with a suction gun. Refill the axle housing with the proper oil. Be sure and clean the area around the drain plug before removing the plug.

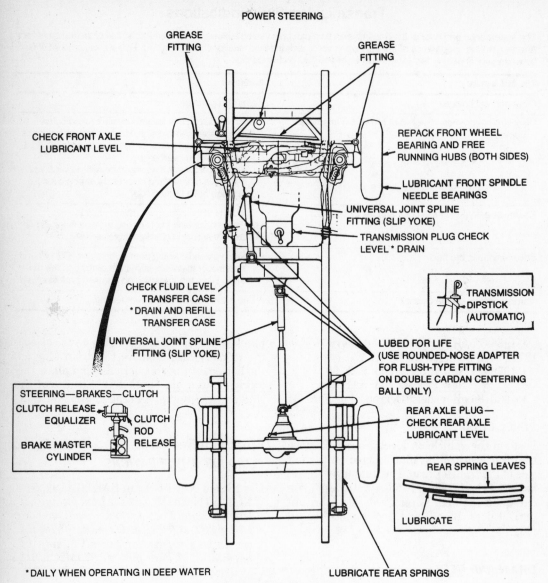

POWER STEERING

GREASE FITTING

GREASE FITTING

CHECK FRONT AXLE LUBRICANT LEVEL

REPACK FRONT WHEEL BEARING AND FREE RUNNING HUBS (BOTH SIDES)

LUBRICANT FRONT SPINDLE NEEDLE BEARINGS

UNIVERSAL JOINT SPLINE FITTING (SLIP YOKE)

TRANSMISSION PLUG CHECK LEVEL * DRAIN

CHECK FLUID LEVEL TRANSFER CASE *DRAIN AND REFILL TRANSFER CASE

UNIVERSAL JOINT SPLINE FITTING (SLIP YOKE)

TRANSMISSION DIPSTICK (AUTOMATIC)

LUBED FOR LIFE (USE ROUNDED-NOSE ADAPTER FOR FLUSH-TYPE FITTING ON DOUBLE CARDAN CENTERING BALL ONLY)

STEERING—BRAKES—CLUTCH

CLUTCH RELEASE EQUALIZER

CLUTCH ROD RELEASE

BRAKE MASTER CYLINDER

REAR AXLE PLUG— CHECK REAR AXLE LUBRICANT LEVEL

REAR SPRING LEAVES

LUBRICATE

*DAILY WHEN OPERATING IN DEEP WATER

LUBRICATE REAR SPRINGS

1980—86 lubrication chart

Cooling System

At least once every 2 years, the engine cooling system should be inspected, flush, and refill with fresh coolant. If the coolant is left in the system too long, it loses its ability to prevent rust and corrosion. If the coolant has too much water, it won't protect against freezing.

The pressure cap should be looked at for signs of age or deterioration. Fan belt and other drive belts should be inspected add adjusted to the proper tension.

Hose clamps should be tightened, and soft or cracked hoses replaced. Damp spots, or accumulations of rust or dye near hoses, water pump or other areas, indicate possible leakage, which must be corrected before filling the system with fresh coolant.

NOTE: *Never remove the radiator cap under any conditions while the engine is hot.*

CHECK THE RADIATOR CAP

While you are checking the coolant level, check the radiator cap for a worn or cracked gasket. If the cap doesn't seal properly, fluid will be lost and the engine will overheat. Worn caps should be replaced.

NOTE: *The locking type radiator cap assembly should not be removed to check the coolant level. If necessary, add coolant to the reservoir only.*

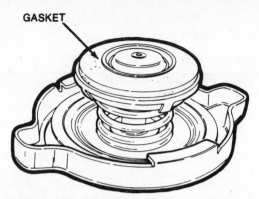

Checking the radiator cap gasket for cracks or wear

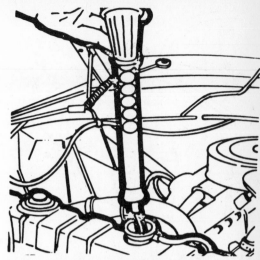

Testing coolant condition with a tester

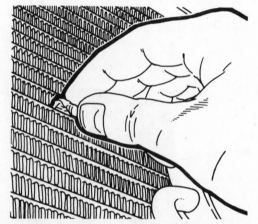

Keep the radiator fins clear of debris for maximum cooling

CLEAN RADIATOR OF DEBRIS

Periodically clean any debris--leaves, paper, insects, etc.--from the radiator fins. Pick the large pieces off by hand. The smaller pieces can be washed away with water pressure from a hose.

Carefully straighten any bent radiator fins with a pair of needle nose pliers. Be careful! The fins are very soft. Don't wiggle the fins back and forth too much. Straighten them once and try not to move them again.

FLUID RECOMMENDATIONS

Coolant mixture in Broncos is 50/50 ethylene glycol and water for year round use. Use a good quality antifreeze with water pump lubricants, rust inhibitors and other corrosion inhibitors along with acid neutralizers.

DRAIN AND REFILL THE COOLING SYSTEM

Completely draining and refilling the cooling system every two years at least will remove accumulated rust, scale and other deposits.

1. Drain the existing antifreeze and coolant. Open the radiator and engine drain petcocks, or disconnect the bottom radiator hose, at the radiator outlet.
NOTE: *Before opening the radiator petcock, spray it with some penetrating lubricant.*
2. Close the petcock or reconnect the lower hose and fill the system with water.
3. Add a can of quality radiator flush.
4. Idle the engine until the upper radiator hose gets hot.
5. Drain the system again.
6. Repeat this process until the drained water is clear and free of scale.
7. Close all petcocks and connect all the hoses.
8. If equipped with a coolant recovery system, flush the reservoir with water and leave empty.
9. Determine the capacity of your cooling system (see capacities specifications). Add a 50/50 mix of quality antifreeze (ethylene glycol) and water to provide the desired protection.
10. Run the engine to operating temperature.
11. Stop the engine and check the coolant level.
12. Check the level of protection with an antifreeze tester, replace the cap and check for leaks.

Brake Master Cylinder

The master cylinder reservoir is located under the hood, on the left side firewall.

FLUID RECOMMENDATIONS

Fill the master cylinder with a good quality Heavy Duty Brake Fluid.

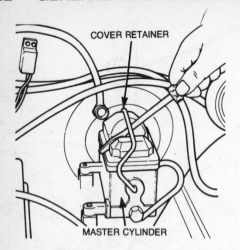

COVER RETAINER

MASTER CYLINDER

LEVEL CHECK

Before removing the master cylinder reservoir cap, make sure the vehicle is resting on level ground and clean all dirt away from the top of the master cylinder. Pry off the retaining clip and remove the cap. The brake fluid level should be within ½" (12.7mm) of the top of the reservoir.

If the level of the brake fluid is less than half the volume of the reservoir, it is advised that you check the brake system for leaks. Leaks in a hydraulic brake system most commonly occur at the wheel cylinder.

There is a rubber diaphragm in the top of the master cylinder cap. As the fluid level lowers in the reservoir due to normal brake shoe wear or leakage, the diaphragm takes up the space. This is t prevent the loss of brake fluid out the vented cap and contamination by dirt. After filling the master cylinder to the proper level with brake fluid, but before replacing the cap, fold the rubber diaphragm up into the cap, then replace the cap on the reservoir and tighten the retaining bolt or snap the retaining clip into place.

Power Steering Reservoir
FLUID RECOMMENDATIONS

Fill the power steering reservoir with a good quality power steering fluid or Auto. Trans. Fluid-Type **F**.

LEVEL CHECK

Position the vehicle on level ground. Run the engine until the fluid is at normal operating temperature. Turn the steering wheel all the way to the left and right several times. Position the wheels in the straight ahead position, then shut off the engine. Check the fluid level on the dipstick which is attached to the reservoir cap. The level should be between the ADD

and FULL marks on the dipstick. Add fluid accordingly. Do not overfill.

Steering Gear
FLUID RECOMMENDATION

Fill the steering gear (manual) housing with a good quality Steering Gear Grease.

LEVEL CHECK

The steering gear is located under the hood, on the left side at the end of the steering shaft. Clean the area around the filler plug of the steering gear, remove the plug and check to see if the level of the lubricant is visible in the filler plug tower. If it is, replace the plug. If it is not, add steering gear lubricant until the level is visible about 1 inch from the top of the hole in filler plug tower. Reinstall the fill plug.

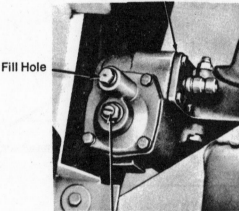

Worm Bearing
Preload Shims

Fill Hole

Worm and Roller
Mesh Adjustment

Chassis Greasing

The preceding charts indicate where the grease fittings are located on the Bronco, and other level checks that should be made at the time of the chassis grease job. The vehicle should be greased according to the Preventive Maintenance Schedule at the end of this chapter, and more often if the vehicle is operating in dusty areas or under heavy duty conditions. If the vehicle is operated in deep water, lubricate the chassis every day.

Body Lubrication
HOOD LATCH AND HINGES

Clean the latch surfaces and apply clean engine oil to the latch pilot bolts and the spring anchor. Also lubricate the hood hinges with engine oil. Use a chassis grease to lubricate all the pivot points in the latch release mechanism.

DOOR HINGES

The gas tank filler door and truck doors should be wiped clean and lubricated with clean engine oil once a year. The door lock cylinders and latch mechanisms should be lubricated periodically with a few drops of graphite lock lubricant or a few shots of silicone spray.

Wheel Bearings

It is recommended that the front wheel bearings be cleaned, inspected and repacked periodically and as soon as possible after the front hubs have been submerged in water.

NOTE: *Sodium based grease is not compatible with lithium based grease. Be careful not to mix the two types. The best way to prevent this is to completely clean all of the old grease from the hub assembly before installing any new grease.*

Before handling the bearings there are a few things that you should remember to do and try to avoid.

Do the following:

1. Remove all outside dirt fro the housing before exposing the bearing.

2. Treat a used bearing as gently as you would a new one.

3. Work with clean tools in clean surroundings.

4. Use clean, dry canvas gloves, or at least clean, dry hands.

5. Clean solvents and flushing fluids are a must.

6. Use a clean paper when laying out the bearings to dry.

7. Protect disassembled bearings from rust and dirt. Cover them up.

8. Use clean rags to wipe bearings.

9. Keep the bearings in oil proof paper when they are to be stored or are not in use.

10. Clean the inside of the housing before replacing the bearing.

Do NOT do the following:

1. Don't work in dirty surroundings.

2. Don't use dirty, chipped, or damaged tools.

3. Try not to work on wooden work benches or use wooden mallets.

4. Don't handle bearings with dirty or moist hands.

5. Do not us gasoline for cleaning; use a safe solvent.

6. Do not spin dry bearings with compressed air. They will be damaged.

7. Do not spin unclean bearings.

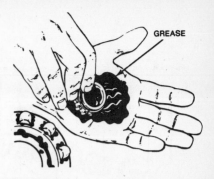

8. Avoid using cotton waste or dirty clothes to wipe bearings.

9. Try not to scratch or nick bearing surfaces.

10. Do not allow the bearing to come in contact with dirt or rust at any time.

FRONT WHEEL BEARINGS WITHOUT FREE RUNNING HUBS

For free running hubs, see Chapter 7.

NOTE: *Sodium based grease is not compatible with lithium based grease. Be careful not to mix the two types. The best way to prevent this is to completely clean all of the old grease from the hub assembly before installing any new grease.*

1. Raise the front of the vehicle and place jackstands under the vehicle. Remove the wheel.

2. Remove the front hub grease cap and driving hub snapring.

3. Remove the splined driving hub and the pressure spring. this may require slight prying.

4. Remove the wheel bearing locknut, lockring and adjusting nut.

5. Drum Brakes: Remove the hub and drum assembly. This may require that the brake adjusting screw be backed off to move the brake shoes away from the brake drum. The outer wheel bearing and spring retainer will slide out as the hub is removed.

Disc Brakes: See the brake section, Chapter 8, for caliper removal. Suspend the caliper out of the way and remove the hub and rotor assembly.

6. Carefully drive out the inner bearing cone and grease seal from the hub.

7. Inspect the bearing caps (races) for cracks and pits. If the cups are excessively worn or there are pits or cracks visible, replace them along with the cones. The cups are removed from the hub by driving them out with a drift pin. They are installed in the same manner.

8. If it is determined that the cups are in satisfactory condition and are to remain in the hub, clean and inspect the cones (bearings).

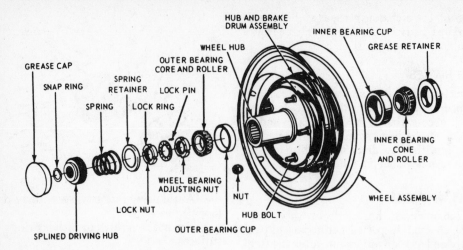

Refer to the bearing diagnosis chart. Replace the bearings if necessary. If it is necessary to replace either the cone or the cup, both parts should be replaced as a unit.

9. Thoroughly clean all components in a suitable solvent and blow them dry with compressed air or allow them to dry while resting on clean paper.

NOTE: *Do not spin the bearings with compressed air while drying them.*

10. Cover the spindle with a cloth and brush all loose dust and dirt from the brake assembly. Remove the cloth and thoroughly clean the inside of the hub and the spindle.

11. Pack the inside of the hub with wheel bearing grease. Add grease to the hub until the grease is flush with the inside diameter of the bearing cup.

12. Pack the bearing cone and roller assembly with wheel bearing grease. A bearing packer is desirable for this operation. If a packer is not available, place a large portion of grease into the palm of your hand and sliding the edge of the roller cage through the grease with your other hand, work as much grease in between the rollers as possible.

13. Position the inner bearing into the inner bearing cup and install the new grease seal.

14. Carefully position the hub assembly onto the spindle. Be careful not to damage the new seal. Install the drum or caliper.

15. Place the outer bearing into position on the spindle and into the bearing cup.

16. Install the bearing adjusting nut and tighten it to 50 ft.lb. while rotating the hub back and forth to seat the bearings.

17. Back off the adjusting nut about 90°.

18. Assemble the lockring by turning the nut to the nearest notch where the dowel pin will enter.

19. Install the outer locknut and torque to 80–100 ft.lb. The final endplay of the wheel on the spindle should be 0.001–0.010″ (0.025–0.254mm).

20. Install the pressure spring retainer,

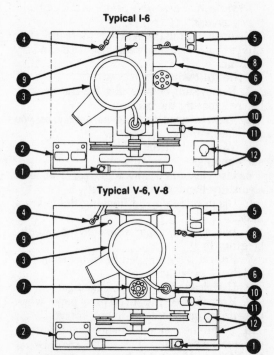

Typical I-6

Typical V-6, V-8

1. Radiator filler cap
2. Battery
3. Air cleaner
4. Automatic transmission dipstick
5. Brake master cylinder
6. Engine oil filter
7. Distributor
8. Engine oil dipstick
9. PCV valve
10. Engine oil filler cap
11. Power steering reservoir
12. Windshield washer reservoir and radiator overflow bottle

Engine compartment service points

spring, and driving hub and driving hub snapring. This is for vehicles without free running hubs.

21. Install the grease cap and adjust the brakes, if they were backed off to remove the hub assembly. Remove the jackstands and lower the vehicle.

TRAILER TOWING

Ford Broncos have long been popular as trailer towing vehicles. Their strong construction, and wide range of engine/transmission combinations make them ideal for towing campers, boat trailers and utility trailers.

Factory trailer towing packages are available on most Ford trucks, if you are installing a trailer hitch and wiring on your Bronco, there are a few thing that you ought to know.

Trailer Weight

Trailer weight is the first, and most important, factor in determining whether or not your vehicle is suitable for towing the trailer you have in mind. The horsepower-to-weight ratio should be calculated. The basic standard is a ratio of 35:1. That is, 35 pounds of GVW for every horsepower.

To calculate this ratio, multiply you engine's rated horsepower by 35, then subtract the weight of the vehicle, including passengers and luggage. The resulting figure is the ideal maximum trailer weight that you can tow. One point to consider: a numerically higher axle ratio can offset what appears to be a low trailer weight. If the weight of the trailer that you have in mind is somewhat higher than the weight you just calculated, you might consider changing your rear axle ratio to compensate.

Hitch Weight

There are three kinds of hitches: bumper mounted, frame mounted, and load equalizing.

Bumper mounted hitches are those which attach solely to the vehicle's bumper. Many states prohibit towing with this type of hitch, when it attaches to the vehicle's stock bumper, since it subjects the bumper to stresses for which it was not designed. Aftermarket rear step bumpers, designed for trailer towing, are acceptable for use with bumper mounted hitches.

Frame mounted hitches can be of the type which bolts to two or more points on the frame, plus the bumper, or just to several points on the frame. Frame mounted hitches can also be of the tongue type, for Class I towing, or, of the receiver type, for classes II and III.

Load equalizing hitches are usually used for large trailers. Most equalizing hitches are welded in place and use equalizing bars and chains to level the vehicle after the trailer is hooked up.

The bolt-on hitches are the most common, since they are relatively easy to install.

Check the gross weight rating of your trailer. Tongue weight is usually figured as 10% of gross trailer weight. Therefore, a trailer with a maximum gross weight of 2,000 lb. will have a maximum tongue weight of 200 lb. Class I tarilers fall into this category. Class II trailers are those with a gross weight rating of 2,000–3,500 lb., while Class III trailers fall into the 3,500–6,000 lb. category. Class IV trailers are those over 6,000 lb. and are for use with fifth wheel trucks, only.

When you've determined the hitch that you'll need, follow the manufacturer's installation instructions, exactly, especially when it comes to fastener torques. The hitch will subjected to a lot of stress and good hitches come with hardened bolts. Never substitute an inferior bolt for a hardened bolt.

Wiring

Wiring the truck for towing is fairly easy. There are a number of good wiring kits available and these should be used, rather than trying to design your own. All trailers will need brake lights and turn signals as well as tail lights and side marker lights. Most states require extra marker lights for overwide trailers. Also, most states have recently required back-up lights for trailers, and most trailer manufacturers have been building trailers with back-up lights for several years.

Additionally, some Class I, most Class II and just about all Class III trailers will have electric brakes.

Add to this number an accessories wire, to operate trailer internal equipment or to charge the trailer's battery, and you can have as many as seven wires in the harness.

Determine the equipment on your trailer and buy the wiring kit necessary. The kit will contain all the wires needed, plus a plug adapter set which included the female plug, mounted on the bumper or hitch, and the male plug, wired into, or plugged into the trailer harness.

When installing the kit, follow the manufacturer's instructions. The color coding of the wires is standard throughout the industry.

One point to note: some domestic vehicles, and most imported vehicles, have separate turn signals. On most domestic vehicles, the brake lights and rear turn signals operate with the same bulb. For those vehicles with separate turn signals, you can purchase an isolation unit so that the brake lights won't blink whenever the turn signals are operated, or, you can go to your local electronics supply house and buy four diodes to wire in series with the brake and turn signal bulbs. Diodes will isolate the brake and turn signals. The choice is yours. The isolation units are simple and quick to install, but far more expensive than the diodes. The diodes, however, require more work to install properly, since they require the cutting of each bulb's wire and soldering in place of the diode.

One, final point, the best kits are those with a spring loaded cover on the vehicle mounted socket. This cover prevent dirt and moisture from corroding the terminals. Never let the vehicle socket hang loosely; always mount it securely to the bumper or hitch.

Cooling
ENGINE

One of the most common, if not THE most common, problems associated with trailer towing is engine overheating.

With factory installed trailer towing packages, a heavy duty cooling system is usually included. Heavy duty cooling systems are available as optional equipment on most Ford vehicles, with or without a trailer package. If you have one of these extra capacity systems, you shouldn't have any overheating problems.

If you have a standard cooling system, without an expansion tank, you'll definitely need to get an aftermarket expansion tank kit, preferably one with at least a 2 quart capacity. These kits are easily installed on the radiator's overflow hose, and come with a pressure cap designed for expansion tanks.

Another helpful accessory is a Flex Fan. These fan are large diameter units are designed to provide more airflow at low speeds, with blades that have deeply cupped surfaces. The blades then flex, or flatten out, at high speed, when less cooling air is needed. These fans are far lighter in weight than stock fans, requiring less horsepower to drive them. Also, they are far quieter than stock fans.

If you do decide to replace your stock fan with a flex fan, note that if your Bronco has a fan clutch, a spacer between the flex fan and water pump hub will be needed.

Aftermarket engine oil coolers are helpful for prolonging engine oil life and reducing overall engine temperatures. Both of these factors increase engine life.

While not absolutely necessary in towing Class I and some Class II trailers, they are recommended for heavier Class II and all Class III towing.

Engine oil cooler systems consist of an adapter, screwed on in place of the oil filter, a remote filter mounting and a multi-tube, finned heat exchanger, which is mounted in front of the radiator or air conditioning condenser.

TRANSMISSION

An automatic transmission is usually recommended for trailer towing. Modern automatics have proven reliable and, of course, easy to operate, in trailer towing.

The increased load of a trailer, however, causes an increase in the temperature of the automatic transmission fluid. Heat is the worst enemy of an automatic transmission. As the temperature of the fluid increases, the life of the fluid decreases.

It is essential, therefore, that you install an automatic transmission cooler. The cooler, which consists of a multi-tube, finned heat exchanger, is usually installed in front of the radiator or air conditioning compressor, and hooked inline with the transmission cooler tank inlet line. Follow the cooler manufacturer's installation instructions.

Select a cooler of at least adequate capacity, based upon the combined gross weights of the truck and trailer.

Cooler manufacturers recommend that you use an aftermarket cooler in addition to, and not instead of, the present cooling tank in your Bronco's radiator. If you do want to use it in place of the radiator cooling tank, get a cooler at least two sizes larger than normally necessary.

One note: transmission cooler can, sometimes, cause slow or harsh shifting in the transmission during cold weather, until the fluid has a chance to come up to normal operating temperature. Some coolers can be purchased with or retrofitted with a temperature bypass valve which will allow fluid flow through the cooler only when the fluid has reached operating temperature, or above.

PUSHING AND TOWING

To push-start your vehicle, (manual transmissions only) follow the procedures below. Check to make sure that the bumpers of both vehicles are aligned so neither will be damaged. Be sure that all electrical system components are turned off (headlights, heater, blower, etc.). Turn on the ignition switch. Place the shift lever in Third or Fourth and push in the clutch pedal. At about 15 mph, signal the driver of the pushing vehicle to fall back, depress the accelerator pedal, and release the clutch pedal slowly. The engine should start.

When you are doing the pushing or pulling, make sure that the two bumpers match so you won't damage the vehicle you are to push. Another good idea is to put an old tire between the two vehicles. If the bumpers don't match, perhaps you should tow the other vehicle. Decide whether or not you are going to use 4-wd or low range. Do the road surface conditions warrant its use? If the other vehicle is just stuck, use First gear to slowly push it out. Tell the driver of the other vehicle to go slowly too. Try to keep your Bronco right up against the other vehicle while you are pushing. If the two vehicles do separate, stop and start over again instead of trying to catch up and ramming the other vehicle. Also try, as much as possible, to avoid ridding or slipping the clutch. Low range makes this easy. When the other vehicle gains enough traction, it should pull away from your vehicle.

If you have to tow the other vehicle, make sure that the tow chain or rope is sufficiently long and strong, and that it is attached securely to both vehicles at a strong place. Attach the chain at a point on the frame or as close to it as possible. Once again, go slowly and tell the other driver to do the same. Warn the other driver not to allow too much slack in the line when he gains traction and can move under his own power. Otherwise he may run over the tow line and damage both vehicles. If your Bronco has to be towed by a tow truck, it can be towed forward for any distance with the driveshaft connected as long as it is done fairly slowly. Otherwise disconnect the driveshaft at the rear axle and tie it up. If your Bronco has to be towed backward, remove the front axle driving hubs, or disengage the lockout hub to prevent the front differential from rotating. If the drive hubs are removed, improvise a cover to keep out dust and dirt.

JUMP STARTING

Jump starting is the only way to start an automatic transmission model with a weak battery, and the best method for a manual transmission model.

CAUTION: *Do not attempt this procedure on a frozen battery; it will probably explode. Do not attempt in a sealed battery showing a light color in the charge indicator.*

1. Turn off all electrical equipment. Place the automatic transmission in Park or the manual in Neutral and set the parking brake.
2. Make sure that the two vehicles are not

touching. It is a good idea to keep the engine running in the booster vehicle.

3. Remove the caps from both batteries and cover the openings with cloths. This isn't necessary on batteries with the sponge type flame arrestor filler/vent caps. It isn't possible on the sealed battery.

4. Attach one end of a jumper cable to the positive (+) terminal of the booster battery. The red cable is usually positive. Attach the other end to the positive terminal of the discharged battery.

CAUTION: *Be very careful about these connections. An alternator and regulator can be destroyed in a remarkably short time if battery polarity is reversed.*

5. Attach one end of the other cable (the black one) to the negative (–) terminal of the booster battery. Attach the other end to a ground point such as the alternator bracket in the engine of the truck being started. Do not connect it to the battery.

CAUTION: *Be careful not to lean over the battery while making this last connection.*

6. If the engine will not start, disconnect the batteries as soon as possible. If this is not done, the two batteries will soon reach a state of equilibrium, with both too weak to start an engine. This is no problem if the engine of the booster vehicle is running fast enough to keep up the charge. Lengthy cranking can also damage the starter.

7. Reverse the procedure exactly to remove the jumper cables. Discard the rags, because they may have acid on them.

NOTE: *It is recognized that some or all of the precautions outlined in this procedure are often ignored with no harmful results. However, the procedure outlined is the only fully safe, foolproof one.*

JACKING AND HOISTING

It is very important to be careful about running the engine, on vehicles equipped with limited slip differentials, while the vehicle is up on a jack. This is because id the drive train is engaged, power is transmitted to the wheel with the best traction and the vehicle will drive off the jack, resulting in possible damage or injury.

Jack the Bronco from under the axles, radius arms, or spring hangers and the frame. Be sure and block the diagonally opposite wheel to prevent the vehicle from moving. Place jackstands under the vehicle at the points mentioned above when you are going to work under the vehicle.

When raising the vehicle on a hoist, position

JUMP STARTING A DEAD BATTERY

The chemical reaction in a battery produces explosive hydrogen gas. This is the safe way to jump start a dead battery, reducing the chances of an accidental spark that could cause an explosion.

Jump Starting Precautions

1. Be sure both batteries are of the same voltage.
2. Be sure both batteries are of the same polarity (have the same grounded terminal).
3. Be sure the vehicles are not touching.
4. Be sure the vent cap holes are not obstructed.
5. Do not smoke or allow sparks around the battery.
6. In cold weather, check for frozen electrolyte in the battery. Do not jump start a frozen battery.
7. Do not allow electrolyte on your skin or clothing.
8. Be sure the electrolyte is not frozen.
CAUTION: *Make certain that the ignition key, in the vehicle with the dead battery, is in the OFF position. Connecting cables to vehicles with on-board computers will result in computer destruction if the key is not in the OFF position.*

Jump Starting Procedure

1. Determine voltages of the two batteries; they must be the same.
2. Bring the starting vehicle close (they must not touch) so that the batteries can be reached easily.
3. Turn off all accessories and both engines. Put both cars in Neutral or Park and set the handbrake.
4. Cover the cell caps with a rag—do not cover terminals.
5. If the terminals on the run-down battery are heavily corroded, clean them.
6. Identify the positive and negative posts on both batteries and connect the cables in the order shown.
7. Start the engine of the starting vehicle and run it at fast idle. Try to start the car with the dead battery. Crank it for no more than 10 seconds at a time and let it cool off for 20 seconds in between tries.
8. If it doesn't start in 3 tries, there is something else wrong.
9. Disconnect the cables in the reverse order.
10. Replace the cell covers and dispose of the rags.

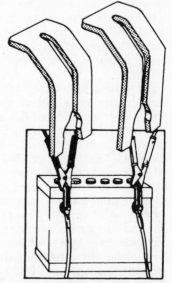

Side terminal batteries occasionally pose a problem when connecting jumper cables. There frequently isn't enough room to clamp the cables without touching sheet metal. Side terminal adaptors are available to alleviate this problem and should be removed after use.

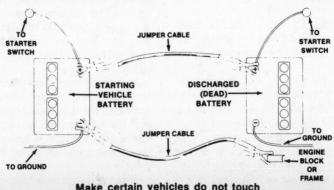

TO STARTER SWITCH   JUMPER CABLE   TO STARTER SWITCH

STARTING VEHICLE BATTERY   DISCHARGED (DEAD) BATTERY

JUMPER CABLE

TO GROUND   TO GROUND   ENGINE BLOCK OR FRAME

Make certain vehicles do not touch

This hook-up for negative ground cars only

Capacities Chart

Year	Engine	Crankcase With Filter (qts)	Tranmission (pts) Manual	Auto-matic ⑥	Transfer Case (pts)	Axle (pts) Front	Rear	Gasoline Tank (gals) Main	Auxilliary	Cooling System (qts)
1966	6-170	7	3.5	—	2.75	3.75	5.0 ①	14.5	—	10.0
	8-289	6	3.5	—	2.75	3.75	5.0 ①	14.5	—	17.0
1967	6-170	7	3.5	—	2.75	3.75	5.0	14.5	11.0	10.0
	8-289	6	3.5	—	2.75	3.75	5.0	14.5	11.0	17.0
1968	6-170	7	3.5	—	2.75	3.75	5.0	14.5	11.0	10.0
	8-289	6	3.5	—	2.75	3.75	5.0	14.5	11.0	16.0
1969	6-170	7	3.5	—	2.75	3.75	6.5	14.5	11.0	10.0
	8-302	6	3.5	—	2.75	3.75	6.5	14.5	11.0	16.0
1970	6-170	7	3.5	—	2.75	4.0	9.0	14.5②	11.5③	10.0
	8-302	6	3.5	—	2.75	4.0	9.0	14.5②	11.5③	16.0
1971	6-170	7	3.5	—	2.75	4.0	9.0	12.75	10.25	10.0
	8-302	6	3.5	—	2.75	4.0	9.0	12.75	10.25	16.0
1972	6-170	7	3.5	—	2.75	3.5	6.0	12.25	7.50	10.0
	8-302	6	3.5	—	2.75	3.5	6.0	12.25	7.50	16.0
1973	6-200	7	4.0	22.0	2.75	3.5④	9.0	12.25	7.50	10.0
	8-302	6	4.0	22.0	2.75	3.5④	9.0	12.25	7.50	16.0
1974	6-200	7	4.0	22.0	2.75	3.5④	9.0	12.25	7.50	10.0
	8-302	6	4.0	22.0	2.75	3.5④	9.0	12.25	7.50	16.0
1975	8-302	6	3.5	17.5	2.75	3.5④	9.0	12.25	7.50	16.0⑤
1976	8-302	6	3.5	22.0	2.75	3.5	9.0	14.0	7.50	16.0⑤
1977	8-302	6	3.5	22.0	2.75	3.5	9.0	14.0	7.50	16.0⑤
1978–79	8-351M	6	7.0	26.4	4.0⑦	5.8	6.5⑭	25.0⑧	—	20.0⑨
	8-400	6	7.0	26.4	4.0⑦	5.8	6.5⑭	25.0⑧	—	22.0⑩
1980–81	6-300	6	7.0⑮	26.8	6.5	4.0	6.5⑭	25.0⑧	—	13.0⑪
	8-302	6	7.0⑮	26.8	6.5	4.0	6.5⑭	25.0⑧	—	13.0⑫
	8-351W	6	7.0⑮	26.8	6.5	4.0	6.5⑭	25.0⑧	—	15.0⑬
1982–86	6-300	6	7.0⑮	26.8	7.0	4.0	6.5⑭	25.0⑧	—	13⑪
	8-302	6	7.0⑮	26.8	7.0	4.0	6.5⑭	25.0⑧	—	13⑫
	8-351W	6	7.0⑮	26.8	7.0	4.0	6.5⑭	25.0⑧	—	15⑬

① 3300 lb.—4.5 pts
② Calif.—11.625 gal
③ Calif.—8.625 gal
④ With locking differential, add 2 oz of friction modifier—Ford part #EST-M2C118-A or equivalent
⑤ With automatic transmission—17.0
⑥ Includes torque converter
⑦ Full-time unit: 9.0
⑧ Optional tank: 32.0
⑨ Extra cooling package, air conditioning, automatic transmission or trailer towing package: 22.0
   Super Cooling package: 24.0
⑩ Super Cooling package: 24.0
⑪ Air conditioning or Super Cooling package: 14.0
⑫ Extra Cooling package with auto trans; air conditioning; Super Cooling package: 14.0
⑬ Air conditioning or Super Cooling package: 16.0
⑭ With locking differential, use Lubricant Ford part #ESW-M2C119-A or equivalent
⑮ 4-speed overdrive available from 1981: 4.5

Preventive Maintenance Schedule

Interval	Item	Service
1966–72		
6mos/6,000 miles	centering yoke sockets and balls 1967–72	MP grease—2 special fittings
	crankcase	change oil and filter
	differentials	check levels
	steering linkage	MP grease—4 fittings
	tires	rotate
	transfer case	check level—50W
	U-joints and splines	MP grease—2 or 4 fittings
	air cleaner element, 1966–67	clean
	air cleaner oil bath	30W
	brake master cylinder	check level
	cooling system	inspect hoses and fluid level
	drive belts	inspect and adjust
	oil filter cap	check and clean
	PCV filter, 1972	replace
	PCV system, 1966–71	test
	power steering reservoir	check level—Type F trans. fluid
	steering column U-joint	MP grease—1 fitting
	steering gear manual	check level—90W gear oil
	automatic transmission	check level—Type F fluid only
12 mos/12,000 miles	hublock hubs	MP—repack
	air cleaner element—1968 6-cyl, 1969–72 all	replace
	cooling system—1966–69	inspect hoses
	distributor	replace points, condenser and rotor
	fuel mixture	check and adjust
	fuel filter	replace
	intake manifold—8 cylinder	torque
	PCV system, 1972	clean system—replace valve
	spark delay valve—1972	replace
	spark plugs	replace
	thermactor air pump filter, 1966–67	replace
	thermostatic air cleaner, 1972	inspect
	throttle and choke linkage	inspect
	valve clearance, 6 cylinder	adjust
24 mos/24,000 miles	brakes	inspect
	front wheel bearings	MP grease—clean and repack
	transfer case and front differential	trnsf. case—SAE 50W; axle—80/90W change lubricant
	air cleaner element—1968 8 cylinder	replace
	cooling system	change coolant, flush system
	distributor	replace cap
	EEC canister and purge hose, 1972	replace
	PCV filter, 1971	replace
	speedometer and parking brake cables	MP grease
	engine	check compression
36 mos/36,000 miles	U-joints without fittings—1966, early 1967	repack with MP grease
	air cleaner element, 1966–67	replace
1973–74		

1973
  4 mos/4,000 miles
1974
  6 mos/6,000 miles
	centering yoke sockets and balls	MP grease—2 fittings

	crankcase	change oil and filter
	differentials	check levels
	steering linkage	MP grease—4 fittings
	transfer case	check level
	automatic transmission	adjust bands and check level
	manual transmission	check level
	U-joints and splines	MP grease—2 or 4 fittings
	master cylinder	check level
	cooling system	check hoses

Preventive Maintenance Schedule (cont.)

Interval	Item	Service
1973–74 (cont.)		
1973	distributor	inspect points
4 mos/4,000 miles	drive belts	inspect and adjust
1974	fuel filter	replace
6 mos/6,000 miles	carburetor	adjust idle speed and mixture
	power steering	check level
	steering column U-joint	MP grease—1 fitting
	steering gear manual—1973	check level—90W gear oil
	throttle and choke linkage	check
	ignition timing	adjust
8 mos/8,000 miles	tires	rotate
	air cleaner-oil bath	clean—30W
	spark plugs—with leaded fuel	replace
	PCV filter, 1973	replace
12 mos/12,000 miles	locking hubs	MP grease—repack
	air cleaner element	replace
	breather cap	clean
	EGR system	inspect
	spark delay valve, 1973	replace
	spark plugs, unleaded fuel	replace
	thermactor system	inspect
18 mos/18,000 miles	distributor cap and rotor	clean and inspect
	intake manifold—8 cylinder	torque
24 mos/24,000 miles	brakes	inspect
	cooling system	change coolant, flush
	EEC canister and purge hose	inspect
	speedometer and parking brake cables	MP grease
	steering gear-manual, 1974	check level—90W
At 24,000 & 36,000	engine	check compression
1975–77		
5 mos/5,000 miles	crankcase	change oil and filter
	centering yoke sockets and balls	MP grease—2 fittings
	differentials	check levels
	steering column U-joint	MP grease—1 fitting
	steering linkage	MP grease—4 fittings
	throttle solenoid off-speed	check
	transfer case	check level—SAE 50W
	automatic transmission	check level; adjust bands
	manual transmission	check level—80/90W
	U-joints and splines	MP grease—2 or 4 fittings
	air cleaner, oil bath	clean and fill—SAE 30W
	carburetor	check carb and fast idle speeds
	power steering reservoir	check level—Type F fuid
Every 6 mos	cooling system	inspect hoses
10 mos/10,000 miles	locking hubs	repack
15 mos/15,000 miles	master cylinder	check level
	parking brake linkage	10W
*Schedule B	air cleaner element	inspect
15 mos/15,000 miles	air cleaner temperature control	inspect
*Schedule A	choke system	inspect
20 mos/20,000 miles	breather cap	clean
	distributor cap and rotor	inspect
	drive belts	adjust
	fuel filter	replace
	carburetor	adjust mixture
	ignition	check timing

Preventive Maintenance Schedule (cont.)

Interval	Item	Service
1975–77 (cont.)		
*Schedule B	intake manifold	torque
15 mos/15,000 miles	PCV system	inspect
*Schedule A	spark plugs	replace
20 mos/20,000 miles	thermactor system	inspect
20 mos/20,000 miles	brakes	inspect
	front wheel bearings	MP grease—clean and repack
Every 24 mos	cooling system	change coolant; flush
25 mos/25,000 miles	manual steering gear	check level—90W gear oil
	transfer case and front differential	change lubricant—transf. case, 50W; axle, 80/90W
	transmission, manual	change lubricant—80/90W
*Schedule A	air cleaner element	replace
20 mos/20,000 miles	crankcase filter in air cleaner	replace
*Schedule B	EEC canister	inspect
30 mos/30,000 miles	gas cap hoses and vapor lines	inspect
Service as Required	tires	rotate
	transmission and clutch linkage	lubricate—MP grease
1978–79		
7 mos/7,500 miles	engine oil & filter	change
	drive belts	check
	idle speed	check
	steering linkage	lubricate—MP grease
	slip yokes	lubricate—MP grease
	wheel lugs	torque
	clutch linkage	lubricate—MP grease
	cooling system	inspect
	automatic transmission bands	adjust
22 mos/22,000 miles	*schedule A spark plugs	replace
	*schedule A PCV valve	replace
	coolant	change
30 mos/30,000 miles	*schedule B spark plugs	replace
	*schedule B PCV valve	replace
	air cleaner element	replace
	brake system components	inspect, clean & lubricate caliper slider rails
	exhaust system	inspect
	master cylinder	check level
	free running hubs	repack
	automatic transmission	drain & refill
1980–81 All US vehicles and Canadian unleaded fuel vehicles		
7 mos/7,500 miles	engine oil & filter	change
	cooling system	check level; inspect hoses
	drive belts	inspect
	steering linkage	lubricate—MP grease
	slip yokes	lubricate—MP grease
	wheel lugs	torque
	clutch linkage	lubricate—MP grease
	automatic transmission bands	adjust
22 mos/22,000 miles	automatic transmission	drain & refill
	coolant	change
30 mos/30,000 miles	spark plugs	replace
	choke plate	clean
	air cleaner element	replace
	crankcase emission filter	replace
	heat riser valve	lubricate—silicone lubricant
	front wheel bearings & spindle	lubricate
	brake system components	inspect, clean and lubricate caliper slider rails

Preventive Maintenance Schedule (cont.)

Interval	Item	Service
1980–81 All US vehicles and Canadian unleaded fuel vehicles (cont.)		
30 mos/30,000 miles (cont.)	exhaust system master cylinder free running hubs	inspect check level clean & repack
1980–81 Leaded fuel Canada exc. 302 V8		
5 mos/5,000 miles	engine oil & filter idle speed chassis fittings wheel lugs automatic transmission bands	change check lubricate torque adjust
15 mos/15,000 miles	drive belts spark plugs fuel filter	inspect change replace
30 mos/30,000 miles	crankcase emission filter air cleaner element PCV valve heat riser valve master cylinder	replace replace replace lubricate—silicone lubricant check level
40 mos/40,000 miles	coolant	replace
1980–81 Leaded fuel Canada 302 V8		
6 mos/6,000 miles	engine oil & filter idle speed ignition timing chassis fittings axle spindle pins automatic transmission bands wheel lugs	change check check lubricate lubricate adjust torque
12 mos/12,000 miles	cooling system	inspect
15 mos/15,000 miles	spark plugs drive belts choke plate crankcase breather cap	replace inspect clean clean
18 mos/18,000 miles	automatic transmission	drain & refill
30 mos/30,000 miles	PCV valve air cleaner element crankcase air filter exhaust system master cylinder brake system components front wheel bearings spindle needle bearings free running hubs	replace replace replace inspect check level clean, inspect and lubricate caliper slider rails clean & repack lubricate clean & repack
1982–86 All US vehicles and Canadian unleaded fuel vehicles		
7 mos/7,500 miles	engine oil & filter cooling system drive belts steering linkage slip yokes wheel lugs clutch linkage automatic trans. linkage U-joints idle speed heat riser valve	change check level; inspect hoses inspect lubricate—MP grease lubricate—MP grease torque lubricate—MP grease lubricate—MP grease lubricate—MP grease check lubricate—silicone lubricant
22 mos/22,000 miles	automatic transmission coolant	drain & refill change

Preventive Maintenance Schedule (cont.)

Interval	Item	Service
1982–86 All US vehicles and Canadian unleaded fuel vehicles (cont.)		
30 mos/30,000 miles	spark plugs	replace
	choke plate & linkage	clean
	air cleaner element	replace
	crankcase emission filter	replace
	front wheel bearings	lubricate
	spindle needle bearings	lubricate
	brake system components	inspect, clean and lubricate caliper slider rails
	exhaust system	inspect
	master cylinder	check level
	free running hubs	clean & repack
1982–83 Leaded fuel Canada exc. 302 & 351 V8		
5 mos/5,000 miles	engine oil & filter	change
	idle speed	check
	chassis fittings	lubricate—MP grease
	wheel lugs	torque
	automatic trans. linkage	lubricate—MP grease
15 mos/15,000 miles	drive belts	inspect
	spark plugs	change
	fuel filter	replace
	automatic choke	inspect
30 mos/30,000 miles	crankcase emission filter	replace
	air cleaner element	replace
	PCV valve	replace
	heat riser valve	lubricate—silicone lubricant
	master cylinder	check fluid level
	front wheel bearings	lubricate
	spindle needle bearings	lubricate
	brake system components	inspect, clean and lubricate slider rails
	exhaust system	inspect
40 mos/40,000 miles	coolant	replace
1982–83 Leaded fuel Canada 302 & 351 V8		
6 mos/6,000 miles	engine oil & filter	change
	idle speed	check
	ignition timing	check
	chassis fittings	lubricate
	automatic trans. linkage	lubricate
	wheel lugs	torque
12 mos/12,000 miles	cooling system	inspect
15 mos/15,000 miles	spark plugs	replace
	drive belts	inspect
	choke plate	clean
	crankcase breather cap	clean
	PCV system, hoses and tubes	inspect
	air cleaner temp. control	inspect
18 mos/18,000 miles	automatic transmission	drain & refill
30 mos/30,000 miles	PCV valve	replace
	air cleaner element	replace
	crankcase air filter	replace
	exhaust system	inspect
	master cylinder	check fluid level
	brake system components	clean, inspect and lubricate caliper slider rails
	front wheel bearings	clean & repack
	spindle needle bearings	lubricate
	free running hubs	clean & repack

*Maintenance schedule code is found on inside of glove compartment door.

NOTE: *When operating under severe conditions, cut maintenance schedules in half. When operating daily in water, repack hubs daily and change axle, transmission and transfer case fluids every 1,000 miles.*

the front end adapters under the center of the lower suspension arm or the spring supports as near to the wheels as practical. The rear hoist adapters should be placed under the spring mounting pads or the rear axle housing. Be careful not to touch the rear shock absorber mounting brackets.

HOW TO BUY A USED TRUCK

Many people believe that a two or three year old used truck is a better buy than a new truck. This may be true; the new truck suffers the heaviest depreciation in the first two years, but is not old enough to present a lot of costly repair problems. Whatever the age of the used truck you might want to buy, this section and a little patience will help you select one that should be safe and dependable.

TIPS

1. First decide what model you want, and how much you want to spend.

2. Check the used truck lots and your local newspaper ads. Privately owned trucks are usually less expensive, however you will not get a warranty that, in most cases, comes with a used truck purchased from a lot.

3. Never shop at night. The glare of the lights make it easy to miss faults on the body caused by accident or rust repair.

4. Try to get the name and phone number of the previous owner. Contact him/her and ask about the truck. If the owner of the lot refuses this information, look for a truck somewhere else.

A private seller can tell you about the truck and maintenance. Remember, however, there's no law requiring honesty from private citizens selling used trucks. There is a law that forbids the tampering with or turning back the odometer mileage. This includes both the private citizen and the lot owner. The law also requires that the seller or anyone transferring ownership of the truck must provide the buyer with a signed statement indicating thé mileage on the odometer at the time of transfer.

5. Write down the year, model and serial number before you buy any used truck. Then dial 1-800-424-9393, the toll free number of the National Highway Traffic Administration, and ask if the truck has ever been included on any manufacturer's recall list. If so, make sure the needed repairs were made.

6. Use the Used truck Checklist in this section and check all the items on the used truck you are considering. Some items are more important than others. You know how much

money you can afford for repairs, and, depending on the price of the truck, may consider doing any needed work yourself. Beware, however, of trouble in areas that will affect operation, safety or emission. Problems in the Used truck Checklist break down as follows:

1–8: Two or more problems in these areas indicate a lack of maintenance. You should beware.

9–13: Indicates a lack of proper trucks, however, these can usually be corrected with a tune-up or relatively simple parts replacement.

14–17: Problems in the engine or transmission can be very expensive. Walk away from any truck with problems in both of these areas.

7. If you are satisfied with the apparent condition of the truck, take it to an independent diagnostic center or mechanic for a complete check. If you have a state inspection program, have it inspected immediately before purchase, or specify on the bill of sale that the sale is conditional on passing state inspection.

8. Road test the truck—refer to the Road Test Checklist in this section. If your original evaluation and the road test agree—the rest is up to you.

USED TRUCK CHECKLIST

NOTE: *The number on the illustrations refer to the numbers on this checklist.*

1. Mileage: Average mileage is about 12,000 miles per year. More than average mileage may indicate hard usage. 1975 and later catalytic converter equipped models may need converter service at 50,000 miles.

2. Paint: Check around the tailpipe, molding and windows for overspray indicating that the truck has been repaired.

3. Rust: Check fenders, doors, rocker panels, window moldings, wheelwells, floorboards, under floormats, and in the truck for signs of rust. Any rust at all will be a problem. There is no way to check the spread of rust, except to replace that part or panel.

4. Body appearance: Check the moldings, bumpers, grille, vinyl roof, glass, doors, trunk lid and body panels for general overall condition. Check for misalignment, loose holdown clips, ripples, scratches in glass, rips or patches in the top. Mismatched paint, weldíng in the trunk, severe misalignment of body panels or ripples may indicate crash work.

5. Leaks: Get down and look under the truck. There are no normal leaks, other than water from the air conditioning condenser.

6. Tires: Check the tire air pressure. A common trick is to pump the tire pressure up to make the truck roll easier. Check the tread wear, open the trunk and check the spare too.

Uneven wear is a clue that the front end needs alignment. See the troubleshooting chapter for clues to the causes of tire wear.

7. Shock absorbers: Check the shock absorbers by forcing downward sharply on each corner of the truck. Good shocks will not allow the truck to bounce more than twice after you let go.

8. Interior: Check the entire interior. You're looking for an interior condition that agrees with the overall condition of the truck. Reasonable wear is expected, but be suspicious of new seatcovers on sagging seats, new pedal pads, and worn armrests. These indicate an attempt to cover up use. Pull back the carpets and look for evidence of water leaks or flooding. Look for missing hardware, door handles, control knobs, etc. Check lights and signal operations. Make sure all accessories (air conditioner, heater, radio, etc.) work. Check windshield wiper operation.

9. Belts and Hoses: Open the hood and check all belts and hoses for wear, cracks or weak spots.

10. Battery: Low electrolyte level, corroded terminals and/or cracked case indicate a lack of maintenance.

11. Radiator: Look for corrosion or rust in the coolant indicating a lack of maintenance.

12. Air filter: A dirty air filter usually means a lack of maintenance.

13. Ignition Wires: Check the ignition wires for cracks, burned spots, or wear. Worn wires will have to be replaced.

14. Oil level: If the oil level is low, chances are the engine uses oil or leaks. Beware of water in the oil (cracked block), excessively thick oil (used to quiet a noisy engine), or thin, dirty oil with a distinct gasoline smell (internal engine problems).

15. Automatic Transmission: Pull the transmission dipstick out when the engine is running. The level should read **Full**, and the fluid should be clear or bright red. Dark brown or black fluid that has distinct burnt odor signals a transmission in need of repair or overhaul.

16. Exhaust: Check the color of the exhaust smoke. Blue smoke indicates, among other problems, worn rings; black smoke can indicate burnt valves or carburetor problems.

Check the exhaust system for leaks; it can be expensive to replace.

17. Spark Plugs: Remove one of the spark plugs (the most accessible will do). And engine in good condition will show plugs with a light tan or gray deposit on the firing tip. See the color Tune-up tips section for spark plug conditions.

ROAD TEST CHECK LIST

1. Engine Performance: The truck should be peppy whether cold or warm, with adequate power and good pickup. It should respond smoothly through the gears.

2. Brakes: They should provide quick, firm stops with no noise, pulling or brake fade.

3. Steering: Sure control with no binding, harshness, or looseness and no shimmy in the wheel should be expected. Noise or vibration from the steering wheel when turning the truck means trouble.

4. Clutch (Manual Transmission): Clutch action should give quick, smooth response with easy shifting. The clutch pedal should have about 1–1½ inches of freeplay before it disengages the clutch. Start the engine, set the parking brake, put the transmission in first gear and slowly release the clutch pedal. The engine should begin to stall when the pedal is ½–¾ of the way up.

5. Automatic Transmission: The transmission should shift rapidly and smoothly, with no noise, hesitation, or slipping.

6. Differential: No noise or thumps should be present. Differentials have no normal leaks.

7. Driveshaft, Universal Joints: Vibration and noise could mean driveshaft problems. Clicking at low speed or coast conditions means worn U-joints.

8. Suspension: Try hitting bumps at different speeds. A truck that bounces has weak shock absorbers. Clunks mean worn bushings or ball joints.

9. Frame: Wet the tires and drive in a straight line. Tracks should show two straight lines, not four. Four tire tracks indicate a frame bent by collision damage. If the tires can't be wet for this purpose, have a friend drive along behind you and see if the truck appears to be traveling in a straight line.

TUNE-UP PROCEDURES

Spark Plugs

SPARK PLUG ANALYSIS

Spark plugs ignite the air and fuel mixture in the cylinder as the piston reaches the top of the compression stroke. The controlled explosion that results forces the piston down, turning the crankshaft and the rest of the drive train.

Ford recommends that spark plugs be changed every 12,000 miles with conventional ignition systems, and every 18,000 miles with electronic ignition systems. Under severe driving conditions, those intervals should be halved. Severe driving conditions are:

1. Extended periods of idling or low speed operation, such as off-road or door-to-door delivery.

2. Driving short distances (less than 10 miles) when the average temperature is below 10°F for 60 days or more.

3. Excessive dust or blowing dirt conditions.

When you remove the spark plugs, check their condition. They are a good indicator of the condition of the engine. It is a good idea to remove the spark plug at regular intervals, such as every 3,000 or 4,000 miles, just so you can keep an eye on the mechanical state of the engine.

A small deposit of light tan or gray material on a spark plug that has been used for any period of time is considered normal. Any other color, or abnormal amounts of deposit, indicate that there is something amiss in the engine.

The gap between the center electrode and the side or ground electrode can be expected to increase not more than 0.001″ (o.025mm) every 1,000 miles under normal conditions. When, and if, a plug fouls and begins to misfire, you will have to investigate, correct the cause of the fouling an either clean or replace the plug.

There are several reasons why a spark plug will foul and you can learn which reason is at

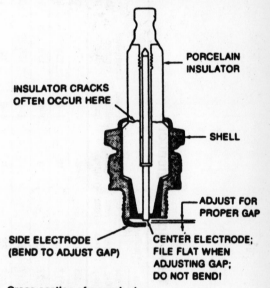

Cross section of a spark plug

fault by just looking at the plug. A few of the most common reasons for plug fouling and a description of fouled plug appearance are listed in the Color Insert section, which also offers solutions to the fouling causes.

SPARK PLUG HEAT RANGE

Spark plug heat range is the ability of the plug to dissipate heat. The longer the insulator (or the farther it extends into the engine), the hotter the plug will operate; the shorter the insulator the cooler it will operate. A plug that absorbs little heat and remains too cool will quickly accumulate deposits of oil and carbon since it is not hot enough to burn them off. This leads to plug fouling and consequently to misfiring. A plug that absorbs too much heat will have no deposits but, due to the excessive heat, the electrodes will burn away quickly and in some instances, preignition may result. Preignition takes place when plug tips get so hot

Tune-Up Specifications

Year	Engine No. Cyl Displacement	Spark Plugs Type	Spark Plugs Gap (in.)	Distributor Point Dwell (deg)	Distributor Point Gap (in.)	Ignition Timing (deg) Manual Trans	Ignition Timing (deg) Auto Trans	Intake Valve Opens (deg)	Fuel Pump Pressure (psi)	Compression Pressure (psi)	Idle Speed Manual Trans	Idle Speed Auto ④ Trans	Clearance (in.) Intake	Clearance (in.) Exhaust
1966–67	6-170	BF82	.034	40	.025	0⑥	—	9	4–6	175	650	—	.018	.018
	8-289	BF42	.034	29	.017	6B	—	16	4–6	155	625	—	Hyd.	Hyd.
1968	6-170	BF82	.034	37	.027	6B	—	9	4–6	175	700	—	.018	.018
	8-289	BF42	.034	29	.017	6B	—	16	4–6	155	625	—	Hyd.	Hyd.
1969	6-170	BF82	.034	37	.027	6B	—	9	4–6	①	750	—	.018	.018
	8-302	BF42	.030	27	.021	6B	—	16	4–6	①	650	—	Hyd.	Hyd.
1970	6-170	BF82	.034	37	.027	6B	—	9	4–6	①	775	—	.018	.018
	8-302	BF42	.034	27	.021	6B	—	16	4–6	①	675	—	Hyd.	Hyd.
1971	6-170	BRF82	.034	36	.027	6B	—	9	4–6	①	775	—	.018	.018
	8-302	BRF42	.030	27	.021	6B	—	16	4–6	①	800/500②	—	Hyd.	Hyd.
1972	6-170	BRF82	.034	36	.027	6B	—	9	4–6	①	750	—	.018	.018
	8-302	BRF42	.034	28	.017	6B	—	16	4–6	①	800/500②	—	Hyd.	Hyd.
1973	6-200	BRF82	.034	37	.027	6B	6B	9	4–6	①	500	600	Hyd.	Hyd.
	8-302	BRF42	.034	27	.017	6B	6B	16③	4–6	①	800/500②	550	Hyd.	Hyd.

1974	6-200	BRF42	.034	37	.027	6B	6B	9	4-6	①	775	675	Hyd.	Hyd.
	8-302	BRF42	.044	27	.017	6B	6B	16③	4-6	①	800/500②	650/500②	Hyd.	Hyd.
1975	8-302	ARF42	.044	Electronic		⑤	⑤	20	5-6	①	900	650	Hyd.	Hyd.
1976	8-302	ARF42	.044	Electronic		⑤	⑤	20	5-6	①	750	650	Hyd.	Hyd.
1977	8-302	ARF42	.044	Electronic		⑥	⑤	20	5-6	①	⑤	⑤	Hyd.	Hyd.
1978	8-351M	ASF42	.042–.046	Electronic		6B	14B	—	6-8	①	650	500	Hyd.	Hyd.
	8-400	ASF42	.042–.046	Electronic		12B	12B	—	6-8	①	650	500	Hyd.	Hyd.
1979	8-351M	ASF42	.042–.046	Electronic		⑤	⑤	—	6-8	①	⑤	⑤	Hyd.	Hyd.
	8-400	ASF42	.042–.046	Electronic		⑤	⑤	—	6-8	①	⑤	⑤	Hyd.	Hyd.
1980–86	6-300	BSF42	.042–.046	Electronic		⑤	⑤	—	6-8	①	⑤	⑤	Hyd.	Hyd.
	8-302	ASF42	.042–.046	Electronic		⑤	⑤	—	6-8	①	⑤	⑤	Hyd.	Hyd.
	8-351W	ASF42	.042–.046	Electronic		⑤	⑤	—	6-8	①	⑤	⑤	Hyd.	Hyd.
	8-351HO	ASF42	.042–.046	Electronic		⑤	⑤	—	6-8	①	⑤	⑤	Hyd.	Hyd.

① Lowest compression ratio should be within 75% of the highest
② Solenoid on/solenoid off
③ With auto trans—20
④ In drive
⑤ See underhood specifications sticker
⑥ Without thermactor air pump: 4B

Should the figures given on the underhood specifications sticker disagree with those given above, use the sticker figures.

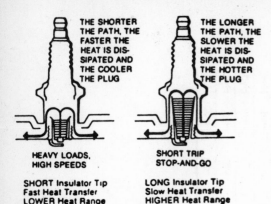

THE SHORTER THE PATH, THE FASTER THE HEAT IS DISSIPATED AND THE COOLER THE PLUG

THE LONGER THE PATH, THE SLOWER THE HEAT IS DISSIPATED AND THE HOTTER THE PLUG

HEAVY LOADS, HIGH SPEEDS

SHORT TRIP STOP-AND-GO

SHORT Insulator Tip
Fast Heat Transfer
LOWER Heat Range
COLD PLUG

LONG Insulator Tip
Slow Heat Transfer
HIGHER Heat Range
HOT PLUG

Spark plug heat range

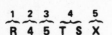

1 2 3   4   5
R 4 5 T S X

1 — R--INDICATES RESISTOR-TYPE PLUG.
2 — "4" INDICATES 14 mm THREADS.
3 — HEAT RANGE
4 — TS--TAPERED SEAT
     S--EXTENDED TIP
5 — SPECIAL GAP

Spark plug type number chart, using the R45TSX as an example

that they glow sufficiently to ignite the fuel/air mixture before the actual spark occurs. this early ignition will usually cause a pinging during low speeds and heavy loads.

The general rule of thumb for choosing the correct heat range when picking a spark plug is: if most of your driving is long distance, high speed travel, use a cooler plug; if most of your driving is stop and go, use a hotter plug. Origi-

Always use a wire gauge to check the electrode gap; a flat feeler gauge may not give the proper reading

Adjust the electrode gap by bending the side electrode

nal equipment plugs are compromise plugs, but most people never have occasion to change their plugs from the factory recommended heat range.

REMOVAL AND INSTALLATION

A set of spark plugs usually requires replacement before about 10,000 miles on Broncos with conventional ignition systems and after about 20,000 to 30,000 miles on Broncos with electronic ignition, depending on your style of driving. In normal operation, plug gap increases about 0.001″ (0.025mm) for every 1,000–2,500 miles. As the gap increases, the plug's voltage requirement also increases. It requires a greater voltage to jump the wider gap and about two to three times as much voltage to fire a plug at high speeds than at idle.

When you're removing spark plugs, you should work on one at a time. Don't start by removing the plug wires all at once, because unless you number them, they may become mixed up. Take a minute before you begin and number the wires with tape. The best location for numbering is near where the wires come out of the cap.

1. Twist the spark plug boot and remove the

Twist and pull on the rubber boot to remove the spark plug wires; never pull on the wire itself

boot and wire from the plug. Do not pull on the wire itself as this will ruin the wire.

2. If possible, use a brush or a rag to clean the area around the spark plug. Make sure that all the dirt is removed so that none will enter the cylinder after the plug is removed.

3. Remove the spark plug using the proper size socket. Turn the socket counterclockwise to remove the plug. Be sure to hold the socket straight on the plug to avoid breaking the plug, or rounding off the hex on the plug.

4. Once the plug is out, check it against the plugs shown in this section to determine engine condition. This is crucial since plug readings are vital signs of engine condition.

5. Use a round wire feeler gauge to check the plug gap. The correct size gauge should pass through the electrode gap with a slight drag. If you're in doubt, try one size smaller and one larger. The smaller gauge should go through easily while the larger one shouldn't go through at all. If the gap is incorrect, use the electrode bending tool on the end of the gauge to adjust the gap. When adjusting the gap, always bend the side electrode. The center electrode is non-adjustable.

6. Squirt a drop of penetrating oil on the threads of the new plug and install it. Don't oil the threads too heavily. Turn the plug in clockwise by hand until it is snug.

7. When the plug is finger tight, tighten it with a wrench.

8. Install the plug boot firmly over the plug. Proceed to the next plug.

Spark Plug Wires
CHECKING AND REPLACING

Visually inspect the spark plug cables for burns, cuts, or breaks in the insulation. Check the spark plug boots and the nipple on the distributor cap and coil. Replace any damaged wiring. If no physical damage is obvious, the wires can be checked with an ohmmeter for excessive resistance. (See the tune-up and troubleshooting section.)

When installing a new set of spark plug cables, replace the cables one at a time so there will be no mixup. Start by replacing the longest cable first. Install the boot firmly over the spark plug. Route the wire exactly the same as the original. Insert the nipple firmly into the tower on the distributor cap. Repeat the process for each cable.

Spark Plug Wires – Dura Spark System

The secondary wires used with the DURA SPARK II system are 8mm to contain the higher output voltage. There are two types of wires used in the system and some engines will have both types. It is important to properly identify the type of wire used for each cylinder before replacements are made.

Both types are blue in color and have silicone jacketing. The insulation material underneath the jacketing may be EPDM or another silicone layer separated by glass braid. The cable incorporating EPDM is used where engine temperatures are cooler and are identified with the letters **SE** with black printing. The silicone jacket silicone insulation type is used where high engine temperatures are present and is identified with the letters **SS** with white printing.

The cables are also marked with the cylinder number, model year and date of cable manufacture (quarter and year). Service replacement wires will not have cylinder numbers, or manufacture date.

NOTE: *On any vehicle equipped with a catalytic converter, never allow the engine to run for more than 30 seconds with a spark plug wire disconnected. Use an oscilloscope for testing and diagnosis. Do not puncture wires or use adapts that can cause misfiring. Unburned fuel in the cylinders will ignite in the converter as it is exhausted and damage the converter.*

REMOVAL

When removing park plug wires, use great care. Grasp and twist the insulator back and forth on the spark plug to free the insulator. Do not pull on the wire directly as it may become separated from the connector inside the insulator.

INSTALLATION

1. Install each wire in or on the proper terminal of the distributor cap. Be sure the terminal connector inside the insulator is fully seated. The No. 1 terminal is identified on the cap. On 6-cylinder engines, install the wires in a clockwise direction.

On 8 cylinder engines, cylinders are numbered from front to rear; right bank 1-2-3-4, left bank 5-6-7-8. On 8 cylinder engines install the wires in a counterclockwise direction in the firing order (1-5-4-2-6-3-7-9) starting at the No. 1 terminal for 4.9L (302 CID) V-8. On 5.8L (351 CID) V-8, and 6.6L (400 CID) V-8 the firing order is 1-3-7-2-6-5-4-8.

2. On 8-cylinder engines, remove the brackets from the old spark plug wire set and install them on the next new set in the same relative position. Install the wires in the brackets on the valve rocker arm covers. Connect the wires

to the proper spark plugs. Install the coil high tension lead.

The wires in the left bank bracket must be positioned in the bracket in a special order to avoid cylinder crossfire. Be sure to position the wires in the bracket in the order from front to rear.

Whenever a DURA SPARK II high tension wire is removed for any reason from a spark plug, coil or distributor terminal housing, silicone grease must be applied to the boot before it is reconnected. Using a small clean tool, coat the entire interior surface of the boot with Ford silicone grease D7AZ 19A331-A or equivalent.

Distributor Wiring Sequences and Firing Orders

Breaker Points

The points function as a circuit breaker for the primary circuit of the ignition system. The ignition coil must boost the 12 volts of electrical pressure supplied by the battery to as much as 25,000 volts in order to fire the plugs. To do this, the coil depends on the points and the condenser to make a clean break in the primary circuit.

The coil has both primary and secondary circuits. When the ignition is turned on, the battery supplies voltage through the coil to the points. The points are connected to ground, completing the primary circuit. As the current passes through the coil, a magnetic field is created in the iron center core of the oil. As the cam in the distributor turns, the points open and the primary circuit collapses. The magnetic field in the primary circuit of the coil cuts through the secondary circuit winding around the iron core. Because of the scientific phenomenon called electromagnetic induction, the battery voltage is increased to a level sufficient to fire the spark plugs.

When the points open, the electrical charge in the primary circuit jumps the gap created between the two open contacts of the points. If this electrical charge were not transferred elsewhere, the metal contacts of the points would melt and the gap between the points would start to change rapidly. If this gap is not maintained, the points will not break the primary circuit. If the primary circuit is not broken, the secondary circuit will not have enough voltage to fire the spark plugs.

NOTE: *1975–86 models have electronic ignition. Breaker points are not used.*

Condenser

The function of the condenser is to absorb excessive voltage from the points when they open

and thus prevent the points from becoming pitted or burned.

NOTE: *1975–86 models have electronic ignition. A condenser is not used.*

It is interesting to note that the above cycle must be completed by the ignition system every time spark fires. In a V8 engine, all of the spark plugs fire once for every two revolutions of the crankshaft. That means that in one revolution, four spark plugs fire. So when the engine is at an idle speed of 800 rpm, the points are opening and closing 3,200 times a minute.

There are two ways to check the breaker point gap: It can be done with a feeler gauge or a dwell meter. Either way you set the points, you are basically adjusting the amount of time that the points remain open. The time is measured in degrees of distributor rotation. When you measure the gap between the breaker points with a feeler gauge, you are setting the maximum amount the points will open when the rubbing block on the points is on a high point of the distributor cam. When you adjust the points with a dwell mete, you are adjusting the number of degrees that the points will remain closed before they start to open as a high point of the distributor cam approaches the rubbing block of the points.

When you replace a set of points, always replace the condenser at the same time.

When you change the point gap or dwell, you will also have the ignition timing. So, if the point gap or dwell is changed, the ignition timing must be adjusted also.

INSPECTION OF THE POINTS

1. Disconnect the high tension wire from the top of the distributor and the coil.
2. Remove the distributor cap by prying off the spring clips on the sides of the cap.
3. Remove the rotor from the distributor shaft by pulling it straight up. Examine the condition of the rotor. If it is cracked or the metal tip is excessively worn or burned it should be replaced.
4. Pry open the contacts of the points with a screwdriver and check the condition of the contacts. If they are excessively worn, burned or pitted, they should be replaced.
5. If the points are in good condition, adjust them, and replace the rotor and the distributor cap. If the points need to be replaced, follow the replacement procedure given below.

REPLACEMENT OF THE BREAKER POINTS AND CONDENSERS

1. Remove the coil high tension wire from the top of the distributor cap. Remove the distributor cap from the distributor and place it out of the way. Remove the rotor from the distributor shaft.

Distributor Wiring Sequences and Firing Orders

NOTE: *To avoid confusion, replace spark plugs and wires one at a time.*

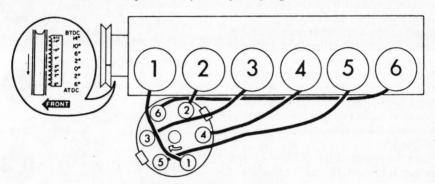

170, 200 6 cylinder 1966–74

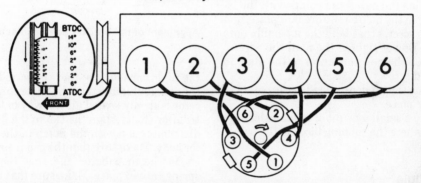

300 6-cylinder, 1980–83

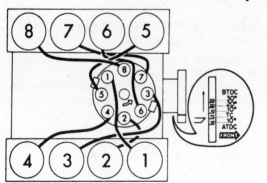

289, 302 V8 through 1974

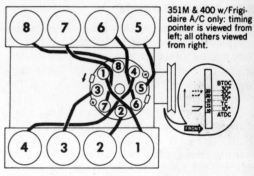

351M & 400 w/Frigidaire A/C only: timing pointer is viewed from left; all others viewed from right.

351W, 351M, 400 V8 1978–86

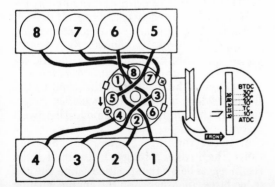

302 V8 1975–83

2. Loosen the screw that holds the condenser lead to the body of the breaker points and remove the condenser lead from the points.

3. Remove the screw that holds and grounds the condenser to the distributor body. Remove the condenser from the distributor and discard it.

4. Remove the points assembly attaching screws and adjustment lockscrews. A screwdriver with a holding mechanism will come in handy here so you don't drop a screw into the distributor and have to remove the entire distributor to retrieve it.

5. Remove the points. Wipe off the cam and apply new cam lubricant. Discard the old set of points.

6. Position the new set of points with the locating peg in the hole on the breaker plate, and install the screws that hold the assembly onto the plate. Do not tighten them all the way.

7. Attach the new condenser to the plate to the ground screw.

8. Attach the condenser lead to the points at the proper place.

9. Apply a small amount of cam lubricant to the shaft where the rubbing block of the points touches.

Dwell Angle

ADJUSTMENT OF THE BREAKER POINTS WITH A FEELER GAUGE

1. If the contact points of the assembly are not parallel, bent the stationary contact so they make contact across across the entire surface of the contacts. Bend only the stationary bracket part of the point assembly, not the movable contact.

2. Turn the engine until the rubbing block of the points is on one of the high points of the distributor cam. You can do this by either turning the ignition switch to the start position and releasing it quickly (bumping the engine) or by using a wrench on the bolt that holds the crankshaft pulley to the crankshaft. Be sure to remove the wrench before starting the engine!

3. Place the correct size feeler gauge between the contacts. Make sure it is parallel with the contact surfaces.

4. With your free hand, insert a screw driver into the notch provided for adjustment or into the eccentric adjusting screw, then twist the screw driver to either increase or decrease the gap to the proper setting.

5. Tighten the adjustment lockscrew and recheck the contact gap to make sure that it didn't change when the lockscrew was tightened.

6. Replace the rotor and distributor cap, and

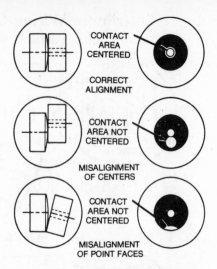

Alignment of the breaker point contacts

the high tension wire that connects the top of the distributor and the coil. Make sure that the rotor is firmly seated all the way onto the distributor shaft. Align the tab in the base of the distributor cap with the notch in the distributor body. Make sure that the cap is firmly seated on the distributor and that the retainer springs are in place. Make sure that the end of the high tension wire is firmly placed in the top of the distributor and the coil.

ADJUSTMENT OF THE BREAKER POINTS WITH A DWELL METER

1. Adjust the points with a feeler gauge as described above.

2. Connect the dwell meter to ignition circuit according to the manufacturer's instructions. One lead of the meter is connected to a ground an the other lead is to be connected to the distributor post on the coil. An adapter is usually provided for this purpose.

3. If the dwell meter has a set line on it, adjust the meter to zero the indicator.

4. Start the engine.

NOTE: *Be careful when working on any vehicle while the engine is running. Make sure that the transmission is in Neutral and that the parking brake is applied. Keep hands, clothing, tools, and the wires of the test instruments clear of the rotating fan blades.*

5. Observe the reading on the dwell meter. If the reading is within the specified range, turn off the engine and remove the dwell meter.

6. If the reading is above the specified range, the breaker point gap is too small. If the reading gets below the specified range, the gap is too large. In either case, the engine must be stopped and the gap adjusted in the manner

previously covered. After making the adjustment, start the engine and check the reading on the dwell meter. When the correct reading is obtained, disconnect the dwell meter.

7. Check the adjustment of the ignition timing.

Electronic Ignition

NOTE: *This book contains simple testing procedures for your Bronco's electronic ignition. More comprehensive testing on this system and other electronic control systems on your Bronco can be found in CHILTON'S GUIDE TO ELECTRONIC ENGINE CONTROLS, book part number 7535, available at your local retailer.*

Ignition System

Two types of ignition systems are used in the Bronco. A conventional system using breaker points and condenser is used on 1966–74 models. A breakerless (solid state) amplifier module located inline between the coil and distributor is installed in all 1975 and later models as standard equipment.

Both systems employ a distributor which is driven by the camshaft at one half crankshaft rpm, a high voltage rotor, distributor cap and spark plug wiring, and an oil filled conventional type coil.

The two systems differ in the manner in which they convert electrical primary voltage (12 volt) from the battery into secondary voltage (20,000 volts or greater) to fire the spark plugs. In the conventional ignition system, the breaker points open and close as the movable breaker arm rides the rotating distributor cam eccentric, thereby opening and closing the current to the ignition coil. When the points open,

they interrupt the flow of primary current to the coil, causing a collapse of the magnetic field in the coil and creating a high tension spark which is used to fire the spark plugs. In the breakerless system, a distributor shaft mounted armature rotates past a magnetic pickup coil assembly fluctuations in the magnetic field generated by the pickup coil current off and on, creating the high tension spark to fire the spark plugs. The amplifier module electrically controls the dwell, which is controlled mechanically in a conventional system by the duration which the points remain closed.

Both the conventional and breakerless ignition systems are equipped and breakerless ignition system are equipped with dual advance distributors. The vacuum advance until governors ignition timing according to engine load, while the centrifugal advance unit governs ignition timing according to engine rpm. Centrifugal advance is controlled by spring mounted weights contained in the distributor, located under the breaker point mounting plate on conventional systems and under the fixed base plate on breakerless systems. As engine speed increases, centrifugal force moves the weights outward from the distributor shaft advancing the position of the distributor cam (conventional) or armature (breakerless), thereby advancing the ignition timing. Vacuum advance is controlled by a vacuum diaphragm which is mounted on the side of the distributor and attached to the breaker point mounting plate (conventional) or the magnetic pickup coil assembly (breakerless) via the vacuum advance link. Under light acceleration, the engine is operating under a low load condition, causing the carburetor vacuum to act on the distributor vacuum diaphragm, moving the breaker

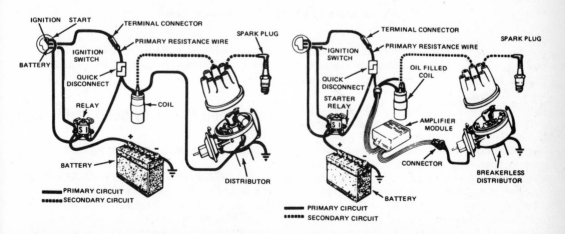

Typical ignition systems

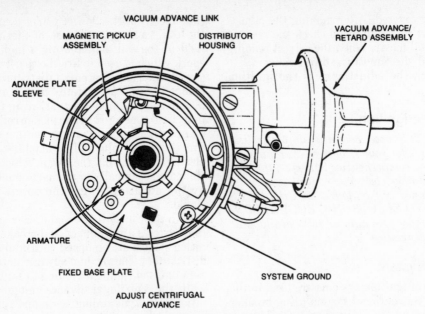

VACUUM ADVANCE LINK

MAGNETIC PICKUP
ASSEMBLY

DISTRIBUTOR
HOUSING

VACUUM ADVANCE/
RETARD ASSEMBLY

ADVANCE PLATE
SLEEVE

ARMATURE

FIXED BASE PLATE

ADJUST CENTRIFUGAL
ADVANCE

SYSTEM GROUND

V8 breakerless distributor, cap and rotor removed

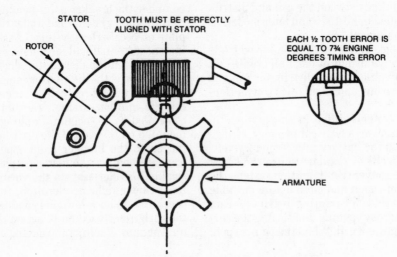

STATOR

TOOTH MUST BE PERFECTLY
ALIGNED WITH STATOR

EACH ½ TOOTH ERROR IS
EQUAL TO 7¾ ENGINE
DEGREES TIMING ERROR

ROTOR

ARMATURE

V8 breakerless distributor, static timing position

point mounting plate (conventional) or pickup coil assembly (breakerless) opposite the direction of distributor shaft rotation, thereby advancing the ignition timing.

The distributors on many models incorporate a vacuum retard mechanism. The retard mechanism is contained in the rear part of the vacuum diaphragm chamber. When the engine is operating under high vacuum conditions (deceleration or idle), intake manifold vacuum is applied to the retard mechanism. The retard mechanism moves the breaker point mounting plate (conventional) or pickup coil assembly (breakerless) in the direction of distributor rotation, thereby retarding the ignition timing. Ignition retard, under these conditions, reduces exhaust emissions of hydrocarbons, although it does reduce engine efficiency somewhat.

Ford Motor Company Solid State Ignition
BASIC OPERATING PRINCIPLES

In mid 1974, Ford Motor Company introduced in selected models its new Solid State Ignition System. In 1975, it became standard equipment in all Bronco models, this system was designed primarily to provide a hotter spark necessary to fire the leaner fuel/air mixtures required by today's emission control standards.

The Ford Solid State Ignition is a pulse triggered, transistor controlled breakerless ignition system. With the ignition switch **ON**, the primary circuit is on and the ignition coil is energized. When the armature spokes approach the magnetic pick-up coil assembly, they induce a voltage which tells the amplifier to turn the coil primary current off. A timing circuit in the amplifier module will turn the current on again after the coil field has collapsed. When the current is on, it flows from the battery through the ignition switch, the primary windings of the ignition coil, and through the amplifier module circuits to ground. When the current is off, the magnetic field built up in the ignition coil is allowed to collapse, inducing a high voltage into the second windings of the coil. High voltage is produced each time the field is thus built up and collapsed.

Although the systems are basically the same, Ford refers to their solid state ignition in several different ways. 1974–76 systems are referred to simply as Breakerless systems. In 1977, Ford named their ignition system Dura Spark I and Dura Spark II. In 1982 Ford dropped the Dura Spark I and introduced the Dura Spark III. This system is based on Electronic Engine Control (EEC). The EEC system controls spark advance in response to various engine sensors. This includes a crankshaft position sensor which replaces the stator and armature assembly in the distributor. Dura Spark II is the version used in all states except California. Dura Spark I and III are the systems used in California V8's only. Basically, the only difference between the two of that the coil charging currents are higher in the California vehicles. This is necessary to fire the leaner fuel/air mixtures required by California's stricter emission laws. The difference in coils alters some of the test values.

Ford has used several different types of wiring harness on their solid state ignition systems, due to internal circuitry changes in the electronic module. Wire continuity and color have not been changed, but the arrangement of the terminals in the connectors is different for each year. Schematics of the different years are included here, but keep in mind that the writing in all diagrams has been simplified and as a result, the routing of your wiring may not match the wiring in the diagram. However, the wire colors and terminal connections are the same.

Wire color coding is critical to servicing the Ford Solid State Ignition. Battery current reaches the electronic module through either the white or red wire, depending on whether the engine is cranking or running. When the engine is cranking, battery current is flowing through the white wire. When the engine is running, battery current flows through the red wire. All distributor signals flow through the orange and purple wires. The green wire carrier primary current from the coil to the module. The black wire is a ground between the distributor and the module. Up until 1975, a blue wire provides transient voltage protection. In 1976, the blue wire was dropped when the zener diode was added to the module. The orange and purple wires which run from the stator to the module must always be connected to the same color wire at the module. If these connections are crossed, polarity will be reversed and the system will be thrown out of phase. Some replacement wiring harnesses were sold with the wiring crossed, which complicates the problem considerably. As previously noted, the black wire is the ground wire. The screw which grounds the black wire, also, of course, grounds the engine primary circuit. If this screw is loose, dirty, or corroded, a seemingly incomprehensible ignition problem will develop. Several other cautions should be noted here. Keep in mind that on vehicles equipped with catalytic converters, any test that requires removal of a spark plug wire while the engine is running should be kept to a thirty second maximum. Any longer than this may damage the converter. In the event you are testing spark plug wires, do not pierce them. Test the wires at their terminals only.

Ignition Timing

Ignition timing is the measurement, in degrees of crankshaft rotation, of the point at which the spark plugs fire in each of the cylinders. It is measured in degrees before or after Top Dead Center (TDC) of the compression

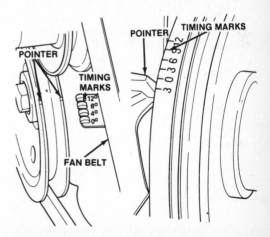

Typical timing marks: left, block mounted; right, pulley mounted

stroke. Ignition timing is controlled by turning the distributor body in the engine.

Ideally, the air/fuel mixture in the cylinder will be ignited by the spark plug just as the piston passes TDC of the compression stroke. If this happens, the piston will be beginning the power stroke just as the compressed and ignited air/fuel mixture starts to expand. The expansion of the air/fuel mixture then forces the piston down on the power stroke and turns the crankshaft.

Because it takes a fraction of a second for the spark plug to ignite the mixture in the cylinder, the spark plug must fire a little before the piston reaches TDC. Otherwise, the mixture will not be completely ignited as the piston passes TDC and the full power of the explosion will not be used by the engine.

The timing measurement is given in degrees of crankshaft rotation before the piston reaches TDC (BTDC). If the setting for the ignition timing is 5° BTDC, the spark plug must fire 5° before each piston reaches TDC. This only holds true, however, when the engine is at idle speed.

As the engine speed increases, the pistons go faster. The spark plugs have to ignite the fuel even sooner if it is to be completely ignited when the piston reaches TDC. To do this, the distributor has a means to advance the timing of the spark as the engine speed increases. This is accomplished by centrifugal weights within the distributor and a vacuum diaphragm mounted on the side of the distributor. It is necessary to disconnect the vacuum line from the diaphragm when the ignition timing is being set.

If the ignition is set too far advanced (BTDC), the ignition and expansion of the fuel in the cylinder will occur too soon and tend to force the piston down while it is still traveling up. This causes engine ping. If the ignition spark is set too far retarded after TDC (ATDC), the piston will have already passed TDC and started on its way down when the fuel is ignited. This will cause the piston to be forced down for only a portion of its travel. This will result in poor engine performance and lack of power.

The timing is best checked with a timing light. This device is connected in series with the No. 1 spark plug. The current that fires the spark plug also causes the timing light to flash.

There is a notch on the crankshaft pulley on the 6 cylinder engines. A scale of degrees of crankshaft rotation is attached to the engine block in such a position that the notches will pass close by the scale. On the V8 engines, the scale is located on the crankshaft and a pointer is attached to the engine block so that the scale will pass close by. When the engine is running, the timing light is aimed at the mark on the crankshaft pulley and the scale.

Ignition Timing
ADJUSTMENTS

1. Locate the timing marks on the crankshaft pulley and the front of the engine.
2. Clean off the timing marks so that you can see them.
3. Mark the timing marks with a piece of chalk or white paint. Color the mark on the scale that will indicate the correct timing when it is aligned with the mark on the pulley or the pointer. It is also helpful to mark the notch in the pulley or the tip of the pointer with a small dab of color.
4. Attach a tachometer to the engine.
5. Attach a timing light according to the manufacturer's instructions.
6. Disconnect the distributor vacuum line at the distributor and plug the vacuum line. A small bolt, center punch or similar object is satisfactory for a plug.
7. Check to make sure that all of the wires clear the fan and then start the engine.
8. Adjust the idle to the correct setting.
9. Aim the timing light at the timing marks. If the marks that you put on the pulley and the engine are aligned when the light flashes, the timing is correct. Turn off the engine and remove the tachometer and the timing light. If the marks are not in alignment, proceed with the following steps.
10. Loosen the distributor lockbolt just enough so that the distributor can be turned with a little effort.
11. With the timing light aimed at the pulley and the marks on the engine, turn the distributor in the direction of rotor rotation to regard the spark, and in the opposite direction of rotor rotation to the advance spark. Align the marks on the pulley and the engine with the flashes of the timing light.
12. When the marks are aligned, tighten the distributor lockbolt and recheck the timing with the timing light to make sure that the distributor did not move when you tightened the lockbolt.
13. Turn off the engine and remove the timing light.

Valve Lash

Valve adjustment determines how far the valves enter the cylinder and how long they stay open and closed.

If the valve clearance is too large, part of the lift of the camshaft will be used in removing the excessive clearance. Consequently, the valve will not be opening as far as it should. This condition has two effects: the valve train components will emit a tapping should as they take up the excessive clearance and the engine will perform poorly because the valves don't open fully and allow the proper amount of gases to flow into and out of the engine.

If the valve clearance is too small, the intake valve and the exhaust valve will open too far and they will not fully seat on the cylinder head when they close. When the valve seats itself on the cylinder head, it does two things; it seals the combustion chamber so that none of the gases in the cylinder escape and it cools itself by transferring some of the heat it absorbs from the combustion in the cylinder to the cylinder head and to the engine's cooling system. If the valve clearance is too small the engine will run poorly because of the gases escape from the combustion chamber. The valves will also become overheated and will warp, since they cannot transfer heat unless they are touching the valve seat in the cylinder head.

NOTE: *While all valve adjustments must be made as accurately as possible, it is better to have the valve adjustment slightly loose than slightly tight as a burned valve may result from overly tight adjustments.*

ADJUSTMENT

6-170 (Solid Lifters)

1. Start the engine and let it run until it has reached operating temperature.

2. Remove the valve corner and gasket.

3. With the engine idling, adjust the valve lash using a step type feeler gauge. This type of feeler gauge is sometimes more commonly known as a "go-no go" type feeler gauge. The proper clearance is reached when the smaller step on the gauge blade will pass through the gap while the larger step on the same blade will not pass through the gap.

Pass the proper size gauge blade between the valve stem and the rocker arm. If the clearance is correct, move on to the next valve. If the clearance is in need of adjustment, turn the adjusting screw on the opposite end of the rocker arm with a wrench until the proper clearance is reached. Turn the screw clockwise to decrease the clearance and counterclockwise to increase the clearance. Use this procedure for all of the valves.

4. After all of the valves have been adjusted, replace the valve cover gasket and cover. If the gasket is made of rubber, and is not torn, squashed or otherwise damaged it can be used again. If the gasket is cork, it is advised that the gasket be replaced.

5. Tighten the valve cover retaining bolts to 3–5 ft.lb.

Adjusting valve clearance on 170 6 Cyl. with solid lifters using step-type feeler gauge

Engines With Hydraulic Lifters

These engines require no periodic adjustments to the valve train. In the event of cylinder head removal or any operation that requires disturbing the rocker arms, the rocker arms will have to be adjusted. For all adjustment procedures, please refer to Chapter 3, Valves and Springs section.

Carburetor

This section contains only tune-up adjustment procedures for the carburetors. Descriptions, adjustments and overhaul procedures of carburetors can be found in the Fuel System section of this book.

When the engine in your Bronco is running, the air/fuel mixture from the carburetor is being drawn into the engine by a partial vacuum created by the downward movement of the pistons on the intake stroke. the amount of air/fuel mixture that enters the engine is controlled by the throttle plate(s) in the bottom of the carburetor. When the engine is not running, the throttle plates are closed, completely blocking off the air/fuel passages at the bottom of the carburetor. The throttle plates are connected by the throttle linkage to the accelerator pedal in the passenger compartment of the Bronco. When you depress the pedal, you open the throttle plates in the carburetor to admit more air/fuel mixture to the engine.

When the engine is idling, it is necessary to have the throttle plates open slightly. To prevent having to hold your foot on the pedal, an idle speed screw is located on the carburetor linkage.

The idle adjusting screw contacts a lever (throttle lever) on the outside of the carburetor. When the screw is turned, it opens or closes the throttle plates of the carburetor, raising or lowering the idle speed of the engine. This screw is called the curb idle adjusting screw.

IDLE SPEED MIXTURE ADJUSTMENT

1966–73

1. With the engine off, turn the idle fuel mixture screw and limiter cap to the full counterclockwise position.

2. Turn the idle speed adjusting screw(s) out until the throttle plate(s) seats in the throttle bore(s).

3. Make certain that the solenoid plunger is not interfering with the throttle lever.

4. Turn the idle speed adjusting screw in until it just contacts the stop on the throttle shaft and lever assembly, then turn the screw inward $1^{1}/_{2}$ turns.

5. Start the engine and warm it up.

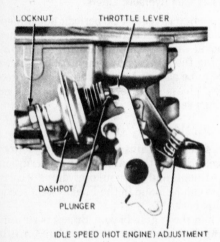

Idle speed adjustment on model 2100 or 2150 2V carburetor installed on early model V8's equipped with a dashpot

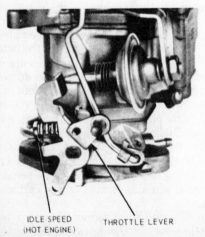

Idle speed adjustment on a Carter YF 1V carburetor

6. Check, and if necessary, adjust the ignition timing.

7. Put the transmission in neutral (manual) or drive (automatic). Set the parking brake. Block the wheels.

8. Check that the choke plate is in the full open position; turn the headlights on high beam.

9. Install a tachometer according to the manufacturer's instructions.

10. If possible leave the air cleaner on while making adjustments.

11. Loosen the solenoid locknut and turn the solenoid in or out to obtain the specified idle speed.

12. Disconnect the solenoid lead wire and place the automatic transmission in neutral.

13. Adjust the carburetor throttle stop screw to obtain 500 rpm.

14. Connect the lead wire and open the throttle slightly by hand.

15. Turn the mixture adjusting screw(s) inward to obtain the smoothest possible idle with the air cleaner installed.

IDLE SPEED ADJUSTMENT

1974–76

1. Remove the air cleaner and plug the vacuum lines.

2. Set the parking brake and block the wheels.

3. Connect a tachometer according to the manufacturer's instructions.

4. Run the engine to normalize underhood temperatures.

5. Check, and if necessary, reset the ignition timing.

6. Make certain that the choke plate is fully open.

7. Place the manual transmission in neutral; the automatic in Drive. Block the wheels.

8. Turn the solenoid adjusting screw in or out to obtain the specified idle speed. The idle speed is the higher of the two rpm figures on the underhood specification sticker.

9. Disconnect the solenoid lead wire. Place the automatic transmission in neutral.

10. Turn the solenoid off adjusting screw to obtain the solenoid off rpm. This is the lower of the two rpm figures on the underhood specifications sticker.

11. Connect the solenoid lead wire and open the throttle slightly to allow the solenoid plunger to extend.

12. Stop the engine, replace the air cleaner and connect the vacuum lines. Check the idle speed. Readjust if necessary with the air cleaner installed.

1977–86

1. Remove the air cleaner and disconnect and plug the vacuum lines.

2. Block the wheels, apply the parking brake, turn off all accessories, start the engine and run it to normalize underhood temperatures.

3. Check that the choke plate is fully open and connect a tachometer according to the manufacturer's instructions.

4. Check the throttle stop positioner (TSP)-off speed as follows:

   a. Collapse the plunger by forcing the throttle lever against it.

   b. Place the transmission in neutral and check the engine speed. If necessary, adjust to specified TSP-Off speed with the throttle adjusting screw. See the underhood sticker.

5. Place the manual transmission in neutral; the automatic in Drive and make certain the TSP plunger is extended.

6. Turn the TSP until the specified idle speed is obtained.

7. Install the air cleaner and connect the vacuum lines. Check the idle speed. Adjust, if necessary, with the air cleaner on.

IDLE MIXTURE ADJUSTMENT

1974–86

NOTE: *For this procedure, Ford recommends a propane enrichment procedure. This requires special equipment not available to the general public. In lieu of this equipment the following procedure may be followed to obtain satisfactory idle mixture.*

1. Block the wheels, set the parking brake and run the engine to bring it to normal operating temperature.

2. Disconnect the hose between the emission canister and the air cleaner.

3. On engines equipped with the Thermactor air injection system, the routing of the vacuum lines connected to the dump valve will have to be temporarily changed. Mark them for reconnection before switching them.

4. For valves with one or two vacuum lines at the side, disconnect and plug the lines.

5. For valves with one vacuum line at the top, check the line to see if it is connected to the intake manifold or an intake manifold source such as the carburetor or distributor vacuum line. If not, remove and plug the line at the dump valve and connect a temporary length of vacuum hose from the dump valve fitting to a source of intake manifold vacuum.

6. Remove the limiter caps from the mixture screws by CAREFULLY cutting them with a sharp knife.

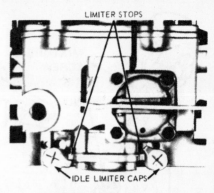

Mixture adjustment screws on the 2100 or 2150 carburetor with the limiter caps in place

Mixture adjustment screws on the Carter YF 1V carburetor with the limiter cap removed

7. Place the transmission in neutral and run the engine at 2500 rpm for 15 seconds.

8. Place the automatic transmission in Drive; the manual in neutral.

9. Adjust the idle speed to the higher of the two figures given on the underhood sticker.

10. Turn the idle mixture screws to obtain the highest possible rpm, leaving the screws in the leanest position that will maintain this rpm.

11. Repeat steps 7 thru 10 until further adjustment of the mixture screws does not increase the rpm.

12. Turn the screws in until the lower of the two idle speed figures is reached. Turn the screws in ¼ turn increments each to insure a balance.

13. Turn the engine off and remove the tachometer. Reinstall all equipment.

NOTE: *Rough idle, that cannot be corrected by normal service procedures on 1977 and later models, may be cause by leakage be-*

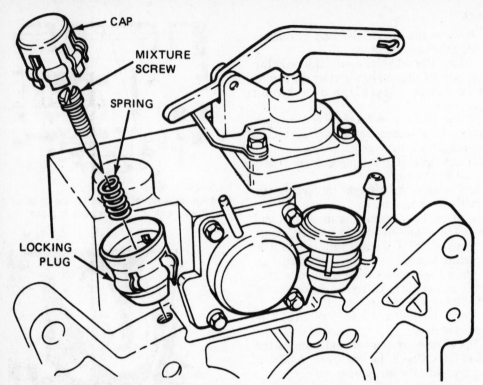

Some 1980 and later 2150 models have 2-piece metal plugs and caps in place of plastic limiter caps on the idle mixture adjusting screws. They should be carefully removed before attempting any adjustments.

tween the EGR valve body and diaphragm. To determine if this is the cause:

1. Tighten the EGR bolts to 15 ft.lb. Connect a vacuum gauge to the intake manifold.

2. Lift to exert a sideways pressure on the diaphragm housing. If the idle changes or the reading on the vacuum gauge varies, replace the EGR valve.

TROUBLESHOOTING THE FORD SOLID STATE IGNITION SYSTEM

NOTE: *Ford has substantially altered their 1978–86 electronic ignition test procedure. Due to the sensitive nature of the system and the complexity of the test procedures, it is recommended that you refer to your dealer if you suspect a problem in your 1978–86 electronic ignition system. The system can, of course, be tested by substituting known good components (module, stator, etc.).*

This system, which at first appears to be extremely complicated, is actually quite simple to diagnose and repair. Diagnosis does, however, require the use of a voltmeter and an ohmmeter. You will also need several jumper wires with both blade ends and alligator clips.

The symptoms of a defective component within the solid state system are exactly the same as those you would encounter in a conventional system. Some of these symptoms are:

- Hard or no starting
- Rough idle
- Poor fuel economy
- Engine misses while under load or while accelerating

If you suspect a problem in your ignition system, first perform a spark intensity test to pinpoint the problem. Using insulated pliers, hold the end of one of the spark plug leads about ½" (12.7mm) away from the engine block or other good ground, and crank the engine. If you have a nice, fat spark, then your problem is not in the ignition system. If you have no spark or a very weak spark, then proceed to the following tests.

Stator Test

To test the stator (also known as the magnetic pickup assembly), you will need an ohmmeter. Run the engine until it reaches operating temperature, then turn the ignition switch to the off position. Disconnect the wire harness from the distributor. Connect the ohmmeter between the orange and purple wires. Resistance should be 400–800Ω. Next, connect t he ohmmeter between the black wire and a good ground on the engine. Operate the vacuum advance either by hand or with an external vacuum source. Resistance should be 0Ω. Finally, connect the ohmmeter between the orange wire and ground, and then purple wire and ground. Resistance should be over 70,000Ω in both cases. If any of your ohmmeter readings differ from the above specifications, then the stator is defective and must be replaced as a unit.

If the stator is good, then either the electronic module or the wiring connections must be checked next. Because of its complicated electronic nature, the module itself cannot be checked, except by substitution. If you have access to a module which you know to be good, then perform a substitution test at this time. If this cures the problem, then the original module is faulty and must be replaced. If it does not

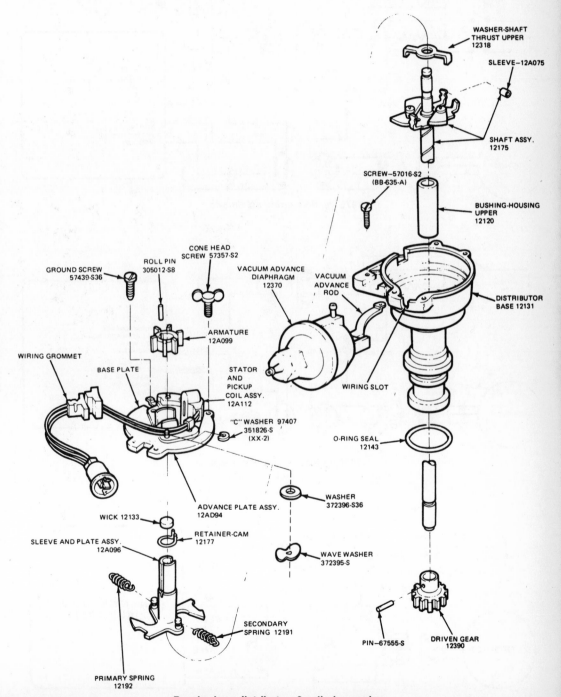

Breakerless distributor, 6-cylinder engine

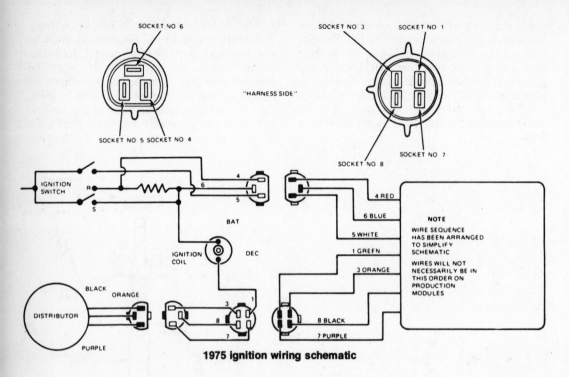

1975 ignition wiring schematic

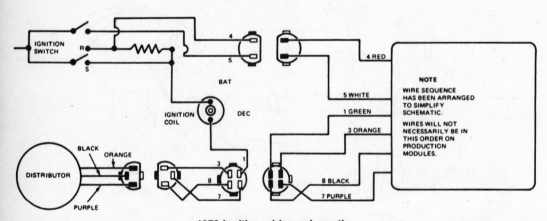

1976 ignition wiring schematic

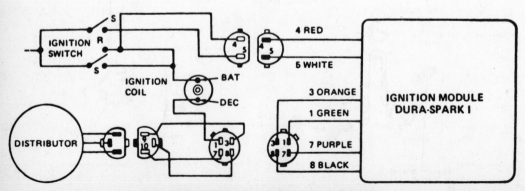

1977–81 Dura-Spark 1 ignition wiring schematic

1975 Test Sequence

	Test Voltage Between	Should Be	If Not, Conduct
Key On	Socket #4 and Engine Ground	Battery Voltage ± 0.1 Volt	Module Bias Test
	Socket #1 and Engine Ground	Battery Voltage ± Volt	Battery Source Test
Cranking	Socket #5 and Engine Ground	8 to 12 volts	Cranking Test
	Jumper #1 to #8 Read #6	more than 6 volts	Starting Circuit Test
	Pin #7 and Pin #8	½ volt minimum AC or any DC volt wiggle	Distributor Hardware Test
Key Off	Socket #7 and #3 Socket #8 and Engine Ground Socket #7 and Engine Ground Socket #3 and Engine Ground	400 to 800 ohms 0 ohms more than 70,000 ohms	Magnetic Pick-up (Stator) Test
	Socket #4 and Coil Tower Socket #1 and Pin #6	7,000 to 13,000 ohms 1.0 to 2.0 ohms	Coil Test
	Socket #1 and Engine Ground	more than 4.0 ohms	Short Test
	Socket #4 and Pin #6	1.0 to 2.0 ohms	Resistance Wire Test

1976 Test Sequence

	Test Voltage Between	Should Be	If Not, Conduct
Key On	Socket #4 and Engine Ground	Battery Voltage ± 0.1 Volt	Battery Source Test
	Socket #1 and Engine Ground	Battery Voltage ± 0.1 Volt	Battery Source Test
Cranking	Socket #5 and Engine Ground	8 to 12 volts	Check Supply Circuit (starting) through Ignition Switch
	Jumper #1 to #8 Read #6	more than 6 volts	Starting Circuit Test
	Pin #3 and Pin #8	½ volt minimum AC or any DC volt wiggle	Distributor Hardware Test
Key Off	Socket #8 and #3 Socket #7 and Engine Ground Socket #8 and Engine Ground Socket #3 and Engine Ground	400 to 800 ohms 0 ohms more than 70,000 ohms more than 70,000 ohms	Magnetic Pick-up (Stator) Test
	Socket #4 and Coil Tower	7,000 to 13,000 ohms	Coil Test
	Socket #1 and Engine Ground	more than 4.0 ohms	Short Test

cure the problem or if you cannot locate a known good module, then disconnect the two wiring harnesses from the module, and, using a voltmeter, check the following circuits.

NOTE: *Make no tests at the module side of the connectors.*

1. Starting circuit: Connect the voltmeter leads to ground and to the corresponding female socket of the white male lead from the module (you will need a jumper wire with a blade end). Crank the engine over. The voltage should be between 8 and 12 volts.

2. Running circuit: Turn the ignition switch to the **ON** position. Connect the voltmeter leads to ground and the corresponding female socket of the red male lead from the module. Voltage should be battery voltage plus or minus 0.1 volts.

3. Coil circuit: Leave the ignition switch **ON**. Connect the voltmeter leads to ground and to the corresponding female socket of the green male lead from the module. Voltage should be battery voltage plus or minus 0.1 volts.

If any of the preceding readings are incorrect, inspect and repair any loose, broken, frayed or dirty connections. If this doesn't solve the problem, perform a battery source test.

1977–80 Test Sequence

	Test Voltage Between	Should Be	If Not, Conduct
Key On	Socket #4 and Engine Ground	Battery Voltage ± 0.1 Volt	Module Bias Test
	Socket #1 and Engine Ground	Battery Voltage ± 0.1 Volt	Battery Source Test
Cranking	Socket #5 and Engine Ground	8 to 12 volts	Cranking Test
	Jumper #1 to #8—Read Coil "Bat" Term & Engine Ground	more than 6 volts	Starting Circuit Test
	Sockets #7 and #3	½ volt minimum wiggle	Distributor Hardware Test
Key Off	Socket #7 and #3 Socket #8 and Engine Ground Socket #7 and Engine Ground Socket #3 and Engine Ground	400 to 800 ohms 0 ohms more than 70,000 ohms more than 70,000 ohms	Magnetic Pick-up (Stator) Test
	Socket #4 and Coil Tower	7,000 to 13,000 ohms	Coil Test
	Socket #1 and Coil "Bat" Term	1.0 to 2.0 ohms Breakerless & Dura-Spark II	
		0.5 to 1.5 ohms Dura-Spark I	
	Socket #1 and Engine Ground	more than 4.0 ohms	Short Test
	Socket #4 and Coil "Bat" Term (Except Dura-Spark I)	1.0 to 2.0 ohms Breakerless	Resistance Wire Test
		0.7 to 1.7 ohms Dura-Spark II	

Battery Source Test

To make this test, do not disconnect the coil.

Connect the voltmeter leads to the BAT terminal at the coil and a good ground. Connect a jumper wire from the DEC terminal at the coil to a good ground. Make sure all lights and accessories are off. Turn the ignition to the **ON** position. Check the voltage. If the voltage is below 4.9 volts (11 volts for Dura Spark I), then check the primary wiring for broken strands, cracked or frayed wires, or loose or dirty terminals. Repair or replace any defects. If, however, the voltage is above 7.9 volts (14 volts for Dura Spark I), then you have a problem in the resistance wiring and it must be replaced.

It should be noted here that if you do have a problem in your electronic ignition system, most of the time it will be a case of loose, dirty or frayed wires. The electronic module, being completely solid state, is not ordinarily subject to failure. It is possible for the unit to fail, of course, but as a general rule, the source of an ignition system probably will be somewhere else in the circuit.

Troubleshooting Engine Performance

Problem	Cause	Solution
Hard starting (engine cranks normally)	• Binding linkage, choke valve or choke piston	• Repair as necessary
	• Restricted choke vacuum diaphragm	• Clean passages
	• Improper fuel level	• Adjust float level
	• Dirty, worn or faulty needle valve and seat	• Repair as necessary
	• Float sticking	• Repair as necessary
	• Faulty fuel pump	• Replace fuel pump
	• Incorrect choke cover adjustment	• Adjust choke cover
	• Inadequate choke unloader adjustment	• Adjust choke unloader
	• Faulty ignition coil	• Test and replace as necessary
	• Improper spark plug gap	• Adjust gap
	• Incorrect ignition timing	• Adjust timing

Troubleshooting Engine Performance (cont.)

Problem	Cause	Solution
	• Incorrect valve timing	• Check valve timing; repair as necessary
Rough idle or stalling	• Incorrect curb or fast idle speed	• Adjust curb or fast idle speed
	• Incorrect ignition timing	• Adjust timing to specification
	• Improper feedback system operation	• Refer to Chapter 4
	• Improper fast idle cam adjustment	• Adjust fast idle cam
	• Faulty EGR valve operation	• Test EGR system and replace as necessary
	• Faulty PCV valve air flow	• Test PCV valve and replace as necessary
	• Choke binding	• Locate and eliminate binding condition
	• Faulty TAC vacuum motor or valve	• Repair as necessary
	• Air leak into manifold vacuum	• Inspect manifold vacuum connections and repair as necessary
	• Improper fuel level	• Adjust fuel level
	• Faulty distributor rotor or cap	• Replace rotor or cap
	• Improperly seated valves	• Test cylinder compression, repair as necessary
	• Incorrect ignition wiring	• Inspect wiring and correct as necessary
	• Faulty ignition coil	• Test coil and replace as necessary
	• Restricted air vent or idle passages	• Clean passages
	• Restricted air cleaner	• Clean or replace air cleaner filler element
	• Faulty choke vacuum diaphragm	• Repair as necessary
Faulty low-speed operation	• Restricted idle transfer slots	• Clean transfer slots
	• Restricted idle air vents and passages	• Clean air vents and passages
	• Restricted air cleaner	• Clean or replace air cleaner filter element
	• Improper fuel level	• Adjust fuel level
	• Faulty spark plugs	• Clean or replace spark plugs
	• Dirty, corroded, or loose ignition secondary circuit wire connections	• Clean or tighten secondary circuit wire connections
	• Improper feedback system operation	• Refer to Chapter 4
	• Faulty ignition coil high voltage wire	• Replace ignition coil high voltage wire
	• Faulty distributor cap	• Replace cap
Faulty acceleration	• Improper accelerator pump stroke	• Adjust accelerator pump stroke
	• Incorrect ignition timing	• Adjust timing
	• Inoperative pump discharge check ball or needle	• Clean or replace as necessary
	• Worn or damaged pump diaphragm or piston	• Replace diaphragm or piston
	• Leaking carburetor main body cover gasket	• Replace gasket
	• Engine cold and choke set too lean	• Adjust choke cover
	• Improper metering rod adjustment (BBD Model carburetor)	• Adjust metering rod
	• Faulty spark plug(s)	• Clean or replace spark plug(s)
	• Improperly seated valves	• Test cylinder compression, repair as necessary
	• Faulty ignition coil	• Test coil and replace as necessary
	• Improper feedback system operation	• Refer to Chapter 4

Troubleshooting Engine Performance (cont.)

Problem	Cause	Solution
Faulty high speed operation	• Incorrect ignition timing • Faulty distributor centrifugal advance mechanism	• Adjust timing • Check centrifugal advance mechanism and repair as necessary
	• Faulty distributor vacuum advance mechanism	• Check vacuum advance mechanism and repair as necessary
	• Low fuel pump volume	• Replace fuel pump
	• Wrong spark plug air gap or wrong plug	• Adjust air gap or install correct plug
	• Faulty choke operation	• Adjust choke cover
	• Partially restricted exhaust manifold, exhaust pipe, catalytic converter, muffler, or tailpipe	• Eliminate restriction
	• Restricted vacuum passages	• Clean passages
	• Improper size or restricted main jet	• Clean or replace as necessary
	• Restricted air cleaner	• Clean or replace filter element as necessary
	• Faulty distributor rotor or cap	• Replace rotor or cap
	• Faulty ignition coil	• Test coil and replace as necessary
	• Improperly seated valve(s)	• Test cylinder compression, repair as necessary
	• Faulty valve spring(s)	• Inspect and test valve spring tension, replace as necessary
	• Incorrect valve timing	• Check valve timing and repair as necessary
	• Intake manifold restricted	• Remove restriction or replace manifold
	• Worn distributor shaft	• Replace shaft
	• Improper feedback system operation	• Refer to Chapter 4
Misfire at all speeds	• Faulty spark plug(s)	• Clean or replace spark plug(s)
	• Faulty spark plug wire(s)	• Replace as necessary
	• Faulty distributor cap or rotor	• Replace cap or rotor
	• Faulty ignition coil	• Test coil and replace as necessary
	• Primary ignition circuit shorted or open intermittently	• Troubleshoot primary circuit and repair as necessary
	• Improperly seated valve(s)	• Test cylinder compression, repair as necessary
	• Faulty hydraulic tappet(s)	• Clean or replace tappet(s)
	• Improper feedback system operation	• Refer to Chapter 4
	• Faulty valve spring(s)	• Inspect and test valve spring tension, repair as necessary
	• Worn camshaft lobes	• Replace camshaft
	• Air leak into manifold	• Check manifold vacuum and repair as necessary
	• Improper carburetor adjustment	• Adjust carburetor
	• Fuel pump volume or pressure low	• Replace fuel pump
	• Blown cylinder head gasket	• Replace gasket
	• Intake or exhaust manifold passage(s) restricted	• Pass chain through passage(s) and repair as necessary
	• Incorrect trigger wheel installed in distributor	• Install correct trigger wheel
Power not up to normal	• Incorrect ignition timing	• Adjust timing
	• Faulty distributor rotor	• Replace rotor
	• Trigger wheel loose on shaft	• Reposition or replace trigger wheel
	• Incorrect spark plug gap	• Adjust gap
	• Faulty fuel pump	• Replace fuel pump
	• Incorrect valve timing	• Check valve timing and repair as necessary
	• Faulty ignition coil	• Test coil and replace as necessary
	• Faulty ignition wires	• Test wires and replace as necessary
	• Improperly seated valves	• Test cylinder compression and repair as necessary

Troubleshooting Engine Performance (cont.)

Problem	Cause	Solution
Power not up to normal (cont.)	• Blown cylinder head gasket • Leaking piston rings • Worn distributor shaft • Improper feedback system operation	• Replace gasket • Test compression and repair as necessary • Replace shaft • Refer to Chapter 4
Intake backfire	• Improper ignition timing • Faulty accelerator pump discharge • Defective EGR CTO valve • Defective TAC vacuum motor or valve • Lean air/fuel mixture	• Adjust timing • Repair as necessary • Replace EGR CTO valve • Repair as necessary • Check float level or manifold vacuum for air leak. Remove sediment from bowl
Exhaust backfire	• Air leak into manifold vacuum • Faulty air injection diverter valve • Exhaust leak	• Check manifold vacuum and repair as necessary • Test diverter valve and replace as necessary • Locate and eliminate leak
Ping or spark knock	• Incorrect ignition timing • Distributor centrifugal or vacuum advance malfunction • Excessive combustion chamber deposits • Air leak into manifold vacuum • Excessively high compression • Fuel octane rating excessively low • Sharp edges in combustion chamber • EGR valve not functioning properly	• Adjust timing • Inspect advance mechanism and repair as necessary • Remove with combustion chamber cleaner • Check manifold vacuum and repair as necessary • Test compression and repair as necessary • Try alternate fuel source • Grind smooth • Test EGR system and replace as necessary
Surging (at cruising to top speeds)	• Low carburetor fuel level • Low fuel pump pressure or volume • Metering rod(s) not adjusted properly (BBD Model Carburetor) • Improper PCV valve air flow • Air leak into manifold vacuum • Incorrect spark advance • Restricted main jet(s) • Undersize main jet(s) • Restricted air vents • Restricted fuel filter • Restricted air cleaner • EGR valve not functioning properly • Improper feedback system operation	• Adjust fuel level • Replace fuel pump • Adjust metering rod • Test PCV valve and replace as necessary • Check manifold vacuum and repair as necessary • Test and replace as necessary • Clean main jet(s) • Replace main jet(s) • Clean air vents • Replace fuel filter • Clean or replace air cleaner filter element • Test EGR system and replace as necessary • Refer to Chapter 4

TROUBLESHOOTING BASIC POINT-TYPE IGNITION SYSTEM PROBLEMS

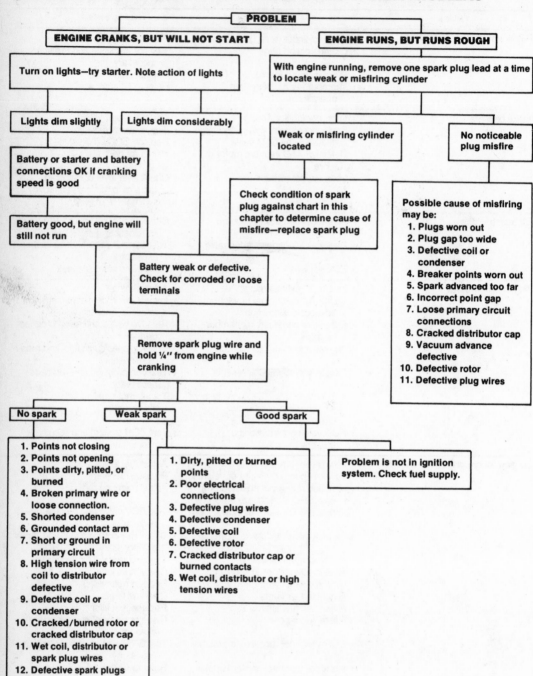

ENGINE ELECTRICAL

NOTE: *This book contains simple testing procedures for your Bronco's electronic ignition. More comprehensive testing on this system and other electronic control systems on your Bronco can be found in CHILTON'S GUIDE TO ELECTRONIC ENGINE CONTROLS, book part number 7535, available at your local retailer.*

Ignition Coil
TESTING

The ignition coil has to be tested separately from the rest of the ignition system.

1. Primary resistance is measured between the two primary (low voltage) coil terminals, with the coil connector disconnected and the ignition switch off. Primary resistance must be 0.71–0.77Ω for Dura Spark I. For Dura Spark II, it must be 1.13–1.23Ω. For TFI systems, the primary resistance should be 0.3–1.0Ω.

2. On Dura Spark ignitions, the secondary the secondary resistance is measured between the BATT and high voltage (secondary) terminals of the ignition coil with the ignition off, and the wiring from the coil disconnected. Secondary resistance must be 7,350–8,250Ω on Dura Spark I systems. Dura Spark II figure is 7,700–9,300Ω. For TFI systems, the primary resistance should be 8,000–11,500Ω.

3. If resistance test are okay, but the coil is still suspected, test the coil on a coil tester by following the test equipment manufacturer's instructions for a standard coil. If the readings differ from the original test, check for a defective harness.

REMOVAL AND INSTALLATION

1. Disconnect the battery.
2. Disconnect and mark the negative and positive terminal wires from the coil.

3. Remove the screws from the bracket that secures the coil to the engine.
4. Remove the coil from the engine.
5. Place the new coil into the bracket.
6. Install the screws that secure the bracket to the engine and tighten.
7. Install the wires to the terminal posts.

Ignition Module
REMOVAL AND INSTALLATION

1. Disconnect the battery.
2. Disconnect and mark the wiring to the ignition module.
3. Remove the bolts which secure the module to the vehicle.
4. Install a new module (if necessary), reconnect the wiring and tighten the bolts.

Distributor
REMOVAL AND INSTALLATION

1. Remove the air cleaner assembly, taking note of the hose locations.
2. On models equipped with a conventional ignition system, disconnect the primary wire at the coil. On models equipped with breakerless ignition, disconnect the distributor wiring connector from the vehicle wiring harness.
3. Noting the position of the vacuum line(s) on the distributor diaphragm, disconnect the lines at the diaphragm. Unsnap the two distributor cap retaining clamps and remove the cap. Position the cap and ignition wires to one side.

NOTE: *If it is necessary to disconnect ignition wires from the cap to get enough room to remove the distributor, make sure to label every wire and the cap for accurate reinstallation.*

4. Using a chalk or paint, carefully mark the position of the distributor rotor in relation to the distributor housing and mark the position of the distributor housing. This is very im-

portant because the distributor must be reinstalled in the exact same location from which it was removed, if correct ignition timing is to be maintained.

5. Remove the distributor holddown bolt and clamp. Remove the distributor from the engine. Make sure that the oil pump (intermediate) driveshaft does not come out with the distributor. If it does, remove it from the distributor shaft, coat its lower end with heavy grease, and reinsert it, making sure that it fully engages the oil pump drive.

NOTE: *Do not disturb the engine while the distributor is removed. If you turn the engine over with the distributor removed, you will have to retime the engine.*

a. If the engine was cranked (disturbed) with the distributor removed, it will now be necessary to retime the engine. If the distributor has been installed incorrectly and the engine will not start, remove the distributor from the engine and start over again. Hold the distributor close to the engine and install the cap on the distributor in its normal position. Locate the No. 1 spark plug tower on the distributor cap. Scribe a mark on the body of the distributor directly below the No.1 spark plug wire tower on the distributor cap. Remove the distributor cap from the distributor and move the distributor and cap to one side. Remove the No. 1 spark plug and crank the engine over until the No. 1 cylinder is on its compression stroke. To accomplish this, place a wrench on the lower engine pulley and turn the engine slowly in a clockwise or counterclockwise (V8) direction until the TDC mark on the crankshaft damper aligns with the timing pointer. If you place your finger in the No. 1 spark plug hole, you will feel air escaping as the piston rises in the combustion chamber. On conventional ignition systems, the rotor must be at the No. 1 firing position to install the distributor. On breakerless ignition systems, one of the armature segments must be aligned with the stator as shown in the accompanying illustration to install the distributor. Make sure that the oil pump intermediate shaft properly engages the distributor shaft. It may be necessary to crank the engine with the starter, after the distributor drive gear is partially engaged, in order to engage the oil pump intermediate shaft. Install, but do not tighten the retaining clamp and bolt. Rotate the distributor to advance the timing to a point where the armature tooth is aligned properly (breakerless ignition) or to a point where the points are just starting to open (conventional ignition). Tighten the clamp.

b. If the engine was not cranked (disturbed) when the distributor was removed, position the distributor in the block with the rotor aligned with the mark previously scribed on the distributor body and the marks on the distributor body and cylinder block in alignment. Install the distributor holddown bolt and clamp fingertight.

6. Install the distributor cap and wires.

7. On models equipped with conventional ignition, connect the primary wire at the coil. On models equipped with breakerless ignition, connect the distributor wiring connector to the wiring harness.

8. Install the Thermactor air pump mounting bolt, if removed, and adjust the air pump drive belt tension, if necessary, as outlined in Chapter 1.

9. Install the air cleaner, if removed.

10. Check the ignition timing as outlined in Chapter 2.

Alternator

The alternator charging system is a negative (–) ground system which consists of a alternator, a regulator, a charge indicator, a storage battery and wiring connecting the components.

The alternator is belt driven from the engine. Energy is supplied from the alternator regulator system to the rotating field through two brushes to two slip rings. The slip rings are mounted on the rotor shaft and are connected to the field coil This energy supplied by the rotating field from the battery is called excitation current and is used to initially energize the field to begin the generation of electricity. Once the alternator starts to generate electricity, the excitation current comes from its own output rather than the battery.

The alternator produces power in the form of alternating current. The alternating current is rectified to direct current by 6 diodes. The direct current is used to charge the battery and power the rest of the electrical system.

ALTERNATOR PRECAUTIONS

To prevent damage to the alternator and regulator, the following precautionary measures must be taken when working with electrical system.

1. Never reverse battery connections. Always check the battery polarity visually. This should be done before any connections are made to be sure that all of the connections correspond to the battery ground polarity of the Bronco.

2. Booster batteries for starting must be connected properly. Make sure that the posi-

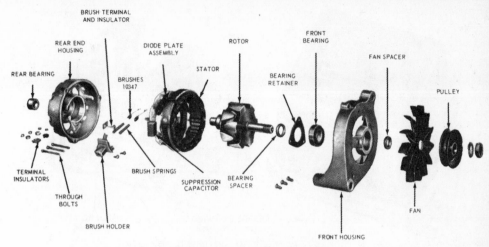

BRUSH TERMINAL
AND INSULATOR

REAR END
HOUSING

ROTOR

FRONT
BEARING

DIODE PLATE
ASSEMBLY

FAN SPACER

REAR BEARING

STATOR

BEARING
RETAINER

BRUSHES
10347

PULLEY

TERMINAL
INSULATORS

BRUSH SPRINGS

SUPPRESSION
CAPACITOR

BEARING
SPACER

THROUGH
BOLTS

BRUSH HOLDER

FAN

FRONT HOUSING

Exploded view of the alternator

Rear terminal alternator contact locations

tive cable of the booster battery is connected to the positive terminal of the battery that is getting the boost. The same applies to the negative cables.

3. Disconnect the battery cables before using a faster charger; the charger has a tendency to force current through the diodes in the opposite direction for which they were designed. This burns out the diodes.

4. Never use a fast charger as a booster for starting the vehicle.

5. Never disconnect the voltage regulator while the engine is running.

6. Do not ground the alternator on an open circuit with the field energized.

8. Do not attempt to polarize an alternator.

REMOVAL AND INSTALLATION

1. Open the hood and disconnect the battery ground cable.

2. From under the vehicle, remove the adjusting arm bolt.

3. Remove the alternator through bolt. Re-

move the drive belt from the alternator pulley and lower the alternator.

4. Label all of the leads to the alternator so that you can install them correctly and disconnect the leads from the alternator.

5. Remove the alternator from the vehicle.

6. To install, reverse the above procedure.

Regulator

The alternator regulator has been designed to control the charging system's rate of charge and to compensate for seasonal temperature changes. The electromechanical regulator on 1968 and later vehicles is calibrated at the factory and is not adjustable. The regulator on 1966–67 models is adjustable.

REMOVAL AND INSTALLATION

1. Disconnect the positive terminal of the battery.

2. Disconnect all of the electrical leads to the regulator. Label them as removed, so you can replace them in the correct order on the replacement unit.

3. Remove all of the holddown screws, then remove the unit from the vehicle.

4. Install the new voltage regulator using the holddown screws from the old one, or on new ones if they are provided with the replacement regulator. Tighten the holddown screws.

5. Connect all the leads to the new regulator.

ADJUSTMENT (1966 and 1967 MODELS ONLY)

To make any adjustments to the voltage regulator, the unit has to be removed from the vehicle. See the removal and installation procedure for instructions.

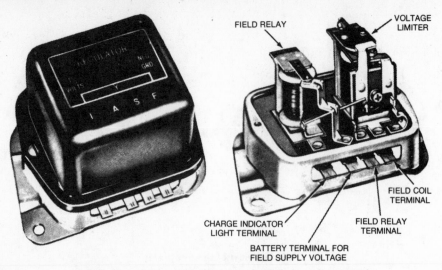

1966–67 regulator with the cover installed, and removed

FIELD RELAY ADJUSTMENT

Air Gap

Place a 0.010–0.018" (0.254–0.457mm) feeler gauge on top of the coil core closest to the contact points. Hold the armature down on the gauge. Do not push down on the contact spring arm. Bend the contact post arm until the bottom contact just touches the upper contact. Remove the feeler gauge.

VOLTAGE LIMITER ADJUSTMENT

The voltage limiter is adjusted by bending the voltage limiter spring arm. To increase the voltage setting, bend the adjusting arm downward. To decrease the voltage setting, bend the adjusting arm upward. Final adjustment of the regulator must be made with the regulator at normal operating temperatures. The voltage limiter should be set to between 13.6 and 15.1 volts read with a voltmeter installed between the battery/alternator terminal of the starter relay and the positive terminal of the battery.

Battery

REMOVAL AND INSTALLATION

1. Loosen the nuts that secure the cable ends to the battery terminals. Lift the battery cables from the terminals with a twisting motion.

2. If there is a battery cable puller available, make use of it.

3. Remove the holddown nuts from the battery holddown bracket and remove the bracket and the battery. Lift the battery straight up and out of the vehicle, being sure to keep the

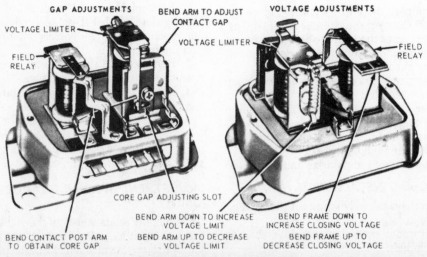

1966–67 regulator adjustments

Alternator Specifications

Year	Color Code	Output		Field Curent Amp	Cut-In rpm	Brush Length Inches	
		Amps	Watts			New	Limit
1966–74	Purple	38	570	2.5	400	½	5/16
	Orange	42	630	2.9	400	½	5/16
1975	Purple	38	570	2.5	400	½	5/16
	Orange	42	630	2.9	400	½	5/16
	Red	55	825	2.9	400	½	5/16
	Green	61	915	2.9	400	½	5/16
1976–81	Orange	40	600	2.9	400	½	5/16
	Green	60	900	2.9	400	½	5/16
	Green*	60	900	4.0	400	½	3/16
1982–86	Orange	40	600	4.3	400	½	5/16
	Green	60	900	4.3	400	½	5/16
	Black	70	1050	4.0	400	½	¼

*Blue ink on pully face

Battery and Starter Specifications

Year	Engine	Battery			Starter						Brush Spring Tension (oz)
		Ampere/ Hour Capacity	Volts	Ground	Lock Test			No Load Test			
					Amps	Volts	Torque (ft. lbs.)	Amps	Volts	RPM	
1966–77	All	45	12	Neg	670	5	15.5	70	12	9500	40
		55	12	Neg	670	5	15.5	70	12	9500	40
		70	12	Neg	670	5	15.5	70	12	9500	40
		80	12	Neg	670	5	15.5	70	12	9500	40
1978	All	41	12	Neg	460	5	9.0	70	12	9500	40
		68	12	Neg	670	5	15.5	80	12	9500	80
					525*	5	17.2	80	11	10,000	50
1979	All	41	12	Neg	460	5	9.0	70	12	9500	40
		53	12	Neg	670	5	15.5	80	12	9500	80
		68	12	Neg							
1980–86	All	36	12	Neg	460	5	9.0	70	12	9500	40
		45	12	Neg	670	5	15.5	80	12	9500	80
		63	12	Neg							
		81	12	Neg							

*Prestolite model with 400 cid engine

battery level so as to not spill out any of the battery acid.

4. Before installing the battery in the vehicle, make sure that the battery terminals are clean and free from corrosion. Use a battery terminal cleaner on the terminals and on the inside of the battery cable ends. If a cleaner is not available, use coarse grade sandpaper to remove the corrosion. A mixture of baking soda and water poured over the terminals and cable ends will help remove and neutralize any acid build up. Before installing the cables onto the terminals onto the terminals, cut apiece of felt cloth or something similar into a circle

about 3″ (76mm) across. Cut a hole in the middle about the size of the battery terminals at their base. Push the cloth pieces over the terminals so they lie flat on the top of the battery. Soak the pieces of cloth with oil. This will keep the formation of oxidized acid to a minimum. Place the battery in the vehicle. Install the cables onto the terminals. Tighten the nuts on the cable ends. Smear a light coating of grease on the cable ends and tops of the terminals. This will further prevent the build up of oxidized acid on the terminals and the cable ends. Install and tighten the nuts of the battery hold bracket.

Starter

REMOVAL AND INSTALLATION

1. Disconnect the positive battery terminal
2. Raise the vehicle and disconnect the starter cable at the starter terminal.
3. Remove all of the starter attaching bolts that attach the starter to the bellhousing.
4. Remove the starter from the engine.
5. Install the starter in the reverse order of removal.

STARTER RELAY REPLACEMENT

The starter relay is mounted on the inside of the left wheel well. To replace it, disconnect the positive battery cable from the battery, disconnect all of the electrical leads from the relay and remove the relay from the fender well. Replace in the reverse order of removal.

STARTER OVERHAUL

Brush Replacement

1. Disconnect the field coil connectors from the starter motor solenoid terminal.

2. Remove the through bolts.
3. Remove the end frame and the field frame from the drive housing.
4. Disassemble the brush assembly from the field frame by releasing the spring and removing the supporting pin. Pull the brushes and the brush holders out and disconnect the wiring.
5. Install the new brushes into the holders.
6. Assemble the brush holder using the spring and position the unit on the supporting pin.
7. Install the unit in the starter motor and attach the wiring.
8. Position the field frame over the armature.
9. Install the through bolts.
10. Connect the field coil connectors to the solenoid.

STARTER DRIVE REPLACEMENT

1. Remove the cover of the starter drive's plunger lever arm, and the brush cover band. Remove the through bolts, starter drive gear housing and the return spring of the driver gear's actuating lever.
2. Remove the pivot pin which retains the starter gear plunger lever and remove the lever.
3. Remove the stopring retainer. Remove and discard the stopring which holds the drive gear to the armature shaft and then remove the drive gear assembly.

To install the drive gear assembly:

4. Lightly Lubriplate® the armature shaft splines and install the starter drive gear assembly on the shaft. Install a new stopring and stopring retainer.
5. Position the starter drive gear plunger le-

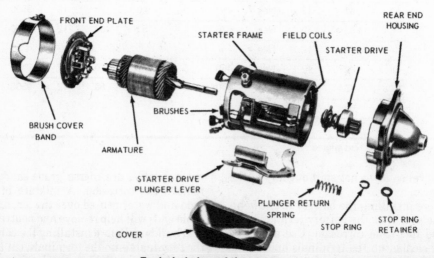

Exploded view of the starter

ver to the frame and starter drive assembly.

6. Install the pivot pin.

7. Position the drive plunger lever return spring and the drive gear housing to the frame, then install and tighten the throughbolts. Be sure that the stopring retainer is properly seated in the drive housing.

8. Position the starter drive plunger lever cover and brush cover band on the starter. Tighten the brush cover band retaining screw.

ENGINE MECHANICAL

Design

6 CYLINDER ENGINES

The 170 cu. in. and 200 cu. in. 6-cylinder engines installed in Broncos are of an inline, overhead valve design.

The exhaust manifold, mounted under the intake manifold, supplies heat to the intake manifold to help vaporize the incoming fuel mixture. To prevent carburetor icing, and to further vaporize the fuel, a spacer connected with the cooling system is installed under the carburetor. Hot coolant circulates through the spacer, warming the incoming fuel mixture.

The cylinder head carries the intake and exhaust valve assemblies and mechanism. Water passages in the cylinder head help keep the valves cool.

The distributor, located on the left side of the engine, is gear driven from the camshaft and also drives the oil pump through an intermediate shaft.

The crankshaft is mounted on 4 main bearings with crankshaft end thrust controlled by the flanged No. 3 bearing.

The camshaft is mounted on 4 bearings and is driven by a sprocket and chain connection with the crankcase. An integral eccentric on the camshaft operates the fuel pump. The intake and exhaust valves are the rotating type. The valve tappets are of the hydraulic type wit solid type tappets installed in early 170 cu. in. engines.

The engines are pressure lubricated by a rotor type oil pump equipped with a pressure relief valve. Oil reaches the rocker arm shaft through No. 6 valve rocker arm shaft support at the rear of the engine.

The engines re equipped with either an open or closed positive crankcase ventilation system. In either case, crankcase fumes are channeled to the intake manifold. From 1967 on, the engines are equipped with the Thermactor exhaust emission control system, otherwise known as the air injection system.

V8 ENGINES

The V8 engines are of the standard, two-bank, V-design with the banks of cylinders opposed to each other at a 90° angle.

To assist in the vaporization of the incoming fuel mixture, the intake manifold contains water passages and an exhaust gas crossover passage. The intake manifold has two separate fuel passages, each with its own inlet passage to the carburetor. One of the fuel passages feeds Nos. 1, 4, 6 and 7 cylinders and the other passage feeds No. 2, 3, 5 and 8 cylinders.

The crankshaft is supported by 5 main bearings, with crankshaft end thrust controlled by the flanged No. 3 bearing.

The camshaft, which is located in the center of the V design of the engine, is mounted on 5 bearings and is driven by a sprocket and chain which are connected to a sprocket on the crankshaft. An eccentric bolted to the front of the camshaft operates the fuel pump. A gear on the front of the camshaft drives the distributor, which drives the oil pump through an intermediate shaft. The oil pump is located in the left front of the oil pan.

The engine is equipped with hydraulic valve lifters.

The engine is equipped with either an open or closed positive crankcase ventilation system which directs crankcase fumes to the intake manifold.

The engine is equipped with the Thermactor exhaust emission control system, otherwise known as the air injection system.

Engine Overhaul Tips

Most engine overhaul procedures are fairly standard. In addition to specific parts replacement procedures and complete specifications for your individual engine, this chapter also is a guide to accept rebuilding procedures. Examples of standard rebuilding practice are shown and should be used along with specific details concerning your particular engine.

Competent and accurate machine shop services will ensure maximum performance, reliability and engine life.

In most instances it is more profitable for the

do-it-yourself mechanic to remove, clean and inspect the component, buy the necessary parts and deliver these to a shop for actual machine work.

On the other hand, much of the rebuilding work (crankshaft, block, bearings, piston rods, and other components) is well within the scope of the do-it- yourself mechanic.

TOOLS

The tools required for an engine overhaul or parts replacement will depend on the depth of your involvement. With a few exceptions, they will be the tools found in a mechanic's tool kit (see Chapter 1). More in-depth work will require any or all of the following:
- a dial indicator (reading in thousandths) mounted on a universal base
- micrometers and telescope gauges
- jaw and screw type pullers
- scraper
- valve spring compressor
- ring groove cleaner
- piston ring expander and compressor
- ridge reamer
- cylinder hone or glaze breaker
- Plastigage®
- engine stand

Use of most of these tools is illustrated in this chapter. Many can be rented for a one time use from a local parts jobber or tool supply house specializing in automotive work.

Occasionally, the use of special tools is called for. See the information on Special Tools and Safety Notice in the front of this book before substituting another tool.

INSPECTION TECHNIQUES

Procedures and specifications are given in this chapter for inspecting, cleaning and assessing the wear limits of most major components. Other procedures such as Magnaflux® and Zyglo® can be used to locate material flaws and stress cracks. Magnaflux® is a magnetic process applicable only to ferrous materials. The Zyglo® process coats the material with a fluorescent dye penetrant and can be used on any material Check for suspected surface cracks can be more readily made using spot check dye. The dye is sprayed onto the suspected area, wiped off and the area sprayed with a developer. Cracks will show up brightly.

OVERHAUL TIPS

Aluminum has become extremely popular for use in engines, due to its low weight. Observe the following precautions when handling aluminum parts:
- Never hot tank aluminum parts (the caustic hot tank solution will eat the aluminum).

- Remove all aluminum parts (identification tag, etc.) from engine parts prior to the tanking.
- Always coat threads lightly with engine oil or anti-seize compounds before installation, to prevent seizure.
- Never over torque bolts or spark plugs especially in aluminum threads.

Stripped threads in any component can be repaired using any of several commercial repair kits (Heli-Coil®, Microdot®, Keenserts®, etc.).

When assembling the engine, any parts that will be frictional contact must be prelubed to provide lubrication at initial start-up. Any product specifically formulated for this purpose can be used, but engine oil is not recommended as a prelube.

When semi-permanent (locked, but removable) installation of bolts or nuts is desired, threads should be cleaned and coated with Loctite® or other similar, commercial non-hardening sealant.

REPAIRING DAMAGED THREADS

Several methods of repairing damaged threads are available. Heli-Coil®, Keenserts® and Microdot® are among the most widely used. All involve basically the same principle—drilling out stripped threads, tapping the hole and in-

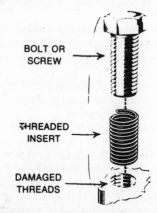

BOLT OR SCREW

THREADED INSERT

DAMAGED THREADS

Damaged bolt holes can be repaired with thread repair inserts

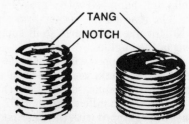

TANG

NOTCH

Standard thread repair insert (left) and spark plug thread insert (right)

Drill out the damaged threads with specified drill. Drill completely through the hole or to the bottom of a blind hole

With the tap supplied, tap the hole to receive the thread insert. Keep the tap well oiled and back it out frequently to avoid clogging the threads

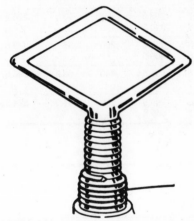

Screw the threaded insert onto the installation tool until the tang engages the slot. Screw the insert into the tapped hole until it is ¼–½ turn below the top surface, After installation break off the tang with a hammer and punch

stalling a prewound insert—making welding, plugging and oversize fasteners unnecessary.

Two types of thread repair inserts are usually supplied—a standard type for most Inch Coarse, Inch Fine, Metric Course and Metric Fine thread sizes and a spark lug type to fit most spark plug port sizes. Consult the individual manufacturer's catalog to determine exact applications. Typical thread repair kits will contain a selection of prewound threaded

inserts, a tap (corresponding to the outside diameter threads of the insert) and an installation tool. Spark plug inserts usually differ because they require a tap equipped with pilot threads and a combined reamer/tap section. Most manufacturers also supply blister packed thread repair inserts separately in addition to a master kit containing a variety of taps and inserts plus installation tools.

Before effecting a repair to a threaded hole, remove any snapped, broken or damaged bolts or studs. Penetrating oil can be used to free frozen threads. The offending item can be removed with locking pliers or with a screw or stud extractor. After the hole is clear, the thread can be repaired, as follows:

Checking Engine Compression

A noticeable lack of engine power, excessive oil consumption and/or poor fuel mileage measured over an extended period are all indicators of internal engine war. Worn piston rings, scored or worn cylinder bores, blown head gaskets, sticking or burnt valves and worn valve seats are all possible culprits here. A check of each cylinder's compression will help you locate the problems.

As mentioned in the Tools and Equipment section of Chapter 1, a screw-in type compression gauge is more accurate that the type you simply hold against the spark plug hole, although it takes slightly longer to use. It's worth it to obtain a more accurate reading. Follow the procedures below for gasoline and diesel engined trucks.

GASOLINE ENGINES

1. Warm up the engine to normal operating temperature.
2. Remove all spark plugs.
3. Disconnect the high tension lead from the ignition coil.
4. On fully open the throttle either by operating the carburetor throttle linkage by hand or by having an assistant floor the accelerator pedal.
5. Screw the compression gauge into the no.1 spark plug hole until the fitting is snug.
NOTE: *Be careful not to crossthread the plug hole. On aluminum cylinder heads use extra care, as the threads in these heads are easily ruined.*
6. Ask an assistant to depress the accelerator pedal fully on both carbureted and fuel injected trucks. Then, while you read the compression gauge, ask the assistant to crank the engine two or three times in short bursts using the ignition switch.
7. Read the compression gauge at the end of

Standard Torque Specifications and Fastener Markings

In the absence of specific torques, the following chart can be used as a guide to the maximum safe torque of a particular size/grade of fastener.

- There is no torque difference for fine or coarse threads.
- Torque values are based on clean, dry threads. Reduce the value by 10% if threads are oiled prior to assembly.
- The torque required for aluminum components or fasteners is considerably less.

U.S. Bolts

SAE Grade Number	1 or 2			5			6 or 7		
Number of lines always 2 less than the grade number.									
Bolt Size (Inches)—(Thread)	Maximum Torque			Maximum Torque			Maximum Torque		
	Ft./Lbs.	Kgm	Nm	Ft./Lbs.	Kgm	Nm	Ft./Lbs.	Kgm	Nm
¼—20	5	0.7	6.8	8	1.1	10.8	10	1.4	13.5
—28	6	0.8	8.1	10	1.4	13.6			
⁵/₁₆—18	11	1.5	14.9	17	2.3	23.0	19	2.6	25.8
—24	13	1.8	17.6	19	2.6	25.7			
⅜—16	18	2.5	24.4	31	4.3	42.0	34	4.7	46.0
—24	20	2.75	27.1	35	4.8	47.5			
⁷/₁₆—14	28	3.8	37.0	49	6.8	66.4	55	7.6	74.5
—20	30	4.2	40.7	55	7.6	74.5			
½—13	39	5.4	52.8	75	10.4	101.7	85	11.75	115.2
—20	41	5.7	55.6	85	11.7	115.2			
⁹/₁₆—12	51	7.0	69.2	110	15.2	149.1	120	16.6	162.7
—18	55	7.6	74.5	120	16.6	162.7			
⅝—11	83	11.5	112.5	150	20.7	203.3	167	23.0	226.5
—18	95	13.1	128.8	170	23.5	230.5			
¾—10	105	14.5	142.3	270	37.3	366.0	280	38.7	379.6
—16	115	15.9	155.9	295	40.8	400.0			
⅞—9	160	22.1	216.9	395	54.6	535.5	440	60.9	596.5
—14	175	24.2	237.2	435	60.1	589.7			
1—8	236	32.5	318.6	590	81.6	799.9	660	91.3	894.8
—14	250	34.6	338.9	660	91.3	849.8			

Metric Bolts

Relative Strength Marking	4.6, 4.8			8.8		
Bolt Markings						
Bolt Size Thread Size x Pitch (mm)	Maximum Torque			Maximum Torque		
	Ft./Lbs.	Kgm	Nm	Ft./Lbs.	Kgm	Nm
6 x 1.0	2–3	.2–.4	3–4	3–6	.4–.8	5–8
8 x 1.25	6–8	.8–1	8–12	9–14	1.2–1.9	13–19
10 x 1.25	12–17	1.5–2.3	16–23	20–29	2.7–4.0	27–39
12 x 1.25	21–32	2.9–4.4	29–43	35–53	4.8–7.3	47–72
14 x 1.5	35–52	4.8–7.1	48–70	57–85	7.8–11.7	77–110
16 x 1.5	51–77	7.0–10.6	67–100	90–120	12.4–16.5	130–160
18 x 1.5	74–110	10.2–15.1	100–150	130–170	17.9–23.4	180–230
20 x 1.5	110–140	15.1–19.3	150–190	190–240	26.2–46.9	160–320
22 x 1.5	150–190	22.0–26.2	200–260	250–320	34.5–44.1	340–430
24 x 1.5	190–240	26.2–46.9	260–320	310–410	42.7–56.5	420–550

each series of cranks, and record the highest of these readings. Repeat this procedure for each of the engine's cylinders. Compare the highest reading of each cylinder to the compression pressure specification in the Tune-Up Specifications chart in Chapter 2. The specs in this chart are maximum values.

A cylinder's compression pressure is usually acceptable if it is not less than 80% of maximum. The difference between each cylinder should be no more than 12–14 pounds.

8. If a cylinder is unusually low, pour a tablespoon of clean engine oil into the cylinder through the spark plug hole and repeat the compression test. If the compression comes up after adding the oil, it appears that the cylinder's piston rings or bore are damaged or worn. If the pressure remains low, the valves may not be seating properly (a valve job is needed), or the head gasket may be blown near that cylinder. If compression in any two adjacent cylinders is low, and if the addition of oil doesn't help the compression, there is leakage past the head gasket. Oil and coolant water in the combustion chamber can result from this problem. There may be evidence of water droplets on the engine dipstick when a head gasket has blown.

Engine
REMOVAL AND INSTALLATION
6–170
6–200

REMOVAL

1. Drain the cooling system and remove the hood.

CAUTION: *When draining the coolant, keep in mind that cats and dogs are attracted by the ethylene glycol antifreeze, and are quite likely to drink any that is left in an uncovered container or in puddles on the ground. This will prove fatal in sufficient quantity. Always drain the coolant into a sealable container. Coolant should be reused unless it is contaminated or several years old.*

2. Remove the air cleaner
3. Disconnect the battery ground cable.
4. Disconnect the upper and lower radiator hoses at the engine.
5. Remove the 4 radiator retaining screws and lift the radiator from the vehicle with the hoses attached.
6. Disconnect the heater hoses at the water pump and at the rear of the carburetor spacer.
7. Remove the retaining screw, and disconnect the battery ground cable and the alternator ground wire from the cylinder block.
8. Remove the fan belt and the alternator and position them to one side.

9. Remove the retaining nut and disconnect the starter cable at the starter.
10. Remove the two retaining screws and remove the starter from the vehicle.
11. Remove the U-bolt clamp holding the exhaust pipe to the cylinder block.
12. Remove the two retaining nuts and disconnect the exhaust pipe from the exhaust manifold.
13. Remove the 4 retaining screws and remove the fan, spacer and the pulley from the water pump.
14. Disconnect the wiring at the ignition coil, and the oil and temperature sending units and position the wires out of the way.
15. Disconnect the throttle cable and the choke cable from the carburetor and position them out of the way.
16. Remove the windshield wiper vacuum hose and the inlet fuel line from the fuel pump.
17. Raise the vehicle and drain the crankcase oil.
18. Remove the retaining screws from the clutch linkage equalizer shaft bracket at the cylinder block and bellhousing, and remove the bracket.
19. Remove the retaining nuts and washers from each of the motor mounts.
20. Remove the retaining screws holding the inspection cover to the bottom of the bellhousing and remove the inspection cover.
21. Loosen the screws that hold the bellhousing to the engine. Do not remove them just yet. Loosen them enough that they can be removed easily with a wrench later on.
22. Replace the drain plug in the oil pan and lower the vehicle.
23. Position a jack under the transmission and remove the screws holding the bellhousing to the engine.
24. Carefully lift the engine from the engine compartment.

INSTALLATION

1. Carefully lower the engine into the engine compartment, aligning the transmission input shaft with he clutch disc splines.
2. Install the two upper bellhousing-to-engine retaining screws securely.
3. Remove the lifting device from the engine and the jack from beneath the transmission.
4. Raise the vehicle and install the remaining two lower bellhousing-to-engine retaining screws.
5. Install the inspection plate cover.
6. Install the washers and nuts onto the motor mounts.
7. Grease the clutch equalizer shaft and mount the bracket to the engine and bellhousing with the proper retaining screws.

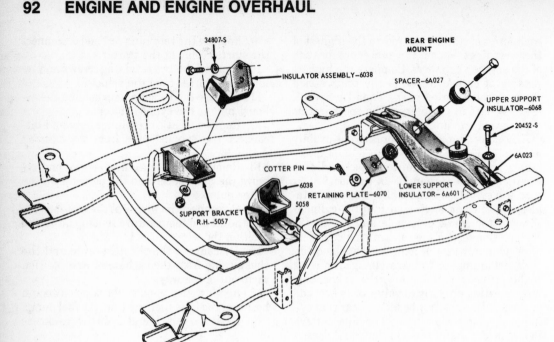

Engine supports for the 6-170, 200

8. Lower the vehicle and install the windshield vacuum hose and the inlet fuel line onto the fuel pump.

9. Connect and adjust the choke and throttle cable at the carburetor.

10. Connect the wiring at the ignition coil and the oil and temperature sending units.

11. Install the water pump pulley, spacer and the fan, alternator and fan belt. Adjust the fan belt tension.

12. Connect the exhaust pipe to the exhaust manifold, using a new gasket. Install the U-bolt clamp that holds the exhaust pipe to the engine block.

13. Position the starter and install the two retaining screws, and install the starter cable.

14. Position the battery ground cable and the alternator ground wire on the engine block and install the retaining screw.

15. Connect the heater hoses at the rear of the carburetor spacer and at the water pump.

16. Install the radiator and connect the upper and lower hoses.

17. Connect the battery ground cable.

18. Install the air cleaner.

19. Fill the crankcase with oil, and the cooling system with coolant.

20. Operate the engine and check for leaks.

21. Install the hood.

8–289, 302 Through 1977

REMOVAL

1. Drain the cooling system and the crankcase.

CAUTION: *When draining the coolant, keep in mind that cats and dogs are attracted by the ethylene glycol antifreeze, and are quite likely to drink any that is left in an uncovered container or in puddles on the ground. This will prove fatal in sufficient quantity. Always drain the coolant into a sealable container. Coolant should be reused unless it is contaminated or several years old.*

2. Disconnect the battery and alternator ground cables from the cylinder block.

3. Remove the air cleaner and intake duct assembly including the crankcase ventilation hose.

4. Disconnect the radiator lower and upper hose at the radiator. If equipped with an automatic transmission disconnect the transmission oil cooler lines.

5. Remove the fan shroud and position it over the fan. Remove the radiator. Remove the fan shroud, fan spacer, belts and pulley.

6. Disconnect the wires at the alternator adjusting bolts and allow the alternator to swing down and out of the way.

7. Disconnect the oil pressure sending unit wire from the sending unit, and the flexible fuel line at the fuel tank line. Plug the fuel tank line. Disconnect the windshield wiper vacuum line at the fuel pump.

8. Disconnect the accelerator rod from the carburetor.

Disconnect the transmission shift rod and remove the retracting spring if so equipped.

9. Disconnect the heater hoses from the wa-

General Engine Specifications

Year	Engine No. Cyl Displacement (cu in.)	Carburetor Type	Advertised Horsepower @ rpm	Advertised Torque @ rpm (ft. lbs.)	Bore x Stroke (in.)	Advertised Compression Ratio	Oil Pressure @ 2000 rpm (psi)
1966–67	6-170	1 bbl	105 @ 4400	158 @ 2400	3.500 x 2.940	9.1:1	45
	8-289	2 bbl	200 @ 4400	282 @ 2400	4.000 x 2.870	9.3:1	35–55
1968	6-170	1 bbl	100 @ 4000	158 @ 2200	3.500 x 2.940	8.7:1	35–60
	8-289	2 bbl	195 @ 4600	288 @ 2600	4.000 x 2.870	8.7:1	35–60
1969	6-170	1 bbl	100 @ 4000	156 @ 2200	3.500 x 2.940	8.7:1	35–60
	8-302	2 bbl	205 @ 4600	300 @ 2600	4.000 x 3.000	8.6:1	35–60
1970	6-170	1 bbl	100 @ 4000	156 @ 2200	3.500 x 2.940	8.7:1	35–60
	8-302	2 bbl	205 @ 4600	300 @ 2600	4.000 x 3.000	8.6:1	35–60
1971	6-170	1 bbl	100 @ 4200	148 @ 2600	3.500 x 2.940	8.7:1	35–60
	8-302	2 bbl	205 @ 4600	300 @ 2600	4.000 x 3.000	8.6:1	35–60
1972	6-170	1 bbl	82 @ 4400	129 @ 1800	3.500 x 2.940	8.3:1	35–60
	8-302	2 bbl	141 @ 4000	242 @ 2000	4.000 x 3.000	8.5:1	35–60
1973	6-200	1 bbl	84 @ 3600	151 @ 1800	3.683 x 3.126	8.3:1	35–55
	8-302	2 bbl	138 @ 4200	234 @ 2200	4.000 x 3.000	8.3:1	40–60
1974	6-200	1 bbl	84 @ 3600	151 @ 1800	3.683 x 3.126	8.3:1	35–55
	8-302	2 bbl	140 @ 3800	230 @ 2600	4.000 x 3.000	8.0:1	40–60
1975	8-302	2 bbl	140 @ 3800	230 @ 2600	4.000 x 3.000	8.0:1	40–60
1976	8-302	2 bbl	134 @ 3600	242 @ 2000	4.000 x 3.000	8.0:1	40–60
1977	8-302	2 bbl	134 @ 3600	242 @ 2000	4.000 x 3.000	8.0:1	40–60
1978–79	8-351M	2 bbl	132 @ 3600 ①	242 @ 1600 ②	4.00 x 3.50	8.0:1	50–75
	8-400	2 bbl	149 @ 3200	300 @ 1400	4.00 x 4.00	8.0:1	50–75
1980–81	6-300	1 bbl	117 @ 3000	243 @ 1600	4.00 x 3.98	8.9:1	40–60
	8-302	2 bbl	135 @ 3400	243 @ 2000	4.00 x 3.00	8.4:1	40–60
	8-351W	2 bbl	132 @ 3600	263 @ 1800	4.00 x 3.50	8.0:1	40–65
1982	6-300	1 bbl	123 @ 3000	257 @ 1600	4.00 x 3.98	8.9:1	40–60
	8-302	2 bbl	132 @ 3400	232 @ 1800	4.00 x 3.00	8.4:1	40–60
	8-351W	2 bbl	139 @ 3600	278 @ 1800	4.00 x 3.50	8.3:1	40–65
1983–86	6-300	1 bbl	120 @ 3200	251 @ 1600	4.00 x 3.98	8.4:1	40–60
	8-302	2 bbl	139 @ 3400	250 @ 2000	4.00 x 3.00	8.4:1	40–60
	8-351W	2 bbl	139 @ 3200	278 @ 1400	4.00 x 3.50	8.3:1	40–65
	8-351HO	4 bbl	210 @ 4000	305 @ 2800	4.00 x 3.50	8.3:1	40–65

① Auto trans: 137 @ 3400
② Auto trans: 257 @ 1800

ter pump and intake manifold. Disconnect the water temperature sending unit wire from the sending unit.

10. Remove the flywheel housing to engine upper bolts.

11. Disconnect the primary wire from the ignition coil. Remove the wire harness from the left rocker arm cover and position the wires out of the way. Disconnect the ground strap from the block.

12. Raise the front of the vehicle. Disconnect the starter cable from the starter. Remove the starter and dust seal.

13. Disconnect the muffler inlet pipes from

Valve Specifications

Year	Engine No. Cyl Displacement (cu in.)	Seat Angle (deg)	Face Angle (deg)	Spring Test Pressure (lbs. @ in.)	Spring Installed Height (in.)	Stem-to Guide Clearance (in.)		Stem Diameter (in.)	
						Intake	Exhaust	Intake	Exhaust
1966–72	6-170	45	44	52 @ 1.6	1⁹⁄₁₆–1³⁹⁄₆₄	.0008–.0025	.0010–.0027	.3103	.3128
1966	8-289	45	44	169 @ 1.39	1²⁵⁄₃₂	.0010–.0027	.0020–.0037	.3420	.3410
1967	8-289	45	44	60 @ 1.64	1²¹⁄₃₂	.0010–.0027	.0010–.0027	.3420	.3420
1968	8-289	45	44	79 @ 1.66	1²¹⁄₃₂	.0010–.0027	.0010–.0027	.3420	.3420
1969	8-302	45	44	75 @ 1.66	1²¹⁄₃₂	.0010–.0027	.0010–.0027	.3420	.3420
1970–71	8-302	45	44	75 @ 1.66	1²¹⁄₃₂	.0020–.0027	.0010–.0027	.3420	.3420
1972	8-302	45	44	75 @ 1.66	1²¹⁄₃₂	.0010–.0027	.0015–.0032	.3420	.3414
1973–74	6-200	45	46	150 @ 1.22	1¹⁹⁄₃₂	.0008–.0025	.0010–.0027	.3104	.3102
1973–76	8-302	45	46	200 @ 1.22	1⁹⁄₁₆	.0010–.0027	.0015–.0032	.3420	.3415
1977	8-302	①	②	200 @ 1.31 ③	1⁹⁄₁₆	.0010–.0027	.0015–.0032	.3420	.3415
1978–79	8-351M	45	44	226 @ 1.39	1¹³⁄₁₆	.0010–.0027	.0015–.0032	.3416–.3423	.3411–.3418
	8-400	45	44	229 @ 1.39	1¹³⁄₁₆	.0010–.0027	.0015–.0032	.3416–.3423	.3411–.3418
1980–86	6-300	45	44	197 @ 1.30 ④	1¹¹⁄₁₆ ⑥	.0010–.0027	.0010–.0027	.3416–.3423	.3416–.3423
	8-302	45	44	204 @ 1.36 ⑤	1⁴³⁄₆₄ ⑦	.0010–.0027	.0015–.0032	.3416–.3423	.3411–.3418
	8-351W	45	44	200 @ 1.36 ⑧	1⁴⁹⁄₆₄ ⑦	.0010–.0027	.0015–.0032	.3416–.3423	.3411–.3418

① 44½–45
② 45½–45¾
③ 1.20—Exhaust
④ Exhaust: 192 @ 1.18

⑤ Exhaust: 200 @ 1.20
⑥ Exhaust: 1⁹⁄₁₆
⑦ Exhaust: 1³⁷⁄₆₄
⑧ Exhaust: 200 @ 1.20

the exhaust manifolds. Disconnect the engine support insulators from the brackets on the frame underbody.

On a vehicle with automatic transmission remove the converter inspection plate. Remove the torque converter to flywheel attaching bolts.

Remove the remaining flywheel housing to engine bolts.

14. Lower the vehicle, and then support the transmission. Install the engine left lifting bracket on the front of the left cylinder head, and install the engine right lifting bracket at the rear of the right cylinder head. Then attach an engine lifting sling.

15. Raise the engine slightly and carefully pull it from the transmission. Carefully lift the engine out of the engine compartment so that the rear cover plate is not bent or other components damaged. Install the engine on a work stand.

INSTALLATION

1. Attach the engine lifting brackets and sling. Remove the engine from the work stand.

2. Lower the engine carefully into the engine compartment. Make sure the exhaust manifolds are properly aligned with the muffler inlet pipes and the dowels in the block are through the rear cover plate and engage the

Crankshaft and Connecting Rod Specifications
(All measurements given in in.)

Year	Engine No Cyl Displacement (cu in.)	Crankshaft				Connecting Rod		
		Main Brg Journal Dia	Main Brg Oil Clearance	Shaft End-play	Thrust on No	Journal Diameter	Oil Clearance	Slide Clearance
1966–72	6-170	2.2482–2.2490	.0005–.0022 ①	.004–.008	3	2.1232–2.1240	.0008–.0024	.0035–.0105
1966–73	8-289 and 8-302	2.2482–2.2490	.0005–.0024 ②	.004–.008	3	2.1228–2.1236	.0008–.0026	.010–.020
1973–74	6-200	2.2482–2.2490	.0005–.0022	.004–.008	5	2.1232–2.1240	.0008–.0024	.003–.010
1973–77	8-302	2.2482–2.2490	.0005–.0024 ③ ④	.004–.008	3	2.1228–2.1236	.0008–.0026	.010–.020
1978–79	8-351M	2.9994–3.0002	.0008–.0015	.004–.008	3	2.3103–2.3111	.0008–.0015	.010–.020
	8-400	2.9994–3.0002	.0008–.0015	.004–.008	3	2.3103–2.3111	.0008–.0015	.010–.020
1980–86	6-300	2.3982–2.3990	.0008–.0015	.004–.008	5	2.1228–2.1236	.0008–.0015	.006–.013
	8-302	2.2482–2.2490	.0005–.0015 ⑤	.004–.008	3	2.1228–2.1236	.0008–.0015	.010–.020
	8-351W	2.9994–3.0002	.0008–.0015	.004–.008	3	2.3103–2.3111	.0008–.0015	.010–.020

① 1970 only, 0.0010–0.0025
② 1970–71 only, 0.0010–0.0025
③ #1 bearing: 0.0001–0.0005
④ 1974–75 0.0005–0.0015
⑤ #1 bearing: .0001–.0015

Camshaft Specifications
(All measurements in inches)

Engine	Journal Diameter					Bearing Clearance	Lobe Lift		Camshaft End Play
	1	2	3	4	5		Intake	Exhaust	
170	1.8095–1.8105	1.8095–1.8105	1.8095–1.8105	1.8095–1.8105	—	.001–.003	.2405	.2390	.001–.007
200	1.8095–1.8105	1.8095–1.8105	1.8095–1.8105	1.8095–1.8105	1.8095–1.8105	.001–.003	.2530	.2320	.001–.007
300	2.0170–2.0180	2.0170–2.0180	2.0170–2.0180	2.0170–2.0180	—	.001–.003	.2490	.2490	.001–.007
289, 302	2.0805–2.0815	2.0655–2.0665	2.0505–2.0515	2.0355–2.0365	2.0205–2.0215	.001–.003	.2303 ①	.2375 ②	.005–.0055
351W	2.0805–2.0815	2.0655–2.0665	2.0505–2.0515	2.0355–2.0365	2.0205–2.0215	.001–.003	.2600	.2600	.001–.007
351M	2.1248–2.1328	2.0655–2.0665	2.0505–2.0515	2.0355–2.0365	2.0205–2.0215	.001–.003	.2350 ③	.2350 ③	.001–.006 ④
400	2.1248–2.1328	2.0655–2.0665	2.0505–2.0515	2.0355–2.0365	2.0505–2.0215	.001–.003	.2474 ③	.2500	.001–.006

① 1977 & 1980–83: .2375
② 1977 & 1980–83: .2470
③ 1979: .2500
④ 1982–86: .001–.007

Piston and Ring Specifications

(All measurements in inches)

Year	Engine	Piston to Bore Clearance	Ring Side Clearance			Ring Gap		
			Top Compression	Bottom Compression	Oil Control	Top Compression	Bottom Compression	Oil Control
1966	170	.0014– .0020	.0009– .0026	.0020– .0040	snug	.0010– .0020	.0010– .0020	.015– .055
	289	.0014– .0022	.0019– .0036	.0020– .0040	snug	.0010– .0020	.0010– .0020	.015– .069
1967	170	.0014– .0020	.0019– .0036	.0020– .0040	snug	.0010– .0020	.0010– .0020	.015– .055
	289	.0018– .0026	.0019– .0036	.0020– .0040	snug	.0010– .0020	.0010– .0020	.015– .066
1968	170	.0014– .0020	.0020– .0040	.0020– .0040	snug	.0010– .0020	.0010– .0020	.015– .055
	289	.0018– .0026	.0020– .0040	.0020– .0040	snug	.0010– .0020	.0010– .0020	.015– .069
1969	170	.0014– .0020	.0020– .0040	.0020– .0040	snug	.0010– .0020	.0010– .0020	.015– .055
	302	.0018– .0026	.0020– .0040	.0020– .0040	snug	.0010– .0020	.0010– .0020	.015– .069
1970	170	.0014– .0020	.0020– .0040	.0020– .0040	snug	.0010– .0020	.0010– .0020	.015– .055
	302	.0018– .0026	.0020– .0040	.0020– .0040	snug	.0010– .0020	.0010– .0020	.015– .069
1971	170	.0014– .0020	.0020– .0040	.0020– .0040	snug	.0010– .0020	.0010– .0020	.015– .055
	302	.0018– .0026	.0020– .0040	.0020– .0040	snug	.0010– .0020	.0010– .0020	.015– .069
1972	170	.0013– .0026	.0020– .0040	.0020– .0040	snug	.0010– .0020	.0010– .0020	.015– .055
	302	.0018– .0026	.0020– .0040	.0020– .0040	snug	.0010– .0020	.0010– .0020	.015– .055
1973–74	200	.0013– .0021	.0020– .0040	.0020– .0040	snug	.0010– .0020	.0010– .0020	.015– .055
1973–77	302	.0018– .0026	.0020– .0040	.0020– .0040	snug	.0010– .0020	.0010– .0020	.015– .055
1978–79	351M, 400	.0014– .0022	.0019– .0036	.0020– .0040	snug	.0010– .0020	.0010– .0020	.015– .055 ①
1980–86	300	.0014– .0022	.0019– .0036	.0020– .0040	snug	.0010– .0020	.0010– .0020	.010– .035 ②
	302, 351W	.0018– .0026	.0019– .0036	.0030– .0040	snug	.0010– .0020	.0010– .0020	.010– .035

① 1979: .015–.035
② 1982–83: .015–.055

rear cover plate and engage the holes in the flywheel housing.

On a vehicle with manual transmission start the transmission main drive gear into the clutch disc. It may be necessary to adjust the position of the transmission in relation to the engine if the input shaft will not enter the clutch disc. If the engine hangs up after the shaft enters, turn the crankshaft slowly (transmission in gear) until the shaft splines mesh with the clutch disc splines.

3. Install the flywheel housing upper bolts.

4. Install the engine support insulator to bracket attaching nuts. Disconnect the engine

Torque Specifications
(All readings in ft. lb.)

Year	Engine	Cylinder Head Bolts	Rod Bearing Bolts	Main Bearing Bolts	Crank-shaft Pulley Bolt	Flywheel-to-Crankshaft Bolts	Manifold	
							Intake	Exhaust
1966–74	170, 200	70–75	19–24	60–70	85–100	75–85	—	13–18
1966–81	289, 302	65–70	19–24	60–70	70–90 ③	75–85	①	12–16 ② ④
1978–79	351M, 400	105	40–45	95–105	70–90	75–85	⑤	18–24
1980–81	300	85	40–45	60–70	130–150	75–85	22–32	28–33
	351W	105–112	40–45	95–105	70–90	75–85	23–25	18–24

—Not Applicable
① 1966–68: 20–22
　1969–73: 23–25
　1974–77: 19–27
　1980–83: 23–25

② 1966–68 only, 15–20 ft. lbs.
③ 1974–77: 35–50
④ 1980–83: 18–24
⑤ ⅜": 22–32
　⁵⁄₁₆": 17–25

Torque Specifications
(All readings in ft. lbs.)

Year	Engine	Cylinder Head Bolts	Rod Bearing Bolts	Main Bearing Bolts	Crank-shaft Pulley Bolt	Flywheel-to-Crankshaft Bolts	Manifold	
							Intake	Exhaust
'83–'86	4-122	①	②	①	100–120	56–64	14–21 ③	16–23 ③
'83–'86	4-134	80–85	50–54	80–85	253–289	95–137	12–17 ③	17–20 ③
'83–'86	4-140	①	②	①	100–120	56–64	14–21 ③	16–23 ③
'83–'86	6-173	④	19–24	65–75	85–96	47–52	15–18 ③	20–30 ③
'82–'84	6-232	⑤	30–36	62–81	85–100	75–85	18	15–22
'79–'86	6-300	70–75	40–45	60–70	130–150	75–85	22–32	28–33
'82	8-255	65–72	19–24	60–70	70–90	75–85	18–20	18–24
'79–'86	8-302	65–70	19–24	60–70	70–90	75–85	23–25	12–16 ⑥
'79–'80	8-351M	95–105	40–45	95–105	70–90	75–85	⑦	18–24
'79–'86	8-351W	105–112	40–45	95–105	70–90	75–85	23–25	18–24
'79–'80	8-400	95–105	40–45	95–105	70–90	75–85	⑦	18–24
'83–'86	420 (diesel)	⑧	46–51 ⑨	95 ⑩	90	44–50 ⑪	24	30
'79–'86	8-460	130–140	40–45	95–105	70–90	75–85	25–30	28–33

① Torque bolts in two steps:
　Step 1: 50–60 ft. lbs.　Step 2: 80–90 ft. lbs.
② Torque nuts in two steps:
　Step 1: 25–30 ft. lbs.　Step 2: 30–36 ft. lbs.
③ Torque in stages, recheck after engine is warmed
④ Torque bolts in three steps:
　Step 1: 29–40 ft. lbs.　Step 2: 40–51 ft. lbs.
　Step 3: 70–85 ft. lbs.
⑤ Tighten in four steps:
　Step 1: 47 ft. lbs.　Step 2: 55 ft. lbs.

Step 3: 63 ft. lbs.　Step 4: 74 ft. lbs.
Back-off all bolts 2–3 turns and retorque in four steps.
⑥ '80 and later: 18–24
⑦ ⅜": 22–32
　⁵⁄₁₆": 17–25
⑧ Refer to text for sequence procedure
⑨ Two steps: 1st—38 ft. lbs, then 46–51 ft. lbs.
⑩ Two steps: 1st—75 ft. lbs, then 95 ft. lbs.
⑪ Apply locking sealer to threads

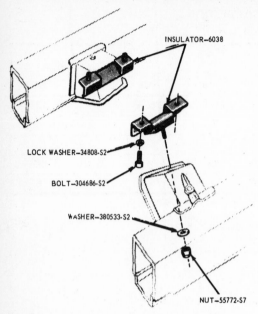

Engine front supports for the 8-289, 302 1966-77

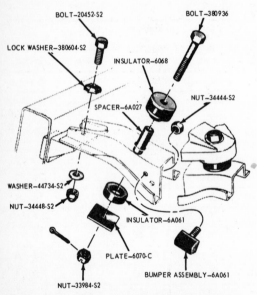

Engine rear supports for the 8-289, 302 1966-77

lifting sling and remove the lifting brackets.

5. Raise the front of the vehicle. Connect both exhaust manifolds to the muffler inlet pipes. Tighten the nuts to 18–22 ft.lb.

6. Position the dust seal and install the starter and the starter cable.

7. Install the remaining flywheel housing to engine bolts. On a vehicle with automatic transmission install the converter to flywheel attaching bolts. Install the converter inspection plate.

8. Remove the support from the transmission and lower the vehicle.

9. Connect the wiring harness to the left valve rocker arm cover and connect the coil wire.

10. Connect the water temperature sending unit wire.

11. Connect the bellcrank to the intake manifold. Connect the transmission shift rod and install the retracting spring.

12. Remove the plug from the fuel tank line and connect the fuel line and the oil pressure sending unit wire.

13. Install the pulley, belt, spacer and fan. Position the fan shroud over the fan.

14. Position the alternator and install the alternator bolts. Connect the alternator and the battery ground cables. Adjust the belt tension.

15. Install the radiator. Connect the radiator upper and lower hoses. Connect the transmission oil cooler lines if so equipped. Install the fan shroud.

16. Connect the heater hose at the water pump. Fill and bleed the cooling system. Fill the crankcase with the proper grade and quantity of oil.

17. Operate the engine at fast idle and check all gaskets and hose connections for leaks.

18. Install the air cleaner and intake duct assembly including the crankcase ventilation hose.

1978–79 8-351M, 400

REMOVAL

The engine removal and installation procedures are for the engine only without the transmission attached.

1. Drain the cooling system and the crankcase.

CAUTION: *When draining the coolant, keep in mind that cats and dogs are attracted by the ethylene glycol antifreeze, and are quite likely to drink any that is left in an uncovered container or in puddles on the ground. This will prove fatal in sufficient quantity. Always drain the coolant into a sealable container. Coolant should be reused unless it is contaminated or several years old.*

2. Disconnect the battery and alternator ground cables from the cylinder block.

3. Remove the air cleaner and intake duct assembly, including the crankcase ventilation hose and carbon canister hose.

4. Disconnect the radiator lower and upper hose at the radiator. If equipped with an automatic transmission, disconnect the transmission oil cooler lines.

5. Remove the fan shroud and position it over the fan. Remove the radiator. Remove the fan shroud, fan spacer, belts and pulley.

6. Disconnect the wires at the alternator ad-

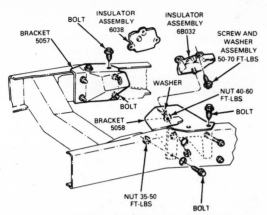

Engine front supports for the 8-351M,400 1978–79

justing bolts and allow the alternator to swing down and out of the way.

7. Disconnect the oil pressure sending unit wire from the sending unit, and the flexible fuel line at the fuel tank line. Plug the fuel tank line.

8. Disconnect the accelerator cable from the carburetor. Disconnect the transmission kickdown rod and remove the retracting spring if so equipped.

9. Disconnect the heater hoses from the water pump and intake manifold. Disconnect the water temperature sending unit wire from the sending unit.

10. Remove the flywheel housing-to-engine upper bolts.

11. Disconnect the primary wire from the ig-nition coil. Remove the wire harness from the left rocker arm cover and position the wires out of the way. Disconnect the ground strap from the cylinder block.

12. Raise the front of the vehicle. Disconnect the starter cable from the starter. Remove the starter.

13. Disconnect the muffler inlet pipes from the exhaust manifolds. Disconnect the engine support insulators from the brackets on the frame underbody.

On a vehicle with automatic transmission, remove the converter inspection plate. Remove the torque converter-to-flywheel attaching bolt.

14. Remove the remaining flywheel housing-to-engine bolts.

15. Lower the vehicle, and then support the transmission. Install the engine lifting eyes on the front of the left cylinder head, and install the engine right lifting bracket at the rear of the right cylinder head. Then attach the engine lifting sling.

16. Raise the engine slightly and carefully pull it from the transmission. Carefully lift the engine out of the engine compartment so that the rear cover plate is not bent or other components damaged. Install the engine on workstand.

INSTALLATION

1. Attach the engine lifting brackets and sling. Remove the engine from the workstand.

2. Lower the engine carefully into the en-

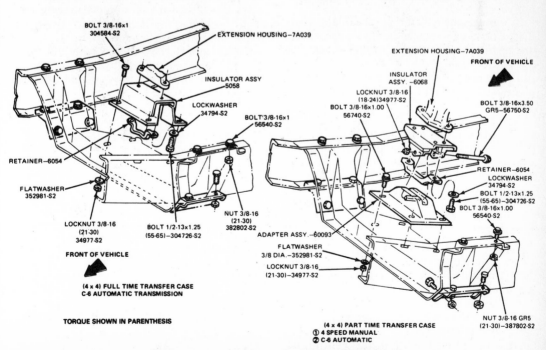

Engine rear supports for the 8-351M,400 1978–79

gine compartment. Make sure the dowels in the block are through the rear cover plate, then engage the holes in the flywheel housing.

On a vehicle with manual transmission, start the transmission main driveshaft into the clutch disc. It may be necessary to adjust the position of the transmission in relation to the engine if the input shaft will not enter the clutch disc. If the engine hangs up after the shaft enters, turn the crankshaft slowly (transmission in gear) until the shaft splines mesh with the clutch disc splines.

3. Install the flywheel housing upper bolts.

4. Install the engine support insulator-to-bracket washers and attaching nuts. Disconnect the engine lifting sling and remove the lifting eyes.

5. Raise the front of the vehicle. Connect both exhaust manifolds to the muffler inlet pipes. Tighten the nuts to 18–24 ft.lb.

6. Position and install the starter and the starter cable.

7. Install the remaining flywheel housing-to-engine bolts.

8. On a vehicle with automatic transmission, install the converter-to-flywheel attaching bolts. Install the converter inspection plate.

9. Remove the support from the transmission and lower the vehicle.

10. Connect the wiring harness to the left valve rocker arm cover and connect the coil wire.

11. Connect the water temperature sending unit wire.

12. Connect the bellcrank to the intake manifold. Connect the transmission kickdown rod and install the retracting spring. Connect the accelerator cable.

13. Remove the plug from the fuel tank line and connect the fuel line and the oil pressure sending unit wire.

14. Install the pulley, belt, spacer and fan. Position the shroud over the fan.

15. Position the alternator and install the alternator bolts. Connect the alternator and battery ground cables. Adjust the belt tension.

16. Install the radiator. Connect the radiator upper and lower hoses. Connect the transmission oil cooler lines if so equipped. Install the fan shroud.

17. Connect the heater hose at the water pump. Fill and bleed the cooling system. Fill the crankcase with the proper grade and quantity of oil.

18. Operate the engine at fast idle and check all gaskets and hose connections for leaks.

19. Install the air cleaner and intake duct assembly including the crankcase ventilation hose and carbon canister hose.

1980–86 6–300

The engine removal and installation procedures are for the engine only without the transmission attached.

CAUTION: *Engine removal requires discharge of the air conditioning system. See Chapter 1 of this book.*

REMOVAL

1. Drain the cooling system and the crankcase. Remove the hood. Remove the air cleaner. Remove air conditioner compressor and condenser.

CAUTION: *When draining the coolant, keep in mind that cats and dogs are attracted by the ethylene glycol antifreeze, and are quite likely to drink any that is left in an uncovered container or in puddles on the ground. This will prove fatal in sufficient quantity. Always drain the coolant into a sealable container. Coolant should be reused unless it is contaminated or several years old.*

2. Disconnect the battery ground cable. Disconnect the heater hose from the water pump and coolant outlet housing. Disconnect the flexible fuel line from the fuel pump.

3. Remove the radiator.

4. Remove the cooling fan, spacer, water pump pulley and fan drive belt.

5. Disconnect the accelerator cable and the choke cable at the carburetor. Remove the cable retracting spring.

On vehicle with power brakes, disconnect the vacuum line at the intake manifold.

On a vehicle with an automatic transmission, disconnect the transmission kickdown rod at the bellcrank assembly.

6. Disconnect the exhaust manifold from the muffler inlet pipe. Disconnect the body ground stop and the battery ground cable at the engine.

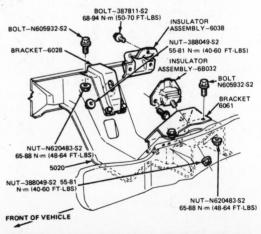

FRONT OF VEHICLE

Engine front supports for the 6-300 1980 and later

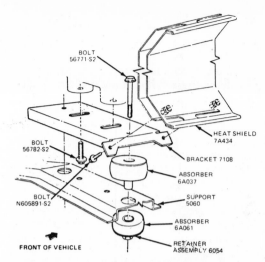

BOLT
56771-S2

HEAT SHIELD
7A434

BOLT
56782-S2

BRACKET 7108

ABSORBER
6A037

BOLT
N605891-S2

SUPPORT
5060

ABSORBER
6A061

FRONT OF VEHICLE

RETAINER
ASSEMBLY 6054

Engine rear supports for the 6-300 1980 and later

7. Disconnect the engine wiring harness at the ignition coil, coolant temperature sending unit and oil pressure sending unit. Position the harness out of the way.

8. Remove the alternator mounting bolts and position the alternator out of the way, leaving the wires attached.

On a vehicle with power steering, remove the power steering pump from the mounting brackets and position it right side up and to one side, leaving the lines attached.

9. Raise the vehicle. Remove the starter (and the automatic transmission fluid filler tube bracket). Remove the engine rear plate upper right bolt.

On a vehicle with a manual shift transmission remove all the flywheel housing lower attaching bolts. disconnect the clutch retracting spring.

On a vehicle with an automatic transmission, remove the converter housing access cover assembly. Remove the flywheel to converter nuts and secure the converter assembly in the housing. Remove the transmission oil cooler lines form the retaining clip at the engine. Remove the converter housing to engine lower attaching bolts. Remove the insulator to intermediate support bracket nut from each engine front support.

10. Lower the vehicle and position a transmission jack under the transmission to support it. Remove the remaining flywheel or converter housing to engine bolts.

11. Attach the engine lifting sling. Raise the engine slightly and carefully pull it from the transmission. Lift the engine out of the chassis.

INSTALLATION

1. Place a new gasket on the muffler inlet pipe.

2. Lower the engine carefully into the chassis. Make sure the dowels in the block engage the holes in the flywheel or converter housing.

On a vehicle with an automatic transmission, start the converter pilot into the crankshaft. Remove the retainer securing the converter in the housing.

On a vehicle with a manual shift transmission, start the transmission input shaft into the clutch disc. It may be necessary to adjust the position of the transmission with relation to the engine if the transmission input shaft will not enter the clutch disc. If the engine hangs up after the shaft enters, turn the crankshaft slowly (with the transmission in gear) until the shaft splines mesh with the clutch disc splines.

3. Install the converter or flywheel housing upper attaching bolts. Remove the jack supporting the transmission.

4. Lower the engine until it rests on the engine support(s) an remove the lifting sling.

5. Tighten the nuts to 40–60 ft.lb. Install the automatic transmission oil cooler lines bracket.

6. Install the remaining converter to flywheel housing attaching bolts. Connect the clutch return spring.

7. Install the starter and connect the starter cable. Attach the automatic transmission fluid filler tube bracket, (if so equipped).

On a vehicle with an automatic transmission, install the transmission oil cooler lines in the bracket at the cylinder block.

8. Install the exhaust manifold to muffler inlet pipe lockwashers and nuts. Tighten the nuts to 25–38 ft.lb.

9. Connect the engine ground strap and the battery ground cable.

10. On a vehicle with an automatic transmission, connect the kickdown rod to the bellcrank assembly on the intake manifold.

Connect the accelerator linkage to the carburetor and install the retracting spring. Connect the choke cable to the carburetor and hand throttle, if so equipped.

On a vehicle with power brakes, connect the brake vacuum line to the intake manifold.

11. Connect the coil primary wire, oil pressure and coolant temperature sending unit wire, flexible fuel line, heater hoses and the battery positive cable.

12. Install the alternator on the mounting bracket.

On a vehicle with power steering install the power steering pump on the mounting brackets.

13. Install the water pump pulley, spacer, cooling fan and drive belt. Tighten the fan bolts to 12–18 ft.lb.

Adjust drive belt tension. Tighten the alternator, power steering pump and air compressor mounting bolts.

14. Install the radiator. Connect the radiator lower hose to the water pump and the radiator upper hose to the coolant outlet housing. If removed, install air conditioner compressor and condenser.

On a vehicle with an automatic transmission, connect the oil cooler lines.

15. If applicable, install and adjust the hood.

16. Fill and bleed the cooling system. Fill the crankcase. Operate the engine at fast idle and check all hose connections and gaskets for leaks.

17. Adjust the carburetor idle speed to Specifications on the Engine Decal.

On a vehicle with standard transmission, adjust the clutch pedal free travel.

On a vehicle with an automatic transmission, adjust the transmission control linkage. Check the fluid level and add as required to bring it to the proper level on the oil indicator.

18. Install the air cleaner.

1980–86 302, 351W
1984–86 351HO

The engine removal and installation procedures are for the engine only without the transmission attached.

CAUTION: *This procedure requires discharge of the air conditioning system. See Chapter 1 of this book.*

REMOVAL

1. Drain the cooling system and the crankcase. Remove the hood.

CAUTION: *When draining the coolant, keep in mind that cats and dogs are attracted by the ethylene glycol antifreeze, and are quite likely to drink any that is left in an uncovered container or in puddles on the ground. This will prove fatal in sufficient quantity. Always drain the coolant into a sealable container. Coolant should be reused unless it is contaminated or several years old.*

2. Disconnect the battery and alternator ground cables from the cylinder block.

3. Remove the air cleaner and intake duct assembly, including the crankcase ventilation hose and carbon canister hose.

4. Disconnect the radiator lower and upper hose at the radiator. If equipped with an automatic transmission, disconnect the transmission oil cooler lines.

5. If so equipped, discharge the A/C system and remove the A/C condenser. Disconnect A/C lines at the compressor.

6. Remove the fan shroud and position it over the fan. Remove the radiator. Remove the fan shroud, fan spacer, belts and pulley.

7. Remove the alternator bolts and allow the alternator to swing down and out of the way.

8. Disconnect the oil pressure sending unit wire from the sending unit, and the flexible fuel line at the fuel tank line. Plug the fuel tank line. Disconnect evaporative emission hoses at the evaporative canister.

9. Disconnect the accelerator cable from the carburetor. Disconnect speed control linkages if so equipped. Disconnect the transmission kickdown rod and remove the retracting spring if so equipped.

10. Disconnect the heater hoses from the water pump and intake manifold. Disconnect the water temperature sending unit wire from the sending unit.

11. Remove the flywheel housing-to-engine upper bolts.

12. Disconnect the primary wire from the ignition coil. Remove the wire harness from the

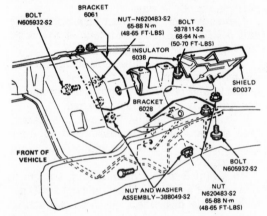

Engine front supports for the 8-302, 8-351W 1980 and later

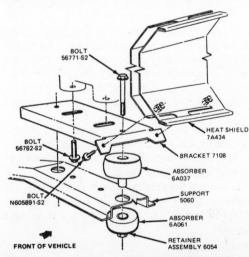

Engine rear supports for the 8-302, 8-351W 1980 and later

left rocker arm cover and position the wires out of the way. Disconnect the ground strap from the cylinder block.

13. Raise the front of the vehicle. Disconnect the starter cable from the starter. Remove the starter.

14. Disconnect the muffler inlet pipes from the exhaust manifolds. Disconnect the engine support insulators from the brackets on the frame underbody.

On a vehicle with automatic transmission, remove the converter inspection plate. Remove the torque converter-to-flywheel attaching bolts.

Remove the remaining flywheel housing-to-engine bolts.

15. If so equipped, disconnect A/C compressor magnetic clutch load wire.

16. Lower the vehicle, and then support the transmission. Install the engine lifting brackets on the front of the left cylinder head, and install the engine right lifting bracket at the rear of the right cylinder head. Then attach an engine lifting sling.

17. Raise the engine slightly and carefully pull it from the transmission. Carefully lift the engine out of the engine compartment so that the rear cover plate is not bent or other components damaged. Install the engine on a workstand.

INSTALLATION

1. Attach the engine lifting brackets and sling. Remove the engine from the workstand.

2. Lower the engine carefully into the engine compartment. Make sure the dowels in the block are through the rear cover plate, then engage the holes in the flywheel housing.

On a vehicle with manual transmission, start the transmission main driveshaft into the clutch disc. It may be necessary to adjust the position of the transmission in relation to the engine if the input shaft will not enter the clutch disc. If the engine hangs up after the shaft enters, turn the crankshaft slowly (transmission in gear) until the shaft splines mesh with the clutch disc splines.

3. Install the flywheel housing upper bolts.

4. Install the engine support insulator-to-bracket washers and attaching nuts. Disconnect the engine lifting sling and remove the lifting eyes.

5. Raise the front of the vehicle. Connect both exhaust manifolds to the muffler inlet pipes. Tighten the nuts to 18–24 ft.lb.

6. Position and install the starter and the starter cable.

7. Install the remaining flywheel housing-to-engine bolts.

8. On a vehicle with automatic transmis-

sion, install the converter-to-flywheel attaching bolts. Install the converter inspection plate.

9. Remove the support from the transmission and lower the vehicle.

10. If so equipped, connect the A/C compressor magnetic clutch lead.

11. Connect the wiring harness to the left valve rocker arm cover and connect the coil wire.

12. Connect the water temperature sending unit wire.

13. Connect the bellcrank to the intake manifold. Connect the transmission shift rod and install the retracting spring. Connect the accelerator rod and speed control linkage, if so equipped.

14. Remove the plug from the fuel tank line and connect the fuel line and the oil pressure sending unit wire. Reconnect evaporative emission hoses at the evaporative canister.

15. Install the pulley, belt, spacer and fan. Position the fan shroud over the fan.

16. Position the alternator and install the alternator bolts. Connect the alternator and the battery ground cables. Adjust the belt tension.

17. If so equipped, connect two A/C lines to the A/C compressor.

18. Install the radiator. Connect the radiator upper and lower hoes. Connect the transmission oil cooler lines if so equipped. Install the fan shroud.

19. If so equipped, install the A/C condenser to the radiator.

20. Connect the heater hose at the water pump. Fill and bleed the cooling system. Fill the crankcase with the proper grade and quantity of oil. Connect the power brake booster vacuum hose, if so equipped.

21. Operate the engine at fast idle and check all gaskets and hose connections for leaks.

22. Install the air cleaner and intake duct assembly including the crankcase ventilation hose and carbon canister hose.

23. Adjust the idle speed and mixture to specifications on engine decal.

24. Evacuate and charge the A/C System (if so equipped).

25. Install hood.

Rocker Arm Cover/Rocker Shaft and Studs

REMOVAL AND INSTALLATION

6–170, 200

1. Remove the air cleaner. Pull the PCV hose and valve out of the rubber grommet in the rocker arm cover and place the hose to the side, out of the way.

2. Disconnect the carburetor air vent tube; then remove the rocker arm cover, discarding the gasket.

3. Remove the rocker arm shaft support bolts by loosening the bolts two turns at a time in sequence.

4. Remove the rocker arm shaft assembly. NOTE: *If the pushrods are removed, they must be replaced in the same position from which they were removed.*

5. Apply Lubriplate® or equivalent to both ends of the pushrods and to the valve stem tip.

6. Install the valve pushrods. Position the valve rocker arm shaft assembly on the cylinder head.

7. Install and tighten all valve rocker arm support bolts, two turns at a time in sequence, until the supports fully contact the cylinder head. Torque the bolts to 30–35 ft.lb.

8. Check the valve clearance and adjust if necessary.

9. If any part which could affect the valve clearance has been changed, check the valve clearance.

10. Clean the valve rocker arm cover and cylinder head gasket surfaces. Install the gasket in the cover making sure that all of the tangs of the gasket are engaged in the notches provided in the cover. Connect all vacuum lines and components to their proper connection. Tighten the cover attaching bolts in two steps. First, torque the bolts to specifications; then, retorque to the same specifications two minutes after initial tightening.

11. Install the crankcase ventilation system and the air cleaner.

DISASSEMBLY AND REASSEMBLY

1. Remove the pin and spring washer from each end of the valve rocker arm shaft.

2. Slide the valve rocker arms, springs and supports off the shaft. Be sure to identify the parts.

3. If it is necessary to remove the plugs from each end of the shaft, drill or pierce the plug on one end. Working from the open end, knock out the remaining plug.

4. On reassembly all valves, valve stems and valve guides are to be lubricated with heavy oil SE. The valve tips are to have Lubriplate® or equivalent applied. The Lubriplate® is to be applied before installation. All rocker arm shafts are to be lubricated with heavy oil SE before installation.

5. If the plugs were removed from the ends of the shaft, use a blunt tool or large diameter pin punch and install a plug, cup side out, in each end of the shaft.

6. Install the spring washer and pin on one end of the shaft.

7. Install the valve rocker arms, supports, and springs in the original order.

NOTE: *Be sure the oil holes in the shaft are facing downward. Complete the assembly by installing the remaining spring, washer and pin.*

6–300

1. Disconnect the inlet air hose at the oil fill cap. Remove the air cleaner.

2. Disconnect the accelerator cable at the carburetor. Remove the cable retracting spring. Remove the accelerator cable bracket from the cylinder head and position the cable and bracket assembly out of the way.

3. Remove the PCV valve from the valve rocker arm cover. Remove the cover bolts and remove the valve rocker arm cover.

4. Remove the valve rocker arm stud nut, fulcrum seat and rocker arm. Inspect the rocker arm cover bolts for worn or damaged seals under the bolt heads and replace as necessary. If it is necessary to remove a rocker arm stud, Tool T79T-6527-A is available. A 0.006" (0.15mm) oversize reamer T62F-6527-B3 or equivalent and a 0.015" (0.38mm) oversize reamer T62F-6527-B5 or equivalent are available. For 0.010" (0.254mm) oversize studs, use reamer T66P-6527-B or equivalent. To press in replacement studs, or use stud replacer T79T-6527-B or equivalent for 6–300.

Rocker arm studs that are broken or have damaged threads may be replaced with standard studs. Loose studs in the head may be replaced with 0.006" (0.152mm), 0.010" (0.254mm) or 0.015" (0.38mm) oversize studs which are available for service.

Standard and oversize studs can be identified by measuring the stud diameter within 1⅛" (28.6mm) from the pilot end of the stud. The stud diameters are:
- 0.006" (0.152mm) oversize: 0.3774–0.3781" (9.586–9.603mm)
- 0.010" (0.254mm) oversize: 0.3814–0.3821" (9.688–9.705mm)
- 0.015" (0.381mm) oversize: 0.3864–0.3871" (9.814–9.832mm)

When going from a standard size rocker arm stud to a 0.010" (0.254mm) or 0.015" (0.38mm) oversize stud, always use the 0.006" (0.152mm) oversize reamer before finish reaming with the 0.010" (0.254mm) or 0.015" (0.381mm) oversize reamer.

5. Position the sleeve of the rocker arm stud remover over the stud with the bearing end down. Thread the puller into the sleeve and over the stud until it is fully bottomed. Hold the sleeve with a wrench; then, rotate the puller clockwise to remove the stud.

If the rocker arm stud was broken off flush

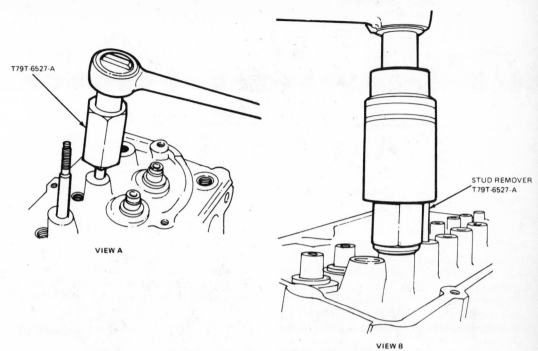

Removing the rocker arm stud on the 6-300

with the stud boss, use an easy-out to remove the broken stud following the instructions of the tool manufacturer.

6. If a loose rocker arm stud is being replaced, ream the stud bore using the proper reamer (or reamers in sequence) for the selected oversize stud. Make sure the metal particles do not enter the valve area.

7. Coat the end of the stud with Lubriplate® or it's equivalent. Align the stud with the stud bore; then, tap the sliding driver until it bottoms. When the driver contacts the stud boss, the stud is installed to its correct height.

8. Apply Lubriplate® or equivalent to the top of the valve stem and at the pushrod guide in the cylinder head.

9. Apply Lubriplate® or equivalent to the rocker arm fulcrum seat and the fulcrum seat socket in the rocker arm. Install the valve rocker arm, fulcrum seat and stud nut. Adjust the valve clearance.

10. Clean the valve rocker arm cover and the cylinder head gasket surface. Place the new gasket in the cover making sure that the tabs of the gasket engage in the notches provided in the cover.

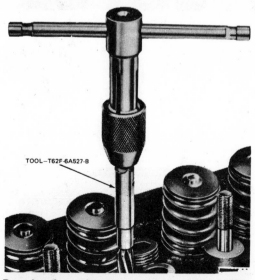

Reaming the rocker arm stud hole on the 6-300

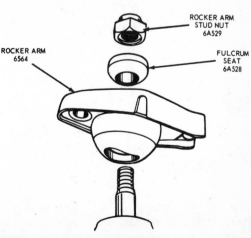

6-300 valve rocker arm assembly

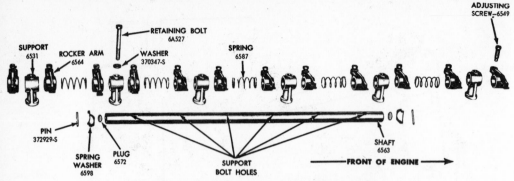

ADJUSTING
SCREW—6549

RETAINING BOLT
6A527

SUPPORT
6531

ROCKER ARM
6564

WASHER
370347-S

SPRING
6587

SPRING
6587

PIN
372929-S

SPRING
WASHER
6598

PLUG
6572

SUPPORT
BOLT HOLES

SHAFT
6563

FRONT OF ENGINE →

Exploded view of the 6-170,200 rocker arm shaft

11. Install the cover on the cylinder head. Make sure the gasket seats evenly all around the head. Partially tighten the cover bolts in sequence, starting at the middle bolts. Then tighten the bolts to 3–5 ft.lb.

12. Install the PCV valve in the rocker arm cover. Install the accelerator cable bracket on the cylinder head and connect the cable to the carburetor.

13. Connect the inlet air hose to the oil fill cap.

14. Install air cleaner.

1966-77 8–289, 302

1. Remove the air cleaner ad intake duct assembly.

2. Remove the PCV valve and hose from the rocker cover. If the engine is equipped with the Thermactor exhaust emission control system, disconnect the air hose and remove the check valve from the right air manifold.

3. Disconnect the spark plug wires from the spark plugs. Remove the wires from the bracket on top of the rocker cover and position them out of the way.

4. If the engine is equipped with the Thermactor exhaust emission control system, disconnect the air hose at the left air manifold.

5. Remove the rocker cover(s).

6. Before removing any of the valve rocker arms, check the torque required to turn the ad-

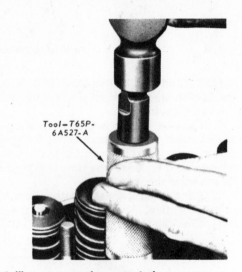

Tool—T65P-
6A527-A

Installing a new rocker arm stud

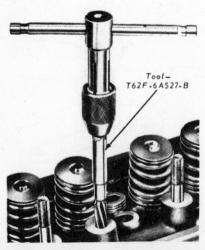

Tool—
T62F-6A527-B

Reaming the rocker arm stud bore on V8 engines

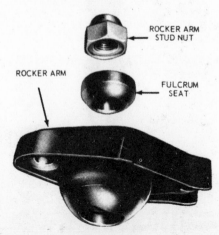

ROCKER ARM
STUD NUT

ROCKER ARM

FULCRUM
SEAT

1966–77 V8 rocker arm assembly

justing nut counterclockwise. It should be between 4.5–15 ft.lb. If it is below these specifications replace the stud and/or the nut.

7. Remove the valve rocker arm stud nut, fulcrum seat and rocker arm.

8. To remove the rocker arm stud, which is pressed into the cylinder head, put spaces over the stud until just enough threads are left showing at the top so a nut can be screwed onto the top of the rocker arm stud and get a full bite. Turn the nut clockwise until the stud is removed, adding spacers under the nut as necessary.

Rocker arm studs that are being replaced because of damaged threads or are broken off, may be replaced with standard size replacement studs. If the stud is being replaced because it is loose in the head, it may be replaced with 0.006″ (0.152mm), 0.010″ (0.254mm) or 0.015″ (0.381mm) oversize studs. Ream the stud mounting hole with a 0.006″ (0.152mm) oversize reamer first, before using the 0.010″ (0.254mm) or 0.015″ (0.381mm) oversize studs. Do not allow metal chips to get down around the valves.

To install the rocker arm studs, it is necessary to have a rocker arm stud installer tool, which is readily available in automotive parts and supply stores. The Ford tool number is shown in the accompanying pictures.

9. Screw the new stud into the installer tool and coat the end of the stud with Lubriplate®. Align the stud and installer with the stud bore and tap the tool until it bottoms against the cylinder head. At this point, the stud is installed to the correct height.

10. Assemble the engine in the reverse order of disassemble. Adjust the valve lash as outlined under Tune-Up and Performance Maintenance.

8–302
1980–86 8–351W
1984–86 8–351HO

1. Remove air cleaner and intake duct assembly, including the closed crankcase ventilation hoses. On 8–302 Canadian Bronco remove vacuum lines and electric solenoid. Remove vacuum solenoid left hand cover only.

2. Remove the PCV valve from the right rocker arm cover.

3. Disconnect the spark plug wires from the spark plugs by grasping, twisting and pulling the molded cap using Tool No. T68P-6666-A or equivalent. Remove the wires and bracket assemblies from the rocker arm cover attaching studs and position out of the way.

4. Remove low voltage wiring clips. Remove rocker arm cover(s).

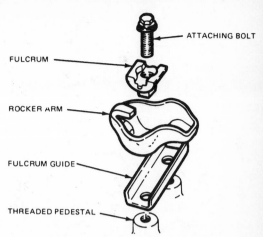

Valve rocker arm assembly for the 8-302, 8-351W 1979 and later

5. Remove the valve rocker arm fulcrum bolt, fulcrum arm and fulcrum guide.

6. Apply Lubriplate® or equivalent to the top of the valve stem, the fulcrum and socket.

7. Install the fulcrum guide, valve rocker arm, fulcrum and fulcrum bolt. Tighten to 18–24 ft.lb.

8. Clean and inspect gasket surfaces. Inspect the gasket sealing surface for damages and distortion due to overtightening of the bolt. Repair and straighten as required.

9. Place the new gaskets in the covers making sure that the tabs of the gasket engage the notches provided in the cover. Position the cover(s) on the cylinder head(s). Install the bolts and tighten to 3–5 ft.lb. Two minutes later tighten the bolts to the same specifications.

10. Install low voltage wiring clips. Insert the spark plug wires and bracket assembly on the attaching stud on the rocker arm cover(s) and connect the wires to the spark plugs.

11. Install the PCV valve into the oil filler cap in the rocker arm cover. Install vacuum solenoid connect vacuum harness and electric connectors.

12. Install air cleaner and intake duct assembly, including the crankcase ventilation hoses.

8–351M, 400

1. Remove the air cleaner and intake duct assembly. Remove the appropriate crankcase ventilation hose(s) at the valve rocker arm cover(s).

2. Disconnect the spark plug wires form the spark plugs by grasping, twisting, and pulling the molded cap with Tool T74P-6666-A or equivalent. Remove the wires from the bracket on the valve rocker arm cover(s) and position the wire out of the way.

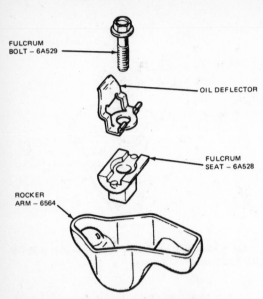

8-351M, 400 valve rocker arm assembly

3. Remove the valve rocker arm cover(s).

4. Remove the valve rocker arm bolt, oil deflector, fulcrum seat and rocker arm.

All rocker arms and fulcrum seats are to be lubricated with heavy engine oil SE before installation.

5. Apply Lubriplate® or equivalent to the top of the valve stem. Lubricate the rocker arm and fulcrum seat with heavy engine oil SE.

6. Position the No. 1 piston on TDC at the end of the compression stroke and install the rocker arm, fulcrum seat, on deflector, and fulcrum bolts on the following valves:
• No. 1 Intake No. 1 Exhaust
• No. 4 Intake No. 3 Exhaust
• No. 8 Intake No. 7 Exhaust
Turn the crankshaft 180° and install the rocker arm, fulcrum seat, oil deflector and fulcrum bolts on the following valves:
• No. 3 Intake No. 2 Exhaust
• No. 7 Intake No. 6 Exhaust
Turn the crankshaft 270° and install the rocker arm, fulcrum seat, oil deflector and fulcrum bolts on the following valves:
• No. 2 Intake No. 4 Exhaust
• No. 5 Intake No. 5 Exhaust
• No. 6 Intake No. 8 Exhaust
Be sure that the fulcrum seat base is seated in its slot on the cylinder head before tightening the fulcrum bolts. Tighten the fulcrum bolt to 18–24 ft.lb. Check the valve clearance.

7. Clean the valve rocker arm cover(s) and the cylinder head gasket surface(s). Apply oil resistant sealer to one side of new cover gasket(s). Lay the cemented side of the gasket(s) in place in the cover(s).

8. Position the cover(s) on the cylinder head(s). Make sure the gasket seats evenly all around the head. Install the bolts. The cover is tightened in two steps. Tighten the bolts to 3–5 lb. Two minutes later, tighten the bolts to the same specification.

9. Reconnect the crankcase ventilation hose(s).

10. Install the air cleaner and intake duct assembly.

11. Install the spark plug wires in the bracket on the valve rocker arm cover(s). Connect the spark plug wires.

12. Start the engine and check for leaks.

Thermostat

REMOVAL AND INSTALLATION

1. Drain the cooling system below the level of the coolant outlet housing. Use the petcock valve at the bottom of the radiator to drain the system. It is not necessary to remove any of the hoses.

CAUTION: *When draining the coolant, keep in mind that cats and dogs are attracted by the ethylene glycol antifreeze, and are quite likely to drink any that is left in an uncovered container or in puddles on the ground. This will prove fatal in sufficient quantity. Always drain the coolant into a sealable container. Coolant should be reused unless it is contaminated or several years old.*

2. Remove the coolant outlet housing retaining bolts and slide the housing with the hose attached to one side.

3. Turn the thermostat counterclockwise to unlock it from the outlet.

4. Remove the gasket from the engine block and clean both mating surfaces.

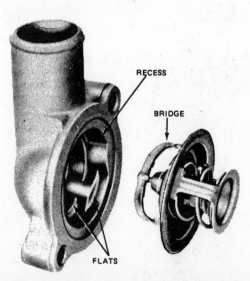

Thermostat spring always faces "down" in all engines

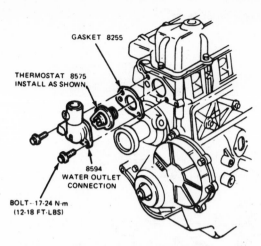

GASKET 8255

THERMOSTAT 8575
INSTALL AS SHOWN

8594
WATER OUTLET
CONNECTION

BOLT - 17-24 N·m
(12-18 FT·LBS)

Inline six cylinder thermostat installation. V8 thermostat mounted vertically on front of engine, diesel is on side of front of intake manifold

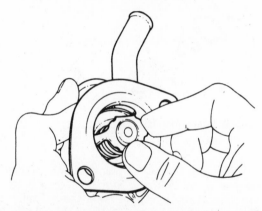

On all gasoline engines, turn the thermostat clockwise to lock it into position on the flats in the outlet elbow

5. To install the thermostat, coat a new gasket with water resistant sealer and position it on the outlet of the engine. The gasket must be in place before the thermostat is installed.

6. Install the thermostat with the bridge (opposite end from the spring) inside the elbow connection and turn it clockwise to lock it in position, with the bridge against the flats cast into the elbow connection.

7. Position the elbow connection onto the mounting surface of the outlet, so that the thermostat flange is resting on the gasket and install the retaining bolts.

8. Fill the radiator and operate the engine until it reaches operating temperature. Check the coolant level and adjust as necessary.

NOTE: *It is a good practice to check the operation of a new thermostat before it is installed in an engine. Place the thermostat in a pan of boiling water. If it does not open more than ¼" (6.35mm), do not install it in the engine.*

Intake Manifold

REMOVAL AND INSTALLATION

6–170, 200

Intake manifold on the 6 cylinder engines is integrally cast on the cylinder head, thus it is removed when the cylinder head is removed.

1966–77 8–289, 302

1. Drain the cooling system, remove the air cleaner and the intake duct assembly.

CAUTION: *When draining the coolant, keep in mind that cats and dogs are attracted by the ethylene glycol antifreeze, and are quite likely to drink any that is left in an uncovered container or in puddles on the ground. This will prove fatal in sufficient quantity. Always drain the coolant into a sealable container. Coolant should be reused unless it is contaminated or several years old.*

2. Disconnect the accelerator rod and choke cable from the carburetor rod and choke cable from the carburetor and remove the accelerator retracting spring. Disconnect the automatic transmission kickdown rod at the carburetor, if so equipped.

3. Disconnect the high tension lead and all other wires from the ignition coil.

4. Disconnect the spark plug wires from the spark plugs by grasping the rubber boots and

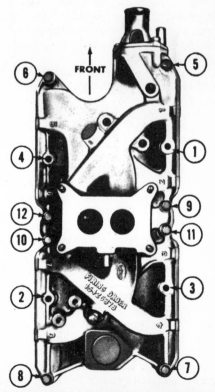

8-289,302,351W intake manifold torque sequence

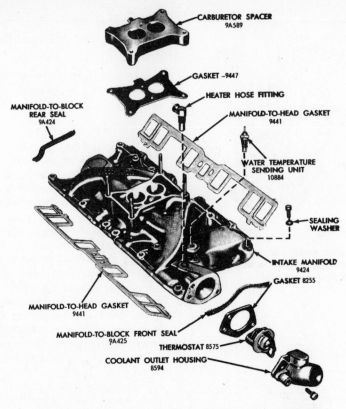

CARBURETOR SPACER
9A589

GASKET -9447

HEATER HOSE FITTING

MANIFOLD-TO-BLOCK
REAR SEAL
9A424

MANIFOLD-TO-HEAD GASKET
9441

WATER TEMPERATURE
SENDING UNIT
10884

SEALING
WASHER

INTAKE MANIFOLD
9424

GASKET 8255

MANIFOLD-TO-HEAD GASKET
9441

MANIFOLD-TO-BLOCK FRONT SEAL
9A425

THERMOSTAT 8575

COOLANT OUTLET HOUSING
8594

Exploded view of the 8-289,302,351W intake manifold

twisting and pulling at the same time. Remove the wires from the brackets on the rocker covers. Remove the distributor cap and spark plug wire assembly.

5. Remove the carburetor fuel inlet line and the distributor vacuum line from the carburetor.

6. Remove the distributor lockbolt and remove the distributor and vacuum line. See Distributor Removal and Installation.

7. Disconnect the upper radiator hose from the coolant outlet housing and the water temperature sending unit wire at the sending unit. Remove the heater hose from the intake manifold.

8. Loosen the clamp on the water pump bypass hose at the coolant outlet housing and slide the hose off the outlet housing.

9. Disconnect the PCV hose at the rocker cover.

10. If the engine is equipped with the Thermactor exhaust emission control system, remove the air pump to left cylinder head air hose at the air pump and position it out of the way. Also remove the air hose at the backfire suppressor valve. Remove the air hose bracket from the right valve rocker arm cover and position the air hose out of the way.

11. Remove the intake manifold and carburetor as an assembly. It may be necessary to pry the intake manifold from the cylinder head. Remove all traces of the intake manifold-to-cylinder head gaskets and to pry the intake manifold from the cylinder head. Remove all traces of the intake manifold-to-cylinder head gaskets and the two end seals from both the manifold and the other mating surfaces of the engine.

12. Clean all mating surfaces with solvent.

13. Apply a ⅛" (3mm) bead of silicone sealer, available at any hardware store, in the crevice formed where the block and head meet. Apply a ¹⁄₁₆" (1.5mm) bead to the outer edge of each intake manifold seal for the full width of the seal. the sealant sets in 15 minutes, so be prompt.

14. Position the seals on the block and new gaskets on the heads, with the gaskets interlocked with the seal tabs. Be sure the holes in the gaskets are aligned with the holes on the heads.

15. Position the manifold on the block and heads.

16. Run a finger around the seal area to make sure the seals are in place. If not, remove the manifold and properly position them.

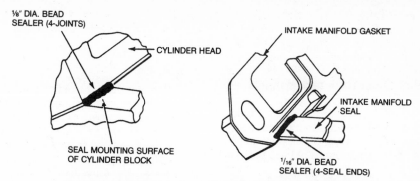

Sealer installation on the 8-289,302,351W intake manifold

17. Install the manifold nuts and bolts and tighten them in two steps, in sequence, to specification.

18. Install all parts in reverse order of removal.

19. Run the engine to normal operating temperature. Retighten manifold bolts in sequence.

8–302
1980–86 8–351W
1984–86 8–351 HO

1. Drain the cooling system. Remove the air cleaner and intake duct assembly, including the crankcase ventilation hose.

CAUTION: *When draining the coolant, keep in mind that cats and dogs are attracted by the ethylene glycol antifreeze, and are quite likely to drink any that is left in an uncovered container or in puddles on the ground. This will prove fatal in sufficient quantity. Always drain the coolant into a sealable container. Coolant should be reused unless it is contaminated or several years old.*

2. Disconnect the accelerator cable and speed control linkage (if so equipped) from the carburetor. Remove the accelerator cable bracket. Disconnect the automatic transmission kickdown rod at the carburetor (if so equipped). Disconnect the electric choke and carburetor solenoid wires, if so equipped.

3. Disconnect the high tension lead and wires form the coil.

4. Disconnect the spark plug wires from the spark plugs by grasping, twisting and pulling the molded cap using Tool No. T74P-6666-A or equivalent. Remove the wires and bracket assembly from the rocker arm cover attaching stud. Remove the distributor cap and spark plug wires as an assembly.

5. Remove the carburetor fuel inlet line.

6. Disconnect the distributor vacuum hoses from the distributor vacuum hoses from the distributor. Remove the distributor hold down bolt and remove the distributor. Disconnect evaporative hoses.

7. Disconnect the radiator upper hose from the coolant outlet housing and the water temperature sending unit wire at the sending unit. Remove the heater hose from the intake manifold.

8. Loosen the clamp on the water pump bypass hose at the coolant outlet housing and slide the hose off the outlet housing.

9. Disconnect the crankcase vent hose at the valve rocker arm cover.

10. Remove the intake manifold and carburetor as an assembly. It may be necessary to pry the intake manifold away from the cylinder heads. Remove the intake manifold gaskets and seals. Discard the intake manifold attaching bolt sealing washers.

11. If the manifold assembly is to be disassembled, identify all vacuum hoses before disconnecting them. Remove the coolant outlet housing gasket and thermostat. Remove the ignition coil, temperature sending unit, carburetor, spacer, gasket, vacuum fitting, accelerator retracting spring bracket and choke cable bracket.

12. If the intake manifold assembly was disassembled, install the temperature sending unit (threads coated with electrical conductive sealer), ignition coil, carburetor, spacer gaskets, vacuum fitting, accelerator retracting spring bracket and choke cable bracket. Position the thermostat in the coolant outlet housing. Coat the thermostat gasket with water resistant sealer and position it on the coolant outlet housing. Install the coolant outlet housing. Connect all vacuum hose.

13. Clean the mating surfaces of the intake manifold, cylinder heads and cylinder block using a solvent such as a spot remover or equivalent. Apply a ⅛″ (3mm) bead of RTV sealer, at the points shown.

14. Apply a ¹⁄₁₆″ (1.5mm) bead of RTV sealer to the outer end of each intake manifold seal for the full width of the seal (4 places).

NOTE: *This seal sets up in 15 minutes, so it is important that assembly be completed promptly. Do not drip any sealer into the en-*

gine valley. Position the seals on the cylinder block and new gaskets on the cylinder heads with the gaskets interlocked with the seal tabs. Be sure the holes in the gaskets are aligned with the holes in the cylinder heads.

15. Carefully lower the intake manifold into position on the cylinder block and cylinder heads. After the intake manifold is in place, run a finger around the seal area to make sure the seals are in place. If the seals are not in place, remove the intake manifold and position the seals.

16. Be sure the holes in the manifold gaskets and manifold are in alignment. Install the intake manifold attaching nuts and bolts. Tighten the nuts and bolts in two steps. Tighten all nuts and bolts in sequence to the specifications listed in the Torque chart at the beginning of this chapter.

After completing the remaining assembly steps, operate the engine until it reaches normal operating temperature, then retighten the manifold nuts and bolts in sequence to specifications.

17. Install the water pump by-pass hose on the coolant outlet housing. Slide the clamp into position and tighten the clamp.

18. Connect the radiator upper hose. Install the heater hose and connect the hose to the intake manifold.

19. Install the carburetor fuel inlet line.

20. Rotate the crankshaft damper until the No. 1 piston is on TDC at the end of the compression stroke. Install the distributor following the procedure in this chapter for breakerless ignition systems.

21. Install the distributor cap. Connect the spark plug wires and bracket assembly to attaching stud on rocker arm cover and connect the wires to the plugs.

22. Connect accelerator cable and accelerator cable bracket. Connect speed control cable, if so equipped. Connect the choke cable. Connect electric choke and carburetor wires, if so equipped. Connect the automatic transmission kickdown rod at the carburetor (if so equipped). Reconnect the evaporative canister hoses.

24. Fill and bleed the cooling system.

25. Start the engine and check and adjust the ignition timing. Connect the distributor vacuum hoses to the distributor.

26. Operate the engine at fast idle and check all hose connections and gaskets for leaks. Operate the engine until engine temperatures have stabilized and adjust the engine idle speed and idle fuel mixture to specifications on engine decal. Retighten the intake manifold bolts to specifications

27. Adjust the transmission throttle linkage.

Install the air cleaner and intake duct assembly, including the closed crankcase ventilation hose.

8–351M, 400

1. Remove the air cleaner and intake duct. If equipped with air conditioning remove the compressor and position it out of the way. Do not disconnect any refrigerant lines!

2. Disconnect the spark plug wires from the spark plugs by grasping, twisting and pulling the molded cap only. Remove the wires from the harness brackets on the valve rocker arm covers. Remove the distributor cap and spark plug wire assembly. Remove the Thermactor by-pass valve and hose from the check valve.

3. Remove the carburetor fuel inlet line.

4. Remove the heater hoses from the retainers and position the hoses out of the way.

5. Remove the ignition coil, vacuum solenoid valve, and bracket.

6. Disconnect the crankcase emission hose at the left rocker arm cover.

7. Disconnect the vacuum lines from the intake manifold.

8. Disconnect the distributor vacuum hoses from the distributor. Remove the distributor hold down bolt and clamp and remove the distributor. Block the distributor hole with a cloth to prevent entry of foreign material into the crankcase.

9. Disconnect the accelerator linkage and transmission downshift linkage, if so equipped, and position out of the way. Disconnect the speed control cable, if so equipped.

10. Remove the carburetor.

11. Remove the manifold attaching bolts. Remove the manifold. Remove and discard the intake manifold valley baffle and seals.

12. If the manifold assembly is to be disassembled, disconnect vacuum hoses.

13. Remove the carburetor spacer, EGR valve and inspect passages in the spacer for erosion. Clean and check the surfaces for flatness.

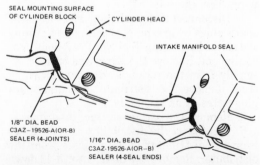

SEAL MOUNTING SURFACE OF CYLINDER BLOCK

CYLINDER HEAD

INTAKE MANIFOLD SEAL

1/8" DIA. BEAD C3AZ–19526-A(OR-B) SEALER (4-JOINTS)

1/16" DIA. BEAD C3AZ-19526-A(OR–B) SEALER (4-SEAL ENDS)

Sealer installation on the 8-351M, 400 intake manifold

14. Clean the mating surfaces of the intake manifold, cylinder heads and cylinder lock, Use a solvent such as lacquer thinner, chlorothane or trichlorethylene. Apply a ⅛" (3mm) bead of silicone rubber sealer at the points shown.

CAUTION: *Do not apply sealer to waffle section of end seals as the sealer will rupture the seal material.*

15. Position new seals on the cylinder block and press the seal locating extensions into the holes in the mating surface.

16. Apply a ¹⁄₁₆" (1.5mm) bead of the above sealer to the outer end of each intake manifold seal for the full width of the seal (4 places).

CAUTION: *DO NOT APPLY SEALER TO WAFFLE SECTION OF END SEALS AS THE SEALER WILL RUPTURE THE SEAL MATERIAL.*

NOTE: *This sealer sets up in 15 minutes, so it is important that assembly be completed promptly. Do not drip any sealer into the engine valley. Position the intake manifold valley baffle onto the block and cylinder heads with the alignment notches under the dowels on the cylinder heads. Be sure the holes in the valley baffle are aligned with the holes in the cylinder head.*

17. Carefully lower the intake manifold into position on the cylinder block and cylinder heads.

18. Be sure the holes in the manifold gaskets and manifold are in alignment. Install the intake manifold attaching bolts. Tighten the intake manifold bolts in three steps to specifications listed in the Torque chart at the beginning of this Chapter.

After completing the remaining assembly steps, operate the engine unit until it reaches normal operating temperature then retighten the manifold bolts in sequence to specifications.

19. Install the spacer, carburetor and new gaskets. If removed, install EGR valve.

20. Install the distributor

21. Install the accelerator linkage and transmission downshift rod, if so equipped. Install speed control cable, if so equipped.

22. Install the vacuum solenoid valve and the ignition coil.

23. If the intake manifold fitting was removed, clean mating surfaces of manifold and fitting with trichlorethylene (or equivalent). Apply Loctite® No. 242 thread locker or equivalent to the threads of the fitting. Install fitting into the manifold. Allow 30 minutes for sealant to cure before operating the vehicle.

24. Connect the vacuum lines at the manifold. Install the Thermactor bypass air supply hose.

25. Position the engine wire harness under the hold down clips on the left rocker arm cover and connect the wires at the ignition coil, water temperature sending unit and throttle solenoid.

26. Connect the crankcase emission line at the left hand rocker arm cover.

27. Install the heater hoses in the retainers.

28. Connect the fuel pump to carburetor fuel line at the carburetor.

29. Install the distributor cap. Position the spark plug wires in the harness brackets on the valve rocker arm covers and connect the wires to the spark plugs. On vehicles equipped with air conditioning, install the compressor.

30. Start the engine and check for leaks.

31. When the engine temperature has stabilized, adjust idle to specifications on engine decal. Retighten the intake manifold bolt to specification.

32. Install the air cleaner and recheck idle speed.

Combination Manifold

REMOVAL

6–300

1. Remove the air cleaner. Disconnect the accelerator cable or rod at the carburetor. Remove the accelerator retracting spring.

2. On a vehicle with automatic transmission, remove the kickdown rod retracting spring. Remove the accelerator rod bellcrank assembly.

3. Disconnect the fuel inlet line.

4. Disconnect and label all vacuum lines from the carburetor.

5. Disconnect the muffler inlet pipe from the exhaust manifold.

6. Disconnect the power brake vacuum line (if so equipped).

7. Remove the bolts and nuts attaching the

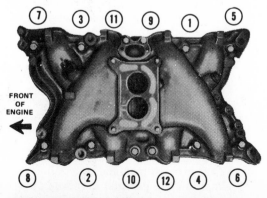

8-351M,400 intake manifold torque sequence

manifolds to the cylinder head. Lift the manifold assemblies from the engine. Remove and discard the gaskets.

8. To separate the manifolds, remove the nuts joining the intake and exhaust manifolds.

INSTALLATION

1. Clean the mating surfaces of the cylinder head and manifold.

2. If one of the manifolds is to be replaced, remove the tube fittings from the discarded manifolds and install them in the new manifold as required. Also install new studs in the new manifold.

3. If the intake and exhaust manifolds have been separated, coat the mating surfaces lightly with graphite grease and place the exhaust manifold over the studs on the intake manifold. Install the lockwashers and nuts. Tighten them finger tight.

4. Install a new intake manifold gasket.

5. Coat the mating surfaces lightly with graphite grease. Place the manifold assemblies in position against the cylinder head. Make sure that the gaskets have not become dislodged. Install the attaching washers, bolts and nuts. Tighten the bolts and nuts to specifications listed in the Torque chart at the beginning of this chapter. If the intake and exhaust manifolds were separated, tighten the nuts joining them.

6. Position a new gasket on the muffler inlet pipe and connect the inlet pipe to the exhaust manifold. Tighten the nuts to specifications.

7. Connect the crankcase vent hose to the intake manifold and position the hose clamp.

8. Connect the fuel inlet line and all vacuum lines to the carburetor.

9. Connect the accelerator cable to the carburetor and install the retracting spring.

10. On a vehicle with an automatic transmission, install the bellcrank assembly and kickdown rod retracting spring. Adjust the transmission control linkage.

11. Install the air cleaner. Adjust the engine idle speed to the specifications on the Engine Decal.

Exhaust Manifold

REMOVAL AND INSTALLATION

1966–77 6- & 8-Cylinder

1. On the V8 engine, it is necessary to remove the air cleaner and intake duct assembly and the oil dipstick tube bracket on the right exhaust manifold.

2. Disconnect the exhaust pipe from the exhaust manifold by removing the retaining nuts at the flange connections. Remove the gasket.

3. Remove the retaining bolts and washers and remove the exhaust manifold from the engine.

4. In preparation for installation, clean the mating surfaces of both the exhaust manifold and the cylinder head. Also clean the mounting flange where the exhaust pipe is connected.

5. Apply graphite grease to the mating surface of the exhaust manifold.

6. Install and tighten the exhaust manifold retaining bolts and washers, working from the center. Tighten to 12–18 ft.lb. on all engines.

7. Connect the exhaust pipe to the exhaust manifold, using a new gasket if necessary.

8. On the V8 engines, install the air cleaner and the intake duct.

9. Start the engine and check for exhaust leaks.

1978–79 8–351M, 400

1. If a right exhaust manifold is being removed, remove the air cleaner, intake duct and heat stove. If a left hand exhaust manifold is being removed, first remove the oil filter. On the left hand exhaust manifold remove the oil dipstick and the tube assembly and the speed control bracket, if so equipped.

2. On vehicles equipped with a column selector and automatic transmission, disconnect the selector lever cross shaft for clearance.

3. Disconnect the muffler inlet pipe or catalytic converter at the exhaust manifold. Remove the spark plug heat shields.

4. Remove the exhaust manifold attaching bolts and remove the manifold.

5. Clean the mating surfaces of the exhaust manifold and cylinder head. Clean the mounting flange of the exhaust manifold and muffler inlet pipe or catalytic converter.

6. Apply graphite grease on the mating surface of the exhaust manifold.

7. Position the exhaust manifold on the head and install the attaching bolts. On the

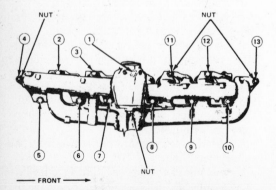

6-300 combination manifold torque sequence

left hand exhaust manifold install the oil dipstick tube assembly and the speed central brackets, if so equipped. Working from the center to the ends, tighten the bolts to specification. Install the spark plug heat shields.

8. Install the spacer between the inlet pipe and the exhaust manifold.

9. Connect the muffler inlet pipe or catalytic converter at the exhaust manifold. Tighten the attaching nuts to 18–24 ft.lb.

10. If a left exhaust manifold is being installed, install the oil filter.

On a vehicle with an automatic transmission and column selector, connect the selector cross shaft at the chassis and cylinder block.

11. If a right exhaust manifold is being replaced, install the air cleaner heat stove. Install the air cleaner and intake duct.

12. Start the engine and check for exhaust leaks.

8–302
1980–86 8–351W
1984–86 8–351 HO

1. Remove the air cleaner and intake duct assembly, including the crankcase ventilation hose.

2. Remove bolts attaching the air cleaner inlet duct.

3. Disconnect muffler inlet pipes.

4. Remove the exhaust manifold heat shields (if so equipped), attaching bolts and flat washers. On the left hand exhaust manifold remove oil dipstick tube assembly and speed control bracket and exhaust heat control valve, if so equipped, then remove the exhaust manifold.

5. Clean the mating surfaces of the exhaust manifold(s) and cylinder head(s). Clean the mounting flange of the exhaust manifold(s) and muffler inlet pipe(s).

6. Position the exhaust manifold(s) on the cylinder head(s) and install attaching bolts and flat washers. On the left hand exhaust manifold install oil dipstick tube assembly and the speed control bracket, if so equipped. Working from the center of the ends, tighten the bolts to specifications listed in the Torque Chart at the beginning of this chapter.

7. Place a new gasket(s) on the muffler inlet pipe(s). Position the muffler inlet pipe(s) and the exhaust heat control valve (if so equipped) into the manifold(s). Install and tighten the attaching nuts to 20–30 ft.lb.

8. Position the air cleaner inlet duct. Install and tighten attaching bolts.

9. Install air cleaner and intake duct assembly, including the crankcase ventilation hose.

Air Conditioning Compressor
REMOVAL AND INSTALLATION

1. Disconnect the negative battery cable.

2. Disconnect the compressor clutch connector.

3. Purge the system of refrigerant.

CAUTION: *Discharging the air conditioning refrigerant should only be attempted by those who have the proper tools and training to do so, as serious personal injury may result. The refrigerant will instantly freeze any surface it comes in contact with, including your eyes.*

4. Remove the belt by releasing the belt tension at the idler pulley.

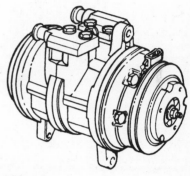

FS-6 compressor

NOTE: *It may be necessary to remove the crankshaft pulley to remove the belt.*

5. Remove the engine cover (if necessary).

6. Remove the air cleaner.

7. Remove the fitting and muffler assembly. Cap and plug all open connections.

8. Remove the compressor bracket.

9. Remove the engine oil tube support bracket bolt and nut.

10. Disconnect the clutch ground lead.

11. Remove the compressor.

12. Drain and measure the oil in the compressor and check for contamination.

13. Replace with fresh oil and reinstall the compressor.

14. Installation is the reverse of the removal procedure.

Radiator
REMOVAL AND INSTALLATION
Six Cylinder Engines

1. Drain the cooling system.

CAUTION: *When draining the coolant, keep in mind that cats and dogs are attracted by the ethylene glycol antifreeze, and are quite*

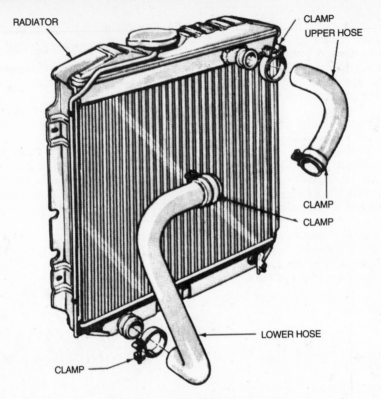

1966–77 6-cylinder radiator assembly

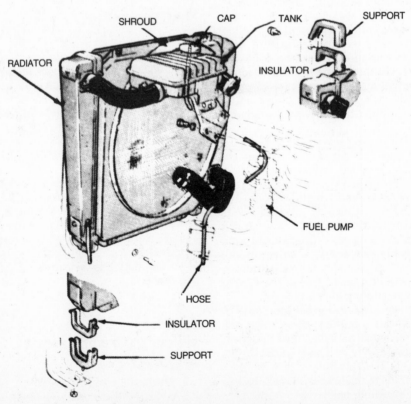

1966–77 V8 radiator assembly

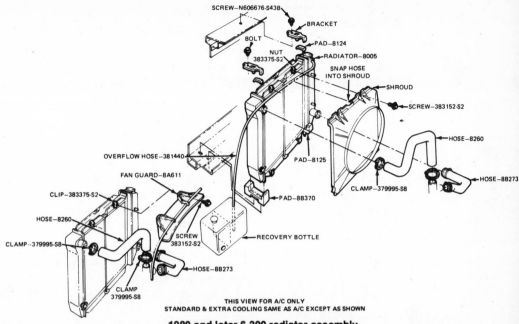

1980 and later 6-300 radiator assembly

likely to drink any that is left in an uncovered container or in puddles on the ground. This will prove fatal in sufficient quantity. Always drain the coolant into a sealable container. Coolant should be reused unless it is contaminated or several years old.

2. Disconnect the transmission cooling lines from the bottom of the radiator, if so equipped.

3. Remove the retaining bolts at each of the 4 corners of the shroud, if so equipped, and position the shroud over the fan, clear of the radiator.

4. Disconnect the upper and lower hoses from the radiator.

5. Remove the radiator retaining bolts or the upper supports and lift the radiator from the vehicle.

6. Install the radiator in the reverse order of removal. Fill the cooling system and check for leaks.

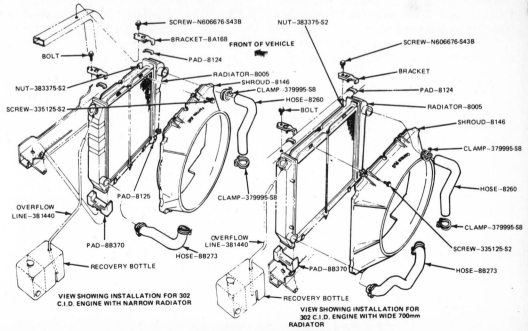

1980 and later 8-302, 8-351W radiator assembly

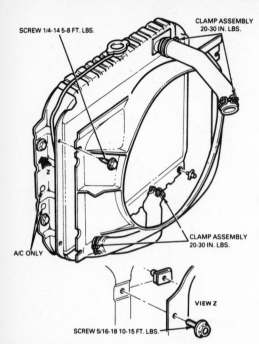

SCREW 1/4-14 5-8 FT. LBS.

CLAMP ASSEMBLY
20-30 IN. LBS.

CLAMP ASSEMBLY
20-30 IN. LBS.

A/C ONLY

VIEW Z

SCREW 5/16-18 10-15 FT. LBS.

1978–79 8-351M,400 radiator assembly

V8 Engines

1. Drain the cooling system.

CAUTION: *When draining the coolant, keep in mind that cats and dogs are attracted by the ethylene glycol antifreeze, and are quite likely to drink any that is left in an uncovered container or in puddles on the ground. This will prove fatal in sufficient quantity. Always drain the coolant into a sealable container. Coolant should be reused unless it is contaminated or several years old.*

2. Remove the bolts securing the fan shroud to the radiator, if so equipped, and position the shroud over the fan.

3. Disconnect the lower radiator hose, heater hose and by-pass hose at the water pump. Remove the drive belts, fan, fan spacer and pulley. Remove the fan shroud, if so equipped.

NOTE: *On the 1978–79, 351M and 400 V8's it is necessary to remove the air conditioning compressor from the pump. Do not disconnect any refrigerant lines! Simply support the compressor out of the way!*

4. Loosen the alternator pivot bolt and the bolt attaching the alternator adjusting arm to the water pump. Remove the power steering pump bracket from the water pump and position it out of the way.

5. Remove the bolts securing the water pump to the timing chain cover and remove the water pump.

6. Install the water pump in the reverse order of removal, using a new gasket.

Water Pump

REMOVAL AND INSTALLATION

6 Cylinder Engines

1. Drain the cooling system.

CAUTION: *When draining the coolant, keep in mind that cats and dogs are attracted by the ethylene glycol antifreeze, and are quite likely to drink any that is left in an uncovered container or in puddles on the ground. This will prove fatal in sufficient quantity. Always drain the coolant into a sealable container. Coolant should be reused unless it is contaminated or several years old.*

2. Disconnect the lower radiator hose from the water pump.

3. Remove the drive belt, fan, fan spacer, fan shroud, if so equipped, and water pump pulley. On the 6–300, remove the alternator pivot arm from the pump.

4. Disconnect the heater hose at the water pump.

5. Remove the water pump.

6. Before installing the old water pump, clean the gasket mounting surfaces on the pump and on the cylinder block. If a new water pump is being installed, remove the heater hose fitting from the old pump and install it on the new one. Coat the new gaskets with sealer on both sides and install the water pump in the reverse order of removal.

8–302 (5.0L)
8–351W/HO (5.8L)

1. Drain the cooling system.

CAUTION: *When draining the coolant, keep in mind that cats and dogs are attracted by the ethylene glycol antifreeze, and are quite likely to drink any that is left in an uncovered container or in puddles on the ground. This will prove fatal in sufficient quantity. Always drain the coolant into a sealable container. Coolant should be reused unless it is contaminated or several years old.*

2. Remove the bolts securing the fan shroud to the radiator, if so equipped, and position the shroud over the fan.

3. Disconnect the lower radiator hose, heater hose and by-pass hose at the water pump. Remove the drive belts, fan, fan spacer and pulley. Remove the fan shroud, if so equipped.

4. Loosen the alternator pivot bolt and the bolt attaching the alternator adjusting arm to the water pump.

5. Remove the bolts securing the water pump to the timing chain cover and remove the water pump.

6. Install the water pump in the reverse order of removal, using a new gasket.

Troubleshooting the Cooling System

Problem	Cause	Solution
High temperature gauge indication— overheating	• Coolant level low	• Replenish coolant
	• Fan belt loose	• Adjust fan belt tension
	• Radiator hose(s) collapsed	• Replace hose(s)
	• Radiator airflow blocked	• Remove restriction (bug screen, fog lamps, etc.)
	• Faulty radiator cap	• Replace radiator cap
	• Ignition timing incorrect	• Adjust ignition timing
	• Idle speed low	• Adjust idle speed
	• Air trapped in cooling system	• Purge air
	• Heavy traffic driving	• Operate at fast idle in neutral inter- mittently to cool engine
	• Incorrect cooling system compo- nent(s) installed	• Install proper component(s)
	• Faulty thermostat	• Replace thermostat
	• Water pump shaft broken or impeller loose	• Replace water pump
	• Radiator tubes clogged	• Flush radiator
	• Cooling system clogged	• Flush system
	• Casting flash in cooling passages	• Repair or replace as necessary. Flash may be visible by remov- ing cooling system components or removing core plugs.
	• Brakes dragging	• Repair brakes
	• Excessive engine friction	• Repair engine
	• Antifreeze concentration over 68%	• Lower antifreeze concentration percentage
	• Missing air seals	• Replace air seals
	• Faulty gauge or sending unit	• Repair or replace faulty component
	• Loss of coolant flow caused by leakage or foaming	• Repair or replace leaking compo- nent, replace coolant
	• Viscous fan drive failed	• Replace unit
Low temperature indication— undercooling	• Thermostat stuck open	• Replace thermostat
	• Faulty gauge or sending unit	• Repair or replace faulty component
Coolant loss—boilover	• Overfilled cooling system	• Reduce coolant level to proper specification
	• Quick shutdown after hard (hot) run	• Allow engine to run at fast idle prior to shutdown
	• Air in system resulting in occa- sional "burping" of coolant	• Purge system
	• Insufficient antifreeze allowing coolant boiling point to be too low	• Add antifreeze to raise boiling point
	• Antifreeze deteriorated because of age or contamination	• Replace coolant
	• Leaks due to loose hose clamps, loose nuts, bolts, drain plugs, faulty hoses, or defective radiator	• Pressure test system to locate source of leak(s) then repair as necessary
	• Faulty head gasket	• Replace head gasket
	• Cracked head, manifold, or block	• Replace as necessary
	• Faulty radiator cap	• Replace cap
Coolant entry into crankcase or cylinder(s)	• Faulty head gasket	• Replace head gasket
	• Crack in head, manifold or block	• Replace as necessary
Coolant recovery system inoperative	• Coolant level low	• Replenish coolant to FULL mark
	• Leak in system	• Pressure test to isolate leak and repair as necessary
	• Pressure cap not tight or seal missing, or leaking	• Repair as necessary
	• Pressure cap defective	• Replace cap
	• Overflow tube clogged or leaking	• Repair as necessary
	• Recovery bottle vent restricted	• Remove restriction

Troubleshooting the Cooling System (cont.)

Problem	Cause	Solution
Noise	• Fan contacting shroud	• Reposition shroud and inspect engine mounts
	• Loose water pump impeller	• Replace pump
	• Glazed fan belt	• Apply silicone or replace belt
	• Loose fan belt	• Adjust fan belt tension
	• Rough surface on drive pulley	• Replace pulley
	• Water pump bearing worn	• Remove belt to isolate. Replace pump.
	• Belt alignment	• Check pulley alignment. Repair as necessary.
No coolant flow through heater core	• Restricted return inlet in water pump	• Remove restriction
	• Heater hose collapsed or restricted	• Remove restriction or replace hose
	• Restricted heater core	• Remove restriction or replace core
	• Restricted outlet in thermostat housing	• Remove flash or restriction
	• Intake manifold bypass hole in cylinder head restricted	• Remove restriction
	• Faulty heater control valve	• Replace valve
	• Intake manifold coolant passage restricted	• Remove restriction or replace intake manifold

NOTE: *Immediately after shutdown, the engine enters a condition known as heat soak. This is caused by the cooling system being inoperative while engine temperature is still high. If coolant temperature rises above boiling point, expansion and pressure may push some coolant out of the radiator overflow tube. If this does not occur frequently it is considered normal.*

8–351M (5.8L)
8–400 (6.6L)

1. Drain the cooling system and remove the fan shroud attaching bolts.

CAUTION: *When draining the coolant, keep in mind that cats and dogs are attracted by the ethylene glycol antifreeze, and are quite likely to drink any that is left in an uncovered container or in puddles on the ground. This will prove fatal in sufficient quantity. Always drain the coolant into a sealable container. Coolant should be reused unless it is contaminated or several years old.*

2. Remove the fan assembly attaching screws and remove the shroud and fan.

3. Loosen the power steering pump attaching bolts.

4. If the truck is equipped with air conditioning, loosen the compressor attaching bolts, and remove the air conditioning compressor and power steering pump drive belts.

5. Loosen the alternator pivot bolt. Remove the two attaching bolts and spacer. Remove the drive belt, then rotate the bracket out of the way.

6. Remove the three air conditioning compressor attaching bolts and secure the compressor out of the way.

7. Remove the power steering pump attaching bolts and position the pump to one side.

8. Remove the air conditioner bracket attaching bolts and remove the bracket.

9. Disconnect the lower radiator hose and heater hose from the water pump.

10. Loosen the by-pass hose clamp at the water pump.

11. Remove the remaining water pump attaching bolts and remove the pump from the front cover. Remove the separator plate from the pump. Discard the gaskets.

12. Remove all gasket material from all of the mating surfaces.

13. Install the water pump in the reverse order of removal, using a new gasket and waterproof sealer. When the water pump is first positioned to the front cover of the engine, install only those bolts not used to secure the air conditioner and alternator brackets.

Cylinder Head
REMOVAL AND INSTALLATION

6–170
6–200

1. Drain the cooling system, remove the air cleaner and disconnect the negative battery cable at the cylinder head.

CAUTION: *When draining the coolant, keep in mind that cats and dogs are attracted by the ethylene glycol antifreeze, and are quite likely to drink any that is left in an uncovered container or in puddles on the ground. This will prove fatal in sufficient quantity. Always*

drain the coolant into a sealable container.
Coolant should be reused unless it is contam-
inated or several years old.

2. Disconnect the exhaust pipe at the exhaust manifold, pull it away from the manifold and remove the gasket.

3. Disconnect the accelerator linkage and the choke linkage at the gasket.

4. Disconnect the accelerator linkage and the choke linkage at the carburetor.

5. Disconnect the fuel inlet line at the fuel filter hose, the distributor vacuum line at the carburetor, and the fuel pump vacuum line at the manifold.

6. Disconnect the coolant lines at the carburetor spacer.

7. Disconnect the distributor vacuum line at the distributor and the carburetor fuel inlet line at the fuel pump. Remove the lines as a unit.

8. Disconnect the spark plug wires at the spark plugs and the temperature sending unit wire at the sending unit.

9. Pull the PCV hose and valve from the rubber grommet in the valve cover, disconnect it from the intake manifold spacer and remove it from the engine.

10. Disconnect the carburetor air vent tube; then remove the valve cover.

11. Remove the valve rocker arm assembly. Remove the rocker arm shaft support bolts by loosening the bolts two turns at a time in sequence.

12. Remove the valve pushrods, identifying them so they can be reinstalled in the same positions from which they were removed.

13. Remove the cylinder head bolts and remove the cylinder head. Do not pry between the cylinder head and the cylinder block because of the possibility of damaging the gasket mating surfaces.

14. Installation is the reverse of removal, noting the following: Clean the head and block surfaces, removing all traces of old gasket material and sealer. If the head was removed because of a gasket failure, check the mating surface of the head and cylinder block for flatness. Apply cylinder head gasket sealer to both sides of the new head gasket. Tighten the cylinder

head bolts in the proper sequence, to the correct torque in three progressive steps: 55 ft.lb., 65 ft.lb., and then to specifications. Install the valve pushrods in the same positions from which they were removed. Coat the ends of the pushrods with Lubriplate※ or equivalent. Check the pushrods for straightness. Discard bent pushrods. Use a new valve cover gasket.

1966–77 8–289
1966–77 8–302

1. Remove the intake manifold and carburetor as an assembly following the procedure given under Intake Manifold Removal and Installation.

2. Remove the rocker arm cover(s). If the left cylinder head is being removed on an engine with Thermactor exhaust emission control system, disconnect the hose from the left cylinder head. Remove the bolts securing the accelerator shaft assembly at the front of the head.

3. If the right cylinder head is to be removed, remove the alternator mounting bracket bolt and spacer, ignition coil and the air cleaner inlet duct from the right cylinder head assembly. If the engine is equipped with Thermactor exhaust emission control system and the right head is being removed, remove the air pump and bracket. Disconnect the hose from the rocker arm cover on the right cylinder head.

4. Disconnect the exhaust pipe(s) from the exhaust manifold(s).

5. Loosen the rocker arm stud nuts to the rocker arms can be rotated to one side. Identify the pushrods so they can be reinstalled in the same position from which they are to be removed and remove the pushrods. Remove the exhaust valve stem caps.

6. Remove the cylinder head bolts and lift the cylinder head off the engine.

7. Installation is the reverse of removal, following the items noted in Step 13 of the 6 cylinder engines Cylinder Head Removal and Installation procedure. Do not use gasket sealer on the head gasket! A specially treated composition gasket should be used.

1978–79 8–351M, 400

1. Remove the intake manifold and carburetor as an assembly following the procedure under Intake Manifold Removal.

2. Remove the rocker arm cover(s).

If the left cylinder head is to be removed on a vehicle with an air conditioner, remove the compressor from its mounts and position it out of the way. Do not disconnect any refrigerant lines!

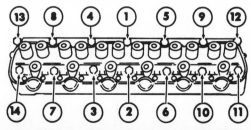

Cylinder head bolt torque sequence, 6-170,200

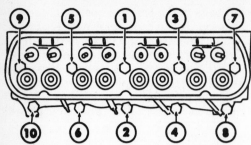

Cylinder head bolt torque sequence, all V8's

If the left cylinder head is to be removed, disconnect the power steering pump bracket from the left cylinder head and remove the drive belt from the pump pulley. Position the power steering pump out of the way and in a position that will prevent the oil from draining out.

3. If the right cylinder head is to be removed, remove the alternator mounting bracket through bolt and air cleaner inlet duct from the right cylinder head assembly. Remove the ground wire at the rear of the cylinder head.

4. Disconnect the exhaust manifold(s) from the muffler inlet pipe(s) or catalytic converter(s).

5. Remove the rocker arm bolts, oil deflectors, fulcrum seats, rocker arms, and pushrods in sequence so that they may be installed in their original positions.

6. Install a cylinder head holding fixture on cylinder head.

7. Remove the cylinder head attaching bolts and lift the cylinder head off the block using the holding fixture. Remove and discard the cylinder head gasket.

8. Clean the cylinder head, intake manifold, valve rocker arm cover and cylinder head gasket surfaces. If the cylinder head was removed for a cylinder head gasket replacement, check the flatness of the cylinder head and block gasket surfaces.

9. Position the new cylinder head gasket over the cylinder dowels on the block. Position the cylinder head on the block and install the attaching bolts. Remove the holding fixture.

10. The cylinder head bolts are tightened in three progressive steps. Tighten all the bolts in sequence to specifications listed at the beginning of this chapter. When cylinder head bolts have been tightened follow this procedure, it is not necessary to retorque the bolts after extended operation. However, the bolts may be checked and retorqued if desired.

11. Clean the pushrods in a suitable solvent. Blow out the oil passage in the pushrod with compressed air. Check the ends of the pushrods for nicks, grooves, roughness or excessive wear. Visually check the pushrods for straightness. If bent discard the rod. Do not attempt to straighten pushrods.

12. Lubricate and install the pushrods in their original positions. Apply Lubriplate® or equivalent to the valve stem tips.

13. Lubricate and install the rocker arms.

14. Connect the exhaust manifold(s) at the muffler inlet pipe(s) or catalytic converter(s). Tighten the nuts to 18–24 ft.lb.

15. If the right cylinder head was removed, install the alternator mounting bracket through bolt and air cleaner inlet duct on the right cylinder head assembly. Connect the ground wire at the rear of the cylinder head. Adjust the drive belt tension.

16. Apply sealer to the rocker cover and cover gasket in place. Position gasket on cover aligning the holes in cover and gasket. Install the valve rocker arm cover(s).

If the left cylinder head was removed, install the drive belt and power steering pump bracket. Install the bracket attaching bolts. Adjust the drive belt.

17. Install the intake manifold and related parts following the procedure under Intake Manifold Installation.

1980–86 6–300

1. Drain the cooling system.
CAUTION: *When draining the coolant, keep in mind that cats and dogs are attracted by the ethylene glycol antifreeze, and are quite likely to drink any that is left in an uncovered container or in puddles on the ground. This will prove fatal in sufficient quantity. Always drain the coolant into a sealable container. Coolant should be reused unless it is contaminated or several years old.*

2. Remove the air cleaner.

3. Remove the PCV valve from the rocker arm cover. Disconnect the vent hose at the intake manifold.

4. Disconnect and remove the carburetor fuel inlet line and the distributor vacuum line.

5. Remove the accelerator cable retracting spring. Disconnect the accelerator cable from the carburetor.

LOCATION FOR 5/16″–18 LIFTING EYES

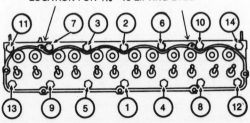

Cylinder head bolt torque sequence, 6-300

On a vehicle with an automatic transmission, disconnect the kickdown rod at the carburetor.

6. Disconnect the radiator upper hose and heater hose at the coolant outlet elbow.

7. Disconnect the muffler inlet pipe from the exhaust manifold. Discard the inlet pipe gasket.

8. Remove the coil bracket attaching bolt and position the coil out of the way.

9. Remove the valve rocker arm cover. Loosen the rocker arm stud nuts so that the rocker arms can be rotated to one side.

10. Remove the valve pushrods in sequence and identify them so that they can be installed in their original position.

11. Disconnect the spark plug wires at the spark plugs.

12. Remove the cylinder head bolts. Install the cylinder head lifting eyes in the locations shown. Position a floor crane and attach the hoist and lifting sling to the lifting eyes. Lift the cylinder head and intake and exhaust manifolds assembly off the engine. Do not pry between the head and block as the gasket surfaces may become damaged.

13. Clean the cylinder had and cylinder block gasket surfaces. Clear the exhaust manifold ad muffler inlet pipe gasket surfaces.

14. If the cylinder head was removed for a cylinder head gasket replacement, check the flatness of the head and block gasket surfaces.

15. Position the gasket over the dowel pins on the cylinder block.

16. Install lifting eyes on the cylinder head in the location shown and use a floor crane and lifting sling to lift the cylinder head over the cylinder block. Lower it carefully until it is properly positioned on the block and dowel pins. Remove the hoist and lifting eyes.

17. Coat the threads with waterproof sealer and install them in the head.

18. Torque the bolts, in sequence to specifications. Once cylinder head bolts have been tightened it is not necessary to retighten the bolts after extended operation.

19. Apply Lubriplate® or equivalent to both ends of the pushrods. Install the pushrods in their original bores, positioning the lower end of the rods in the valve lifter sockets.

20. Apply Lubriplate® or equivalent to the rocker arm fulcrum seat and the fulcrum seat socket in the rocker arm. Position the rocker arms and tighten the stud nuts just enough to hold the pushrods in position. Adjust the valve clearance.

21. Clean the valve rocker arm cover. Place the new gasket in the cover making sure that the tabs of the gasket engage the notches provided in the cover. Position the cover, making sure that the gasket seats evenly around the cylinder head. Install the cover bolts and tighten in sequence (starting in the center) to 3–7 ft.lb.

22. Connect the spark plug wires to the spark plugs.

23. Connect the crankcase vent hose to the inlet tube in the intake manifold. Install the PCV valve in the valve rocker arm cover.

24. Position the fuel inlet line and the distributor vacuum line on the engine. Connect the distributor vacuum line to the distributor and carburetor. connect the carburetor fuel inlet line to the carburetor and fuel pump.

25. Connect the accelerator cable to the carburetor. Install the accelerator cable retracting spring.

26. On a vehicle with an automatic transmission, connect the kickdown rod to the carburetor.

27. Connect the radiator upper hose to the coolant outlet housing. Connect the heater hose to the coolant outlet housing, but do not tighten the clamp.

28. Fill and bleed the cooling system, then tighten the heater hose clamp.

8-302
1980–86 8-351W
1984–86 8-351 HO

1. Remove the intake manifold and carburetor as an assembly.

2. Remove the rocker arm cover(s).

3. If the right cylinder head is to be removed, loosen the alternator and air pump adjusting arm bolt and remove the alternator and air pump mounting bracket bolt and spacer. Swing the alternator down and out of the way. Remove the air cleaner inlet duct from the right cylinder head assembly.

If the left cylinder head is being removed, remove the bolts fastening the air conditioning compressor bracket at the front of the cylinder head and position the compressor out of the way. Do not disconnect any refrigerant lines! Remove oil dipstick and tube assembly and speed control bracket, if so equipped.

4. Disconnect the exhaust manifold(s) from the muffler inlet pipe(s).

5. Loosen the rocker arm fulcrum bolts so that the rocker arms can be rotated to the side. Remove the pushrods in sequence so that they may be installed in their original positions.

6. Disconnect the thermactor air supply hoses at the check valves and plug the check valves.

7. Remove the exhaust valve stem caps.

8. Install the cylinder head holding fixtures.

9. Remove the cylinder head attaching bolts

and lift the cylinder head off the block. Remove and discard the cylinder head gasket.

10. Clean the cylinder head, intake manifold, valve rocker arm cover and cylinder head gasket surfaces. If the cylinder head was removed for a cylinder head gasket replacement, check the flatness of the cylinder head and block gasket surfaces.

11. A specially treated composition gasket is used. Do not apply sealer to a composition gasket. Position the new cylinder head gasket over the cylinder dowels on the block. Position the cylinder head on the block and install the attaching bolts. Remove the holding fixtures.

12. The cylinder head bolts are tightened in three progressive steps. Tighten all the bolts in sequence to the specifications listed in the Torque Specifications Chart at the beginning of this Chapter. When cylinder head bolts have been tightened following this procedure, it is not necessary to retighten the bolts after extended operation. However, the bolts may be checked and retightened if desired.

13. Clean the pushrods in a suitable solvent. Blow out the oil passage in the pushrod with compressed air. Check the ends of the pushrods for nicks, grooves, roughness or excessive wear. Visually check the pushrods for straightness or check pushrod run out with a dial indicator. If runout exceeds the maximum limit at any point, discard the rod. Do not attempt to straighten pushrods.

14. Lubricate the end of the pushrods with Lubriplate® or equivalent and install them in their original positions. Apply Lubriplate® or equivalent to the valve stem tips. Install the exhaust valve stem cap.

15. Lubricate the rocker arms and fulcrum seats with Lubriplate® or equivalent, then install the rocker arms.

16. Position a new gasket(s) on the muffler inlet pipe(s). Connect the exhaust manifold(s) at the muffler inlet pipe(s). Tighten the nuts to 18–24 ft.lb.

17. If the right cylinder head was removed, swing the air pump into position ad install the alternator attaching bolt and spacer, and air cleaner inlet duct on the right cylinder head. Adjust the drive belt tension.

If the left cylinder head was removed, install the air conditioning compressor and bracket, if so equipped, at the front of the cylinder head. Install the oil dipstick and tube assembly and speed control bracket, if so equipped.

18. Clean the valve rocker arm cover and cylinder head gasket surfaces. Place the new gaskets in the covers making sure that the tabs of the gasket engage the notches provided in the cover. Install the valve rocker arm cover(s).

19. Install the intake manifold and related parts, following the procedure under Intake Manifold Installation.

20. Unplug the check valves and connect the thermactor air supply hose.

CLEANING AND INSPECTION

1. With the valves installed to protect the valve seats, remove deposits from the combustion chambers and valve heads with a scraper and a wire brush. Be careful not to damage the cylinder head gasket surface. After the valves are removed, clean the valve guide bores with a valve guide cleaning tool. Using cleaning solvent to remove dirt, grease and other deposits, clean all bolt holes; be sure the oil passage is clean (V-8 engines).

2. Remove all deposits from the valves with a fine wire brush or buffing wheel.

3. Inspect the cylinder heads for cracks or excessively burned areas in the exhaust outlet ports.

4. Check the cylinder head for cracks and inspect the gasket surfaces for burrs and nicks. Replace the head if it is cracked.

5. On cylinder heads that incorporate valve seat inserts, check the inserts for excessive wear, cracks or looseness.

RESURFACING

Cylinder Head Flatness

When a cylinder head is removed because of gasket leaks, check the flatness of the cylinder head gasket surface.

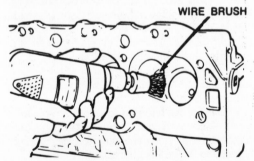

Remove the carbon from the cylinder head with a wire brush and electric drill

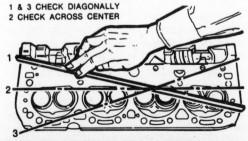

Check the cylinder head for warpage

1. Place a straightedge across the gasket surface of the cylinder head. Using feeler gauges, determine the clearance at the center of the straightedge.

2. If warpage exceeds 0.003" (0.0762mm) in a 6" (152mm) span, or 0.006" (0.152mm) over the total length, the cylinder head must be resurfaced.

3. If necessary to refinish the cylinder head gasket surface, do not plane or grind off more than 0.254mm (0.010") from the original gasket surface.

NOTE: *When milling the cylinder heads of V-8 engines, the intake manifold mounting position is altered, and must be corrected by milling the manifold flange a proportionate amount.*

Valves and Springs

VALVE LASH

Valve adjustment determines how far the valves enter the cylinder and how long they stay open and closed.

If the valve clearance is too large, part of the lift of the camshaft will be used in removing the excessive clearance. Consequently, the valve will not be opening as far as it should. This condition has two effects: the valve train components will emit a tapping sound as they take up the excessive clearance and the engine will perform poorly because the valves don't open fully and allow the proper amount of gases to flow into and out of the engine.

If the valve clearance is too small, the intake valve and the exhaust valves will open too far and they will not fully seat on the cylinder head when they close. When a valve seats itself on the cylinder head, it does two things: it seals the combustion chamber so that none of the gases in the cylinder escape and it cools itself by transferring some of the heat it absorbs from the combustion in the cylinder to the cylinder head and to the engine's cooling system. If the valve clearance is too small, the engine will run poorly because of the gases escaping from the combustion chamber. The valves will also become overheated and will warp, since they cannot transfer heat unless they are touching the valve seat in the cylinder head.

NOTE: *While all valve adjustments must be made as accurately as possible, it is better to have the valve adjustment slightly loose than slightly tight as a burned valve may result from overly tight adjustments.*

ADJUSTMENT

6-170 (Solid Lifters)

1. Start the engine and let it run until it has reached operating temperature.

Adjusting valve clearance on 170 6 Cyl. with solid lifters using step-type feeler gauge

2. Remove the valve cover and gasket.

3. With the engine idling, adjust the valve lash using a step-type feeler gauge. This type of feeler gauge is sometimes more commonly known as a "go-no-go" type feeler gauge. The proper clearance is reached when the smaller step on the gauge blade will pass through the gap while the larger step on the same blade will not pass through the gap.

Pass the proper size gauge blade between the valve stem and the rocker arm. If the clearance is correct, move on to the next valve. If the clearance is in need of adjustment, turn the adjusting screw on the opposite end of the rocker arm with a wrench until the proper clearance is reached. Turn the screw clockwise to decrease the clearance and counterclockwise to increase the clearance. Use this procedure for all of the valves.

4. After all of the valves have been adjusted, replace the valve cover gasket and cover. If the gasket is made of rubber, and is not torn, squashed or otherwise damaged it can be used again. If the gasket is cork, it is advised that the gasket be replaced.

5. Tighten the valve cover retaining bolts to 3–5 ft.lb.

Engines with Hydraulic Lifters

These engines require no periodic adjustment to the valve train. In the event of cylinder head removal or any operation that requires disturbing the rocker arms, the rocker arms will have to be adjusted.

6-200
6-300

1. Crank the engine until the TDC mark on the crankshaft damper is aligned with timing pointer on the cylinder front cover.

STEP 1—SET NO. 1 PISTON ON T.D.C. AT END OF
COMPRESSION STROKE ADJUST NO. 1
INTAKE AND EXHAUST

STEP 4— ADJUST NO. 6 INTAKE AND EXHAUST

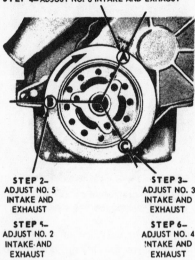

STEP 2—	STEP 3—
ADJUST NO. 5	ADJUST NO. 3
INTAKE AND	INTAKE AND
EXHAUST	EXHAUST
STEP 5—	STEP 6—
ADJUST NO. 2	ADJUST NO. 4
INTAKE AND	INTAKE AND
EXHAUST	EXHAUST

**Position of crankshaft for valve adjustment, 200 &
300 6 cyl. engine**

2. Scribe a mark on the damper at this point.

3. Scribe two more marks on the damper, each equally spaced from the first mark (see illustration).

4. With the engine on TDC of the compression stroke, (mark A aligned with the pointer) back off the rocker arm adjusting nut until there is endplay in the pushrod. Tighten the adjusting nut until all clearance is removed, then tighten the adjusting nut one additional turn. To determine when all clearance is removed from the rocker arm, turn the pushrod with the fingers. When the pushrod can no longer be turned, all clearance has been removed.

5. Repeat this procedure for each valve, turning the crankshaft $\frac{1}{3}$ turn to the next mark each time and following the engine firing order of 1-5-3-6-2-4.

8–289
8–302

Some early models of the 8–302 are equipped with adjustable rockers whereas the later models are equipped with positive stop type rocker mounting studs. Positive stop equipped rockers are adjusted by turning the adjusting nut down until it stops. You can identify a positive stop mounting stud by determining whether or not the shank portion of the stud that is exposed just above the cylinder head is the same diameter as the threaded portion at the top of the stud, to which the rocker arm retaining

Inspect the rocker arms, balls, studs, and nuts:

SMALL
FRACTURES

Stress cracks in the rocker nuts

nut attaches. If the shank portion is larger than the threaded area, it is a positive stop mounting stud. Use the procedure given below for adjusting the valve lash on positive stop type mounting stud equipped vehicles.

There are two different procedures for adjusting the valves on the V8 engines. One is a preferred procedure and one is an alternate procedure. The preferred procedure is recommended, but the alternate procedure may be used.

NOTE: *These procedures are not tune-up procedures, but rebuild procedures to be performed only after valve train reassembly.*

PREFERRED PROCEDURE THROUGH 1969

1. Position the piston(s) on TDC of the compression stroke, using the timing mark on the crankshaft pulley as a reference for starting with the No. 1 cylinder. You can tell if a piston is coming up on its compression stroke by removing the spark plug of the cylinder you are working on and placing your thumb over the hole while the engine is cranked over. Air will try to force its way past your thumb when the piston comes upon the compression stroke. Make sure that the high tension coil wire leading to the distributor is removed before cranking the engine. Remove the valve covers.

2. Starting with No. 1 cylinder, and the piston in the position as mentioned above, apply

Tool – 6513-AC

Checking valve clearance on engines with hydraulic lifters

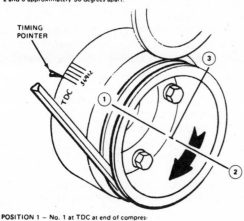

With No. 1 at TDC at end of compression stroke make a chalk mark at points 2 and 3 approximately 90 degrees apart.

TIMING POINTER

POSITION 1 — No. 1 at TDC at end of compression stroke.
POSITION 2 — Rotate the crankshaft 180 degrees (one half revolution) clockwise from POSITION 1.
POSITION 3 — Rotate the crankshaft 270 degrees (three quarter revolution clockwise from POSITION 2.

Position of the crankshaft for checking and adjusting valve clearance

pressure to slowly bleed down the valve lifter until the plunger is completely bottomed.

3. While holding the valve lifter in the fully collapsed position, check the available clearance between the rocker arm and the valve stem tip. Use a feeler gauge.

4. If the clearance is not within the specified amount, rotate the rocker arm stud nut clockwise to decrease the clearance and counterclockwise to increase the clearance. Normally, one turn of the rocker arm stud nut will vary the clearance by 0.066" (1.676mm). Check the break-away torque of each stud nut with a torque wrench, turning it counterclockwise. It should be anywhere from 4.5 to 15 ft.lb. Replace the nut and/or the stud as necessary.

5. When both valves for the No. 1 cylinder have been adjusted, proceed on to the other valves, following the firing order sequence 1-5-4-2-6-3-7-8.

6. Replace the valve covers and gaskets.

ALTERNATE PROCEDURE THROUGH 1969

Follow Step 1 of the preferred procedure given above, but instead of collapsing the lifter as in Step 2, loosen the rocker retaining nut until there is endplay present in the pushrod; then tighten the nut to remove all pushrod-to-rocker arm clearance. When the pushrod-to-rocker arm clearance has been eliminated, tighten the stud nut an additional ¾ turn to place the lifter plunger in the desired operating range.

Repeat this procedure for all of the cylinders, using the firing order sequence as a guide. It takes ¼ turn of the crankshaft to bring the

next piston in the firing order sequence up to TDC at the end of its compression stroke. Collapsed Tappet Gap Clearance:
- Allowable: 0.071–0.193" (1.8–4.9mm)
- Desired: 0.096–0.165" (2.4–4.2mm)

POSITIVE STOP TYPE MOUNTING STUD FROM 1970

8–351, 400
1970 and Later 8–302

1. Crank the engine until no. 1 cylinder is at TDC of the compression stroke and the timing pointer is aligned with the mark on the crankshaft damper.

2. Scribe a mark on the damper at this point.

3. Scribe two additional marks on the damper (see illustration).

4. With the timing pointer aligned with mark 1 on the damper, tighten the following valves to 18–20 ft.lb.
- 302: no. 1,7, and 8 Intake; no. 1, 5, and 4 Exhaust
- 351, 400: no. 1, 4, and 8 Intake; no. 1, 3, and 7 Exhaust

5. Rotate the crankshaft 180° to point 2 and tighten the following valves:
- 302: no. 5 and 4 Intake; no. 2 and 6 Exhaust.
- 351, 400: no. 3 and 7 Intake; no. 2 and 6 Exhaust.

6. Rotate the crankshaft 270° to point 3 and tighten the following valves:
- 302: no. 2, 3 and 6 Intake; no. 7, 3, and 8 Exhaust
- 351, 400: no. 2, 5, and 6 Intake; no. 4, 5, and 8 Exhaust.

7. Rocker arm tighten specifications are: 302, 351 W and 351HO, tighten nut until it contacts the rocker shoulder, then torque to 18-20 ft.lb.; 351M, 400, tighten bolt to 18–25 ft.lb.

Valve Spring, Retainer And Seal
REMOVAL AND INSTALLATION

Broken valve springs or damaged valve stem seals and retainers may be replaced without removing the cylinder head, provided damage to the valve or valve seat has not occurred.

NOTE: *The following procedure requires the use of special tools: air compressor, air line adapter tool to fit the spark plug hole, and a valve spring compressor tool designed to be used with the head on the engine. If the head has been removed from the engine the procedure will only require the use of a valve spring compressor tool designed to be used with the head off.*

1. Remove the valve rocker arm cover.

2. Remove the applicable spark plug and bring the piston to top of the bore to prevent accidental loss of the valve into the cylinder.

3. Remove the valve rocker arm fulcrum bolts, fulcrum seats, rocker arms and pushrods from the applicable cylinder.

4. Install an air line with an adapter in the spark plug hole and apply air pressure to hold the valve(s) in the closed position. Failure to hold the valve(s) closed is an indication of valve seat damage and requires removal of the cylinder head.

5. Install the fulcrum bolt or the stud nut and position the compressor tool. Compress the valve spring and remove the retainer locks, spring retainer and valve spring.

6. Remove and discard the valve stem seal.

7. If air pressure has forced the piston to the bottom of the cylinder, any removal of air pressure will allow the valve(s) to fall into the cylinder. A rubber band wrapped around the end

of the valve stem will prevent this condition and will still allow enough travel to check the valve for binds.

8. Inspect the valve stem for damage. Rotate the valve and check the valve stem tip for eccentric movement during rotation. Move the valve up and down through normal travel in the valve guide and check the stem for binds.

NOTE: *If the valve has been damaged, it will be necessary to remove the cylinder head.*

9. If the valve condition proves satisfactory, lubricate the valve stem with engine oil. Hold the valve in the closed position and apply air pressure within the cylinder.

10. Install a new valve stem seal. Place the spring in position over the valve and install the valve spring retainer. Compress the valve spring and install the valve spring retainer locks. Remove the valve spring compressor tool.

11. Lubricate the pushrod ends with Lubriplate® or equivalent and install the pushrod. Apply Lubriplate® or equivalent to the tip of the valve stem.

12. Apply Lubriplate® or equivalent to the tip of the rocker arm, fulcrum seat and stud nut or bolt.

13. Turn off the air and remove the air line and adapter. Install the spark plug and connect the spark plug wire.

14. Clean and install the rocker arm cover.

INSPECTING VALVES

Minor pits, grooves, etc., may be removed. Discard valves that are severely damaged, or if the face runout cannot be corrected by refinishing or if the stem clearance exceeds specifications. Discard any worn or damaged valve train parts.

REFACING THE VALVES

NOTE: *The valve seat refacing operation should be coordinated with the valve refacing operations so that the finished angles of the valve seat and valve face will be to specifications and provide a compression tight fit.*

If the valve face runout is excessive and/or to remove pits and grooves, reface the valves to a true 44° angle. Remove only enough stock to correct the runout or to clean up the grooves and pits.

If the edge of the head is less than 0.794mm ($\frac{1}{32}$″) thick after grinding, replace the valve because the valve will run too hot for the engine. The interference fit of the valve and seat should not be lapped out.

Remove all grooves or score marks from the end of the valve stem, and chamfer it as necessary. Do not remove more than 0.254mm (0.010″) from the end of the valve stem.

VALUE SPRING COMPRESSOR TOOL   AIR LINE ADAPTER TOOL

ROCKER ARM STUD NUT   FULCRUM SEAT

Compressing valve spring with cylinder head on the engine

AIR LINE ADAPTER TOOL

OIL SEAL

Removing or installing valve stem seals

FOR DIMENSIONS, REFER TO SPECIFICATIONS

CHECK FOR BENT STEM

DIAMETER

VALVE FACE ANGLE

1/32″ MINIMUM

THIS LINE PARALLEL WITH VALVE HEAD

Critical valve dimensions

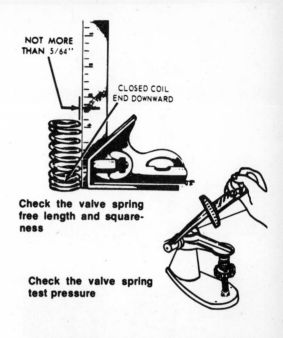

NOT MORE THAN 5/64″

CLOSED COIL END DOWNWARD

Check the valve spring free length and square-ness

Check the valve spring test pressure

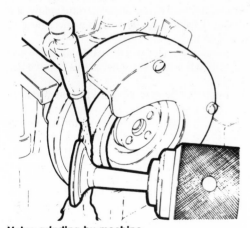

Valve grinding by machine

If the valve and/or valve seat has been refaced, it will be necessary to check the clearance between the rocker arm pad and the valve stem tip with the valve train assembly installed in the engine.

CHECKING VALVE SPRINGS

Check the valve spring for proper pressure at the specified spring lengths using valve spring pressure tool. Weak valve springs cause poor performance; therefore, if the pressure of any spring is lower than the service limit, replace the spring. Springs should be ±5 lbs. of all other springs.

Check each valve spring for squareness. Stand the spring on a flat surface next to a square. Measure the height of the spring, and rotate the spring slowly and observe the space between the top coil of the spring and the square. If the spring is out of square more than $5/64''$ (2mm) or the height varies (by comparison) by more than $1/16''$ (1.5mm), replace the spring.

Valve Seats

CUTTING THE SEATS

NOTE: *The valve refacing operation should be coordinated with the refacing of the valve seats so that the finished angles of the valve seat and valve face will be to specifications and provide a compression tight fit.*

Grind the valve seats of all engines to a true 45° angle. Remove only enough stock to clean up pits and grooves or to correct the valve seat runout.

The finished valve seat should contact the approximate center of the valve face. It is good practice to determine where the valve seat contacts the valve face. To do this, coat the seat with Prussian blue and set the valve in place. Rotate the valve with light pressure. If the blue is transferred to the top edge of the valve face, lower the valve seat. If the blue is transferred to the bottom edge of the valve face, raise the valve seat.

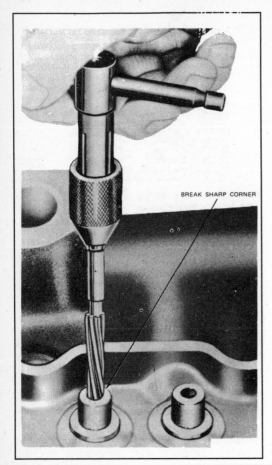

Reaming valve guides

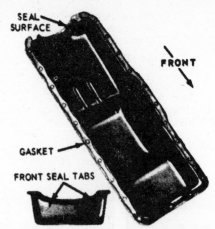

Inline six cylinder pan gasket and oil seal installation

Valve Guides

REAMING VALVE GUIDES

If it becomes necessary to ream a valve guide to install a valve with an oversize stem, a reaming kit is available which contains an oversize reamer and pilot tools.

When replacing a standard size valve with an oversize valve always use the reamer in sequence (smallest oversize first, then next smallest, etc.) so as not to overload the reamers. Always reface the valve seat after the valve guide has been reamed, and use a suitable scraper to break the sharp corner at the top of the valve guide.

Oil Pan

REMOVAL AND INSTALLATION

6–170, 200

1. Drain the crankcase and cooling system. Remove the oil level dipstick.
CAUTION: *When draining the coolant, keep in mind that cats and dogs are attracted by the ethylene glycol antifreeze, and are quite likely to drink any that is left in an uncovered container or in puddles on the ground. This will prove fatal in sufficient quantity. Always drain the coolant into a sealable container. Coolant should be reused unless it is contaminated or several years old.*
2. Remove the fan and water pump pulley.
3. Disconnect the radiator upper hose at the coolant outlet elbow.
4. Disconnect the flexible fuel line at the fuel pump.
5. Raise the vehicle and remove the air deflector shield (if so equipped) from below the radiator. Disconnect the radiator lower hose at the radiator.
6. Disconnect the starter cable at the starter. Remove the retaining bolts and remove the starter.
7. Remove the attaching nuts and washers from the motor mounts, raise the front of the engine with a transmission jack and a block of wood. Place 2″ (51mm) thick wood blocks between the motor mounts on the engine and the mounting brackets. Lower the engine and remove the transmission jack.
8. Remove the oil pan retaining bolts. Remove the oil pump inlet tube retaining bolts, and remove the inlet tube and screen assembly from the oil pump. Leave it in the bottom of the oil pan. Remove the oil pan and gaskets. Remove the inlet tube and screen from the oil pan.
9. In preparation for installation, clean the gasket surfaces of the oil pump, oil pan and cylinder block. Remove the rear main bearing cap-to-oil pan seal and engine front cover-to-oil pan seal. Clean the seal grooves.
10. Position the oil pan front and rear seal on the engine front cover and the rear main bearing cap, respectively. Be sure that the tabs on the seals are over the oil pan gasket.

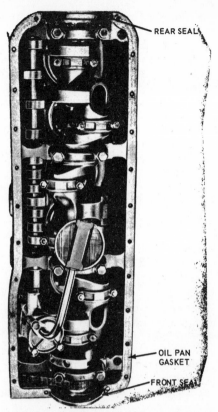

Typical oil pan gasket and seals for a 6-170,200

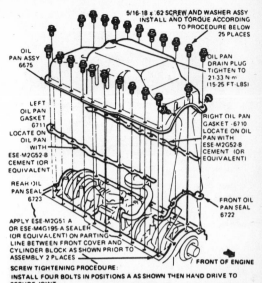

5/16-18 x .62 SCREW AND WASHER ASSY
INSTALL AND TORQUE ACCORDING
TO PROCEDURE BELOW
25 PLACES

OIL
PAN ASSY
6675

OIL PAN
DRAIN PLUG
TIGHTEN TO
21-33 N·m
(15-25 FT·LBS)

LEFT
OIL PAN
GASKET
6711
LOCATE ON
OIL PAN
WITH
ESE-M2G52-B
CEMENT (OR
EQUIVALENT)

RIGHT OIL PAN
GASKET 6710
LOCATE ON OIL
PAN WITH
ESE-M2G52-B
CEMENT (OR
EQUIVALENT)

REAR OIL
PAN SEAL
6723

FRONT OIL
PAN SEAL
6722

APPLY ESE-M2G51 A
OR ESE-M4G195-A SEALER
(OR EQUIVALENT) ON PARTING
LINE BETWEEN FRONT COVER AND
CYLINDER BLOCK AS SHOWN PRIOR TO
ASSEMBLY 2 PLACES

FRONT OF ENGINE

SCREW TIGHTENING PROCEDURE:
INSTALL FOUR BOLTS IN POSITIONS A AS SHOWN THEN HAND DRIVE TO
SECURE JOINT

INSTALL THE REMAINING BOLTS EXCEPT X, Y & Z AND TORQUE
SIMULTANEOUSLY TO 14-16 N·m (120-144 IN·LBS)

INSTALL BOLTS X, Y, AND Z LAST AND TORQUE TO 14-16 N·m (120-144 IN·LBS)

240 and 300 inline six oil pan removal

11. Clean the inlet tube and screen assembly and place it in the oil pan.

12. Position the oil pan under the engine and install the inlet tube and screen assembly on the oil pump with a new gasket. Position the oil pan against the cylinder block and install the retaining bolts.

13. Assemble the rest of the engine in the reverse order of disassembly, starting with Step 7.

6–300

1. Drain the crankcase, also drain the cooling system.

CAUTION: *When draining the coolant, keep in mind that cats and dogs are attracted by the ethylene glycol antifreeze, and are quite likely to drink any that is left in an uncovered container or in puddles on the ground. This will prove fatal in sufficient quantity. Always drain the coolant into a sealable container. Coolant should be reused unless it is contaminated or several years old.*

2. Remove the radiator.

3. Raise the vehicle on a hoist. Disconnect the starter cable at the starter and remove the starter.

4. Remove the engine front support insula-

tor to support bracket nuts and washers on both supports. Raise the front of the engine with a transmission jack and wood block and place 1″ (25.4mm) thick wood blocks between the front support insulators and support brackets. Lower the engine and remove the transmission jack.

5. Remove the oil pan attaching bolts and lower the pan to the crossmember. Remove the 2 oil pump inlet tube and screw assembly bolts and drop the assembly in the pan. Remove the oil pan. Remove the oil pump inlet tube attaching bolts. Remove the inlet tube and screen assembly from the oil pump and leave it in the bottom of the oil pan. Remove the oil pan gaskets. Remove the inlet tube and screen from the oil pan.

6. Clean the gasket surfaces of the oil pump, oil pan and cylinder block. Remove the rear main bearing cap to oil pan seal and cylinder front cover to oil pan seal. Clan the seal grooves.

7. Apply oil resistant sealer in the cavities between the bearing cap and cylinder block. Install a new seal in the rear main bearing cap and apply a bead of oil resistant sealer to the tapered ends of the seal.

8. Install new side gaskets on the oil pan with oil resistant sealer. Position a new oil pan to cylinder front cover seal on the oil pan.

9. Clean the inlet tube and screen assembly and place it in the oil pan.

10. Position the oil pan under the engine. Install the inlet tube and screen assembly on the oil pump with a new gasket. Tighten the

Oil pan rear seal installation on inline six cylinder engines

240 and 300 inline six rear oil seal installation using special tool

screws to 5–7 ft. lb. Position the oil pan against the cylinder block and install the attaching bolts. Tighten the bolts in sequence to 10–12 ft.lb.

11. Raise the engine with a transmission jack and remove the wood blocks from the engine front supports. Lower the engine until the front support insulators are positioned on the support brackets. Install the washers and nuts on the insulator studs and tighten the nuts.

12. Install the starter and connect the starter cable.

13. Lower the vehicle. Install the radiator.

14. Fill the crankcase and cooling system.

15. Start the engine and check for coolant and oil leaks.

1966–77 8–289, 302

1. Remove the air cleaner and the air cleaner duct. Remove the oil dipstick and dipstick tube.

2. Drain the crankcase and remove the oil pan retaining bolts. Remove the oil pan, seals and gasket.

3. Remove the oil pump pick-up tube and screen assembly.

4. Clean the oil pump pick-up tube and screen assembly and the oil pan and cylinder block mating surfaces before reassembling the engine.

5. Position the new oil pan gasket and end seals to the cylinder block then install the oil pump pick-up tube and screen assembly with the retaining bolts and nut.

6. Position the oil pan onto the block and then install the retaining bolts.

7. Install the oil dipstick tube and the dipstick. Install the air cleaner duct and the air cleaner.

8–302
1980–86 8–351W
1984–86 8–351 HO

1. Remove the oil dipstick (on pan entry models only).

2. Remove the bolts attaching the fan shroud to the radiator and position the shroud over the fan.

3. Remove the nuts and lockwashers attaching the engine support insulators to the chassis bracket.

4. If equipped with an automatic transmis-

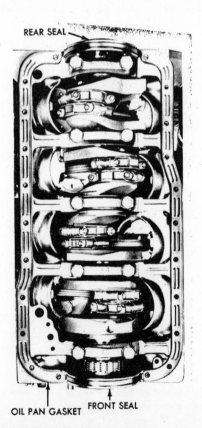

Oil pan gasket and seals for a V8

sion, disconnect the oil cooler line at the left side of the radiator.

5. Raise the engine and place wood blocks under the engine supports.

6. Drain the crankcase.

7. Remove the oil pan attaching bolts and lower the oil pan onto the crossmember.

8. Remove the two bolts attaching the oil pump pickup tube to the oil pump. Remove nut attaching oil pump pickup tube to the number 3 main bearing cap stud. Lower the pick-up tube and screen into the oil pan.

9. Remove the oil pan from the vehicle.

10. Clean oil pan, inlet tube and gasket surfaces. Inspect the gasket sealing surface for damages and distortion due to overtightening of the bolts. Repair and straighten as required.

11. Position a new oil pan gasket and seals to the cylinder block.

12. Position the oil pick-up tube and screen to the oil pump, and install the lower attaching bolt and gasket loosely. Install nut attaching to number 3 main bearing cap stud.

13. Place the oil pan on the crossmember. Install the upper pick-up tube bolt. Tighten the pick-up tube bolts.

14. Position the oil pan to the cylinder block and install the attaching bolts. Tighten to 10–12 ft.lb.

15. Raise the engine and remove the wood blocks. Lower the engine and install the insulator-to-chassis bracket nuts and washers. Tighten the nuts.

16. If equipped with an automatic transmission, connect the oil cooler line at the radiator.

17. Install the fan shroud attaching bolts.

18. Fill the crankcase with the proper grade and quantity of engine oil. Install the oil dipstick. Start the engine and operate it until it reaches normal operating temperature, then check for leaks.

1978–79 8–351M, 400

1. Remove the oil level dipstick.

2. Remove the fan shroud attaching bolts and position the fan shroud over the fan.

3. Raise the vehicle.

4. Drain the crankcase.

5. Disconnect the starter cable and remove the starter.

6. Support the engine with a jack and a wood block placed under the oil pan.

7. Remove the engine front support through bolts.

8. Raise the engine and place wood blocks between the engine supports and chassis brackets. Remove the jack.

9. Remove the oil pan attaching bolts.

10. If equipped with an automatic transmission, position the oil cooler lines out of the way.

11. Remove the oil pan.

12. Clean the gasket surfaces of the block and oil pan. The oil pan has a two-piece gasket.

13. Clean the oil pump pick-up tube and screen.

14. Coat the block surface and the oil pan gasket with sealer. Position the oil pan gaskets on the cylinder block.

15. Position the oil pan front seal on the cylinder front cover plate. Be sure the tabs on the seal are over the oil pan gasket.

16. Position the oil pan rear seal on the rear main bearing cap. Be sure the tabs on the seal are over the oil pan gasket.

17. Position the oil pan against the block and install a bolt, finger tight, on each side of the block. Install the remaining bolts. Tighten the bolts from the center outward in each direction to 10–12 ft.lb. Support the engine with a jack.

18. Raise the engine and remove the wood blocks from between the engine supports and chassis brackets. Lower the engine and install the engine support through bolts. Tighten the bolts.

19. Remove the jack and wood block supporting the engine.

20. Install the starter and connect the starter cable.

21. Lower the vehicle.

22. Install the fan shroud attaching bolts.

23. Install the oil level dipstick. Fill the crankcase with the proper grade and quantity of engine oil. Start the engine and operate at idle speed until it reaches normal operating temperature. Check for oil leaks.

Oil Pump

REMOVAL AND INSTALLATION

1. Remove the oil pan.

2. Remove the oil pump inlet tube and screen assembly.

3. Remove the oil pump attaching bolts and remove the oil pump gasket and intermediate driveshaft.

4. Before installing the oil pump, prime it by filling the inlet and outlet port with engine oil and rotating the shaft of the pump to distribute it.

5. Position the intermediate driveshaft into the distributor socket.

6. Position the new gasket on the pump body and insert the intermediate driveshaft into the pump body.

7. Install the pump and intermediate driveshaft as an assembly. Do not force the pump if it does not seat readily. The driveshaft may be misaligned with the distributor shaft. To align it, rotate the intermediate driveshaft into a new position.

6-170,200 oil pump with the inlet tube attached

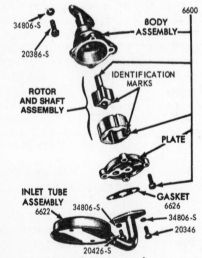

6-170,200 oil pump exploded view

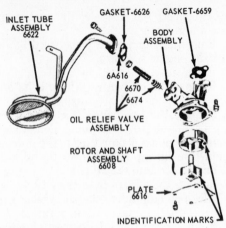

Typical V8 oil pump

pressure relief valve chamber. Be sure all dirt and metal particles are removed.

2. Check the inside of the pump housing and the outer race and rotor for damage or excessive wear or scoring.

3. Check the mating surface of the pump cover for wear. If the cover mating surface is worn, scored or grooved, replace the pump.

4. Measure the inner rotor tip clearance.

5. With the rotor assembly installed in the housing, place a straight edge over the rotor assembly and the housing. Measure the clearance (rotor end play) between the straight edge and the rotor and the outer race.

6. Check the driveshaft to housing bearing clearance by measuring the OD of the shaft and the ID of the housing bearing.

7. Components of the oil pump are not serviced. If any part of the oil pump requires replacement, replace the complete pump assembly.

8. Install the oil pump attaching bolts and torque them to 12–15 ft.lb. on the 6 cylinder engines and to 20–25 ft.lb. on the V8 engines.

9. Install the oil pan.

OVERHAUL

1. Wash all parts in a solvent and dry them thoroughly with compressed air. Use a brush to clean the inside of the pump housing and the

NOTE: INNER TO OUTER ROTOR TIP CLEARANCE MUST NOT EXCEED .012 WITH FEELER GAUGE INSERTED 1/2" MINIMUM AND ROTORS REMOVED FROM PUMP HOUSING.

Checking inner rotor tip clearance

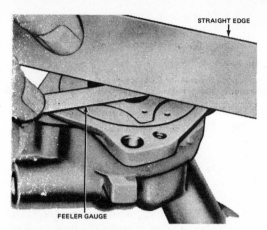

STRAIGHT EDGE

FEELER GAUGE

Checking rotor end play

Tool—T58P-6316-A
or 6306-A J

Tool—T62F-6316-B
or ⅜ inch Jackscrew

Removing the crankshaft vibration damper, typical of all engines

8. Inspect the relief valve spring to see if it is collapsed or worn.

9. Check the relief valve piston for scores and free operation in the bore.

Crankshaft Damper

REMOVAL AND INSTALLATION

Torsional damper puller tool Ford T58P-6316-D or equivalent is required to perform this procedure.

1. Remove the fan belts, fan and pulley.
2. Remove the fan shroud assembly.
3. Remove the accessory drive pulley.
4. Remove the torsional damper bolt.
5. Remove the torsional damper using tool T58P-6316-D.

NOTE: *Make sure you do not loose the crankshaft key, if it has been removed.*

6. Install the vibration damper using vibration damper replacer tool T52L-6306-AEE.
7. Installation is the reverse of the removal procedure.

Timing Gear Cover Oil Seal

REPLACEMENT

6-170, 200

1. Drain the cooling system and disconnect the radiator upper hose at the coolant outlet elbow and remove the two upper radiator retaining bolts.

CAUTION: *When draining the coolant, keep in mind that cats and dogs are attracted by the ethylene glycol antifreeze, and are quite likely to drink any that is left in an uncovered container or in puddles on the ground. This will prove fatal in sufficient quantity. Always drain the coolant into a sealable container. Coolant should be reused unless it is contaminated or several years old.*

2. Raise the vehicle and drain the crankcase.

3. Remove the splash shield and the automatic transmission oil cooling lines, if so equipped, then remove the radiator.

4. Loosen and remove the fan belt, fan and pulley.

5. Use a gear puller to remove the crankshaft pulley damper.

6. Remove the cylinder front cover retaining bolts and gently pry the cover away from the block. Remove the gasket.

7. Drive out the old seal with a pin punch from the rear of the cover. Clean out the recess in the cover.

8. Coat the new seal with grease and drive it into the cover until it is fully seated. Check the seal to make sure that the spring around the seal is in the proper position.

9. Clean the cylinder front cover and the gasket surface of the cylinder block. Apply an oil resistant sealer in the new front cover gasket and install the gasket onto the cover.

10. Install the cylinder front cover onto the engine.

NOTE: *Trim away the exposed portion of the old oil pan gasket flush with the front of the engine block. Cut and position the required portion of a new gasket to the oil pan, applying sealer to both sides.*

11. Lubricate the hub of the crankshaft damper pulley with Lubriplate® to prevent damage to the seal during installation or the initial starting of the engine.

12. Install and assemble the remaining components in the reverse order of removal, starting from Step 4. Start the engine and check for leaks.

6–300

1. Drain the cooling system.

CAUTION: *When draining the coolant, keep in mind that cats and dogs are attracted by the ethylene glycol antifreeze, and are quite likely to drink any that is left in an uncovered container or in puddles on the ground. This will prove fatal in sufficient quantity. Always drain the coolant into a sealable container. Coolant should be reused unless it is contaminated or several years old.*

2. Remove the shroud and radiator.

3. Remove the alternator adjusting arm bolt, loosen the drive belt and swing the adjusting arm aside. Remove the fan, drive belts, spacer and pulleys.

4. Remove the screw and washer from the end of the crankshaft and remove the damper.

5. Remove the front oil pan and front cover attaching screws.

CAUTION: *Avoid foreign material from entering the crankcase during service work or the crankcase oil will have to be changed.*

6. Remove the cylinder front cover and discard the gasket. It is a good practice to replace the crankshaft oil seal when the cylinder front cover is removed.

7. Drive out the oil seal with a pin punch. Clean the seal bore in the cover.

8. Coat a new crankshaft oil seal with grease and install the seal in the cover. Drive the seal in until it is fully seated in the seal bore.

9. Cut the old front oil pan seal flush at the cylinder block/pan junction. Remove the old seal material.

10. Clean all gasket surfaces: front cover, block, and oil pan.

11. Cut and fit the new pan seal flush to the cylinder block/pan junction. (old seal may be helpful as a pattern.)

12. Coat the gasket surfaces of the block and cover with oil resistant sealer. Position a new front cover gasket on the block.

13. Align the pan seal locating tabs with the pan holes, pull the seal tabs through until the seal is completely seated. Apply RTV silicone sealer or equivalent to the block/pan junction.

14. Position the front cover assembly over the end of the crankshaft and against the cylinder block. Start the cover and pan attaching screws. Slide the cover alignment tool over the crank stub and into the seal bore of the cover. Install alternator adjusting arm, tighten all attaching oil pan and front cover screws to 17–23 ft.lb.

NOTE: *Tighten the oil pan screws first (compress pan seal) to obtain proper cover alignment.*

15. Lubricate the crank stub, damper hub I.D. and the seal rubbing surface with Lubriplate. Align the damper keyway with the key on the crankshaft and install the damper.

16. Install the washer and capscrew. Tighten to 130–150 ft.lb.

17. Install the pulley(s), drive belt(s), spacer (if used) and fan. Adjust all drivebelt tensions.

18. Install the shroud, radiator, and hoses.

19. Fill and bleed the cooling system. If foreign material has not entered the crankcase during the service work, it is not necessary to change the engine oil.

20. Operate the engine at fast idle and check for coolant and oil leaks.

8–289, 302, 351W and 351HO

1. Drain the cooling system and the crankcase.

CAUTION: *When draining the coolant, keep in mind that cats and dogs are attracted by the ethylene glycol antifreeze, and are quite likely to drink any that is left in an uncovered container or in puddles on the ground. This will prove fatal in sufficient quantity. Always drain the coolant into a sealable container. Coolant should be reused unless it is contaminated or several years old.*

2. Disconnect the upper and lower radiator hoses from the water pump and remove the radiator.

3. Disconnect the heater hose from the water pump. Slide the water pump by-pass hose clamp toward the water pump.

4. Loosen the alternator pivot bolt and the bolt which secures the alternator adjusting arm to the water pump.

5. Remove the bolts holding the fan shroud to the radiator, if so equipped. Remove the fan, spacer, pulley and drive belts.

6. Remove the crankshaft pulley from the crankshaft damper. Remove the damper attaching bolt and washer and remove the damper with a puller.

7. Disconnect the fuel pump outlet line at the fuel pump. Disconnect the vacuum inlet and outlet lines from the fuel pump. Remove the fuel pump attaching bolts and lay the pump to one side with the fuel inlet line still attached.

8. Remove the oil level dipstick and the bolt holding the dipstick tube to the exhaust manifold.

9. Remove the oil pan-to-cylinder front cover attaching bolts. Use a sharp, thin cutting blade to cut the oil pan gasket flush with the cylinder block. Remove the front cover and water pump as an assembly.

10. Discard the front cover gasket.

11. See Steps 7 and 8 of the procedure for 6–170, 200 engines for replacing the front cover oil seal.

12. Assemble the engine in the reverse order of disassembly, referring to Steps 9, 10 and 12 of the procedure for 6–170, 200 engines. It may be necessary to force the cover downward slightly to compress the pan gasket and align the attaching bolt holes in the cover and the

cylinder block. This operation can be accomplished by inserting a dowel or drift pin in the holes and aligning the cover with the block.

Cylinder Front Cover Plate and Timing Chain

REMOVAL AND INSTALLATION

8–351M, 400

1. Remove the water pump.
2. Remove the heater hose and lower radiator hose from the water pump.
3. Remove the crankshaft pulley from the crankshaft vibration damper. Remove the vibration damper attaching screw. Install a puller on the crankshaft vibration damper and remove the vibration damper.
4. Remove the timing pointer.
5. Remove the bolts attaching the front cover plate to the cylinder block. Remove the front cover plate and water pump assembly.
6. Disconnect the fuel pump outlet line from the fuel pump. Remove the fuel pump attaching bolt and nut and lay the pump to one side with the flexible fuel line still attached.
7. Discard the cylinder front cover plate gasket and oil pan seal.
8. Crank the engine until the timing marks on the sprockets are positioned as shown.
9. Remove the camshaft sprocket cap screw, washer and two piece fuel pump eccentric. Slide both sprockets and the timing chain forward, and remove them as an assembly.
10. Position the sprockets and timing chain on the camshaft and crankshaft. Be sure the timing marks on the sprockets are positioned as shown.
11. Install the two-piece fuel pump eccentric, washers and camshaft sprocket cap screw. Tighten the sprocket cap screw to 40–45 ft.lb. Be sure the outer eccentric sleeve rotates freely.
12. Coat a new fuel pump gasket with oil resistant sealer and position the fuel pump and gasket on the cylinder block with pump arm resting on the eccentric outer sleeve. Install the pump attaching bolt and nut and tighten to 15–20 ft.lb. Connect the fuel pump outlet line.
13. Place the front seal removing tool onto the front cover plate over the front seal as shown.
14. Alternately tighten the four puller bolts a half turn at a time to pull the oil seal from the front cover.
15. Clean the cylinder front cover plate and the engine block gasket surfaces.
16. Coat the gasket surfaces of the block and cover with sealer and position a new gasket on the cylinder block alignment dowels.
17. Position the cylinder front cover plate

8-351M,400 front crankshaft seal installation

and water pump assembly on the cylinder block alignment dowels.
18. Coat the threads of the attaching bolts with oil resistant sealer and install the timing pointer and attaching bolts.
19. Install the front crankshaft seal into the cylinder front cover plate with the tool shown.
20. Coat a new front cover plate oil seal with Lubriplate® or equivalent and place it onto the front oil seal and alignment and installation sleeve as shown. Place the sleeve and seal onto the end of the crankshaft and push the seal toward the engine until the seal starts into the front cover.
21. Place the installation screw, washer and nut onto the end of the crankshaft. Thread the screw into the crankshaft. Tighten the nut against the washer and installation sleeve to force the seal into the front cover plate. Remove the installation tool from the crankshaft.
22. Apply Lubriplate® or equivalent to the oil seal rubbing surface of the vibration damper inner hub to prevent damage to the seal. Apply a white lead and oil mixture to the front of the crankshaft for damper installation.

8-351M,400 vibration damper installation

23. Line up the crankshaft vibration damper keyway with the key on the crankshaft using Tool T52L-6306-AEE (or 6306-AJ) or equivalent. Install the cap screw and washer. Tighten the cap screw to 70–90 ft.lb. Install the crankshaft pulley.

24. Connect the heater hose and the radiator lower hose at the water pump.

25. Refer to Water Pump Installation in this chapter, completely fill and bleed the cooling system.

26. Raise the vehicle. Remove the oil pan and install new gaskets and seals following procedures under Oil Pan Removal and Installation in this chapter.

27. Lower the vehicle.

28. Fill the crankcase with the proper grade and quantity of engine oil.

29. Connect the battery. Operate the engine until normal operating temperature has been reached and check for leaks.

Timing Chain

REMOVAL AND INSTALLATION

6–170 200
8–289, 302, 351W, 351HO

1. Remove the front cover and the crankshaft front oil slinger.

2. With a socket wrench of the proper size on the crankshaft pulley bolt, gently rotate the crankshaft in a clockwise direction until all slack is removed from the left side of the timing chain. Scribe a mark on the engine block parallel to the present position of the left side of the chain. Next, turn the crankshaft in a counterclockwise direction to remove all slack from the right side of the chain. Force the left side of the chain outward with the fingers and measure the distance between the reference point and the present position of the chain. If the distance is more than ½″ (12.7mm), replace the chain and/or the sprockets.

3. Crank the engine until the timing marks are aligned.

TIMING MARKS

Timing mark alignment, all V8's

FUEL PUMP ECCENTRIC   DOWEL

CRANKSHAFT FRONT OIL SLINGER

Installation of the fuel pump eccentric and oil slinger, all V8's

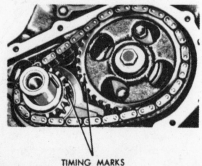

TIMING MARKS

Timing mark alignment, 6-170,200

4. Remove the camshaft sprocket capscrew, washers and fuel pump eccentric on V8 engines. Slide both sprockets and the timing chain forward and remove them as an assembly.

Removing or installing the timing chain sprockets on the 6-170,200; V8's are similar

5. Install the sprockets and chain the reverse order of removal, making sure that when they are positioned onto the camshaft and crankshaft, the timing marks are aligned.

Timing Gears

To prevent possible damage to the camshaft lobes, do not rotate the camshaft or crankshaft in the engine without the timing gears installed.

REMOVAL AND INSTALLATION

6-300

CAMSHAFT GEAR

1. Drain the cooling system and crankcase. CAUTION: *When draining the coolant, keep in mind that cats and dogs are attracted by the ethylene glycol antifreeze, and are quite likely to drink any that is left in an uncovered container or in puddles on the ground. This will prove fatal in sufficient quantity. Always drain the coolant into a sealable container. Coolant should be reused unless it is contaminated or several years old.*
2. Remove the cylinder front cover following the procedures under Cylinder Front Cover Removal.

6-300 timing mark alignment

TOOL—OTC-943

Removing the camshaft gear from the 6-300

TOOL—T64T-6306-A

TOOL—T65L-6306-A

Installing the camshaft gear on the 6-300

3. Crank the engine until the timing marks are aligned as shown.
4. Install a gear puller as shown and remove the camshaft gear.
5. Be sure the key spacer and thrust plate are properly installed. Align the gear keyway with the key and install the gear on the camshaft as shown. Be sure that the timing marks line up on the camshaft and crankshaft gears.
6. Install the cylinder front cover and related parts.
7. Fill the crankcase and cooling system. Start the engine and adjust the ignition timing. Operate the engine at fast idle and check all hose connections and gaskets for leaks. Reset curb idle to specifications on underhood decal.

CRANKSHAFT GEAR

1. Drain the cooling system and crankcase. Remove the radiator.
CAUTION: *When draining the coolant, keep in mind that cats and dogs are attracted by the ethylene glycol antifreeze, and are quite likely to drink any that is left in an uncovered container or in puddles on the ground. This*

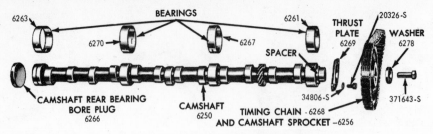

6-170,200 camshaft and related parts

will prove fatal in sufficient quantity. Always drain the coolant into a sealable container. Coolant should be reused unless it is contaminated or several years old.

2. Remove the cylinder front cover.

3. Crank the engine until the timing marks are aligned as shown.

4. Use the gear puller as shown and remove the crankshaft gear. Remove the key from the crankshaft.

5. Install the key in the crankshaft keyway. Install the crankshaft gear using the tool shown. Be sure the timing marks are aligned properly. Install the oil slinger.

6. Replace the crankshaft front oil seal and install the cylinder front cover, following the procedures under Cylinder Front Cover.

7. Install the radiator.

8. Fill the crankcase and the cooling systems. Start the engine and check all gaskets and hose connections for leaks. Adjust the ignition timing and curb idle to the specifications.

Camshaft

REMOVAL AND INSTALLATION

6-Cylinder Engines

1. Remove the front cover, timing gear, timing chain and related parts as stated before.

2. Remove the cylinder head as previously outlined.

3. Disconnect the distributor primary wire at the ignition coil. Loosen the distributor lockbolt and remove the distributor.

4. Disconnect and plug the fuel inlet line at the fuel pump. Remove the fuel pump and gasket.

5. Remove the valve tappets with a magnet. Note that the tappets must be replaced in the same positions from which they are removed.

6. Remove the oil level dipstick.

7. Disconnect the light ground wires and the screws. Disconnect the headlights and parking lights.

8. Remove the grille and hood lock as an assembly.

9. Remove the camshaft thrust plate.

10. Carefully withdraw the camshaft from the engine.

11. In preparation for installing the camshaft, clean the passage that feeds the rocker arm shaft by blowing compressed air into the opening in the block. Oil the camshaft journals and apply Lubriplate® to all of the camshaft lobes. If a new camshaft is being installed, the spacer and dowel from the old camshaft must be used. Carefully slide the camshaft through the bearings.

12. Assemble the engine in the reverse order of disassembly.

V8 Engines

1. Remove the timing cover and chain as described earlier.

2. Remove the intake manifold as described earlier.

3. Remove the valve pushrods in sequence so they can be reinstalled in the same positions from which they are removed.

4. Remove the lifters and place them in order so they too can be reinstalled in their original positions. Use either a magnet, or if the lifters are coated with varnish, a pair of pliers to remove them.

5. Remove the camshaft thrust plate and carefully remove the camshaft by sliding it out of the front of the engine.

6. In preparation for installation, oil the camshaft journal and apply Lubriplate® to the lobes. Carefully slide the camshaft through the bearings and install the camshaft thrust plate.

NOTE: *Do not drive the camshaft sprocket gear onto the camshaft because you might drive the plug out of the rear of the engine and cause an oil leak.*

7. Assemble the rest of the engine in the reverse order of disassembly.

CHECKING CAMSHAFT

Camshaft Lobe Lift

Check the lift of each lobe in consecutive order and make a note of the reading.

1. Remove the fresh air inlet tube and the air cleaner. Remove the heater hose and crankcase ventilation hoses. Remove valve rocker arm cover(s).

2. Remove the rocker arm stud nut or fulcrum bolts, fulcrum seat and rocker arm.

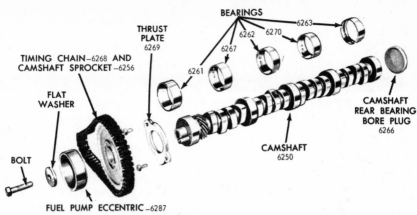

BEARINGS

THRUST PLATE 6269

TIMING CHAIN–6268 AND CAMSHAFT SPROCKET –6256

FLAT WASHER

BOLT

FUEL PUMP ECCENTRIC –6287

6261 6267 6262 6270 6263

CAMSHAFT 6250

CAMSHAFT REAR BEARING BORE PLUG 6266

V8 camshaft and related parts

3. Make sure the pushrod is in the valve tappet socket. Install a dial indicator D78P-4201-B (or equivalent) so that the actuating point of the indicator is in the pushrod socket (or the indicator ball socket adapter Tool 6565-AB is on the end of the pushrod) and in the same plane as the pushrod movement.

4. Disconnect the I terminal and the S terminal at the starter relay. Install an auxiliary starter switch between the battery and S terminals of the starter relay. Crank the engine with the ignition switch off. Turn the crankshaft over until the tappet is on the base circle of the camshaft lobe. At this position, the pushrod will be in its lowest position.

5. Zero the dial indicator. Continue to rotate

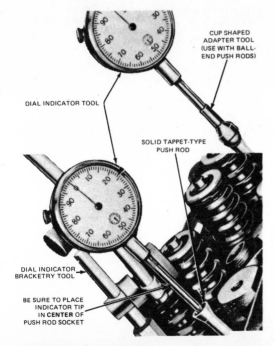

CUP SHAPED ADAPTER TOOL (USE WITH BALL-END PUSH RODS)

DIAL INDICATOR TOOL

SOLID TAPPET-TYPE PUSH ROD

DIAL INDICATOR BRACKETRY TOOL

BE SURE TO PLACE INDICATOR TIP IN **CENTER** OF PUSH ROD SOCKET

Checking camshaft lobe lift

the crankshaft slowly until the pushrod is in the fully raised position.

6. Compare the total lift recorded on the dial indicator with the specification shown on the Camshaft Specification Chart.

7. To check the accuracy of the original indicator reading, continue to rotate the crankshaft until the indicator reads zero. If the lift on any lobe is below specified wear limits listed, the camshaft and the valve tappet operating on the worn lobe(s) must be replaced.

8. Remove the dial indicator and auxiliary starter switch.

9. Install the rocker arm, fulcrum seat and stud nut or fulcrum bolts. Check the valve clearance. Adjust if required (refer to procedure in this chapter).

10. Install the valve rocker arm cover(s) and the air cleaner.

Camshaft End Play

NOTE: *On all V-8 engines, prying against the aluminum/nylon camshaft sprocket, with the valve train load on the camshaft, can break or damage the sprocket. Therefore, the rocker arm adjusting nuts must be backed off, or the rocker arm and shaft assembly must be loosened sufficiently to free the camshaft. After checking the camshaft end play, check the valve clearance. Adjust if required (refer to procedure in this chapter).*

1. Push the camshaft toward the rear of the engine. Install a dial indicator (Tools D78P-4201-F, -G or equivalent so that the indicator point is on the camshaft sprocket attaching screw.

2. Zero the dial indicator. Position a prybar between the camshaft gear and the block. Pull the camshaft forward and release it. Compare the dial indicator reading with the specifications.

3. If the end play is excessive, check the

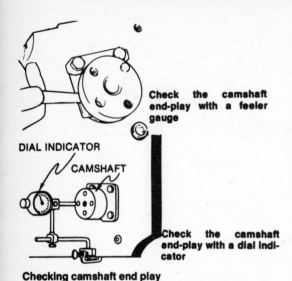

Check the camshaft end-play with a feeler gauge

DIAL INDICATOR

CAMSHAFT

Check the camshaft end-play with a dial indicator

Checking camshaft end play

spacer for correct installation before it is removed. If the spacer is correctly installed, replace the thrust plate.

4. Remove the dial indicator.

CAMSHAFT BEARING REPLACEMENT

1. Remove the engine following the procedures in this chapter and install it on a work stand.

2. Remove the camshaft, flywheel and crankshaft, following the appropriate procedures. Push the pistons to the top of the cylinders.

3. Remove the camshaft rear bearing bore plug. Remove the camshaft bearings with Tool T65L-6250-A or equivalent.

4. Select the proper size expanding collet and back-up nut and assemble on the mandrel. With the expanding collet collapsed, install the collet assembly in the camshaft bearing and tighten the back-up nut on the expanding mandrel until the collet fits the camshaft bearing.

5. Assemble the puller screw and extension (if necessary) and install on the expanding mandrel. Wrap a cloth around the threads of the puller screw to protect the front bearing or journal. Tighten the pulling nut against the thrust bearing and pulling plate to remove the camshaft bearing. Be sure to hold a wrench on the end of the puller screw to prevent it from turning.

6. To remove the front bearing, install the puller from the rear of the cylinder block.

7. Position the new bearings at the bearing bores, and press them in place with Tool T65L-6250-A or equivalent. Be sure to center the pulling plate and puller screw to avoid damage to the bearing. Failure to use the correct expanding collet can cause severe bearing damage. Align the oil holes in the bearings with the oil holes in the cylinder block before pressing bearings into place. Be sure the front bearing is installed 0.51–0.89mm (0.020–0.035") for the 6 cylinder engines or 0.127–0.508mm (0.005–0.020") for the 8 cylinder, below the front face of the cylinder block.

8. Install the camshaft rear bearing bore plug.

9. Install the camshaft, crankshaft, flywheel and related parts, following the appropriate procedures.

10. Install the engine in the Bronco, following the appropriate procedure in this chapter.

Pistons and Connecting Rods
REMOVAL AND INSTALLATION
6-Cylinder

1. Drain the cooling system and the crankcase.

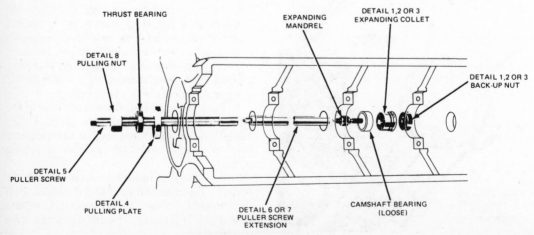

THRUST BEARING

EXPANDING MANDREL

DETAIL 1,2 OR 3 EXPANDING COLLET

DETAIL 8 PULLING NUT

DETAIL 1,2 OR 3 BACK-UP NUT

DETAIL 5 PULLER SCREW

DETAIL 4 PULLING PLATE

DETAIL 6 OR 7 PULLER SCREW EXTENSION

CAMSHAFT BEARING (LOOSE)

Camshaft bearing replacement

CAUTION: *When draining the coolant, keep in mind that cats and dogs are attracted by the ethylene glycol antifreeze, and are quite likely to drink any that is left in an uncovered container or in puddles on the ground. This will prove fatal in sufficient quantity. Always drain the coolant into a sealable container. Coolant should be reused unless it is contaminated or several years old.*

2. Remove the cylinder head.

3. Remove the oil pan, the oil pump inlet tube and the oil pump.

4. Turn the crankshaft until the piston to be removed is at the bottom of its travel and place a cloth on the piston head to collect fillings. Using a ridge reaming tool, remove any ridge of carbon or any other deposit from the upper cylinder walls where piston travel ends. Do not cut into the piston ring travel area more than $\frac{1}{32}$" (0.8mm) while removing the ridge.

5. Identify all of the connecting rod caps so that they can be reinstalled in the original positions from which they are removed and remove the connecting rod bearing cap. Also identify the piston assemblies as they, too, must be reinstalled in the same cylinder from which removed.

6. Push the connecting rod and piston assembly out the top of the cylinder with a stick of wood or the handle end of a hammer. Be careful to avoid damaging the crankpin or the cylinder wall when removing the piston and rod assembly.

7. Before installing the piston/connecting rod assembly, be sure to clean all gasket mating surfaces, oil the pistons, piston rings and the cylinder walls with light engine oil.

8. Be sure to install the pistons in the cylinders from which they were removed. The connecting rod and bearing caps are numbered from 1 to 6 beginning at the front of the engine. The numbers on the connecting rod and bearing cap must be on the same side when installed in the cylinder bore. If a connecting rod is ever transposed from one engine or cylinder to another, new bearings should be fitted and the connecting rod should be numbered to correspond with the new cylinder number. The notch on the piston head goes toward the front of the engine.

9. Make sure the ring gaps are properly spaced around the circumference of the piston. Fit a piston ring compressor around the piston and slide the piston and connecting rod assembly down into the cylinder bore, pushing it in with the wooden hammer handle. Push the piston down until it is only slightly below the top of the cylinder bore. Guide the connecting rods onto the crankshaft bearing journals carefully, to avoid damaging the crankshaft.

Proper spacing of the piston ring gaps around the circumference of the piston

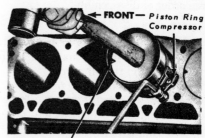

Installing the piston and connecting rod assembly into the block on a 6-170,200

Checking the connecting rod side clearance on the crankshaft bearing journal of a 6-170

10. Check the bearing clearance of all the rod bearings, fitting them to the crankshaft bearing journals.

11. After the bearings have been fitted, apply a light coating of engine oil to the journals and bearings.

12. Turn the crankshaft until the appropriate bearing journal is at the bottom of its stroke, then push the piston assembly all the way down until the connecting rod bearing seats on the crankshaft journal. Be careful not to allow the bearing cap screws to strike the crankshaft bearing journals and damage them.

13. After the piston and connecting rod assemblies have been installed, check the con-

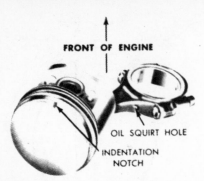

FRONT OF ENGINE

OIL SQUIRT HOLE

INDENTATION NOTCH

Connecting rod and piston assembly for a 6-cylinder engine

necting rod side clearance on each crankshaft journal.

14. Prime and install the oil pump and the oil pump intake tube, then install the oil pan.

15. Reassemble the rest of the engine in the reverse order of disassembly.

V8 Engines

1. Drain the cooling system and the crankcase. Remove the intake manifold, cylinder heads, oil pan and the oil pump.

CAUTION: *When draining the coolant, keep in mind that cats and dogs are attracted by the ethylene glycol antifreeze, and are quite*

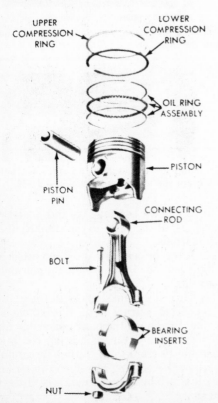

UPPER COMPRESSION RING

LOWER COMPRESSION RING

OIL RING ASSEMBLY

PISTON

PISTON PIN

CONNECTING ROD

BOLT

BEARING INSERTS

NUT

Exploded view of a typical piston and connecting rod assembly

likely to drink any that is left in an uncovered container or in puddles on the ground. This will prove fatal in sufficient quantity. Always drain the coolant into a sealable container. Coolant should be reused unless it is contaminated or several years old.

2. Turn the crankshaft until the piston to be removed is at the bottom of its travel, then place a cloth on the piston head to collect fillings. Remove any ridge of deposits at the end of the piston travel from the upper cylinder bore, using a ridge reaming tool. Do not cut into the piston ring travel area more than $\frac{1}{32}''$ (0.8mm) when removing the ridge.

3. Make sure that all of the connecting rod bearing caps can be identified, so they will be reinstalled in their original positions.

4. Turn the crankshaft until the connecting rod that is to be removed is at the bottom of its stroke and remove the connecting rod nuts and bearing cap.

5. Push the connecting rod and piston assembly out the top of the cylinder bore with the wooden end of a hammer handle. Be careful not to damage the crankshaft bearing journal or the cylinder wall when removing the piston and rod assembly.

6. Remove the bearing inserts from the connecting rod and cap if the bearings are to be replaced, and place the cap onto the piston/rod assembly from which it was removed.

7. Install the piston/rod assemblies in the same manner as that for the 6 cylinder engines.

NOTE: *The connecting rod and bearing caps are numbered from 1 to 4 in the right bank and from 5 to 8 in the left bank, beginning at the front of the engine. The numbers on the rod and cap must be on the same side when they are installed in the cylinder bore. Also, the largest chamfer at the bearing end of the rod should be positioned toward the crank pin thrust face of the crankshaft and the notch in the head of the piston faces toward the front of the engine.*

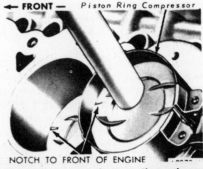

← FRONT — *Piston Ring Compressor*

NOTCH TO FRONT OF ENGINE

Installing the piston and connecting rod assembly on a V8

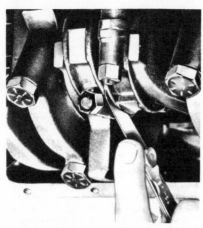

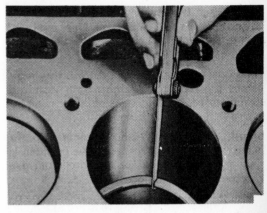

Checking piston ring gap

Measuring the connecting rod side clearance and the crankshaft journal on a V8

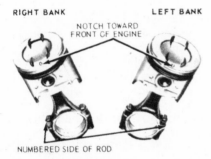

V8 piston and rod assembly

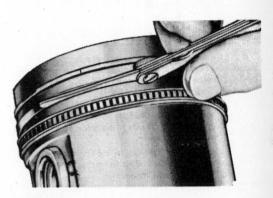

Checking piston ring side clearance

8. Assemble the engine in the reverse order of disassembly.

PISTON RING REPLACEMENT

1. Select the proper ring set for the size cylinder bore.

2. Position the ring in the bore in which it is going to be used.

3. Push the ring down into the bore area where normal ring wear is not encountered.

4. Use the head of the piston to position the ring in the bore so that the ring is square with the cylinder wall. Use caution to avoid damage to the ring or cylinder bore.

5. Measure the gap between the ends of the ring with a feeler gauge. Ring gap in a worn cylinder is normally greater than specification. If the ring gap is greater than the specified limits, try an oversize ring set.

6. Check the ring side clearance of the compression rings with a feeler gauge inserted between the ring and its lower land according to specification. The gauge should slide freely around the entire ring circumference without binding. Any wear that occurs will form a step at the inner portion of the lower land. If the

lower lands have high steps, the piston should be replaced.

CLEANING AND INSPECTION

Connecting Rods

1. Remove the bearings from the rod and cap. Identify the bearings if they are to be used again. Clean the connecting rod in solvent, including the rod bore and the back of the bearing inserts. Do not use a caustic cleaning solution. Blow out all passages with compressed air.

2. The connecting rods and related parts should be carefully inspected and checked for conformance to specifications. Various forms of engine wear caused by these parts can be readily identified.

3. A shiny surface on the pin boss side of the piston usually indicates that a connecting rod is bent or the piston pin hole is not in proper relation to the piston skirt and ring grooves.

4. Abnormal connecting rod bearing wear can be caused by either a bent connecting rod, an improperly machined journal, or a tapered connecting rod bore.

5. Twisted connecting rods will not create

an easily identifiable wear pattern, but badly twisted rods will disturb the action of the entire piston, rings, and connecting rod assembly and may be the cause of excessive oil consumption.

6. Inspect the connecting rods for signs of fractures and the bearing bores for out-of-round and taper. If the bore exceeds the maximum limit and/or if the rod is fractured, it should be replaced.

7. Check the ID of the connecting rod piston pin bore. Install oversize piston pin if the pin bore is not within specifications. Replace worn or damaged connecting rod nuts and bolts.

8. After the connecting rods are assembled to the piston, check the rods for bends or twists on a suitable alignment fixture. Follow the instructions of the fixture manufacturer. If the bend and/or twist exceeds specifications, the rod must be straightened or replaced.

Pistons, Pins and Rings

1. Remove deposits from the piston surfaces. Clean gum or varnish from the piston skirt, piston pins and rings with solvent. Do not use a caustic cleaning solution or a wire brush to clean pistons. Clean the ring groove with a ring groove cleaner. Make sure the oil ring slots (or holes) are clean.

2. Carefully inspect the pistons for fractures at the ring lands, skirts and pin bosses, and for scuffed, rough, or scored skirts. If the lower inner portion of the ring grooves have high steps, replace the piston. The step will interfere with ring operation and cause excessive ring side clearance.

3. Spongy, eroded areas near the edge of the piston top are usually caused by detonation or pre-ignition. A shiny surface on the thrust surface of the piston, offset from the centerline between the piston pin holes, can be caused by a bent connecting rod. Replace pistons that show signs of excessive wear, wavy ring lands or fractures, or damage from detonation or pre-ignition.

4. Check the piston to cylinder bore clearance by measuring the piston and bore diameters. Measure the OD of the piston with micrometers at the centerline of the piston pin bore, and at 90° to the pin bore axis. Check the ring side clearance following the procedure under Piston Ring Replacement in this Chapter.

5. Replace piston pins showing signs of fracture, etching or wear. Check the piston pin fit in the piston and rod.

6. Check the OD of the piston pin and the ID of the pin bore in the piston. Replace any piston pin or piston that is not within specifications.

7. Replace all rings that are scored, chipped

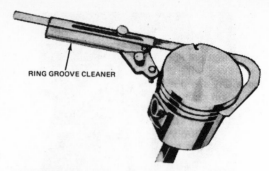

RING GROOVE CLEANER

Cleaning piston ring grooves

or cracked. Check the end gap and side clearance. It is good practice to always install new rings when overhauling an engine. Rings should not be transferred from one piston to another regardless of mileage.

PISTON PIN REPLACEMENT

1. Remove the bearing inserts from the connecting rod and cap.

2. Mark the pistons to assure assembly with the same rod, rod position and installation in the same cylinders from which they were removed.

3. Using an Arbor press and tool T68P-6135-A or equivalent, press the piston pin from the piston and connecting rod. Remove the piston rings if they are to be replaced.

NOTE: *Check the fit of a new piston in the cylinder bore before assembling the piston and piston pin to the connecting rod.*

4. Apply a light coat of engine oil to all parts. Assemble the piston to the connecting rod with the indentation or notch in the original position.

5. Start the piston pin in the connecting rod (this may require a very light tap with a mallet). Using an Arbor press and tool T68P-6135-A or equivalent, press the piston pin through the piston and connecting rod until the pin is centered in the piston.

6. Install the piston rings using a piston ring installation tool of the proper size (refer to Piston Ring Replacement in this chapter).

7. Be sure the bearing inserts and the bearing bore in the connecting rod and cap are clean. Foreign material under the inserts will distort the bearing and cause it to fail.

ROD BEARING REPLACEMENT

1. Drain the crankcase. Remove the oil level dipstick. Remove the oil pan and related parts, following the procedure under Oil Pan Removal and Installation in this chapter.

2. Remove the oil pump inlet tube assembly and the oil pump.

3. Turn the crankshaft until the connecting

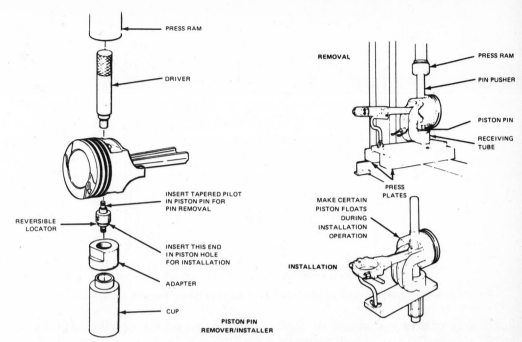

Removal and installation of piston pins

rod to which new bearings are to be fitted is down. Remove the connecting rod cap. Remove the bearing inserts from the rod and cap.

4. Be sure the bearing inserts and the bearing bore in the connecting rod and cap are clean. Foreign material under the inserts will distort the bearing and cause failure.

5. Clean the crankshaft journal. Inspect journals for nicks, burrs or bearing pick-up that would cause premature bearing wear.

6. Install the bearing inserts in the connecting rod and cap with the tangs fitting in the slots provided.

7. Pull the connecting rod assembly down firmly on the crankshaft journal.

8. Select fit the bearing using the following procedures.

a. Place a piece of Plastigage® or it's equivalent, on the bearing surface across the full width of the bearing cap and about 6.35mm (¼") off center.

b. Install cap and tighten bolts to specifications. Do not turn crankshaft while Plastigage® is in place.

c. Remove cap. Using Plastigage® scale, check width of Plastigage® at widest point to get minimum clearance. Check at narrowest point to get maximum clearance. Difference between readings is taper of journal.

d. If clearance exceed specified limits, try a 0.001" (0.025mm) or 0.002" (0.051mm) undersize bearing in combination with the standard bearing. Bearing clearance must be within specified limits. If standard and 0.002" (0.051mm) undersize bearing does not bring clearance within desired limits, refinish crankshaft journal, then use undersize bearings.

9. After bearing has been fitted, apply light coat of engine oil to journal and bearings. Install bearing cap. Tighten cap bolts to specifications.

10. Repeat procedures for remaining bearings that require replacement.

11. Clean the oil pump inlet tube screen. Prime the oil pump by filling the inlet opening with oil and rotating the pump shaft until oil emerges from the outlet opening. Install the oil pump and inlet tube assembly.

12. Install the oil pan and related parts, following the procedure under Oil Pan Removal and Installation in this chapter. Install the oil level dipstick.

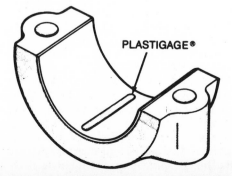

PLASTIGAGE®

Plastigage® installed on the lower bearing shell

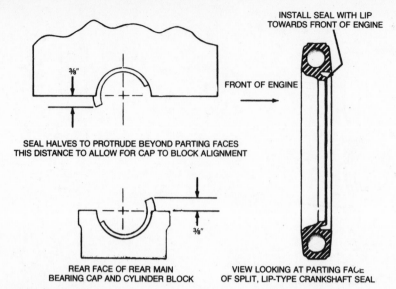

INSTALL SEAL WITH LIP
TOWARDS FRONT OF ENGINE

FRONT OF ENGINE →

SEAL HALVES TO PROTRUDE BEYOND PARTING FACES
THIS DISTANCE TO ALLOW FOR CAP TO BLOCK ALIGNMENT

REAR FACE OF REAR MAIN
BEARING CAP AND CYLINDER BLOCK

VIEW LOOKING AT PARTING FACE
OF SPLIT, LIP-TYPE CRANKSHAFT SEAL

Proper positioning of the replacement rear main oil seal for all engines except the 6-300

13. Fill the crankcase with engine oil. Start the engine and check for oil pressure. Operate the engine at fast idle and check for oil leaks.

Rear Main Oil Seal

REMOVAL AND INSTALLATION

All Engines 1966–73

1. Drain the crankcase and remove the oil pan, and, if necessary, the oil pump.

2. Remove the lower half of the rear main bearing cap and, after removing the old seal from the cap, drive out the pin in the bottom of the seal groove with a punch.

3. Loosen all the main bearing caps and allow the crankshaft to lower slightly.

NOTE: *Do not allow the crankshaft to drop more than* $\frac{1}{32}$" *(0.8mm).*

4. With a 6" (152mm) length of $\frac{3}{16}$" (4.76mm) brazing rod, drive up on either exposed end of the top half of the oil seal. When the opposite end of the seal starts to protrude, grasp it with a pair of pliers and gently pull, while the driven end is being tapped.

5. After removing both halves of the old original rope seal and the retaining pin from the lower half of the bearing cap, carefully clean the seal grooves in the cap and block with solvent.

6. Soak the new rubber replacement seals in clean engine oil.

7. Install the upper half of the seal in the block with the undercut side of the seal toward the front of the engine. Slide the seal around the crankshaft journal until $\frac{3}{8}$" (9.5mm) protrudes beyond the base of the block.

8. Repeat the above procedure for the lower seal, allowing an equal amount of the seal to

protrude beyond the opposite end of the bearing cap.

9. Install the rear bearing cap and torque all the main bearings to the proper specification. Apply sealer only to the rear of the seals.

10. Dip the bearing cap side seals in oil, then immediately install them. Do not use any sealer on the side seals. Tap the seals into place and do not clip the protruding ends.

11. Install the oil pump and oil pan. Fill the crankcase with oil, start the engine and check for leaks.

All Engines 1974–86 Except 6–300

1. Remove the oil pan and the oil pump (if required).

2. Loosen all the main bearing cap bolts, thereby lowering the crankshaft slightly but not to exceed $\frac{1}{32}$" (0.8mm).

3. Remove the rear main bearing cap, and remove the oil seal from the bearing cap and cylinder block. On the block half of the seal use a seal removal tool, or install a small metal screw in one end of the seal, and pull on the screw to remove the seal. Exercise caution to prevent scratching or damaging the crankshaft seal surfaces.

4. Remove the oil seal retaining pin from the bearing cap if so equipped. The pin is not used with the split lip seal.

5. Carefully clean the seal groove in the cap and block with a brush and solvent such as lacquer thinner, spot remover, or equivalent, or trichorethylene. Also, clean the area where sealer is later to be applied. Dry the area thoroughly, so that no solvent touches the seal.

6. Dip the split lip type seal halves in clean engine oil.

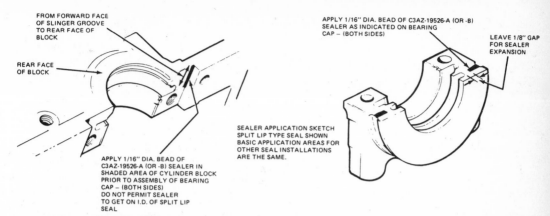

FROM FORWARD FACE OF SLINGER GROOVE TO REAR FACE OF BLOCK

REAR FACE OF BLOCK

APPLY 1/16" DIA. BEAD OF C3AZ-19526-A (OR -B) SEALER IN SHADED AREA OF CYLINDER BLOCK PRIOR TO ASSEMBLY OF BEARING CAP – (BOTH SIDES) DO NOT PERMIT SEALER TO GET ON I.D. OF SPLIT LIP SEAL

APPLY 1/16" DIA. BEAD OF C3AZ-19526-A (OR -B) SEALER AS INDICATED ON BEARING CAP – (BOTH SIDES)

LEAVE 1/8" GAP FOR SEALER EXPANSION

SEALER APPLICATION SKETCH SPLIT LIP TYPE SEAL SHOWN BASIC APPLICATION AREAS FOR OTHER SEAL INSTALLATIONS ARE THE SAME.

Applying RTV sealant to the main bearing cap and block on all 1974–83 engines except the 6-300

7. Carefully install the upper seal (cylinder block) into its groove with undercut side of seal toward the FRONT of the engine, by rotating it on the seal journal of the crankshaft until approximately 3/8″ (9.5mm) protrudes below the parting surface.

Be sure no rubber has been shaved from the outside diameter of the seal by the bottom edge of the groove. Do not allow oil to get on the sealer area.

8. Tighten the remaining bearing cap bolts to the specifications listed in the Torque chart at the beginning of this chapter.

9. Install the lower seal in the rear main bearing cap with undercut side of seal toward the FRONT of the engine, allow the seal to protrude approximately 3/8″ (9.5mm) above the parting surface to mate with the upper seal when the cap is installed.

10. Apply an even 1/16″ (1.5mm) bead of TRV silicone rubber sealer, to the areas shown, following the procedure given in the illustration.

NOTE: *This sealer sets up in 15 minutes.*

Install the rear main bearing cap. Tighten the cap bolts to specifications.

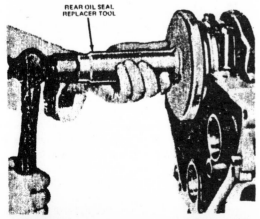

REAR OIL SEAL REPLACER TOOL

240 and 300 inline six rear oil seal installation using special tool

11. Install the oil pump and oil pan. Fill the crankcase with the proper amount and type of oil.

12. Operate the engine and check for oil leaks.

6–300

If the crankshaft rear oil seal replacement is the only operation being performed, it can be done in the vehicle as detailed in the following procedure. If the oil seal is being replaced in conjunction with a rear main bearing replacement, the engine must be removed from the vehicle and installed on a work stand.

1. Remove the starter.

2. Remove the transmission from the vehicle, following the procedures in Chapter 6.

3. On a manual shift transmission, remove the pressure plate and cover assembly and the clutch disc following the procedure in Chapter 6.

4. Remove the flywheel attaching bolts and remove the flywheel and engine rear cover plate.

5. Use an awl to punch two holes in the crankshaft rear oil seal. Punch the holes on opposite sides of the crankshaft and just above the bearing cap to cylinder block split line. Install a sheet metal screw in each hole. Use two large screwdrivers or small pry bars and pry against both screws at the same time to remove the crankshaft rear oil seal. It may be necessary to place small blocks of wood against the cylinder block to provide a fulcrum point for the pry bars. Use caution throughout this procedure to avoid scratching or otherwise damaging the crankshaft oil seal surface.

6. Clean the oil seal recess in the cylinder block and main bearing cap.

7. Clean, inspect and polish the rear oil seal rubbing surface on the crankshaft. Coat a new oil seal and the crankshaft with a light film of engine oil. Start the seal in the recess with the

seal lip facing forward and install it with a seal driver. Keep the tool straight with the center-line of the crankshaft and install the seal until the tool contacts the cylinder block surface. Remove the tool and inspect the seal to be sure it was not damaged during installation.

8. Install the engine rear cover plate. Position the flywheel on the crankshaft flange. Coat the threads of the flywheel attaching bolts with oil resistant sealer and install the bolts. Tighten the bolts in sequence across from each other to the specifications listed in the Torque chart at the beginning of this Chapter.

9. On a manual shift transmission, install the clutch disc and the pressure plate assembly following the procedure in Chapter 6.

10. Install the transmission, following the procedure in Chapter 6.

Crankshaft and Main Bearings

REMOVAL AND INSTALLATION

1. With the engine removed from the vehicle and placed in a work stand, disconnect the spark plug wires from the spark plugs and remove the wires and bracket assembly from the attaching stud on the valve rocker arm cover(s) if so equipped. Disconnect the coil to distributor high tension lead at the coil. Remove the distributor cap and spark plug wires as an assembly. Remove the spark plugs to allow easy rotation of the crankshaft.

2. Remove the fuel pump and oil filter. Slide the water pump by-pass hose clamp (if so equipped) toward the water pump. Remove the alternator and mounting brackets.

3. Remove the crankshaft pulley from the crankshaft vibration damper. Remove the cap-screw and washer from the end of the crank-shaft. Install a universal puller, Tool T58P-6316-D or equivalent on the crankshaft vibration damper and remove the damper.

4. Remove the cylinder front cover and crankshaft gear, refer to Cylinder Front Cover and Timing Chain in this chapter.

5. Invert the engine on the work stand. Remove the clutch pressure plate and disc (manual shift trans.). Remove the flywheel and engine rear cover plate. Remove the oil pan and gasket. Remove the oil pump.

6. Make sure all bearing caps (main and connecting rod) are marked so that they can be installed in their original locations. Turn the crankshaft until the connecting rod from which the cap is being removed is down, and remove the bearing cap. Push the connecting rod and piston assembly up into the cylinder. Repeat this procedure until all the connecting rod bearing caps are removed.

7. Remove the main bearing caps.

8. Carefully lift the crankshaft out of the block so that the thrust bearing surfaces are not damaged. Handle the crankshaft with care to avoid possible fracture to the finished surfaces.

9. Remove the rear journal oil seal from the block and rear main bearing cap.

10. Remove the main bearing inserts from the block and bearing caps.

11. Remove the connecting rod bearing inserts from the connecting rods and caps.

12. If the crankshaft main bearing journals have been refinished to a definite undersize, install the correct undersize bearings. Be sure the bearing inserts and bearing bores are clean. Foreign material under the inserts will distort the bearing and cause a failure.

13. Place the upper main bearing inserts in position in bores with the tang fitting in the slot. Be sure the oil holes in the bearing inserts are aligned with the oil holes in the cylinder block.

14. Install the lower main bearing inserts in the bearing caps.

15. Clean the rear journal oil seal groove and the mating surfaces of the block and rear main bearing cap.

16. Dip the lip type seal halves in clean engine oil. Install the seals in the bearing cap and block with the undercut side of the seal toward the front of the engine.

NOTE: *This procedure applies only to engines with two piece rear main bearing oil seals. Those having one piece seals (6–200 engine) will be installed after the crankshaft is in place.*

17. Carefully lower the crankshaft into place. Be careful not to damage the bearing surfaces.

18. Check the clearance of each main bearing by using the following procedure:

    a. Place a piece of Plastigage® or its equivalent, on bearing surface across full width of bearing cap and about ¼" (6.35mm) off center.

    b. Install cap and tighten bolts to specifications. Do not turn crankshaft while Plastigage® is in place.

    c. Remove the cap. Using Plastigage® scale, check width of Plastigage® at widest point to get the minimum clearance. Check at narrowest point to get maximum clearance. Difference between readings is taper of journal.

    d. If clearance exceeds specified limits, try a 0.001" (0.0254mm) or 0.002" (0.051mm) undersize bearing in combination with the standard bearing. Bearing clearance must be within specified limits. If standard and

0.002″ (0.051mm) undersize bearing does not bring clearance within desired limits, refinish crankshaft journal, then install undersize bearings.

NOTE: *Refer to Rear Main Oil Seal Removal and Installation, for special instructions in applying RTV sealer to rear main bearing cap.*

19. Apply engine oil to the journals and bearings.

20. Install all the bearing caps except the thrust bearing cap (no. 3) bearing on all except the 6–200, 300 which use the no. 5 as the thrust bearing). Be sure the main bearing caps are installed in their original locations. Tighten the bearing cap bolts to specifications.

21. Install the thrust bearing cap with the bolts finger tight.

22. Pry the crankshaft forward against the thrust surface of the upper half of the bearing.

23. Hold the crankshaft forward and pry the thrust bearing cap to the rear. This will align the thrust surfaces of both halves of the bearing.

24. Retain the forward pressure on the crankshaft. Tighten the cap bolts to specifications.

25. Check the crankshaft end play using the following procedures:

a. Force the crankshaft toward the rear of the engine.

b. Install a dial indicator (tools D78P-4201-F, -G or equivalent) so that the contact point rests against the crankshaft flange and the indicator axis is parallel to the crankshaft axis.

c. Zero the dial indicator. Push the crankshaft forward and note the reading on the dial.

d. If the end play exceeds the wear limit listed in the Crankshaft and Connecting Rod Specifications chart, replace the thrust bearing. If the end play is less than the minimum limit, inspect the thrust bearing faces for scratches, burrs, nicks, or dirt. If the thrust faces are not damaged or dirty, then they probably were not aligned properly. Lubricate and install the new thrust bearing and align the faces following procedures 21 through 24.

26. On 6–300 engine with one piece rear main bearing oil seal, coat a new crankshaft rear oil seal with oil and install using Tool T65P-6701-A or equivalent. Inspect the seal to be sure it was not damaged during installation.

27. Install new bearing inserts in the connecting rods and caps. Check the clearance of each bearing, following the procedure (18.a through d).

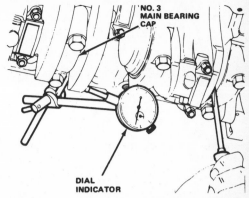

Check the crankshaft end-play with a dial indicator

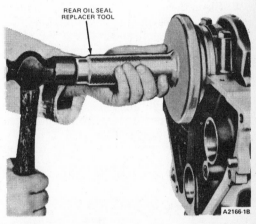

Installing rear main oil seal on 300 6 cyl. engine

28. After the connecting rod bearings have been fitted, apply a light coat of engine oil to the journals and bearings.

29. Turn the crankshaft throw to the bottom of its stroke. Push the piston all the way down until the rod bearing seats on the crankshaft journal.

30. Install the connecting rod cap. Tighten the nuts to specifications.

31. After the piston and connecting rod assemblies have been installed, check the side clearance with a feeler gauge between the connecting rods on each connecting rod crankshaft journal. Refer to Crankshaft and Connecting Rod Specifications chart in this chapter.

32. Install the timing chain and sprockets or gears, cylinder front cover and crankshaft pulley and adapter, following steps under Cylinder Front Cover and Timing Chain Installation in this chapter.

33. Coat the threads of the flywheel attaching bolts with Loctite® or equivalent. Position the flywheel on the crankshaft flange. Install and tighten the bolts to specifications. On a

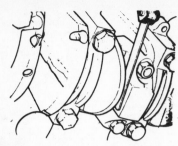

Check the connecting rod side clearance with a feeler gauge

flywheel for manual shift transmission, use a clutch alignment tool to locate the clutch disc. Install the pressure plate and tighten to specifications.

34. Clean the oil pan, oil pump and oil pump screen. Prime the oil pump by filling the inlet port with engine oil and rotating the pump shaft to distribute oil within the housing. Install the oil pump and oil pan by following procedures under Oil Pan removal and installation in this chapter.

35. Install the oil filter, fuel pump and connect the fuel lines. Install the alternator, shield and mounting bracket.

36. Install the spark plugs, distributor cap and spark plug wires.

37. Install the engine in the vehicle.

CLEANING AND INSPECTION

Crankshaft

NOTE: *Handle the crankshaft carefully to avoid damage to the finish surfaces.*

1. Clean the crankshaft with solvent, and blow out all oil passages with compressed air. On the 6–300 engine, clean the oil seal contact surface at the rear of the crankshaft with solvent to remove any corrosion, sludge or varnish deposits.

2. Use crocus cloth to remove any sharp edges, burrs, or other imperfections which might damage the oil seal during installation or cause premature seal wear.

NOTE: *Do not use crocus cloth to polish the seal surfaces. A finely polished surface may produce poor sealing or cause premature seal wear.*

3. Inspect the main and connecting rod journals for cracks, scratches, grooves or scores.

4. Measure the diameter of each journal at least four places to determine out-of-round, taper or undersize condition.

5. On an engine with a manual transmission, check the fit of the clutch pilot bearing in the bore of the crankshaft. A needle roller bearing and adapter assembly is used as a clutch pilot bearing. It is inserted directly into the engine crank shaft. The bearing and adapter assembly cannot be serviced separately. A new bearing must be installed whenever a bearing is removed.

6. Inspect the pilot bearing, when used, for roughness, evidence of overheating or loss of lubricant. Replace if any of these conditions are found.

7. On the 6–300 engine, inspect the rear oil seal surface of the crankshaft for deep grooves, nicks, burrs, porosity, or scratches which could damage the oil seal lip during installation. Remove all nicks and burrs with crocus cloth.

Main Bearings

1. Clean the bearing inserts and caps thoroughly in solvent, and dry them with compressed air.

NOTE: *Do not scrape varnish or gum deposits from the bearing shells.*

2. Inspect each bearing carefully. Bearings that have a scored, chipped, or worn surface should be replaced.

3. The copper/lead bearing base may be visible through the bearing overlay in small localized areas. This may not mean that the bearing is excessively worn. It is not necessary to replace the bearing if the bearing clearance is within recommended specifications.

4. Check the clearance of bearings that appear to be satisfactory with Plastigage® or its equivalent. Fit the new bearings following the procedure Crankshaft and Main Bearings Removal and Installation in this chapter.

REGRINDING JOURNALS

1. Dress minor scores with an oil stone. If the journals are severely marred or exceed the service limit, they should be reground to size for the next undersize bearing.

2. Regrind the journals to give the proper clearance with the next undersize bearing. If the journal will not clean up to maximum undersize bearing available, replace the crankshaft.

3. Always reproduce the same journal shoulder radius that existed originally. Too small a radius will result in fatigue failure of the crankshaft. Too large a radius will result in bearing failure due to radius ride of the bearing.

4. After regrinding the journals, chamfer the oil holes, then polish the journals with a no. 320 grit polishing cloth and engine oil. Crocus cloth may also be used as a polishing agent.

Flywheel and Ring Gear
REMOVAL AND INSTALLATION

1. Remove the transmission, following the procedures in Chapter 6.

2. On a manual shift transmission, remove the clutch pressure plate and cover assembly and clutch disc, following the procedures in Chapter 6.

3. Remove the flywheel attaching bolts and remove the flywheel.

4. Position the flywheel on the crankshaft flange. Coat the threads of the flywheel attaching bolts with Loctite® or equivalent and install the bolts. Tighten the bolts in sequence across from each other to 75–85 ft.lb.

5. On a manual shift transmission, install the clutch disc and pressure plate and cover assembly following the procedures in Chapter 6.

6. Install the transmission following the procedure in Chapter 6.

RING GEAR REPLACEMENT

NOTE: *This procedure is for manual shift transmission only. On automatic transmission if the ring gear has worn, chipped or cracked teeth, replace the flywheel assembly.*

1. Heat the ring gear with a blow torch on the engine side of the gear, and knock it off the flywheel. Do not hit the flywheel when removing the ring gear.

2. Heat the new ring gear evenly until the gear expands enough to slip onto the flywheel. Make sure the gear is properly seated against the shoulder. Do not heat any part of the gear more than 500°F (260°C). If this limit is exceeded, the hardness will be removed from the ring gear teeth.

Exhaust System

SAFETY PRECAUTIONS

For a number of reasons, exhaust system work can be the most dangerous type of work you can do on your Bronco. Always observe the following precautions:

1. Support the van extra securely. Not only will you often be working directly under it, but you'll frequently be using a lot of force, say, heavy hammer blows, to dislodge rusted parts. This can cause a van that's improperly supported to shift and possibly fall.

2. Wear goggles. Exhaust system parts are always rusty. Metal chips can be dislodged, even when you're only turning rusted bolts. Attempting to pry pipes apart with a chisel makes the chips fly even more frequently.

3. If you're using a cutting torch, keep it a great distance from either the fuel tank or lines. Stop what you're doing and feel the temperature of the fuel bearing pipes on the tank frequently. Even slight heat can expand and/or vaporize fuel, resulting in accumulated vapor, or even a liquid leak, near your torch.

4. Watch where your hammer blows fall.

You could easily tap a brake or fuel line when you hit an exhaust system part with a glancing blow. Inspect all lines and hoses in the area where you've been working.

Special Tools

A number of special exhaust system tools can be rented from auto supply houses or local stores that rent special equipment. A common one is a tail pipe expander, designed to enable you to join pipes of identical diameter.

It may also be quite helpful to use solvents designed to loosen rusted bolts or flanges. Soaking rusted parts the night before you do the job can speed the work of freeing rusted parts considerably. Remember that these solvents are are often flammable. Apply only to parts after they are cool!

Exhaust Manifold

REMOVAL AND INSTALLATION

Exhaust manifolds rarely rust, but they may crack due to road damage or thermal shock. The first step is to disconnect the exhaust pipe or crossover pipe by removing the nuts from the manifold studs. Then slide the collar or pull the flanged portion of the exhaust pipe or crossover away. In some cases, you may have to loosen the crossover pipe on the other side in order to gain clearance for easy manifold removal. Make sure you remove and replace seals. If the Early Fuel Evaporation valve is involved remove it and install it later with all new seals.

CAUTION: *Be extremely careful not to contact the hot exhaust pipe, while working underneath the truck.*

Remove parts that are in the way. These may include the hot air shroud, or various accessory brackets on the engine. You may have to disconnect the steering shaft on certain vehicles. Disconnect the oxygen sensor, if it's on the manifold.

You'll have to bend back locking tabs that ensure that mounting nuts remain tight. Then, after the mounting nuts are soaked with solvent, loosen and remove them. Finally, remove the manifold and seal. Clean the surface of the block.

Install in reverse order, being careful to ensure that seals are installed facing in the proper direction so all exhaust ports are fully open and all bolt or stud holes or slots are in proper position. Install nuts loosely and then tighten in several stages, going around the manifold, until you reach the specified torque. Take your time here as even and proper torquing helps prevent leaks. If necessary, torque nuts further to align a flat with the locking tab. Then,

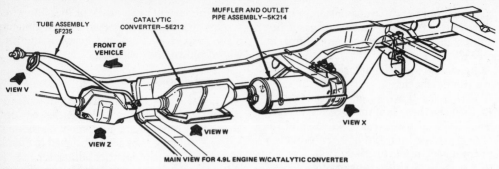

MAIN VIEW FOR 4.9L ENGINE W/CATALYTIC CONVERTER

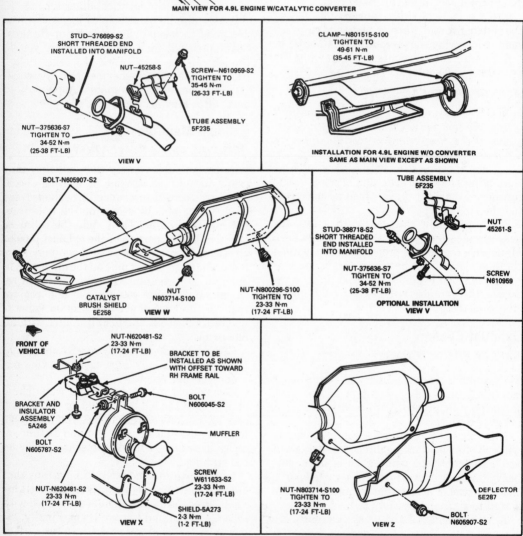

Bronco 4.9L (300 CID) I-6 engine exhaust system

make sure to bend all tabs over to prevent loosened nuts and leaks.

If the manifold has an oxygen sensor installed in it, you'll have to remove it and install it into the new manifold, using a high temperature sealer on the threads. Make sure you don't forget to reconnect the sensor when the manifold is in place.

Crossover Pipe

REMOVAL AND REPLACEMENT

The crossover pipe (used on V-type engines only) is typically connected to the manifolds by flanged connections or collars. In some cases, bolts that are unthreaded for part of their length are used in conjunction with springs.

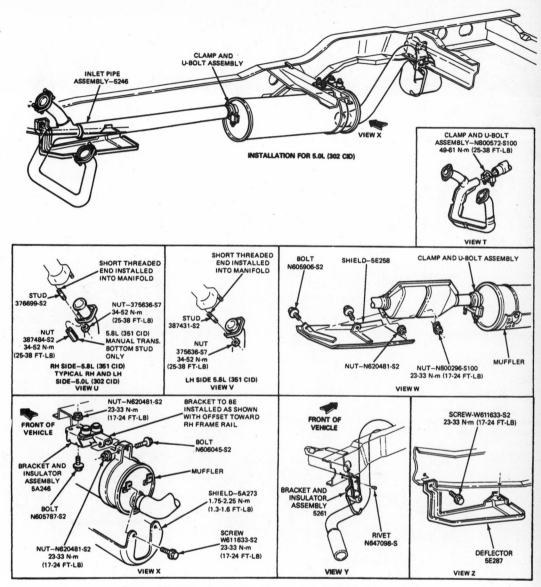

Bronco V8 engine exhaust system—without catalytic converter

Make sure you install the springs and that they are in good mechanical condition (no broken coils) when installing the new pipe. Replace ring type seals, also.

Headpipe

REMOVAL AND REPLACEMENT

The headpipe is typically attached to the rear of one exhaust manifold with a flange or collar type connector and flagged to the front of the catalytic converter. Remove nuts and bolts and, if springs are used to maintain the seal, the springs. The pipe may then be separated from the rest of the system at both flanges.

Replace ring seals; inspect springs and replace them if any coils are broken.

Catalytic Converter

REMOVAL AND REPLACEMENT

CAUTION: *Be very careful when working on or near the converter. External temperatures can reach +1,500°F (+816°C) and more, causing severe burns. Removal or installation should only be performed on a cold exhaust system.*

Remove bolts at the flange at the rear end. Then, loosen nuts and remove U-clamp to remove the catalyst. Slide the catalyst out of the

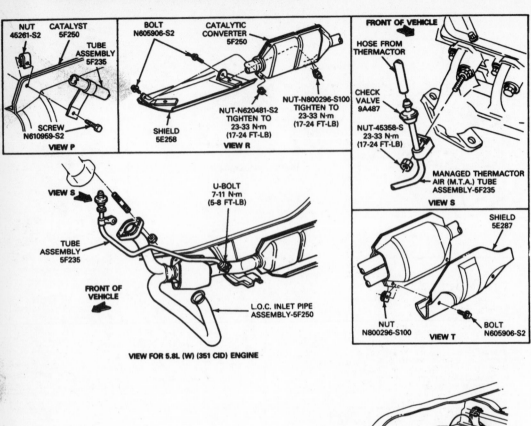

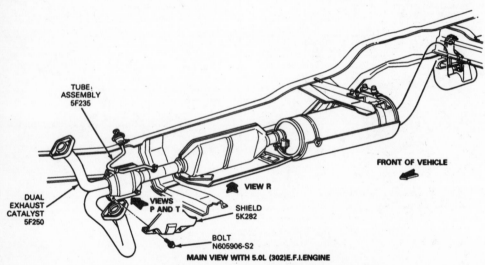

Bronco V8 engine exhaust system—with catalytic converter

Muffler and Tailpipes
REMOVAL AND INSTALLATION

outlet pipe. Replace all ring seals. In some cases, you'll have to disconnect an air line coming from the engine compartment before catalyst removal. In some cases, a hanger supports the converter via one of the flange bolts. Make sure the hanger gets properly reconnected. Also, be careful to retain all parts used to heat shield the converter and reinstall them. Make sure the converter is replaced for proper direction of flow and air supply connections.

These units are typically connected by flanges at the rear of the converter and at either end of mufflers either by an original weld or by U-clamps working over a pipe connection in which one side of the connection is slightly larger than the other. You may have to cut the original connection and use the pipe expander to allow the original equipment exhaust pipe to be fitted over the new muffler. In this case, you'll have to purchase new U-clamps to fasten the joints. Ford recommends that whenever you replace a muffler, all parts to the rear of the muffler in the exhaust system must be replaced. Also, all slip joints rearward of the converter should be coated with sealer before they are assembled.

Be careful to connect all U-clamps or other hanger arrangements so the exhaust system will not flex. Assemble all parts loosely and rotate parts inside one another or clamps on the pipes to ensure proper routing of all exhaust system parts to avoid excessive heating of the floorpan, fuel lines and tank, etc. Also, make sure there is clearance to prevent the system from rattling against spring shackles, the differential, etc. You may be able to bend long pipes slightly by hand to help get enough clearance, if necessary.

While disassembling the system, keep your eye open for any leaks or for excessively close clearance to any brake system parts. Inspect the brake system for any sort of heat damage and repair as necessary.

Troubleshooting Engine Mechanical Problems

Problem	Cause	Solution
External oil leaks	• Fuel pump gasket broken or improperly seated	• Replace gasket
	• Cylinder head cover RTV sealant broken or improperly seated	• Replace sealant; inspect cylinder head cover sealant flange and cylinder head sealant surface for distortion and cracks
	• Oil filler cap leaking or missing	• Replace cap
	• Oil filter gasket broken or improperly seated	• Replace oil filter
	• Oil pan side gasket broken, improperly seated or opening in RTV sealant	• Replace gasket or repair opening in sealant; inspect oil pan gasket flange for distortion
	• Oil pan front oil seal broken or improperly seated	• Replace seal; inspect timing case cover and oil pan seal flange for distortion
	• Oil pan rear oil seal broken or improperly seated	• Replace seal; inspect oil pan rear oil seal flange; inspect rear main bearing cap for cracks, plugged oil return channels, or distortion in seal groove
	• Timing case cover oil seal broken or improperly seated	• Replace seal
	• Excess oil pressure because of restricted PCV valve	• Replace PCV valve
	• Oil pan drain plug loose or has stripped threads	• Repair as necessary and tighten
	• Rear oil gallery plug loose	• Use appropriate sealant on gallery plug and tighten
	• Rear camshaft plug loose or improperly seated	• Seat camshaft plug or replace and seal, as necessary
	• Distributor base gasket damaged	• Replace gasket
Excessive oil consumption	• Oil level too high	• Drain oil to specified level
	• Oil with wrong viscosity being used	• Replace with specified oil
	• PCV valve stuck closed	• Replace PCV valve
	• Valve stem oil deflectors (or seals) are damaged, missing, or incorrect type	• Replace valve stem oil deflectors
	• Valve stems or valve guides worn	• Measure stem-to-guide clearance and repair as necessary
	• Poorly fitted or missing valve cover baffles	• Replace valve cover
	• Piston rings broken or missing	• Replace broken or missing rings
	• Scuffed piston	• Replace piston
	• Incorrect piston ring gap	• Measure ring gap, repair as necessary
	• Piston rings sticking or excessively loose in grooves	• Measure ring side clearance, repair as necessary

Troubleshooting Engine Mechanical Problems (cont.)

Problem	Cause	Solution
Excessive oil consumption (cont.)	• Compression rings installed upside down	• Repair as necessary
	• Cylinder walls worn, scored, or glazed	• Repair as necessary
	• Piston ring gaps not properly staggered	• Repair as necessary
	• Excessive main or connecting rod bearing clearance	• Measure bearing clearance, repair as necessary
No oil pressure	• Low oil level	• Add oil to correct level
	• Oil pressure gauge, warning lamp or sending unit inaccurate	• Replace oil pressure gauge or warning lamp
	• Oil pump malfunction	• Replace oil pump
	• Oil pressure relief valve sticking	• Remove and inspect oil pressure relief valve assembly
	• Oil passages on pressure side of pump obstructed	• Inspect oil passages for obstruction
	• Oil pickup screen or tube obstructed	• Inspect oil pickup for obstruction
	• Loose oil inlet tube	• Tighten or seal inlet tube
Low oil pressure	• Low oil level	• Add oil to correct level
	• Inaccurate gauge, warning lamp or sending unit	• Replace oil pressure gauge or warning lamp
	• Oil excessively thin because of dilution, poor quality, or improper grade	• Drain and refill crankcase with recommended oil
	• Excessive oil temperature	• Correct cause of overheating engine
	• Oil pressure relief spring weak or sticking	• Remove and inspect oil pressure relief valve assembly
	• Oil inlet tube and screen assembly has restriction or air leak	• Remove and inspect oil inlet tube and screen assembly. (Fill inlet tube with lacquer thinner to locate leaks.)
	• Excessive oil pump clearance	• Measure clearances
	• Excessive main, rod, or camshaft bearing clearance	• Measure bearing clearances, repair as necessary
High oil pressure	• Improper oil viscosity	• Drain and refill crankcase with correct viscosity oil
	• Oil pressure gauge or sending unit inaccurate	• Replace oil pressure gauge
	• Oil pressure relief valve sticking closed	• Remove and inspect oil pressure relief valve assembly
Main bearing noise	• Insufficient oil supply	• Inspect for low oil level and low oil pressure
	• Main bearing clearance excessive	• Measure main bearing clearance, repair as necessary
	• Bearing insert missing	• Replace missing insert
	• Crankshaft end play excessive	• Measure end play, repair as necessary
	• Improperly tightened main bearing cap bolts	• Tighten bolts with specified torque
	• Loose flywheel or drive plate	• Tighten flywheel or drive plate attaching bolts
	• Loose or damaged vibration damper	• Repair as necessary
Connecting rod bearing noise	• Insufficient oil supply	• Inspect for low oil level and low oil pressure
	• Carbon build-up on piston	• Remove carbon from piston crown
	• Bearing clearance excessive or bearing missing	• Measure clearance, repair as necessary
	• Crankshaft connecting rod journal out-of-round	• Measure journal dimensions, repair or replace as necessary

Troubleshooting Engine Mechanical Problems (cont.)

Problem	Cause	Solution
Connecting rod bearing noise (cont.)	• Misaligned connecting rod or cap • Connecting rod bolts tightened improperly	• Repair as necessary • Tighten bolts with specified torque
Piston noise	• Piston-to-cylinder wall clearance excessive (scuffed piston) • Cylinder walls excessively tapered or out-of-round • Piston ring broken • Loose or seized piston pin • Connecting rods misaligned • Piston ring side clearance excessively loose or tight • Carbon build-up on piston is excessive	• Measure clearance and examine piston • Measure cylinder wall dimensions, rebore cylinder • Replace all rings on piston • Measure piston-to-pin clearance, repair as necessary • Measure rod alignment, straighten or replace • Measure ring side clearance, repair as necessary • Remove carbon from piston

Valve actuating component noise	• Insufficient oil supply
	
	• Push rods worn or bent
	• Rocker arms or pivots worn
	
	• Foreign objects or chips in hydraulic tappets
	• Excessive tappet leak-down
	• Tappet face worn
	
	• Broken or cocked valve springs
	
	• Stem-to-guide clearance excessive
	
	• Valve bent
	• Loose rocker arms
	• Valve seat runout excessive
	• Missing valve lock
	• Push rod rubbing or contacting cylinder head
	• Excessive engine oil (four-cylinder engine)
		• Check for:
		  (a) Low oil level
		  (b) Low oil pressure
		  (c) Plugged push rods
		  (d) Wrong hydraulic tappets
		  (e) Restricted oil gallery
		  (f) Excessive tappet to bore clearance
		• Replace worn or bent push rods
		• Replace worn rocker arms or pivots
		• Clean tappets
		
		• Replace valve tappet
		• Replace tappet; inspect corresponding cam lobe for wear
		• Properly seat cocked springs; replace broken springs
		• Measure stem-to-guide clearance, repair as required
		• Replace valve
		• Tighten bolts with specified torque
		• Regrind valve seat/valves
		• Install valve lock
		• Remove cylinder head and remove obstruction in head
		• Correct oil level

Emission Controls and Fuel System

4

EMISSION CONTROLS

There are three types of automobile pollutants that concern automotive engineers: crankcase fumes, exhaust gases and gasoline vapors from evaporation. The devices and systems used to limit these pollutants are commonly called emission control equipment.

Crankcase Emission Controls

The crankcase emission control equipment consists of a positive crankcase ventilation (PCV) valve, a closed or open oil filler cap and the hoses that connect this equipment.

When the engine is running, a small portion of the gases which are formed in the combustion chamber leak by the piston rings and enter the crankcase. Since these gases are under pressure they tend to escape from the crankcase and enter into the atmosphere. If these gases were allowed to remain in the crankcase for any length of time, they would contaminate the engine oil and cause sludge to build up. If the gases are allowed to escape into the atmosphere, they would pollute the air, as they contain unburned hydrocarbons. The crankcase emission control equipment recycles these gases back into the engine combustion chamber, where they are burned.

Crankcase gases are recycled in the following manner. While the engine is running, clean filtered air is drawn into the crankcase either directly through the oil filler cap or through the carburetor air filter and then through a hose leading to the oil filler cap. As the air passes through the crankcase it picks up the combustion gases and carries them out of the crankcase, up through the PCV valve and into the intake manifold. After they enter the intake manifold they are drawn into the combustion chamber and are burned.

The most critical component of the system is the PCV valve. This vacuum controlled valve

regulates the amount of gases which are recycled into the combustion chamber. At low engine speeds the valve is partially closed, limiting the flow of gases into the intake manifold. As engine speed increases, the valve opens to admit greater quantities of the gases into the intake manifold. If the valve should become blocked or plugged, the gases will be prevented from escaping the crankcase by the normal route. Since these gases are under pressure, they will find their own way out of the crankcase. This alternate route is usually a weak oil seal or gasket in the engine. As the gas escapes by the gasket, it also crates an oil leak. Besides causing oil leaks, a clogged PCV valve also allows these gases to remain in the crankcase for an extended period of time, promoting the formation of sludge in the engine.

The above explanation and the troubleshoot-

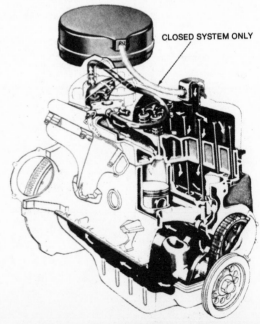

CLOSED SYSTEM ONLY

A cutaway of the typical 6-cylinder PCV system

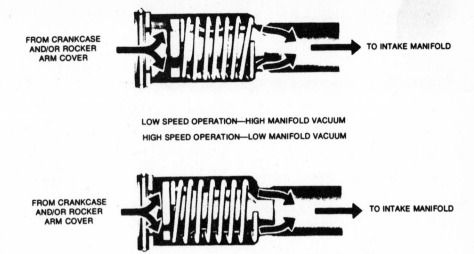

FROM CRANKCASE AND/OR ROCKER ARM COVER → → TO INTAKE MANIFOLD

LOW SPEED OPERATION—HIGH MANIFOLD VACUUM

HIGH SPEED OPERATION—LOW MANIFOLD VACUUM

FROM CRANKCASE AND/OR ROCKER ARM COVER → → TO INTAKE MANIFOLD

A cutaway of a PCV valve showing its operation

ing procedure which follows applies to all of the engines installed in Ford Bronco, since all are equipped with PCV systems.

TROUBLESHOOTING

With the engine running, pull the PCV valve and hose from the valve rocker cover rubber grommet. Block off the end of the valve with your finger. A strong vacuum should be felt. Shake the valve; a clicking noise indicates it is free. Replace the valve if it is suspected of being blocked.

REMOVAL AND INSTALLATION

1. Pull the PCV valve and hose from the rubber grommet in the rocker cover.

2. Remove the PCV valve from the hose. Inspect the inside of the PCV valve. If it is dirty, disconnect it from the intake manifold and clean it in a suitable, safe solvent.

To install, proceed as follows:

1. If the PCV valve hose was removed, connect it to the intake manifold.

2. Connect the PCV valve to its hose.

3. Install the PCV valve into the rubber grommet in the valve rocker cover.

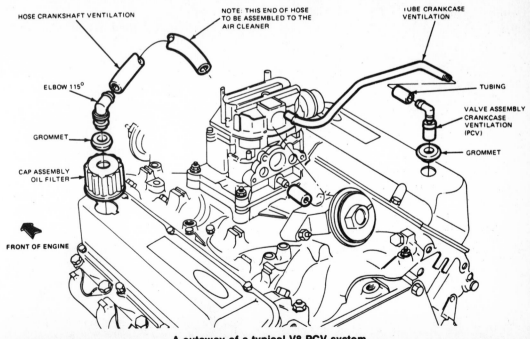

HOSE CRANKSHAFT VENTILATION

NOTE: THIS END OF HOSE TO BE ASSEMBLED TO THE AIR CLEANER

TUBE CRANKCASE VENTILATION

ELBOW 115°

TUBING

GROMMET

VALVE ASSEMBLY CRANKCASE VENTILATION (PCV)

CAP ASSEMBLY OIL FILTER

GROMMET

FRONT OF ENGINE

A cutaway of a typical V8 PCV system

Evaporative Emission Controls

Beginning 1970, Ford Broncos produced for sale in California were equipped with evaporative emission controls on the fuel system. For 1971, the system was modified somewhat and used on all Ford Broncos as standard equipment.

Changes in atmospheric temperature cause fuel tanks to breathe; that is, the air within the tank expands and contracts with outside temperature changes. As the temperature rises, air escapes through the tank vent tube or the vent in the tank cap. The air which escapes contains gasoline vapors. In a similar manner, the gasoline which fills the carburetor float bowl expands when the engine is stopped. Engine heat causes this expansion. The vapors escape through the carburetor and air cleaner.

The Evaporative Emission Control System provides a sealed fuel system with the capability to store and condense fuel vapors. The system has three parts: a fill control vent system; a vapor vent and storage system; and a pressure and vacuum relief system (special fill cap).

The fill control vent system is a modification to the fuel tank. It uses an air space within the tank which is 10–12% of the tank's volume. The air space is sufficient to provide for the thermal expansion of the fuel. The space also serves as part of the in-tank vapor vent system.

The in-tank vent system consists of the air space previously described and a vapor separator assembly. The separator assembly is mounted to the top of the fuel tank and is secured by a cam-locking, similar to the one which secures the fuel sending unit. Foam material fills the vapor separator assembly. The foam material separates raw fuel and vapors, thus retarding the entrance of fuel into the vapor line.

The sealed filler cap has a pressure vacuum relief valve. Under normal operating conditions, the filler cap operates as a check valve, allowing air to enter the tank to replace the fuel consumed. At the same time, it prevents vapors from escaping through the cap. In case of excessive pressure within the tank, the filler cap valve opens to relieve the pressure.

Because the filler cap is sealed, fuel vapors have but one place through which they may escape: the vapor separator assembly at the top of the fuel tank. The vapors pass through the foam material and continue through a single vapor line which leads in a canister in the engine compartment. The canister is filled with activated charcoal.

Another vapor line runs from the top of the carburetor float chamber to the charcoal canister.

As the fuel vapors (hydrocarbons), enter the charcoal canister, they are absorbed by the charcoal. The air is dispelled through the open bottom of the charcoal canister, leaving the hydrocarbons trapped within the charcoal. When the engine is started, vacuum causes fresh air to be drawn into the canister from its open bottom. The fresh air passes through the charcoal picking up the hydrocarbons which are trapped there and feeding them into the carburetor for burning with the fuel mixture.

EVAPORATIVE EMISSION CONTROL SYSTEM CHECK

Other than a visual check to determine that none of the vapor lines are broken, there is no test for this equipment.

Thermactor System

All 1967 models equipped with manual transmission, all 1974 models manufactured for sale in California, and most 1975–86 models are equipped with a Thermactor emission control system.

The Thermactor emission control system makes use of a belt driven air pump to inject fresh air into the hot exhaust stream through the engine exhaust ports. The result is the extended burning of those fumes which were not completely ignited in the combustion chamber, and the subsequent reduction of some of the hydrocarbon and carbon monoxide content of the exhaust emissions into harmless carbon dioxide and water.

The Thermactor system is composed of the following components:

1. Air supply pump (belt driven)
2. Air by-pass valve.
3. Check valves
4. Air manifolds (internal or external)
5. Air supply tubes (on external manifolds only).

Air for the Thermactor system is cleaned by means of a centrifugal filter fan mounted on the air pump driveshaft. The air filter does not require a replaceable element.

To prevent excessive pressure, the air pump is equipped with a pressure relief valve which uses a replaceable plastic plug to control the pressure setting.

The Thermactor air pump has sealed bearings which are lubricated for the life of the unit, and preset rotor vane and bearing clearances, which do not require any periodic adjustments.

The air supply from the pump is controlled by the air by-pass valve, sometimes called a

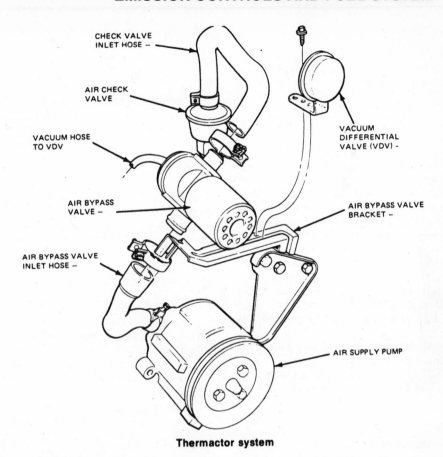

Thermactor system

dump valve. During deceleration, the air by-pass valve opens, momentarily diverting the air supply through a silencer and into the atmosphere, thus preventing backfires within the exhaust system.

A check valve is incorporated in the air inlet side of the air manifolds. Its purpose is to prevent exhaust gases from backing up into the Thermactor system. This valve is especially important in the event of drive belt failure, and during deceleration, when the air by-pass valve is dumping the air supply.

The air manifolds and air supply tubes channel the air from the Thermactor air pump into the exhaust ports of each cylinder, thus completing the cycle of the Thermactor system.

REPLACEMENT

Air By-Pass Valve

1. Disconnect the air and vacuum hoses at the air by-pass valve body.
2. Position the air by-pass valve and connect the respective hoses.

Check Valve

1. Disconnect the air supply hose at the valve. Use a 1¼" crowfoot wrench. The valve has a standard, right hand pipe thread.

2. Clean the threads on the air manifold adapter (air supply tube on the V8 engines) with a wire brush. Do not blow compressed air through the check valve in either direction.
3. Install the check valve and tighten.
4. Connect the air supply hose.

Air Manifold

6-CYLINDER ENGINES ONLY

1. Disconnect the air supply hose at the check valve, position the hose out of the way and remove the valve.
2. Loosen all of the air manifold-to-cylinder head tube coupling nuts (compression fittings). Inspect the air manifold for damaged threads and fittings and for leaking connections. Repair or replace as required. Clean the manifold and associated parts with kerosene. Do not dry the parts with compressed air.
3. Position the air manifold on the cylinder head. Be sure that all of the tube coupling nuts are aligned with the cylinder head.
4. Screw each coupling nut into the cylinder head, one or two threads. Tighten the tube coupling nuts.
5. Install the check valve and tighten it.
6. Connect the air supply hose to the check valve.

Air Supply Tube

V8 ENGINE ONLY

1. Disconnect the air supply hose at the check valve and position the hose out of the way.
2. Remove the check valve.
3. Remove the air supply tube bolt and seal washer.
4. Carefully remove the air supply tube and seal washer from the cylinder head. Inspect the air supply tube for evidence of leaking threads or seal surfaces. Examine the attaching bolt head, seal washers, and supply tube surface for leaks. Inspect the attaching bolt and cylinder head threads for damage. Clean the air supply tube, seal washers, and bolt with kerosene. Do not dry the parts with compressed air.
5. Install the seal washer and air supply tube on the cylinder head. Be sure that it is positioned in the same manner as before removal.
6. Install the seal washer and mounting bolt. Tighten the bolt.
7. Install the check valve and tighten it.
8. Connect the air supply hose to the check valve.

Air Nozzle

6-CYLINDER ENGINES ONLY

Normally, air nozzles should be replaced during cylinder head reconditioning. A nozzle may be replaced, however, without removing the cylinder head, by removing the air manifold and using a hooked tool.

Clean the nozzle with kerosene and a stiff brush. Inspect the air nozzles for eroded tips.

Air Pump and Filter Fan

1. Loosen the air pump attaching bolts.
2. Remove the drive pulley attaching bolts and pull the pulley off the air pump shaft.
3. Pry the outer disc loose, then remove the centrifugal filter fan. Care must be used to prevent foreign matter from entering the air intake hole, especially if the fan breaks during removal. Do not attempt to remove the metal drive hub.
4. Install the new filter fan by drawing it into position with the pulley bolts.

NOTE: *Some 1966–67 air pumps have air filters with replaceable, non-cleanable elements.*

Air Pump

1. Disconnect the air outlet hose at the air pump.
2. Loosen the pump belt tension adjuster.
3. Disengage the drive belt.

4. Remove the mounting bolt and air pump.
5. Position the air pump on the mounting bracket and install the mounting bolt.
6. Place the drive belt in the pulley and attach the adjusting arm to the air pump.
7. Adjust the drive belt tension and tighten the adjusting arm and mounting bolts.
8. Connect the air outlet hose to the air pump.

Relief Valve

Do not disassemble the air pump on the truck to replace the relief valve, but remove the pump from the engine.

1. Remove the relief valve on the pump housing and hold it in position with a block of wood.
2. Use a hammer to lightly tap the wood block until the relief valve is seated.

Relief Valve Pressure Setting Plug

1. Compress the locking tabs inward (together) and remove the plastic pressure setting plug.
2. Before installing the new plug, be sure that the plug is the correct one. The plugs are color coded.
3. Insert the plug in the relief valve hole and push in until it snaps into place.

Catalytic Converter

Starting 1975, most models have an exhaust system catalytic converter. The converter is in the exhaust system ahead of the muffler. It contains a catalytic agent made of platinum and palladium, used to oxidize hydrocarbons (HC) and carbon monoxide (CO). The catalyst is expected to function without service of any kind for at least 50,000 miles. Use of leaded fuel would quickly cause catalyst failure; for this reason, a tank filler restriction prevents the entry of service station leaded fuel nozzles.

Exhaust Gas Recirculation System (EGR)

In this system, a vacuum operated EGR flow valve is attached to the carburetor spacer. A passage in the carburetor spacer mates with a hole in the mounting face of the EGR valve or the intake manifold. The most common system allows exhaust gases to flow from the exhaust crossover, through the control valve and through the spacer into the intake manifold below the carburetor. For those engines where exhaust gases cannot be picked up from the exhaust crossover (6 cylinder) as described above, the gases are picked up from the choke stove located on the exhaust manifold or directly from the exhaust manifold. The exhaust

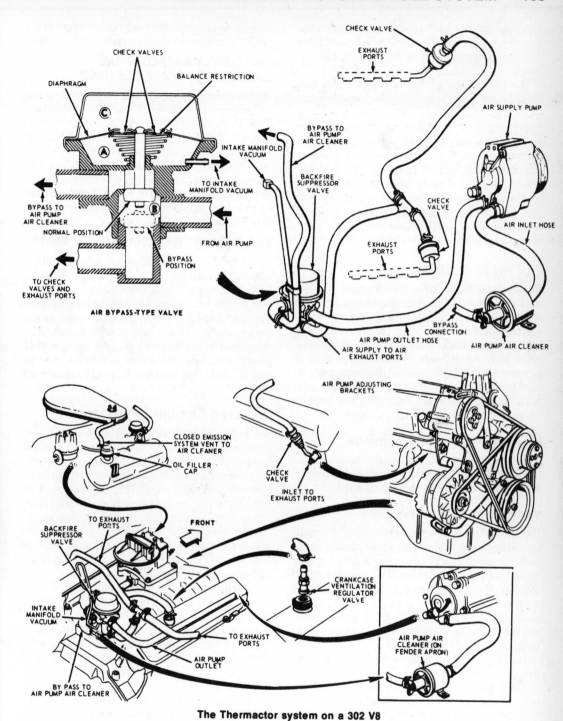

The Thermactor system on a 302 V8

gases are routed to the carburetor spacer through steel tubing.

The vacuum signal which operates the EGR valve originates at the EGR vacuum port in the carburetor. This signal is controlled by at least one, and sometimes two, series of valves.

A water temperature sensing valve (the EGR PVS) which is closed until the water temperature reaches either 60°F (15.5°C) or 125°F

(52°C), depending on application, is always used.

The position of the EGR vacuum port in the carburetor and calibration of the EGR valve can be varied to give the required modulation of EGR during acceleration and low speed cruise conditions. However, a more complicated system using a second series valve is sometimes needed to provide control of EGR for engine operation at high speed cruise conditions. The second valve, the high speed modulator valve, is controlled as a function of vehicle speed.

The high speed EGR modulator subsystem consists of a speed sensor, an electronic module and a solenoid vacuum valve. The speed sensor, driven by the speedometer cable, provides an AC signal in relation to engine speed, to the electronic module. The electronic module processes the information from the speed sensor and sends a signal to the high speed modulator (vacuum solenoid) valve. When the vehicle speed exceeds the module trigger speed, the solenoid vacuum valve closes which, in turn, causes the EGR valve to close.

EGR VALVE CLEANING

Remove the EGR valve for cleaning. Do not strike or pry on the valve diaphragm housing or supports, as this may damage the valve operating mechanism and/or change the valve calibration. Check orifice hole in the EGR valve body for deposits. A small hand drill of no more than 0.060″ (1.5mm) diameter may be used to clean the hole if plugged. Extreme care must be taken to avoid enlarging the hole or damaging the surface of the orifice plate.

Valves Which Cannot Be Disassembled

Valves which are riveted or otherwise permanently assembled should be replaced if highly contaminated; they cannot be cleaned.

Valves Which Can Be Disassembled

Separate the diaphragm section from the main mounting body. Clean the valve plates, stem, and the mounting plate, using a small power driven rotary type wire brush. Take care not to damage the parts. Remove deposits between stem and valve disc by using a steel blade or shim approximately 0.028″ (0.7mm) thick in a sawing motion around the stem shoulder at both sides of the disc.

The poppet must wobble and move axially before reassembly.

Clean the cavity and passages in the main body of the valve with a power driven rotary wire brush. If the orifice plate has a hole less than 0.450″ (1.14mm) it must be removed for cleaning. Remove all loosened debris using shop compressed air. Reassemble the diaphragm section on the main body using a new gasket between them. Torque the attaching screws to specification. Clean the orifice plate and the counterbore in the valve body. Reinstall the orifice plate using a small amount of contact cement to retain the plate in place during assembly of the valve to the carburetor

spacer. Apply cement to only outer edges of the orifice plate to avoid restriction of the orifice.

EGR SUPPLY PASSAGES AND CARBURETOR SPACE CLEANING

Remove the carburetor and carburetor spacer on engines so equipped. Clean the supply tube with a small power driven rotary type wire brush or blast cleaning equipment. Clean the exhaust gas passages in the spacer using a suitable wire brush and/or scraper. The machined holes in the spacer can be cleaned by using a suitable round wire brush. Hard encrusted material should be probed loose first, then brushed out.

EGR EXHAUST GAS CHANNEL CLEANING

Clean the exhaust gas channel, where applicable, in the intake manifold, using a suitable carbon scraper. Clean the exhaust gas entry port in the intake manifold by hand passing a suitable drill bit through the holes to auger out the deposits. Do not use a wire brush. The manifold riser bore(s) should be suitably plugged during the above action to prevent any of the residue from entering the induction system.

Improved Combustion System

All 1968 Broncos equipped with automatic transmission, all 1969 models and all 1970 and later models (regardless of other exhaust emission control equipment) are equipped with the Improved Combustion (IMCO) system. The IMCO system controls emissions arising from the incomplete combustion of the air/fuel mixture in the cylinders. The IMCO system incorporates a number of modifications to the distributor spark control system, the fuel system, and the internal design of the engine.

Internal engine modifications include the following: elimination of surface irregularities and crevices as well as a low surface area-to-volume ratio in the combustion chambers, a high velocity intake manifold combined with short exhaust ports, selective valve timing and a higher temperature and capacity cooling system.

Modifications to the fuel system include the following: recalibrated carburetors to achieve a leaner air/fuel mixture, more precise calibration of the choke mechanism, the installation of idle mixture limiter caps and a heated air intake system.

Modifications to the distributor spark control system include the following: a modified centrifugal advance curve, the use of dual diaphragm distributors in most applications, a ported vacuum switch, a deceleration valve and a spark delay valve.

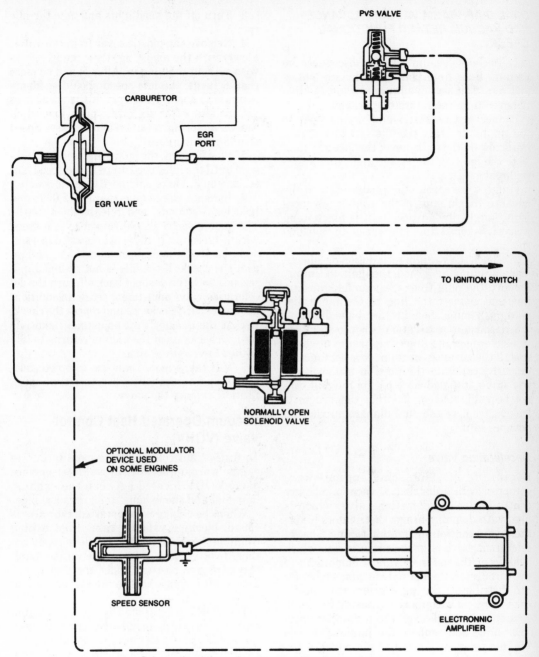

PVS VALVE

CARBURETOR

EGR
PORT

EGR VALVE

TO IGNITION SWITCH

NORMALLY OPEN
SOLENOID VALVE

OPTIONAL MODULATOR
DEVICE USED
ON SOME ENGINES

SPEED SENSOR

ELECTRONNIC
AMPLIFIER

Schematic of the exhaust gas recirculation system

Spark Delay Valve

The spark delay valve is a plastic spring loaded, color coded valve in the vacuum line to the distributor vacuum advance chamber on some 1972 models. Under heavy throttle application, the valve will close, blocking carburetor vacuum to the distributor vacuum advance mechanism. After the designated period of time, the valve opens, restoring normal carburetor vacuum to the distributor.

Dual Diaphragm Distributor

The dual diaphragm distributor has two diaphragms which operate independently. The outer (primary) diaphragm makes use of carburetor vacuum to advance the ignition timing. The inner (secondary) diaphragm uses intake manifold vacuum to provide additional retardation of ignition timing during closed throttle deceleration and idle, resulting in the reduction of hydrocarbon emissions.

DUAL DIAPHRAGM VACUUM ADVANCE AND VACUUM RETARD FUNCTIONAL CHECK

1. To check vacuum advance, disconnect the vacuum lines from both the advance (outer) and retard (inner) diaphragms. Plug the line removed from the retard diaphragm.

Connect a tachometer and timing light to the engine. Increase the idle speed by setting the screw on the first step of the fast idle cam. Note the ignition timing setting, using a timing light.

Connect the carburetor vacuum line to the advance diaphragm. If the timing advances immediately, the advance unit is functioning properly. Adjust the idle speed to 550–600 rpm.

2. Check the vacuum retardation as follows: using a timing light, note the ignition timing. Remove the plug from the manifold vacuum line and connect the line to the inner diaphragm. Timing should retard immediately.

3. If vacuum retardation is not to specifications, replace the dual diaphragm advance unit. If the advance (vacuum) does not function properly, calibrate the unit on a distributor test stand. If the advance part of the unit cannot be calibrated, or if either diaphragm is leaking, replace the dual diaphragm vacuum advance unit.

Deceleration Valve

Beginning in 1969, some engines were equipped with a distributor vacuum advance control valve (deceleration valve) which is used with dual diaphragm distributors to further aid in controlling ignition timing. The deceleration valve is in the vacuum line which runs from the outer (advance) diaphragm to the carburetor, the normal vacuum supply for the distributor. During deceleration, the intake manifold vacuum rises causing the deceleration valve to close off the carburetor vacuum source and connect the intake manifold vacuum source to the distributor advance diaphragm. The increase in vacuum provides maximum ignition timing advance, thus providing more complete fuel combustion and decreasing exhaust system backfiring.

DISTRIBUTOR DECELERATION VACUUM CONTROL VALVE TEST

1. Connect a tachometer to the engine and bring the engine to the normal operating temperature.

2. Check the idle speed and set it to specifications with the headlights on high beam, as necessary.

3. Turn off the headlights and note the idle rpm.

4. Remove the plastic cover from the valve. Slowly turn the adjusting screw counterclockwise without pressing in. After 5, and no more than 6 turns, the idle speed should suddenly increase to about 1,000 rpm. If the speed does not increase after six turns, push inward on the valve spring retainer and release. Speed should now increase.

5. Slowly turn the adjusting screw clockwise until the idle speed drops to the speed noted in Step 3. Make one more turn clockwise.

6. Increase the engine speed to 2,000 rpm, hold for 5 seconds, and release the throttle. The engine speed should return to idle speed within 4 seconds. If idle is not resumed in 4 seconds, back off the dashpot adjustment and repeat the check. If the idle is not resumed in 3 seconds with the dashpot back off, turn the deceleration valve adjustment screw an additional quarter turn clockwise and repeat the check. Repeat the quarter turn adjustment and idle return checks until the engine returns to idle within the required time.

7. If it takes more than one complete turn from Step 5 to meet the idle return time specification, replace the valve.

Vacuum Operated Heat Control Valve (VOHV)

To further aid cold start driveability during engine warmup, most 1975 and later engines use a VOHV located between the exhaust manifold and the exhaust inlet (header) pipe.

When the engine is first started, the valve is closed, blocking exhaust gases from exiting from one bank of cylinders. These gases are then diverted back through the intake manifold crossover passage under the carburetor. The result is quick heat to the carburetor and choke.

The VOHV is controlled by a ported vacuum switch which uses manifold vacuum to keep the vacuum motor on the valve closed until the coolant reaches a predetermined warm-up valve. When the engine is warmed up, the PVS shuts off vacuum to the VOHV, and a strong return spring opens the VOHV butterfly.

Carburetor

The carburetors used on engines equipped with emission controls have specific flow characteristics that differ from the carburetors used on vehicles not equipped with emission control devices. Also, since 1968, all carburetors have limiter caps installed on the idle fuel mixture adjustment screws. These limiter caps prevent an overly rich mixture adjustment from being made. The correct adjustment can usually be reached within the range of the limiter caps. These carburetors are identified by number. The same type carburetor should be used when replacement is necessary.

Thermostatically Controlled Air Cleaner System (TAC)

This system consists of a heat shroud which is integral with the right side exhaust manifold, a hot air hose and a special air cleaner assembly equipped with a thermal sensor and vacuum motor and air valve assembly.

The temperature of the carburetor intake air is thermostatically controlled by means of a valve plate and a vacuum override built into a duct assembly attached to the air cleaner. The exhaust manifold shroud tube is attached to the shroud over the exhaust manifold for the source of heated air.

The thermal sensor is attached to the air valve actuating lever, along with the vacuum motor lever, both of which control the position of the air valve to supply either heated air from the exhaust manifold or cooler air from the engine compartment.

During the warm-up period, when the under-the-hood temperatures are low, the thermal sensor doesn't exert enough tension on the air valve actuating lever to close (heat off) the air valve. Thus, the carburetor receives heated air from around the exhaust manifold.

As the temperature of the air entering the air cleaner approaches approximately 110°F (43°C), the thermal sensor begins to push on the air valve actuating lever and overcome the spring tension which holds the air valve in the open (heat on) position. The air valve begins to move to the closed (heat off) position, allowing only under-the-hood air to enter the air cleaner.

The air valve in the air cleaner will also open, regardless of the air temperature, during heavy acceleration to obtain maximum airflow through the air cleaner. The extreme decrease in intake manifold vacuum during heavy ac-

celeration permits the vacuum motor to override the thermostatic control. This opens the system to both heated air and air from the engine compartment.

HEATED AIR INTAKE TEST

1. With the engine completely cold, look inside the cold air duct and make sure that the valve plate is fully in the up position (closing the cold air duct).

2. Start the engine and bring it to operating temperature.

3. Stop the engine and look inside the cold air duct again. The valve plate should be down, allowing an opening from the cold air duct into the air cleaner.

4. If the unit appears to be malfunctioning, remove it and examine it to make sure that the springs are not broken or disconnected, and replace the thermostat if all other parts appear intact and properly connected.

EGR/Coolant Spark Control (CSC) System

The EGR/CSC system is used on most 1974 and later models. It regulates both distributor spark advance and the EGR valve operation according to coolant temperature by sequentially switching vacuum signals.

The major EGR/CSC system components are:

1. 95°F (35°C) EGR/PVS valve;
2. Spark Delay Valve (SDV);
3. Vacuum check valve.

When the engine coolant temperature is below 82°F (28°C), the EGR/PVS valve admits carburetor EGR port vacuum (occurring at about 2,500 rpm) directly to the distributor advance diaphragm, through the one-way check valve.

At the same time, the EGR/PVS valve shuts off carburetor EGR vacuum to the EGR valve and transmission diaphragm.

When engine coolant temperature is 95°F (35°C) and above, the EGR/PVS valve is actuated and directs carburetor EGR vacuum to

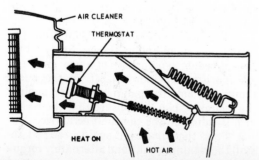

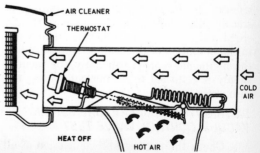

Temperature-operated duct and valve assembly

the EGR valve and transmission instead of the distributor. At temperatures between 82–95°F (28–35°C), the EGR/PVS valve may be open, closed, or in mid-position.

The SDV valve delay carburetor spark vacuum to the distributor advance diaphragm by restricting the vacuum signal through the SDV valve for a predetermined time. During normal acceleration, little or not vacuum is admitted to the distributor advance diaphragm until acceleration is completed, because of (1) the time delay of the SDV valve and (2) the re-routing of EGR port vacuum if the engine coolant temperature is 95°F (35°C) or higher.

The check valve blocks off vacuum signal from the SDV to the EGR/PVS so that carburetor spark vacuum will not be dissipated when the EGR/PVS is actuated above 95°F (35°C).

The 235°F (113°C) PVS is not part of the EGR/CSC system, but is connected to the distributor vacuum advance to prevent engine overheating while idling (as on previous models). At idle speed, no vacuum is generated at either the carburetor spark port or EGR port and engine timing is fully retarded. When engine coolant temperature reaches 235°F (113°C), however, the valve is actuated to admit intake manifold vacuum to the distributor advance diaphragm. This advances the engine timing and speeds up the engine. The increase in coolant flow and fan speed lowers engine temperature.

Ported Vacuum Switch Valve (PVS)

The PVS valve is a temperature sensing valve found on the distributor vacuum advance line, and is installed in the coolant outlet elbow. During prolonged periods of idle, or any other situation which causes engine operating temperatures to be higher than normal, the valve, which under normal conditions simply connects the vacuum advance diaphragm to its vacuum source within the carburetor, closes the normal source vacuum port and engages an alternate source vacuum port. This alternate source is from the intake manifold which, under idle conditions, maintains a high vacuum. This increase in vacuum supply to the distributor diaphragm advances the timing, increasing the idle speed. The increase in idle speed causes a directly proportional increase in the operation of the cooling system. When the engine has cooled sufficiently, the vacuum supply is returned to its normal source, the carburetor.

DISTRIBUTOR TEMPERATURE SENSING VACUUM CONTROL VALVE TEST

1. Check the routing and connection of all the vacuum hoses.

2. Attach a tachometer to the engine.
3. Bring the engine up to the normal operating temperature. The engine must not be overheated.
4. Note the engine rpm, with the transmission in Neutral, and the throttle at curb idle.
5. Disconnect the vacuum hose from the intake manifold at the temperature sensing valve. Plug or clamp the hose.
6. Note the idle rpm with the hose disconnected. If there is no change in rpm, the valve is good. If there is a drop of 100 or more rpm, the valve should be replaced. Replace the vacuum line.
7. Check to make sure that the all season coolant mixture meets specifications and that the correct radiator cap is in place and functioning.
8. Block the radiator airflow to induce a higher-than-normal temperature condition.
9. Continue to operate the engine until the temperature or heat indicator shows above normal.

If the engine speed, by this time, has increased 100 or more rpm, the temperature sensing valve is satisfactory. If not, it should be replaced.

CARBURETED FUEL SYSTEM

Fuel Pump

Ford Bronco engines use a camshaft eccentric actuated combination fuel pump located on the lower left side of the engine block on both 6-cylinder and V8 engines.

REMOVAL

1. Disconnect the fuel inlet and outlet lines at the fuel pump. Discard the fuel inlet retaining clamp.
2. Remove the pump retaining bolts then remove the pump assembly and gasket from the engine. Discard the gasket.

INSTALLATION

1. If a new pump is to be installed, remove the fuel line connector fitting from the old pump and install it in the new pump.
2. Remove all gasket material from the mounting pad and pump flange. Apply oil resistant sealer to both sides of a new gasket.
3. Position the new gasket on the pump flange and hold the pump in position against the mounting pad. Make sure that the rocker arm is riding on the camshaft eccentric.
4. Press the pump tight against the pad, install the retaining bolts and alternately torque them to 12–15 ft.lb. on 6 cylinder engines and

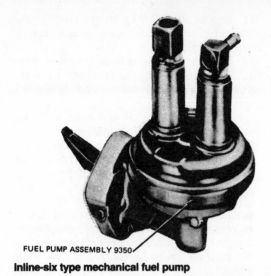

FUEL PUMP ASSEMBLY 9350

Inline-six type mechanical fuel pump

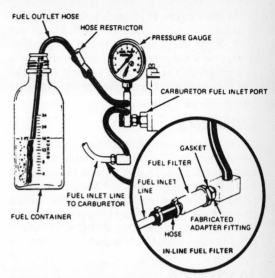

Typical fuel pump and capacity test equipment

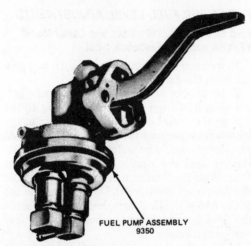

FUEL PUMP ASSEMBLY
9350

Gasoline V8 type fuel pump

20–24 ft.lb. on the V8. Connect the fuel lines. Use a new clamp on the fuel inlet line.

5. Operate the engine and check for leaks.

TESTING

Incorrect fuel pump pressure and low volume (flow rate) are the two most likely fuel pump troubles that will affect engine performance. Low pressure will cause a lean mixture and fuel starvation at high speeds and excessive pressure will cause high fuel consumption and carburetor flooding.

To determine that the fuel pump is in satisfactory operating condition, tests for both fuel pump pressure and volume should be performed.

The tests are performed with the fuel pump installed on the engine and the engine at normal operating temperature and at idle speed.

Before the test, make sure that the replaceable fuel filter has been changed at the proper mileage interval. If in doubt, install a new filter.

Pressure Test

1. Remove the air cleaner assembly. Disconnect the fuel inlet line of the fuel filter at the carburetor. Use care to prevent fire, due to fuel spillage. Place an absorbent cloth under the connection before removing the line to catch any fuel that might flow out of the line.

2. Connect a pressure gauge, a restrictor and a flexible hose between the fuel filter and the carburetor.

3. Position the flexible hose and the restrictor so that the fuel can be discharged into a suitable graduated container.

4. Before taking a pressure reading, operate the engine at the specified idle rpm and vent the system into the container by opening the hose restrictor momentarily.

5. Close the hose restrictor, allow the pressure to stabilize and note the reading. The pressure should be as specified in the Tune Up Charts earlier in this book.

If the pump pressure is not within 4–6 psi and the fuel lines and filter are in satisfactory condition, the pump is defective and should be replaced.

If the pump pressure is within the proper range, perform the test for fuel volume.

Volume Test

1. Operate the engine at the specified idle rpm.

2. Open the hose restrictor and catch the fuel in the container while observing the time it takes to pump 1 pint. It should take 30 seconds for 1 pint to be expelled on all vehicles

made prior to the 1974 model year. On 1974–86 vehicles, 1 pint should be expelled in 20 seconds. If the pump does not pump to specifications, check for proper fuel tank venting or a restriction in the fuel line leading from the fuel tank to the carburetor before replacing the fuel pump.

Carburetors

The carburetor identification tag is attached to the carburetor. The basic part number for all carburetors is 9510. To obtain replacement parts, it is necessary to know the part number prefix, suffix and, in some cases, the design change code. If the carburetor is ever replaced by a new unit, make sure that the identification tag stays with the new carburetor and the vehicle.

ADJUSTMENTS

Idle Mixture

NOTE: *For this procedure, Ford recommends a propane enrichment procedure. This requires special equipment not available to the general public. In lieu of this equipment the following procedure may be followed to obtain a satisfactory idle mixture.*

1. Block the wheels, set the parking brake and run the engine to bring it to normal operating temperature.
2. Disconnect the hose between the emission canister and the air cleaner.
3. On engines equipped with the Thermactor air injection system, the routing of the vacuum lines connected to the dump valve will have to be temporarily changed. Mark them for reconnection before switching them.
4. For valves with one or two vacuum lines at the side, disconnect and plug the lines.
5. For valves with one vacuum line at the top, check the line to see if it is connected to the intake manifold or an intake manifold source such as the carburetor or distributor vacuum line. If not, remove and plug the line at the dump valve and connect a temporary length of vacuum hose from the dump valve fitting to a source of intake manifold vacuum.
6. Remove the limiter caps from the mixture screws by CAREFULLY cutting them with a sharp knife.
7. Place the transmission in neutral and run the engine at 2,500 rpm for 15 seconds.
8. Place the automatic transmission in Drive; the manual in neutral.
9. Adjust the idle speed to the higher of the two figures given on the underhood sticker.
10. Turn the idle mixture screw(s) to obtain the highest possible rpm, leaving the screw(s) in the leanest position that will maintain this rpm.

11. Repeat Steps 7 thru 10 until further adjustment of the mixture screw(s) does not increase the rpm.
12. Turn the screw(s) in until the lower of the two idle speed figures is reached. Turn the screw(s) in ¼ turn increments each to insure a balance.
13. Turn the engine off and remove the tachometer. Reinstall all equipment.

NOTE: *Rough idle, that cannot be corrected by normal service procedures may be caused by leakage between the EGR valve body and diaphragm. To determine if this is the cause: Tighten the EGR bolts to 15 ft.lb. Connect a vacuum gauge to the intake manifold. Lift to exert a sideways pressure on the diaphragm housing. If the idle changes or the reading on the vacuum gauge varies, replace the EGR valve.*

FLOAT AND FUEL LEVEL ADJUSTMENTS

Ford Model 1100, 1101 1-bbl and Carter Model YF, YFA and YFA Feedback 1-bbl

1. Remove the carburetor air horn and gasket from the carburetor.
2. Invert the air horn assembly, and check the clearance from the top of the float to the bottom of the air horn. Hold the air horn at eye level when gauging the float level. The float arm (lever) should be resting on the needle pin. Do not load the needle when adjusting the float. Bend the float arm as necessary to adjust the float level (clearance). Do not bend the tab at the end of the float arm, because it prevents the float from striking the bottom of the fuel bowl when empty.
3. Turn the air horn over and hold it upright and let the float hang free. Measure the maximum clearance from the top of the float to the bottom of the air horn with the float gauge. Hold the air horn at eye level when gauging the dimension. To adjust the float drop, bend the tab at the end of the float arm.
4. Install the carburetor air horn with a new gasket.

Autolite (Motorcraft) Model 2100, 2150 2-bbl (Wet Adjustment)

1. Operate the engine until it reaches normal operating temperature. Place the vehicle on a level surface and stop the engine.
2. Remove the carburetor air cleaner assembly.
3. Remove the air horn attaching screws and the carburetor identification tag. Temporarily, leave the air horn and gasket in position on the carburetor main body and start the engine. Let the engine idle for a few minutes, then rotate the air horn out of the way and re-

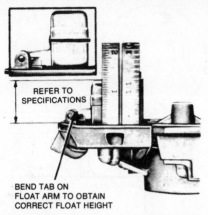

Float level adjustment for the Autolite (Ford) model 1100 1-bbl

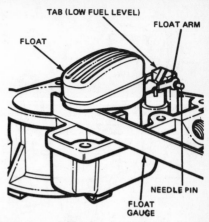

Float level adjustment for the Carter YF, YFA and YFA Feedback 1-bbl carburetor

move the air horn gasket to provide access to the float assembly.

4. While the engine is idling, use a scale to measure the vertical distance from the top machined surface of the carburetor main body to the level of the fuel in the fuel bowl. The measurement must be made at least ¼" (6mm) away from any vertical surface to assure an accurate reading, because the surface of the fuel is concave, being higher at the edges than in the center. Care must be exercised to measure the fuel level at the point of contact with the float.

5. If any adjustment is required, stop the engine to minimize the hazard of fire due to spilled gasoline. To adjust the fuel level, bend the float tab contacting the fuel inlet valve upward in relation to the original position to raise the fuel level, and downward to lower it. Each time the float is adjusted, the engine must be started and permitted to idle for a few

minutes to stabilize the fuel level. Check the fuel level after each adjustment, until the specified level is obtained.

6. Assemble the carburetor in the reverse order of disassembly, using a new gasket between the air horn and the main carburetor body.

Motorcraft Model 7200 VV Feedback 2-bbl

1. Remove the upper body assembly and the gasket.

2. Fabricate a gauge to the specified dimensions.

3. With the upper body inverted, place the fuel level gauge on the cast surface of the upper body and measure the vertical distance from the cast surface of the upper body and the bottom of the float.

4. To adjust, bend the float operating lever away from the fuel inlet needle to decrease the setting and toward the needle to increase the setting.

5. Check and/or adjust the float drop using the following procedures.

   a. Fabricate a gauge to the specified dimension.

   b. With the upper body assembly held in the upright position, place the gauge against the cast surface of the upper body and measure the vertical distance between the cast surface of the upper body and the bottom of the float.

   c. To adjust, bend the stop tab on the float lever away from the hinge pin to increase the setting and toward the hinge pin to decrease the setting.

6. Reinstall the upper body assembly and new gasket.

Holley Model 4180-C 4-V (Dry Adjustment)

The float adjustment is a preliminary fuel level adjustment only. The final adjustment (Wet)

Float level adjustment for the Autolite 2100 and 2150 2-bbl carburetor

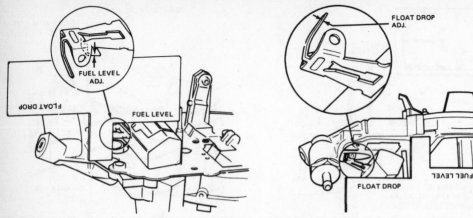

Float level adjustment for the Motorcraft 7200 VV 2-bbl. carburetor

Float drop adjustment for the Motorcraft 7200 VV 2-bbl. carburetor

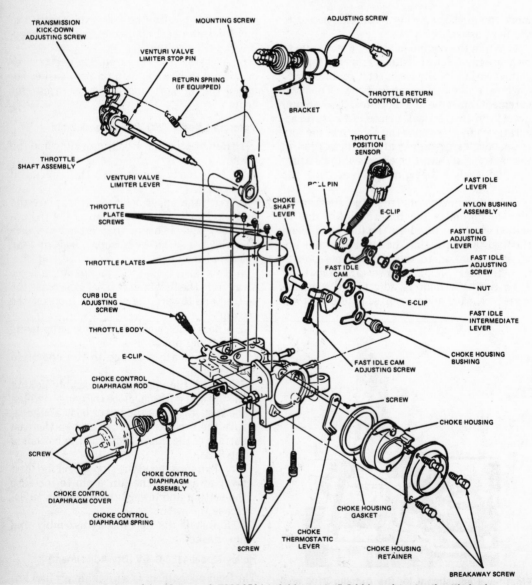

An exploded view of the Motorcraft 7200 VV (variable venturi) 2-bbl. carburetor throttle body

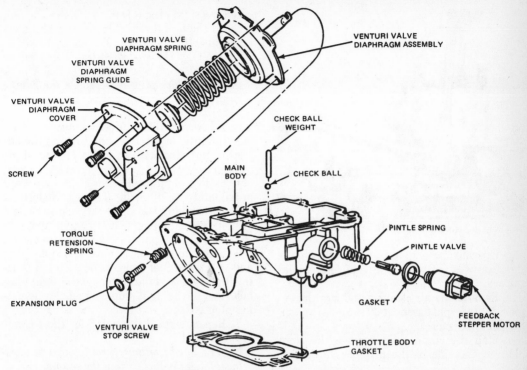

An exploded view of the Motorcraft 7200 VV (variable venturi) 2-bbl. carburetor main body

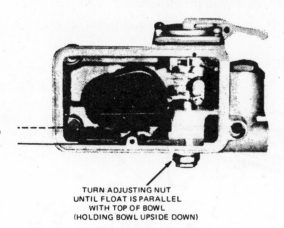

TURN ADJUSTING NUT
UNTIL FLOAT IS PARALLEL
WITH TOP OF BOWL
(HOLDING BOWL UPSIDE DOWN)

Dry float adjustment Holley 4180-C

must be performed after the carburetor has been installed on the engine.

With the fuel bowls and the float assemblies removed, hold the fuel bowls upside down and turn the adjusting nuts until the floats are parallel with the top of the fuel bowls.

SECONDARY THROTTLE PLATE ADJUSTMENT

This adjustment must be performed before the carburetor is installed on the engine and before the float level wet adjustment.

1. With the carburetor off the engine, hold the secondary throttle plates closed.

2. Turn the secondary throttle shaft lever adjusting screw (stop screw) out (counterclockwise) until the secondary throttle plates seat in the throttle bores.

3. Turn the screw in clockwise until the screw just contacts the secondary lever, then turn the screw in (clockwise) $3/8$ turn.

Holley Model 4180-C 4-V (Wet Adjustment)

NOTE: *The fuel pump pressure and volume must be to specifications prior to performing the following adjustments. Refer to the fuel pump specifications in this chapter.*

Secondary throttle plate adjustment

Wet float adjustment Holley 4180-C

1. Operate the engine to normalize engine temperatures and place the vehicle on a flat surface.

2. Remove the air cleaner, and run the engine at 1,000 rpm for about 30 seconds to stabilize the fuel level.

3. Stop the engine and remove the sight plug on the side of the primary carburetor bowl.

4. Check the fuel level. It should be at the bottom of the sight plug hole. If fuel spills out when the sight plug is removed, lower the fuel level. If the fuel level is below the sight glass hole, raise the fuel level.

CAUTION: *Do not loosen the lock screw or nut, or attempt to adjust the fuel level with the sight glass plug removed or the engine running as fuel may spray out creating a fire hazard.*

5. Adjust the front level as necessary by loosening the lock screw, and turning the adjusting nut clockwise to lower fuel level, or counterclockwise to raise fuel level. A $\frac{1}{16}$ turn of the adjusting nut will change fuel level approximately $\frac{1}{32}''$ (0.8mm). Tighten the locking screw and install the sight plug, using the old gasket. Start the engine and run for about 30 seconds at 1,000 rpm to stabilize the fuel level.

6. Stop the engine, remove the sight plug and check the fuel level. Repeat step 5 until the fuel level is at the bottom of the sight plug hole, install the sight plug using a new adjusting plug gasket.

7. Repeat steps 3 through 6 for the secondary fuel bowl.

NOTE: *The secondary throttle must be used to stabilize the fuel level in the secondary fuel bowl.*

8. Install the air cleaner.

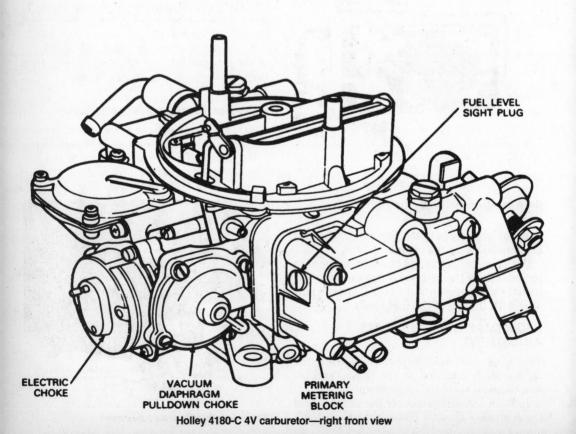

Holley 4180-C 4V carburetor—right front view

IDLE SPEED ADJUSTMENT

CARBURETORS

Through 1982

1. Remove the air cleaner and disconnect and plug the vacuum lines.

2. Block the wheels, apply the parking brake, turn off all accessories, start the engine and run it to normalize underhood temperatures.

3. Check that the choke plate is fully open and connect a tachometer according to the manufacturer's instructions.

4. Check the throttle stop positioner (TSP) off speed as follows: Collapse the plunger by forcing the throttle lever against it. Place the transmission in neutral and check the engine speed. If necessary, adjust to specified TSP Off speed with the throttle adjusting screw. See the underhood sticker.

5. Place the manual transmission in neutral; the automatic in Drive and make certain the TSP plunger is extended.

6. Turn the TSP until the specified idle speed is obtained.

7. Install the air cleaner and connect the vacuum lines. Check the idle speed. Adjust, if necessary, with the air cleaner on.

1983 and Later 6-300 (4.9L) YFA–IV & YFA–IV–FB

1. Block the wheels and apply the parking brake. Place the transmission in Neutral or Park.

2. Bring engine to normal operating temperature.

3. Place A/C Heat Selector to Off position.

4. Place transmission in specified gear.

5. Check/adjust curb idle RPM as follows: TSP dashpot. Insure that TSP is activated using a ⅜″ open end wrench, adjust curb idle RPM by rotating the nut directly behind the dashpot housing. Adjust curb idle RPM by turning the idle RPM speed screw. Front mounted TSP (same as A/C kicker on all other calibrations) insure that TSP is activated. After loosening lock nut, adjust curb idle RPM by rotating TSP solenoid until specified RPM is obtained. Tighten locknut.

6. Check/adjust anti-diesel (TSP Off). Manually collapse the TSP by rotating the carb throttle shaft lever until the TSP Off adjusting screw contacts the carburetor body. If adjustment is required, turn the TSP Off adjusting screw while holding the lever adjustment screw against the stop.

7. Place the transmission in Neutral or Park. Rev the engine momentarily. Place the transmission in specified position and recheck curb idle rpm. Readjust if required.

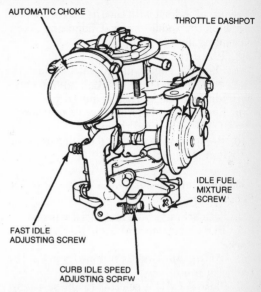

Carburetor speed adjustments for the Carter YF 1-bbl carburetor

8. Check/adjust dashpot clearance to 0.120″ ± 0.030″ (3mm ± 0.76mm).

9. If a final curb idle speed adjustment is required, the bowl vent setting must be checked as follows: Stop the engine and turn the ignition key to the On position, so that the TSP dashpot or TSP is activated but the engine is not running (where applicable). Secure the choke plate in the wide open position. Open the throttle, so that the throttle vent lever does not touch the fuel bowl vent rod. Close the throttle, and measure the travel of the fuel bowl vent rod from the open throttle position. Travel of the fuel bowl vent rod should be 0.100–0.150″ (2.54–3.81mm). If out of specification, bend the throttle vent lever to obtain the required travel. Remove all test equipment, and tighten the air cleaner holddown bolt to specification.

10. Whenever it is required to adjust engine idle speed by more than 50 rpm, the adjustment screw on the AOD linkage lever at the carburetor should also be readjusted.

1983 and Later 8–302 (5.0L) 2150–2V FB (FEEDBACK)

1. Set parking brake and block wheels.

2. Place the transmission in Park.

3. Bring the engine to normal operating temperature.

4. Disconnect the electric connector on the EVAP purge solenoid.

5. Disconnect and plug the vacuum hose to the VOTM kicker.

6. Place the transmission in Drive position.

7. Check/adjust curb idle rpm, if adjustment

is required: Adjust with the the curb idle speed screw or the saddle bracket adjusting screw, depending on how equipped.

8. Place the transmission in Neutral or Park. Rev the engine momentarily. Place the transmission in Drive position and recheck curb idle rpm. Readjust if required.

9. Remove the plug from the vacuum hose to the VOTM kicker and reconnect.

10. Reconnect the electrical connector on the EVAP purge solenoid.

1983 and Later 8–302 (5.0L) 2150–2V (NON-FEEDBACK)

1. Set parking brake and block wheels.
2. Place the transmission in Neutral or Park.
3. Bring engine to normal operating temperature.
4. Place A/C Heat selector to Off position.
5. Disconnect and plug vacuum hose to thermactor air bypass valve.
6. Place the transmission in specified gear.
7. Check curb idle rpm. Adjust to specification by using the curb idle rpm speed screw or the saddle bracket adjusting screw, depending on how equipped.
8. Place the transmission in Neutral or Park. Rev the engine momentarily. Place the transmission in specified position, and recheck curb idle rpm. Readjust if required.
9. Remove plug from vacuum hose to thermactor air bypass valve and reconnect.
10. Whenever it is required to adjust engine idle speed by more than 50 rpm, the adjustment screw on the AOD linkage lever at the carburetor should also be readjusted.

1983 and Later 8–351 (5.8L) 2150–2V OR 7200 VV

1. Block the wheels and apply parking brake. Place the transmission in Neutral or Park.
2. Bring the engine to normal operating temperature.
3. Disconnect purge hose on canister side of evaporator purge solenoid. Check to ensure that purge vacuum is present (solenoid has opened and will require 3 to 5 minute wait after starting engine followed by a short time at part throttle). Reconnect purge hose.
4. Disconnect and plug the vacuum hose to the VOTM kicker.
5. Place the transmission in specified position.
6. Check/adjust curb idle rpm. If adjustment is required, adjust with the curb idle speed screw or the saddle bracket adjusting screw (ensure curb idle speed screw is not touching throttle shaft lever).

7. Place the transmission in Neutral or Park. Rev the engine momentarily. Place the transmission in specified position and recheck curb idle rpm. Readjust if required.

8. Check/adjust throttle position sensor (TPS).

9. Remove the plug from the vacuum hose to the VOTM kicker and reconnect.

10. Apply a slight pressure on top of the nylon nut located on the accelerator pump to take up the linkage clearance.

11. Turn the nylon nut on the accelerator pump rod clockwise until a 0.010″ ± 0.005″ (0.254–0.127mm) clearance is obtained between the top of the accelerator pump and the pump lever.

12. Turn the accelerator pump rod nut one turn counterclockwise to set the lever lash preload.

13. If curb idle adjustment exceeds 50 rpm, adjust automatic transmission TV linkage.

1983 and Later 8–302 (5.0L) & 351 (5.8L) CANADA 2150–2V

1. Place the transmission in Neutral or Park.
2. Bring engine to normal operating temperature.
3. Place A/C Heat Selector to Off position.
4. Place the transmission in specified gear.
5. Check curb idle rpm. Adjust to specification using the curb idle speed screw or the hex head on the rear of the solenoid or the saddle bracket adjustment screw depending on how equipped.
6. Place the transmission in Neutral or Park. Rev the engine momentarily. Place the transmission in specified position and recheck curb idle rpm. Readjust if required.
7. TSP Off: With transmission in specified gear, collapse the solenoid plunger, and set specified TSP Off speed on the speed screw.
8. Disconnect vacuum hose to decel throttle control modulator and plug (if so equipped).
9. Connect a slave vacuum from manifold vacuum to the decel throttle control modulator (if so equipped).
10. Check/adjust decel throttle control rpm. Adjust if necessary.
11. Remove slave vacuum hose.
12. Remove plug from decel throttle control modulator hose and reconnect.

1983 and Later Holley Model 4180-C 4V

1. Block the wheels and apply parking brake.
2. Run engine until normal operating temperature is reached.

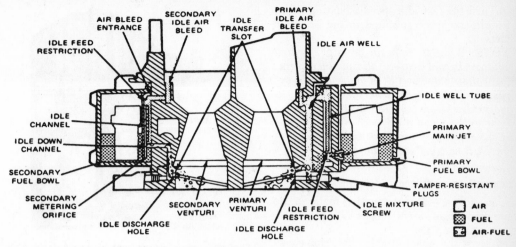

Idle system—4180-C carburetor

3. Place the vehicle in Park or Neutral, A/C in Off position, and set parking brake.

4. Remove air cleaner.

5. Disconnect and plug decel throttle control kicker diaphragm vacuum hose.

6. Connect a slave vacuum hose from an engine manifold vacuum source to the decel throttle control kicker.

7. Run engine at approximately 2,500 rpm for 15 seconds, then release the throttle.

8. If decel throttle control rpm is not within ± 50 rpm of specification, adjust the kicker.

9. Disconnect the slave vacuum hose and allow engine to return to curb idle.

10. Adjust curb idle, if necessary, using the curb idle adjusting screw.

11. Rev the engine momentarily, recheck curb idle and adjust if necessary.

12. Reconnect the decel throttle control vacuum hose to the diaphragm.

13. Reinstall the air cleaner.

FAST IDLE SPEED ADJUSTMENT

Ford Model 1100, 1101 1-bbl

The fast idle is controlled by the idle adjusting screw bearing against the bottom of the choke cam and lever during idle or closed throttle conditions. The choke cam and lever opens the throttle slightly, through contact of the idle adjusting screw with the cam, as the manual choke position is selected. Higher engine idle speeds are automatically provided through contact of the idle adjusting screw with the cam. The curb idle must be adjusted correctly for the fast idle to be proper during application of the choke.

Carter Model YF 1-bbl

1966–74

1. Position the fast idle screw on the kickdown step of the fast idle cam against the shoulder of the high step.

2. Adjust by bending the choke plat connecting rod to obtain the specified clearance between the lower edge of the choke plate and the carburetor air horn. Use a drill bit inserted between the lower edge of the choke plate and the carburetor air horn.

3. With the engine at operating temperature, air cleaner removed and a tachometer attached according to the manufacturer's instructions, manually rotate the fast idle cam to the top or second step as specified while holding the choke plate fully open. Turn the fast idle adjustment screw inward or outward as required to obtain the specified speed.

4. When setting the fast idle speed, all distributor vacuum and EGR controls must be disconnected and plugged to insure proper speeds during cold operation.

Carter YF, and YFA 1-bbl

1975–86

1. Run the engine to normal operating temperature.

2. Remove the air cleaner and attach a tachometer to the engine according to the manufacturer's instructions.

3. Manually rotate the fast idle to the top step while holding the choke plate fully opened.

4. Rotate the cam until the fast idle adjusting screw rests on the cam step specified on the underhood emissions sticker.

5. Turn the fast idle speed adjusting screw to obtain the speed specified in the Tune-Up Charts.

NOTE: *When this operation is performed outdoors in cold weather, all vacuum controls to the distributor and EGR valve must be by-passed. This can be done by connecting a jumper hose from the DIST port on the carburetor to the vacuum advance port of the distributor and by disconnecting and plugging the EGR vacuum source hose.*

Autolite (Motorcraft) Model 2100, 2150 2-bbl

The fast idle speed adjustment is made in the same manner as for the Model YF carburetor, starting at Step 3.

To adjust the model 2100 fast idle cam clearance, follow the procedure given below:

1. Rotate the choke thermostatic spring housing 90° in the rich direction.

2. Position the idle speed screw on the high step of the cam.

3. Depress the choke pulldown diaphragm against the diaphragm stop screw to place the choke in the pulldown position.

4. While holding the choke pulldown diaphragm depressed, open the throttle slightly and allow the fast idle cam to fall.

5. Close the throttle and check the position of the fast idle cam. The screw should contact the cam at the V mark on the cam.

6. Adjust the fast idle cam adjusting screw to obtain the proper setting.

Motorcraft Model 7200 VV 2-bbl

1. Place the transmission in Park or Neutral.

2. Bring the engine to normal operating temperature.

3. Disconnect the purge hose on the canister side of the evaporator purge solenoid. Check to see that purge vacuum is present (solenoid has opened--will require 3 to 5 minute wait after starting the engine) followed by a short time at part throttle. Reconnect the purge hose.

4. Disconnect and plug the vacuum hose at the EGR and purge valves.

5. Place the fast idle lever on the second step of the fast idle cam. (Third step on Calif. models.)

6. Adjust the fast idle rpm to specifiations.

7. Reconnect the EGR and purge vacuum hoses.

Holley 4180-C 4V

1. Set the parking brake, block the wheels, place the transmission in neutral or park and remove the air cleaner.

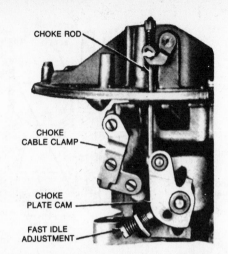

Fast idle speed adjustment for the Autolite 2100, 2150 2-bbl. carburetor

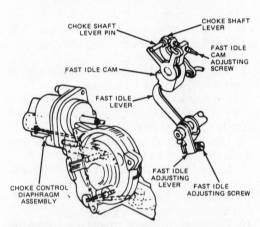

Fast idle speed adjustment for the Motorcraft 7200 VV 2-bbl. carburetor

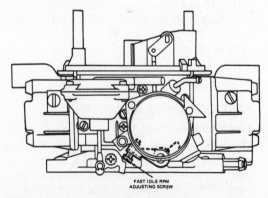

Holley 4180C 4-bbl fast idle adjustment

2. Bring the engine to normal operating temperature.

3. Disconnect the vacuum hoses at the EGR valve and the purge control valves and plug.

4. Place the fast idle adjustment on the specified step of the fast idle cam. Check and adjust the fast idle rpm to the specifications found on the Exhaust Emission Control Decal on the engine.

5. Rev the engine momentarily, place the fast idle adjustment on the specified step and recheck the fast idle rpm.

6. Remove the plug from the EGR valve and the purge control valves and reconnect.

DASHPOT ADJUSTMENT

1. Remove the air cleaner.
2. Loosen the anti-stall dashpot locknut.
3. With the choke plate open, hold the throttle plate closed (idle position), and check the clearance between the throttle lever and the dashpot plunger tip with a feeler gauge.

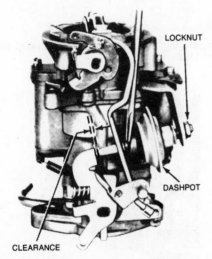

Anti-stall dashpot adjustment on the Carter YF carburetor

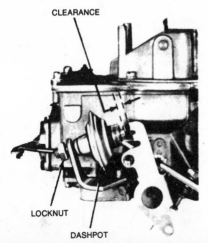

Anti-stall dashpot adjustment on the Autolite 2100 2-bbl carburetor

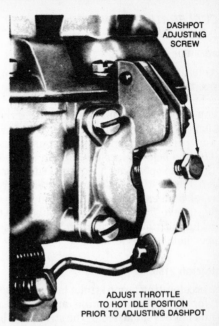

Anti-stall dashpot adjustment on the Autolite (Ford) 1100 1-bbl carburetor

NOTE: *On the Ford Model 1100 1-bbl carburetor, turn the adjusting screw 3 turns in after the screw contacts the diaphragm assembly.*

ACCELERATING PUMP CLEARANCE ADJUSTMENT

Ford 1100

1. Insert the roll pin in the lower hole (HI position in the lever stop hold).

2. Position the throttle and choke linkage so that the throttle plate will seat in the throttle bore. Hold the throttle plates in the closed position. Position a gauge or drill of the specified thickness between the roll pin and the cover surface. Bend the accelerating pump actuating rod to obtain the specified gauge or drill clearance between the pump cover and the roll pin in the pump lever.

Holley 4180-C

1. Using a feeler gauge and with the primary throttle plates in the wide open position, there should be 0.015" (0.381mm) clearance between the accelerator pump operating lever adjustment screw head and the pump arm when the pump arm is depressed manually.

2. If adjustment is required, hold the adjusting screw locknut and turn the adjusting screw inward to increase the clearance and out to decrease the clearance. One half turn on the adjusting screw is approximately 0.015" (0.381mm).

ACCELERATING PUMP STROKE ADJUSTMENTS

Ford 1100

Acceleration requirements in various climates are satisfied by controlling the amount of fuel discharged by the accelerating pump. The pump stroke is controlled by changing the location of the roll pin in the lever stop hole.

For operation in ambient temperatures 50°F (10°C) and below, place the roll pin in the hole of the pump operating lever marked HI (lower hole). For best performance and economy at normal ambient temperatures and high altitude, (above 50°F [10°C] and/or above 5,000' [1,524m] altitude), place the roll pin in the LO (upper hole) of the lever.

Motorcraft 2150

The accelerating pump stroke has been factory set for a particular engine application and should not be readjusted. If the stroke has been changed from the specified hole reset to specifications by following these procedures.

1. To release the rod from the retaining clip, lift upward on the portion of the clip that snaps over the shaft and then disengage the rod.

2. Position the clip over the specified hole in the overtravel lever and insert the operating rod through the clip and the overtravel lever. Snap the end of the clip over the rod to secure.

Holley 4180-C 4V

The accelerator pump stroke has been set to help keep the exhaust emission level of the engine within the specified limits. The additional holes provided (if any) for pump stroke adjustment are for adjusting the stroke for specific engine applications. The stroke should not be changed from the specified setting.

CHOKE PULLDOWN ADJUSTMENT

Ford 1100

1. Insert a drill or gauge of the specified size between the choke plate and the inside of the air horn, and place the choke linkage in the full choke position.

2. While maintaining the full choke position, adjust the nut on the choke connector (pulldown) rod to just contact the swivel on the cam lever.

Carter YF, YFA

1. Remove the air cleaner. Remove the choke thermostatic spring housing from the carburetor.

2. Bend a 0.026" (0.66mm) diameter wire gauge at a 90° angle approximately ⅛" (3mm)

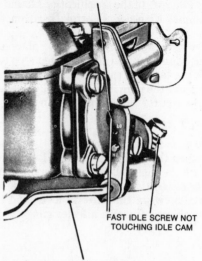

WITH THROTTLE PLATE CLOSED, INSERT A GAUGE THAT EQUALS THE SPECIFIED CLEARANCE BETWEEN THE PIN AND COVER

FAST IDLE SCREW NOT TOUCHING IDLE CAM

BEND ROD FOR CLEARANCE ADJUSTMENT

Accelerating pump clearance adjustment on the Ford 1100

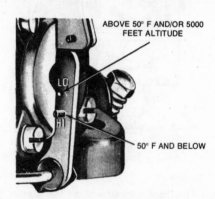

ABOVE 50° F AND/OR 5000 FEET ALTITUDE

LO

HI

50° F AND BELOW

Accelerating pump lever adjustment on the Ford 1100

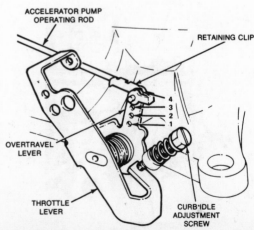

ACCELERATOR PUMP OPERATING ROD

RETAINING CLIP

4
3
2
1

OVERTRAVEL LEVER

THROTTLE LEVER

CURB·IDLE ADJUSTMENT SCREW

Accelerating pump stroke adjustment on the Motorcraft 2150

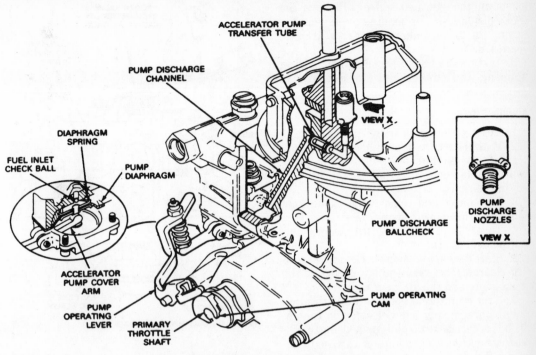

Accelerator pump system—4180-C carburetor

from one end. Insert the bent end of the gauge between the choke piston slot and the right hand slot in the choke housing. Rotate the choke piston lever counterclockwise until the gauge is snug in the piston slot.

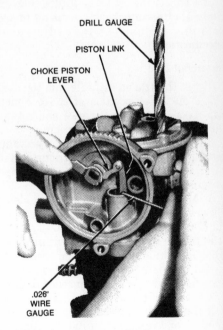

Carter YF choke pulldown adjustment

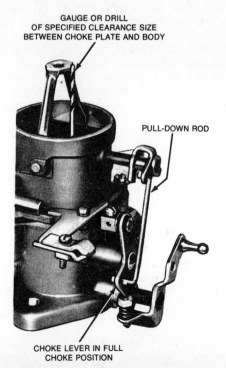

Ford 1100 choke pulldown adjustment

3. Exert a light pressure on the choke piston lever to hold the gauge in place, then use a drill gauge with a diameter equal to the specified clearance between the lower edge of the choke plate and the carburetor bore to check clearance.

4. To adjust the choke plate pulldown clearance, bend the choke piston lever as required

to obtain the specified setting. Remove the choke piston lever for bending to prevent distorting the piston link, causing erratic choke operation.

5. Install the choke thermostatic spring housing and gasket. Set the housing to specifications.

Autolite 2100

1. Remove the air cleaner.

2. With the engine at normal operating temperature, loosen the choke thermostatic spring housing retainer screws and set the housing 90° in the rich direction.

3. Disconnect and remove the choke heat tube from the choke housing.

4. Turn the fast idle adjusting screw outward one full turn.

5. Start the engine, then check for the specified clearance between the lower edge of the choke plate and the air horn wall.

6. If the clearance is not within specification the diaphragm stop screw (located on the underside of the choke diaphragm housing) clockwise to decrease or counterclockwise to increase the clearance.

7. Connect the choke heat tube and set the choke thermostatic spring housing to specifications. Adjust the fast idle speed to specifications.

Motorcraft 2150

1. Set throttle on fast idle cam top step.

2. Note index position of choke bimetallic cap. Loosen retaining screws and rotate cap 90° in the rich (closing) direction.

3. Activate pulldown motor by manually forcing pulldown control diaphragm link in the direction of applied vacuum or by applying vacuum to external vacuum tube.

4. Measure vertical hard gauge clearance between choke plate and center of carburetor air horn wall nearest fuel bowl.

Pulldown setting should be within specifications for minimum choke plate opening.

If choke plate pulldown is found to be out of specification, reset by adjusting diaphragm stop on end of choke pulldown diaphragm.

If pulldown is reset, cam clearance should be checked and reset if required.

After pulldown check is completed, reset choke bimetallic cap to recommend index position as specified in the Carburetor Specifications Chart. Check and reset fast idle speed to specifications if necessary.

Holley 4180-C

1. Remove the air cleaner. Then remove the carburetor from the vehicle and cover the intake manifold.

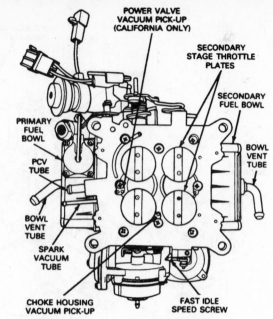

4180-C 4V carburetor—bottom view

2. Place the carburetor on a stand which allows access to the pulldown diaphgram vacuum passage on the underside of the throttle body.

3. Mark the choke cap and housing. Then remove the choke cap, gasket and retainer.

4. Reinstall the choke cap temporarily with a standard choke cap gasket. Line up the marks made previously on the cap and the housing and rotate the cap 90° counterclockwise from that position. Secure with one screw.

5. With the choke plate in the full closed position, actuate the choke pulldown motor using an outside vacuum source, 17 in.Hg minimum.

6. Using a drill gauge of the specified size check the clearence between the upper edge of the choke plate and the air horn wall.

NOTE: *The gauge should fit in such a manner that it contacts the air horn and choke plate but does not move the plate.*

7. If the pulldown dimension is out of specification, carefully remove the diaphgagm adjustment screw cap with a small sharp punch or screw driver.

8. Turn the adjustment screw with a $^5/_{16}$" Allen wrench clockwise to decrease the pulldown set or counterclockwise to increase the pulldown set.

NOTE: *Maintain a minimum of 17 in.Hg to the pulldown diaphgram during adjustment. Cycle vacuum from 0–17 in.Hg to verify proper set.*

9. Apply RTV sealant to the adjustment screw cavity and check the fast idle cam index adjustment.

To adjust the fast idle cam index:

1. With the choke cap still wrapped, and with vacuum applied to the diaphragm, cycle the trottle. The fast idle screw should rest on the No. 2 step of the fast idle cam.

2. If the fast idle cam requires adjustment, turn the Allen adjustment screw clockwise to position the fast idle screw higher on the No. 2 step or counterclockwise to position the fast idle screw lower on the No. 2 step.

3. Remove the temporary choke plate gasket, install the original locking gasket, choke cap and choke cap retainer. Secure with breakaway screws and check the dechoke adjustment.

To adjust the dechoke:

1. Reinstall the choke cap at the proper index using one screw.

2. Hold the throttle in the wide open position.

3. Apply light closing pressure to the choke plate and measure the gap between the lower edge of the choke plate and the air horn wall.

4. To adjust, bend the pawl on the fast idle lever.

DECHOKE ADJUSTMENT

All Except Holley 4180C-4V

1. Remove the air cleaner.

2. Hold the throttle plate fully open and close the choke plate as far as possible without forcing it. Use a drill of the proper diameter to check the clearance between the choke plate and air horn.

3. If the clearance is not within specification, adjust by bending the arm on the choke trip lever. Bending the arm downward will increase the clearance, and bending it upward will decrease the clearance. Always recheck the clearance after making any adjustment.

4. If the choke plate clearance and fast idle cam linkage adjustment was performed with the carburetor on the engine, adjust the engine idle speed and fuel mixture. Adjust the dashpot (if so equipped).

REMOVAL AND INSTALLATION

1. Remove the air cleaner.

2. Remove the throttle cable or rod from the throttle lever. Disconnect the distributor vacuum line, EGR vacuum line, if so equipped, the inline filter and the choke heat tube at the carburetor.

3. Disconnect the choke clean air tube from the air horn. Disconnect the choke actuating cable, if so equipped.

4. Remove the carburetor retaining nuts then remove the carburetor. Remove the carburetor mounting gasket, spacer (if so equipped), and the lower gasket from the intake manifold.

5. Before installing the carburetor, clean the gasket mounting surfaces of the spacer and carburetor. Place the spacer between two new gaskets and position the spacer and the gaskets on the intake manifold. Position the carburetor on the spacer and gasket and secure it with the retaining nuts. To prevent leakage, distortion or damage to the carburetor body flange, snug the nuts, then alternately tighten each nut in a criss-cross pattern.

6. Connect the inline fuel filter, throttle cable, choke heat tube, distributor vacuum line, EGR vacuum line and choke cable.

7. Connect the choke clean air line to the air horn.

8. Adjust the engine idle speed, the idle fuel mixture and anti-stall dashpot (if so equipped). Install the air cleaner.

TROUBLESHOOTING

The best way to diagnose a bad carburetor is to eliminate all other possible sources of the problem. If the carburetor is suspected to be the problem, first perform all of the adjustments given in this Section. If this doesn't correct the difficulty, then check the following. Check the ignition system to make sure that the spark plugs, breaker points, and condenser are in good condition and adjusted to the proper specifications. Examine the emission control equipment to make sure that all the vacuum lines are connected and none are blocked or clogged. See the first half of this Chapter. Check the ignition timing adjusting. Check all the vacuum lines on the engine for loose connections, splits or breaks. Torque the carburetor and intake manifold attaching bolts to the proper specifications. If, after performing all of these checks and adjustments, the problem is still not solved, then you can safely assume that the carburetor is the source of the problem.

OVERHAUL

Efficient carburetion depends greatly on careful cleaning and inspection during overhaul since dirt, gum, water or varnish in or on the carburetor parts are often responsible for poor performance.

Overhaul the carburetor in a clean, dustfree area. Carefully disassemble the carburetor, referring often to the exploded views. Keep all similar and look-alike parts segregated during disassembly and cleaning to avoid accidental interchange during assembly. Make a note of all jet sizes.

When the carburetor is disassembled, wash

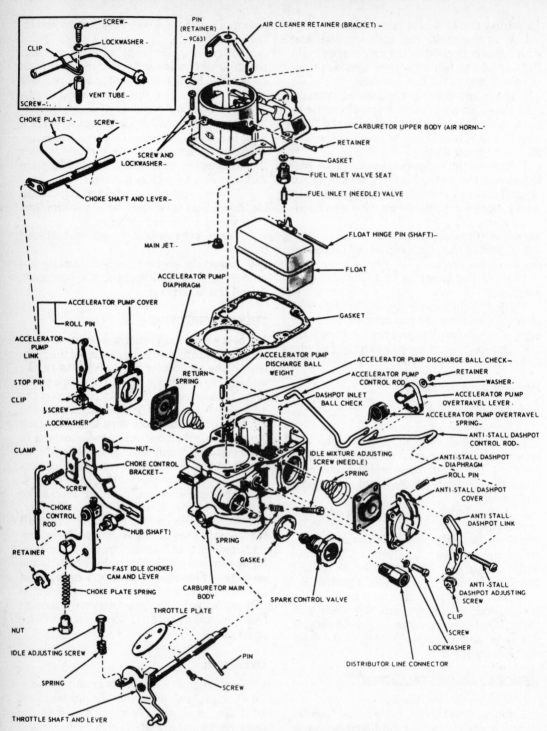

An exploded view of the Ford 1100 1-bbl carburetor

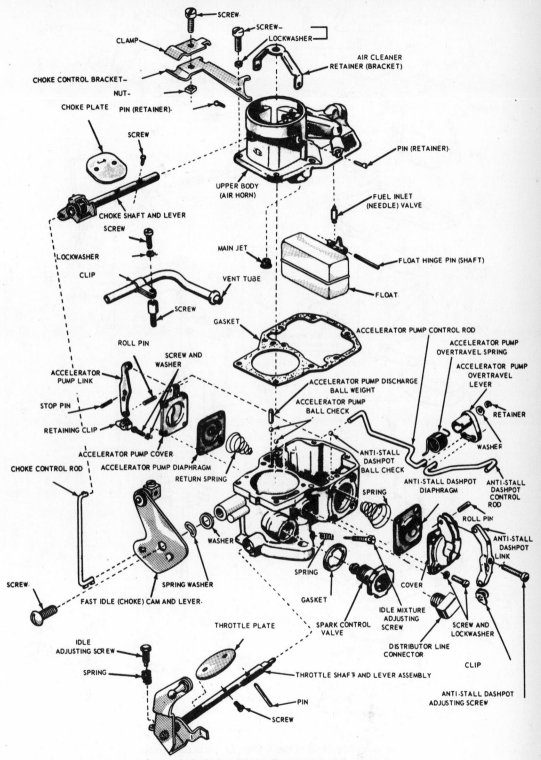

An exploded view of the Ford 1101 1-bbl carburetor

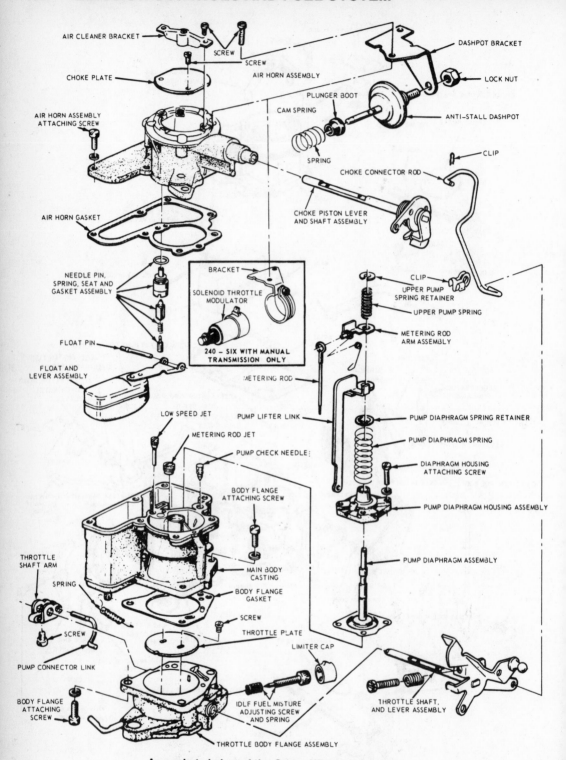

An exploded view of the Carter YF 1-bbl carburetor

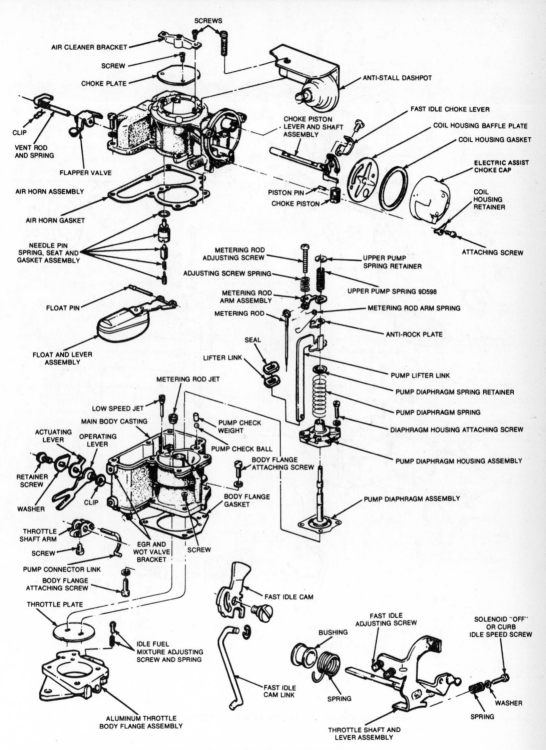

An exploded view of the Carter YFA 1-bbl carburetor

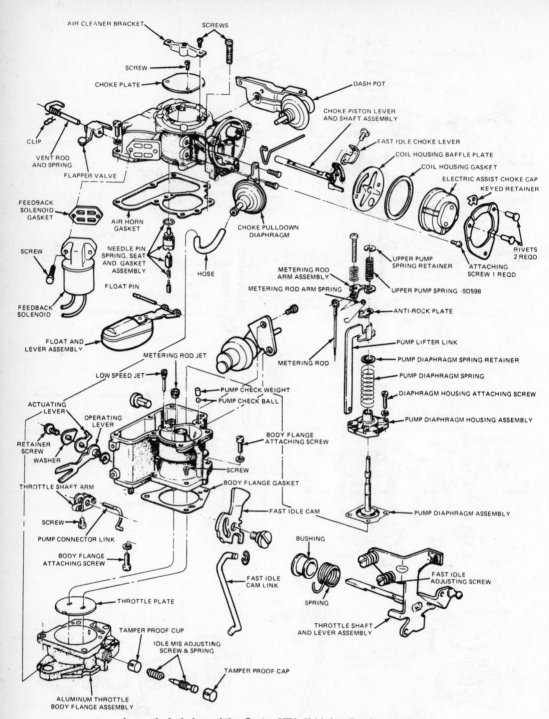

An exploded view of the Carter YFA 1bbl. feedback carburetor

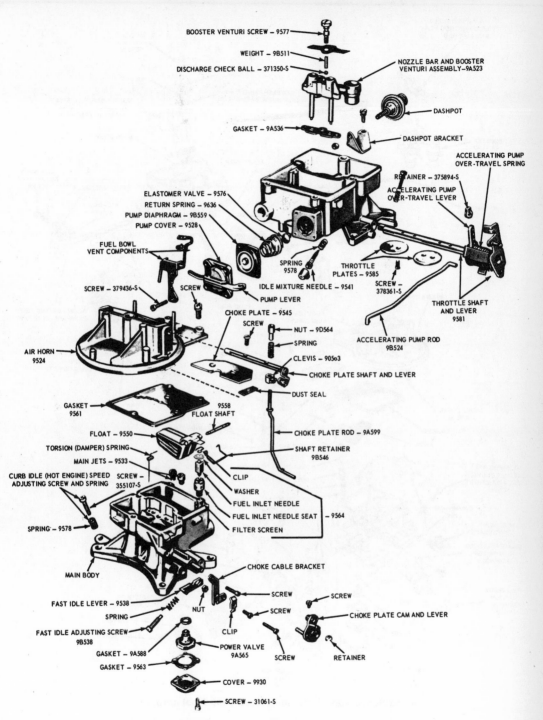

BOOSTER VENTURI SCREW – 9577

WEIGHT – 9B511

DISCHARGE CHECK BALL – 371350-S

NOZZLE BAR AND BOOSTER
VENTURI ASSEMBLY–9A523

DASHPOT

GASKET – 9A536

DASHPOT BRACKET

ACCELERATING PUMP
OVER-TRAVEL SPRING

RETAINER – 375894-S

ACCELERATING PUMP
OVER-TRAVEL LEVER

ELASTOMER VALVE – 9576
RETURN SPRING – 9636
PUMP DIAPHRAGM – 9B559
PUMP COVER – 9528

FUEL BOWL
VENT COMPONENTS

SPRING
9578

THROTTLE
PLATES – 9585

IDLE MIXTURE NEEDLE – 9541

SCREW –
378361-S

SCREW – 379436-S

SCREW

PUMP LEVER

THROTTLE SHAFT
AND LEVER
9581

ACCELERATING PUMP ROD
9B524

CHOKE PLATE – 9545

SCREW

NUT – 9D564

SPRING

CLEVIS – 905o3

AIR HORN
9524

CHOKE PLATE SHAFT AND LEVER

DUST SEAL

GASKET
9561

9558
FLOAT SHAFT

CHOKE PLATE ROD – 9A599

FLOAT – 9550

TORSION (DAMPER) SPRING

MAIN JETS – 9533

SHAFT RETAINER
9B546

CLIP

CURB IDLE (HOT ENGINE) SPEED
ADJUSTING SCREW AND SPRING

SCREW –
355107-S

WASHER

FUEL INLET NEEDLE

FUEL INLET NEEDLE SEAT

SPRING – 9578

9564

FILTER SCREEN

MAIN BODY

CHOKE CABLE BRACKET

FAST IDLE LEVER – 9538

SCREW

SCREW

SPRING

NUT

SCREW

CHOKE PLATE CAM AND LEVER

FAST IDLE ADJUSTING SCREW
9B538

CLIP

GASKET – 9A588

POWER VALVE
9A565

SCREW

RETAINER

GASKET – 9563

COVER – 9930

SCREW – 31061-S

An exploded view of the Autolite 2100 2-bbl carburetor

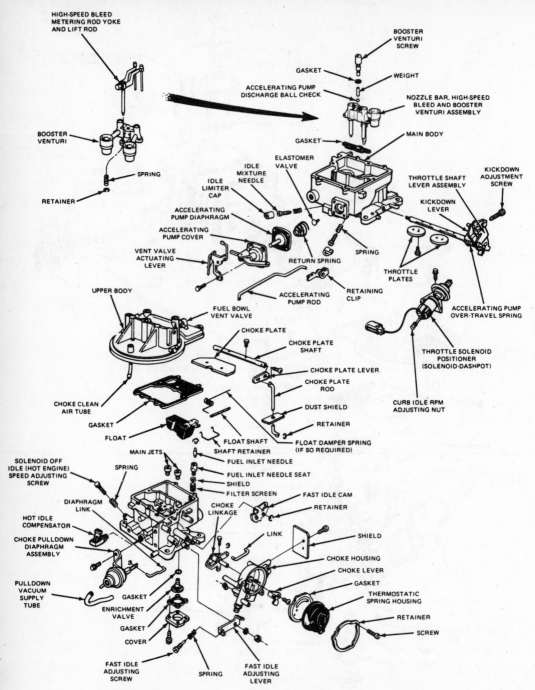

An exploded view of the Motorcraft 2150 2-bbl carburetor

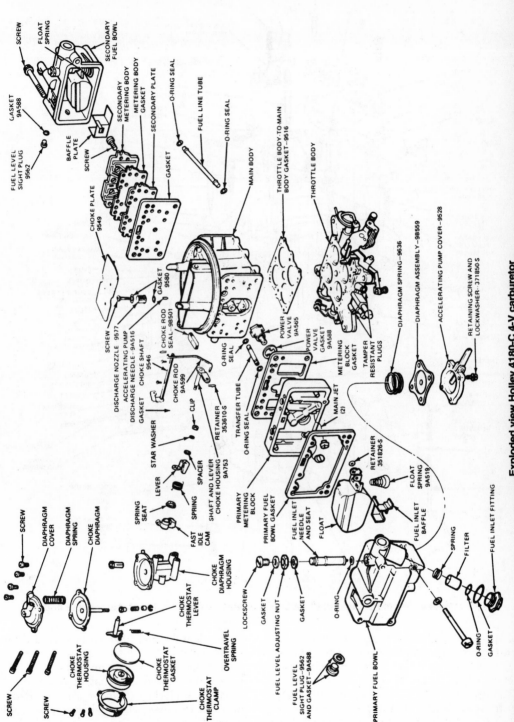

Exploded view Holley 4180-C 4-V carburetor

SCREW

FLOAT SPRING

SECONDARY FUEL BOWL

GASKET 9A588

SECONDARY METERING BODY

METERING BODY GASKET

SECONDARY PLATE

O-RING SEAL

FUEL LINE TUBE

O-RING SEAL

FUEL LEVEL SIGHT PLUG 9562

BAFFLE PLATE

SCREW

GASKET

MAIN BODY

THROTTLE BODY-TO-MAIN BODY GASKET—9516

THROTTLE BODY

CHOKE PLATE 9549

DISCHARGE NOZZLE 9577

ACCELERATING PUMP DISCHARGE NEEDLE—9A516

GASKET   CHOKE SHAFT 9546

GASKET 9580

SCREW

CHOKE ROD SEAL—9B501

CHOKE ROD 9A599

CLIP

RETAINER 353610-S

TRANSFER TUBE

O-RING SEAL

O-RING SEAL

POWER VALVE 9A565

POWER VALVE GASKET 9A588

METERING BLOCK GASKET

TAMPER RESISTANT PLUGS

MAIN JET (2)

DIAPHRAGM SPRING—9636

DIAPHRAGM ASSEMBLY—9B559

ACCELERATING PUMP COVER—9528

RETAINING SCREW AND LOCKWASHER—371850 S

STAR WASHER

LEVER

SPACER

SHAFT AND LEVER CHOKE HOUSING 9A753

SPRING SEAT

FAST IDLE CAM

SPRING

PRIMARY METERING BLOCK

PRIMARY FUEL BOWL GASKET

FUEL INLET NEEDLE AND SEAT

FLOAT

RETAINER 351826-S

FLOAT SPRING 9A519

FUEL INLET BAFFLE

SPRING

FILTER

FUEL INLET FITTING

SCREW

DIAPHRAGM COVER

DIAPHRAGM SPRING

CHOKE DIAPHRAGM

CHOKE DIAPHRAGM HOUSING

CHOKE THERMOSTAT LEVER

OVERTRAVEL SPRING

LOCKSCREW

FUEL LEVEL ADJUSTING NUT

GASKET

GASKET

O-RING

FUEL LEVEL SIGHT PLUG—9562 AND GASKET—9A588

PRIMARY FUEL BOWL

O-RING

GASKET

SCREW

SCREW

CHOKE THERMOSTAT HOUSING

CHOKE THERMOSTAT GASKET

CHOKE THERMOSTAT CLAMP

SCREW

SCREW

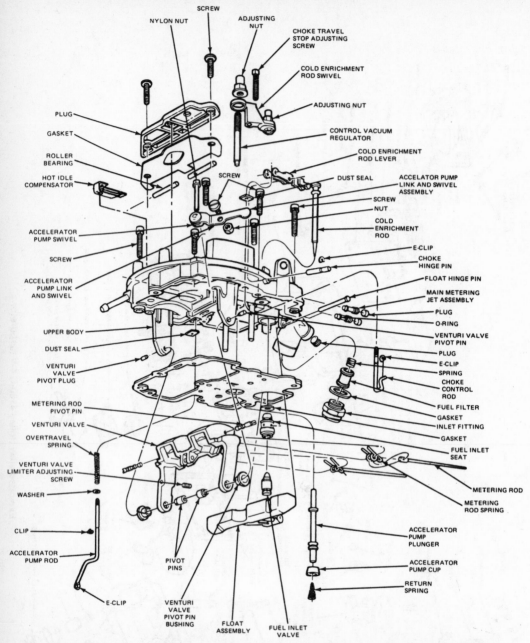

An exploded view of the Motorcraft 7200 VV (variable venturi) 2-bbl. carburetor upper body

all parts (except diaphragms, electric choke unit, pump plunger and any other plastic, leather, fiber, or rubber parts) in clean carburetor solvent. Do not leave the parts in the solvent any longer than is necessary to sufficiently loosen the dirt and deposits. Excessive cleaning may remove the special finish from the float bowl and choke valve bodies, leaving these parts unfit for service. Rinse all parts in clean solvent and blow them dry with compressed air or allow them to air dry, while resting on clan, lintless paper. Wipe clean all cork,

plastic, leather and fiber parts with a clean, lint-free cloth.

Blow out all passages and jets with compressed air and be sure that there are no restrictions or blockages. Never use wire or similar tools to clean jets, fuel passages or air bleeds. Clean all jets and valves separately to avoid accidental interchange.

Examine all parts for wear or damage. If wear or damage is found, replace the defective parts. Especially, inspect the following:

1. Check the float needle and seat for wear.

If wear is found, replace the complete assembly.

2. Check the float hinge pin for wear and the float(s) for dents or distortion. Replace the float if fuel has leaked into it.

3. Check the throttle and choke shaft bores for wear or an out-of-round condition. Damage or wear to the throttle arm, shaft or shaft bore will often require replacement of the throttle body. These parts require a close tolerance of fit; wear may allow air leakage, which could affect starting and idling.

NOTE: *Throttle shafts and bushings are not normally included in overhaul kits. They can be purchased separately.*

4. Inspect the idle mixture adjusting needles for burrs or grooves. Any such condition requires replacement of the needle, since you will not be able to obtain a satisfactory idle.

5. Test the accelerator pump check valves. They should pass air one way, but not the other. Test for proper seating by blowing and sucking on the valve. Replace the valve as necessary. If the valve is satisfactory, wash the valve again to remove moisture.

6. Check the bowl cover for warped surfaces with a straightedge.

7. Closely inspect the valves and seats for wear and damage, replacing as necessary.

8. After the carburetor is assembled, check the choke valve for freedom of operation.

Carburetor overhaul kits are recommended for each overhaul. These kits contain all gaskets and new parts to replace those which deteriorate most rapidly. Failure to replace all of the parts supplied with the kit (especially gaskets) can result in poor performance later.

NOTE: *Most carburetor rebuilding kits include specific procedures which should be following during overhaul.*

Most carburetor manufacturers supply overhaul kits of these basic types: minor repair; major repair; and gasket kits. Basically, they contain the following:

Minor Repair Kits:
- All gaskets
- Float needle valve
- Mixture adjusting screws
- All diaphragms
- Spring for the pump diaphragm

Major Repair Kits:
- All jets and gaskets
- All diaphragms
- Float needle valve
- Mixture adjusting screws
- Pump ball valve
- Main jet carrier
- Float
- Some float bowl cover holddown screws and washer

Gasket Kits:
- All gaskets

After cleaning and checking all components, reassemble the carburetor, using new parts and referring to the exploded view. When reassembling, make sure that all screws and jets are tight in their seats, but do not overtighten, as the tips will be distorted. Tighten all screws gradually, in rotation. Do not tighten needle valves into their seats; uneven jetting will result. Always use new gaskets. Be sure to adjust the float level.

GASOLINE FUEL INJECTION SYSTEM

NOTE: *This book contains simple testing and service procedures for your Bronco's fuel injection system. More comprehensive testing and diagnosis procedures may be found in CHILTON'S GUIDE TO FUEL INJECTION AND FEEDBACK CARBURETORS, BOOK PART NUMBER 7488, available in Sears stores, most book stores and auto parts stores, or aviable directly from Chilton Co.*

Mechanical Fuel Pump

REMOVAL & INSTALLATION

1. Loosen the threaded fittings to the fuel pump (use the proper size flare wrench), do not remove the lines at this time.

2. Loosen the fuel pump mounting bolts one or two turns. Loosen the pump and gasket from the engine or front cover. Rotate the engine, in the proper direction, while checking the tension on the fuel pump. When the cam or eccentric lobe is near the low point pressure on the fuel pump arm will be greatly reduced. This is especially important on engines using an aluminum front cover to help prevent thread stripping.

3. Have a rag handy to catch fuel spill and disconnect all lines from the fuel pump. Dispose of the rag safely.

4. Remove the fuel pump mounting bolts, the fuel pump and mounting gasket.

5. Clean all mounting surfaces. Apply oil resistant sealer to mounting surfaces. Install the fuel pump and new gasket in the reverse order of removal. Start the engine and check for leaks.

TESTING

Incorrect fuel pump pressure and low volume (flow rate) are the two most likely fuel pump troubles that will affect engine performance. Low pressure will cause a lean mixture and fuel starvation at high speeds and excessive

1966–78 Carburetor Specifications

AUTOLITE 2100

Year	Engine	Float Setting (in.)	Fuel Level (in.)	Fast Idle Cam Clearance (in.)	Choke Pulldown (in.)	Dechoke Minimum (in.)	Choke Cap Setting
1966–69	289, 302	3/8	3/4	—	1/4	—	—
1970	302 AT	7/16	13/16	.140	3/16	1/16	Index
	302 MT	7/16	13/16	.150	3/16	1/16	2 Rich
1971	302 MT	7/16	13/16	.140	5/32	1/16	Index
	302 AT	7/16	13/16	.140	5/32	1/16	1 Rich
1972–73	302	7/16	13/16	see text	see text	—	2 Rich
1974	302	7/16	13/16	see text	see text	—	2 Rich

MOTORCRAFT 2150

Year	Engine	Float Setting (in.)	Fuel Level (in.)	Fast Idle Cam Clearance (in.)	Choke Pulldown (in.)	Accelerator Pump Rod Location	Choke Cap Setting
1975–76	302 MT	31/64	7/8	see text	5/32	#3	1 NR ②
	302 AT	31/64	7/8	see text	5/32	#3	3 NR
1977	302 MT	7/16	13/16	see text	3/16	#3	3 NR
	302 AT	7/16	13/16	see text	3/16	#2	3 NR
1978	351M AT	31/64	7/8	see text	7/32	#4	Index
	351M MT	31/64	7/8	see text	3/16	#3	Index
	400	31/64	7/8	see text	7/32	#3	Index

① with Thermactor
② California: 3NR
49s: 49 states (except Calif.)

MT: Manual Transmission
AT: Automatic Transmission
NR: Notches Rich

FORD 1100, 1101

Year	Engine	Float Setting (in.)	Accelerator Pump Clearance (in.)	Choke Plate Pulldown Clearance (in.)	Dashpot Clearance (in.)	Idle Mixture Adjustment	Spark Control Valve Closes (in. Hg)
1966	170 MT	1 1/32	3/16	3/8	—	1½ turns out	8.5
	170 AT	1 1/32	3/16	3/8	3½ turns in	1½ turns out	8.5
1967–68	170 MT	1 3/32	3/16	3/8	—	1½ turns out	—
	170 AT	1 3/32	3/16	3/8	3½ turns in	1½ turns out	—
	170 ①	1 3/32	3/16	3/8	2 turns in	1½ turns out	—

CARTER YF

Year	Engine	Float Setting (in.)	Dechoke Minimum (in.)	Choke Pulldown (in.)	Dashpot Clearance (in.)	Throttle Plate Fast Idle Clearance (in.)	Fast Idle Speed (rpm)
1969–70	170	7/32	5/64	7/32	7/64	3/64	—
1971	170	3/8	9/32	8/32	—	—	1750
1972–73	170, 200	3/8	9/32	8/32	—	—	1750
1974	200	3/8	9/32	8/32	—	6/32	—

55 WAYS TO IMPROVE FUEL ECONOMY

CHILTON'S
FUEL ECONOMY
& TUNE-UP TIPS

Tune-up • Spark Plug Diagnosis • Emission Controls

Fuel System • Cooling System • Tires and Wheels

General Maintenance

CHILTON'S FUEL ECONOMY & TUNE-UP TIPS

Fuel economy is important to everyone, no matter what kind of vehicle you drive. The maintenance-minded motorist can save both money and fuel using these tips and the periodic maintenance and tune-up procedures in this Repair and Tune-Up Guide.

There are more than 130,000,000 cars and trucks registered for private use in the United States. Each travels an average of 10-12,000 miles per year, and, and in total they consume close to 70 billion gallons of fuel each year. This represents nearly ⅔ of the oil imported by the United States each year. The Federal government's goal is to reduce consumption 10% by 1985. A variety of methods are either already in use or under serious consideration, and they all affect you driving and the cars you will drive. In addition to "down-sizing", the auto industry is using or investigating the use of electronic fuel delivery, electronic engine controls and alternative engines for use in smaller and lighter vehicles, among other alternatives to meet the federally mandated Corporate Average Fuel Economy (CAFE) of 27.5 mpg by 1985. The government, for its part, is considering rationing, mandatory driving curtailments and tax increases on motor vehicle fuel in an effort to reduce consumption. The government's goal of a 10% reduction could be realized — and further government regulation avoided — if every private vehicle could use just 1 less gallon of fuel per week.

How Much Can You Save?

Tests have proven that almost anyone can make at least a 10% reduction in fuel consumption through regular maintenance and tune-ups. When a major manufacturer of spark plugs sur-

TUNE-UP

1. Check the cylinder compression to be sure the engine will really benefit from a tune-up and that it is capable of producing good fuel economy. A tune-up will be wasted on an engine in poor mechanical condition.

2. Replace spark plugs regularly. New spark plugs alone can increase fuel economy 3%.

3. Be sure the spark plugs are the correct type (heat range) for your vehicle. See the Tune-Up Specifications.

Heat range refers to the spark plug's ability to conduct heat away from the firing end. It must conduct the heat away in an even pattern to avoid becoming a source of pre-ignition, yet it must also operate hot enough to burn off conductive deposits that could cause misfiring.

The heat range is usually indicated by a number on the spark plug, part of the manufacturer's designation for each individual spark plug. The numbers in bold-face indicate the heat range in each manufacturer's identification system.

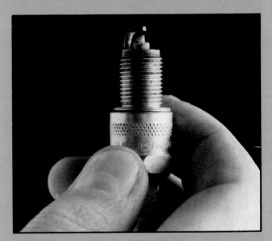

Periodically, check the spark plugs to be sure they are firing efficiently. They are excellent indicators of the internal condition of your engine.

Manufacturer	Typical Designation
AC	R **45** TS
Bosch (old)	WA **145** T30
Bosch (new)	HR **8** Y
Champion	RBL **15** Y
Fram/Autolite	4**15**
Mopar	P-**62** PR
Motorcraft	BRF-**42**
NGK	BP **5** ES-15
Nippondenso	W **16** EP
Prestolite	14GR **5** 2A

On AC, Bosch (new), Champion, Fram/Autolite, Mopar, Motorcraft and Prestolite, a higher number indicates a hotter plug. On Bosch (old), NGK and Nippondenso, a higher number indicates a colder plug.

4. Make sure the spark plugs are properly gapped. See the Tune-Up Specifications in this book.

5. Be sure the spark plugs are firing efficiently. The illustrations on the next 2 pages show you how to "read" the firing end of the spark plug.

6. Check the ignition timing and set it to specifications. Tests show that almost all cars have incorrect ignition timing by more than 2°.

veyed over 6,000 cars nationwide, they found that a tune-up, on cars that needed one, increased fuel economy over 11%. Replacing worn plugs alone, accounted for a 3% increase. The same test also revealed that 8 out of every 10 vehicles will have some maintenance deficiency that will directly affect fuel economy, emissions or performance. Most of this mileage-robbing neglect could be prevented with regular maintenance.

Modern engines require that all of the functioning systems operate properly for maximum efficiency. A malfunction anywhere wastes fuel. You can keep your vehicle running as efficiently and economically as possible, by being aware of your vehicle's operating and performance characteristics. If your vehicle suddenly develops performance or fuel economy problems it could be due to one or more of the following:

PROBLEM	POSSIBLE CAUSE
Engine Idles Rough	Ignition timing, idle mixture, vacuum leak or something amiss in the emission control system.
Hesitates on Acceleration	Dirty carburetor or fuel filter, improper accelerator pump setting, ignition timing or fouled spark plugs.
Starts Hard or Fails to Start	Worn spark plugs, improperly set automatic choke, ice (or water) in fuel system.
Stalls Frequently	Automatic choke improperly adjusted and possible dirty air filter or fuel filter.
Performs Sluggishly	Worn spark plugs, dirty fuel or air filter, ignition timing or automatic choke out of adjustment.

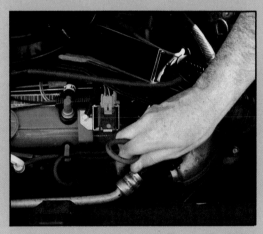

Check spark plug wires on conventional point type ignition for cracks by bending them in a loop around your finger.

Be sure that spark plug wires leading to adjacent cylinders do not run too close together. (Photo courtesy Champion Spark Plug Co.)

7. If your vehicle does not have electronic ignition, check the points, rotor and cap as specified.

8. Check the spark plug wires (used with conventional point-type ignitions) for cracks and burned or broken insulation by bending them in a loop around your finger. Cracked wires decrease fuel efficiency by failing to deliver full voltage to the spark plugs. One misfiring spark plug can cost you as much as 2 mpg.

9. Check the routing of the plug wires. Misfiring can be the result of spark plug leads to adjacent cylinders running parallel to each other and too close together. One wire tends to

pick up voltage from the other causing it to fire "out of time".

10. Check all electrical and ignition circuits for voltage drop and resistance.

11. Check the distributor mechanical and/or vacuum advance mechanisms for proper functioning. The vacuum advance can be checked by twisting the distributor plate in the opposite direction of rotation. It should spring back when released.

12. Check and adjust the valve clearance on engines with mechanical lifters. The clearance should be slightly loose rather than too tight.

SPARK PLUG DIAGNOSIS

Normal

APPEARANCE: This plug is typical of one operating normally. The insulator nose varies from a light tan to grayish color with slight electrode wear. The presence of slight deposits is normal on used plugs and will have no adverse effect on engine performance. The spark plug heat range is correct for the engine and the engine is running normally.

CAUSE: Properly running engine.

RECOMMENDATION: Before reinstalling this plug, the electrodes should be cleaned and filed square. Set the gap to specifications. If the plug has been in service for more than 10-12,000 miles, the entire set should probably be replaced with a fresh set of the same heat range.

Oil Deposits

APPEARANCE: The firing end of the plug is covered with a wet, oily coating.

CAUSE: The problem is poor oil control. On high mileage engines, oil is leaking past the rings or valve guides into the combustion chamber. A common cause is also a plugged PCV valve, and a ruptured fuel pump diaphragm can also cause this condition. Oil fouled plugs such as these are often found in new or recently overhauled engines, before normal oil control is achieved, and can be cleaned and reinstalled.

RECOMMENDATION: A hotter spark plug may temporarily relieve the problem, but the engine is probably in need of work.

Incorrect Heat Range

APPEARANCE: The effects of high temperature on a spark plug are indicated by clean white, often blistered insulator. This can also be accompanied by excessive wear of the electrode, and the absence of deposits.

CAUSE: Check for the correct spark plug heat range. A plug which is too hot for the engine can result in overheating. A car operated mostly at high speeds can require a colder plug. Also check ignition timing, cooling system level, fuel mixture and leaking intake manifold.

RECOMMENDATION: If all ignition and engine adjustments are known to be correct, and no other malfunction exists, install spark plugs one heat range colder.

Photos Courtesy Fram Corporation

Carbon Deposits

APPEARANCE: Carbon fouling is easily identified by the presence of dry, soft, black, sooty deposits.

CAUSE: Changing the heat range can often lead to carbon fouling, as can prolonged slow, stop-and-start driving. If the heat range is correct, carbon fouling can be attributed to a rich fuel mixture, sticking choke, clogged air cleaner, worn breaker points, retarded timing or low compression. If only one or two plugs are carbon fouled, check for corroded or cracked wires on the affected plugs. Also look for cracks in the distributor cap between the towers of affected cylinders.

RECOMMENDATION: After the problem is corrected, these plugs can be cleaned and reinstalled if not worn severely.

MMT Fouled

APPEARANCE: Spark plugs fouled by MMT (Methycyclopentadienyl Maganese Tricarbonyl) have reddish, rusty appearance on the insulator and side electrode.

CAUSE: MMT is an anti-knock additive in gasoline used to replace lead. During the combustion process, the MMT leaves a reddish deposit on the insulator and side electrode.

RECOMMENDATION: No engine malfunction is indicated and the deposits will not affect plug performance any more than lead deposits (see Ash Deposits). MMT fouled plugs can be cleaned, regapped and reinstalled.

High Speed Glazing

APPEARANCE: Glazing appears as shiny coating on the plug, either yellow or tan in color.

CAUSE: During hard, fast acceleration, plug temperatures rise suddenly. Deposits from normal combustion have no chance to fluff-off; instead, they melt on the insulator forming an electrically conductive coating which causes misfiring.

RECOMMENDATION: Glazed plugs are not easily cleaned. They should be replaced with a fresh set of plugs of the correct heat range. If the condition recurs, using plugs with a heat range one step colder may cure the problem.

Ash (Lead) Deposits

APPEARANCE: Ash deposits are characterized by light brown or white colored deposits crusted on the side or center electrodes. In some cases it may give the plug a rusty appearance.

CAUSE: Ash deposits are normally derived from oil or fuel additives burned during normal combustion. Normally they are harmless, though excessive amounts can cause misfiring. If deposits are excessive in short mileage, the valve guides may be worn.

RECOMMENDATION: Ash-fouled plugs can be cleaned, gapped and reinstalled.

Detonation

APPEARANCE: Detonation is usually characterized by a broken plug insulator.

CAUSE: A portion of the fuel charge will begin to burn spontaneously, from the increased heat following ignition. The explosion that results applies extreme pressure to engine components, frequently damaging spark plugs and pistons.

Detonation can result by over-advanced ignition timing, inferior gasoline (low octane) lean air/fuel mixture, poor carburetion, engine lugging or an increase in compression ratio due to combustion chamber deposits or engine modification.

RECOMMENDATION: Replace the plugs after correcting the problem.

Photos Courtesy Champion Spark Plug Co.

EMISSION CONTROLS

13. Be aware of the general condition of the emission control system. It contributes to reduced pollution and should be serviced regularly to maintain efficient engine operation.

14. Check all vacuum lines for dried, cracked or brittle conditions. Something as simple as a leaking vacuum hose can cause poor performance and loss of economy.

15. Avoid tampering with the emission control system. Attempting to improve fuel econ-

FUEL SYSTEM

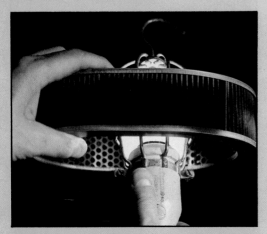

Check the air filter with a light behind it. If you can see light through the filter it can be reused.

Extremely clogged filters should be discarded and replaced with a new one.

18. Replace the air filter regularly. A dirty air filter richens the air/fuel mixture and can increase fuel consumption as much as 10%. Tests show that ⅓ of all vehicles have air filters in need of replacement.

19. Replace the fuel filter at least as often as recommended.

20. Set the idle speed and carburetor mixture to specifications.

21. Check the automatic choke. A sticking or malfunctioning choke wastes gas.

22. During the summer months, adjust the automatic choke for a leaner mixture which will produce faster engine warm-ups.

COOLING SYSTEM

29. Be sure all accessory drive belts are in good condition. Check for cracks or wear.

30. Adjust all accessory drive belts to proper tension.

31. Check all hoses for swollen areas, worn spots, or loose clamps.

32. Check coolant level in the radiator or expansion tank.

33. Be sure the thermostat is operating properly. A stuck thermostat delays engine warm-up and a cold engine uses nearly twice as much fuel as a warm engine.

34. Drain and replace the engine coolant at least as often as recommended. Rust and scale

TIRES & WHEELS

38. Check the tire pressure often with a pencil type gauge. Tests by a major tire manufacturer show that 90% of all vehicles have at least 1 tire improperly inflated. Better mileage can be achieved by over-inflating tires, but never exceed the maximum inflation pressure on the side of the tire.

39. If possible, install radial tires. Radial tires deliver as much as ½ mpg more than bias belted tires.

40. Avoid installing super-wide tires. They only create extra rolling resistance and decrease fuel mileage. Stick to the manufacturer's recommendations.

41. Have the wheels properly balanced.

omy by tampering with emission controls is more likely to worsen fuel economy than improve it. Emission control changes on modern engines are not readily reversible.

16. Clean (or replace) the EGR valve and lines as recommended.

17. Be sure that all vacuum lines and hoses are reconnected properly after working under the hood. An unconnected or misrouted vacuum line can wreak havoc with engine performance.

---

23. Check for fuel leaks at the carburetor, fuel pump, fuel lines and fuel tank. Be sure all lines and connections are tight.

24. Periodically check the tightness of the carburetor and intake manifold attaching nuts and bolts. These are a common place for vacuum leaks to occur.

25. Clean the carburetor periodically and lubricate the linkage.

26. The condition of the tailpipe can be an excellent indicator of proper engine combustion. After a long drive at highway speeds, the inside of the tailpipe should be a light grey in color. Black or soot on the insides indicates an overly rich mixture.

27. Check the fuel pump pressure. The fuel pump may be supplying more fuel than the engine needs.

28. Use the proper grade of gasoline for your engine. Don't try to compensate for knocking or "pinging" by advancing the ignition timing. This practice will only increase plug temperature and the chances of detonation or pre-ignition with relatively little performance gain.

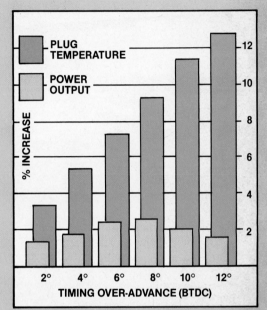

Increasing ignition timing past the specified setting results in a drastic increase in spark plug temperature with increased chance of detonation or preignition. Performance increase is considerably less. (Photo courtesy Champion Spark Plug Co.)

---

that form in the engine should be flushed out to allow the engine to operate at peak efficiency.

35. Clean the radiator of debris that can decrease cooling efficiency.

36. Install a flex-type or electric cooling fan, if you don't have a clutch type fan. Flex fans use curved plastic blades to push more air at low speeds when more cooling is needed; at high speeds the blades flatten out for less resistance. Electric fans only run when the engine temperature reaches a predetermined level.

37. Check the radiator cap for a worn or cracked gasket. If the cap does not seal properly, the cooling system will not function properly.

---

42. Be sure the front end is correctly aligned. A misaligned front end actually has wheels going in differed directions. The increased drag can reduce fuel economy by .3 mpg.

43. Correctly adjust the wheel bearings. Wheel bearings that are adjusted too tight increase rolling resistance.

Check tire pressures regularly with a reliable pocket type gauge. Be sure to check the pressure on a cold tire.

GENERAL MAINTENANCE

Check the fluid levels (particularly engine oil) on a regular basis. Be sure to check the oil for grit, water or other contamination.

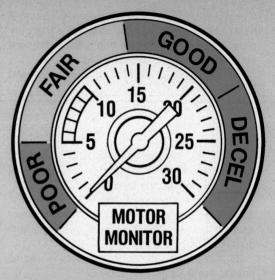

A vacuum gauge is another excellent indicator of internal engine condition and can also be installed in the dash as a mileage indicator.

44. Periodically check the fluid levels in the engine, power steering pump, master cylinder, automatic transmission and drive axle.

45. Change the oil at the recommended interval and change the filter at every oil change. Dirty oil is thick and causes extra friction between moving parts, cutting efficiency and increasing wear. A worn engine requires more frequent tune-ups and gets progressively worse fuel economy. In general, use the lightest viscosity oil for the driving conditions you will encounter.

46. Use the recommended viscosity fluids in the transmission and axle.

47. Be sure the battery is fully charged for fast starts. A slow starting engine wastes fuel.

48. Be sure battery terminals are clean and tight.

49. Check the battery electrolyte level and add distilled water if necessary.

50. Check the exhaust system for crushed pipes, blockages and leaks.

51. Adjust the brakes. Dragging brakes or brakes that are not releasing create increased drag on the engine.

52. Install a vacuum gauge or miles-per-gallon gauge. These gauges visually indicate engine vacuum in the intake manifold. High vacuum = good mileage and low vacuum = poorer mileage. The gauge can also be an excellent indicator of internal engine conditions.

53. Be sure the clutch is properly adjusted. A slipping clutch wastes fuel.

54. Check and periodically lubricate the heat control valve in the exhaust manifold. A sticking or inoperative valve prevents engine warm-up and wastes gas.

55. Keep accurate records to check fuel economy over a period of time. A sudden drop in fuel economy may signal a need for tune-up or other maintenance.

© 1980 Chilton Book Company, Radnor, PA 19089

1979 Carburetor Specifications

Calibration Number•	Choke Plate Pulldown Setting (inches)	Time for Choke Plate to Rotate (Come Off) (Seconds—Maximum)	Air Flow (Pounds Per Minute)	Choke Setting	Fast Idle RPM		Curb Idle RPM		TSP Off RPM		Timing RPM
					High Cam	Kick Down	⊕A/C Off/On	Non-AC	AC	Non-AC	
9-51G-RO	.230	80	.06	Index	—	1600	700	700	500	500	500
9-51J-RO	.230	80	.06	Index	—	1600	700	700	500	500	500
9-51K-RO	.230	80	.06	Index	—	1600	700	700	500	500	500
9-51L-RO	.230	80	.06	Index	—	1600	700	700	500	500	500
9-51M-RO	.230	80	.06	Index	—	1600	700	700	500	500	500
9-51S-RO	.230	80	.06	Index	—	1600	700	700	500	500	500
9-51T-RO	.230	80	.06	Index	—	1600	700	700	500	500	500
9-52G-RO	.230	80	.06	Index	—	1600	550	550	500	500	500
9-52J-RO	.230	80	.06	Index	—	1600	550	550	500	500	500
9-52L-RO	.230	80	.06	Index	—	1600	550	550	500	500	500
9-52M-RO	.230	80	.06	Index	—	1600	550	550	500	500	500
9-53G-RO	.140	235	.085	3 Rich	2000	—	700	700	—	—	550
9-53H-RO	.140	125	.085	3 Rich	2000	—	700	700	—	—	550
9-54G-RO	.145	150	.079	3 Rich	2000	—	600	700	—	—	550
R-54H-RO	.145	150	.079	3 Rich	2000	—	600	600	550	550	550
9-54J-RO	.145	135	.079	2 Rich	2000	—	600	600	550	550	550
9-54R-RO	.145	135	.079	3 Rich	2000	—	600	600	550	550	550
9-54S-RO	.136	75	.080	1 Rich	2400	—	650	650	550	550	550
9-54T-RO	.145	150	.079	3 Rich	2000	—	600	600	550	550	550
9-54U-RO	.136	75	.080	1 Rich	2400	—	650	600	550	550	550
9-59H-RO	.135	84	.074	Index	2000	—	650	650	—	—	650
9-59J-RO	.145	84	.074	Index	2000	—	650	650	—	—	650
9-59K-RO	.145	84	.074	Index	2000	—	650	650	—	—	650

1979 Carburetor Specifications

Calibration Number	Choke Plate Pulldown Setting (inches)	Time for Choke Plate to Rotate (Come Off) (Seconds—Maximum)	Air Flow (Pounds Per Minute)	Choke Setting	Fast Idle RPM		Curb Idle RPM		TSP Off RPM		Timing RPM
					High Cam	Kick Down	① A/C Off/On	Non-AC	AC	Non-AC	
9-59S-RO	.135	84	.07	Index	2000	—	650	650	—	—	650
9-59T-RO	.150	84	.07	Index	2000	—	650	650	—	—	650
9-60G-RO	.145	84	.079	Index	2000	—	550	550	—	—	500
9-60H-RO	.150	84	.08	Index	2000	—	550	550	—	—	500
9-60J-RO	.140	84	.079	Index	2000	—	550	550	—	—	500
9-60L-RO	.150	84	.08	Index	2000	—	550	550	—	—	500
9-60M-RO	.150	84	.08	Index	2000	—	550	550	—	—	500
9-60S-RO	.150	84	—	3 Rich	2100	—	550	550	—	—	500
9-61G-RO	.145	84	.074	Index	2000	—	650	650	—	—	650
9-61H-RO	.135	84	.076	Index	2000	—	650	650	—	—	650
9-62J-RO	.145	85	.079	Index	1900	—	550	550	—	—	550
9-62M-RO	.145	85	.079	Index	1900	—	550	550	—	—	500
9-63H-RO	.190	77	.06	Index	—	1500	800	800	500	500	500
9-64G-RO	.200	67	.06	Index	2200	—	600	600	500	500	500
9-64H-RO	.200	67	.06	Index	2200	—	600	600	500	500	500
9-64S-RO	.200	67	.06	Index	2200	—	600	600	500	500	500
9-66G-RO	.210	130	.09	5 Rich	—	1600	650②	650	800③	800	650 TSP Off

① Only for A/C-TSP equipped, A/C compressor electromagnetic clutch de-energized
② Energize A/C electromagnetic clutch
③ De-energize A/C electromagnetic clutch
• Refer to engine calibration code on underhood emissions sticker.

1980 Carburetor Specifications

CARTER YFA

Check the carburetor part number tag to determine which specifications to use for your vehicle.

Engine	Part Number	Choke Pulldown Setting	Fast Idle Cam Setting	Dechoke Setting	Choke Plate Come-Off Time	Float Setting (Dry)	Primary Jet Dia.	Choke Cap Setting	Fast Idle
6-300	EOTE-9510-ALA	.230	.140	.280	100 sec.	.690	.104	Index	1600
	EOTE-9510-AHA	.230	.140	.280	80 sec.	.690	.104	Index	1600
	EOTE-9510-ATA	.230	.140	.280	80 sec.	.690	.104	Index	1600
	EOUE-9510-GA	.230	.140	.280	80 sec.	.690	.104	Index	1600

MOTORCRAFT 2150

Check the carburetor part number tag to determine which specifications to use for your vehicle.

Engine	Part Number	Choke Pulldown Setting	Fast Idle Cam Setting	Dechoke Setting	Fuel Level (Wet)	Accelerator Pump Lever Location	Fuel Bowl Vent Clearance	Choke Cap Setting	Fast Idle
8-302	EOTE-9510-BGA	.140	V-notch	.200	.810	#2	.080	3 Rich	2000
	EOTE-9510-BHA	.135	V-notch	.200	.810	#2	.050	3 Rich	2000
	EOTE-9510-BRA	.128	V-notch	.200	.875	#3	.050	3 Rich	2000
	EOTE-9510-CFA	.128	V-notch	.250	.810	#2	—	2 Rich	2000
	EOTE-9510-CVA	.105	V-notch	.200	.875	#2	—	1 Rich	2400
	EOTE-9510-CYA	.140	V-notch	.200	.810	#2	.050	3 Rich	2000
	EOTE-9510-CZA	.140	V-notch	.200	.810	#2	.080	3 Rich	2000
	EOTE-9510-DDA	.128	V-notch	.200	.875	#3	.050	1 Rich	2400
	EOUE-9510-ABA	.140	V-notch	.200	.810	#2	.080	3 Rich	2000
	EOUE-9510-NA	.105	V-notch	.200	.810	#3	—	Index	2100
	EOTE-9510-BEA	.140	V-notch	.200	.810	#2	—	Index	2100
8-351	EOUE-9510-AAA	.185	V-notch	.250	.810	#2	.050	3 Rich	2000
	EOTE-9510-BLA/BFA	.148	V-notch	.250	.875	#3	.050	2 Rich	2400
	EOTE-9510-BSA ①	.140	V-notch	.115	.875	#2	.050	1 Rich	2000
	EOTE-9510-BSA ②	.140	V-notch	.200	.875	#2	.050	2 Rich	2000
	EOTE-9510-BZA	.148	V-notch	.250	.875	#3	.050	3 Rich	2100
	EOTE-9510-CCA/CBA	.159	V-notch	.250	.875	#3	.050	3 Rich	2000
	EOUE-9510-PA/RA	.185	V-notch	.250	.810	#4	.050	2 Rich	2400
	EOUE-9510-SA/TA	.185	V-notch	.250	.810	#2	.050	3 Rich	2000
	EOUE-9510-VA	.185	V-notch	.250	.810	#4	.050	3 Rich	2000

① Calibration code 0-59G-R10
② Calibration codes 0-59H-R10, 0-59J-R10

1981 Carburetor Specifications

CARTER YFA
Check the carburetor part number tag to determine which specifications to use for your vehicle.

Engine	Part Number	Choke Pulldown Setting	Fast Idle Cam Setting	Dechoke Setting	Choke Plate Come-Off Time	Float Setting (Dry)	Choke Cap Setting	Fast Idle
6-300	D9TE-9510-CA,VA E0TE-9510-AMA,FA	.290	.140	.280	—	.690	Index	1400
	E1TE-9510-UA,ARA, ARB	.230	.140	.280	110 sec.	.780	Index	1400
	E1TE-9510-EA,DA, ANA,TA,EB,ANB	.300	.140	.280	110 sec.	.780	Index	1400

MOTORCRAFT 2150
Check the carburetor part number tag to determine which specifications to use for your vehicle.

Engine	Part Number	Choke Pulldown Setting	Fast Idle Cam Setting	Dechoke Setting	Float Level (Wet)	Float Level (Dry)	Accelerator Pump Lever Location	Choke Cap Setting	Fast Idle
8-302	E1TE-9510-CNA,CMA	.125	V-notch	.200	.810	7/16	#2	V-notch	1500
	E1TE-9510-CPA,CRA	.125	V-notch	.200	.810	7/16	#2	V-notch	1500
8-351	E1TE-9510-CCA	.155	V-notch	.250	.875	31/64	#4	V-notch	2000
	E1TE-9510-BHA	.140	V-notch	.200	.875	31/64	#2	3NR	2000
	E1TE-9510-BFA	.140	V-notch	.200	.875	31/64	#2	V-notch	2000
	E1UE-9510-FA	.120	V-notch	.200	.875	31/64	#3	Index	2000
	E1UE-9510-CA, JA	.120	V-notch	.200	.875	31/64	#3	V-notch	2000

1982 Carburetor Specifications

CARTER YFA
Check the carburetor part number tag to determine which specifications to use for your vehicle

Engine	Part Number	Choke Pulldown Setting	Fast Idle Cam Setting	Dechoke Setting	Choke Plate Come-Off Time	Float Setting (Dry)	Choke Cap Setting	Fast Idle
6-300	E2TE-BZA E2TE-BVA	.270	.140	.280	110 sec.	.780	Index	1400
	E2TE-9510-BZB E2TE-9510-BVB	.270	.140	.280	110 sec.	.780	2NR	1400
	E2TE-AMA E2UE-EA	.230	.140	.280	110 sec.	.780	Index	1400
	E2TE-CEA	.320	.140	.330	110 sec.	.780	2NR	1600
	E2TE-JA	.320	.140	.330	110 sec.	.780	2NR	1600
	E2TE-YA	.300	.140	.280	110 sec.	.780	Index	1600
	E2TE-AAA	.300	.140	.280	110 sec.	.780	Index	1400
	E2TE-MA	.300	.140	.280	110 sec.	.780	2NR	1400
	E2TE-ANA	.300	.140	.280	110 sec.	.780	2NR	1400

1982 Carburetor Specifications (Cont.)

CARTER YFA

Check the carburetor part number tag to determine which specifications to use for your vehicle

Engine	Part Number	Choke Pulldown Setting	Fast Idle Cam Setting	Dechoke Setting	Choke Plate Come-Off Time	Float Setting (Dry)	Choke Cap Setting	Fast Idle
6-300	E2TE-KA	.320	.140	.330	110 sec.	.780	2NR	1400
	E2UE-DA	.320	.140	.330	110 sec.	.780	2NR	1400

MOTORCRAFT 2150

Engine	Part Number	Choke Pulldown Setting	Fast Idle Cam Setting	Dechoke Setting	Float Level (Wet)	Float Level (Dry)	Accelerator Pump Lever Location	Choke Cap Setting	Fast Idle
8-302	E2TE-AYA E1UE-9510-GA	.130	V-notch	.200	.810	7/16	#2	V-notch	2000
	E2TE-BEA E1TE-9510-BVA	.130	V-notch	.200	.810	7/16	#2	V-notch	2000
	E2TE-CJA	.130	V-notch	.200	.810	7/16	#2	V-notch	2000
	E2TE-BFA	.125	V-notch	.200	.810	7/16	#2	V-notch	2000
	E2TE-9510-DRA	.125	V-notch	.200	.810	7/16	#2	V-notch	2000
	E2TE-JA	.130	V-notch	.200	.875	31/64	#2	V-notch	2000
	E2UE-9510-AHA	.130	V-notch	.200	.875	31/64	#2	V-notch	2000
	E2TE-BBA E1TE-9510-CKA	.125	V-notch	.200	.810	7/16	#2	V-notch	2000
	E2TE-BAA E1TE-9510-CMA	.125	V-notch	.200	.810	7/16	#2	V-notch	2000
	E2TE-CKA	.120	V-notch	.200	.810	7/16	#2	V-notch	2100
8-351	E2UE-FA E1UE-JA	.120	V-notch	.200	.875	31/64	#3	V-notch	2000
	E1UE-KA	.120	V-notch	.200	.875	31/64	#2	V-notch	2000

MOTORCRAFT 7200

Engine	Part Number	Fast Idle Cam Setting	Float Drop	Float Level (Dry)	Accelerator Pump Lever Lash	Choke Cap Setting	Fast Idle
8-302	E1TE-ABA E2TE-CBA	.355–.365	1.490–1.430	1.070–1.010	.010 ③	Index	1350 ②
	E2TE-9510-DLA E2TE-9510-DGB	.355–.365	1.490–1.430	1.070–1.010	.010 ③	2NR	1350 ②
	E1TE-YA D2TE-CAA	.355–.365 ①	1.490–1.430	1.070–1.010	.010 ③	Index	1350
	E2TE-9510-DKA	.355–.365	1.490–1.430	1.070–1.010	.010 ③	2NR	1350 ②
8-351	E1TE-ZA E2TE-CDA,DJA	.355–.365 ①	1.490–1.430	1.070–1.010	.010 ③	Index	1700 ①
	E2TE-9510-CDB E2TE-9510-CDD	.355–.365	1.490–1.430	1.070–1.010	.010 ③	Index	1700 ①

1982 Carburetor Specifications (Cont.)

MOTORCRAFT 7200

Engine	Part Number	Fast Idle Cam Setting	Float Drop	Float Level (Dry)	Accelerator Pump Lever Lash	Choke Cap Setting	Fast Idle
	E1TE-AHA E2TE-CCA E2TE-9510-DHA	.355–.365 ①	1.490–1.430	1.070–1.010	.010 ③	Index	1650 ①
	E2TE-9510-CCB	.355–.365	1.490–1.430	1.070–1.010	.010 ③	Index	1650 ①

① 2nd highest step
② 3rd highest step
③ Plus 1 turn counter clockwise

1983 Carburetor Specifications

CARTER YFA

Check the carburetor part number tag to determine which specifications to use for your vehicle

Engine	Part Number	Choke Pulldown Setting	Fast Idle Cam Setting	Dechoke Setting	Choke Plate Come-Off Time	Float Setting (Dry)	Choke Cap Setting	Fast Idle
6-300	E3TE-9510-YA	.270	.140	.280	90–140 sec.	.780	Red	1600
	E3TE-9510-AHA E3TE-9510-AJA	.270	.140	.280	90–140 sec.	.780	Red	1600
	E3TE-9510-BNA	.320	.140	.330	90–140 sec.	.780	Red	1600
	E3TE-9510-GA	.320	.140	.330	90–140 sec.	.780	Red	1600
	E3TE-9510-BDA	.320	.140	.330	90–140 sec.	.780	Red	1600
	E3TE-9510-ZA	.300	.140	.280	90–140 sec.	.780	White	1600
	E3TE-9510-AFA E3TE-9510-ANA	.270	.140	.280	90–140 sec.	.780	Red	1600
	E3TE-9510-AAA E3TE-9510-ARA	.300	.140	.280	90–140 sec.	.780	Red	1600
	E3TE-9510-ALA	.320	.140	.330	90–140 sec.	.780	Red	1600
	E3TE-9510-FA	.320	.140	.330	90–140 sec.	.780	Red	1600
	E3TE-9510-BKA	.320	.140	.330	90–140 sec.	.780	Red	1600
	E3TE-9510-ABA	.300	.140	.280	90–140 sec.	.780	White	1600
	E3TE-9510-BRA	.300	.140	.280	90–140 sec.	.780	White	1600
	E3TE-9510-AKA	.300	.140	.280	90–140 sec.	.780	White	1600

MOTORCRAFT 2150

Engine	Part Number	Choke Pulldown Setting	Fast Idle Cam Setting	Dechoke Setting	Float Level (Wet)	Float Level (Dry)	Accelerator Pump Lever Location	Choke Cap Setting	Fast Idle
8-302	E3TE-9510-AUA	.142	V-notch	.200	.810	7/16	#3	V-notch	2100
	E3TE-9510-BHA	.152	V-notch	.200	.810	7/16	#3	V-notch	2100
	E3TE-9510-AYA	.137	V-notch	.250	.810	7/16	#4	V-notch	2250
	E3TE-9510-AVA	.149	V-notch	.250	.810	7/16	#3	V-notch	2250

1983 Carburetor Specifications (Cont.)

MOTORCRAFT 2150

Engine	Part Number	Choke Pulldown Setting	Fast Idle Cam Setting	Dechoke Setting	Float Level (Wet)	Float Level (Dry)	Accelerator Pump Lever Location	Choke Cap Setting	Fast Idle
	E3TE-9510-BJA	.157	V-notch	.200	.810	7/16	#4	V-notch	2000
	E3TE-9510-BLA E3TE-9510-BPA	.157	V-notch	.200	.810	7/16	#3	V-notch	2000
	E3TE-9510-BEA	.149	V-notch	.200	.810	7/16	#3	V-notch	2250
	E3TE-9510-BMA	.150	V-notch	.200	.810	7/16	#4	V-notch	2250
8-351W	E3UE-9510-CA E2UE-9510-FA	.120	V-notch	.200	.875	31/64	#3	V-notch	2000
	E3UE-9510-BA E3UE-9510-KA	.120	V-notch	.200	.875	31/64	#2	V-notch	2000

MOTORCRAFT 7200

Engine	Part Number	Fast Idle Cam Setting	Float Drop	Float Level (Dry)	Accelerator Pump Lever Lash	Choke Cap Setting	Fast Idle
8-351	E2TE-9510-CDD E2TE-9510-CDB	.355 – .365 ①	1.430 – 1.490	1.010 – 1.070	.010 ②	Index	1700
	E2TE-9510-CCC E2TE-9510-CCB	.355 – .365	1.430 – 1.490	1.010 – 1.070	.010 ②	Index	1650

① 2nd highest step
② Plus 1 turn counter clockwise

1984 Carburetor Specifications

CARTER YFA

Check the carburetor part number tag to determine which specifications to use for your vehicle

Engine	Part Number	Choke Pulldown Setting	Fast Idle Cam Setting	Dechoke Setting	Choke Plate Come-Off Time	Float Setting (Dry)	Choke Cap Setting	Fast Idle
6-300	E4TE-9510-VA, HA,FA,UA,AAA, GA,EA,ZA	.360	.140	.330	90–141 sec.	.780	Red	①
	D5TE-9510-AGB	.230	1NR	.280	—	.375	—	①
	D5TE-9510-AMB, FE	.290	Index	.280	—	.690	Index	①

① Refer to underhood emission sticker

Models YF/YFA
(All measurements in inches)

Year	Carburetor Number	Float Level	Float Drop	Choke Unloader Setting	Choke Setting	Dash Pot Plunger	Initial Choke Opening
'85–'86	E5TE-9510 DA	.65	—	.270	Gray ①	—	.320
	VA,UA,TA, BA,RA,SA, JA	.78	—	.330	Red ①	—	.360
	FA	.78	—	.330	Red ①	—	.340
	HA	.78	—	.330	Red ①	—	.320
	DA,MA,CA ②	.78	—	.330	Red ①	—	.360
	D5TE-9510 AGB	⅜	—	.280	—		.230
	EOTE-9510 AMB,FB	.69	—	.280	Index	—	.290

① Choke cap index plate color
② Feedback carburetor

Model 2150
(All measurements in inches)

Year	Carburetor Number	Float Level (Dry)	Choke Unloader Setting	Choke Setting	Accelerator Pump Rod Location	Fuel Level (Wet)	Choke Pulldown Setting (Min)
'85–'86	E57E-9510 BA,CA	¹⁄₁₆	.250	3-Rich	4	.810 ④	.136
	E5TE-9510			V-notch	4	.875	.150
	YA	⁹⁄₃₂	.220				
	ACA	⁹⁄₃₂	.200	3 Rich	4	.875	.150
	AAA	¼	.200	V-notch	4	.810	.155
	PA	¼	.200	3 Rich	4	.810	.152
	E3UE-9510 EA,DA	³¹⁄₆₄	.250	V-notch	3	.875	.180

Motorcraft 2150

Engine	Part Number	Choke Pulldown Setting	Fast Idle Cam Setting	Dechoke Setting	Float Level (Wet)	Float Level (Dry)	Accelerator Pump Lever Location	Choke Cap Setting	Fast Idle
8-302	E4TE-9510-AMA	.140	V-notch	.250	.875	³¹⁄₆₄	#3	V-notch	①
	E4TE-9510-AEA	.142	V-notch	.250	.875	³¹⁄₆₄	#3	V-notch	①
	E4TE-9510-ALA	.125	V-notch	.250	.875	³¹⁄₆₄	#3	V-notch	①
	E4TE-9510-APA	.145	V-notch	.250	.875	³¹⁄₆₄	#3	V-notch	①
	E4TE-9510-AKA	.137	V-notch	.250	.875	³¹⁄₆₄	#3	V-notch	①
	E4TE-9510-AHA	.150	V-notch	.250	.875	³¹⁄₆₄	#4	V-notch	①
	E4TE-9510-AJA	.150	V-notch	.250	.875	³¹⁄₆₄	#3	V-notch	①
	E4TE-9510-AFA	.144	V-notch	.250	.875	³¹⁄₆₄	#3	V-notch	①
	E3TE-9510-BAA, AZA	.130	V-notch	.250	.875	³¹⁄₆₄	#3	V-notch	①

Motorcraft 2150 (cont.)

Engine	Part Number	Choke Pulldown Setting	Fast Idle Cam Setting	Dechoke Setting	Float Level (Wet)	Float Level (Dry)	Accelerator Pump Lever Location	Choke Cap Setting	Fast Idle
8-351	E4TE-9510-ADA	.152	V-notch	.250	.810	$7/16$	#4	V-notch	①
	E4TE-9510-ACA	.155	V-notch	.250	.810	$7/16$	#4	V-notch	①
	E3UE-9510-EA, DA	.180	V-notch	.250	.875	$31/64$	#3	V-notch	①

① Refer to underhood emission sticker

Model 4180C
(All measurements in inches)

Year	Carburetor Number	Fuel Level (Wet)	Choke Pulldown Setting	Choke Unloader Setting	Choke Setting	Pump Level Location	Enrichment Valve Indent.
'84–'86	E4TE-9510-ARA	①	.185	.300	Index	#1	13
	E3TE-9510 PD	①	.220	.295–.335	3 Rich	#1	8
	TC	①	.210–.230	.300–.330	3 Rich	#1	8
	RD	①	.200	.315	3 Rich	#1	8A
	SC	①	.210–.230	.315	3 Rich	#1	8A

① At bottom of sight plug

pressure will cause high fuel consumption and carburetor flooding.

To determine that the fuel pump is in satisfactory operating condition, tests for both fuel pump pressure and volume should be performed.

The tests are performed with the fuel pump installed on the engine and the engine at normal operating temperature and at idle speed.

Before the test, make sure that the replaceable fuel filter has been changed at the proper mileage interval. If in doubt, install a new filter.

Pressure Test

1. Remove the air cleaner assembly. Disconnect the fuel inlet line of the fuel filter at the carburetor. Use care to prevent fire, due to fuel spillage. Place an absorbent cloth under the connection before removing the line to catch any fuel that might flow out of the line.

2. Connect a pressure gauge, a restrictor and a flexible hose between the fuel filter and the carburetor.

3. Position the flexible hose and the restrictor so that the fuel can be discharged into a suitable, graduated container.

4. Before taking a pressure reading, operate the engine at the specified idle rpm and vent the system into the container by opening the hose restrictor momentarily.

5. Close the hose restrictor, allow the pressure to stabilize and note the reading. The pressure should be 5 psi. If the pump pressure is not within 4–6 psi and the fuel lines and filter are in satisfactory condition, the pump is defective and should be replaced. If the pump pressure is within the proper range, perform the test for fuel volume.

Volume Test

1. Operate the engine at the specified idle rpm.

2. Open the hose restrictor and catch the fuel in the container while observing the time it takes to pump 1 pint. 1 pint should be pumped in 20 seconds. If the pump does not pump to specifications, check for proper fuel tank venting or a restriction in the fuel line leading from the fuel tank to the carburetor before replacing the fuel pump.

Electric Fuel Pump

Two electric pumps are used on injected models; a low pressure boost pump mounted in the

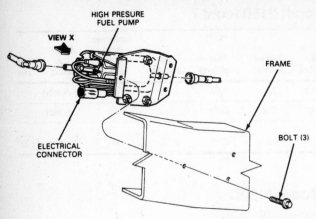

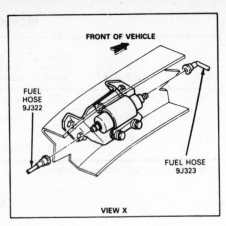

High pressure fuel pump

gas tank and a high pressure pump mounted on the vehicle frame.

On injected models the low pressure pump is used to provide pressurized fuel to the inlet of the high pressure pump and helps prevent noise and heating problems. The externally mounted high pressure pump is capable of supplying 15.9 gallons of fuel an hour. System pressure is controlled by a pressure regulator mounted on the engine.

On internal fuel tank mounted pumps tank removal is required. Frame mounted models can be accessed from under the vehicle. Prior to servicing release system pressure (see proceeding Fuel Supply Manifold details). Disconnect the negative battery cable prior to pump removal.

REMOVAL AND INSTALLATION

In-Tank Pump

1. Disconnect the negative battery cable.
2. Depressurize the system and drain as

much gas from the tank by pumping out through the filler neck.

3. Raise the back of the vehicle and safely support on jackstands.

4. Disconnect the fuel supply, return and vent lines at the right and left side of the frame.

5. Disconnect the wiring harness to the fuel pump.

6. Support the gas tank, loosen and remove the mounting straps. Remove the gas tank.

7. Disconnect the lines and harness at the pump flange.

8. Clean the outside of the mounting flange and retaining ring. Turn the fuel pump lock ring counterclockwise and remove.

9. Remove the fuel pump.

10. Clean the mounting surfaces. Put a light coat of grease on the mounting sufaces and on the new sealing ring. Install the new fuel pump.

11. Installation is in the reverse order of removal. Fill the tank with at least 10 gals. of gas. Turn the ignition key ON for three seconds. Repeat 6 or 7 times until the fuel system is pressurized. Check for any fitting leaks. Start the engine and check for leaks.

External Pump

1. Disconnect the negative battery cable.
2. Depressurize the fuel system.
3. Raise and support the rear of the vehicle on jackstands.
4. Disconnect the inlet and outlet fuel lines.
5. Remove the pump from the mounting bracket.
6. Install in reverse order, make sure the pump is indexed correctly in the mounting bracket insulator.

Low pressure fuel pump

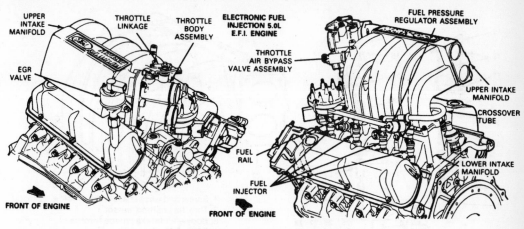

Ford EFI-V8 engine component location

Air Intake And Throttle Body
REMOVAL AND INSTALLATION

1. Disconnect the air intake hose.
2. Disconnect the throttle position sensor and air by-pass valve connectors.
3. Remove the four throttle body mounting nuts and carefully separate the air throttle body from the upper intake manifold.
4. Remove and discard the mounting gasket. Clean all mounting surfaces using care not to damage the gasket surfaces of the throttle body and manifold. Do not allow any material to drop into the intake manifold.
5. Install the throttle body in the reverse order of removal. The mounting nuts are tightened to 12–15 ft.lb.

Quick-Connect Line Fittings
REMOVAL AND INSTALLATION

NOTE: *Quick-Connect (push) type fittings must be disconnected using proper procedures or the fitting may be damaged. Two types of retainers are used on the push con-*

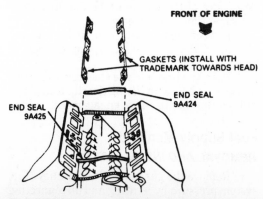

Ford EFI-V8 lower manifold gasket installation

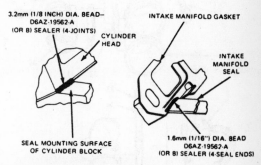

NOTE: THIS SEALER SETS UP WITHIN 15 MINUTES AFTER APPLICATION. TO ASSURE EFFECTIVE SEALING, ASSEMBLY SHOULD PROCEED PROMPTLY.

Ford EFI-V8 lower manifold seal installation

nect fittings. Line sizes of ⅜″ and ⁵⁄₁₆″ use a "hairpin" clip retainer. ¼″ line connectors use a "duck bill" clip retainer.

Hairpin Clip

1. Clean all dirt and/or grease from the fitting. Spread the two clip legs about an ⅛″ (3mm) each to disengage from the fitting and pull the clip outward from the fitting. Use finger pressure only, do not use any tools.
2. Grasp the fitting and hose assembly and pull away from the steel line. Twist the fitting and hose assembly slightly while pulling, if necessary, when a sticking condition exists.
3. Inspect the hairpin clip for damage, replace the clip if necessary. Reinstall the clip in position on the fitting.
4. Inspect the fitting and inside of the connector to insure freedom of dirt or obstruction. Install fitting into the connector and push together. A click will be heard when the hairpin snaps into proper connection. Pull on the line to insure full engagement.

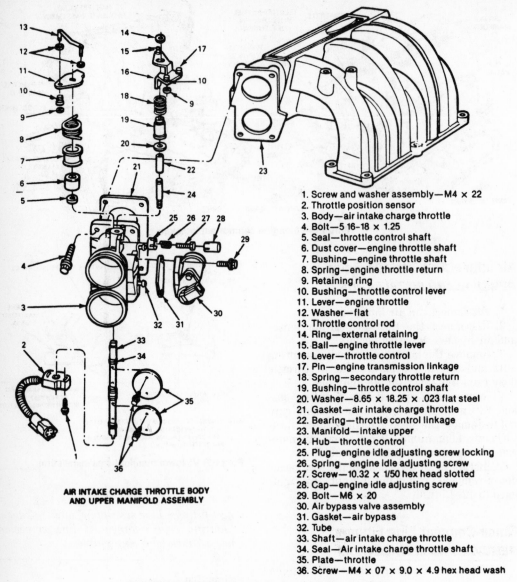

1. Screw and washer assembly—M4 × 22
2. Throttle position sensor
3. Body—air intake charge throttle
4. Bolt—5 16–18 × 1.25
5. Seal—throttle control shaft
6. Dust cover—engine throttle shaft
7. Bushing—engine throttle shaft
8. Spring—engine throttle return
9. Retaining ring
10. Bushing—throttle control lever
11. Lever—engine throttle
12. Washer—flat
13. Throttle control rod
14. Ring—external retaining
15. Ball—engine throttle lever
16. Lever—throttle control
17. Pin—engine transmission linkage
18. Spring—secondary throttle return
19. Bushing—throttle control shaft
20. Washer—8.65 × 18.25 × .023 flat steel
21. Gasket—air intake charge throttle
22. Bearing—throttle control linkage
23. Manifold—intake upper
24. Hub—throttle control
25. Plug—engine idle adjusting screw locking
26. Spring—engine idle adjusting screw
27. Screw—10.32 × 1/50 hex head slotted
28. Cap—engine idle adjusting screw
29. Bolt—M6 × 20
30. Air bypass valve assembly
31. Gasket—air bypass
32. Tube
33. Shaft—air intake charge throttle
34. Seal—Air intake charge throttle shaft
35. Plate—throttle
36. Screw—M4 × 07 × 9.0 × 4.9 hex head wash

**AIR INTAKE CHARGE THROTTLE BODY
AND UPPER MANIFOLD ASSEMBLY**

Ford EFI-V8 air intake throttle body and upper manifold

Duck Bill Clip

1. A special tool is available from Ford for removing the retaining clips (Ford Tool No. T82L–9500–AH). If the tool is not on hand see Step 2. Align the slot on the push connector disconnect tool with either tab on the retaining clip. Pull the line from the connector.

2. If the special clip tool is not available, use a pair of narrow 6″ (152mm) channel lock pliers with a jaw width of 0.2″ (5mm) or less. Align the jaws of the pliers with the openings of the fitting case and compress the part of the retaining clip that engages the case. Compressing the retaining clip will release the fitting which may be pulled from the connector.

Both sides of the clip must be compressed at the same time to disengage.

3. Inspect the retaining clip, fitting end and connector. Replace the clip if any damage is apparent.

4. Push the line into the steel connector until a click is heard, indicting the clip is in place. Pull on the line to check engagement.

Fuel Supply Manifold
REMOVAL AND INSTALLATION

1. Remove the gas tank fill cap. Relieve fuel system pressure by locating and disconnecting the electrical connection to either the fuel

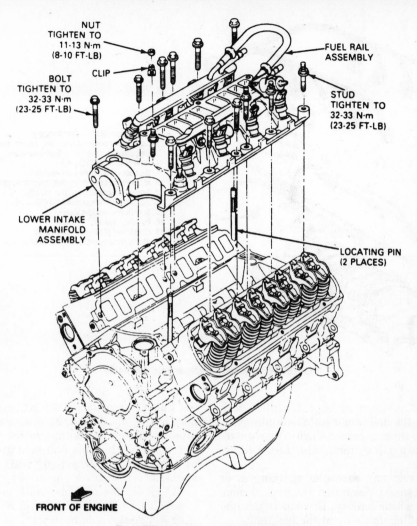

NUT
TIGHTEN TO
11-13 N·m
(8-10 FT-LB)

CLIP

BOLT
TIGHTEN TO
32-33 N·m
(23-25 FT-LB)

FUEL RAIL
ASSEMBLY

STUD
TIGHTEN TO
32-33 N·m
(23-25 FT-LB)

LOWER INTAKE
MANIFOLD
ASSEMBLY

LOCATING PIN
(2 PLACES)

FRONT OF ENGINE

Ford EFI-V8 lower manifold installation

pump relay, the inertia switch or the in-line high pressure fuel pump. Crank the engine for about ten seconds. If the engine starts, crank for an additional five seconds after the engine stalls. Reconnect the connector. Disconnect the negative battery cable. Remove the upper intake manifold assembly.

NOTE: *Special tool T81P-19623-G or equivalent is necessary to release the garter springs that secure the fuel line/hose connections.*

2. Disconnect the fuel crossover hose from the fuel supply manifold. Disconnect the fuel supply and return line connections at the fuel supply manifold.

3. Remove the fuel supply manifold retaining bolts. Carefully disengage the manifold from the fuel injectors and remove the manifold.

4. When installing: Make sure the injector caps are clean and free of contamination. Place the fuel supply manifold over each injector and seat the injectors into the manifold. Make sure the caps are seated firmly.

5. Torque the fuel supply manifold retaining bolts to 23–25 ft.lb. Install the remaining components in the reverse order of removal.

INJECTOR REPLACEMENT

Fuel injectors may be serviced after the fuel supply manifold is removed. Carefully disconnect the electrical harness connectors from individual injectors as required. Grasp the injector and pull up on it while gently rocking injector from side to side. Inspect the mounting O-rings and replace any that show deterioration.

Fuel Tank

REMOVAL AND INSTALLATION

NOTE: *This procedure will apply to either the main or auxiliary tank.*

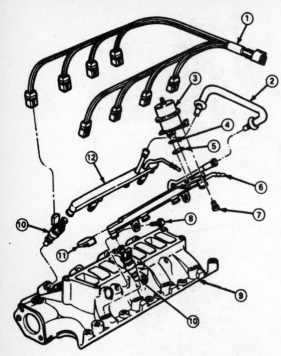

1. Wiring harness—fuel charging
2. Connector assembly—fuel injector manifold
3. Regulator assembly—fuel pressure
4. Seal 5 16 × .070 O-ring
5. Gasket—fuel pressure regulator
6. Manifold assembly—fuel injector fuel supply-LH
7. Screw—Socket head 5.0 × 0.8 × 10
8. Bolt—hex flange head 1 4-20 × .75
9. Manifold—intake lower
10. Injector assembly—fuel
11. Shield—fuel supply manifold
12. Manifold assembly—fuel injector fuel supply-RH

Ford EFI-V8 fuel charging manifold assembly

1. Insert a siphon through the filler neck and drain the fuel into a suitable container.

2. Raise the rear of the vehicle. If you are removing the auxiliary tank, raise the left side of the vehicle.

3. To avoid any chance of sparking at or near the tank(s), disconnect the ground cable from the vehicle battery. Disconnect the fuel gauge sending unit wire at the fuel tank.

4. Loosen the clamp on the fuel filler pipe hose at the filler pipe and disconnect the hose from the pipe.

5. Loosen the hose clamps, slide the clamps forward and disconnect the fuel line at the fuel gauge sending unit.

6. If the fuel gauge sending unit is to be removed, turn the unit retaining ring, and gasket, and remove the unit from the tank.

7. Remove the strap attaching nut at each tank mounting strap, swing the strap down, and lower the tank enough to gain access to the tank vent hose.

8. Disconnect the fuel tank vent hose at the top of the tank. Disconnect the fuel tank-to-separator tank lines at the fuel tank.

9. Lower the fuel tank and remove it from under the vehicle.

To install the fuel tank:

10. Position the forward edge of the tank to the frame crossmember, and connect the vent hose to the top of the tank. Connect the fuel tank-to-separator tank lines at the fuel tank.

11. Position the tank and mounting straps, and install the attaching nuts and flat washers.

NOTE: *On the auxiliary tank installation, the nuts on the J-bolts should be threaded 1.25" (32mm) in on the bolts.*

12. If the fuel gauge sending unit was removed, make sure that all of the old gasket material has been removed from the unit mounting surface on the fuel tank. Using a new gasket, position the fuel gauge sending unit to the fuel tank and secure it with the retaining ring.

13. Connect the fuel line at the fuel gauge sending unit and tighten the hose clamps securely. Install the drain plug, if so equipped.

14. Connect the fuel gauge sending unit wire to the sending unit.

15. Connect the filler pipe-to-tank hose at the filler pipe and install the hose clamp.

16. Connect the vehicle battery ground cable.

17. Fill the tank and check all connections for leaks.

18. Lower the vehicle.

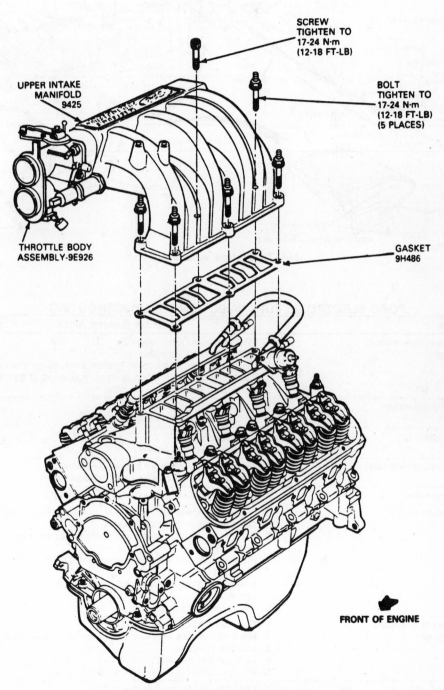

SCREW
TIGHTEN TO
17-24 N·m
(12-18 FT-LB)

BOLT
TIGHTEN TO
17-24 N·m
(12-18 FT-LB)
(5 PLACES)

UPPER INTAKE
MANIFOLD
9425

THROTTLE BODY
ASSEMBLY-9E926

GASKET
9H486

FRONT OF ENGINE

Ford EFI-V8 upper manifold and throttle body assembly

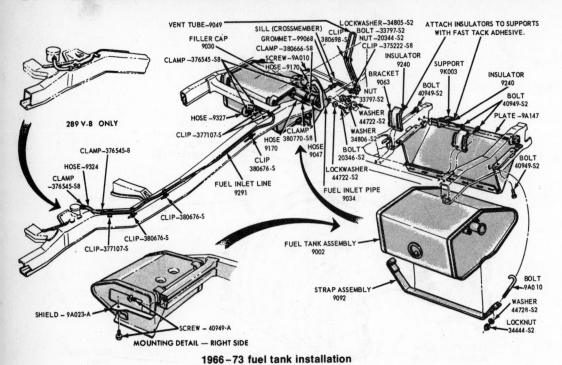

289 V-8 ONLY

1966-73 fuel tank installation

FORD ELECTRONIC FUEL INJECTION TROUBLESHOOTING

Symptom	Possible Problem Areas
Surging, backfire, misfire, runs rough	1. EEC distributor rotor registry 2. EGR solenoid(s)defective 3. Distributor, cap, body, rotor, ignition wires, plugs, coil defective 4. Pulse ring behind vibration damper misaligned or damaged 5. Spark plug fouling
Stalls on deceleration	1. EGR solenoid(s) or valve defective 2. EEC distributor rotor registry
Stalls at idle	1. Idle speed wrong 2. Throttle kicker not working
Hesitates on acceleration	1. Acceleration enrichment system defective 2. Fuel pump ballast bypass relay not working
Fuel pump noisy	1. Fuel pump ballast bypass relay not working
Engine won't start	1. Fuel pump power relay defective, no spark, EGR system defective, no or low fuel pressure 2. Crankshaft position sensor not seated, clearance wrong, defective 3. Pulse ring behind vibration damper misaligned, sensor tabs damaged 4. Power and ground wires open or shorted, poor electrical connections 5. Inertia switch tripped
Engine starts and stalls or runs rough	1. Fuel pump ballast wire defective 2. Manifold absolute pressure (MAP) sensor circuit not working 3. Low fuel pressure 4. EGR system problem 5. Microprocessor and calibration assembly faulty
Starts hard when cold	1. Cranking signal circuit faulty

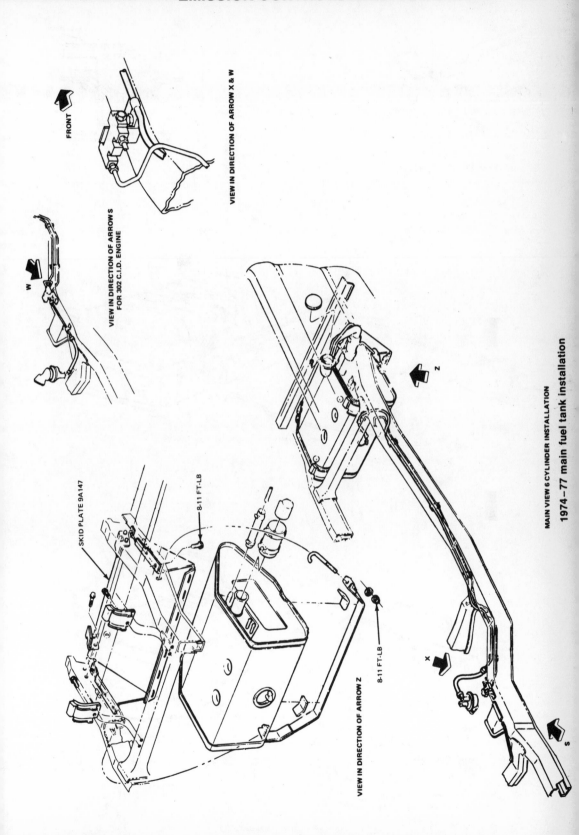

FRONT

VIEW IN DIRECTION OF ARROW X & W

VIEW IN DIRECTION OF ARROWS
FOR 302 C.I.D. ENGINE

W

Z

X

S

SKID PLATE 9A147

8-11 FT-LB

8-11 FT-LB

VIEW IN DIRECTION OF ARROW Z

MAIN VIEW 6 CYLINDER INSTALLATION

1974–77 main fuel tank installation

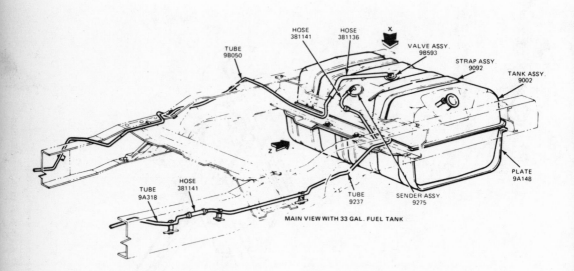

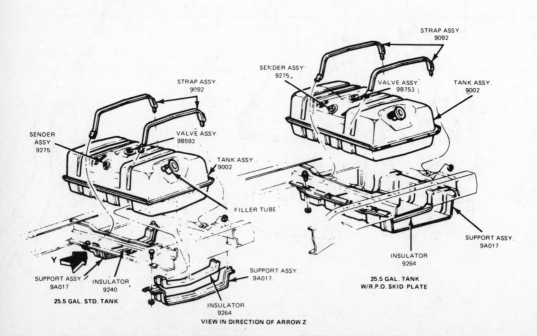

1978–79 fuel tank installation, standard or optional tanks

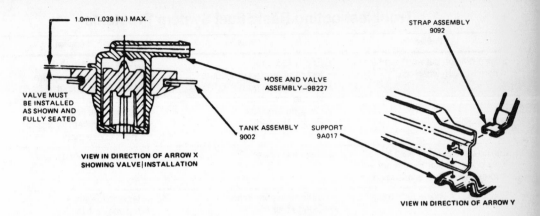

1.0mm (.039 IN.) MAX.

VALVE MUST
BE INSTALLED
AS SHOWN AND
FULLY SEATED

HOSE AND VALVE
ASSEMBLY—9B227

TANK ASSEMBLY
9002

SUPPORT
9A017

STRAP ASSEMBLY
9092

**VIEW IN DIRECTION OF ARROW X
SHOWING VALVE INSTALLATION**

VIEW IN DIRECTION OF ARROW Y

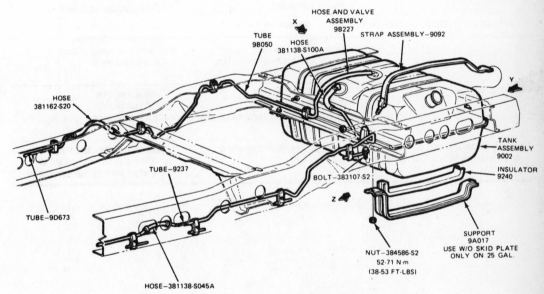

TUBE
9B050

HOSE AND VALVE
ASSEMBLY
9B227

HOSE
381138-S100A

X

STRAP ASSEMBLY—9092

Y

HOSE
381162-S20

HOSE
381138-S045A

TUBE—9237

TUBE—9D673

BOLT—383107-S2

Z

TANK
ASSEMBLY
9002

INSULATOR
9240

NUT—384586-S2
52-71 N·m
(38-53 FT-LBS)

SUPPORT
9A017
USE W/O SKID PLATE
ONLY ON 25 GAL.

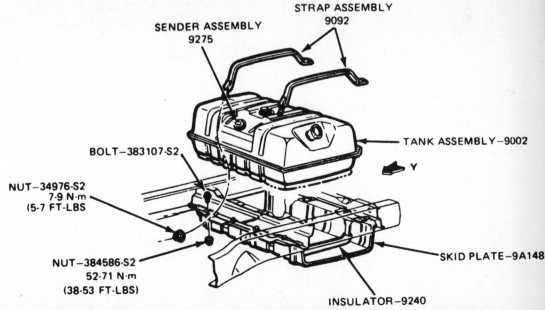

STRAP ASSEMBLY
9092

SENDER ASSEMBLY
9275

BOLT—383107-S2

NUT—34976-S2
7-9 N·m
(5-7 FT-LBS

NUT—384586-S2
52-71 N·m
(38-53 FT-LBS)

INSULATOR—9240

TANK ASSEMBLY—9002

Y

SKID PLATE—9A148

VIEW IN DIRECTION OF ARROW Z

1980 and later fuel tank installation, standard or optional tanks

Troubleshooting Basic Fuel System Problems

Problem	Cause	Solution
Engine cranks, but won't start (or is hard to start) when cold	• Empty fuel tank • Incorrect starting procedure • Defective fuel pump • No fuel in carburetor • Clogged fuel filter • Engine flooded • Defective choke	• Check for fuel in tank • Follow correct procedure • Check pump output • Check for fuel in the carburetor • Replace fuel filter • Wait 15 minutes; try again • Check choke plate
Engine cranks, but is hard to start (or does not start) when hot— (presence of fuel is assumed)	• Defective choke	• Check choke plate
Rough idle or engine runs rough	• Dirt or moisture in fuel • Clogged air filter • Faulty fuel pump	• Replace fuel filter • Replace air filter • Check fuel pump output
Engine stalls or hesitates on acceleration	• Dirt or moisture in the fuel • Dirty carburetor • Defective fuel pump • Incorrect float level, defective accelerator pump	• Replace fuel filter • Clean the carburetor • Check fuel pump output • Check carburetor
Poor gas mileage	• Clogged air filter • Dirty carburetor • Defective choke, faulty carburetor adjustment	• Replace air filter • Clean carburetor • Check carburetor
Engine is flooded (won't start accompanied by smell of raw fuel)	• Improperly adjusted choke or carburetor	• Wait 15 minutes and try again, without pumping gas pedal • If it won't start, check carburetor

Chassis Electrical

5

UNDERSTANDING AND TROUBLESHOOTING ELECTRICAL SYSTEMS

For any electrical system to operate, it must make a complete circuit. This simply means that the power flow from the battery must make a complete circle. When an electrical component is operating, power flows from the battery to the component, passes through the component causing it to perform its function (lighting a light bulb, for example) and then returns to the battery through the ground of the circuit. This ground is usually (but not always) the metal part of the vehicle on which the electrical component is mounted.

Perhaps the easiest way to visualize this is to think of connecting a light bulb with two wires attached to it to your vehicle battery. The battery in your vehicle has two posts (negative and positive). If one of the two wires attached to the light bulb was attached to the negative post of the battery and the other wire was attached to the positive post of the battery, you would have a complete circuit. Current from the battery would flow out one post, through the wire attached to it and then to the light bulb, causing it to light. It would then leave the light bulb, travel through the other wire, and return to the other post of the battery.

The normal automotive circuit differs from this simple example in two ways. First, instead of having a return wire from the bulb to the battery, the light bulb returns the current to the battery through the chassis of the vehicle. Since the negative battery cable is attached to the chassis and the chassis is made of electrically conductive metal, the chassis of the vehicle can serve as a ground wire to complete the circuit. Secondly, most automotive circuits contain switches to turn components on and off as required.

There are many types of switches, but the most common simply serves to prevent the passage of current when it is turned off. Since the switch is a part of the circle necessary for a complete circuit, it operates to leave an opening in the circuit, and thus an incomplete or open circuit, when it is turned off.

Some electrical components which require a large amount of current to operate also have a relay in their circuit. Since these circuits carry a large amount of current, the thickness of the wire (gauge size) in the circuit is also greater. If this large wire were connected from the component to the control switch on the instrument panel, and then back to the component, a voltage drop would occur in the circuit. To prevent this potential drop in voltage, an electromagnetic switch (relay) is used. The large wires in the circuit are connected from the vehicle battery to one side of the relay, and from the opposite side of the relay to the component. The relay is normally open, preventing current from passing through the circuit. An additional, smaller, wire is connected from the relay to the control switch to the circuit. When the control switch is turned on, it completes the circuit. This closes the relay and allows current to flow from the battery to the component. The horn, headlight, and starter circuits are three which use relays.

You have probably noticed how the vehicle's instrument panel lights get brighter the faster you rev the engine. This happens because you alternator (which supplies the battery) puts out more current at speeds above idle. This is normal. However, it is possible for larger surges of current to pass through the electrical system of your car. If this surge of current were to reach an electrical component, it could burn the component out. To prevent this from happening, fuses are connected into the current supply wires of most of the major electrical systems of your vehicle. The fuse serves to head off the surge at the pass. When an electrical current of excessive power passes through the component's fuse, the fuse blows out and breaks the circuit, saving it from destruction.

The fuse also protects the component from damage if the power supply wire to the component is grounded before the current reaches the component.

There is another important rule to the complete circle circuit. Every complete circuit from a power source must include a component which is using the power from the power source. If you were to disconnect the light bulb (from the previous example of a light bulb being connected to the battery by two wires together (take our word for it – don't try it) the result would literally be shocking. A similar thing happens (on a smaller scale) when the power supply wire to a component or the electrical component itself becomes grounded before the normal ground connection for the circuit. To prevent damage to the system, the fuse for the circuit blows to interrupt the circuit, protecting the components from damage. Because grounding a wire from a power source makes a complete circuit, less the required component to use the power, this phenomenon is called a short circuit. The most common causes of short circuits are: the rubber insulation on a wire breaking or rubbing through to expose the current carrying core of the wire to a metal part of the vehicle, or a short switch.

Some electrical systems on the vehicle are protected by a circuit breaker which is, basically, a self-repairing fuse. When either of the above described events takes place in a system which is protected by a circuit breaker, the circuit breaker opens the circuit the same way a fuse does. However, when either the short is removed from the circuit or the surge subsides, the circuit breaker resets itself and does not have to be replaced as a fuse does.

The final protective device in the chassis electrical system is a fuse link. A fuse link is a wire that acts as a fuse. It is connected between the starter relay and the main wiring harness for the car. This connection is under the hood, very near a similar fuse link which protects all the chassis electrical components. It is the probable cause of trouble when none of the electrical components function, unless the battery is disconnected or dead.

Electrical problems generally fall into one of three areas:

1. The component that is not functioning is not receiving current.
2. The component itself is not functioning.
3. The component is not properly grounded.

Problems that fall into the first category are by far the most complicated. It is the current supply system to the component which contains all the switches, relays, fuses, etc.

The electrical system can be checked with a test light and a jumper wire. A test light is a device that looks like a pointed screwdriver with a wire attached to it. It has a light bulb in its handle. A jumper wire is a piece of insulated wire with an alligator clip attached to each end.

If a light bulb is not working, you must follow a systematic plan to determine which of the three causes is the villain.

1. Turn on the switch that controls the inoperable bulb.
2. Disconnect the power supply wire from the bulb.
3. Attach the ground wire on the test light to a good metal ground.
4. Touch the probe end of the test light to the end of the power supply wire that was disconnected from the bulb. If the bulb is receiving current, the test light will go on.

NOTE: *If the bulb is one which works only when the ignition key is turned on (turn signal), make sure the key is turned on.*

If the test light does not go on, then the problem is in the circuit between the battery and the bulb. As mentioned before, this includes all the switches, fuses, and relays in the system. The problem is an open circuit between the battery and the bulb. If the fuse is blown and, when replaced, immediately blows again, there is a short circuit in the system which must be located and repaired. If there is a switch in the system, bypass it with a jumper wire. This is done by connecting one end of the jumper wire to the power supply wire into the switch, and the other end of the jumper wire to the wire coming out of the switch. If the test light lights with the jumper wire installed, the switch or whatever was bypassed is defective.

NOTE: *Never substitute the jumper wire for the bulb, as the bulb is the component required to use the power from the power source.*

5. If the bulb in the test light goes on, then the current is getting to the bulb that is not working in the vehicle. This eliminates the first of the three possible causes. Connect the power supply wire and connect a jumper wire from the bulb to a good metal ground. Do this with the switch which controls the bulb turned on, and also the ignition switch turned on if it is required for the light to work. If the bulb works with the jumper wire installed, then it has a bad ground. This is usually caused by the metal area on which the bulb mounts to the car being coated with some type of foreign matter or rust.

6. If neither test located the source of the

trouble, then the light bulb itself is defective.

The above test procedure can be applied to any of the components of the chassis electrical system by substituting the component that is not working for the light bulb. Remember that for any electrical system to work, all connections must be clean and tight.

HEATING AND AIR CONDITIONING

Heater, A/C Blower Motor

REMOVAL AND INSTALLATION

1966–77

1. Disconnect the electrical connectors and the ground wire from the top of the heater.

2. Remove the screws retaining the motor to the plenum chamber and remove the motor assembly.

3. Loosen the blower wheel allen screw and remove the wheel.

4. Remove the motor from the mounting plate.

5. Install the motor to the mounting plate.

6. Install the blower wheel.

7. Position the motor to the plenum chamber. Install the retaining screws.

8. Connect the electrical lead and the ground wire.

9. Check the operation of the blower motor.

1978–79 Standard Heater, Without Air Conditioning

REMOVAL

1. Disconnect the temperature and function control Bowden cables from the heater housing. This must be done to prevent damage to the cables.

2. Disconnect the wires from the blower resistor.

3. Remove five screws attaching the air inlet (vent) duct to the heater housing.

4. Disconnect the blower wires.

5. Drain the radiator and remove the heater hoses from the heater core.

6. Remove three heater stud retaining nuts and remove heater.

7. Remove gasket between the heater hose ends and the dash panel at core tubes.

8. Remove two screws and two nuts attaching blower to heater.

9. Remove blower fan from motor shaft, and remove motor from mounting plate.

INSTALLATION

1. Install new motor on mounting plate and install blower fan on motor shaft.

2. Install blower and motor in heater.

3. Position heater assembly in vehicle and install three stud retaining nuts.

4. Connect heater hoses to heater core and fill radiator.

5. Connect blower motor wires.

6. Place defroster nozzle on heater so that the defroster and heater openings are in the up position and there is no air leak around the seal.

7. Install air inlet (vent) duct to heater. Plush duct firmly against seal on side cowl and tighten five attaching screws.

8. Connect wires in blower motor resistor.

9. Connect temperature and function control cables to heater, and adjust the cables.

10. Reinstall gasket between the heater hose ends and the dash panel at core ends.

11. Fill cooling system.

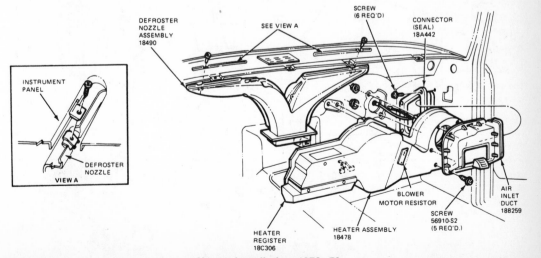

Heater installation, 1978–79

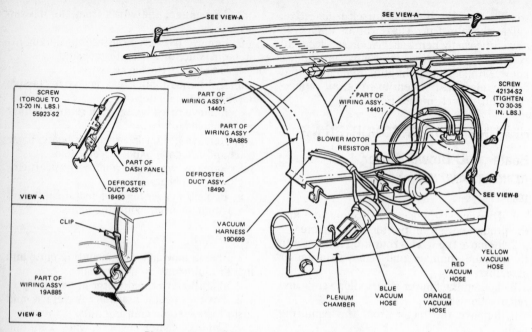

Plenum chamber and nozzle assembly, 1978–79

1978–79 Deluxe Hi-Lo Heater, Without Air Conditioning

REMOVAL

1. Disconnect the battery cable, remove the carburetor air cleaner and partially drain the coolant system.

2. Remove the heater hoses from the heater core.

3. Remove the glove box liner and remove the register duct by pulling from the instrument panel register and releasing the clip at the plenum.

4. Disconnect the right cowl outside air inlet vacuum hose from the outside/recirculating door vacuum motor.

5. Remove the rear housing from under the instrument panel. Remove the outside air inlet duct from the rear housing (4 nuts and 1 bolt)

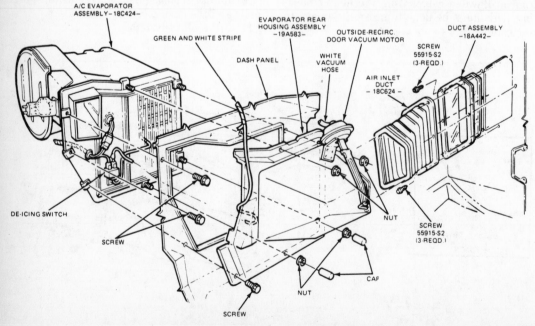

Evaporator rear housing, 1978–79

and install one upper nut to retain heater housing-to-dash after rear housing is removed.

6. Remove two screws retaining plenum-to-dash (above transmission tunnel) and two screws to heater housing and remove the plenum.

7. Install a piece of protective tape on A-pillar inner cowl panel, at lower right corner of instrument panel.

8. Remove the lower right instrument panel-to-A-pillar bolt to hold the panel in the rearward position.

9. Remove the heater core (3 screws retaining 2 plates).

10. Remove the temperature blend door (snaps off).

11. Remove the temperature blend door arm support (2 screws) and pivot arm retainer (1 screw).

12. Remove blower motor (2 screws) and remove blower wheel.

INSTALLATION

1. Transfer blower to blower motor and panel assembly.

2. Install door arm pivot retainer (1 screw) and door arm support (2 screws).

3. Install the temperature blend door (snaps on).

4. Install heater core.

5. Install the plenum (4 screws).

6. Connect blower wires.

7. Remove heater housing upper retaining nut and install the heater outlet (4 nuts and 1 bolt). Position the air inlet duct.

8. Connect the white vacuum hose to the outside/recirculating door vacuum motor.

9. Reposition the instrument panel, install the retaining bolts and remove the protective tape at the A-pillar inner cowl panel, lower right corner of instrument panel.

10. Install the right register duct assembly and install the glove box liner.

11. Connect heater hoses to the heater core assembly.

12. Fill cooling system, install the air cleaner and connect the battery cable to the battery.

13. Check blower motor operation.

1978–79 With Air Conditioning

REMOVAL (Without Discharging the A/C System)

1. Disconnect the battery cable, remove the carburetor air cleaner and partially drain the coolant system.

2. Remove the heater hoses from the heater core.

3. From under the hood, remove A/C hose support bracket from the cowl (one screw).

4. Remove the insulation tape from the expansion valve and sensing bulb. Then remove the cover plate and seal from the evaporator housing at the expansion valve (two screws).

5. Remove the glove box liner and remove the A/C duct by pulling from the instrument panel register and releasing the clip at the plenum.

6. Disconnect the right cowl fresh air inlet vacuum hose from the fresh air door vacuum motor.

7. Remove the evaporator rear housing from under the instrument panel. Then, remove the fresh air inlet tube from the evaporator rear housing (4 nuts and 1 bolt) and install one upper nut to retain evaporator housing-to-dash after rear housing is removed.

8. Disconnect wires from the de-icing switch and pull capillary tube out of evaporator core. Remove the de-icing switch mounting plate (four screws).

9. Remove two screws retaining plenum-to-dash (above transmission tunnel) and two screws to evaporator case and remove the plenum.

10. Install a piece of protective tape on A-pillar inner cowl panel, at lower right corner of instrument panel.

11. Then, remove the lower right instrument panel-to-A-pillar bolt and lower the center instrument panel brace, bolt and nut.

12. Position the instrument panel rearward and install the A-pillar bolt to hold the panel in the rearward position.

13. Remove four evaporator retaining screws.

14. Position the evaporator away from the case and secure it rearward and upward. Remove evaporator sealing grommet.

15. Remove heater core (3 screws retaining 2 plates).

16. Remove A/C-heat door (snaps off).

17. Remove A/C-heat door arm support (2 screws) and pivot arm retainer (1 screw).

18. Remove blower motor (2 screws) and remove blower wheel.

INSTALLATION

1. Transfer blower wheel to blower motor and panel assembly.

2. Install door arm pivot retainer (1 screw) and door arm support (2 screws).

3. Install A/C/heat door (snaps on).

4. Install heater core.

5. Remove the retainer that held the evaporator away from the case, install evaporator and tube sealing grommet.

6. Install the plenum (4 screws).

7. Install the de-icing switch mounting plate, install de-icing switch capillary tube back into evaporator core and position blower wire grommet.

8. Connect blower and de-icing switch wires.

9. Remove upper evaporator case retaining nut and install the evaporator outlet (4 nuts and 1 bolt). Then, position the air inlet bellows.

10. Connect the right cowl fresh air inlet vacuum hose to the fresh air door vacuum motor.

11. Reposition the instrument panel, install the retaining bolts and remove the protective tape at the A-pillar inner cowl panel, lower right corner of instrument panel.

12. Install the right A/C duct assembly and install the glove box liner.

13. Install seal and cover plate to the evaporator case at the expansion valve.

14. Install insulation tape over the expansion valve and sensing bulb.

15. Install the A/C hose support bracket-to-cowl.

16. Connect heater hoses to the heater core assembly.

17. Fill cooling system, install the carburetor air cleaner and connect the battery cable to the battery.

18. Check blower motor operation.

1980–81 Comfort Vent Heaters, Without Air Conditioning

REMOVAL

1. Disconnect the motor wires at the hard shell connectors.

2. Disconnect the blower motor air cooling tube from the motor.

3. Remove four (4) blower motor mounting plate attaching screws and remove the motor and wheel assembly from the blower housing.

4. Remove the hub clamp spring from the blower wheel hub and the retainer from the motor shaft. Then, remove the blower wheel from the motor shaft.

INSTALLATION

1. Position the blower wheel on the blower motor shaft. Then, install a new hub clamp spring on the blower hub as shown. The hub clamp spring is included with a new blower wheel but not with the blower motor.

2. Install a new flange gasket on the blower motor flange.

3. Position the blower motor and wheel assembly in the blower housing and install the four (4) attaching screws.

NOTE: *The wire clamp should be installed under the screw closest to the resistor assembly.*

4. Cement the blower motor air tube on the nipple of the blower housing with RTV silicone adhesive.

5. Connect the blower motor wires at the hard shell connectors.

6. Check the blower motor for proper operation.

1980–86 Standard & High Output Heaters, Without Air Conditioning

REMOVAL

1. Disconnect the motor wire at the hard shell connector and the ground wire at the ground screw.

2. Remove four (4) screws attaching the blower motor and wheel to the heater case.

3. Remove the blower motor and wheel from the heater case.

4. Remove the blower wheel hub clamp spring and the tab lock washer from the motor shaft. Then, pull the blower wheel from the motor shaft.

INSTALLATION

1. Install the blower wheel on the blower motor shaft.

2. Install the hub clamp spring on the blower hub.

3. Position the blower motor and wheel to the heater case, and install the four (4) attaching screws.

4. Connect the blower motor wires and check the blower motor for proper operation.

1980–86 With Air Conditioning

REMOVAL (WITHOUT DISCHARGING THE A/C SYSTEM)

1. Disconnect the motor wires at the hard shell connectors.

2. Disconnect the blower motor air cooling tube from the motor.

3. Remove four (4) blower motor mounting plate attaching screws and remove the motor and wheel assembly from the blower housing.

4. Remove the hub clamp spring from the blower wheel hub and the retainer from the motor shaft. Then, remove the blower wheel from the motor shaft.

INSTALLATION

1. Position the blower wheel on the blower motor shaft to the dimension shown. Then, install a new hub clamp spring on the blower hub as shown. The hub clamp spring is included with a new blower wheel but not with the blower motor.

2. Install a new flange gasket on the blower motor flange.

3. Position the blower motor and wheel assembly in the blower housing and install the four (4) attaching screws.

Note: *The wire clamp should be installed under the screw closest to the resistor assembly.*

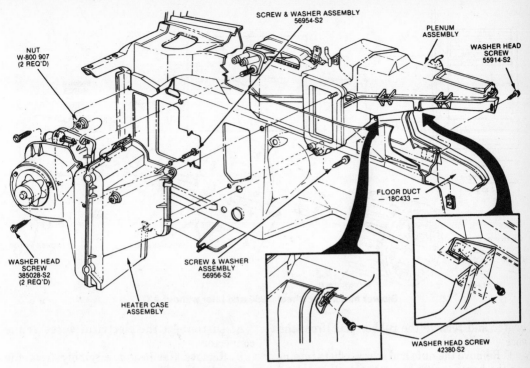

NUT
W-800 907
(2 REQ'D)

SCREW & WASHER ASSEMBLY
56954-S2

PLENUM
ASSEMBLY

WASHER HEAD
SCREW
55914-S2

FLOOR DUCT
— 18C433 —

WASHER HEAD
SCREW
385028-S2
(2 REQ'D)

SCREW & WASHER
ASSEMBLY
56956-S2

HEATER CASE
ASSEMBLY

WASHER HEAD SCREW
42380-S2

Heater case and plenum assemblies, 1980–81

4. Cement the blower motor air tube on the nipple of the blower housing with RTV silicone adhesive.

5. Connect the blower motor wires at the hard shell connectors.

6. Check the blower motor for proper operation.

Heater Core
REMOVAL AND INSTALLATION

1966–77

1. Drain the cooling system.
2. Disconnect the two heater hoses at the

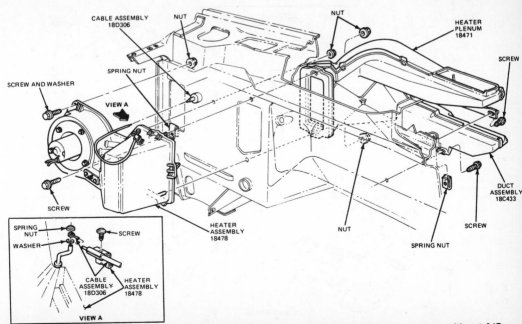

CABLE ASSEMBLY
18D306

NUT

NUT

HEATER
PLENUM
18471

SCREW AND WASHER

SPRING NUT

SCREW

VIEW A

SCREW

HEATER
ASSEMBLY
18478

NUT

DUCT
ASSEMBLY
18C433

SCREW

SPRING NUT

SPRING
NUT

SCREW

WASHER

CABLE
ASSEMBLY
18D306

HEATER
ASSEMBLY
18478

VIEW A

Heater case and plenum assemblies, 1980 and later standard and high output units without A/C

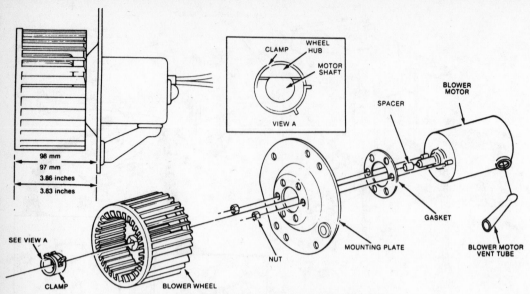

Blower motor and wheel, 1980 and later without A/C

heater and remove the rubber pads from the core.

3. Remove the nuts and star washers retaining the heater assembly to the dash panel.

4. Disconnect the right and left defroster hoses at the plenum.

5. Disconnect the fresh air inlet at the cowl. Rest the heater on the floor.

6. Disconnect the heat/defrost door cable at the door crank arm.

7. Disconnect the outside air door cable at the crank arm.

8. Disconnect the electrical wires at the connector.

9. Remove the heater assembly from the vehicle.

10. Remove the screws retaining the rear cover. Remove the clip retaining the core in the case and remove the core.

11. Transfer the seals from the old heater core to the new heater core.

12. Position the core in the case. Install the retaining clip. Position the cover and install the retaining screws.

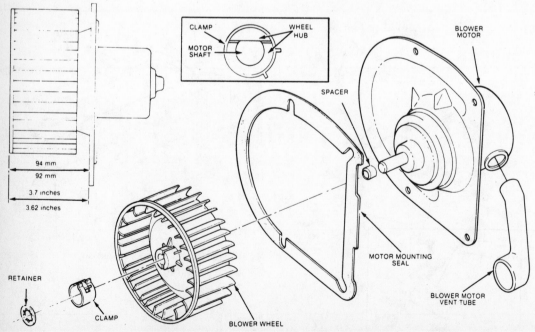

Blower motor and wheel, 1980 and later with A/C

13. Position the heater assembly on the floor in the vehicle. Connect the wire connectors.

14. Connect and adjust the outside air door control cable.

15. Connect and adjust the heat/defrost door control cable.

16. Position the heater assembly to the dash and install the nuts and washers.

17. Position the heater core pads over the core and connect both hoses.

18. Connect the defroster hoses and fresh air intake.

19. Fill the cooling system with the proper coolant mixture.

20. Check the heater operation and check for leaks.

1978–79 Without Air Conditioning

REMOVAL

1. Disconnect the temperature and function control Bowden cables from the heater housing. This must be done to prevent damage to the cables.

2. Disconnect the wires from the blower resistor.

3. Remove five screws attaching the air inlet (vent) duct to the heater housing.

4. Disconnect the blower wires.

5. Drain the radiator and remove the heater hoses from the heater core.

6. Remove three heater stud retaining nuts and remove heater.

7. Remove gasket between the heater hose ends and the dash panel at core tubes.

8. Remove heater core cover and gasket (four screws).

9. Pull heater core and lower support from heater.

INSTALLATION

1. Install foam gaskets on heater core and install in heater assembly.

2. Install the core seal and cover plate.

3. Position heater assembly in vehicle and install three stud retaining nuts.

4. Connect heater hoses to heater core and fill radiator.

5. Connect blower motor wires.

6. Place defroster nozzle on heater so that the defroster and heater openings are in the up position, and there is no air leak around the seal.

7. Install air inlet (vent) duct to heater. Push duct firmly against seal on side cowl and tighten five attaching screws.

8. Connect wires to blower motor resistor.

9. Connect temperature and function control cables to heater, and adjust the cables.

10. Reinstall gasket between the heater hose ends and the dash panel at core ends.

11. Fill Cooling System.

1978–79 Deluxe HI-LO Heater, Without Air Conditioning

REMOVAL

1. Disconnect the battery cable, remove the carburetor air cleaner and partially drain the coolant system.

2. Remove the heater hoses from the heater core.

3. Remove the glove box liner and remove the register duct by pulling from the instrument panel register and releasing the clip at the plenum.

4. Disconnect the right cowl outside air inlet vacuum hose from the outside/recirculating door vacuum motor.

5. Remove the rear housing from under the instrument panel. Remove the outside air inlet duct from the rear housing (4 nuts and 1 bolt) and install one upper nut to retain heater housing-to-dash after rear housing is removed.

6. Remove two screws retaining plenum-to-dash (above transmission tunnel) and two screws to heater housing and remove the plenum.

7. Install a piece of protective tape on A-pillar inner cowl panel, at lower right corner of instrument panel.

8. Remove the lower right instrument panel-to-A-pillar bolt and lower the center instrument panel brace, bolt and nut.

9. Position the instrument panel rearward and install the A-pillar bolt to hold the panel in the rearward position.

10. Remove heater core (3 screws retaining 2 plates).

11. Remove the temperature blend door (snaps off).

12. Remove the temperature blend door arm support (2 screws) and pivot arm retainer (1 screw).

13. Remove blower motor (2 screws) and remove blower wheel.

INSTALLATION

1. Transfer blower wheel to blower motor and panel assembly.

2. Install door arm pivot retainer (1 screw) and door arm support (2 screws).

3. Install the temperature blend door (snaps on).

4. Install heater core.

5. Install the plenum (4 screws).

6. Connect blower wires.

7. Remove heater housing upper retaining

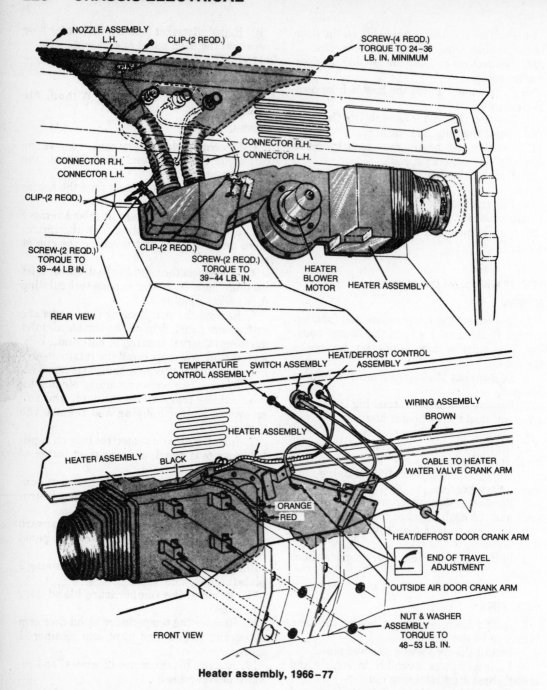

Heater assembly, 1966–77

nut and install the heater outlet (4 nuts and 1 bolt). Position the air inlet duct.

8. Connect the white vacuum hose to the outside/recirculating door vacuum motor.

9. Reposition the instrument panel, install the retaining bolts and remove the protective tape at the A-pillar inner cowl panel, lower right corner of instrument panel.

10. Install the right register duct assembly and install the glove box liner.

11. Connect heater hoses to the heater core assembly.

12. Fill cooling system, install the air cleaner and connect the battery cable to the battery.

13. Check blower motor operation.

1978–79 With Air Conditioning

REMOVAL (WITHOUT DISCHARGING A/C SYSTEM)

1. Disconnect the battery cable, remove the carburetor air cleaner and partially drain the coolant system.

2. Remove the heater hoses from the heater core.

3. From under the hood, remove A/C hose support bracket from the cowl (one screw).

4. Remove the insulation tape from the expansion valve and sensing bulb. Then remove the cover plate and seal from the evaporator housing at the expansion valve (two screws).

5. Remove the glove box liner and remove the A/C duct by pulling from the instrument panel register and releasing the clip at the plenum.

6. Disconnect the right cowl fresh air inlet vacuum hose from the fresh air door vacuum motor.

7. Remove the evaporator rear housing from under the instrument panel. Then, remove the fresh air inlet tube from the evaporator rear housing (4 nuts and 1 bolt) and install one upper nut to retain evaporator housing-to-dash after rear housing is removed.

8. Disconnect wires from the de-icing switch and pull capillary tube out of evaporator core. Remove the de-icing switch mounting plate (four screws).

9. Remove two screws retaining plenum-to-dash (above transmission tunnel) and two screws to evaporator case and remove the plenum.

10. Install a piece of protective tape on A-pillar inner cowl panel, at lower right corner of instrument panel.

11. Then, remove the lower right instrument panel-to-A-pillar bolt and lower the center instrument panel brace, bolt and nut.

12. Position the instrument panel rearward and install the A-pillar bolt to hold the panel in the rearward position.

13. Remove four evaporator retaining screws.

14. Position the evaporator away from the case and secure it rearward and upward. Remove evaporator sealing grommet.

15. Remove heater core (3 screws retaining 2 plates).

16. Remove A/C-heat door (snaps off).

17. Remove A/C-heat door arm support (2 screws) and pivot arm retainer (1 screw).

INSTALLATION

1. Install door arm pivot retainer (1 screw) and door arm support (2 screws).

2. Install A/C-heat door (snaps on).

3. Install heater core.

4. Remove the retainer that held the evaporator away from the case, install evaporator and tube sealing grommet.

5. Install the plenum (4 screws).

6. Install the de-icing switch mounting plate, install de-icing switch capillary tube back into evaporator core and position blower wire grommet.

7. Connect blower and de-icing switch wires.

8. Remove upper evaporator case retaining nut and install the evaporator outlet (4 nuts and 1 bolt). Then, position the air inlet bellows.

9. Connect the right cowl fresh air inlet vacuum hose to the fresh air door vacuum motor.

10. Reposition the instrument panel, install the retaining bolts and remove the protective tape at the A-pillar inner cowl panel, lower right corner of instrument panel.

11. Install the right A/C duct assembly and install the glove box liner.

12. Install seal and cover plate to the evaporator case at the expansion valve.

13. Install insulation tape over the expansion valve and sensing bulb.

14. Install the A/C hose support bracket-to-cowl.

15. Connect heater hoses to the heater core assembly.

16. Fill cooling system, install the carburetor air cleaner and connect the battery cable to the battery.

17. Check blower motor operation.

1980–81 Comfort Vent Heaters, Without Air Conditioning

REMOVAL

1. Disconnect the heater hoses from the heater core tubes and plug the hoses with suitable 5/8" (16mm) plugs.

2. Remove the glove compartment liner.

3. Remove two (2) spring clips attaching the heater core cover to the plenum along the top edge of the heater core cover.

4. Remove eight (8) screws attaching the heater core cover to the plenum and remove the cover.

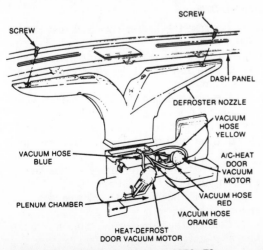

A/C-heater control connections, 1978–79

5. Remove the heater core from the plenum taking care not to spill coolant from the core.

INSTALLATION

1. Install the heater core in the plenum.
2. Install the heater core cover (eight (8) screws and two (2) spring clips along the top edge of the cover).
3. Install the glove compartment liner.
4. Connect the heater hoses to the heater core. Tighten the hose clamps.
5. Add coolant to raise the coolant level to specification.
6. Check the system for proper operation and for coolant leaks.

1980–81 Standard & High Output Heaters, Without Air Conditioning

REMOVAL

1. Disconnect the temperature cable from the temperature blend door and the mounting bracket on top of the heater case.
2. Disconnect the wires from the blower motor resistor and the blower motor.
3. Disconnect the heater hoses from the heater core and plug the hoses with suitable 5/8" (16mm) plugs.
4. Working under the instrument panel, remove two (2) nuts retaining the left end of the heater case and the right end of the plenum to the dash panel.
5. In the engine compartment, remove one (1) screw attaching the top center of the heater case to the dash panel.
6. Remove two (2) screws attaching the right end of the heater case to the dash panel, and remove the heater case from the vehicle.
7. Remove nine (9) screws and one (1) bolt and nut attaching the heater housing plate to the heater case, and remove the heater housing plate.
8. Remove three (3) screws attaching the heater core frame to the heater case and remove the frame.
9. Remove the heater core and seal from the heater case.

INSTALLATION

1. Position the heater core and seal in the heater case.
2. Install the heater core frame (3 screws).
3. Position the heater housing plate on the heater case and install the nine (9) screws and one (1) bolt and nut.
4. Position the heater case to the dash panel and install the three (3) attaching screws.
5. Working in the passenger compartment, install two (2) nuts to retain the heater case and plenum right end to the dash panel.

6. Connect the heater hoses to the heater core. Tighten the hose clamps.
7. Connect the wires to the blower motor resistor assembly.
8. Connect the blower motor wires.
9. Position (slide) the self-adjusting clip on the temperature cable to a position approximately one 1" (25.4mm) from the cable end loop.
10. Snap the temperature cable on the cable mounting bracket of the heater case. Then, position the self-adjusting clip on the door crank arm.
11. Adjust the temperature cable.
12. Check the system for proper operation.

1982–86 Standard & High Output Heaters, Without Air Conditioning

REMOVAL

1. Disconnect the temperature cable from the temperature blend door and the mounting bracket on top of the heater case.
2. Disconnect the wires from the blower motor resistor and the blower motor.
3. Disconnect the heater hoses from the heater core and plug the hoses with suitable 5/8" (16mm) plugs.
4. Working under the instrument panel, remove three nuts retaining the left end of the heater case and the right end of the plenum in the dash panel.
5. Remove two screws attaching the right end of the heater case to the dash panel, and remove the heater case from the vehicle.
6. Remove eleven screws and one bolt and nut attaching the heater housing plate to the heater case, and remove the heater housing plate.
7. Remove the heater core and seal from the heater case.

INSTALLATION

1. Position the heater core and seal in the heater case.
2. Position the heater housing plate on the heater case and install the eleven screws and one bolt and nut.
3. Position the heater case to the dash panel and install the two attaching screws.
4. Working in the passenger compartment, install three nuts to retain the heater case and plenum right end to the dash panel.
5. Connect the heater hoses to the heater core. Tighten the hose clamps.
6. Connect the wires to the blower motor resistor assembly.
7. Connect the wire harness connector to the blower motor.
8. Position the temperature cable pigtail on

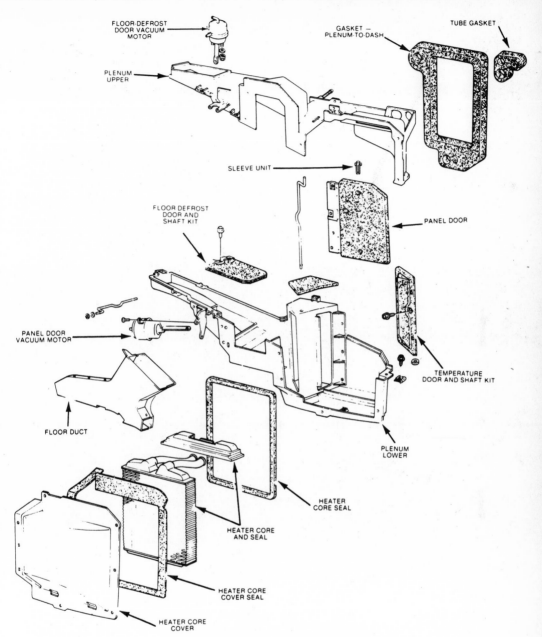

Comfort Vent heater plenum, 1980–81

the temperature door crank arm with the pigtail up. Be sure a flat washer is placed under the pigtail. Then, install a new pushnut to retain the pigtail on the crank arm.

9. Position the temperature cable flag to the mounting bracket and install the attaching screw.

10. Check the system for proper operation.

1980–86 With Air Conditioning

REMOVAL (WITHOUT DISCHARGING THE A/C SYSTEM)

1. Disconnect the heater hoses from the heater core tubes and plug the hoses with suitable ⅝" (16mm) plugs.

2. Remove the glove compartment liner.

3. Remove eight (8) screws attaching the heater core cover to the plenum and remove the cover.

4. Remove the heater core from the plenum taking care not to spill coolant from the core.

INSTALLATION

1. Install the heater core in the plenum.

2. Install the heater core cover (eight screws).

3. Install the glove compartment liner.

4. Connect the heater hoses to the heater core. Tighten the hose clamps.

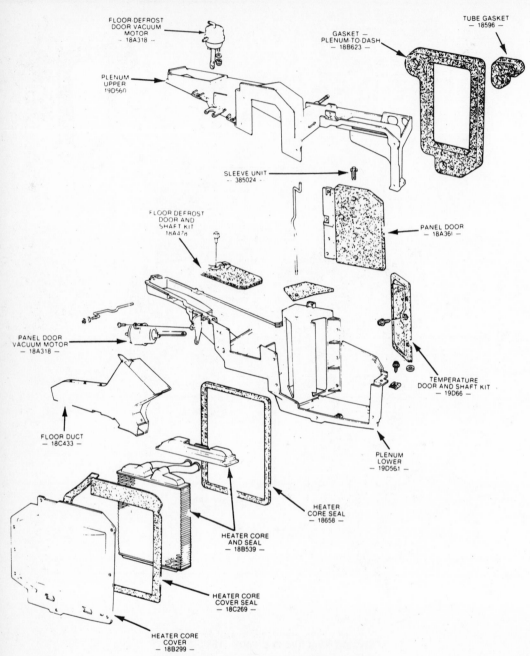

FLOOR DEFROST DOOR VACUUM MOTOR — 18A318 —

GASKET — PLENUM-TO-DASH — 18B623 —

TUBE GASKET — 18596 —

PLENUM UPPER 19D560

SLEEVE UNIT — 385024 —

FLOOR DEFROST DOOR AND SHAFT KIT 18A478

PANEL DOOR — 18A361 —

PANEL DOOR VACUUM MOTOR — 18A318 —

TEMPERATURE DOOR AND SHAFT KIT — 19D66 —

FLOOR DUCT — 18C433 —

PLENUM LOWER — 19D561 —

HEATER CORE SEAL — 18658 —

HEATER CORE AND SEAL — 18B539 —

HEATER CORE COVER SEAL — 18C269 —

HEATER CORE COVER — 18B299 —

Manual A/C—heater plenum, 1980 and later

5. Add coolant to raise the coolant level to specification.

RADIO

REMOVAL and INSTALLATION

1966–77

1. Disconnect the radio lead wire at the receptacle on the fuse panel.

2. Disconnect the speaker leads at the receptacle on the underside of the radio chassis.

3. Disconnect the antenna lead at the receptacle on the right side of the radio chassis.

4. Remove (pull) the volume control and the manual tuning control knobs from the shafts.

5. Remove the screws that retain the dial assembly to the instrument panel and remove the dial assembly.

6. Remove the retaining nuts and the retaining plates that secure the radio to the instrument panel.

7. Remove the radio bottom support bracket retaining screw and remove the radio assembly from the instrument panel.

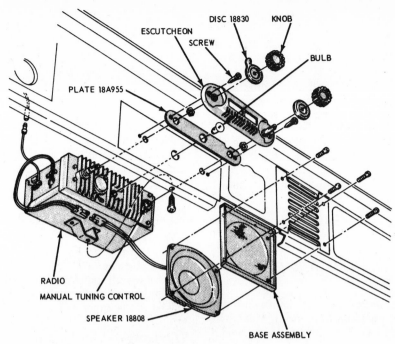

1966–77 radio installation

To install the radio:

8. Position the radio to the inner side of the instrument panel, and install the right and left support bracket to the radio retaining nuts.

9. Position the retaining plate to the outer side of the instrument panel over the pilot light and control shafts, and install the retaining nuts.

10. Position the dial assembly, install the retaining screw and seat the knobs on the control shafts.

11. Connect the speaker leads, the antenna lead, and the radio power lead wire at the fuse panel.

12. Calibrate the dial pointer with the tuner by rotating the tuning knob until the dial pointer reaches the end of its travel at the right side of the dial.

13. Check the operation of the radio and adjust the antenna trimmer.

1978–86

1. Disconnect the battery ground cable.

2. On 1978–79 models, remove the ash tray and bracket.

3. Disconnect the antenna, speakers and radio lead.

4. Remove the bolt attaching the radio rear

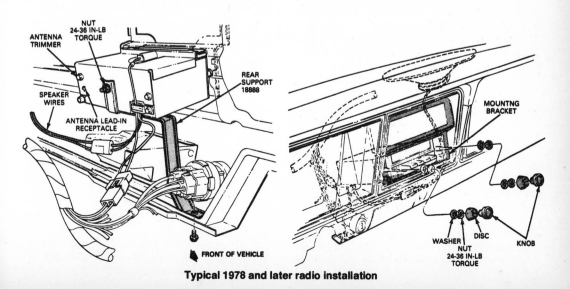

Typical 1978 and later radio installation

support to the lower edge of the instrument panel.

5. On 1978 models equipped with air conditioning, disconnect the left A/C duct hose from the A/C plenum.

6. Remove the knobs and discs from the radio control shafts.

7. Remove the retaining nuts from the control shafts and remove the bezel.

8. Remove the nuts and washers from the control shafts and remove the radio from the panel.

9. Installation is the reverse of removal.

WINDSHIELD WIPERS

Wiper Arm Assembly

REMOVAL AND INSTALLATION

1966–79

Bend the arm backward at the joint next to the pivot. Now, pull the arm straight off the splined pivot shaft. To replace the arm, hold it in the bent position and slide it on the pivot.

1980–86

Raise the blade end of the arm off of the windshield and move the slide latch away from the pivot shaft. This will unlock the wiper arm from the pivot shaft and hold the blade end of the arm off of the glass at the same time. The wiper arm can now be pulled off of the pivot shaft without the aid of any tools.

Blade Assembly to Wiper Arm

REMOVAL AND INSTALLATION

1978–79

Wiper blades are used from two different manufacturers.

Trico® and Anco® blades come in two types. With a bayonet type, the blade saddle slides over the end of the arm and is engaged by a locking stud. With the bottom type, a screw and nut is used to retain the blade on the arm.

Bayonet Type

To remove a Trico® type blade, press down on the arm to unlatch the top stud. Depress the tab on the saddle and pull the blade from the arm.

To remove an Anco type blade, press inward on the tab and pull the blade from the arm.

To install a new blade assembly, slide the blade saddle over the end of the wiper arm so that the locking stud snaps into place.

Side Saddle Pin Type

To remove a pin type Trico® type blade, insert an appropriate tool into the spring release opening of the blade saddle, depress the spring clip and pull the blade from the arm.

To install, push the blade saddle on to the pin, so that the spring clip engages the pin. Be sure the blade is securely attached to the arm.

1980–86

1. Cycle arm and blade assembly to a position on the windshield where REMOVAL of blade assembly can be performed without difficulty. Turn ignition key off at desired position.

2. With blade assembly resting on windshield, grasp either end of the wiper blade frame and pull away from windshield, then pull blade assembly from pin.

NOTE: *Rubber element extends past frame. To prevent damage to the blade element, be sure to grasp blade frame and not the end of the blade element.*

3. To install, push blade assembly onto pin until fully seated. Be sure blade is securely attached to the wiper arm.

Windshield Wiper Motor

REMOVAL AND INSTALLATION

Vacuum Type

NOTE: *All Broncos from 1968 have electric windshield wipers.*

1. Pull the wiper arm and blade assembly off the motor pivot shaft. Remove the grommet from the shaft with a puller.

2. If the vehicle has a padded header, loosen the set screw in the windshield wiper switch knob and remove the knob. Remove the header pad assembly.

3. Disconnect the vacuum hoses to the motor. Remove the screws retaining the motor to the header and remove the motor.

4. Position the new motor to the header and install the retaining screws. Connect the vacuum hoses.

5. Tap the grommet in place around the motor pivot shaft and stake it. Install the wiper arm and blade assembly.

6. Install the padded header assembly and windshield wiper switch knob, if so equipped.

7. Check the operation of the wiper motor and adjust the blade parking position if necessary.

Electric Type, 1968–77

1. The motor is mounted on the left side of the windshield header. To remove the motor it will be necessary to first remove the cover and disconnect the linkage arm and pivot shaft assembly from the motor driving arm by removing the retaining clip.

2. Disconnect the motor electrical leads at the multiple connector. Remove the two bolts

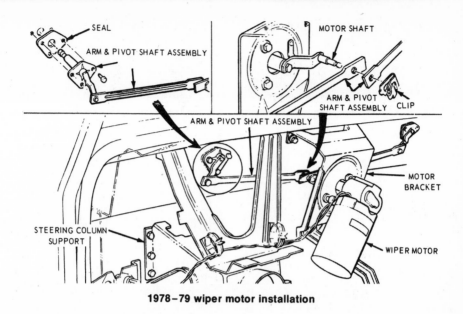

1978-79 wiper motor installation

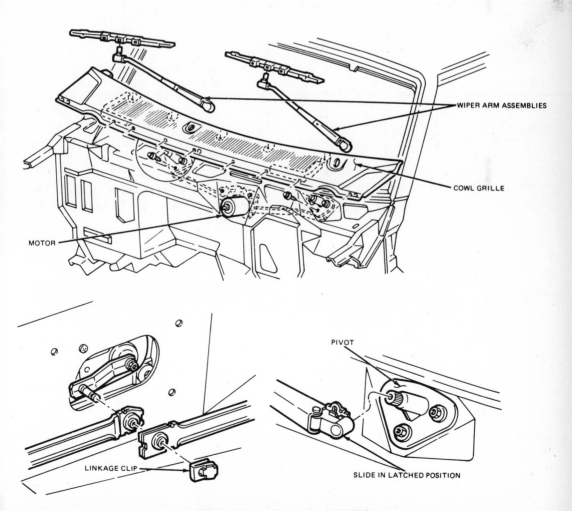

1980 and later wiper motor installation

and nuts that attach the motor mounting bracket to the windshield header, and remove the bracket and motor assembly.

3. Install the windshield wiper motor in the reverse order of REMOVAL. When installing the motor, tighten the motor bracket-to-windshield header bolts to 48–72 in.lb. and the nuts to 20–30 in.lb.

1978–79

1. Disconnect the battery ground cable.
2. Remove the radio.
3. Remove the engine components attached to the lower wiper bracket bolt, if so equipped.
4. Remove the wiper motor bracket attaching bolts.
5. Disconnect the wiper motor wires. Then, disconnect the wiper arm linkage from the motor shaft.
6. Connect the linkage to motor and install motor bracket attaching bolts. Tighten bolts to 8–12 ft.lb., and install engine components to lower bracket bolts.
7. Connect wiper motor wires.
8. Install radio.
9. Connect battery cable and check wiper motor operation.

1980–86

1. Disconnect the battery ground cable.
2. Remove both wiper arm and blade assemblies.
3. Remove the cowl grille attaching screws and lift the cowl grille slightly.
4. Disconnect the washer nozzle hose and remove the cowl grille assembly.
5. Remove the wiper linkage clip from the motor output arm.
6. Disconnect the wiper motor's wiring connector.
7. Remove the wiper motor's three attaching screws and remove the motor.
8. Install the motor and attach the three attaching screws. Tighten to 60–85 in.lb.
9. Connect wiper motor's wiring connector.
10. Install wiper linkage clip to the motor's output arm.
11. Connect the washer nozzle hose and install the cowl assembly and attaching screws.
12. Install both wiper arm assemblies.
13. Connect battery ground cable.

Wiper Linkage
REMOVAL AND INSTALLATION
1966–77 (Electric Type Only)

1. Remove the windshield wiper arm and blade assemblies from their pivot shafts.
2. Disconnect the linkage arm from the motor drive arm by removing the retaining clip.

3. The right and left pivot shaft assemblies are each retained to the windshield header by two mounting screws and a nut. Remove these mounting screws and the nut, and remove the pivot shafts and linkage as an assembly.

4. Install the linkage in the reverse order of REMOVAL.

1978–79
REMOVAL

1. Open the hood and disconnect the battery ground cable. Remove the arm and blade assemblies from the pivot shafts.
2. Reach under the instrument panel and disconnect the speedometer cable from the rear of the instrument cluster.
3. Remove the instrument cluster bezel.
4. Loosen the three bolts retaining the wiper motor bracket to the cowl. This will allow access between the cowl panel and the link assembly.
5. Remove the clip retaining the motor drive arm to the link assemblies.
6. Through the cluster bezel opening, remove the retaining bolts from the left pivot assembly. Remove the left pivot and link assembly from under the instrument panel.
7. Remove the glove box assembly.
8. Remove the three bolts retaining the right pivot and link assembly to the cowl panel.
9. Disconnect the right link assembly from the drive arm and remove the right pivot and link assembly.

INSTALLATION

1. Place gaskets on the pivot shafts and position the shafts to the cowl panel and install the retaining bolts.
2. Install the glove box assembly.
3. Position the link assemblies to the motor drive arm and install the retaining clip.
4. Tighten the bolts retaining the motor bracket to the cowl and then install engine components to lower bracket bolt.
5. Install the wiper arm and blade assemblies.
6. Position and install the instrument cluster bezel.
7. Connect the speedometer cable.
8. Connect the battery ground cable and close the hood and check the operation of the wipers.

1980–86
REMOVAL

1. Disconnect the battery ground cable.
2. Remove both wiper arm assemblies.
3. Remove the cowl grille attaching screws and lift the cowl grille slightly.

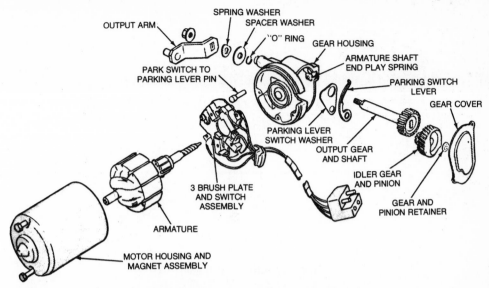

1966–77 wiper motor and transmission

4. Disconnect the washer nozzle hose and remove the cowl grille assembly.

5. Remove the wiper linkage clip from the motor output arm and pull the linkage from the output arm.

6. Remove the pivot body to cowl screws and remove the linkage and pivot shaft assembly (three screws on each side). The left and right pivots and linkage are independent and can be serviced separately.

INSTALLATION

1. Attach the linkage and pivot shaft assembly to cowl with attaching screws.

2. Replace the linkage to the output arm and attach the linkage clip.

3. Connect the washer nozzle hose and cowl grille assembly.

4. Attach cowl grille attaching screws.

5. Replace both wiper arm assemblies.

6. Connect battery ground cable.

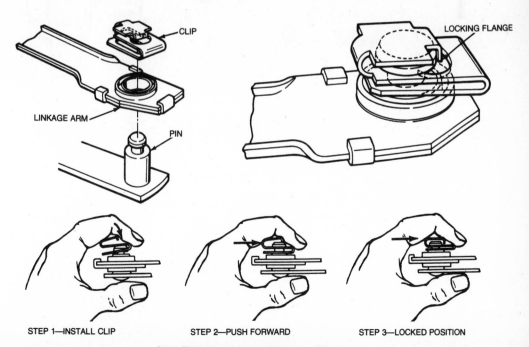

Installing the wiper arm connecting clip

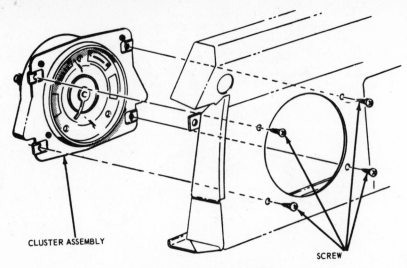

CLUSTER ASSEMBLY

SCREW

1966–77 instrument cluster

INSTRUMENTS AND SWITCHES

Instrument Cluster
REMOVAL AND INSTALLATION

1966–77

1. Disconnect the battery ground cable and disconnect the speedometer cable from the speedometer head.

2. Remove the screws retaining the instru-ment cluster assembly to the instrument panel.

3. Remove the cluster from behind the in-strument panel.

4. Disconnect the feed wires to the instru-ments and the instrument voltage regulator and remove the light sockets from the cluster back, noting their positions. Remove the two clips that retain the wiring harness to the clus-ter back and pull the harness away from the

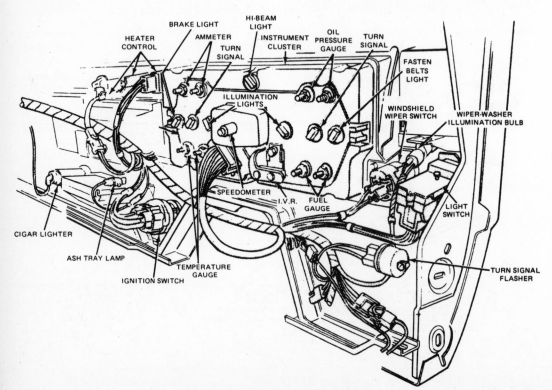

1978–79 instrument cluster rear view

cluster. Remove the instrument cluster assembly.

5. Mount the wiring harness to the lower edge of the cluster back by installing the two retaining clips.

6. Connect the instrument voltage regulator and the instrument wires to the cluster assembly and install the light sockets. Be sure that the ammeter wire is routed through the ammeter loop of the charge indicator correctly to prevent reverse gauge indications.

7. Connect the speedometer cable and tighten the nut.

8. Carefully move the instrument cluster into position from behind the instrument panel, guiding all wiring and cables into position to prevent damage. Be careful not to kink the speedometer cable.

9. Install the screws retaining the instrument cluster to the instrument panel.

10. Connect the battery ground cable and check the operation of all gauges, lights and signals.

1978–79

REMOVAL

1. Disconnect the battery ground cable.

2. Remove the radio knobs from the radio shafts (if so equipped).

3. Remove the fuel gauge switch knob (if so equipped), heater control knobs and wiper/washer knob. Use a hook-shaped tool to release each knob lock tab.

4. Remove the knob and shaft from the light switch.

5. Remove one nut and washer from each radio control shaft, and remove the radio bezel.

6. Remove the cluster trim cover. The attaching screws are located as follows: four screws along top of bezel; one screw between the lights and wiper/washer switch, and two screws below the radio. Then, disconnect the A/C duct (if so equipped), and illumination light from the bezel. The illumination light is located between the lights and wiper/washer switches. Remove four cluster attaching screws, disconnect the speedometer cable and wire connector from the printed circuit, and remove the cluster.

INSTALLATION

1. Position cluster to opening and connect the multiple connector and the speedometer cable. Connect the A/C duct and A/C illumination light (if so equipped) and install the four cluster retaining screws.

2. Install the trim cover.

3. Install the radio bezel (if so equipped).

4. Install the light switch knob and shaft.

5. Install the heater control knobs and the wiper/washer control knobs.

6. Install the radio knobs, (if so equipped).

7. Connect the battery cable, and check the operation of all gauges, lights and signals.

1980–86

REMOVAL

1. Disconnect the battery ground cable.

2. Remove the fuel gauge switch knob (if so equipped), and wiper/washer knob. Use a hook tool to release each knob lock tab.

3. Remove the knob from the headlamp and windshield wiper switch. Remove the fog lamp switch knob, if so equipped.

4. Remove steering column shroud. Care must be taken not to damage transmission control selector indicator (PRNDL) cable on vehicles equipped with automatic transmission.

5. On vehicles equipped with automatic transmission, remove loop on indicator cable assembly from retainer pin. Remove bracket screw from cable bracket and slide bracket out of slot in tube.

6. Remove the cluster trim cover. Remove four cluster attaching screws, disconnect the speedometer cable, wire connector from the printed circuit, 4 x 4 indicator light and remove the cluster.

INSTALLATION

1. Position cluster to opening and connect the multiple connector, the speedometer cable and 4 × 4 indicator light. Install the four cluster retaining screws.

2. If so equipped, place loop on transmission indicator cable assembly over retainer on column.

3. Position the tab on steering column bracket into slot on column. Align and attach screw.

4. Place transmission selector lever on steering column into **D** position.

5. Adjust slotted bracket so the pin is within the letter band.

6. Install the trim cover.

7. Install the headlamp switch knob. If so equipped, install the fog lamp switch.

8. Install the wiper/washer control knobs.

9. Connect the battery cable, and check the operation of all gauges, lights and signals.

Windshield Wiper/Washer Switch
REMOVAL AND INSTALLATION

1. Disconnect the battery cable.

2. Remove the switch knob, bezel nut and bezel.

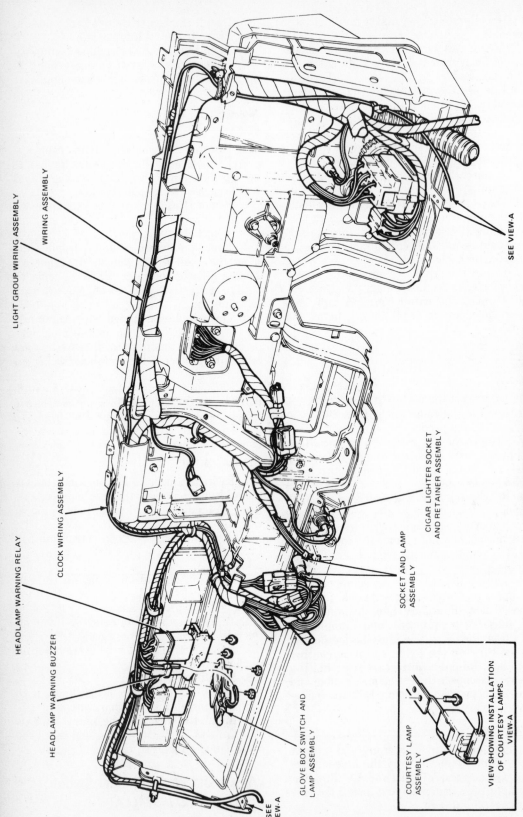

LIGHT GROUP WIRING ASSEMBLY

WIRING ASSEMBLY

HEADLAMP WARNING RELAY

HEADLAMP WARNING BUZZER

CLOCK WIRING ASSEMBLY

GLOVE BOX SWITCH AND LAMP ASSEMBLY

SEE VIEW-A

SEE VIEW-A

SOCKET AND LAMP ASSEMBLY

CIGAR LIGHTER SOCKET AND RETAINER ASSEMBLY

COURTESY LAMP ASSEMBLY

VIEW SHOWING INSTALLATION OF COURTESY LAMPS. VIEW-A

1980 and later instrument cluster view

3. Pull out the switch from under the instrument panel. Disconnect the plug connector from the switch and remove the switch.

4. Installation is the reverse of the removal procedure.

Headlight Switch

REMOVAL AND INSTALLATION

1. Disconnect the battery ground cable.

2. Depending on the year and model remove the wiper/washer and fog lamp switch knob if they will interfere with the headlight switch knob removal. Check the switch body (behind dash, see Step 3) for a release button. Press in on the button and remove the knob and shaft assembly. If not equipped with a release button, a hook tool may be necessary for knob removal.

3. Remove the steering column shrouds and cluster panel finish panel if they interfere with the required clearance for working behind the dash.

4. Unscrew the switch mounting nut from the front of the dash. Remove the switch from the back of the dash and disconnect the wiring harness.

5. Install in reverse order.

Neutral Safty And Back-up Light switch

REMOVAL AND INSTALLATION

Manual Transmission

The switch is located on the left side of the transmission case. To remove:

1. Disconnect the negative battery cable.

2. Disconnect the back-up switch harness.

3. Remove the back-up switch and the seal.

4. Installation is the reverse of the removal procedure.

Automatic Transmission

The switch is located on the left side of the transmission case. To remove:

1. Disconnect the negative battery cable.

2. Disconnect the back-up switch assembly harness.

3. Place the gear selector in neutral.

4. Squeeze the switch tangs together and lift out the switch assembly.

5. Installation is the reverse of the removal procedure.

Ignition Switch

REMOVAL AND INSTALLATION

1966–79

1. Disconnect the battery ground cable.

2. Turn the ignition key to Accessories and slightly depress the release pin in the face of the lock cylinder.

3. Turn the key counterclockwise and pull the key and lock assembly out of the switch.

4. From under the instrument panel, press in on the rear of the switch 1/8 turn counterclockwise.

5. Remove the bezel and switch. Remove the retainer and spring.

6. Remove the nut from the back of the switch.

7. Remove the accessory and gauge feed wires from the accessory terminal of the switch. Pull the insulated plug from the rear of the switch.

To install:

8. Insert a screwdriver into the lock opening of the switch and turn the slot in the switch to the full counterclockwise position.

9. Connect the insulated plug and wires to the back of the switch. Connect the accessory and gauge wires to the switch and install the retaining nut.

10. Place the bezel and switch in the switch opening, press the switch toward the instrument panel and rotate it 1/8 turn to lock it.

11. Position the spring and retainer on the switch with the open face of the retainer away from the switch. Place the switch in the opening.

12. Press the switch toward the instrument panel and install the bezel.

13. Place the key in the cylinder and turn the key to the accessory position. Place the lock and key in the switch, depress the release pin slightly, and turn the key counterclockwise. Push the new lock cylinder into the switch. Turn the key to check the operation.

14. Connect the battery.

1980–86

1. Disconnect the battery ground cable.

2. Remove steering column shroud and lower the steering column.

3. Disconnect the switch wiring at the multiple plug.

4. Remove the two nuts that retain the switch to the steering column.

5. Lift the switch vertically upward to disengage the actuator rod from the switch and remove switch.

6. When installing the ignition switch, both the locking mechanism at the top of the column and the switch itself must be in LOCK position for correct adjustment.

To hold the mechanical parts of the column in LOCK position, move the shift lever into PARK (with automatic transmissions) or REVERSE (with manual transmissions), turn the key to LOCK position, and remove the key.

New replacement switches, when received, are already pinned in LOCK position by a metal shipping pin inserted in a locking hole on the side of the switch.

7. Engage the actuator rod in the switch.

8. Position the switch on the column and install the retaining nuts, but do not tighten them.

9. Move the switch up and down along the column to locate the mid-position of rod lash, and then tighten the retaining nuts.

10. Remove the locking pin, connect the battery cable, and check for proper start in PARK or NEUTRAL.

Also check to make certain that the start circuit cannot be actuated in the DRIVE and REVERSE position.

11. Raise the steering column into position at instrument panel. Install steering column shroud.

Speedometer Cable Core
REMOVAL AND INSTALLATION

1. Reach up behind the cluster and disconnect the cable by depressing the quick disconnect tab and pulling the cable away.

2. Remove the cable from the casing. If the cable is broken, raise the vehicle on a hoist and disconnect the cable from the transmission.

3. Remove the cable from the casing.

4. To remove the casing from the vehicle, pull it through the floor pan.

5. To replace the cable, slide the new cable into the casing and connect it at the transmission.

6. Route the cable through the floor pan and position the grommet in its groove in the floor.

7. Push the cable onto the speedometer head.

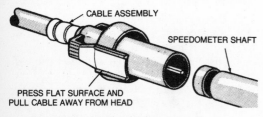

Speedometer cable quick-disconnect

LIGHTING

Headlights
REMOVAL AND INSTALLATION

1966–77 All
1978 Except Ranger And XLT Options

1. Remove the screws retaining the headlight trim ring and remove the trim ring.

2. Loosen the headlight retaining ring screws, rotate the ring counterclockwise and remove it. Do not disturb the adjusting screw settings.

3. Pull the headlight bulb forward and disconnect the wiring assembly plug from the hub.

4. Connect the wiring assembly plug to the new bulb. Place the bulb in position, making sure that the locating tabs of the bulb are fitted in the positioning slots.

5. Install the headlight retaining ring, slipping the ring tabs over the screws and rotating the ring clockwise as far as possible. Tighten the screws.

6. Place the headlight trim ring into position, and install the retaining screws.

7. Check the operation of the headlight.

1978 Ranger and XLT Option
All 1979 And Later Models

1. Remove the attaching screws and remove the headlamp door attaching screws and remove the headlamp door.

2. Remove the headlight retaining ring screws, and remove the retaining ring. Do not disturb the adjusting screw settings.

3. Pull the headlight bulb forward and disconnect the wiring assembly plug from the bulb.

4. Connect the wiring assembly plug to the new bulb. Place the bulb in position, making sure that the locating tabs of the bulb are fitted in the positioning slots.

5. Install the headlight retaining ring.

6. Place the headlight trim ring or door into position, and install the retaining screws.

HEADLIGHT AIMING

The headlights must be properly aimed to provide the best, safest road illumination. The lights should be checked for proper aim, and adjusted if necessary, after installing a new sealed beam unit or if the front end sheet metal has been replaced. Certain state and local authorities have requirements for headlight aiming and you should check these before adjusting.

NOTE: *The truck's fuel tank should be about half full when adjusting the headlights. Tires should be properly inflated, and if a heavy load is carried, it should remain there.*

Horizontal and vertical aiming of each sealed beam unit is provided by two adjusting screws, which move the mounting ring in the body against the tension of the coil spring. There is no adjustment for focus; this is done during headlight manufacturing.

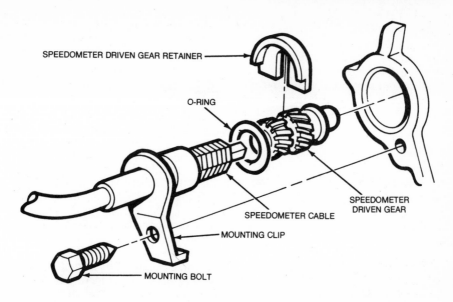

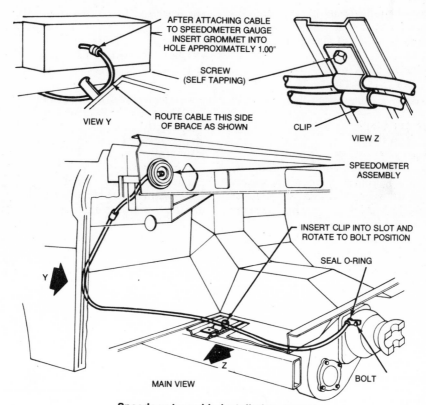

Speedometer cable installation, typical

Signal and Marker Lights
REMOVAL AND INSTALLATION

Front Turn Signal and Parking Lights

1. Disconnect the negative battery cable.
2. Remove the four bezel retaining screws.
3. Remove the bezel.
4. Remove the three park lamp retaining screws.
5. Remove the parking lamp.
6. Disconnect the electrical connector from the parking lamp and install a new bulb.
7. Installation is the reverse of the removal procedure.

Front Side Marker Lights

1. Disconnect the negative battery cable.
2. Remove the two retaining screws.
3. Remove the side marker lamp.
4. Remove the bulb from the lamp and install a new bulb.
5. Installation is the reverse of the removal procedure.

Rear Side Marker Lights

1. Disconnect the negative battery cable.
2. Remove the housing retaining screws.
3. Remove the housing.
4. Gently pull out the bulb socket.
5. Remove the bulb.
6. Installation is the reverse of the removal procedure.

Rear Turn Signal, Brake and Parking Lights

1. Disconnect the negative battery cable.
2. Remove the lens housing retaining screws.
3. Remove the lamp housing.
4. Remove the bulb socket by squeezing the retention lock and rotating the socket counterclockwise.
5. Remove the bulb.
6. Installation is the reverse of the removal procedure.

TRAILER TOWING

Broncos have long been popular as trailer towing vehicles. Their strong construction, and wide range of engine/transmission combinations make them ideal for towing campers, boat trailers and utility trailers.

Factory trailer towing packages are available on most Ford vehicles. However, if you are installing a trailer hitch and wiring on your Bronco, there are a few thing that you ought to know.

Trailer Weight

Trailer weight is the first, and most important, factor in determining whether or not your vehicle is suitable for towing the trailer you have in mind. The horsepower-to-weight ratio should be calculated. The basic standard is a ratio of 35:1. That is, 35 pounds of GVW for every horsepower.

To calculate this ratio, multiply you engine's rated horsepower by 35, then subtract the weight of the vehicle, including passengers and luggage. The resulting figure is the ideal maximum trailer weight that you can tow. One point to consider: a numerically higher axle ratio can offset what appears to be a low trailer weight. If the weight of the trailer that you have in mind is somewhat higher than the weight you just calculated, you might consider changing your rear axle ratio to compensate.

Hitch Weight

There are three kinds of hitches: bumper mounted, frame mounted, and load equalizing.

Bumper mounted hitches are those which attach solely to the vehicle's bumper. Many states prohibit towing with this type of hitch, when it attaches to the vehicle's stock bumper, since it subjects the bumper to stresses for which it was not designed. Aftermarket rear step bumpers, designed for trailer towing, are acceptable for use with bumper mounted hitches.

Frame mounted hitches can be of the type which bolts to two or more points on the frame, plus the bumper, or just to several points on the frame. Frame mounted hitches can also be of the tongue type, for Class I towing, or, of the receiver type, for classes II and III.

Load equalizing hitches are usually used for large trailers. Most equalizing hitches are welded in place and use equalizing bars and chains to level the vehicle after the trailer is hooked up.

The bolt-on hitches are the most common, since they are relatively easy to install.

Check the gross weight rating of your trailer. Tongue weight is usually figured as 10% of gross trailer weight. Therefore, a trailer with a maximum gross weight of 2,000 lb. will have a maximum tongue weight of 200 lb. Class I trailers fall into this category. Class II trailers are those with a gross weight rating of 2,000–3,500 lb., while Class III trailers fall into the 3,500–6,000 lb. category. Class IV trailers are those over 6,000 lb. and are for use with fifth wheel trucks, only.

When you've determined the hitch that you'll need, follow the manufacturer's installation instructions, exactly, especially when it comes to fastener torques. The hitch will subjected to a lot of stress and good hitches come with hardened bolts. Never substitute an inferior bolt for a hardened bolt.

Trailer Wiring

Wiring the Bronco for towing is fairly easy. There are a number of good wiring kits available and these should be used, rather than trying to design your own. All trailers will need brake lights and turn signals as well as tail lights and side marker lights. Most states require extra marker lights for overwide trailers. Also, most states have recently required backup lights for trailers, and most trailer manufacturers have been building trailers with back-up lights for several years.

Additionally, some Class I, most Class II and just about all Class III trailers will have electric brakes.

Add to this number an accessories wire, to operate trailer internal equipment or to charge the trailer's battery, and you can have as many as seven wires in the harness.

Determine the equipment on your trailer and buy the wiring kit necessary. The kit will contain all the wires needed, plus a plug adapter set which included the female plug, mounted on the bumper or hitch, and the male plug, wired into, or plugged into the trailer harness.

When installing the kit, follow the manufacturer's instructions. The color coding of the wires is standard throughout the industry.

One point to note: some domestic vehicles, and most imported vehicles, have separate turn signals. On most domestic vehicles, the brake lights and rear turn signals operate with the same bulb. For those vehicles with separate turn signals, you can purchase an isolation unit so that the brake lights won't blink whenever the turn signals are operated, or, you can go to your local electronics supply house and buy four diodes to wire in series with the brake and turn signal bulbs. Diodes will isolate the brake and turn signals. The choice is yours. The isolation units are simple and quick to install, but far more expensive than the diodes. The diodes, however, require more work to install properly, since they require the cutting of each bulb's wire and soldering in place of the diode.

One, final point, the best kits are those with a spring loaded cover on the vehicle mounted socket. This cover prevents dirt and moisture from corroding the terminals. Never let the vehicle socket hang loosely; always mount it securely to the bumper or hitch.

Cooling
ENGINE

One of the most common, if not THE most common, problems associated with trailer towing is engine overheating.

With factory installed trailer towing packages, a heavy duty cooling system is usually included. Heavy duty cooling systems are available as optional equipment on most Ford vehicles, with or without a trailer package. If you have one of these extra capacity systems, you shouldn't have any overheating problems.

If you have a standard cooling system, without an expansion tank, you'll definitely need to get an aftermarket expansion tank kit, preferably one with at least a 2 quart capacity. These

kits are easily installed on the radiator's overflow hose, and come with a pressure cap designed for expansion tanks.

Another helpful accessory is a Flex Fan. These fan are large diameter units are designed to provide more airflow at low speeds, with blades that have deeply cupped surfaces. The blades then flex, or flatten out, at high speed, when less cooling air is needed. These fans are far lighter in weight than stock fans, requiring less horsepower to drive them. Also, they are far quieter than stock fans.

If you do decide to replace your stock fan with a flex fan, note that if your Bronco has a fan clutch, a spacer between the flex fan and water pump hub will be needed.

Aftermarket engine oil coolers are helpful for prolonging engine oil life and reducing overall engine temperatures. Both of these factors increase engine life.

While not absolutely necessary in towing Class I and some Class II trailers, they are recommended for heavier Class II and all Class III towing.

Engine oil cooler systems consist of an adapter, screwed on in place of the oil filter, a remote filter mounting and a multi-tube, finned heat exchanger, which is mounted in front of the radiator or air conditioning condenser.

TRANSMISSION

An automatic transmission is usually recommended for trailer towing. Modern automatics have proven reliable and, of course, easy to operate, in trailer towing.

The increased load of a trailer, however, causes an increase in the temperature of the automatic transmission fluid. Heat is the worst enemy of an automatic transmission. As the temperature of the fluid increases, the life of the fluid decreases.

It is essential, therefore, that you install an automatic transmission cooler.

The cooler, which consists of a multi-tube, finned heat exchanger, is usually installed in front of the radiator or air conditioning compressor, and hooked inline with the transmission cooler tank inlet line. Follow the cooler manufacturer's installation instructions.

Select a cooler of at least adequate capacity, based upon the combined gross weights of the Bronco and trailer.

Cooler manufacturers recommend that you use an aftermarket cooler in addition to, and not instead of, the present cooling tank in your Bronco's radiator. If you do want to use it in place of the radiator cooling tank, get a cooler at least two sizes larger than normally necessary.

One note, transmission cooler can, sometimes, cause slow or harsh shifting in the transmission during cold weather, until the fluid has a chance to come up to normal operating temperature. Some coolers can be purchased with or retrofitted with a temperature bypass valve which will allow fluid flow through the cooler only when the fluid has reached operating temperature, or above.

CIRCUIT PROTECTION

Turn Signal and Hazard Flasher Locations

The turn signal flasher unit is mounted in a clip on the left side of the instrument panel brace, between the top of the instrument cluster and the steering column. The 1978–81 turn signal flasher unit is attached to the left side cowl.

The 19676–77 hazard flasher unit is clipped to the rear of the hazard flasher switch. The 1978–81 hazard flasher unit is taped to the wiring harness.

Both the turn signal flasher and the hazard warning flasher are mounted on the fuse panel on the 1982–86 Bronco. The turn signal flasher is mounted on the front of the fuse panel, and the hazard warning flasher is mounted on the rear of the fuse panel.

Fuse Link

The fuse link is a short length of special, Hypalon (high temperature) insulated wire, integral with the engine compartment wiring harness and should not be confused with standard wire. It is several wire gauges smaller than the circuit which it protects. Under no circumstances should a fuse link replacement repair be made using a length of standard wire cut from bulk stock or from another wiring harness.

To repair any blown fuse link use the following procedure:

1. Determine which circuit is damaged, its location and the cause of the open fuse link. If the damaged fuse link is one of three fed by a common No. 10 or 12 gauge feed wire, determine the specific affected circuit.

2. Disconnect the negative battery cable.

3. Cut the damaged fuse link from the wiring harness and discard it. If the fuse link is one of three circuits fed by a single feed wire, cut it out of the harness at each splice end and discard it.

4. Identify and procure the proper fuse link and butt connectors for attaching the fuse link in the harness.

5. To repair any fuse link in a 3-link group with one feed:

   a. After cutting the open link out of the harness, cut each of the remaining undamaged fuse links close to the feed wire weld.

   b. Strip approximately ½" (12.7mm) of insulation from the detached ends of the two good fuse links. Then insert two wire ends into one end of a butt connector and carefully push one stripped end of the replacement fuse link into the same end of the butt connector and crimp all three firmly together. NOTE: *Care must be taken when fitting the three fuse links into the butt connector as the internal diameter is a snug fit for three wires. Make sure to use a proper crimping tool. Pliers, side cutters, etc. will not apply the proper crimp to retain the wires and withstand a pull test.*

   c. After crimping the butt connector to the three fuse links, cut the weld portion from the feed wire and strip approximately ½" (12.7mm) of insulation from the cut end. Insert the stripped end into the open end of the butt connector and crimp very firmly.

   d. To attach the remaining end of the replacement fuse link, strip approximately ½" (12.7mm) of insulation from the wire end of the circuit from which the blown fuse link was removed, and firmly crimp a butt connector or equivalent to the stripped wire. Then, insert the end of the replacement link into the other end of the butter connector and crimp firmly.

   e. Using rosin core solder with a consistency of 60 percent tin and 40 percent lead, solder the connectors and the wires at the repairs and insulate with electrical tape.

6. To replace any fuse link on a single circuit in a harness, cut out the damaged portion, strip approximately ½" (12.7mm) of insulation from the two wire ends and attach the appropriate replacement fuse link to the stripped wire ends with two proper size butt connectors. Solder the connectors and wires and insulate with tape.

7. To repair any fuse link which has an eyelet terminal on one end such as the charging circuit, cut off the open fuse link behind the weld, strip approximately ½" (12.7mm) of insulation from the cut end and attach the appropriate new eyelet fuse link to the cut stripped wire with an appropriate size butt connector. Solder the connectors and wires at the repair and insulate with tape.

8. Connect the negative battery cable to the battery and test the system for proper operation. NOTE: *Do not mistake a resistor wire for a fuse link. The resistor wire is generally long-*

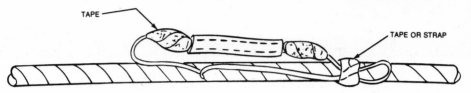

REMOVE EXISTING VINYL TUBE SHIELDING
REINSTALL OVER FUSE LINK BEFORE CRIMPING
FUSE LINK TO WIRE ENDS

TAPE

TAPE OR STRAP

TYPICAL REPAIR USING THE SPECIAL #17 GA. (9.00' LONG-YELLOW) FUSE LINK REQUIRED FOR THE AIR/COND.
CIRCUITS (2) #687E and #261A LOCATED IN THE ENGINE COMPARTMENT

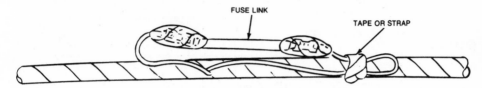

FUSE LINK

TAPE OR STRAP

TYPICAL REPAIR FOR ANY IN-LINE FUSE LINK USING THE SPECIFIED GAUGE FUSE LINK FOR THE SPECIFIC CIRCUIT

TAPE

TYPICAL REPAIR USING THE EYELET TERMINAL FUSE LINK OF THE SPECIFIED GAUGE FOR ATTACHMENT TO A CIRCUIT WIRE END

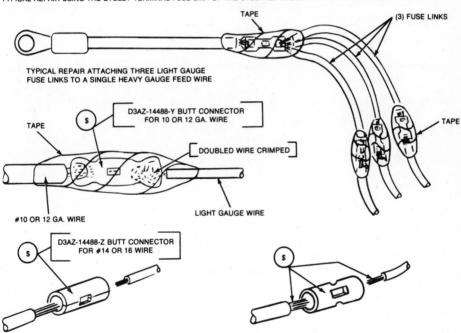

TAPE

(3) FUSE LINKS

TYPICAL REPAIR ATTACHING THREE LIGHT GAUGE
FUSE LINKS TO A SINGLE HEAVY GAUGE FEED WIRE

D3AZ-14488-Y BUTT CONNECTOR
FOR 10 OR 12 GA. WIRE

TAPE

TAPE

DOUBLED WIRE CRIMPED

#10 OR 12 GA. WIRE

LIGHT GAUGE WIRE

D3AZ-14488-Z BUTT CONNECTOR
FOR #14 OR 16 WIRE

FUSIBLE LINK REPAIR PROCEDURE

General fuse link repair procedure

er and has print stating, "Resistor: don't cut or splice." When attaching a single No. 16, 17, 18 or 20 gauge fuse link to a heavy gauge wire, always double the stripped wire end of the fuse link before inserting and crimping it into the butt connector for positive wire retention.

WIRING DIAGRAMS

Wiring diagrams have been left out of this book. As Broncos have become more complex, and available with longer and longer option lists, wiring diagrams have grown in size and complexity also. It has become virtually impossible to provide a readable reproduction in a reasonable number of pages. Information on ordering wiring diagrams from the vehicle manufacturer can be obtained from your dealer.

Fuses and Circuit Breakers 1966–77

Circuit	Location	Type of Device
Back-up Lights, W/S Washer, Turn Signal and Radio	Fuse Panel	SFE 14 Fuse
Dome, Courtesy, Map or Cargo Lights and Cigarette Lighter	Fuse Panel	AGW Fuse
Emergency Flasher System	Fuse Panel	SFE 20 Fuse
Headlights	Headlight Switch	12 Amp C.B.
Heater	Fuse Panel	SFE 20 Fuse
Horns, Park, License, Marker and Stop Lights	Headlight Switch	15 Amp C.B.
Instrument Panel Light	Fuse Panel	AGA 2 Fuse

Fuses and Circuit Breakers 1978–79

Circuit	Location	Type of Device
Instrument Panel & Cluster Lamps, Ash Tray, Trans. Ind., Radio Lamp, A/C Lamp, Headlight Switch Lamp, Wiper/Washer Switch Lamp	Fuse Panel	AGA 3 Fuse
Heater/Defroster and/or A/C	Fuse Panel	AGC 35 Fuse
Seat Belt Buzzer	Fuse Panel	SFE 7.5 Fuse
Throttle Solenoid, Emission Control Circuitry	Fuse Panel	AGC 7.5 Fuse
Dome, Cargo, Courtesy Lamps, Cigar Lighter, Glove Box Lamp, Engine Compartment Lamp	Fuse Panel	SFE 15 Fuse
Emergency Flashers, Stop Lights	Fuse Panel	SFE 20 Fuse
Turn Signal Flasher	Fuse Panel	SFE 15 Fuse
Accessory Feed, Speed Control, 4 x 4 Ind. Light, Dual Battery Relay, Power Life-gate Window	Fuse Panel	SFE 20 Fuse
Back-up Lamps, Windshield Washer	Fuse Panel	SFE 15 Fuse
Radio, CB Radio	Fuse Panel	SFE 7.5 Fuse
Cargo Shell Switch & Lamp	In-line	SFE 7.5 Fuse
Headlights and Hi-Beam Ind.	In Switch	18 amp CB
Roof Markers, Rear Markers Trailer Exterior Lamps, Parking Lights, License Plate Light, Front & Rear Side Markers, Relay Coil Feed	In Headlight Switch	15 amp CB
Windshield Wipers (STD)	In Wiper Switch	7 amp CB
Windshield Wipers (Intermittant)	In Wiper Switch	7 amp CB
#22 Electric Trailer Brakes	At Starter Relay	16 ga. Fuse Link
#37 Trailer Lights (Relay Feed)	Engine Compartment Junction Block	16 ga. Fuse Link
#888 A/C Blower Motor	At Starter Relay	SFE 35 Fuse
#198 Accessory Safety Relay, Dual Battery	At Safety Relay	14 ga. Fuse Link
#38 Alternator	At Starter Relay	16 ga. Fuse Link
#666 Dome Lamp (Camper) w/Dual Battery	Engine Compartment Junction Block	16 ga. Fuse Link
#526 Marker Lamps Relay	Engine Compartment Junction Block	20 ga. Fuse Link
#4 Electric Carburetor Choke	In Harness Near Starter Relay	20 ga. Fuse Link
Power Window Liftgate	At Starter Relay	20 amp CB

Fuses and Circuit Breakers 1980–81

Circuit	Location	Type of Device
Turn Signal Flasher	Fuse Panel	SFE 15 Fuse
Windshield Washer, Back-up Lights	Fuse Panel	SFE 15 Fuse
Throttle Positioner, Seat Belt Buzzer	Fuse Panel	SFE 10 Fuse
Fuel Tank Selector Switch	Fuse Panel	SFE 10 Fuse
Emergency Flasher, Stop Lights	Fuse Panel	SFE 10 Fuse

Fuses and Circuit Breakers 1980–81 (cont.)

Circuit	Location	Type of Device
Radio, CB Radio	Fuse Panel	SFE 10 Fuse
Heater-A/C Mode Switch & Blower Motor	Fuse Panel	SFE 30 Fuse
Instrument Panel, Cluster and Interior Illumination, Headlight Switch, Wiper Switch, Heater-A/C Switch, Clock Light, Radio Dial Light, Trans. Ind. Light, Ash Tray	Fuse Panel	SFE 4 Fuse
Speed Control Relay, Control Amplifier, 4 x 4 Ind. Light, Accessory Safety Relay, Convenience Group	Fuse Panel	SFE 10 Fuse
Courtesy Lights Under Dash, Dome, Glove Box, Cigar Lighter, Clock, Engine Compartment Lamp, Visibility Group, Cargo Light, CB Memory Circuit	Fuse Panel	SFE 15 Fuse
Headlights, Hi-Beam Indicator	In Switch	18 amp CB
Roof Markers, Rear Markers, Trailer Lights, Parking Lights, License Plate Lights, Side Markers, Relay Coil Feed	In Headlight Switch	15 amp CB
Windshield Wipers	In Switch	7 amp CB
#22 Electric Trailer Brakes	At Starter Relay	16 ga. Fuse Link
#37 Trailer Lamp Relay Feed	Engine Compartment Junction Block	14 ga. Fuse Link
#883 A/C Blower Motor	Fuse Panel	SFE 35 Fuse
#198 Accessory Safety Relay, Dual Battery	At Safety Relay	14 ga. Fuse Link
#38 Alternator	At Starter Relay	18 ga. Fuse Link
#666 Dome Lamp Camper w/o Dual Battery	Engine Compartment Junction Block	16 ga. Fuse Link
#526 Marker Lamps Relay	Engine Compartment Junction Block	20 ga. Fuse Link
#4 Electric Carburetor Choke	In Harness Near Starter Relay	20 ga. Fuse Link
Power Window Liftgate	At Starter Relay	20 amp CB

Fuses and Circuit Breakers 1982–86

Circuit	Location	Type of Device
Hazard warning flasher, stop lamps	Fuse Panel	ATC 15 Fuse
Tail lamps, parking lamps, marker lamps, "Headlamps on" warning buzzer, trailer lamps relay, instrument illumination	Fuse Panel	ATC 15 Fuse
Turn signals, back-up lamps	Fuse Panel	ATC 15 Fuse
Acc., clock, 4-wheel drive indicator lamp, speed control, auxiliary battery relay, engine solenoids, rear window device relay, auxiliary heater	Fuse Panel	ATC 15 Fuse
Courtesy lamps, cargo lamps, clock, radio memory, engine compartment lamp visibility group	Fuse Panel	ATC 15 Fuse
Heater—A/C blower motor	Fuse Panel	ATC 30 Fuse
Radio	Fuse Panel	ATC 15 Fuse
Power door locks, electric mirror, power tailgate (Key Switch)	Fuse Panel	30 amp CB
Power windows	Fuse Panel	20 amp CB
Horn, cigar lighter	Fuse Panel	ATC 20 Fuse
Instrument illumination	Fuse Panel	ATC 5 Fuse
Warning lamps, seat belt buzzer, carburetor circuits, tachometer, choke heater, upshift indicator lamp	Fuse Panel	ATC 15 Fuse
Headlamp	Integral w/light switch	22 amp CB
Electric mirror	harness near fuse panel	5 amp Fuse (in-line)
Auxiliary battery	Near R.H. fender apron and dash panel	14 ga. Fuse Link
Alternator (40 or 60 amp)	Starter motor relay	16 ga. Fuse Link
(70 amp)	Starter motor relay	14 ga. Fuse Link
Headlamp switch and fuse panel feed	Near R.H. fender apron and dash panel	16 ga. Fuse Link
Ignition switch and fuse panel feed	Near R.H. fender apron and dash panel	14 ga. Fuse Link
Electronic engine controls	Starter motor relay	18 ga. Fuse Link

Troubleshooting Basic Turn Signal and Flasher Problems

Most problems in the turn signals or flasher system, can be reduced to defective flashers or bulbs, which are easily replaced. Occasionally, problems in the turn signals are traced to the switch in the steering column, which will require professional service.

F = Front   R = Rear   ● = Lights off   ○ = Lights on

Problem		Solution
Turn signals light, but do not flash		• Replace the flasher
No turn signals light on either side		• Check the fuse. Replace if defective. • Check the flasher by substitution • Check for open circuit, short circuit or poor ground
Both turn signals on one side don't work		• Check for bad bulbs • Check for bad ground in both housings
One turn signal light on one side doesn't work		• Check and/or replace bulb • Check for corrosion in socket. Clean contacts. • Check for poor ground at socket
Turn signal flashes too fast or too slow		• Check any bulb on the side flashing too fast. A heavy-duty bulb is probably installed in place of a regular bulb. • Check the bulb flashing too slow. A standard bulb was probably installed in place of a heavy-duty bulb. • Check for loose connections or corrosion at the bulb socket
Indicator lights don't work in either direction		• Check if the turn signals are working • Check the dash indicator lights • Check the flasher by substitution

One indicator light doesn't light		• On systems with 1 dash indicator: See if the lights work on the same side. Often the filaments have been reversed in systems combining stoplights with taillights and turn signals.
		  Check the flasher by substitution
		• On systems with 2 indicators: Check the bulbs on the same side
		  Check the indicator light bulb
		  Check the flasher by substitution

Troubleshooting Basic Lighting Problems

Problem	Cause	Solution
Lights		
One or more lights don't work, but others do	• Defective bulb(s) • Blown fuse(s) • Dirty fuse clips or light sockets • Poor ground circuit	• Replace bulb(s) • Replace fuse(s) • Clean connections • Run ground wire from light socket housing to car frame
Lights burn out quickly	• Incorrect voltage regulator setting or defective regulator • Poor battery/alternator connections	• Replace voltage regulator • Check battery/alternator connections
Lights go dim	• Low/discharged battery • Alternator not charging • Corroded sockets or connections • Low voltage output	• Check battery • Check drive belt tension; repair or replace alternator • Clean bulb and socket contacts and connections • Replace voltage regulator
Lights flicker	• Loose connection • Poor ground • Circuit breaker operating (short circuit)	• Tighten all connections • Run ground wire from light housing to car frame • Check connections and look for bare wires
Lights "flare"—Some flare is normal on acceleration—if excessive, see "Lights Burn Out Quickly"	• High voltage setting	• Replace voltage regulator
Lights glare—approaching drivers are blinded	• Lights adjusted too high • Rear springs or shocks sagging • Rear tires soft	• Have headlights aimed • Check rear springs/shocks • Check/correct rear tire pressure
Turn Signals		
Turn signals don't work in either direction	• Blown fuse • Defective flasher • Loose connection	• Replace fuse • Replace flasher • Check/tighten all connections
Right (or left) turn signal only won't work	• Bulb burned out • Right (or left) indicator bulb burned out • Short circuit	• Replace bulb • Check/replace indicator bulb • Check/repair wiring
Flasher rate too slow or too fast	• Incorrect wattage bulb • Incorrect flasher	• Flasher bulb • Replace flasher (use a variable load flasher if you pull a trailer)
Indicator lights do not flash (burn steadily)	• Burned out bulb • Defective flasher	• Replace bulb • Replace flasher
Indicator lights do not light at all	• Burned out indicator bulb • Defective flasher	• Replace indicator bulb • Replace flasher

Troubleshooting Basic Dash Gauge Problems

Problem	Cause	Solution
Coolant Temperature Gauge		
Gauge reads erratically or not at all	• Loose or dirty connections • Defective sending unit	• Clean/tighten connections • Bi-metal gauge: remove the wire from the sending unit. Ground the wire for an instant. If the gauge registers, replace the sending unit.
	• Defective gauge	• Magnetic gauge: disconnect the wire at the sending unit. With ignition ON gauge should register COLD. Ground the wire; gauge should register HOT.
Ammeter Gauge—Turn Headlights ON (do not start engine). Note reaction		
Ammeter shows charge Ammeter shows discharge Ammeter does not move	• Connections reversed on gauge • Ammeter is OK • Loose connections or faulty wiring • Defective gauge	• Reinstall connections • Nothing • Check/correct wiring • Replace gauge
Oil Pressure Gauge		
Gauge does not register or is inaccurate	• On mechanical gauge, Bourdon tube may be bent or kinked	• Check tube for kinks or bends preventing oil from reaching the gauge
	• Low oil pressure	• Remove sending unit. Idle the engine briefly. If no oil flows from sending unit hole, problem is in engine.
	• Defective gauge	• Remove the wire from the sending unit and ground it for an instant with the ignition ON. A good gauge will go to the top of the scale.
	• Defective wiring	• Check the wiring to the gauge. If it's OK and the gauge doesn't register when grounded, replace the gauge.
	• Defective sending unit	• If the wiring is OK and the gauge functions when grounded, replace the sending unit
All Gauges		
All gauges do not operate	• Blown fuse • Defective instrument regulator	• Replace fuse • Replace instrument voltage regulator
All gauges read low or erratically	• Defective or dirty instrument voltage regulator	• Clean contacts or replace
All gauges pegged	• Loss of ground between instrument voltage regulator and car • Defective instrument regulator	• Check ground • Replace regulator
Warning Lights		
Light(s) do not come on when ignition is ON, but engine is not started	• Defective bulb • Defective wire • Defective sending unit	• Replace bulb • Check wire from light to sending unit • Disconnect the wire from the sending unit and ground it. Replace the sending unit if the light comes on with the ignition ON.
Light comes on with engine running	• Problem in individual system • Defective sending unit	• Check system • Check sending unit (see above)

Troubleshooting the Heater

Problem	Cause	Solution
Blower motor will not turn at any speed	• Blown fuse • Loose connection • Defective ground • Faulty switch • Faulty motor • Faulty resistor	• Replace fuse • Inspect and tighten • Clean and tighten • Replace switch • Replace motor • Replace resistor
Blower motor turns at one speed only	• Faulty switch • Faulty resistor	• Replace switch • Replace resistor
Blower motor turns but does not circulate air	• Intake blocked • Fan not secured to the motor shaft	• Clean intake • Tighten security
Heater will not heat	• Coolant does not reach proper temperature • Heater core blocked internally • Heater core air-bound • Blend-air door not in proper position	• Check and replace thermostat if necessary • Flush or replace core if necessary • Purge air from core • Adjust cable
Heater will not defrost	• Control cable adjustment incorrect • Defroster hose damaged	• Adjust control cable • Replace defroster hose

Troubleshooting Basic Windshield Wiper Problems

Problem	Cause	Solution
Electric Wipers		
Wipers do not operate— Wiper motor heats up or hums	• Internal motor defect • Bent or damaged linkage • Arms improperly installed on linking pivots	• Replace motor • Repair or replace linkage • Position linkage in park and reinstall wiper arms
Wipers do not operate— No current to motor	• Fuse or circuit breaker blown • Loose, open or broken wiring • Defective switch • Defective or corroded terminals • No ground circuit for motor or switch	• Replace fuse or circuit breaker • Repair wiring and connections • Replace switch • Replace or clean terminals • Repair ground circuits
Wipers do not operate— Motor runs	• Linkage disconnected or broken	• Connect wiper linkage or replace broken linkage
Vacuum Wipers		
Wipers do not operate	• Control switch or cable inoperative • Loss of engine vacuum to wiper motor (broken hoses, low engine vacuum, defective vacuum/fuel pump) • Linkage broken or disconnected • Defective wiper motor	• Repair or replace switch or cable • Check vacuum lines, engine vacuum and fuel pump • Repair linkage • Replace wiper motor
Wipers stop on engine acceleration	• Leaking vacuum hoses • Dry windshield • Oversize wiper blades • Defective vacuum/fuel pump	• Repair or replace hoses • Wet windshield with washers • Replace with proper size wiper blades • Replace pump

Troubleshooting the Ignition Switch

Problem	Cause	Solution
Ignition switch electrically inoperative	• Loose or defective switch connector • Feed wire open (fusible link) • Defective ignition switch	• Tighten or replace connector • Repair or replace • Replace ignition switch
Engine will not crank	• Ignition switch not adjusted properly	• Adjust switch
Ignition switch wil not actuate mechanically	• Defective ignition switch • Defective lock sector • Defective remote rod	• Replace switch • Replace lock sector • Replace remote rod
Ignition switch cannot be adjusted correctly	• Remote rod deformed	• Repair, straighten or replace

Troubleshooting the Turn Signal Switch

Problem	Cause	Solution
Turn signal will not cancel	• Loose switch mounting screws • Switch or anchor bosses broken • Broken, missing or out of position detent, or cancelling spring	• Tighten screws • Replace switch • Reposition springs or replace switch as required
Turn signal difficult to operate	• Turn signal lever loose • Switch yoke broken or distorted • Loose or misplaced springs • Foreign parts and/or materials in switch • Switch mounted loosely	• Tighten mounting screws • Replace switch • Reposition springs or replace switch • Remove foreign parts and/or material • Tighten mounting screws
Turn signal will not indicate lane change	• Broken lane change pressure pad or spring hanger • Broken, missing or misplaced lane change spring • Jammed wires	• Replace switch • Replace or reposition as required • Loosen mounting screws, reposition wires and retighten screws
Turn signal will not stay in turn position	• Foreign material or loose parts impeding movement of switch yoke • Defective switch	• Remove material and/or parts • Replace switch
Hazard switch cannot be pulled out	• Foreign material between hazard support cancelling leg and yoke	• Remove foreign material. No foreign material impeding function of hazard switch—replace turn signal switch.
No turn signal lights	• Inoperative turn signal flasher • Defective or blown fuse • Loose chassis to column harness connector • Disconnect column to chassis connector. Connect new switch to chassis and operate switch by hand. If vehicle lights now operate normally, signal switch is inoperative • If vehicle lights do not operate, check chassis wiring for opens, grounds, etc.	• Replace turn signal flasher • Replace fuse • Connect securely • Replace signal switch • Repair chassis wiring as required
Instrument panel turn indicator lights on but not flashing	• Burned out or damaged front or rear turn signal bulb • If vehicle lights do not operate, check light sockets for high	• Replace bulb • Repair chassis wiring as required

Troubleshooting the Turn Signal Switch (cont.)

Problem	Cause	Solution
Instrument panel turn indicator lights on but not flashing (cont.)	resistance connections, the chassis wiring for opens, grounds, etc.	
	• Inoperative flasher	• Replace flasher
	• Loose chassis to column harness connection	• Connect securely
	• Inoperative turn signal switch	• Replace turn signal switch
	• To determine if turn signal switch is defective, substitute new switch into circuit and operate switch by hand. If the vehicle's lights operate normally, signal switch is inoperative.	• Replace turn signal switch
Stop light not on when turn indicated	• Loose column to chassis connection	• Connect securely
	• Disconnect column to chassis connector. Connect new switch into system without removing old.	• Replace signal switch
Stop light not on when turn indicated (cont.)	Operate switch by hand. If brake lights work with switch in the turn position, signal switch is defective.	
	• If brake lights do not work, check connector to stop light sockets for grounds, opens, etc.	• Repair connector to stop light circuits using service manual as guide
Turn indicator panel lights not flashing	• Burned out bulbs	• Replace bulbs
	• High resistance to ground at bulb socket	• Replace socket
	• Opens, ground in wiring harness from front turn signal bulb socket to indicator lights	• Locate and repair as required
Turn signal lights flash very slowly	• High resistance ground at light sockets	• Repair high resistance grounds at light sockets
	• Incorrect capacity turn signal flasher or bulb	• Replace turn signal flasher or bulb
	• If flashing rate is still extremely slow, check chassis wiring harness from the connector to light sockets for high resistance	• Locate and repair as required
	• Loose chassis to column harness connection	• Connect securely
	• Disconnect column to chassis connector. Connect new switch into system without removing old. Operate switch by hand. If flashing occurs at normal rate, the signal switch is defective.	• Replace turn signal switch
Hazard signal lights will not flash— turn signal functions normally	• Blow fuse	• Replace fuse
	• Inoperative hazard warning flasher	• Replace hazard warning flasher in fuse panel
	• Loose chassis-to-column harness connection	• Conect securely
	• Disconnect column to chassis connector. Connect new switch into system without removing old. Depress the hazard warning lights. If they now work normally, turn signal switch is defective.	• Replace turn signal switch
	• If lights do not flash, check wiring harness "K" lead for open between hazard flasher and connector. If open, fuse block is defective	• Repair or replace brown wire or connector as required

Drive Train

+6

MANUAL TRANSMISSION

From 1966–77 the only manual transmission offered with the Ford 3.03 3-speed unit with column mounted shifter.

In 1978, the Bronco was available with a New Process 435 4-speed unit only, with floor mounted shifter.

In 1979, the Warner T-18 4-speed, floor mounted shifter was the standard unit in all states except California, where the standard unit was the NP 435.

In 1980, the NP 435 joined the T-18 in being available nationwide.

In 1981 the Ford single rail overdrive 4-speed became an option.

During the 1982–86 model years, the T-18 was the standard unit, with the Ford single rail overdrive offered optionally. The NP 435 was offered as an option to fleet buyers, only.

Adjustments

LINKAGE

3.03 3-Speed

1. Place the shifter in the Neutral position and insert a $\frac{3}{16}$" (4.8mm) gauge pin diameter through the steering column shift levers and the locating hole in the spacer.

2. If the shift rods at the transmission are equipped with threaded sleeves, adjust the sleeves so that they enter the shift levers on the transmission easily with the shift levers in the Neutral position. Now lengthen the rods seven turns of the sleeves and insert them into the shift levers.

3. If the shift rods are slotted, loosen the attaching nut, make sure that the transmission shift levers are in the Neutral position, then retighten the attaching nuts.

4. Remove the gauge pin and check the operation of the shift linkage.

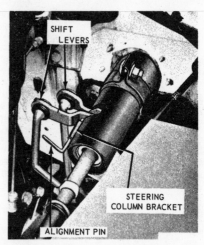

Shift linkage adjustment, 3.03 3-speed

4-Speed Overdrive w/External Linkage

1. Attach the shift rods to the levers.

2. Rotate the output shaft to determine that the transmission is in neutral.

3. Insert an alignment pin into the shift control assembly alignment hole.

4. Attach the slotted end of the shift rods over the flats of the studs in the shift control assembly.

5. Install the locknuts and remove the alignment pin.

Neutral Safety And Back-up Light switch

REMOVAL AND INSTALLATION

Manual Transmission

The switch is located on the left side of the transmission case. To remove:

1. Disconnect the negative battery cable.

2. Disconnect the back-up switch harness.

3. Remove the back-up switch and the seal.

4. Installation is the reverse of the removal procedure.

Automatic Transmission
The switch is located on the left side of the transmission case. To remove:

1. Disconnect the negative battery cable.
2. Disconnect the back-up switch assembly harness.
3. Place the gear selector in neutral.
4. Squeeze the switch tangs together and lift out the switch assembly.
5. Installation is the reverse of the removal procedure.

Transmission

REMOVAL AND INSTALLATION

1966–77 Ford 3.03 3-speed

1. Shift the transfer case into Neutral.
2. Remove the bolts attaching the fan shroud to the radiator support, if so equipped.
3. Raise the vehicle on a hoist.
4. Support the transfer case shield with a jack and remove the bolts that attach the shield to the frame side rails. Remove the shield.
5. Drain the transmission and transfer case lubricant. To drain the transmission lubricant, remove the lower extension housing-to-transmission bolt.
6. Disconnect the front and rear driveshafts at the transfer case.
7. Disconnect the speedometer cable at the transfer case.
8. Disconnect the T.R.S. switch, if so equipped.
9. Disconnect the shift rods from the transmission shift levers. Place the First/Reverse gear shift lever into the First gear position and insert the fabricated tool. The tool consists of a length of rod, the same diameter as the holes in the shift levers, which is bent in such a way to fit in the holes in the two shift levers and hold them in the position stated above. More important, this tool will prevent the input shaft roller bearings from dropping into the transmission and output shaft. THIS TOOL IS A MUST.
10. Support the engine with a jack.
11. Remove the two cotter pins, bolts, washers, plate and insulators that secure the crossmember to the transfer case adapter.
12. Remove the crossmember-to-frame side support attaching bolts.
13. Position a transmission jack under the transfer case and remove the upper insulators from the crossmember. Remove the crossmember.
14. Roll back the boot enclosing the transfer case shift linkage. Remove the threaded cap holding the shift lever assembly to the shift bracket. Remove the shift lever assembly.

15. Remove the two lower bolts attaching the transmission to the flywheel housing.
16. Reposition the transmission jack under the transmission and secure it with a chain.
17. Remove the two upper bolts securing the transmission to the flywheel housing. Move the transmission and transfer case rearward and downward out of the vehicle.
18. Move the assembly to a bench and remove the transfer case-to-transmission attaching bolts.
19. Slide the transmission assembly off the transfer case.

To install the transmission:

20. Position the transfer case to the transmission. Apply an oil resistant sealer to the bolt threads and install the attaching bolts. Tighten to 42–50 ft.lb.
21. Position the transmission and transfer case on a transmission jack and secure them with a chain.
22. Raise the transmission and transfer case assembly into position and install the transmission case to the flywheel housing.
23. Install the two upper and two lower transmission attaching bolts and torque them to 37–42 ft.lb.
24. Position the transfer case shift lever and install the threaded cap to the shift bracket. Reposition the rubber boot.
25. Raise the transmission and transfer case high enough to provide clearance for installing the crossmember. Position the upper insulators to the crossmember and install the crossmember-to-frame side support attaching bolts.
26. Align the bolt holes in the transfer case adapter with those in the crossmember, then lower the transmission and remove the jack.
27. Install the crossmember-to-transfer case adapter bolts, nuts, insulators, plates and washers. Tighten the nuts and secure them with cotter pins.
28. Remove the engine jack.
29. Remove the fabricated tool and connect each shift rod to its respective lever on the transmission. Adjust the linkage.
30. Connect the speedometer cable.
31. Connect the T.R.S. switch, if so equipped.
32. Install the front and rear driveshafts to the transfer case.
33. Fill the transmission and transfer case to the bottom of the filler hole with the recommended lubricant.
34. Position the transfer case shield to the frame side rails and install the attaching bolts.
35. Lower the vehicle.
36. Install the fan shroud, if so equipped.
37. Check the operation of the transfer case and transmission shift linkage.

1978–86 NP435

1. Remove the rubber boot and floor mat.
2. Remove the weather pad. It may be necessary first to remove the seat assembly.
3. Disconnect the back-up light switch located in the rear of the gearshift housing cover.
4. Raise the vehicle and position safety stands. Position a transmission jack under the transmission, and disconnect the speedometer cable.
5. Disconnect the parking brake lever from its linkage, and remove the gearshift housing.
6. Disconnect the driveshaft or coupling shaft. Remove the bolts that attach the coupling shaft center support to the crossmember and wire the coupling shaft and driveshaft to one side. Remove the transfer case.
7. Remove the transmission attaching bolts at the clutch housing, and remove the transmission.

Before installing the transmission apply a light film of chassis lubricant to the release lever fulcrum and fork. Do not apply a thick coat of grease to these parts, as it will work out and contaminate the clutch disc.

1. Place the transmission on a transmission jack, and raise the transmission until the input shaft splines are aligned with the clutch disc splines. The clutch release bearing and hub must be properly positioned in the release lever fork.
2. Install guide studs in the clutch housing and slide the transmission forward on the guide studs until it is in position on the clutch housing. Install the attaching bolts or nuts, and tighten them to the following torques:
   - $7/16$–14; 40–50 ft.lb.
   - $5/8$–11; 120–150 ft.lb.
   - $9/16$–12; 90–115 ft.lb.
   - $5/8$–18C; 120–150 ft.lb.
   - $9/16$–18C; 90–115 ft.lb.

Remove the guide studs and install the two lower attaching bolts.
3. Install the bolts attaching the coupling shaft center support to the crossmember. Tighten the bolts to 40–50 ft.lb.
4. Connect the driveshaft or coupling shaft and the speedometer cable. Tighten the U-joint nuts.
5. Connect the back-up light switch wire.
6. Install the transmission cover plate. Install the seat assembly if it was removed.
7. Install weather pad, pad retainer, floor mat, and rubber boot.

1979 T-18

1. Open door cover seat.
2. Remove shift knobs.
3. Remove the four screws attaching the transmission shift lever boot assembly.
4. Remove the four screws holding the floor mat.
5. Remove the eleven screws holding the access cover to the floor pan. Place the shift lever in the reverse position and remove the cover.
6. Remove the insulator and dust cover.
7. Remove the transfer case shift lever.
8. Remove the eight bolts holding the shift cover and gasket.
9. Use cardboard or heavy paper to fabricate a suitable cover for the shift cover opening to protect the transmission from dirt during removal.
10. Raise the vehicle on a hoist.
11. Remove the drain pan and drain the transmission.
12. Disconnect the rear driveshaft from the transfer case and wire it out of the way.
13. Disconnect the front driveshaft from the transfer case and wire it out of the way.
14. Remove the cotter key that holds the shift link in place and remove the shift link.
15. Remove the speedometer cable from the transfer case.
16. Position a transmission jack under the transfer case. Remove the six bolts holding the transfer case to the transmission and lower the transfer case from the vehicle.
17. Remove the eight bolts that hold the rear support bracket to the transmission.
18. Position a transmission jack under the transmission and remove the rear support bracket and brace.
19. Remove the four bolts that hold the transmission tot he bell housing.
20. Remove the transmission from the vehicle.

To Install:

1. Place the transmission on a transmission jack and install it in the vehicle installing two guide studs in the bell housing top holes, to guide the transmission into position.
2. Install the two lower bolts. Remove the guide studs and install the upper bolts.
3. Place the rear support bracket in position and install the eight retaining bolts.
4. Install the two bolts at the rear support insulator bracket. Remove the transmission jack.
5. Position the transfer case on the transmission jack and install the six retaining bolts and gasket. Position the transfer case on the transmission and tighten the bolts to 50–60 ft.lb.
6. Install the transfer case shift link and cotter pin.
7. Position and install the speedometer cable.
8. Remove wire and connect front driveshaft.
9. Remove wire and connect rear driveshaft.

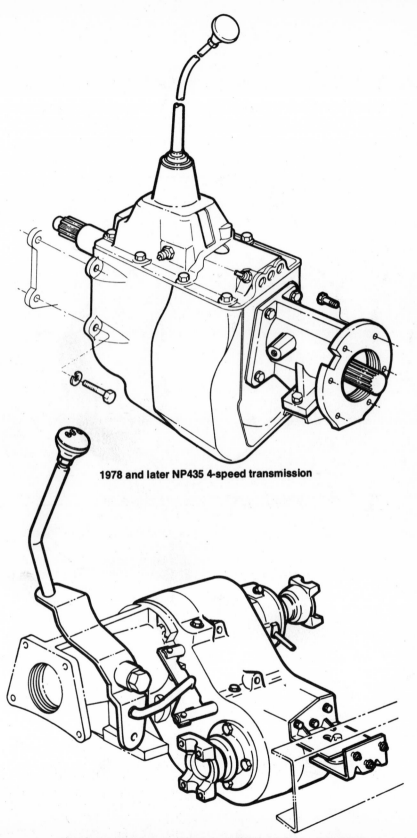

1978 and later NP435 4-speed transmission

1978 and later NP435 transmission-to-transfer case mounting

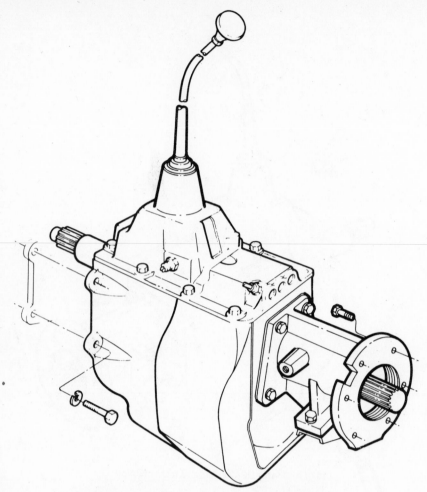

1979 and later Warner T-18 4-speed transmission

10. Fill transfer case and manual transmission with lubricant.

11. Lower vehicle.

12. Remove fabricated dirt shield and prepare gasket area.

13. Position gasket and shift cover.

14. Install two pilot bolts, then install remaining shift cover retaining bolts.

15. Install transfer case shift handle.

16. Install dust cover and insulator.

17. Install access cover to floor pan screws.

18. Install the four floor mat screws.

19. Install the four boot area screws.

20. Install the shift knobs.

1980–86 T-18

1. Open door cover seat.

2. Remove shift knobs.

3. Remove the four screws attaching the transmission shift lever boot assembly.

4. Remove the four screws holding the floor mat.

5. Remove the eleven screws holding the access cover to the floor pan. Place the shift lever in the reverse position and remove the cover.

6. Remove the insulator and dust cover.

7. Remove the transfer case shift lever.

8. Remove transmission shift lever.

9. Raise the vehicle on a hoist.

10. Remove the drain plug and drain the transmission.

11. Disconnect the rear driveshaft from the transfer case and wire it out of the way.

12. Disconnect the front driveshaft from the transfer case and wire it out of the way.

13. Remove the retainer ring that holds the shift link in place and remove the shift link from transfer case.

14. Remove the speedometer cable from the transfer case.

15. Position a transmission jack under the transfer case. Remove the six bolts holding the transfer case to the transmission and lower the transfer case from the vehicle.

16. Remove the eight bolts that hold the rear support bracket to the transmission.

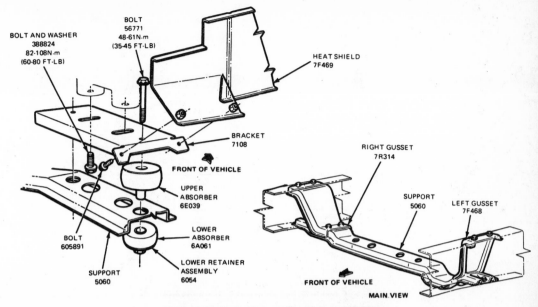

1980 and later T-18 crossmember installation

17. Position a transmission jack under the transmission and remove the rear support bracket and brace.

18. Remove the four bolts that hold the transmission to the bell housing.

19. Remove the transmission from the vehicle.

To Install:

1. Place the transmission on a transmission jack and install it in the vehicle installing two guide studs in the bell housing top holes, to guide the transmission into position.

2. Install the two lower bolts. Remove the guide studs and install the upper bolts.

3. Place the rear support bracket in position and install the eight retaining bolts. Torque to 35–50 ft.lb.

4. Install the two bolts at the rear support insulator bracket. Remove the transmission jack.

5. Position the transfer case on the transmission jack and install the six retaining bolts and gasket. Position the transfer case on the transmission and tighten the bolts to 28–33 ft.lb.

6. Install the transfer case shift link and retainer ring.

7. Position and install the speedometer cable.

8. Remove wire and connect front driveshaft.

9. Remove wire and connect rear driveshaft.

10. Fill transfer case and transmission.

11. Lower vehicle.

12. Remove fabricated dirt shield and prepare gasket area.

13. Position gasket and shift cover.

14. Install two pilot bolts, then install remaining shift cover retaining bolts.

15. Install transfer case shift handle and transmission shift lever.

16. Install dust cover and insulator.

17. Install access cover to floor pan screws.

18. Install the four floor mat screws.

19. Install the four boot area screws.

20. Install the shift knobs.

Ford Single Rail Overdrive

1. Raise the vehicle and support it on jackstands.

2. Mark the driveshaft so that it may be installed in the same relative position. Disconnect the driveshaft from the rear U-joint flange. Slide the driveshaft off the transmission output shaft and install an extension housing seal installation tool, or rags into the extension housing to prevent lubricant leakage.

3. Disconnect the speedometer cable from the extension housing.

4. Remove three screws securing shift lever to turret assembly.

5. Remove shift lever from turret assembly.

6. Support the engine with a transmission jack and remove the extension housing-to-engine rear support attaching bolts.

7. Raise the rear of the engine high enough to remove the weight from the crossmember. Remove the bolts retaining the crossmember to the frame side supports and remove the crossmember.

8. Support the transmission on a jack and

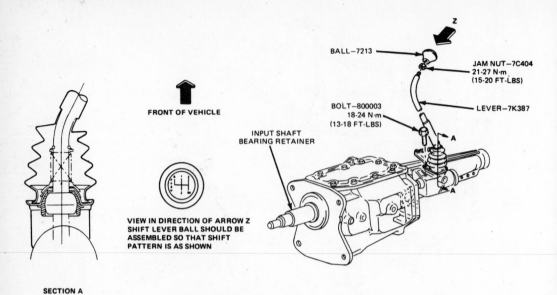

FRONT OF VEHICLE

BALL—7213

JAM NUT—7C404
21-27 N·m
(15-20 FT-LBS)

BOLT—800003
18-24 N·m
(13-18 FT-LBS)

LEVER—7K387

INPUT SHAFT
BEARING RETAINER

A

A

VIEW IN DIRECTION OF ARROW Z
SHIFT LEVER BALL SHOULD BE
ASSEMBLED SO THAT SHIFT
PATTERN IS AS SHOWN

SECTION A

Single rail 4-speed overdrive transmission

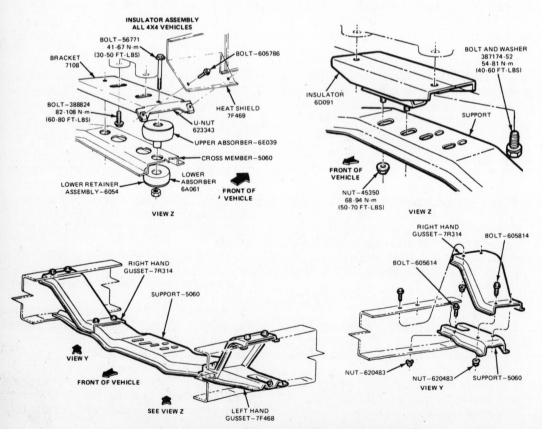

INSULATOR ASSEMBLY
ALL 4X4 VEHICLES

BOLT—56771
41-67 N·m
(30-50 FT-LBS)

BOLT—605786

BRACKET
7108

BOLT AND WASHER
387174-S2
54-81 N·m
(40-60 FT-LBS)

BOLT—388824
82-108 N·m
(60-80 FT-LBS)

HEAT SHIELD
7F469

U-NUT
623343

INSULATOR
6D091

SUPPORT

UPPER ABSORBER—6E039

CROSS MEMBER—5060

FRONT OF
VEHICLE

LOWER RETAINER
ASSEMBLY—6054

LOWER
ABSORBER
6A061

FRONT OF
VEHICLE

NUT—45350
68-94 N·m
(50-70 FT-LBS)

VIEW Z

VIEW Z

RIGHT HAND
GUSSET—7R314

BOLT—605814

RIGHT HAND
GUSSET—7R314

BOLT—605614

SUPPORT—5060

VIEW Y

FRONT OF VEHICLE

SEE VIEW Z

LEFT HAND
GUSSET—7F468

NUT—620483

NUT—620483

SUPPORT—5060

VIEW Y

Single rail 4-speed overdrive transmission mounting points

remove the bolts that attach the transmission to the flywheel housing.

9. Move the transmission and jack rearward until the transmission input shaft clears the flywheel housing. If necessary, lower the engine enough to obtain clearance for transmission removal.

CAUTION: *Do not depress the clutch pedal while the transmission is removed.*

To Install:

1. Make sure that the mounting surface of the transmission and the flywheel housing are free of dirt, paint, and burrs. Install two guide pins in the flywheel housing lower mounting bolt holes. Move the transmission forward on the guide pins until the input shaft splines enter the clutch hub splines and the case is positioned against the flywheel housing.

2. Install the two upper transmission to flywheel housing mounting bolts snug, and then remove the two guide pins. Install the two lower mounting bolts. Torque all mounting bolts to specifications.

3. Raise the rear of the engine and install the crossmember. Install and torque the crossmember attaching bolts to specifications, then lower the engine.

4. With the transmission extension housing resting on the engine rear support, install the transmission extension housing attaching bolts. Torque the bolts to specifications.

5. Position shift tower to extension housing and secure with three screws.

6. Connect the speedometer cable to the extension housing.

7. Remove the extension housing installation tool and slide the forward end of the driveshaft over the transmission output shaft. Connect the driveshaft to the rear U-joint flange.

8. Fill the transmission to the proper level with the specified lubricant.

9. Lower the car. Check the shift and crossover motion for full shift engagement and smooth crossover operation.

CLUTCH

Broncos are equipped with a single plate, dry disc, mechanically actuated clutch. There have been 3 different diameters available since 1966: 9″ (229mm) and 9⅜″ (238mm) for the 1966–74 6 cyl. and 11″ (279mm) for all other engines. The 9″ clutch was dropped for the 1970 model year. The color code (paint dab) for the clutches was: green, blue, orange, respectively, with the orange changed to bronze in 1970.

Adjustments

FREEPLAY AND MANUAL LINKAGE ADJUSTMENT

1. Measure the clutch pedal freeplay by depressing the pedal slowly until the freeplay between the release bearing assembly and the pressure plate is removed. Note this measurement. The difference between this measurement and when the pedal is not depressed is the freeplay measurement.

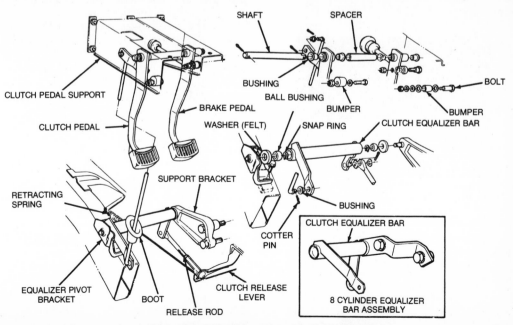

Exploded view of the 1966–77 clutch linkage

2. If the freeplay measurement is less than ½–¾" (12.7–19.05mm), the clutch linkage must be adjusted.

3. Loosen the two jam nuts on the release rod under the truck and back off both nuts several turns.

4. Loosen or tighten the first jam nut (nearest the release lever) against the bullet (rod extension) until a freeplay measurement of ¾–1½" (19.05–38.1mm) is obtained. A freeplay measurement closer to 1½" (38.1mm) is more desirable.

5. When the correct freeplay measurement is obtained, hold the first jam nut in position and securely tighten the other nut against the first.

6. Recheck the freeplay adjustment. Total pedal travel is fixed and is not adjustable.

PEDAL HEIGHT

1966–77

1. Measure the total travel of the pedal. If the total travel is less than 6¾" (171½mm) or more than 6¼" (158¾mm), move the clutch pedal bumper and bracket up or down until the travel is within these limits.

2. To check and adjust the pedal free travel, slowly apply the clutch pedal until the clutch fingers contact the clutch release bearing. The distance the clutch pedal moves is the free travel dimension. The free travel should be 1¼ to 1⅞" (47⅝mm). If it is not within these limits, loosen the nut at the bullet on the clutch release rod and adjust the bullet until the free travel is within the specified range.

3. Tighten the nut at the turnbuckle.

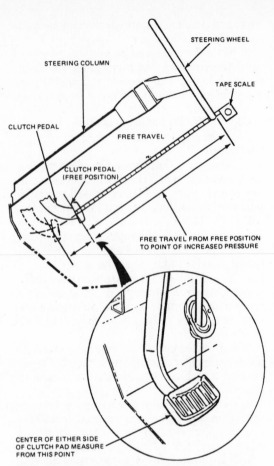

TOTAL   FREE
TRAVEL   TRAVEL

Measuring the clutch pedal free travel, 1966–77

1978–79

1. Measure the clutch pedal free travel using a steel tape. Measure the distance from the clutch pedal pad to the steering wheel rim. Depress the pedal slowly until the free travel between the release bearing assembly and the

Measuring clutch pedal free travel, 1978 and later

pressure plate assembly is taken up. Note this measurement. The difference between the two measurements is the free travel.

2. If the free travel measurement is less than ½" (12.7mm) 1978; ¾" (19.05mm) 1979 or greater than 2" (51mm) 1978; 1½" (38mm) 1979, the clutch linkage must be adjusted.

3. With retracting spring removed, hold the release rod firmly against release lever, eliminating lever free play.

4. Position first jam nut 0.062" (1.6mm) from the bar while holding needle firmly against release lever.

5. Position second jam nut finger tight against the first nut, while holding second nut. Lock the first nut with 15–20 ft.lb. torque. This gives ¾–1½" (19–38mm) at pedal pad with 1½" (38mm) preferred.

6. Check adjustment with retracting spring in place.

1980–86

1. Measure the clutch pedal free travel using a steel tape. Measure the distance from the clutch pedal pad to the steering wheel rim. De-

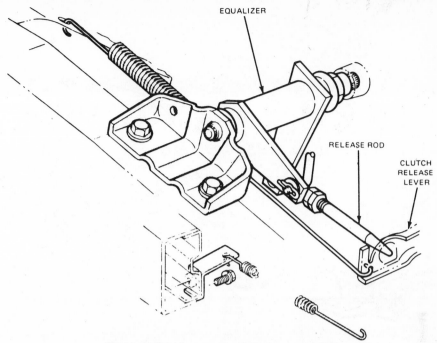

Clutch pedal free travel adjustment, 1978–79

press the pedal slowly until the free travel between the release bearing assembly and the pressure plate assembly is taken up. Note this measurement. The difference between the two measurements is the free travel.

2. If the free travel measurement is less than ½" (12.7mm) or more than 2" (51mm), the clutch linkage must be adjusted.

3. Remove the retracting spring.

4. Loosen the two jam nuts on the release rod assembly and back off both nuts several turns.

5. Slide the release rod extension (bullet) firmly against the release lever. Push the release rod forward against the equalizer bar le-

ver to eliminate all freeplay from the linkage system.

6. Insert 0.135" (3.4mm) thick gauge between the jam nut and bullet. Tighten the first jam nut finger tight against the gauge with all freeplay eliminated.

7. Tighten the second jam nut finger tight against the first jam nut. Hold the first nut and tighten the second jam nut to 15–20 ft.lb. Freeplay should measure ¾–1½" (19–38mm) at the pedal.

8. With the recommended free travel obtained, and holding the first jam nut, position and securely tighten the second jam nut against the first jam nut.

9. Recheck the pedal free travel.

Driven Disc And Pressure Plate

REMOVAL AND INSTALLATION

CAUTION: *The clutch driven disc contains asbestos, which has been determined to be a cancer causing agent. Never clean clutch surfaces with compressed air! Avoid inhaling any dust from clutch surface! When cleaning clutch surfaces, use a commercially available brake cleaning fluid.*

1966–77

1. Disconnect the cable from the starter and remove the starter.

2. Remove the transmission and transfer case.

Clutch pedal free travel adjustment, 1980 and later

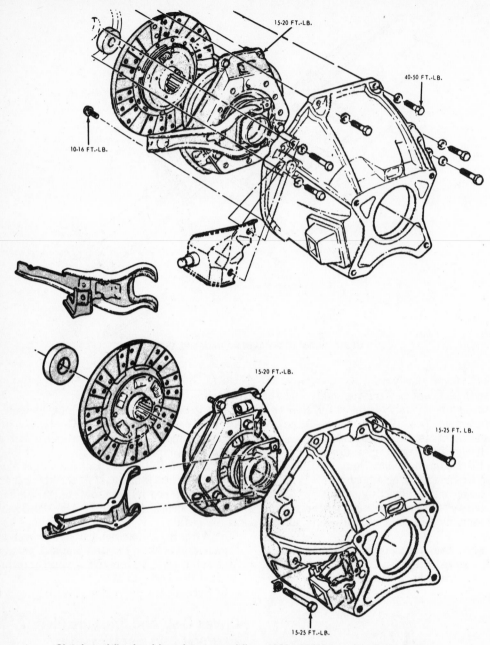

Clutch and flywheel housing assemblies, 1966–77 V8 top, 6-cylinder bottom

3. Disconnect the release lever retracting spring and the release rod.

4. Remove the hub and release bearing assembly.

5. Remove the flywheel housing-to-engine bolts and lower the flywheel housing.

6. Remove the pressure plate and disc from the flywheel. Unscrew the attaching bolts a few turns at a time, in a staggered sequence to prevent distortion of the pressure plate.

To install the clutch:

7. Wash the flywheel surface with alcohol.

Do not use an oil base cleaner, carbon tetrachloride or gasoline.

8. Place the clutch disc and the pressure plate and cover assembly in position on the flywheel. Start the retaining bolts until fingertight.

9. Align the clutch disc with an aligning tool (an old mainshaft works well), and then evenly torque the bolts to 23–28 ft.lbs.

10. Lightly lubricate the release lever fulcrum and ends with lithium base grease and position the release lever in the flywheel hous-

ing. Crimp the dust seal tabs flush against the flywheel housing. Attach the springs of the release bearing hub to the ends of the release fork. Be careful not to distort the springs.

11. Fill the groove in the clutch release bearing hub with lithium base grease. Wipe the excess grease from the hub.

12. Position the flywheel housing and release lever assembly, and install the mounting bolts. Make sure that the muffler front hanger is in place on the flywheel housing. Install the dust cover, and tighten the attaching bolts.

13. Remove any dirt, paint or burrs from the mounting surfaces of the flywheel housing and the transmission.

14. Install the transmission and transfer case.

15. Install the starter and connect the starter cable.

16. Adjust the clutch pedal free travel and check the operation of the clutch.

1978–79

1. Disconnect the release lever retracting spring and pushrod assembly at the lever.

2. Refer to the appropriate transmission part of this chapter for instructions and remove the transmission from the vehicle.

3. If the clutch housing is not provided with a dust cover, remove the starting motor. Remove the flywheel housing attaching bolts and remove the housing.

4. If the flywheel housing is provided with a dust cover, remove it from the housing. Remove the release lever and release bearing from the clutch housing.

5. Mark the pressure plate and cover assembly and the flywheel, so that the parts can be reinstalled in the same relative position.

6. Loosen the pressure plate and cover attaching bolts evenly until the pressure plate springs are expanded, and remove the bolts.

7. Remove the pressure plate and cover assembly and the clutch disc from the flywheel or through the opening in the bottom of the clutch housing. Remove the pilot bearing only for replacement.

To Install:

1. Position the clutch disc on the flywheel so that the pilot tool can enter the clutch pilot bearing and align the disc.

2. When installing the original pressure plate and cover assembly, align the assembly and flywheel according to the marks made during the removal operations. Position the pressure plate and cover assembly on the flywheel, align the pressure plate and disc, and install the retaining bolts that fasten the assembly to the flywheel. Tighten the bolts to 20–30 ft.lb. and remove the clutch disc pilot tool.

3. With the clutch fully released, apply a light film of lithium base grease ESA-M1C75-B or equivalent on the sides of the driving lugs.

4. Position the clutch release bearing and

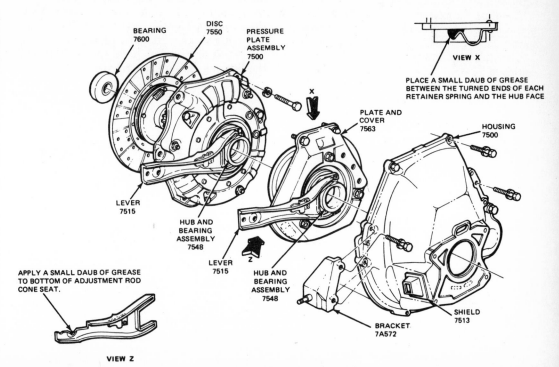

Clutch installation, 8-351, 400

ALIGNING TOOL   CLUTCH DISC

PRESSURE PLATE

Installing the clutch to the flywheel

the bearing hub on the release lever. Install the release lever on the trunnion in the flywheel housing. Apply a light film of lithium base grease ESA-M1C75-B or equivalent to the release lever fingers and to the lever trunnion or fulcrum. Fill the annular groove of the release bearing hub with grease.

5. If the flywheel housing has been removed, position it against the engine rear cover plate, and install the attaching bolts. Tighten the bolts to 40–50 ft.lb.

6. Install the starter motor. Install the transmission assembly on the clutch housing. Tighten the bolts to 50–60 ft.lb.

7. Install the slave cylinder on vehicles so equipped, and tighten the bolts.

8. Adjust the release lever pushrod assembly. Connect the release lever retracting spring.

9. Install the clutch housing dust cover if so equipped.

1980–86

1. Disconnect the release lever retracting spring and pushrod assembly at the lever. Remove starter.

2. Refer to the appropriate transmission part of this chapter for instructions and remove the transmission from the vehicle.

3. If the clutch housing is not provided with a dust cover, remove the starter. Remove the flywheel housing attaching bolts and remove the housing.

4. If the flywheel housing is provided with a dust cover, remove it from the housing. Remove the release lever and release bearing from the clutch housing.

5. Loosen the pressure plate and cover attaching bolts evenly until the pressure plate springs are expanded, and remove the bolts.

6. Remove the pressure plate and cover assembly and the clutch disc from the flywheel or through the opening in the bottom of the clutch housing. Remove the pilot bearing only for replacement.

To Install:

1. Position the clutch disc on the flywheel so that the pilot tool can enter the clutch pilot bearing and align the disc.

2. When installing the original pressure plate and cover assembly, align the assembly and flywheel according to the marks made during the removal operations. Position the pressure plate and cover assembly on the flywheel, align the pressure plate and disc, and install the retaining bolts that fasten the assembly to the flywheel. Tighten the bolts to 20–30 ft.lb., and remove the clutch disc pilot tool.

3. Position the clutch release bearing and the bearing hub on the release lever. Install

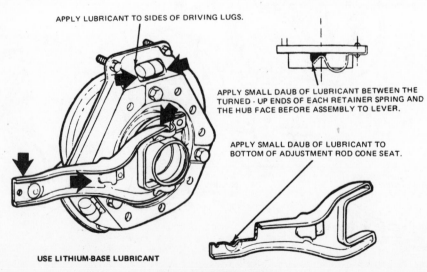

APPLY LUBRICANT TO SIDES OF DRIVING LUGS.

APPLY SMALL DAUB OF LUBRICANT BETWEEN THE TURNED - UP ENDS OF EACH RETAINER SPRING AND THE HUB FACE BEFORE ASSEMBLY TO LEVER.

APPLY SMALL DAUB OF LUBRICANT TO BOTTOM OF ADJUSTMENT ROD CONE SEAT.

USE LITHIUM-BASE LUBRICANT

Clutch lubrication points

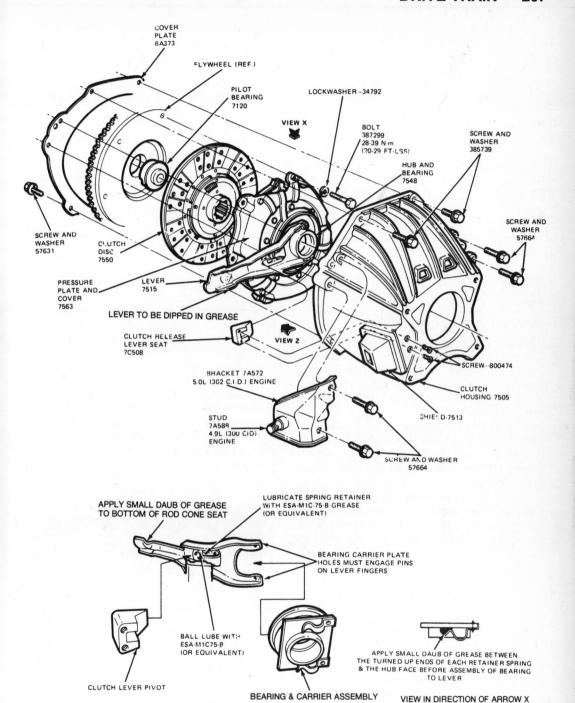

COVER
PLATE
6A373

FLYWHEEL (REF.)

PILOT
BEARING
7120

LOCKWASHER –34792

VIEW X

BOLT
387299
28-39 N·m
(20-29 FT-LBS)

SCREW AND
WASHER
385739

HUB AND
BEARING
7548

SCREW AND
WASHER
57664

SCREW AND
WASHER
57631

CLUTCH
DISC
7550

PRESSURE
PLATE AND
COVER
7563

LEVER
7515

LEVER TO BE DIPPED IN GREASE

CLUTCH RELEASE
LEVER SEAT
7C508

VIEW Z

BRACKET 7A572
5.0L (302 C.I.D.) ENGINE

STUD
7A588
4.9L (300 CID)
ENGINE

SCREW–800474

CLUTCH
HOUSING 7505

SHIELD-7513

SCREW AND WASHER
57664

APPLY SMALL DAUB OF GREASE
TO BOTTOM OF ROD CONE SEAT

LUBRICATE SPRING RETAINER
WITH ESA-M1C-75-B GREASE
(OR EQUIVALENT)

BEARING CARRIER PLATE
HOLES MUST ENGAGE PINS
ON LEVER FINGERS

BALL LUBE WITH
ESA-M1C75-B
(OR EQUIVALENT)

CLUTCH LEVER PIVOT

BEARING & CARRIER ASSEMBLY

APPLY SMALL DAUB OF GREASE BETWEEN
THE TURNED UP ENDS OF EACH RETAINER SPRING
& THE HUB FACE BEFORE ASSEMBLY OF BEARING
TO LEVER

VIEW IN DIRECTION OF ARROW X

VIEW IN DIRECTION OF ARROW Z

Clutch installation, 1980 and later 6-300, 8-302, 8-351W

the release lever on the pivot bar pedestal in the flywheel housing. Apply a light film of lithium base grease ESA-M1C75-B or equivalent to the release lever fingers and to the lever pivot ball. Fill the annular groove of the release bearing hub with grease.

4. If the flywheel housing has been removed, position it against the engine rear cover plate and install the attaching bolts. Tighten the bolts to 40–50 ft.lb.

5. Install the starter motor. Install the transmission assembly on the clutch housing. Tighten the bolts.

6. Adjust the release lever pushrod assembly. Connect the release lever retracting spring.

7. Install the clutch housing dust cover if so equipped.

AUTOMATIC TRANSMISSION

The automatic transmission installed in the 1966–77 Bronco is the C4 model. In the 1978–86 models, the C6 is the only unit used. The only adjustments that can be made on the C4 are the Intermediate and Low/Reverse bands. On the C6, only the intermediate band is adjustable.

NOTE: *Driveline vibration in 1973 models with automatic transmission may be caused by a lifting eye attached to the transfer case on the rear bearing retainer. This contacts the floor causing vibration. Remove and discard the lifting eye and replace the bolt.*

Pan

REMOVAL AND INSTALLATION

NOTE: *The torque converter on all of the transmissions has a drain plug. If the converter is drained, refill the C4 with 5 quarts of fluid and the C6 with 8 quarts of fluid.*

1. Raise the vehicle so the transmission oil pan is readily accessible.

2. On the C4 disconnect the fluid filler tube from the pan and allow the fluid to drain into an appropriate container. On the C6 start removing the pan bolts so that the fluid drains from one corner.

NOTE: *It is not recommended that the drained fluid be used over again; refill the transmission with new fluid. However, in an emergency situation, the old fluid can be reused. The old fluid should be strained through a #100 screen or a fine mesh cloth before being reinstalled.*

3. Remove the transmission oil pan attaching bolts, pan and gasket.

4. Clean the transmission oil pan and transmission mating surfaces.

5. Install the transmission oil pan in the reverse order of removal, torquing the attaching bolts to 12–16 ft.lb. and using a new gasket. Fill the transmission with 3 qts. of the correct type fluid, check the operation of the transmission and check for leakage.

NOTE: *The C4 automatic transmission uses Type F automatic transmission fluid only. The C6 uses type CJ or Dexron® II. When starting the engine after the transmission fluid has been drained, do not race the engine. Move the gear shift selector through all of the ranges before moving the vehicle.*

FILTER SERVICE

1. Remove the transmission oil pan and gasket.

2. Remove the fine mesh oil screen by removing the machine screws holding it to the lower valve body.

CAUTION: *When removing the filter on C4 transmissions, be careful not to lose the throttle pressure limit valve and spring when separating the filter from the valve body.*

3. Install the new filter screen and transmission oil pan gasket in the reverse order of removal.

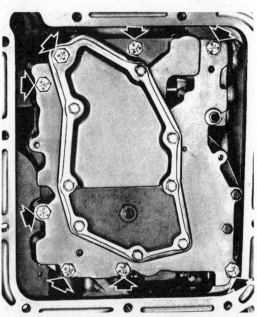

View showing the filter screen, which is attached to the lower valve body. Bolts indicated by arrows are holding the valve body. Do not remove these if the screen only is being serviced

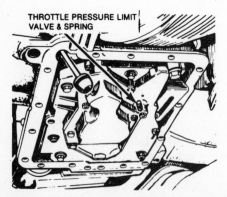

THROTTLE PRESSURE LIMIT VALVE & SPRING

C4 throttle pressure limit valve which is held in place in the valve body by the filter. The valve is installed with the large end toward the valve body; the spring fits over the valve stem

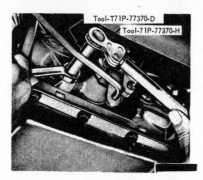

Tool-T71P-77370-D
Tool-71P-77370-H

Adjusting the intermediate band

Adjustments

FRONT BAND (INTERMEDIATE) ADJUSTMENT

C4, C6

1. Clean all dirt from the adjusting screw and remove and discard the locknut.
2. Install a new locknut on the adjusting screw. Using a torque wrench, tighten the adjusting screw to 10 ft.lb.
3. Back off the adjusting screw EXACTLY 1¾ TURNS FOR THE C4, 1½ TURNS FOR THE C6.
4. Hold the adjusting screw steady and tighten the locknut to 35–45 ft.lb.

REAR BAND (LOW/REVERSE) ADJUSTMENT

C4 Only

1. Clean all dirt from around the band adjusting screw and remove and discard the locknut.
2. Install a new locknut on the adjusting screw. Using a torque wrench, tighten the adjusting screw to 10 ft.lb.
3. Back off the adjusting screw EXACTLY 3 FULL TURNS.
4. Hold the adjusting screw steady and tighten the locknut to 35–45 ft.lb.

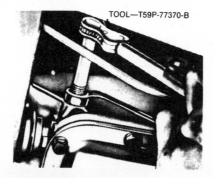

TOOL—T59P-77370-B

Adjusting the low-reverse band

SHIFT LINKAGE ADJUSTMENT

1966–77

1. Place the selector lever in Drive and hold it against the D stop.
2. Loosen the shift rod adjusting nut at point A.
3. Move the transmission lever into Drive by pushing it all the way rearward and then forward two detents.
4. Tighten the adjusting nut, taking care not to disturb the adjustment.
5. Operate the linkage. Error in the adjustment must not exceed ⅛ of a detent.

1978–86

1. With the engine stopped and the parking brake applied, place the transmission selector lever at the steering column in the D (DRIVE) position and hold against the D stop by applying an eight pound weight to the selector lever knob.
2. Loosen the shift rod adjusting nut at point A.
3. Shift the manual lever at the transmission into the D (DRIVE) position, by moving the lever all the way rearward, then forward two detents.
4. With the selector lever and transmission manual lever in the D position, tighten the nut at point A 12–18 ft.lb. torque. Use care to prevent motion between the stud and rod.
5. Remove the eight pound weight from the steering column selector lever knob.
6. Operate the shift lever in all positions to make certain that the manual lever at the transmission is in full detent in all gear ranges. Re-adjust the linkage if required.
7. Verify neutral start switch adjustment. Error must not exceed ⅛ detent. Under no circumstances will it be permissible to adjust linkage in any position other than the D position.

DOWNSHIFT LINKAGE ADJUSTMENT

1. Rotate the throttle plate to the full open position.
2. Insert a 0.060″ (1.5mm) spacer between the throttle lever and the adjusting screw.
3. Move the transmission kickdown lever until it touches the internal stop.
4. Turn the adjusting screw until it contacts the 0.060″ (1.5mm) spacer. Remove the spacer.

NEUTRAL START SWITCH ADJUSTMENT

1. Loosen the two switch adjusting screws.
2. Place the transmission lever in Neutral.
3. Rotate the switch and insert a #43 drill

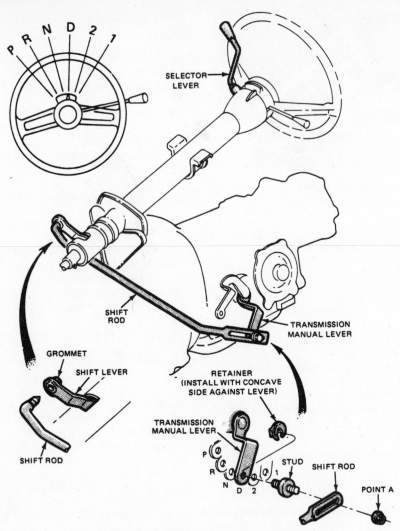

1966–77 C4 shift linkage adjustment

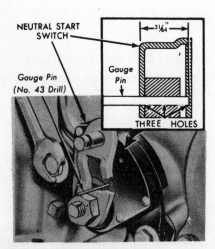

Neutral start switch adjustment

bit, shank end into the gauge pin holes of the switch.

4. The gauge pin must be inserted ½" (12.7mm) into the three holes.

5. Tighten the attaching bolts and remove the drill bit.

Transmission

REMOVAL AND INSTALLATION

C4, 1966–77

1. Disconnect the fan shroud from the radiator.

2. Raise and support the vehicle on jackstands.

3. Remove the transfer case skid plate.

4. Remove the transmission filler tube and drain the fluid.

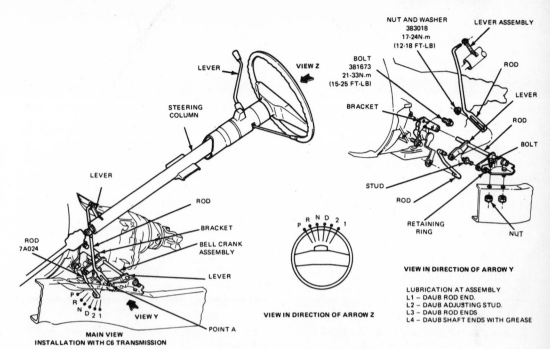

1978 and later C6 shift linkage adjustment

5. Drain the transfer case.

6. Remove the converter drain plug access cover from the lower end of the converter housing.

7. Remove the convert-to-flywheel attaching nuts. Place a wrench on the crankshaft pulley attaching bolt to turn the converter, thereby giving access to the nuts.

8. Turn the converter to gain access to the drain plug and remove it.

9. When the fluid has drained, replace the plug.

10. Disconnect the rear driveshaft.

11. Remove the front driveshaft.

12. Remove the complete exhaust system.

13. Remove the speedometer cable.

14. Disconnect the transmission oil cooler lines.

15. Disconnect the transmission linkage.

16. Remove the starter.

17. Disconnect the vacuum lines from the transmission.

18. Disconnect the transfer case adapter from the crossmember.

19. Remove the crossmember-to-frame side support attaching bolts.

20. Support the transmission and transfer case on a jack.

21. Raise the jack slightly, to take up the weight and remove the four bolts securing the left side support bracket, crossmember and upper crossmember insulators.

22. Disconnect the shift rod from the transfer case shift lever bracket.

23. Remove the bolts that attach the shift lever bracket to the transfer case adapter and allow the assembly to hang by the shift lever.

24. Make sure the transmission is secure on the jack and remove the six converter housing-to-engine bolts.

25. Remove the transmission assembly from the engine by rolling the jack backwards and letting it down slowly.

26. When installing the transmission, turn the converter so that the studs and drain plug are aligned with their holes in the flywheel.

27. Roll the assembly forward into position.

CAUTION: *Make certain that the converter rests squarely against the flywheel. This ensures that the converter pilot is not binding in the engine crankshaft.*

28. Install the six mounting bolts and torque to 30 ft.lb.

29. Install the shift lever bracket.

30. Install the shift rod, spring washer, flat washer and cotter pin.

31. Install the crossmember and insulators.

32. Lower the transmission assembly onto the crossmember and remove the jack.

33. Bolt the transfer case to the crossmember.

34. Install the flywheel-to-converter nuts and torque to 30 ft.lb.

35. Install the starter and torque the bolts to 30 ft.lb.

36. Connect the filler tube and oil cooler lines.

37. Install the vacuum lines.

38. Install the speedometer cable.
39. Connect the transmission linkage rods to the levers.
40. Adjust the linkage.
41. Install the exhaust system.
42. Connect the rear driveshaft.
43. Connect the front axle driveshaft.
44. Install the converter drain plug access cover.
45. Fill the transfer case with lubricant as outlined in the first chapter and install the skid plate.
46. Lower the vehicle, install the fan shroud and fill the transmission with type F fluid.
47. Adjust the manual and downshift linkage.

C6, 1978–86

1. Drive the vehicle on a hoist, but do not raise at this time.
2. Remove the two upper converter housing-to-engine bolts.
3. Remove the bolt securing the fluid filler tube to the engine cylinder head.
4. Raise the vehicle on a hoist or stands.
5. Place the drain pan under the transmission fluid pan. Starting at the rear of the pan and working toward the front, loosen the attaching bolts and allow the fluid to drain. Finally remove all of the pan attaching bolts except two at the front, to allow the fluid to further drain. With fluid drained, install two bolts on the rear side of the pan to temporarily hold it in place.
6. Remove the converter drain plug access cover from the lower end of the converter housing.
7. Remove the converter-to-flywheel attaching nuts. Place a wrench on the crankshaft pulley attaching bolt to turn the converter to gain access to the nuts.
8. With the wrench on the crankshaft pulley attaching bolt, turn the converter to gain access to the converter drain plug and remove the plug. Place a drain pan under the converter to catch the fluid. After the fluid has been drained, install the plug.
9. Disconnect the driveshaft from the rear axle and slide shaft rearward from the transmission. Install a seal installation tool in the extension housing to prevent fluid leakage.
10. Disconnect the speedometer cable from the extension housing.
11. Disconnect the throttle and manual linkage rods from the levers at the transmission.
12. Disconnect the oil cooler lines from the transmission.
13. Remove the vacuum hose from the vacuum unit. Remove the vacuum line retaining clip.

14. Disconnect the cable from the terminal on the starter motor. Remove the three attaching bolts and remove the starter motor.
15. Remove the transfer case.
16. Loosen the radius arm brackets and rotate them outward and downward to clear the transmission rear support. Remove the nuts from the crossmember-to-frame and crossmember-to-transmission bolts, leaving the bolts loose in the frame.

NOTE: *Shipping screws may appear between the two studs attaching the crossmember to the frame. They are not required and must be loosened to allow the crossmember to drop.*

17. Remove the transfer case steady-rest absorber and frame side bracket.
18. Force the transmission support downward to clear the transfer case and move it rearward taking care to avoid damage to the left frame rail fuel or brake lines. Some force may be required to clear the converter.
19. The frame opens to the rear to permit the crossmember to be moved downward, free of the frame rails.
20. Secure the transmission to the jack with the safety chain.
21. Remove the remaining converter housing-to-engine attaching bolts.
22. Move the transmission away from the engine. Lower the jack and remove the converter and transmission assembly from under the vehicle.

To Install:

1. Tighten the converter drain plug to 14–28 ft.lb.
2. Position the converter on the transmission making sure the converter drive flats are fully engaged in the pump gear.
3. With the converter properly installed, place the transmission on the jack. Secure the transmission to the jack with the chain.
4. Rotate the converter until the studs and drain plug are in alignment with their holes in the flywheel.
5. Move the converter and transmission assembly forward into position, using care not to damage the flywheel and the converter pilot. The converter must rest squarely against the flywheel. This indicates that the converter pilot is not binding in the engine crankshaft.
6. Install and tighten the converter housing-to-engine attaching bolts to 40–50 ft.lb.
7. Remove the transmission jack safety chain from around the transmission.
8. Position the No. 2 crossmember to the frame side rails. Install and tighten the attaching bolts to 55–65 ft.lb.
9. Install transfer case.
10. Position the engine rear support cross-

member to the frame side rails. Install the rear support-to-extension housing mounting bolts and tighten the bolts to 50–60 ft.lb.

11. Lower the transmission and remove the jack.

12. Secure the engine rear support crossmember to the frame side rails with the attaching bolts and tighten them to 50–60 ft.lb.

13. Connect the vacuum line to the vacuum diaphragm making sure that the line is in the retaining clip.

14. Connect the oil cooler lines to the transmission.

15. Connect the throttle and manual linkage rods to their respective levers on the transmission.

16. Connect the speedometer cable to the bearing retainer.

17. Secure the starter motor in place with the attaching bolts. Connect the cable to the terminal on the starter.

18. Install a new O-ring on the lower end of the transmission filler tube and insert the tube in the case.

19. Secure the converter-to-flywheel attaching nuts and tighten them to 20–30 ft.lb.

20. Install the converter housing dust shield and secure it with the attaching bolts.

21. Connect the driveshaft.

22. Adjust the shift linkage as required.

23. Lower the vehicle. Then install the two upper converter housing-to-engine bolts and tighten them to 20–30 ft.lb.

24. Position the transmission fluid filler tube to the cylinder head and secure with the attaching bolt.

25. Fill the transmission to the correct level with Ford type CJ fluid.

TRANSFER CASE

The transfer case used in 1966–77 models is the Dana 20 2-speed unit. In 1978–79 models, the New Process 205 part time and the new Process 203 full time units were available. In 1980–86 models, the only unit used is the New Process 208 part time.

Adjustments

SHIFT LEVER

NOTE: *The NP-205 and 208 do not require adjustment.*

DANA 20, 1966–72

1. Shift the transfer case selector lever into the 4L position and raise the vehicle on a hoist.

2. Loosen the pawl plate attaching bolt.

3. Press inward on the shift rail link to be sure that the two shift rails are indexed to their respective detents.

4. Tighten the pawl plate attaching bolt to 20–30 ft.lb.

5. Lower the vehicle and check the shift operation. The pawl assembly must index against the sides of the pawl plate notches in all positions. If the pawl assembly plunger requires more travel to lock and unlock easily, remove the T-handle and rotate the plunger ½ turns counterclockwise.

NOTE: *No adjustment is possible on 1973–77 models.*

NP-203

1. Place shift lever in neutral position.

2. Remove two adjusting stud nuts.

3. Install ¼" (6.35mm) diameter alignment pin, 1¼" (31¾mm) long, through shifter assembly.

4. Align the two transfer case levers as follows:

   a. Bottom lever, (Lock lever): Rotate clockwise to the forward position.

   b. Top lever, (Range lever): Place in the Mid-position or Neutral position.

5. Reposition the two shift rods and tighten new adjusting stud nuts to 15–20 ft.lb.

6. Remove alignment pin from shifter assembly.

Transfer Case

REMOVAL AND INSTALLATION

Dana 20

1. Shift the transfer case into Neutral.

2. Remove the bolts attaching the fan shroud to the radiator support.

3. Raise the vehicle on a hoist.

4. Support the transfer case shield with a jack and remove the bolts that attach the shield to the frame side rails. Remove the shield.

5. Drain the transmission and transfer case lubricant.

6. Disconnect the front and rear driveshafts at the transfer case.

7. Disconnect the speedometer cable at the transfer case.

8. If equipped with a manual transmission, disconnect the shift rods from the transmission shift lever. Then, place the First/Reverse gear shift lever in to the First gear position and insert the fabricated tool. (See transmission removal and installation.) This tool will prevent the input shaft roller bearings from dropping into the transmission case when separating the transfer case from the transmission and output shaft.

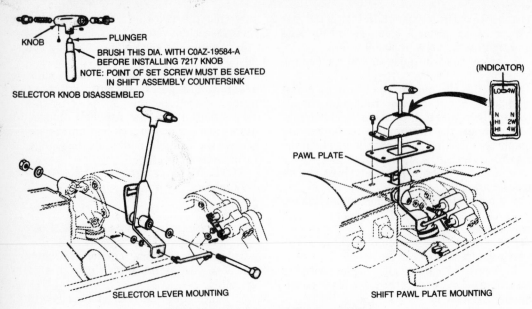

KNOB — PLUNGER

BRUSH THIS DIA. WITH C0AZ-19584-A
BEFORE INSTALLING 7217 KNOB
NOTE: POINT OF SET SCREW MUST BE SEATED
IN SHIFT ASSEMBLY COUNTERSINK

SELECTOR KNOB DISASSEMBLED

(INDICATOR)

PAWL PLATE

SELECTOR LEVER MOUNTING

SHIFT PAWL PLATE MOUNTING

1966–72 transfer case shifter assemblies

9. Support the engine with a jack.

10. Remove the two cotter pins, bolts, washers, plates and insulators that secure the crossmember to the transfer case adapter.

11. Remove the crossmember to frame side support attaching bolts.

12. Raise the transmission and remove the upper insulators from the crossmember. Remove the crossmember.

NOTE: *For vehicles built before Nov. 1, 1974 use step 13. For those built on or after Nov. 1, 1974 use 13A.*

13. Roll back the boot enclosing the transfer case shift linkage. Remove the threaded cap holding the shift lever assembly to the shift bracket. Remove the shift lever assembly.

13A. Remove the carpet from around the shift levers. Remove the bolts holding the shifter to the transmission adapter. Remove the boot from the bottom of the shifter. Bend up the left side of the floor opening as required to remove the shifter assembly.

14. Secure the transfer case to a transmission jack and remove the transfer case adapter-to-transmission attaching bolts.

15. Move the transfer case and jack rearward until it clears the transmission output shaft. Lower the transfer case.

16. Installation is the reverse of the removal procedure.

NOTE: *A loose shift feel may occur in some 1973–74 models with automatic transmission and U-shift transfer case pattern. This is caused by the transfer case shift lever fulcrum ball braze separating from the lever. Install a new lever as follows:*

1. Remove the right and left door sill plates and roll back the floor mat.

2. Remove the shift lever post (3 screws) and knob.

3. Remove the through bolt and nut, disconnect the spring and remove the lever.

4. Install a new lever and knob.

New Process 205

1. Drain the transfer case. Disconnect the rear axle driveshaft and front driveshaft from the flange at the transfer case.

2. Disconnect the shift selector rod steady rest and the speedometer cable at the transfer case.

3. Secure the transfer case to a transmission jack, and remove the mounting bolts.

4. Remove transfer case, and place it on a floor stand or work bench.

To Install:

1. Remove the transfer case from the floor stand or bench and place it on the transmission jack.

2. Raise the transfer case into position and attach the mounting bolts. Tighten the bolts and nuts to 20–40 ft.lb.

3. Connect the shift selector rod, the speedometer cable, and steady rest.

4. Connect the front and rear axle driveshafts and tighten the universal joint U-bolt nuts.

5. Fill the transfer case to filler plug level with SAE 80W/90 oil. Tighten drain plug to 25–35 ft.lb.

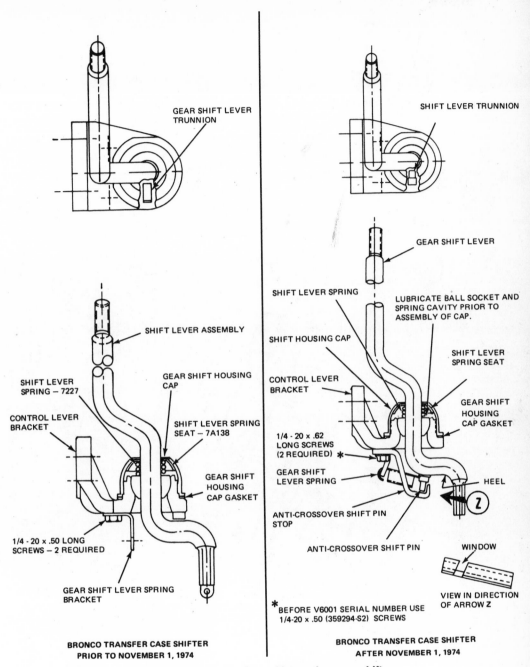

Differences in the Dana 20 transfer case shifter

New Process 203

1. Drain the transfer case by removing the power take-off lower bolts and the front output rear cover lower bolts.

2. Disconnect the front axle driveshaft from the flange at the transfer case.

3. Disconnect the shift rods from the transfer case.

4. Disconnect the speedometer cable and lockout lamp switch wire from the transfer case rear output shaft housing.

5. Remove the transfer case-to-transmission adapter attaching bolts. Disconnect the rear axle driveshaft at the transfer case flange.

6. Position a transmission jack under the transfer case and secure it to the jack.

7. Remove the transfer case mounting bracket support to frame crossmember nuts, bolts, spacers and upper absorbers and remove the transfer case.

8. Using a chain fall, place the transfer case on a suitable work bench.

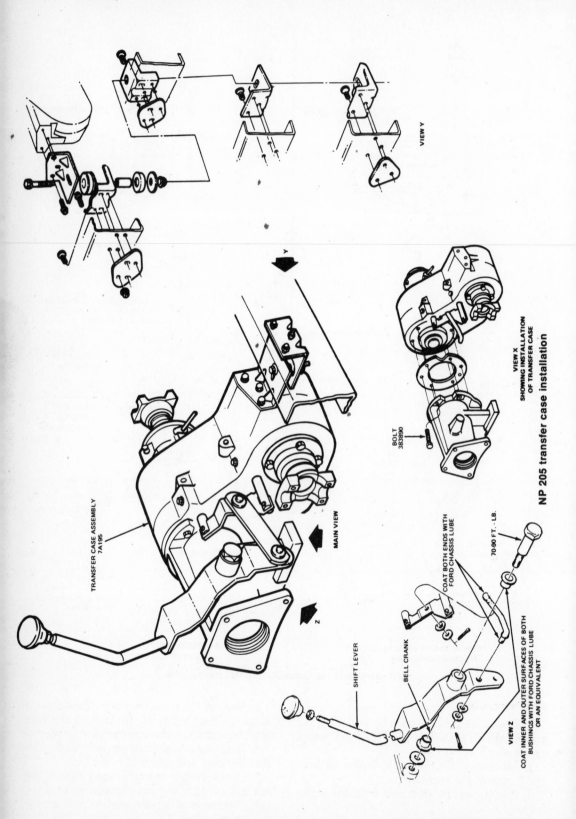

VIEW V

TRANSFER CASE ASSEMBLY
7A195

MAIN VIEW

BOLT
383890

VIEW X
SHOWING INSTALLATION
OF TRANSFER CASE

NP 205 transfer case installation

SHIFT LEVER

Z

BELL CRANK

COAT BOTH ENDS WITH
FORD CHASSIS LUBE

70-90 FT. - LB.

VIEW Z
COAT INNER AND OUTER SURFACES OF BOTH
BUSHINGS WITH FORD CHASSIS LUBE
OR AN EQUIVALENT

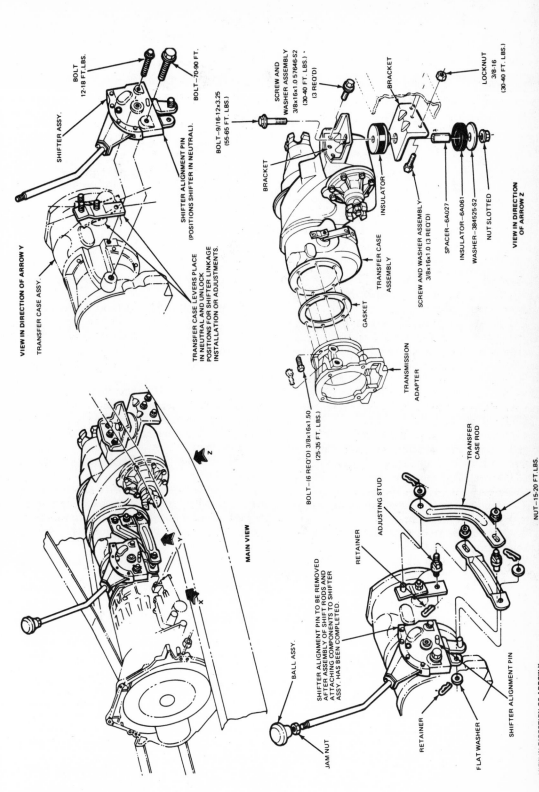

VIEW IN DIRECTION OF ARROW Y

TRANSFER CASE ASSY.

SHIFTER ASSY.

BOLT
12-18 FT.LBS.

BOLT—70-90 FT.

SHIFTER ALIGNMENT PIN
(POSITIONS SHIFTER IN NEUTRAL).

TRANSFER CASE LEVERS PLACE
IN NEUTRAL AND UNLOCK
POSITIONS FOR SHIFTER LINKAGE
INSTALLATION OR ADJUSTMENTS.

BOLT—9/16-12x3.25
(55-65 FT. LBS.)

SCREW AND
WASHER ASSEMBLY
3/8x16x1.0 57646-S2
(30-40 FT. LBS.)
(3 REQ'D)

BRACKET

BRACKET

INSULATOR

TRANSFER CASE
ASSEMBLY

GASKET

SCREW AND WASHER ASSEMBLY
3/8x16x1.0 (3 REQ'D)

SPACER—6A027

INSULATOR—6A061

WASHER—38452S-S2

NUT SLOTTED

LOCKNUT
3/8-16
(30-40 FT. LBS.)

VIEW IN DIRECTION
OF ARROW Z

TRANSMISSION
ADAPTER

BOLT—(6 REQ'D) 3/8x16x1.50
(25-35 FT. LBS.)

MAIN VIEW

Z

Y

X

SHIFTER ALIGNMENT PIN TO BE REMOVED
AFTER ASSEMBLY OF SHIFT RODS AND
ATTACHING COMPONENTS TO SHIFTER
ASSY. HAS BEEN COMPLETED.

BALL ASSY.

JAM NUT

RETAINER

ADJUSTING STUD

TRANSFER
CASE ROD

NUT—15-20 FT.LBS.

RETAINER

FLAT WASHER

SHIFTER ALIGNMENT PIN

VIEW IN DIRECTION OF ARROW X

NP 203 transfer case installation

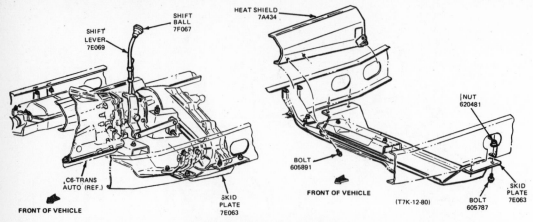

NP 208 transfer case installation

To Install:

1. Using a chain fall, secure the transfer case on a transmission jack.

2. Position the transfer case in the truck, aligning the mounting bracket supports with the lower absorbers. Align the transfer case-to-transmission attaching bolts.

3. Install the transfer case mounting bracket support to frame crossmember bolts with upper absorbers and spacers. Tighten all mounting bolts to 40–50 ft.lb.

4. Remove the transmission jack.

5. Connect the speedometer cable and the lockout switch wire to the transfer case.

6. Connect the rear axle driveshaft to the transfer case rear output flange.

7. Install the shift rods on the transfer case and adjust the shift linkage.

8. Connect the front axle driveshaft to the transfer case flange.

9. Fill the transfer case with SAE 80W/90 oil. Tighten the filler plug to 25–35 ft.lb.

New Process 208

1. Raise vehicle on a hoist.

2. Place a drain pan under transfer case, remove drain plug and drain fluid from transfer case.

3. Disconnect four wheel drive indicator switch wire connector at transfer case.

4. Disconnect speedometer driven gear from transfer case rear bearing retainer.

5. Remove nut retaining transmission shift lever assembly to transfer case.

6. If so equipped, remove skid plate from frame.

7. Remove heat shield from frame.

CAUTION: *Catalytic converter is located beside the heat shield. Be careful when working around catalytic converter because of the extremely high temperatures generated by the converter.*

8. Support transfer case with transmission jack.

9. Disconnect front driveshaft from front output shaft yoke.

10. Disconnect rear driveshaft from rear output shaft yoke.

11. Remove the bolts retaining transfer case to transmission adapter. Remove gasket between transfer case and adapter.

12. Lower transfer case from vehicle.

To Install:

1. Place a new gasket between transfer case and adapter.

2. Raise transfer case with transmission jack so transmission output shaft aligns with splined transfer case input shaft. Install bolts retaining transfer case to adapter. Tighten bolts to 30–40 ft.lb.

3. Connect rear driveshaft to rear output shaft yoke.

4. Connect front driveshaft to front output yoke.

5. Remove transmission jack from transfer case.

6. Position heat shield to frame crossmember and mounting lug on transfer case. Install and tighten bolts and screw to 11–16 ft.lb.

7. Install skid plate to frame. Tighten nuts and bolts.

8. Install shift lever to transfer case. Install retaining nut.

9. Connect speedometer driven gear to transfer case.

10. Connect 4-wheel drive indicator switch wire connector at transfer case.

11. Install drain plug. Remove filler plug, and install 2.8 liters (six pints) of automatic transmission fluid Ford type CJ or Dexron®II, Series D or equivalent. Install filler plug.

12. Lower vehicle.

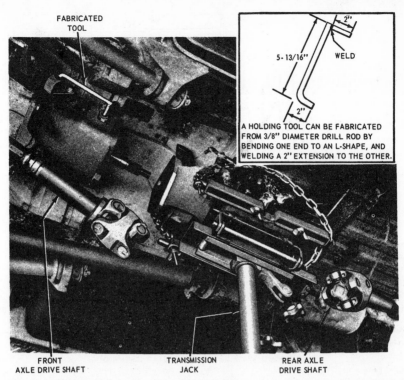

FABRICATED
TOOL

5- 13/16"   WELD

2"

2"

A HOLDING TOOL CAN BE FABRICATED
FROM 3/8" DIAMETER DRILL ROD BY
BENDING ONE END TO AN L-SHAPE, AND
WELDING A 2" EXTENSION TO THE OTHER.

FRONT
AXLE DRIVE SHAFT

TRANSMISSION
JACK

REAR AXLE
DRIVE SHAFT

Removal or installation of the Dana 20 transfer case and the dimensions of the holding tool which must be used when removing the transfer case or transmission

DRIVE LINE

Front and Rear Driveshafts

The Bronco driveshaft assemblies are of the double Cardan type, which incorporate two universal joints, a centering socket yoke and a center yoke at the transfer case end of each shaft. A single universal joint is used at the axle end of the shafts.

The universal joint spiders and sliding splines are equipped with lubrication fittings.

All driveshafts are balanced; therefore care should be taken to maintain the balance.

REMOVAL AND INSTALLATION

1. To remove the rear driveshaft, disconnect the double Cardan joint from the flange at the transfer case and the single U-joint from the flange at the rear axle. Remove the driveshaft.

2. To remove the front driveshaft, disconnect the double Cardan joint from the flange at the transfer case and the single U-joint from the flange at the front axle. Remove the driveshaft.

3. To install the front and rear driveshafts, position the single U-joint end of the driveshaft to the front axle and install the U-bolts and nuts. Torque the nuts to 10–17 ft.lb.

4. Position the double Cardan joint to the transfer case and install the 4 bolts and lock washers. Torque the bolts to 20–25 ft.lb.

U-Joints

DISASSEMBLY AND ASSEMBLY

1. Mark the position of the spiders, the center yoke, and the centering socket as related to the stud yoke which is welded to the front of the driveshaft tube. The spiders must be assembled with the bosses in their original positions to provide proper clearance.

2. Remove the snaprings that secure the bearings in the front of the center yoke.

3. Position the driveshaft in a vise so that the bearing caps that are pressed into the center yoke can be pressed or driven out with a drift and hammer. Do this for all of the spiders.

4. Clean all the serviceable parts in cleaning solvent. If you are using a repair kit, install all of the parts supplied with the kit.

NOTE: *If the driveshaft is damaged in any way, replace the complete driveshaft to insure a balanced assembly.*

5. Assemble the U-joints in the reverse order of disassembly.

REAR AXLE

A Ford conventional, removable carrier type rear axle is used on the Bronco through 1984. A integral carrier C-Lock type rear axle is used on the Bronco from 1984–86. A Traction-

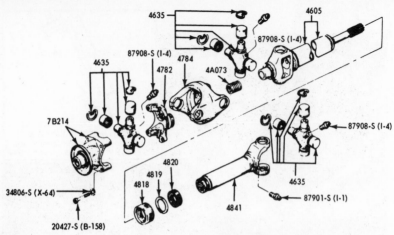

87901. Grease fitting
87908. Grease fitting
4635. Universal joint spider assembly—bearing caps with needle bearings, bearing journals, bearing cap retainers
4841. Front yoke at the axle end of the driveshaft
4820. Seal
4819. Washer
4818. Dust cap

4605. Shaft assembly
4A073. Centering socket yoke spring
4784. Center yoke
4782. Centering socket yoke pivot
7B214. Transfer case output shaft flange
20427. Flange-to-centering socket yoke pivot attaching bolt
34806. Washer

Exploded view of the driveshaft assembly

Lok® differential is available as optional equipment. An axle identification tag, showing the axle ratio as the lower left side number, is attached by one of the housing bolts.

Axle Shaft, Bearing and Seal
REMOVAL AND INSTALLATION

Removable Carrier

NOTE: *The following procedure requires the use of special tools, including a shop press.*

1. Jack up the vehicle and support it on jackstands.
2. Remove the wheel.
3. Working through the hole in the flange, remove the nuts that secure the wheel bearing retainer.
4. Pull the axle assembly out of the axle housing.
5. Whenever an axle shaft is removed the oil seal should be replaced. Install one nut to hold the brake backing plate in place and remove

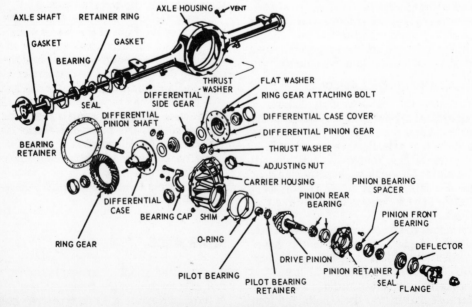

Exploded view of the Ford rear axle

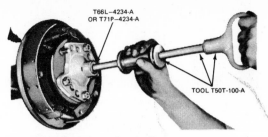

T66L—4234-A
OR T71P—4234-A

TOOL T50T-100-A

Removing the rear axle shaft

the oil seal with a slide hammer and adapter.

6. If the wheel bearing is to be replaced, the inner retaining ring must be loosened. Never use heat to do this.

7. Nick the retaining ring deeply with a cold chisel in several places. It will then slide off the axle.

8. The use of a shop press is necessary for the removal of the bearing.

To install:

9. Lightly coat the wheel bearing bores with axle lubricant.

10. Press the bearing and then the inner retaining ring onto the shaft until the retainer seats against the bearing.

11. Install the oil seal with a seal installing tool.

12. Place a new gasket between the housing flange and the backing plate, then carefully slide the axle shaft into the housing so that the rough forging of the shaft will not damage the oil seal.

13. Start the axle splines into the side gear and push the shaft in until it bottoms in the housing.

14. Install the bearing retainer plate and nuts.

15. Install the brake drum and wheel.

Integral Carrier C-Lock Type

1. Raise and safely support the vehicle on jackstands.

2. Remove the wheels and tires from the brake drums.

3. Place a drain pan under the housing and drain the lubricant by loosening the housing cover.

4. Remove the locks securing the brake drums to the axle shaft flanges and remove the drums.

5. Remove the housing cover and gasket.

6. Remove the side gear pinion shaft lockbolt and the side gear pinion shaft.

7.. Push the axle shafts inward and remove the C-locks from the inner end of the axle shafts. Temporarily replace the shaft and lockbolt to retain the differential gears in position.

8. Remove the axle shafts with a slide ham-

mer. Be sure the seal is not damaged by the splines on the axle shaft.

9. Remove the bearing and oil seal from the housing. Both the seal and bearing can be removed with a slide hammer

10. Two types of bearings are used on some axles, one requiring a press fit and the other a loose fit. A loose fitting bearing does not necessarily indicate excessive wear.

11. Inspect the axle shaft housing and axle shafts for burrs or other irregularities. Replace any work or damaged parts. A light yellow color on the bearing journal of the axle shaft is normal, and does not require replacement of the axle shaft. Slight pitting and wear is also normal.

12. Lightly coat the wheel bearing rollers with axle lubricant. Install the bearings in the axle housing until the bearing seats firmly against the shoulder.

13. Wipe all lubricant from the oil seal bore, before installing the seal.

14. Inspect the original seals for wear. If necessary, these may be replaced with new seals, which are prepacked with lubricant and do not require soaking.

15. Install the oil seal.

16. Remove the lockbolt and pinion shaft. Carefully slide the axle shafts into place. Be careful that you do not damage the seal with the splined end of the axle shaft. Engage the splined end of the shaft with the differential side gears.

17. Install the axle shaft C-locks on the inner end of the axle shafts and seat the C-locks in the counterbore of the differential side gears.

18. Rotate the differential pinion gears until the differential pinion shaft can be installed. Install the differential pinion shaft lockbolt. Tighten to 15–22 ft.lb.

19. Install the brake drum on the axle shaft flange.

20. Install the wheel and tire on the brake drum and tighten the attaching nuts.

21. Clean the gasket surface of the rear housing and install a new cover gasket and the housing cover. Some covers do not use a gasket. On these models, apply a bead of silicone sealer on the gasket surface. The bead should run inside of the bolt holes.

22. Raise the rear axle so that it is in the running position. Add the amount of specified lubricant to bring the lubricant level to ½" (12.7mm) below the filler hole.

Differential Carrier

REMOVAL

Removable Type Carrier Only

NOTE: *The C-Lock type carrier is not removable.*

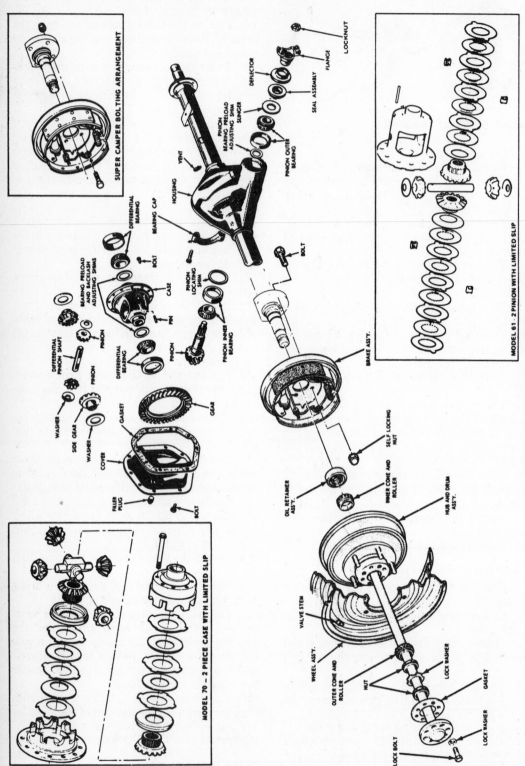

SUPER CAMPER BOLTING ARRANGEMENT

VENT

HOUSING

DIFFERENTIAL BEARING

BEARING CAP

BOLT

BEARING PRELOAD AND BACKLASH ADJUSTING SHIMS

CASE

PIN

PINION LOCATING SHIM

PINION BEARING PRELOAD ADJUSTING SHIM

SLINGER

DEFLECTOR

FLANGE

LOCKNUT

SEAL ASSEMBLY

PINION OUTER BEARING

BOLT

DIFFERENTIAL PINION SHAFT

PINION

DIFFERENTIAL BEARING

PINION

PINION INNER BEARING

PINION

WASHER

SIDE GEAR

WASHER

COVER

GASKET

GEAR

FILLER PLUG

BOLT

BRAKE ASS'Y.

SELF LOCKING NUT

OIL RETAINER ASS'Y.

INNER CONE AND ROLLER

HUB AND DRUM ASS'Y.

VALVE STEM

WHEEL ASS'Y.

OUTER CONE AND ROLLER

NUT

LOCK WASHER

GASKET

LOCK WASHER

LOCK BOLT

MODEL 70 – 2 PIECE CASE WITH LIMITED SLIP

MODEL 61 - 2 PINION WITH LIMITED SLIP

Exploded view of a Dana integral carrier type axle

1. Raise the vehicle on a hoist and remove the two rear wheel and tire assemblies.

2. Remove the brake drums from the axle shaft flange studs (back off the brake shoes to make drum removal easier).

3. Working through the access hole provided in each axle shaft flange, remove the nuts that secure the rear wheel bearing retainer plate. Pull each axle shaft assembly out of the axle housing using axle shaft puller adapter, Tool T66L-4234-A or equvalent. Wire the brake backing plate to the frame rail. Remove the gasket and discard, if so equipped.

NOTE: *Whenever a rear axle is replaced, The wheel bearing oil seals must be replace. Remove the seals with seal remover, Tool 1175-AC or equivalent (if roller bearing equipped this need not be done).*

4. Make scribe marks on the driveshaft end yoke and the axle companion flange to insure proper position at assembly. Disconnect the driveshaft at the rear axle U-joint. Hold the cups on the spider with tape. Mark the cups so that they will be in their original position relative to the flange when they are assembled. Remove the driveshaft from the transmission extension housing. Install an oil seal replacer tool in the housing to prevent transmission leakage.

5. Clean area around carrier to housing surfaces with a wire brush and wipe clean, to prevent dirt entry into the housing. Place a drain pan under the carrier and housing, remove the carrier attaching nuts and washers, and drain the axle. Remove the carrier assembly from the axle housing.

NOTE: *Synthetic Type wheel bearing seals must not be cleaned, soaked or washed in cleaning solvent.*

INSTALLATION

1. Clean the axle housing and shaft using kerosene and swabs. To avoid contamination of the of the grease in the sealed ball bearings, do not allow any quantity of solvent directly on the wheel bearings. Clean the mating surfaces of the axle housing and carrier.

2. Position the differential carrier on the studs in the axle housing using a new gasket between the carrier and the housing. To insure a good seal, apply a bead of Silicone Rubber Sealant (D6AZ-19562-A or B). to the gasket. Install the carrier to housing attaching nuts and washers, tighten them to 25–40 ft.lb.

3. Remove the oil seal replacer tool from the transmission extension housing. Position the driveshaft so that the U-joint slip yoke splines to the transmission output shaft.

4. Connect the driveshaft to the axle U-joint flange, aligning the scribe marks made on the

driveshaft end yoke and the axle U-joint flange during the removal procedure. Install the U-bolts and nuts and tighten them to specifications.

5. Install the two axle shaft assemblies in the axle housing. Care must be exercised to prevent damage to the oil seals. Carefully slide the axle shaft into the housing so that the rough forging of the shaft will not damage the oil seal. Timken bearing axle shafts do not require a gasket. Start the axle splines into the differential side gear, and push the shaft in until the bearing bottoms in the housing.

6. Install the bearing retainer plates on the attaching bolts and alternately tighten them to 20–40 ft.lb.

7. Install the two rear brake drums.

8. Install the rear wheel and tire assemblies.

9. If the rear brake shoes were backed off, adjust the brakes. (Refer to the brake chapter for procedures)

10. Fill the rear axle with the specified lubricant.

Axle Housing
REMOVAL AND INSTALLATION

1. Remove the carrier assembly from the axle housing as outlined in the above procedure.

2. Position safety stands under the rear frame members, and support the housing with either a floor jack or hoist.

3. Disengage the brake line from the clips that retain the line to the housing.

4. Disconnect the vent tube from the housing.

5. Remove the brake backing plate from the housing, and support them with wire. Do not disconnect the brake line.

6. Disconnect each rear shock absorber from the mounting bracket stud on the housing.

7. Lower the axle slightly to reduce some of the spring tension. At each rear spring, remove the spring clip (U-bolt) nuts, spring clips, and spring seat caps.

8. Remove the housing from under the vehicle.

To Install:

1. Position the axle housing under the rear springs. Install the spring clips (U-bolts), spring seat clamps and nuts. Tighten the spring clamps evenly to specifications.

2. If a new axle housing is being installed, remove the bolts that attach the brake backing plate and bearing retainer from the old housing flanges. Position the bolts in the new housing flanges to hold the brake backing plates in position.

3. Connect the vent tube to the housing.

4. Position the brake line to the housing, and secure it with the retaining clips.

5. Raise the axle housing and springs enough to allow connecting the rear shock absorbers to the mounting bracket studs on the housing.

6. Install the carrier assembly and the two axle shaft assemblies in the housing as described in the previous procedure.

FRONT AXLE

The front axle installed in Broncos is a Dana Model 30AF (1966–70), the Dana Model 44-1F (1971–77), the Dana 44-9F (1978–79) or the Dana 44-1FS (1980–86). Limited slip differentials are optional in all models. Dana front driving axles are of the integral carrier type.

NOTE: *There has been some problem with leakage in early Dana axles due to porosity, sand holes or small cracks. This type of leakage can be repaired with metallic plastic epoxy as follows:*

1. Clean the surface to be repaired by grinding to a bright metal surface. Chamfer or undercut the hole or porosity to a greater depth than the surrounding area. Solid metal must surround the hole. Openings larger than ¼" (6.35mm) must be repaired using a threaded plug.

2. Mix the epoxy as directed on the container.

3. Apply the repair mixture with a clean tool.

4. Allow the repair mixture to harden by drying with a heat lamp placed 12" (305mm) from the surface for 5 minutes or by air drying at above 50°F for 3–4 hours.

5. Grind the area to blend with the surroundings.

Manual Free Running Hub
REMOVAL AND INSTALLATION
1966–79

1. Remove the free running hub bolts and washers.

2. Remove the hub ring and the knob. Wipe the parts clean.

3. Remove the internal snapring from the groove in the hub.

4. Remove the cam body ring and clutch retainer, axle shaft sleeve, and inner clutch ring (as an assembly) from the hub. Disassemble the parts.

5. Remove the large spring. The spring collar may come out at this time. If not, you will remove it later.

6. Remove the axle shaft snapring. For easier snapring removal, push outward on the shaft at the U-joint, while pushing inward on the gear.

7. Remove the gear from the axle shaft.

8. Remove the spring collar if you didn't remove it earlier.

To Install:

1. Grease the hub inner spline with Moly grease or equivalent.

2. Install the spring retainer ring, positioned as shown with recessed undercut area

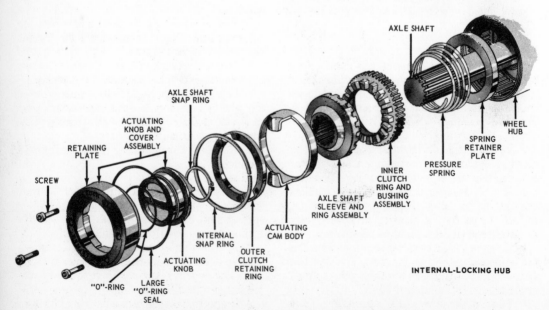

Typical internal locking hub used on 1966–79 models

going in first. Be sure ring seats against the bearing.

3. Grease with Moly grease or equivalent and install the axle shaft gear.

4. Install the axle shaft snapring. Push inward on gear and, if necessary, push out axle shaft to allow groove clearance on shaft for the snapring. Be sure snapring is fully seated in the snapring groove on the shaft. Tapping it with a punch can insure full seating.

5. Install the coil spring with large end entering first.

6. Install the clutch ring and actuating cam as an assembly, meshing the clutch ring with the hub and shaft gear. Slide the assembly into position, flush with the shaft gear and hold it there.

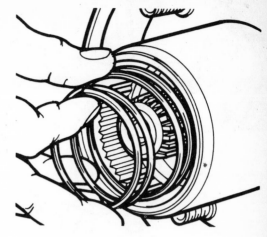

Coil spring installation

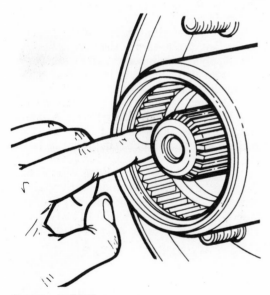

Grease application

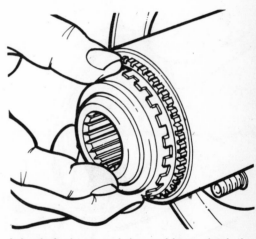

Axle shaft sleeve and ring and inner clutch ring installation

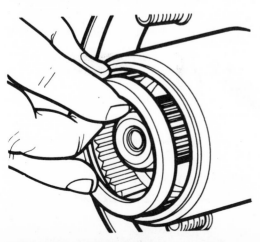

Spring retainer ring installation

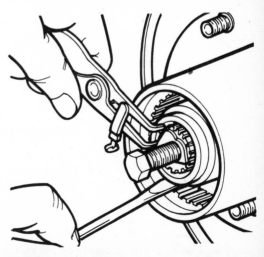

Installing axle shaft snap ring

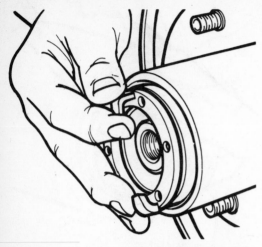

Installing the cam body ring into the clutch retaining ring

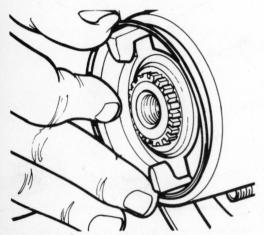

Installing the internal snap ring

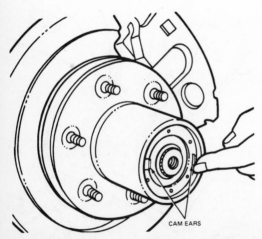

CAM EARS

Applying a small amount of grease on the ears of the cam

Lubricating the selector knob

7. Install the outer clutch retaining ring and snap ring.

8. Apply a small amount of Moly grease or equivalent on the ears of the cam.

9. Apply a small amount of Parker O-ring lube or an equivalent lube in groove of actuating knob before assembling outer O-ring.

10. Assemble knob in hub ring and assemble to axle with knob in **LOCK** position. Assemble screws and washers alternately and evenly, making sure the retainer ring is not cocked in the hub.

11. Tighten the six hub bolts to 30 to 35 in.lb. Be sure the washers are under each retaining screw. Each free running hub will fit either wheel. Do not drive vehicle until you are sure that both free running hubs are functioning properly.

1980–86

1. To remove hub, first separate cap assembly from body assembly by removing the six (6) socket head capscrews from the cap assembly and slip apart.

2. Remove snapring (retainer ring) from the end of the axle shaft.

3. Remove the lock ring seated in the groove of the wheel hub. The body assembly will now slide out of the wheel hub. If necessary, use an appropriate puller to remove the body assembly.

4. Install hub in reverse order of removal. Torque socket head capscrews to 30–35 in.lb.

Automatic Locking Hubs
REMOVAL AND INSTALLATION

1. Remove capscrews and remove hub cap assembly from spindle.

2. Remove capscrew from end of axle shaft.

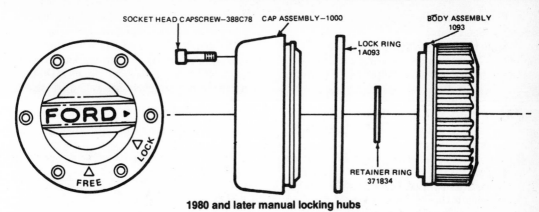

1980 and later manual locking hubs

3. Remove lock ring seated in the groove of the wheel hub with a knife blade or with a small sharp awl with the tip bent in a hook.

4. Remove body assembly from spindle. If body assembly does not slide out easily, use an appropriate puller.

5. Unscrew all three set in the spindle locknut until the heads are flush with the edge of the locknut. Remove outer spindle locknut with tool T8OT-4000-V, Automatic Hub Lock Nut Wrench.

6. Reinstall in reverse order of removal. Tighten the outer spindle locknut to 15–20 ft.lb. with special tool T8OT-4000-V, Automatic Hub Lock Nut Wrench. Tighten down all three set screws. Firmly push in body assembly until the friction shoes are on top of the spindle outer locknut.

7. Install capscrew into the axle shaft and tighten to 35–50 ft.lb.

8. Place cap on spindle and install capscrews. Tighten to 35–50 in.lb. Turn dial firmly from stop to stop, causing the dialing mechanism to engage the body spline.

NOTE: *Be sure both hub dials are in the same position,* **AUTO** *or* **LOCK**.

Front Wheel Bearing

REPLACEMENT OR REPACKING

1966–86

1. Raise the vehicle and install safety stands.

2. If equipped with free running hubs refer to Manual or Automatic Free Running Hub Removal and Installation and remove the hub assemblies.

3. Remove the wheel bearing lock nut, using Tool T59T-1197-B, or equivalent.

4. Remove the lock ring from the bearing adjusting nut. This can be done with your finger tips or a screwdriver.

5. Using Tool T59T-1197-B, or equivalent, remove the bearing adjusting nut.

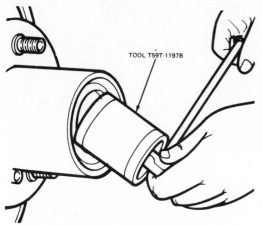

Lock nut, lock ring and adjusting nut removal

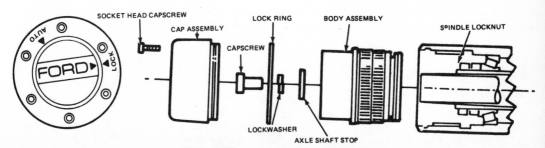

1980 and later automatic locking hubs

6. Remove the caliper and suspend it out of the way. See Chapter 8.

7. Slide the hub and disc assembly off of the spindle. The outer wheel bearing will slide out as the hub is removed, so be prepared to catch it.

8. Lay the hub on a clean work surface. Carefully drive the inner bearing cone and grease seal out of the hub using Tool T69L-1102-A, or equivalent.

9. Inspect the bearing cups for pits or cracks. If necessary, remove them with a drift. If new cups are installed, install new bearings.

10. Lubricate the bearings with Multi-Purpose Lubricant Ford Specification, ESA-MIC7-B or equivalent. Clean all old grease from the hub. Pack the cones and rollers. If a bearing packer is not available, work as much lubricant as possible between the rollers and the cages.

11. Drive new cups into place with a driver, making sure that they are fully seated.

12. Position the inner bearing cone and roller in the inner cup and install the grease retainer.

13. Carefully position the hub and disc assembly on the spindle.

14. Install the outer bearing cone and roller, and the adjusting nut.

NOTE: *The adjusting nut has a small dowel on one side. This dowel faces outward to engage the locking ring.*

15. Using Tool T59T-1197-B and a torque wrench, tighten the bearing adjusting nut to 50 ft.lb., while rotating the wheel back and forth to seat the bearings.

16. Back off the adjusting nut approximately 90°.

17. Install the lock ring by turning the nut to the nearest hole and inserting the dowel pin.

NOTE: *The dowel pin must seat in a lock ring hole for proper bearing adjustment and wheel retention.*

18. Install the outer lock nut and tighten to 50–80 ft.lb. Final end play of the wheel on the spindle should be 0.001–0.010" (0.025–0.25mm).

19. Assemble the hub parts.

20. Install the caliper.

21. Remove the safety stands and lower the vehicle.

Axle Shaft
REMOVAL AND INSTALLATION
30AF, 44-1F, 44-9F

1. Raise the vehicle and support it on jackstands.

2. Remove the front wheels.

3. On drum brake models, remove the hub, brake drum, backing plate and spindle. Tie the backing plate up to avoid damage to the hose.

4. On disc brake models, remove the hubs, calipers and rotors. Tie up the calipers to avoid damage to the hoses. Remove the nuts that attach the brake support bracket, dust shield and spindle.

5. Pull the axle shaft from the housing, carefully working the U-joint through the steering knuckle.

6. Install the shaft in reverse order of removal.

Spindle
REMOVAL AND INSTALLATION
All Except the 44-IFS

1. Raise the vehicle and install safety stands.

2. If equipped with free running hubs refer to Manual or Automatic Free Running Hub Removal and Installation and remove the hub assemblies.

3. Remove the wheel bearing lock nut, using Tool T59T-1197-B, or equivalent.

4. Remove the lock ring from the bearing adjusting nut. This can be done with your finger tips or a screwdriver.

5. Using Tool T59T-1197-B, or equivalent, remove the bearing adjusting nut.

6. Remove the caliper and suspend it out of the way. See Chapter 8.

7. Slide the hub and disc assembly off of the spindle. The outer wheel bearing will slide out as the hub is removed, so be prepared to catch it.

8 Remove the spindle retaining nuts, then carefully remove the spindle from the knuckle studs and axle shaft.

NOTE: *The spindle will probably be VERY difficult to remove. First try whacking on the outer end of the spindle with a plastic mallet. If that doesn't break it loose, thread the wheel bearing locking nut on the end of the spindle and assemble a large 2-jawed puller, with the jaws on the locking ring and the threaded stud in the recess in the end of the axle shaft. Tighten the puller while hammering on the back side of the spindle.*

9. Clean all old grease from the needle bearings and wipe clean the spindle face that mates with the spindle bore seal.

10. Remove the spindle bore seal, V-seal, and thrust washer from the outer axle shaft. Clean any old grease or dirt from these parts and replace those that show signs of excessive wear. The spindle bearing can be removed with a slide hammer or driven out with a long drift. Install the new bearing with a bearing driver.

11. Using Multi-Purpose Lubricant, Ford

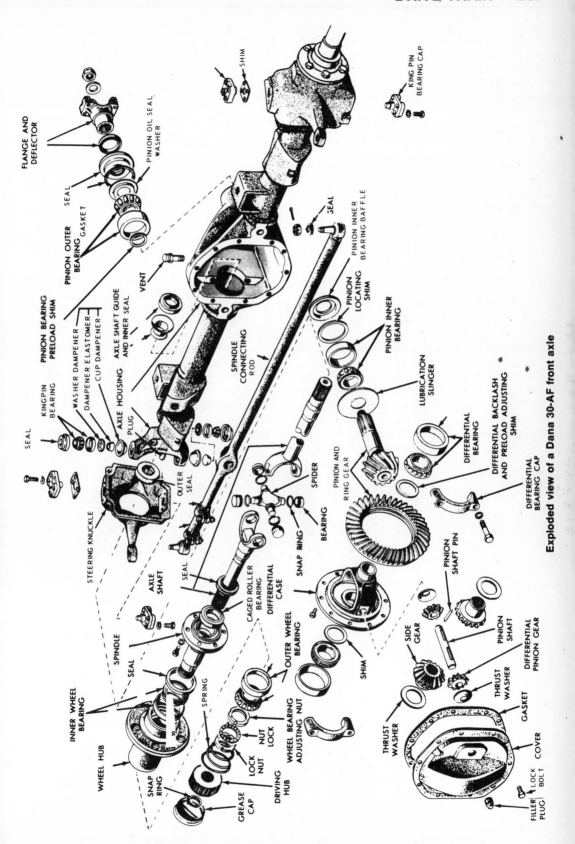

Exploded view of a Dana 30-AF front axle

SHIM

KING PIN BEARING CAP

FLANGE AND DEFLECTOR

PINION OIL SEAL WASHER

SEAL

SEAL

PINION OUTER BEARING GASKET

PINION INNER BEARING BAFFLE

VENT

SEAL

PINION BEARING PRELOAD SHIM

PINION LOCATING SHIM

PINION INNER BEARING

LUBRICATION SLINGER

SEAL

KINGPIN BEARING

WASHER DAMPENER

DAMPENER ELASTOMER

CUP DAMPENER

AXLE SHAFT GUIDE AND INNER SEAL

SPINDLE CONNECTING ROD

DIFFERENTIAL BEARING

DIFFERENTIAL BACKLASH AND PRELOAD ADJUSTING SHIM

DIFFERENTIAL BEARING CAP

AXLE HOUSING

PLUG

SEAL

OUTER SEAL

STEERING KNUCKLE

SPIDER

PINION AND RING GEAR

BEARING

PINION SHAFT PIN

AXLE SHAFT

CAGED ROLLER BEARING

DIFFERENTIAL CASE

SNAP RING

SIDE GEAR

PINION SHAFT

DIFFERENTIAL PINION GEAR

SPINDLE

SEAL

OUTER WHEEL BEARING

SHIM

THRUST WASHER

INNER WHEEL BEARING

SPRING

WHEEL BEARING ADJUSTING NUT

THRUST WASHER

GASKET

WHEEL HUB

NUT LOCK

LOCK NUT

COVER

SNAP RING

DRIVING HUB

LOCK BOLT

GREASE CAP

FILLER PLUG

Specification ESA-M1C75-B or equivalent, thoroughly lubricate the needle bearing and pack the spindle face that mates with the spindle bore seal.

12. Assemble the V-seal in the spindle bore next to the needle bearing. Assemble the spindle bore seal on the axle shaft.

13. Assemble the spindle with the axle shaft on the knuckle studs. Adjust the retaining nuts to 50–60 ft.lb.

14. Carefully position the hub and disc assembly on the spindle.

15. Install the outer bearing cone and roller, and the adjusting nut.

16. Using Tool T59T-1197-B and a torque wrench, tighten the bearing adjusting nut to 50 ft.lb., while rotating the wheel back and forth to seat the bearings.

17. Back off the adjusting nut approximately 90°.

18. Assemble the lock ring by turning the nut to the nearest hole and inserting the dowel pin.

NOTE: *The dowel pin must seat in a lock ring hole for proper bearing adjustment and wheel retention.*

19. Install the outer lock nut and tighten to 50–80 ft.lb. Final end play of the wheel on the spindle should be 0.001–0.010″ (0.025–0.25mm).

20. Install the pressure spring and riving hub snapring.

21. Apply non-hardening sealer to the seating edge of the grease cap, and install the grease cap.

22. Adjust the brake if it was backed off.

23. Remove the safety stands and lower the vehicle.

Axle Shaft and Steering Knuckle
REMOVAL AND INSTALLATION
1980–86 44-IFS

NOTE: *This procedure requires the use of special tools. See Chapter 1 for tool availability.*

1. Remove spindle nuts and remove spindle. It may be necessary to tap the spindle with a rawhide or plastic hammer to break the spindle loose. Remove spindle, splash shield and axle shaft assembly.

2. Place the spindle in a vise with a shop towel around the spindle to protect the spindle from damage. Using a slide hammer T50-T-100-A and seal remover, Tool 1175-AC remove the axle shaft seal and then the needle bearing from the spindle bar.

3. If the tie rod has not been removed, then

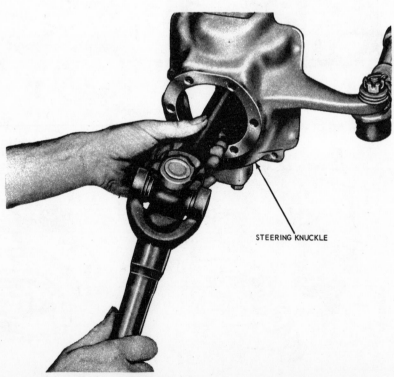

STEERING KNUCKLE

Typical removal or installation of a front axle shaft, 1966–79 models

remove cotter key from the tie rod nut and then remove nut. Tap on the tie rod stud to free it from the steering arm.

4. Remove the cotter pin from the top ball joint stud. Loosen the nut on the top stud and the bottom nut inside the knuckle. Remove the top nut.

5. Sharply hit the top stud with a plastic or rawhide hammer to free the knuckle from the tube yoke. Remove and discard bottom nut. Use new nut upon assembly.

6. Remove camber adjuster with Pitman arm puller T64P-3590-F.

7. Place knuckle in vise and remove snapring from bottom ball joint socket if so equipped.

8. Press the bottom ball joint socket from the knuckle with the special tools Receiver Cup Tool (P79P-3010-AG) and C1 Clamp Tool (D79T-3010-A)-B. Remove the top ball joint in the same manner.

NOTE: *Always remove bottom ball joint first.*

9. Pull out the seal with the appropriate puller tool. Remove and discard seal.

10. Install a new seal on the Differential Seal Replacer Tool T80T-4000-H.

11. Slide the seal and tool into the carrier housing bore. Seat the seal with a plastic or rawhide hammer.

12. Place lower ball joint (stud does not have a cotter key hole in stud) in knuckle and press into position using ball joint installation set T80T-3010-A.

13. Install upper ball joint (stud has cotter key hole) in knuckle with ball joint installation set T80T-2010-A.

14. Assemble knuckle to tube and yoke assembly. Install camber adjuster on top ball joint stud with the arrow pointing outboard for positive camber, pointed inboard for negative camber.

15. Install new nut on bottom socket finger tight. Install and tighten nut on top socket finger tight. Tighten bottom nut to 90–110 ft.lb.

16. Tighten top nut to 100 ft.lb., then advance nut until castellation aligns with cotter pin hole. Install cotter pin.

NOTE: *Do not loosen top nut to install cotter pin.*

17. Remove and install a new needle to bearing in the spindle bore with T80T-4000-R or S Spindle Bearing replacer and driver handle, T80T-4000-W. Install a new seal with tool T80T-400-T or U, Sealer Replacer and T90T-4000-W Driven Handle.

18. Install the axle shaft assembly into the housing. Install the splash shield and spindle. Install and tighten the spindle attaching nuts.

Steering Knuckle and Ball Joint
REPLACEMENT
30AF, 44-1F, 44-9F

NOTE: *The following procedure requires the use of special tools available from Ford or most parts and tools suppliers.*

1. Follow the axle shaft removal outlined above.

2. Disconnect the steering connecting rod end from the knuckle.

3. Remove the cotter key from the upper ball joint.

4. Loosen the nuts from the upper and lower ball joints.

5. The lower ball joint nut must be discarded after removal since it is a self-torquing nut.

6. Remove the knuckle from the yoke.

7. If the upper ball joint should remain in the yoke, hit it with a plastic or rawhide hammer to remove it.

8. Obtain a puller, and remove the clamps and puller jaws. Remove the bottom ball joint using the tool's forcing screw to push out the joint. Remove and discard the adjusting sleeve.

9. If the top ball joint remained in the knuckle, drive it from the knuckle at this point.

10. Place the knuckle in a vise. Position the new lower ball joint in the knuckle and force the ball joint into the knuckle.

11. Make sure that the ball joint shoulder is seated against the knuckle. Try placing a 0.0015″ (0.038mm) feeler gauge between the ball joint and the knuckle. The feeler should not enter at the area of minimum contact.

12. Install the snapring.

13. In a similar manner, press the new top ball joint into place.

14. Assemble a new adjusting sleeve into the top of the yoke. Install a new nut onto the bottom socket. Tighten the nut finger tight.

15. Place a spanner wrench and step plate over the adjusting sleeve. Locate the puller exactly as shown and turn the forcing screw. This will pull the knuckle assembly into the yoke. With torque still applied, tighten the lower ball joint nut to 70–90 ft.lb.

16. If the bottom stud should turn with the nut, add more torque to the forcing screw. Remove the puller, step plate and holding plate.

17. Tighten the adjusting sleeve to 40 ft.lb.

18. Install the upper ball joint nut and torque it to 100 ft.lb. Line up the cotter key hole in the nut with the hole in the stud by tightening, not loosening the nut.

19. Install a new cotter key.

20. Attach a pull scale to the knuckle and

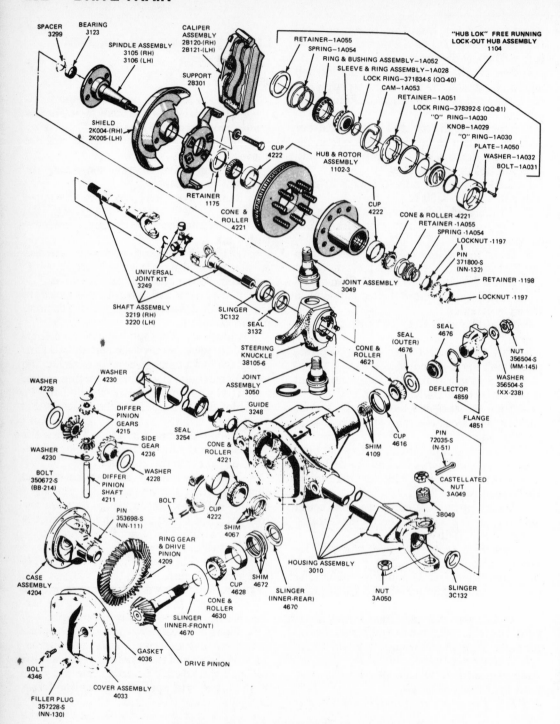

Exploded view of a Dana 44-9F front axle

check the turning effort. Pull should not exceed 26 lb. If it does, the ball joints will have to be replaced.

21. Connect the steering linkage to the knuckle.

22. Make sure that the seal and deflector are

properly installed on the axle shaft assembly. Assemble the seal on the shoulder of the deflector. Position the wheel bearing spacer and apply a small amount of wheel bearing lubricant to the exposed face of the spacer.

23. Slide the axle shaft back into the hous-

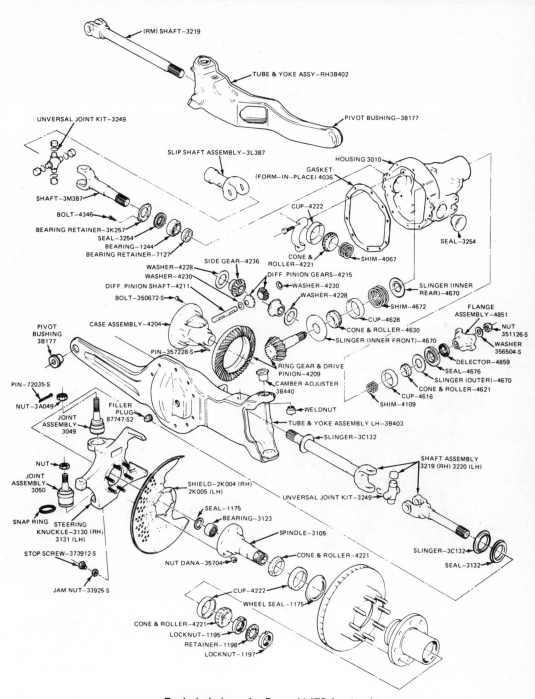

Exploded view of a Dana 44-IFS front axle

ing, taking great care to avoid damage to the seal.

24. Install the backing plate and other parts as explained in the axle shaft procedure given previously.

Axle Shaft Bearing

This procedure requires the use of special tools.

REMOVAL AND INSTALLATION

Dana 30 Axles Only

With Dana 44 Axles, the spindle bearing serves as the outer axle bearing.

1. Remove the axle shaft assembly as described in this part under Axle Shaft and Steering Knuckle.

2. Remove the stub assembly by removing 3

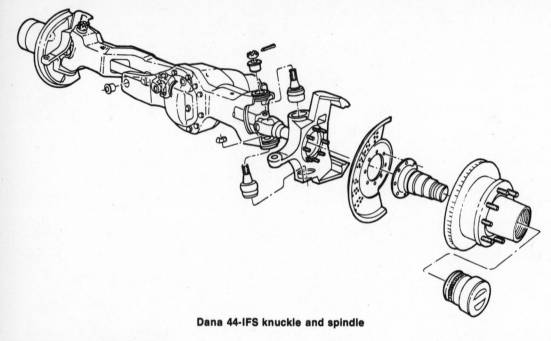

Dana 44-IFS knuckle and spindle

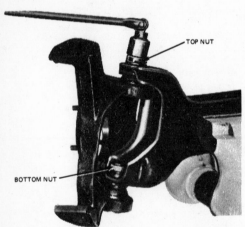

Removing the steering knuckle nut, Dana 44-IFS

Removing the camber bushing, Dana 44-IFS

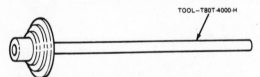

Inner axle seal installation tool, Dana 44-IFS

bolts attaching retainer plate to carrier housing.

3. Place the axle shaft in a vise and drill a 6.35mm (¼") hole in the outside of the Bearing retaining ring to a depth ¾ the thickness of the ring.

NOTE: *Do not drill through the ring because this will damage the axle shaft.*

4. With a chisel placed across the hole, strike sharply with a hammer to remove the retaining ring. Replace bearing retaining ring upon assembly.

5. Press the bearing from the axle shaft with the special tools, T80 Axle Bearing Remover T80T-4000-M and Sleeve T8OT-4000-L.

NOTE: *Do not use a torch to aid in bearing removal or the stub shaft will be damaged.*

6. Remove the seal and retainer plate from the stub shaft. Discard seal and replace with new seal upon assembly.

7. Inspect the retainer plate and stub shaft for distortion, nicks or burrs. Replace if necessary.

8. Install retainer plate and new seal on shaft. Coat oil seal with ESA-M175B or equivalent.

9. Place the bearing on the shaft. The large

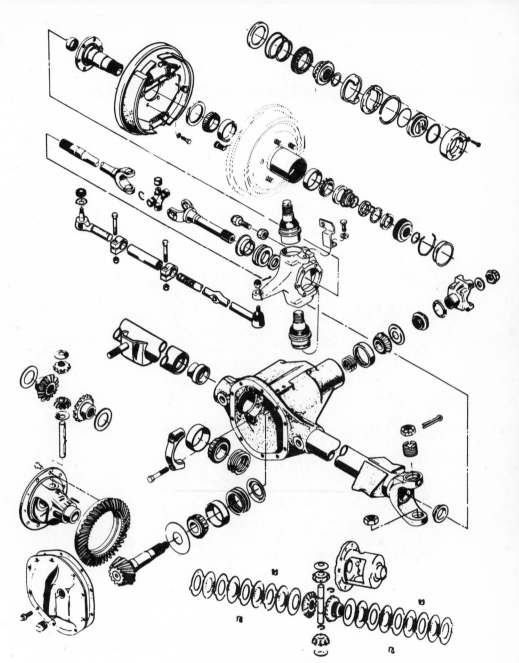

"TRAC-LOK" LIMITED SLIP DIFFERENTIAL

Exploded view of a Dana 44-1F front axle

radius on the inner race must face the yoke end of the shaft.

10. Use Axle Bearing Replacer T8OT-4000-N and Pinion Bearing Cone Remover T71P-4621-B to press the bearing onto the shaft until completely seated. A 0.038mm (0.0015″) feeler gauge should not fit between the bearing seat and bearing.

11. Use Axle Bearing Replacer T8OT-4000-N and Pinion Bearing Cone Remover T71P-4612-B to press the bearing retainer ring onto

the stub shaft. Press the bearing retainer ring until completely seated. A 0.038mm (0.0015″) feeler gauge should not fit between the ring and bearing. There must be one point between the bearing and ring where the feeler gauge cannot enter. If feeler gauge enters completely around the circumference press the retainer further onto the shaft.

12. Push the seal and retainer plate away from the bearing to form a space between the seal and bearing. Fill the space with wheel

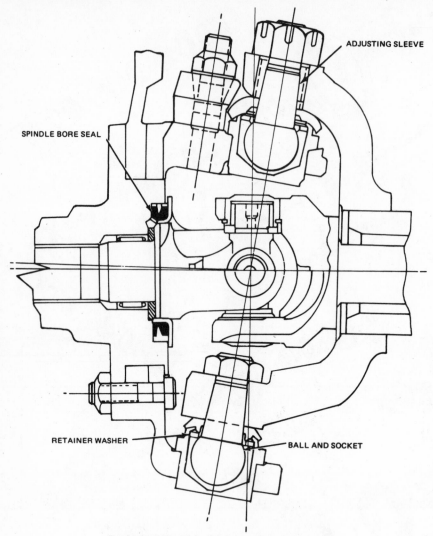

ADJUSTING SLEEVE

SPINDLE BORE SEAL

RETAINER WASHER

BALL AND SOCKET

Typical 1966–79 ball joint and seal assembly

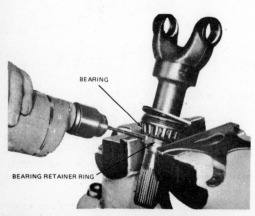

BEARING

BEARING RETAINER RING

Drilling the stub shaft bearing retainer ring, Dana 44-IFS

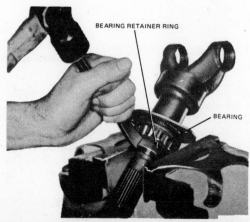

BEARING RETAINER RING

BEARING

Removing the bearing retainer ring, Dana 44-IFS

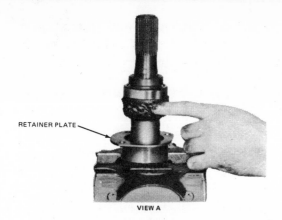

RETAINER PLATE

VIEW A

VIEW B

VIEW C

Lubricating the axle bearing, Dana 44-IFS

bearing grease meeting Ford specification ESA-MIC75B or equivalent, View A.

13. With the space filled with grease, wrap tape around the space, View B.

14. Pull the seal towards the bearing until it contacts the inner race, View C. This will force grease between the rollers and cup. Remove tape.

NOTE: *If grease is not visible on the small end of the rollers, repeat steps 6 through 8 until grease is visible. Install the slip yoke and U-joint to stub shaft.*

15. Install the stub shaft in the carrier and install 3 retainer bolts. Torque to 30–40 ft.lb. Install right hand axle shaft assembly into slip yoke.

16. Install splash shield and spindle.

AXLE SHAFT U-JOINT OVERHAUL

Follow the procedures outlined under Axle Shaft Removal and Installation to gain access to the U-joints. Overhaul them as described under U-Joints at the beginning of this chapter.

Troubleshooting the Manual Transmission and Transfer Case

Problem	Cause	Solution
Transmission shifts hard	• Clutch adjustment incorrect • Clutch linkage or cable binding • Shift rail binding	• Adjust clutch • Lubricate or repair as necessary • Check for mispositioned selector arm roll pin, loose cover bolts, worn shift rail bores, worn shift rail, distorted oil seal, or extension housing not aligned with case. Repair as necessary.
	• Internal bind in transmission caused by shift forks, selector plates, or synchronizer assemblies	• Remove, dissemble and inspect transmission. Replace worn or damaged components as necessary.

Troubleshooting the Manual Transmission and Transfer Case (cont.)

Problem	Cause	Solution
Transmission shifts hard (cont.)	• Clutch housing misalignment	• Check runout at rear face of clutch housing
	• Incorrect lubricant	• Drain and refill transmission
	• Block rings and/or cone seats worn	• Blocking ring to gear clutch tooth face clearance must be 0.030 inch or greater. If clearance is correct it may still be necessary to inspect blocking rings and cone seats for excessive wear. Repair as necessary.
Gear clash when shifting from one gear to another	• Clutch adjustment incorrect	• Adjust clutch
	• Clutch linkage or cable binding	• Lubricate or repair as necessary
	• Clutch housing misalignment	• Check runout at rear of clutch housing
	• Lubricant level low or incorrect lubricant	• Drain and refill transmission and check for lubricant leaks if level was low. Repair as necessary.
	• Gearshift components, or synchronizer assemblies worn or damaged	• Remove, disassemble and inspect transmission. Replace worn or damaged components as necessary.
Transmission noisy	• Lubricant level low or incorrect lubricant	• Drain and refill transmission. If lubricant level was low, check for leaks and repair as necessary.
	• Clutch housing-to-engine, or transmission-to-clutch housing bolts loose	• Check and correct bolt torque as necessary
	• Dirt, chips, foreign material in transmission	• Drain, flush, and refill transmission
	• Gearshift mechanism, transmission gears, or bearing components worn or damaged	• Remove, disassemble and inspect transmission. Replace worn or damaged components as necessary.
	• Clutch housing misalignment	• Check runout at rear face of clutch housing
Jumps out of gear	• Clutch housing misalignment	• Check runout at rear face of clutch housing
	• Gearshift lever loose	• Check lever for worn fork. Tighten loose attaching bolts.
	• Offset lever nylon insert worn or lever attaching nut loose	• Remove gearshift lever and check for loose offset lever nut or worn insert. Repair or replace as necessary.
	• Gearshift mechanism, shift forks, selector plates, interlock plate, selector arm, shift rail, detent plugs, springs or shift cover worn or damaged	• Remove, disassemble and inspect transmission cover assembly. Replace worn or damaged components as necessary.
	• Clutch shaft or roller bearings worn or damaged	• Replace clutch shaft or roller bearings as necessary
	• Gear teeth worn or tapered, synchronizer assemblies worn or damaged, excessive end play caused by worn thrust washers or output shaft gears	• Remove, disassemble, and inspect transmission. Replace worn or damaged components as necessary.
	• Pilot bushing worn	• Replace pilot bushing
Will not shift into one gear	• Gearshift selector plates, interlock plate, or selector arm, worn, damaged, or incorrectly assembled	• Remove, disassemble, and inspect transmission cover assembly. Repair or replace components as necessary.
	• Shift rail detent plunger worn, spring broken, or plug loose	• Tighten plug or replace worn or damaged components as necessary

Troubleshooting the Manual Transmission and Transfer Case (cont.)

Problem	Cause	Solution
Will not shift into one gear (cont.)	• Gearshift lever worn or damaged • Synchronizer sleeves or hubs, damaged or worn	• Replace gearshift lever • Remove, disassemble and inspect transmission. Replace worn or damaged components.
Locked in one gear—cannot be shifted out	• Shift rail(s) worn or broken, shifter fork bent, setscrew loose, center detent plug missing or worn • Broken gear teeth on countershaft gear, clutch shaft, or reverse idler gear Gearshift lever broken or worn, shift mechanism in cover incorrectly assembled or broken, worn damaged gear train components	• Inspect and replace worn or damaged parts • Inspect and replace damaged part • Disassemble transmission. Replace damaged parts or assemble correctly.
Transfer case difficult to shift or will not shift into desired range	• Vehicle speed too great to permit shifting • If vehicle was operated for extended period in 4H mode on dry paved surface, driveline torque load may cause difficult shifting • Transfer case external shift linkage binding • Insufficient or incorrect lubricant • Internal components binding, worn, or damaged	• Stop vehicle and shift into desired range. Or reduce speed to 3–4 km/h (2–3 mph) before attempting to shift. • Stop vehicle, shift transmission to neutral, shift transfer case to 2H mode and operate vehicle in 2H on dry paved surfaces • Lubricate or repair or replace linkage, or tighten loose components as necessary • Drain and refill to edge of fill hole with SAE 85W-90 gear lubricant only • Disassemble unit and replace worn or damaged components as necessary
Transfer case noisy in all drive modes	• Insufficient or incorrect lubricant	• Drain and refill to edge of fill hole with SAE 85W-90 gear lubricant only. Check for leaks and repair if necessary. Note: If unit is still noisy after drain and refill, disassembly and inspection may be required to locate source of noise.
Noisy in—or jumps out of four wheel drive low range	• Transfer case not completely engaged in 4L position • Shift linkage loose or binding • Shift fork cracked, inserts worn, or fork is binding on shift rail	• Stop vehicle, shift transfer case in Neutral, then shift back into 4L position • Tighten, lubricate, or repair linkage as necessary • Disassemble unit and repair as necessary
Lubricant leaking from output shaft seals or from vent	• Transfer case overfilled • Vent closed or restricted • Output shaft seals damaged or installed incorrectly	• Drain to correct level • Clear or replace vent if necessary • Replace seals. Be sure seal lip faces interior of case when installed. Also be sure yoke seal surfaces are not scored or nicked. Remove scores, nicks with fine sandpaper or replace yoke(s) if necessary.
Abnormal tire wear	• Extended operation on dry hard surface (paved) roads in 4H range	• Operate in 2H on hard surface (paved) roads

Troubleshooting Basic Clutch Problems

Problem	Cause
Excessive clutch noise	Throwout bearing noises are more audible at the lower end of pedal travel. The usual causes are: • Riding the clutch • Too little pedal free-play • Lack of bearing lubrication A bad clutch shaft pilot bearing will make a high pitched squeal, when the clutch is disengaged and the transmission is in gear or within the first 2″ of pedal travel. The bearing must be replaced. Noise from the clutch linkage is a clicking or snapping that can be heard or felt as the pedal is moved completely up or down. This usually requires lubrication. Transmitted engine noises are amplified by the clutch housing and heard in the passenger compartment. They are usually the result of insufficient pedal free-play and can be changed by manipulating the clutch pedal.
Clutch slips (the car does not move as it should when the clutch is engaged)	This is usually most noticeable when pulling away from a standing start. A severe test is to start the engine, apply the brakes, shift into high gear and SLOWLY release the clutch pedal. A healthy clutch will stall the engine. If it slips it may be due to: • A worn pressure plate or clutch plate • Oil soaked clutch plate • Insufficient pedal free-play
Clutch drags or fails to release	The clutch disc and some transmission gears spin briefly after clutch disengagement. Under normal conditions in average temperatures, 3 seconds is maximum spin-time. Failure to release properly can be caused by: • Too light transmission lubricant or low lubricant level • Improperly adjusted clutch linkage
Low clutch life	Low clutch life is usually a result of poor driving habits or heavy duty use. Riding the clutch, pulling heavy loads, holding the car on a grade with the clutch instead of the brakes and rapid clutch engagement all contribute to low clutch life.

Troubleshooting Basic Automatic Transmission Problems

Problem	Cause	Solution
Fluid leakage	• Defective pan gasket	• Replace gasket or tighten pan bolts
	• Loose filler tube	• Tighten tube nut
	• Loose extension housing to transmission case	• Tighten bolts
	• Converter housing area leakage	• Have transmission checked professionally
Fluid flows out the oil filler tube	• High fluid level	• Check and correct fluid level
	• Breather vent clogged	• Open breather vent
	• Clogged oil filter or screen	• Replace filter or clean screen (change fluid also)
	• Internal fluid leakage	• Have transmission checked professionally
Transmission overheats (this is usually accompanied by a strong burned odor to the fluid)	• Low fluid level	• Check and correct fluid level
	• Fluid cooler lines clogged	• Drain and refill transmission. If this doesn't cure the problem, have cooler lines cleared or replaced.
	• Heavy pulling or hauling with insufficient cooling	• Install a transmission oil cooler
	• Faulty oil pump, internal slippage	• Have transmission checked professionally

Troubleshooting Basic Automatic Transmission Problems (cont.)

Problem	Cause	Solution
Buzzing or whining noise	• Low fluid level • Defective torque converter, scored gears	• Check and correct fluid level • Have transmission checked professionally
No forward or reverse gears or slippage in one or more gears	• Low fluid level • Defective vacuum or linkage controls, internal clutch or band failure	• Check and correct fluid level • Have unit checked professionally
Delayed or erratic shift	• Low fluid level • Broken vacuum lines • Internal malfunction	• Check and correct fluid level • Repair or replace lines • Have transmission checked professionally

Lockup Torque Converter Service Diagnosis

Problem	Cause	Solution

No lockup	• Faulty oil pump
	• Sticking governor valve
	• Valve body malfunction
	  (a) Stuck switch valve
	  (b) Stuck lockup valve
	  (c) Stuck fail-safe valve
	• Failed locking clutch
	• Leaking turbine hub seal
	• Faulty input shaft or seal ring
		• Replace oil pump
		• Repair or replace as necessary
		• Repair or replace valve body or its internal components as necessary
		
		• Replace torque converter
		• Replace torque converter
		• Repair or replace as necessary

Will not unlock	• Sticking governor valve
	• Valve body malfunction
	  (a) Stuck switch valve
	  (b) Stuck lockup valve
	  (c) Stuck fail-safe valve
		• Repair or replace as necessary
		• Repair or replace valve body or its internal components as necessary

Stays locked up at too low a speed in direct	• Sticking governor valve
	• Valve body malfunction
	  (a) Stuck switch valve
	  (b) Stuck lockup valve
	  (c) Stuck fail-safe valve
		• Repair or replace as necessary
		• Repair or replace valve body or its internal components as necessary

Locks up or drags in low or second	• Faulty oil pump
	• Valve body malfunction
	  (a) Stuck switch valve
	  (b) Stuck fail-safe valve
		• Replace oil pump
		• Repair or replace valve body or its internal components as necessary

Sluggish or stalls in reverse	• Faulty oil pump
	• Plugged cooler, cooler lines or fittings
	• Valve body malfunction
	  (a) Stuck switch valve
	  (b) Faulty input shaft or seal ring
		• Replace oil pump as necessary
		• Flush or replace cooler and flush lines and fittings
		• Repair or replace valve body or its internal components as necessary

Loud chatter during lockup engagement (cold)	• Faulty torque converter • Failed locking clutch • Leaking turbine hub seal	• Replace torque converter • Replace torque converter • Replace torque converter
Vibration or shudder during lockup engagement	• Faulty oil pump • Valve body malfunction • Faulty torque converter • Engine needs tune-up	• Repair or replace oil pump as necessary • Repair or replace valve body or its internal components as necessary • Replace torque converter • Tune engine

Lockup Torque Converter Service Diagnosis (cont.)

Problem	Cause	Solution
Vibration after lockup engagement	• Faulty torque converter • Exhaust system strikes underbody • Engine needs tune-up • Throttle linkage misadjusted	• Replace torque converter • Align exhaust system • Tune engine • Adjust throttle linkage
Vibration when revved in neutral Overheating: oil blows out of dip stick tube or pump seal	• Torque converter out of balance • Plugged cooler, cooler lines or fittings • Stuck switch valve	• Replace torque converter • Flush or replace cooler and flush lines and fittings • Repair switch valve in valve body or replace valve body
Shudder after lockup engagement	• Faulty oil pump • Plugged cooler, cooler lines or fittings • Valve body malfunction • Faulty torque converter • Fail locking clutch • Exhaust system strikes underbody • Engine needs tune-up • Throttle linkage misadjusted	• Replace oil pump • Flush or replace cooler and flush lines and fittings • Repair or replace valve body or its internal components as necessary • Replace torque converter • Replace torque converter • Align exhaust system • Tune engine • Adjust throttle linkage

Transmission Fluid Indications

The appearance and odor of the transmission fluid can give valuable clues to the overall condition of the transmission. Always note the appearance of the fluid when you check the fluid level or change the fluid. Rub a small amount of fluid between your fingers to feel for grit and smell the fluid on the dipstick.

If the fluid appears:	It indicates:
Clear and red colored	• Normal operation
Discolored (extremely dark red or brownish) or smells burned	• Band or clutch pack failure, usually caused by an overheated transmission. Hauling very heavy loads with insufficient power or failure to change the fluid, often result in overheating. Do not confuse this appearance with newer fluids that have a darker red color and a strong odor (though not a burned odor).
Foamy or aerated (light in color and full of bubbles)	• The level is too high (gear train is churning oil) • An internal air leak (air is mixing with the fluid). Have the transmission checked professionally.
Solid residue in the fluid	• Defective bands, clutch pack or bearings. Bits of band material or metal abrasives are clinging to the dipstick. Have the transmission checked professionally.
Varnish coating on the dipstick	• The transmission fluid is overheating

Troubleshooting Basic Driveshaft and Rear Axle Problems

When abnormal vibrations or noises are detected in the driveshaft area, this chart can be used to help diagnose possible causes. Remember that other components such as wheels, tires, rear axle and suspension can also produce similar conditions.

BASIC DRIVESHAFT PROBLEMS

Problem	Cause	Solution
Shudder as car accelerates from stop or low speed	• Loose U-joint • Defective center bearing	• Replace U-joint • Replace center bearing
Loud clunk in driveshaft when shifting gears	• Worn U-joints	• Replace U-joints
Roughness or vibration at any speed	• Out-of-balance, bent or dented driveshaft • Worn U-joints • U-joint clamp bolts loose	• Balance or replace driveshaft • Replace U-joints • Tighten U-joint clamp bolts
Squeaking noise at low speeds	• Lack of U-joint lubrication	• Lubricate U-joint; if problem persists, replace U-joint
Knock or clicking noise	• U-joint or driveshaft hitting frame tunnel • Worn CV joint	• Correct overloaded condition • Replace CV joint

BASIC REAR AXLE PROBLEMS

First, determine when the noise is most noticeable.

Drive Noise: Produced under vehicle acceleration.

Coast Noise: Produced while the car coasts with a closed throttle.

Float Noise: Occurs while maintaining constant car speed (just enough to keep speed constant) on a level road.

Road Noise

Brick or rough surfaced concrete roads produce noises that seem to come from the rear axle. Road noise is usually identical in Drive or Coast and driving on a different type of road will tell whether the road is the problem.

Tire Noise

Tire noises are often mistaken for rear axle problems. Snow treads or unevenly worn tires produce vibrations seeming to originate elsewhere. **Temporarily** inflating the tires to 40 lbs will significantly alter tire noise, but will have no effect on rear axle noises (which normally cease below about 30 mph).

Engine/Transmission Noise

Determine at what speed the noise is most pronounced, then stop the car in a quiet place. With the transmission in Neutral, run the engine through speeds corresponding to road speeds where the noise was noticed. Noises produced with the car standing still are coming from the engine or transmission.

Front Wheel Bearings

While holding the car speed steady, lightly apply the footbrake; this will often decease bearing noise, as some of the load is taken from the bearing.

Rear Axle Noises

Eliminating other possible sources can narrow the cause to the rear axle, which normally produces noise from worn gears or bearings. Gear noises tend to peak in a narrow speed range, while bearing noises will usually vary in pitch with engine speeds.

Suspension and Steering

FRONT SUSPENSION

The front suspension consists of a driving axle which is attached to the vehicle frame with two coil springs, two radius arms, and a track bar. The 1980–86 front suspension consists of a two-piece driving axle assembly, two coil spring and two radius arms. The front axle consists of two independent yoke and tube assemblies. One end of each assembly is anchored to the frame, the other end is supported by the spring and radius arm.

> NOTE: *The 1966–79 radius arm and cap are matched sets and should never be mixed with other sets. They are identified by numbers 1 through 100. The numbers should be together when installing the radius arm and cap.*

Springs
REMOVAL AND INSTALLATION
1966–77

1. Raise the vehicle until the tires are a few inches off the ground and place jackstands under the frame side rails. Position a hydraulic floor jack under the center of the front axle housing.
2. Remove the shock absorber-to-lower bracket attaching bolt and nut.
3. Remove the spring lower retainer attaching bolts from the inside of the spring coil.
4. Lower the axle enough to relieve tension from the spring.
5. Remove the spring upper retainer attaching bolts and nuts and remove the upper retainer.
6. Remove the spring, lower retainer and the lower seat from the vehicle.

To install the front spring:

7. Position the upper retainer over the spring coil and loosely install the attaching bolts and nuts.

8. Position the spring lower seat, and the lower retainer to the frame spring pocket and the radius arm.
9. Raise the axle up into position and install the two lower retainer attaching bolts and tighten them.
10. Tighten the upper retainer attaching bolts.
11. Position the shock absorber to the lower bracket and install the attaching bolt and nut.
12. Remove the jackstands and lower the vehicle.

1978–79

1. Raise the vehicle and remove the shock absorber-to-lower bracket attaching bolt and nut.
2. Remove two spring lower retainer attaching bolts from inside of the spring coil.
3. Remove two spring upper retainer attaching bolts and nuts and remove the upper retainer.
4. Position safety stands under the frame side rails and lower the axle enough to relieve tension from the spring. Remove the spring, lower retainer, and lower the spring from the vehicle.
5. Position the spring, spring lower seat, and lower retainer to the frame spring pocket and the radius arm. Position the spring seat and the lower retainer.
6. Position the upper retainer over the spring coil and loosely install the two attaching bolts and nuts.
7. Install the two lower retainer attaching bolts and tighten to 80–120 ft.lb.
8. Tighten the upper retainer attaching bolts to 20–30 ft.lb.
9. Position the shock absorber to the lower bracket and install the attaching bolt and nut. Tighten the bolt and nut to 40–60 ft.lb. Remove safety stands and lower the vehicle.

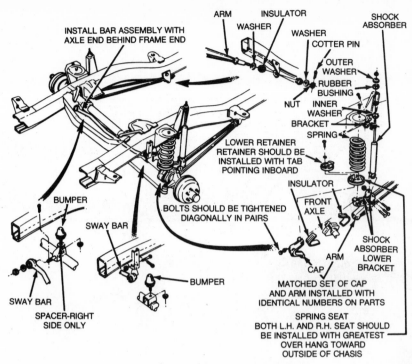

INSTALL BAR ASSEMBLY WITH
AXLE END BEHIND FRAME END

ARM INSULATOR
WASHER
WASHER
COTTER PIN
SHOCK
ABSORBER
OUTER
WASHER
RUBBER
BUSHING
NUT INNER
WASHER
BRACKET
SPRING
LOWER RETAINER
RETAINER SHOULD BE
INSTALLED WITH TAB
POINTING INBOARD
INSULATOR
FRONT
AXLE
SHOCK
ABSORBER
LOWER
BRACKET
ARM
CAP
BUMPER
BOLTS SHOULD BE TIGHTENED
DIAGONALLY IN PAIRS
SWAY BAR
BUMPER
SWAY BAR
SPACER-RIGHT
SIDE ONLY
MATCHED SET OF CAP
AND ARM INSTALLED WITH
IDENTICAL NUMBERS ON PARTS
SPRING SEAT
BOTH L.H. AND R.H. SEAT SHOULD
BE INSTALLED WITH GREATEST
OVER HANG TOWARD
OUTSIDE OF CHASIS

1966–75 front suspension assembly

1980–86

1. Raise the vehicle and remove the shock absorber-to-lower bracket attaching bolt and nut.

2. Remove spring lower retainer attaching nuts from inside of the spring coil.

3. Remove spring upper retainer attaching screw and remove the upper retainer.

4. Position safety stands under the frame side rails and lower the axle enough to relieve tension from the spring.

NOTE: *The axle must be supported on the jack throughout spring removal and installation, and must not be permitted to hang by the brake hose. If the length of the brake hose is not sufficient to provide adequate clearance for removal and installation of the spring, the disc brake caliper must be removed from the spindle according to the procedures in Chapter 8. After removal, the caliper must be placed on the frame or otherwise supported to prevent suspending the caliper from the caliper hose. These precautions are absolutely necessary to prevent serious damage to the tube portion of the caliper hose assembly.*

Remove the spring, lower retainer, and lower the spring from the vehicle.

5. Place the spring in position and slowly raise the front axle. Ensure springs are positioned correctly in the upper spring seats.

6. Position the spring lower retainer over the stud and lower seat and torque the attaching nut to 30–70 ft.lb.

7. Position the upper retainer over the spring coil and torque the attaching screws 13–18 ft.lb.

8. Position the shock absorber to the lower bracket and install the attaching bolt and nut. Tighten the bolt and nut to 48–65 ft.lb. Remove safety stands and lower the vehicle.

Shock Absorbers

TESTING

1. Visually check the shock absorbers for the presence of fluid leakage. A thin film of fluid is acceptable. Anything more than that means that the shock absorber must be replaced.

2. Disconnect the lower end of the shock absorber. Compress and extend the shock fully as fast as possible. If the action is not smooth in both directions, or there is no pressure resistance, replace the shock absorber. Shock absorbers should be replaced in pairs if they have accumulated more than 20,000 miles of wear. In the case of relatively new shock absorbers, where one has failed, that one, along, may be replaced.

REMOVAL AND INSTALLATION

NOTE: *Prior to installing a new shock absorber, hold it upright and extend it fully. In-*

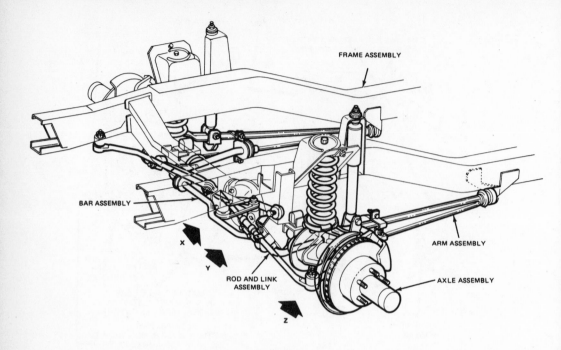

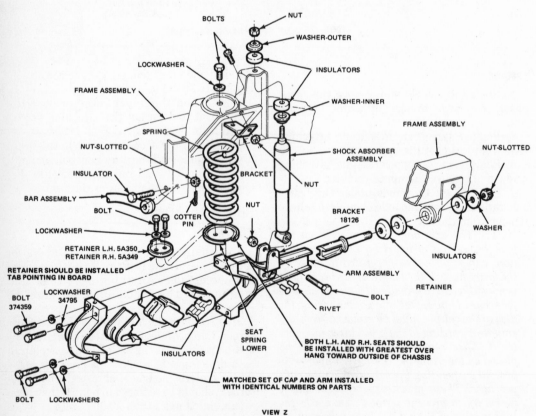

VIEW Z

1976–77 front suspension assembly

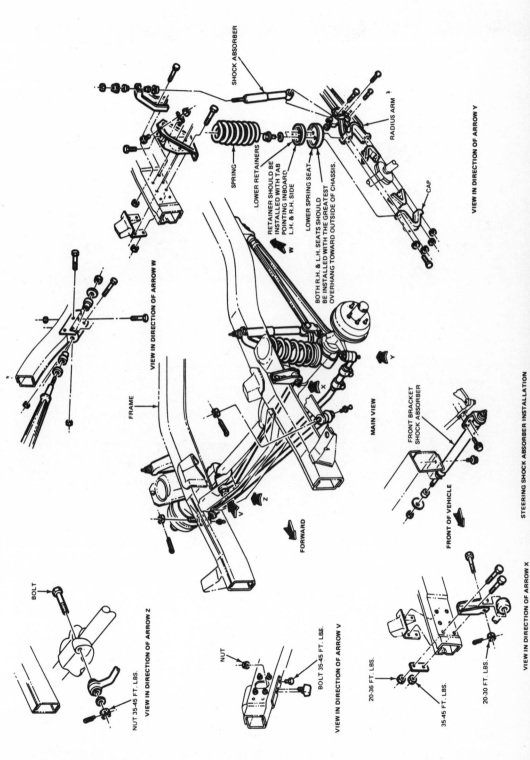

SHOCK ABSORBER

SPRING

LOWER RETAINERS

RETAINER SHOULD BE
INSTALLED WITH TAB
POINTING INBOARD
L.H. & R.H. SIDE

LOWER SPRING SEAT

BOTH R.H. & L.H. SEATS SHOULD
BE INSTALLED WITH THE GREATEST
OVERHANG TOWARD OUTSIDE OF CHASSIS.

RADIUS ARM

CAP

VIEW IN DIRECTION OF ARROW Y

VIEW IN DIRECTION OF ARROW W

FRAME

MAIN VIEW

FRONT BRACKET
SHOCK ABSORBER

FRONT OF VEHICLE

STEERING SHOCK ABSORBER INSTALLATION

FORWARD

BOLT

NUT 35-45 FT. LBS.

VIEW IN DIRECTION OF ARROW Z

NUT

BOLT 35-45 FT. LBS.

VIEW IN DIRECTION OF ARROW V

20-36 FT. LBS.

35-45 FT. LBS.

20-30 FT. LBS.

VIEW IN DIRECTION OF ARROW X

1978–79 front suspension assembly

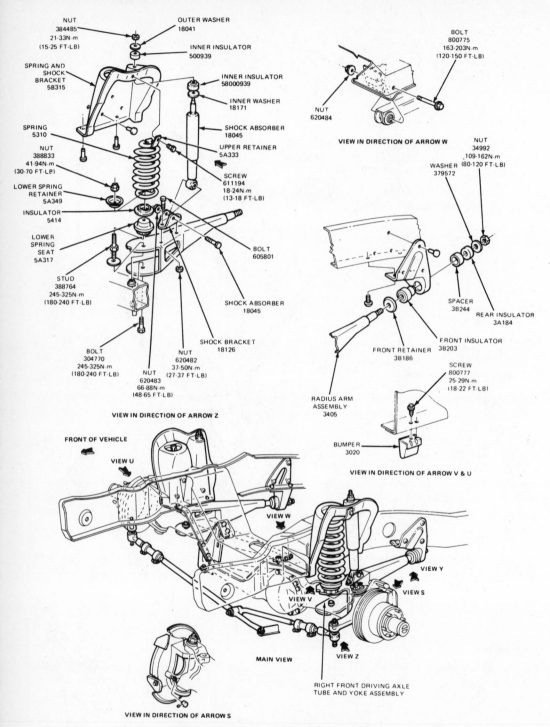

1980 and later front suspension assembly

*vert it and fully compress and extend it at
least three times. This will bleed trapped air.*

1. Raise the vehicle to provide additional access and remove the bolt and nut attaching the
shock absorber to the lower bracket on the radius arm.

2. Remove the nut, washer and insulator

from the shock absorber at the frame bracket
and remove the shock absorber.

To install the front shock absorber:

3. Position the washer and insulator on the
shock absorber rod and position the shock absorber to the frame bracket.

4. Position the insulator and washer on the

shock absorber rod and install the attaching nut loosely.

5. Position the shock absorber to the lower bracket and install the attaching bolt and nut loosely.

6. Tighten the lower attaching bolts to 40–60 ft.lb., and the upper attaching bolts to 15–25 ft.lb.

Radius Arm
REMOVAL AND INSTALLATION
1966–77

1. Raise the vehicle and position safety stands under the frame side rails.

2. Remove the shock absorber-to-lower bracket attaching bolt and nut and pull the shock absorber free of the radius arm.

3. Remove the two spring lower retainer attaching bolts from inside of the spring coil.

4. Remove the cotter pin and nut attaching the radius arm to the frame bracket and remove the radius arm rear insulator.

5. Remove the four bolts attaching the radius arm cap to the radius arm and remove the cap and insulator. The cap and radius arm are a matched set with identical numbers on each part and should not be mixed.

6. Move the axle forward and remove the radius arm and insulator from the axle. Then, pull the radius arm from the frame bracket.

The radius arm and cap must be identified by a T on each piece in addition to a number (1 through 100).

7. Position the washer and insulator on the rear of the radius arm and insert the radius arm and insulator into the frame bracket.

8. Position the rear insulator and washer on the radius arm and loosely install the attaching nut.

9. Position the insulator on the axle and position the radius arm to the insulator and axle.

10. Position the front insulator to the axle and install the radius arm cap with the numbers on the radius arm and cap together. Torque the attaching bolts diagonally in pairs to 90–100 ft.lb.

11. Position the spring lower seat and retainer to the spring and axle. Install the two attaching bolts. Torque the bolts to 45–55 ft.lb.

12. Torque the radius rod rear attaching nut to 80–120 ft.lb. Advance the nut as required and install the cotter pin.

13. Position the shock absorber to the lower bracket and install the attaching bolt and nut. Torque the nut to 40–60 ft.lb. Remove safety stands and lower the vehicle.

1978–79

1. Raise the vehicle and position safety stands under the frame side rails.

2. Remove the shock absorber-to-lower bracket attaching bolt and nut and pull the shock absorber free of the radius arm.

3. Remove two spring lower retainer attaching bolts from inside of the spring coil.

4. Remove the nut attaching the radius arm to the frame bracket and remove the radius arm rear insulator.

5. Remove four bolts attaching the radius arm cap to the radius arm and remove the cap and insulator. The cap and radius arm are a matched set with identical numbers on each part and should not be mixed.

6. Move the axle forward and remove the radius arm and insulator from the axle. Then, pull the radius arm from the frame bracket.

The radius arm and cap must be identified by a T on each piece in addition to a number (1 through 100).

7. Position the washer and insulator on the rear of the radius arm and insert the radius arm and insulator into the frame bracket.

8. Position the rear insulator and washer on the radius arm and loosely install the attaching nut.

9. Position the insulator on the axle and position the radius arm to the insulator and axle.

10. Position the front insulator to the axle and install the radius arm cap with the numbers on the radius arm and cap together. Tighten the attaching bolts diagonally in pairs to 90–110 ft.lb.

11. Position the spring lower seat and retainer to the spring and axle. Install the two attaching bolts. Tighten the bolts to 45–55 ft.lb.

12. Tighten the radius rod rear attaching nut to 80–120 ft.lb.

13. Position the shock absorber to the lower bracket and install the attaching bolt and nut. Tighten the nut to 40–60 ft.lb. Remove safety stands and lower the vehicle.

1980–86

1. Raise the vehicle and position safety stands under the frame side rails.

2. Remove the shock absorber-to-lower bracket attaching bolt and nut and pull the shock absorber free of the radius arm.

3. Remove spring lower retainer attaching bolt from inside the spring coil.

4. Remove the nut attaching the radius arm to the frame bracket and remove the radius arm rear insulator. Lower the axle and allow axle to move forward.

NOTE: *The axle must be supported on the jack throughout spring removal and installation, and must not be permitted to hang by the brake hose. If the length of the brake hose is not sufficient to provide adequate clearance for removal and installation of the spring, the disc brake caliper must be removed from the spindle according to the procedures specified in Chapter 8. After removal, the caliper must be placed on the frame or otherwise supported to prevent suspending the caliper from the caliper hose. These precautions are absolutely necessary to prevent serious damage to the tube portion of the caliper hose assembly.*

5. Remove the bolt and stud attaching radius arm to axle.

6. Move the axle forward and remove the radius arm from the axle. Then, pull the radius arm from the frame bracket.

7. Position the washer and insulator on the rear of the radius arm and insert the radius arm to the frame bracket.

8. Position the rear insulator and washer on the radius arm and loosely install the attaching nut.

9. Position the radius arm to the axle.

10. Install new bolts and stud type bolt attaching radius arm to axle. Tighten to 180–240 ft.lb.

11. Position the spring lower seat, spring insulator and retainer to the spring and axle. Install the two attaching bolts. Tighten the nuts to 30–70 ft.lb.

12. Tighten the radius rod rear attaching nut to 80–120 ft.lb.

13. Position the shock absorber to the lower bracket and install the attaching bolt and nut. Tighten the nut to 40–60 ft.lb. Remove safety stands and lower the vehicle.

Stabilizer Bar

REMOVAL AND INSTALLATION

1978–79

1. Remove locknut, washers, and insulator to remove link assemblies from stabilizer bar. Remove nuts, bolts, and washers connecting link assemblies to frame.

2. Remove nuts on U-bolts to remove stabilizer bar from retainers. Remove stabilizer bar. Remove U-bolts, brackets and retainers.

3. Place bracket assemblies on axle aligning holes in brackets with alignment pins on axles.

4. Install U-bolts through bracket assembly. Position stabilizer bar on brackets. Install retainer and tighten nuts to 35–55 ft.lb.

5. Install link assemblies on frame. Connect link assemblies to stabilizer bar. Tighten link to stabilizer bar nuts to 18–25 ft.lb. Tighten link to frame nuts to 40–60 ft.lb.

1980–86

1. Remove nuts, bolts and washers connecting the stabilizer bar to connecting links. Remove nuts and bolts of the stabilizer bar retainer.

2. Remove stabilizer bar insulator assembly.

3. To remove the stabilizer bar mounting bracket, the coil spring must be removed as described above under spring removal. Remove the lower spring seat. The bracket attaching stud and bracket can now be removed.

4. To install the stabilizer bar mounting brackets, locate the brackets so that the locating tang is positioned in the radius arm notch (or quad shock bracket notch if vehicle has quad shocks). Install a new stud. Torque to 180–220 ft.lb.

NOTE: *A new stud is required because of the adhesive on the threads.*

Reposition the spring lower seat and reinstall the spring and retainers.

5. To reinstall the stabilizer bar insulator assembly, assemble all nuts, bolts and washers to the bar, brackets, retainers and links loosely. With the bar positioned correctly, torque retainer nuts to 32–35 ft.lb. with retainer around the insulator. Then torque all remaining nuts at the link assemblies to 41–50 ft.lb.

Front End Alignment

CASTER AND CAMBER ADJUSTMENT

The caster and camber angles on the Bronco are designed into the front axle assembly and cannot be adjusted. Toe-in, however, is adjustable and the procedure is given in later paragraphs.

If you should start to notice abnormal tire wear patterns and handling (steering wheel is hard to return to straight ahead position after negotiating a turn on pavement in 2WD), and misalignment of caster and camber are suspected, make the following checks:

1. Check the air pressure in all the tires. Make sure that the pressures agree with those specified for the tires and vehicle model being checked.

2. Raise the front of the vehicle off the ground. Grasp each front tire at the front and rear, and push the wheel inward and outward. If any freeplay is noticed adjust the wheel bearings.

NOTE: *There is supposed to be a very, very small amount of freeplay present where the wheel bearings are concerned. Replace the bearings if they are worn or damaged.*

3. Check all steering linkage for wear or maladjustment. Adjust and/or replace all worn parts.

4. Check the steering gear mounting bolts and tighten if necessary.

5. Rotate each front wheel slowly, and observe the amount of lateral or side runout. If the wheel runout exceeds ⅛" (3mm), replace the wheel or install the wheel on the rear.

6. Inspect the radius arms to be sure they are not bent or damaged. Inspect the bushings

Wheel Alignment Specifications 1966–79

Year	Caster		Camber		Toe-in (in.)	Steering Axis Inclination (deg)
	Range (deg)	Preferred (deg)	Range	Preferred (deg)		
1966–77	2¾P to 4¼P	3½P	1P to 2P	½P	1/16–¼	—
1978–79*	6½P to 9½P	8P	1P to 3P	1½P	3/32	8½

Wheel Alignment Specifications 1980–86

Ride Height (in.)	Camber (deg)	Caster (deg)	Toe-in (in.)	Kin Pin Angle (deg)
2¾–3¼	2½N to ¼N	6P to 9P	1/32 out-5/32 in	13
3¼–3½	1¾N to ½P	5P to 8P	1/32 out-5/32 in	13
3½–4	¾N to 1½P	4P to 7P	1/32 out-5/32 in	13
4–4¼	0 to 2¼P	3P to 6P	1/32 out-5/32 in	13
4¼–4¾	1P to 3¼P	2P to 5P	1/32 out-5/32 in	13
4¾–5	1¾P to 4P	1P to 4P	1/32 out-5/32 in	13

*1978–79 caster measured at 3½ inches ride height. Subtract 2° for each inch increase in ride height.

at the radius arm-to-axle attachment and radius arm-to-frame attachment points for wear or looseness. Repair or replace parts as required.

TOE-IN ADJUSTMENT

Toe-in can be measured by either a front end alignment machine or by the following method:

With the front wheels in the straight ahead position, measure the distance between the extreme front and the extreme rear of the front wheels. In other words, measure the distance across the undercarriage of the vehicle between the two front edges and the two rear edges of the two front wheels. Both of these measurements (front and rear of the two wheels) must be taken at an equal distance from the floor and at the approximate centerline of the spindle. The difference between these two distances is the amount that the wheels toe-in or toe-out. The wheels should always be adjusted to toe-in according to specifications.

1. Loosen the clamp bolts at each end of the left tie rod, seen from the front of the vehicle. Rotate the connecting rod tube until the correct toe-in is obtained, then tighten the clamp bolts.

2. Recheck the toe-in to make sure that no changes occurred when the bolts were tightened.

NOTE: *The clamps should be positioned 3/16" (4.8mm) from the end of the rod with the clamp bolts in a vertical position in front of the tube, with the nut down.*

REAR SUSPENSION

Semi-eliptic leaf springs are used on the rear suspension for all models. The springs are mounted outside the frame members, and are attached to the axle with two U-bolts. The front end of each spring is attached to a hanger, which is part of the frame side member, with a bolt and nut. The rear end of the spring is attached to a shackle assembly with a bolt and nut and the shackle assembly is attached to a hanger.

The shock absorbers are attached to a bracket which is part of the axle tube and extend up to an upper bracket at a slight rearward angle.

Springs

REMOVAL AND INSTALLATION

1. Raise the vehicle and install jackstands under the frame. The vehicle must be supported in such a way that the rear axle hangs free with the tire a few inches off the ground. Place a hydraulic floor jack under the center of the axle housing.

2. Disconnect the shock absorber from the axle.

3. Remove the U-bolt attaching nuts and remove the two U-bolts and the spring clip plate.

4. Lower the axle to relieve the spring tension and remove the nut from the spring front attaching bolt.

5. Remove the spring front attaching bolt from the spring and hanger with a drift.

6. Remove the nut from the shackle-to-hanger attaching bolt and drive the bolt from

the shackle and hanger with a drift and remove the spring from the vehicle.

7. Remove the nut from the spring rear attaching bolt. Drive the bolt out of the spring and shackle with a drift.

To install the rear spring:

8. Position the shackle (closed section facing toward the front of the vehicle) to the spring rear eye and install the bolt and nut.

9. Position the spring front eye and bushing to the spring front hanger, and install the attaching bolt and nut.

10. Position the spring rear eye and bushing to the shackle, and install the attaching bolt and nut.

11. Raise the axle to the spring and install the U-bolts and spring clip plate.

12. Torque the U-bolt nuts and spring front and rear attaching bolt nuts to 45–60 ft.lb.

13. Remove the jackstands and lower the vehicle.

NOTE: *Squeaky rear springs can be corrected by tightening the front and rear eye bolts to 150–204 ft.lb., then raising and supporting the rear of the vehicle so that the rear springs hang, spreading the leaves. Apply a silicone based lubricant for a distance of 3″ (76mm) in from each leaf tip.*

Shock Absorbers

TESTING

1. Visually check the shock absorbers for the presence of fluid leakage. A thin film of fluid is acceptable. Anything more than that means that the shock absorber must be replaced.

2. Disconnect the lower end of the shock absorber. Compress and extend the shock fully, as fast as possible. If the action is not smooth in both directions, or there is no pressure resistance, replace the shock absorber. Shock absorbers should be replaced in pairs if they have accumulated more than 20,000 miles of wear. In the case of relatively new shock absorbers, where one has failed, that one, alone, may be replaced.

REMOVAL AND INSTALLATION

NOTE: *Prior to installing a new shock absorber, hold it right side up and extend it fully. Turn it upside down and fully compress and extend it at least three times. This will bleed any trapped air.*

1. Raise the vehicle and place jackstands under the frame.

2. Remove the shock absorber-to-upper bracket attaching nut and washers, and bushing from the shock absorber rod.

3. Remove the shock absorber-to-axle attaching bolt. Drive the bolts from the axle bracket and shock absorber with a brass drift and remove the shock absorber.

4. Position the washers and bushing on the shock absorber rod and position the shock absorber at the upper bracket.

5. Position the bushing and washers on the shock absorber rod and install the attaching nut loosely.

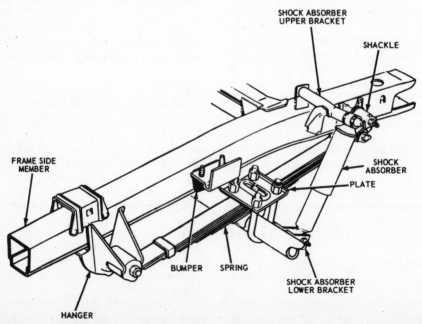

Typical rear suspension. On 1978–80 models, the shock absorber is outboard of the spring

6. Position the shock absorber at the axle housing bracket and install the attaching bolt and nut. Tighten the lower nut to 40–60 ft.lb., and the upper nut to 15–25 ft.lb.

STEERING

Steering Wheel

REMOVAL AND INSTALLATION

1966–74

1. Disconnect the battery and depress the horn button or horn ring and rotate it counterclockwise to remove it. Remove the horn spring.

2. Mark the steering wheel position on the steering column.

3. Remove the steering wheel attaching nut. Remove the steering wheel with a puller.

4. Remove the spring from around the end of the steering shaft.

5. Install the steering wheel in the revere order of removal.

1975–86

1. Disconnect the battery ground and mark the steering wheel-to-column alignment.

2. Remove once screw from the underside of each spoke and lift the horn assembly from the wheel. On vehicles with a sport wheel option, pry the button cover off with a screwdriver.

3. Disconnect the horn switch wires by pulling the spade terminal from the blade connector. Squeeze or pinch the J-clip ground wire terminal fully and pull it out of the hole in the steering wheel. Do not pull the ground terminal out of the threaded hole without squeezing the clip to remove the spring tension.

4. Remove the horn switch assembly.

5. Remove the steering wheel retaining nut.

6. Using a steering wheel puller, remove the wheel.

7. Position the steering wheel in alignment with the marks.

8. Tighten the retaining nut to 50 ft.lb.

9. Connect the wires, install the horn assembly and connect the battery ground.

Turn Signal Switch

REPLACEMENT

1966–77

1. Disconnect the horn and turn signal wires at the connectors located behind the instrument panel. Remove the steering column wires and terminals from the connectors by inserting a small screwdriver or similar tool in the opposite end from which the wire is inserted and depress the tang on the wire. The wire can then be removed from the connector.

NOTE: *Be sure to record the color code and location of each wire before removing it from the connector plug. Tape a pull-through wire or cord to one of the wire ends.*

2. Remove the steering wheel.

3. Turn the signal switch lever counterclockwise to remove it. Remove the screws and retainer which hold the turn signal switch and wire assembly to the steering column, and pull the assembly from the column. Disconnect the pull-through wire or cord from the end of the wire to which it was taped.

To install the switch:

4. Tape the loose ends of the new turn signal switch wires to the pull-through wire or cord. Carefully pull the wires through the steering column, while guiding the turn signal switch into position. Install the switch retainer screws.

5. Assemble the rest of the steering column in the reverse order of disassembly.

1978–86

1. Disconnect the battery ground cable.

2. Remove the horn switch.

3. Remove the steering wheel retaining nut and using Tool 3600AA or equivalent, remove the steering wheel from the shaft.

4. Remove the turn signal switch lever by unscrewing it from the steering column.

5. Disconnect the turn indicator switch wiring connector plug by lifting up on the tabs and separating and removing the screws that secure the switch assembly to the column.

6. Remove the wires and terminals from the steering column wiring connector plug. Record the color code and location of each wire before removing it from the connector plug.

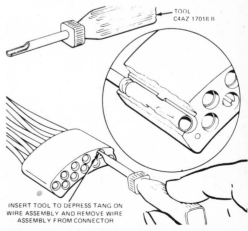

INSERT TOOL TO DEPRESS TANG ON WIRE ASSEMBLY AND REMOVE WIRE ASSEMBLY FROM CONNECTOR

TOOL C4AZ 17018 B

Turn signal switch wiring connector removal, 1978 and later

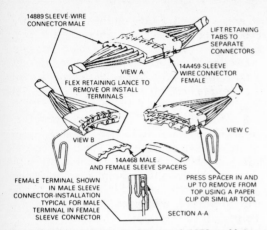

14889 SLEEVE-WIRE CONNECTOR MALE

LIFT RETAINING TABS TO SEPARATE CONNECTORS

VIEW A

14A459-SLEEVE WIRE CONNECTOR FEMALE

FLEX RETAINING LANCE TO REMOVE OR INSTALL TERMINALS

VIEW C

VIEW B

14A468 MALE AND FEMALE SLEEVE SPACERS

FEMALE TERMINAL SHOWN IN MALE SLEEVE CONNECTOR-INSTALLATION TYPICAL FOR MALE TERMINAL IN FEMALE SLEEVE CONNECTOR

PRESS SPACER IN AND UP TO REMOVE FROM TOP USING A PAPER CLIP OR SIMILAR TOOL

SECTION A-A

Turn signal switch terminal removal, 1978 and later

7. Connect and pull the wire through to the end of wiring harness. Secure it with tape.

8. Remove the protective wire cover from the wiring harness and remove the switch and wires through the top of the column.

9. Tape the loose ends of the new turn signal switch wires to the pull-through wire or cord. Carefully pull the wires through the steering column while guiding the turn signal switch into position.

10. Install switch assembly retaining screws to column.

11. Install wires into steering column wire connector terminal and connect terminals.

12. Install turn signal lever. Hand tighten the lever (on flat side) to 10–20 in.lb. Test turn signal operation, hazard signal operation and PRND21 dial lamp (if so equipped).

13. Install steering wheel.

14. Install horn switch.

15. Connect battery ground cable.

Ignition Switch And Lock Cylinder
REMOVAL AND INSTALLATION
1966–79

1. Disconnect the battery ground cable.

2. Turn the ignition key to Accessories and slightly depress the release pin in the face of the lock cylinder.

3. Turn the key counterclockwise and pull the key and lock assembly out of the switch.

4. From under the instrument panel, press in on the rear of the switch ⅛ turn counterclockwise.

5. Remove the bezel and switch. Remove the retainer and spring.

6. Remove the nut from the back of the switch.

7. Remove the accessory and gauge feed wires from the accessory terminal of the switch. Pull the insulated plug from the rear of the switch.

8. To install: insert a screwdriver into the lock opening of the switch and turn the slot in the switch to the full counterclockwise position.

9. Connect the insulated plug and wires to the back of the switch. Connect the accessory and gauge wires to the switch and install the retaining nut.

10. Place the bezel and switch in the switch opening, press the switch toward the instrument panel and rotate it ⅛ turn to lock it.

11. Position the spring and retainer on the switch with the open face of the retainer away from the switch. Place the switch in the opening.

12. Press the switch toward the instrument panel and install the bezel.

13. Place the key in the cylinder and turn the key to the accessory position. Place the lock and key in the switch, depress the release pin slightly, and turn the key counterclockwise. Push the new lock cylinder into the switch. Turn the key to check the operation.

14. Connect the battery.

1980–86

1. Disconnect the battery ground cable.

2. Remove steering column shroud and lower the steering column.

3. Disconnect the switch wiring at the multiple plug.

4. Remove the two nuts that retain the switch to the steering column.

5. Lift the switch vertically upward to disengage the actuator rod from the switch and remove switch.

6. When installing the ignition switch, both the locking mechanism at the top of the column and the switch itself must be in LOCK position for correct adjustment.

To hold the mechanical parts of the column in LOCK position, move the shift lever into PARK (with automatic transmissions) or REVERSE (with manual transmissions), turn the key to LOCK position, and remove the key. New replacement switches, when received, are already pinned in LOCK position by a metal shipping pin inserted in a locking hole on the side of the switch.

7. Engage the actuator rod in the switch.

8. Position the switch on the column and install the retaining nuts, but do not tighten them.

9. Move the switch up and down along the column to locate the mid-position of rod lash, and then tighten the retaining nuts.

10. Remove the locking pin, connect the bat-

tery cable, and check for proper start in PARK or NEUTRAL.

Also check to make certain that the start circuit cannot be actuated in the DRIVE and REVERSE position.

11. Raise the steering column into position at instrument panel. Install steering column shroud.

Steering Cloumn

REMOVAL

1. Set the parking brake and disconnect the battery. Remove the bolt and nut attaching the intermediate shaft to the steering column.

2. Disconnect the shift linkage rods from the column.

3. Remove the steering wheel as described previously. If a tilt steering column is being serviced, the steering wheel must be in the full **UP** position when it is removed.

4. Remove the steering column floor opening cover plate screws.

5. Remove the shroud by loosening the screw at the bottom, selecting position **1** on manual 3-speeds and automatics and spreading shroud open, withdrawing out of instrument panel opening, while pulling up and away from column.

6. Remove PRND21 indicator actuation cable (automatics).

7. Remove the instrument panel column opening cover.

8. Remove the bolts attaching the column support bracket to the pedal support bracket.

9. Disconnect the turn signal/hazard warning and ignition switch wiring harnesses.

10. Remove the column from the vehicle.

INSTALLATION

1. Attach the steering column support bracket making sure that the turn signal/hazard warning wiring is on the outboard side of the column. Tighten the nuts to 13–38 ft.lb.

2. Start the floor opening cover clamp bolt and press the plate until the clamp flats touch the stops on the column outer tube.

3. Load the column into the vehicle through the opening in the floor.

4. Connect the turn signal/hazard warning and ignition switch wiring harnesses.

5. Raise the column up to the pedal support bracket and hand start the two bolts.

6. Fasten the floor opening cover plate to the floor. Tighten to 6–10 ft.lb.

7. Tighten the two support bracket bolts 19–27 ft.lb.

8. Tighten the cover plate clamp bolt 8–18 ft.lb.

9. Install and adjust the PRND21 indicator actuator cable (automatics).

10. Install the instrument panel steering column opening cover.

11. Mount the shroud by selecting position **1** on 3-speed manuals and automatic transmissions, spreading shroud around steering column and through the opening in the instrument panel. Post on the interior will index shroud when properly positioned.

12. Tighten the screw at the bottom of the shroud 10–15 in.lb.

13. Attach the shift linkage rods to the column.

14. Fasten the intermediate shaft to the steering column and tighten to 45–59 ft.lb.

Steering Linkage Connecting Rods

Replace the drag link if a ball stud is excessively loose or if the drag link is bent. Do not attempt to straighten a drag link.

Replace the connecting rod if the ball stud is excessively loose, if the connecting rod is bent or if the threads are stripped. Do not attempt to straighten connecting rod. Always check to insure that the adjustment sleeve and clamp stops are correctly installed on the Bronco.

REMOVAL AND INSTALLATION

1966–75

1. Disconnect the connecting rods from the spindles and drag link.

2. Place the connecting rods in a vise and loosen the tube clamps. Disassemble the rods. The right one is shorter than the left one.

3. Clean and oil all threads on components to be reused.

4. Install the left tube and clamps on the left spindle rod end. Do not tighten clamps.

5. Install the right end in the tube and remove the assembly from the vise.

6. Install new dust seal and attach the assembly to the spindles. Torque the nuts to 40 ft.lb. aligning the cotter pin holes as the nut is tightened.

7. Install new seals on the drag link stud and attach it to the connecting rod. Torque the nut to 40 ft.lb.

8. Check and adjust toe in and tighten the tube clamps.

1976–77

1. Raise vehicle and support on jackstands.

2. Disconnect connecting rod ends from spindles.

3. Remove U-bolts securing left connecting rod to brace.

4. Disconnect right connecting rod end from steering arm.

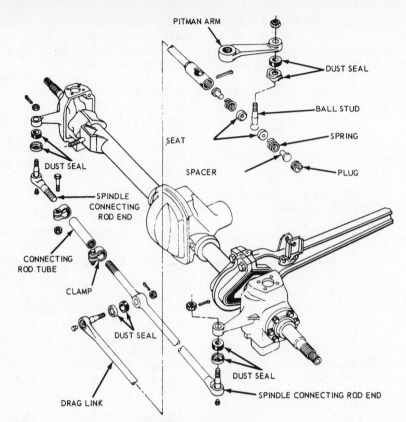

PITMAN ARM

DUST SEAL

BALL STUD

SEAT

SPRING

SPACER

PLUG

DUST SEAL

SPINDLE CONNECTING ROD END

CONNECTING ROD TUBE

CLAMP

DUST SEAL

DUST SEAL

SPINDLE CONNECTING ROD END

DRAG LINK

1966–74 steering linkage

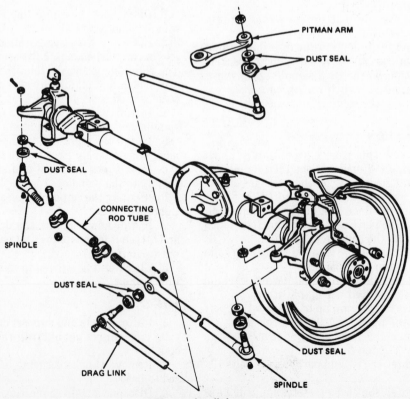

PITMAN ARM

DUST SEAL

DUST SEAL

CONNECTING ROD TUBE

SPINDLE

DUST SEAL

DUST SEAL

DRAG LINK

SPINDLE

1975 steering linkage

5. Mount the assembly in a vise and disconnect the right and left rod assemblies.

6. Mark the position of the clamp on the left connecting halves.

7. Clean and oil all threaded parts.

8. Assemble left connecting rod halves in clamp at about the same position marked.

9. Attach right and left connecting rods, but do not tighten nut.

10. Attach connecting rods to the spindles. Torque the nuts to 40 ft.lb.

11. Check and adjust toe-in by turning the left connecting rod halves. Tighten lamp bolts.

12. Attach the left connecting rod to the brace by tightening the two U-bolts evenly to 20 ft.lb.

1978–79

1. Remove the cotter pins and nuts from the drag link, ball studs and from the right connecting rod ball stud.

2. Remove the right connecting rod hall stud from the drag link.

3. Remove the drag link ball studs from the spindle and the Pitman arm.

4. Position the new drag link, ball studs in the spindle, and Pitman arm and install nuts.

5. Position the right connecting rod ball stud in the drag link and install nut.

6. Tighten the nuts as follows and install the cotter pins. Drag link studs, 50–75 ft.lb. Ball studs, 50–60 ft.lb. Connecting rod studs, 35–45 ft.lb.

7. Remove the cotter pin and nut from the connecting rod.

8. Remove the ball stud from the mating part.

9. Loosen the clamp bolt and turn the rod out of the adjustment sleeve.

10. Lubricate the threads of the new connecting rod, and turn it into the adjustment sleeve to about the same distance the old rods were

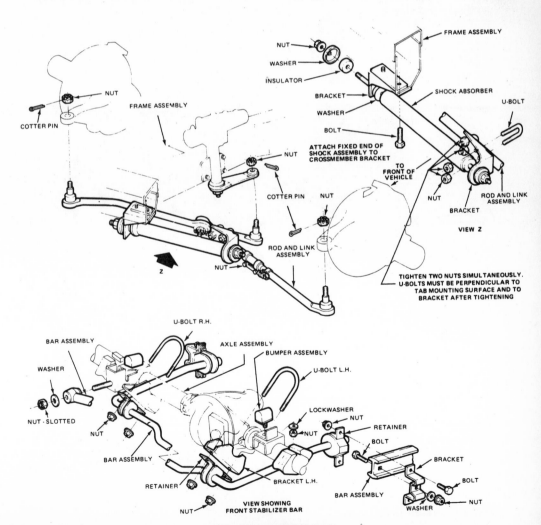

1976–77 steering linkage

installed. This will provide an approximate toe-in setting. Position the connecting rod ball studs in the spindle arms.

11. Install the nuts on to the connecting rod ball studs, tighten the nut to specification and install the cotter pin.

12. Check the toe-in and adjust, if necessary. After checking or adjusting toe-in, center the adjustment sleeve clamps between the locating nubs, positions the clamps and tighten the nuts to 35–45 ft.lb.

1980–86

1. Remove the cotter pins and nuts from the drag link, ball studs and from the right connecting rod ball studs.

2. Remove the right connecting rod ball stud from the right spindle assembly and Pitman arm.

3. Remove the drag link ball studs from the spindle and the connecting rod assembly.

4. Loosen the clamp bolt and turn the rod out of the adjustment sleeve.

5. Lubricate the threads of the new connecting rod, and turn it into the adjustment sleeve to about the same distance the old rods were installed. This will provide an approximate toe-in setting. Position the connecting rod ball studs in the spindle arms.

6. Position the new drag link, ball studs in the spindle, and connecting rod assembly and install nuts.

7. Position the right connecting rod ball stud in the drag link and install nut.

8. Tighten all the nuts to 50–75 ft.lb. and install the cotter pins.

9. Remove the cotter pin and nut from the left connecting rod.

10. Install the nuts on the connecting rod ball studs, tighten the nut to 50–75 ft.lb. and install the cotter pin.

11. Check the toe-in and adjust, if necessary. After checking or adjusting toe-in, center the adjustment sleeve clamps between the locating nubs, position the clamps and tighten the nuts to 29–41 ft.lb.

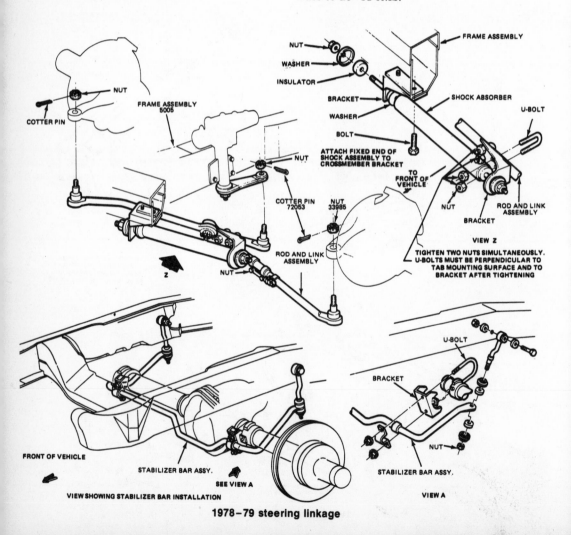

1978–79 steering linkage

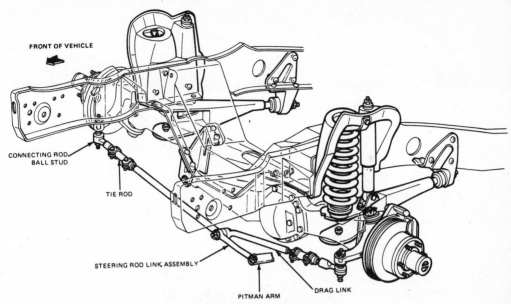

FRONT OF VEHICLE

CONNECTING ROD
BALL STUD

TIE ROD

STEERING ROD LINK ASSEMBLY

PITMAN ARM

DRAG LINK

1980 and later steering linkage

Manual Steering Gear

REMOVAL AND INSTALLATION

1966–79

1. Raise the vehicle on a hoist and remove the Pitman arm attaching nut and lockwasher.

2. Remove the Pitman arm from the sector shaft using Tool T64P-3590-F.

3. Remove bolts, nuts and flat washers that attach the steering gear to the frame side rail, and lower the vehicle.

4. Remove the flex coupling bolt and nut from the coupling clamp. Loosen the clamp from the coupling at the end of the steering column and separate the coupling from the steering gear input shaft by pushing the steering shaft toward the steering column. Discard the clamp, bolt, and nut.

5. Remove and discard the flex coupling clamp from the steering gear input shaft, and remove the steering gear from the frame side rail.

6. Place the steering gear on the frame side rail and install the attaching bolts, nuts, and flat washers.

7. Place the flex coupling and a new clamp on the steering gear input shaft and install the clamp bolt and nut. Tighten the bolt and nut to 28–35 ft.lb.

8. Install a new steering shaft clamp at the end of the steering column and tighten the bolt and nut to 20–30 ft.lb.

9. Raise the vehicle and tighten the steering gear attaching bolts and nuts to 60–80 ft.lb.

10. Place the Pitman arm on the sector shaft and install the washer and attaching nut.

Tighten the nut to 170–230 ft.lb., lower the vehicle, and fill the gear with lubricant SAE-90EP Oil.

ADJUSTMENTS

1. Be sure that the steering column is properly aligned and is not causing excessive turning effort.

2. The steering gear must be removed from the truck.

3. Be sure that the ball nut assembly and the sector gear are properly adjusted as follows to maintain minimum steering shaft endplay and backlash between the sector gear and ball nut (preload adjustment).

4. Loosen the sector shaft adjusting screw locknut and tighten worm bearing adjuster screw until all endplay is removed.

5. Measure the worm bearing preload by attaching an in.lb. torque wrench to the input shaft. Measure the torque required to rotate the input shaft all the way to the right and then turn back about one half turn. The worm bearing preload should be 10–16 in.lb.

6. Turn the sector shaft adjusting screw clockwise until the specified pull is obtained to rotate the worm past its center. With the steering gear in the center position, hold the sector shaft to prevent rotation and check the lash between the ball nuts, balls and worm shaft by applying a 15 in.lb. torque on the steering gear input shaft, in both right and left turn directions. Total travel of the wrench should not exceed 1¼" (32mm) when applying a 15 in.lb. torque on the steering shaft.

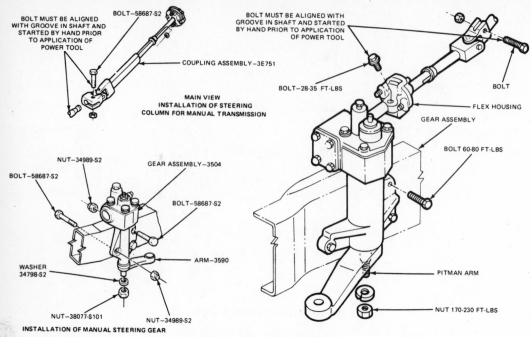

INSTALLATION OF MANUAL STEERING GEAR

1966–79 steering gear installation

7. Tighten the sector shaft adjusting screw locknut, and recheck the backlash adjustment.

Power Steering Gear

REMOVAL AND INSTALLATION

Through 1977

When servicing the steering gear, label hoses before disconnecting them so they can be easily identified for reassembly.

Service the steering gear as follows:

1. Position a drain pan under the steering gear. Disconnect the pressure and the return lines from the steering gear and plug the lines and ports in the gear to prevent entry of dirt.

2. Raise the vehicle on a hoist and remove the Pitman arm attaching nut and lock washer.

3. Remove the Pitman arm from the sector shaft using Tool T64P-3590-F.

4. Remove the bolts and nuts that attach the steering gear to the frame side rail. Lower the vehicle.

5. Remove the pinch bolt from the flange and insulator assembly.

6. Loosen the nut holding the horn and turn the horn outward.

7. Remove the steering gear attaching bolts and remove the steering gear, shaft, and joint assemblies as a unit.

8. Remove the pinch bolt and nut from the shaft and joint assembly.

9. Remove the shaft and joint assembly from the steering gear.

10. Before installing the gear in the vehicle, attach the shaft and joint assembly to the steering gear. Install the pinch bolt and torque the nut to 45 to 60 ft.lb.

11. Raise the vehicle on a hoist. Place the steering gear on the frame side rail and loosely attach the forward attaching bolt and nut.

12. Center the steering gear input shaft.

13. Insert the shaft end of the shaft and joint assembly into the flange and insulator assembly while supporting the rear of the steering gear.

14. Install the remaining steering gear attaching bolts through the steering gear flange, through the frame side rail.

15. Install the remaining steering gear attaching nuts and torque all three attaching nuts to 52 to 90 ft.lb.

16. Make sure the wheels are in the straight ahead position and install the Pitman arm, lock washer and nut. Torque the nut to 170–230 ft.lb. Lower the vehicle.

17. Install the pinch bolt in the flange and insulator assembly, and torque to 28 to 35 ft.lb.

18. Remove the plugs from the pressure and return lines and ports of the steering gear. Connect the lines to gar and torque to 16 to 25 ft.lb.

19. Turn the horn inward and tighten the retaining nut. Disconnect the coil wire. Fill the power steering pump reservoir. Turn on the ignition and turn the steering wheel to distribute the fluid. Check the fluid level and add fluid, if necessary. Connect the coil wire, start the

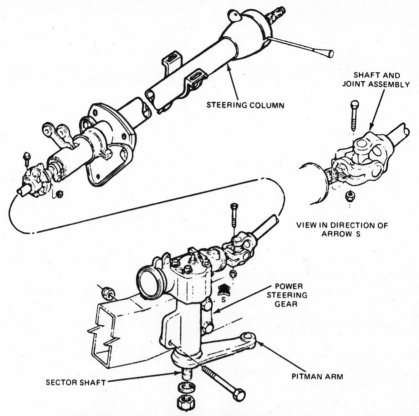

Power steering gear installation through 1977

engine and turn the steering wheel from side to side. Check for fluid leaks.

1978–86

Service the steering gear as follows:

1. Disconnect the pressure and return lines from the steering gear. Plug the lines and the ports in the gear to prevent entry of dirt. Disconnect brake lines from the steering gear bracket.

2. Remove the bolts that secure the flex coupling to the steering gear and to the column steering shaft assembly.

3. Raise the vehicle and remove the Pitman arm attaching nut, and washer.

4. Remove the Pitman arm from the sector shaft using Tool T64P-3590-F. Remove the tool from the Pitman arm. Do not damage the seals.

5. On vehicles with standard transmission remove the clutch release lever retracting spring to provide clearance for removing the steering gear.

6. Support the steering gear, and remove the steering gear attaching bolts.

7. Work the steering gear free of the flex coupling. Remove the steering gear from the vehicle.

8. Slide the flex coupling into place on the steering shaft assembly. Turn the steering wheel so the spokes are in the horizontal position.

9. Center the steering gear input shaft.

10. Slide the steering gear input shaft into the flex coupling and into place on the frame side rail. Install the attaching bolts and tighten to 60–80 ft.lb.

11. Be sure the wheels are in the straight ahead position, then install the Pitman arm on the sector shaft. Install the Pitman arm attaching washer and nut. Tighten nut to 170–230 ft.lb.

12. Connect and tighten the pressure and the return lines to the steering gear. Reinstall the brake lines on the steering gear bracket.

13. Disconnect the coil wire. Fill the reservoir. Turn on the ignition and turn the steering wheel from left to right to distribute the fluid.

14. Recheck fluid level and add fluid, if necessary. Connect the coil wire, start the engine and turn the steering wheel from side to side. Inspect for fluid leaks.

ADJUSTMENTS

Steering Gear Meshload

1. Make sure that the steering column is correctly aligned.

2. Disconnect the steering linkage from the Pitman arm on the steering gear. Remove the horn pad as explained under Steering Wheel Removal and Installation.

3. Disconnect the fluid reservoir return line and cap the reservoir return line tube. Place the end of the return line in a clean container and turn the steering wheel back and forth several times to empty the steering gear.

4. Turn the steering wheel nut with an inch pound torque wrench slowly. Find the torque required at ½ turn off right and left stops, ½ turn off center both right and left, and overcenter (full turn). The overcenter torque should be 4–6 in.lb. more than the end readings, but the total overcenter torque must not exceed 14 in.lb.

5. To correct, back off the Pitman shaft adjuster all the way, then back in ½ turn. Recheck the overcenter torque. Loosen the locknut and tighten the sector shaft adjusting screw until the overcenter torque reads 4–6 in.lb. higher, but doesn't exceed 14 in.lb. Tighten the adjusting screw locknut and recheck.

6. Refill the system with the fluid specified. Bleed the system of air by turning the steering wheel all the way to the right and left several times with the engine warmed up. Do not hold the steering against the stops or pump damage will result.

Power Steering Pump
REMOVAL AND INSTALLATION

1. Position a drain pan under the power steering pump.

2. Disconnect the pressure and return lines at the pump. Disconnect the cooler hoses over the pump.

NOTE: *If the power steering pump is being removed from the engine in order to facilitate the removal of some other component, and it is not necessary for the pump to be completely removed from the vehicle, it is not necessary and is not recommended that the pressure and return hoses be disconnected from the pump.*

3. Loosen the one pivot bolt and one adjustment bolt. Remove the drive belt.

4. Remove the two water pump bolts from the adjusting bracket attached to the front cover.

5. While holding the pump, use a jam nut and remove the through bolt from the cylinder head. Remove the pump with both brackets from the vehicle.

6. If installing a new pump, transfer the pump support brackets to the new unit.

7. Insert the through bolt from the rear of the pump bracket. Install the pump in the vehicle without the adjusting bracket, inserting the through bolt into the block.

8. Position the adjusting bracket to the water pump and torque the two retaining bolts to 11–16 ft.lb.

9. Install the bolt. Install and torque the bolts, retaining the support bracket to the pump and block, to 30–40 ft.lb. Check the belt tension.

10. Connect the cooler hoses over the pump and tighten the hose clamp to 10–18 in.lb. Connect the pressure and return lines to the pump.

11. Fill the power steering system with the proper type power steering fluid. Perform the system bleeding operation.

12. Remove the drain pan.

SYSTEM BLEEDING

1. Disconnect the coil wire.

2. Crank the engine and continue adding fluid until the level stabilizes.

3. Continue to crank the engine and rotate the steering wheel about 30° to either side of center.

4. Check the fluid level and add as required.

5. Connect the coil wire and start the engine. Allow it to run for several minutes.

6. Rotate the steering wheel from stop to stop.

7. Shut off the engine and check the fluid level. Add fluid as necessary.

Noise Diagnosis

The Noise Is	Most Probably Produced By
• Identical under Drive or Coast	• Road surface, tires or front wheel bearings
• Different depending on road surface	• Road surface or tires
• Lower as the car speed is lowered	• Tires
• Similar with car standing or moving	• Engine or transmission
• A vibration	• Unbalanced tires, rear wheel bearing, unbalanced driveshaft or worn U-joint
• A knock or click about every 2 tire revolutions	• Rear wheel bearing
• Most pronounced on turns	• Damaged differential gears
• A steady low-pitched whirring or scraping, starting at low speeds	• Damaged or worn pinion bearing

Noise Diagnosis (cont.)

The Noise Is	Most Probably Produced By
• A chattering vibration on turns	• Wrong differential lubricant or worn clutch plates (limited slip rear axle)
• Noticed only in Drive, Coast or Float conditions	• Worn ring gear and/or pinion gear

Troubleshooting Basic Steering and Suspension Problems

Problem	Cause	Solution
Hard steering (steering wheel is hard to turn)	• Low or uneven tire pressure	• Inflate tires to correct pressure
	• Loose power steering pump drive belt	• Adjust belt
	• Low or incorrect power steering fluid	• Add fluid as necessary
	• Incorrect front end alignment	• Have front end alignment checked/adjusted
	• Defective power steering pump	• Check pump
	• Bent or poorly lubricated front end parts	• Lubricate and/or replace defective parts
Loose steering (too much play in the steering wheel)	• Loose wheel bearings	• Adjust wheel bearings
	• Loose or worn steering linkage	• Replace worn parts
	• Faulty shocks	• Replace shocks
	• Worn ball joints	• Replace ball joints
Car veers or wanders (car pulls to one side with hands off the steering wheel)	• Incorrect tire pressure	• Inflate tires to correct pressure
	• Improper front end alignment	• Have front end alignment checked/adjusted
	• Loose wheel bearings	• Adjust wheel bearings
	• Loose or bent front end components	• Replace worn components
	• Faulty shocks	• Replace shocks
Wheel oscillation or vibration transmitted through steering wheel	• Improper tire pressures	• Inflate tires to correct pressure
	• Tires out of balance	• Have tires balanced
	• Loose wheel bearings	• Adjust wheel bearings
	• Improper front end alignment	• Have front end alignment checked/adjusted
	• Worn or bent front end components	• Replace worn parts
Uneven tire wear	• Incorrect tire pressure	• Inflate tires to correct pressure
	• Front end out of alignment	• Have front end alignment checked/adjusted
	• Tires out of balance	• Have tires balanced

Troubleshooting the Steering Column

Problem	Cause	Solution
Will not lock	• Lockbolt spring broken or defective	• Replace lock bolt spring
High effort (required to turn ignition key and lock cylinder)	• Lock cylinder defective	• Replace lock cylinder
	• Ignition switch defective	• Replace ignition switch
	• Rack preload spring broken or deformed	• Replace preload spring
	• Burr on lock sector, lock rack, housing, support or remote rod coupling	• Remove burr
	• Bent sector shaft	• Replace shaft
	• Defective lock rack	• Replace lock rack
	• Remote rod bent, deformed	• Replace rod
	• Ignition switch mounting bracket bent	• Straighten or replace

Troubleshooting the Steering Column (cont.)

Problem	Cause	Solution
High effort (required to turn ignition key and lock cylinder) (cont.)	• Distorted coupling slot in lock rack (tilt column)	• Replace lock rack
Will stick in "start"	• Remote rod deformed • Ignition switch mounting bracket bent	• Straighten or replace • Straighten or replace
Key cannot be removed in "off-lock"	• Ignition switch is not adjusted correctly • Defective lock cylinder	• Adjust switch • Replace lock cylinder
Lock cylinder can be removed without depressing retainer	• Lock cylinder with defective retainer • Burr over retainer slot in housing cover or on cylinder retainer	• Replace lock cylinder • Remove burr
High effort on lock cylinder between "off" and "off-lock"	• Distorted lock rack • Burr on tang of shift gate (automatic column) • Gearshift linkage not adjusted	• Replace lock rack • Remove burr • Adjust linkage
Noise in column	• One click when in "off-lock" position and the steering wheel is moved (all except automatic column) • Coupling bolts not tightened • Lack of grease on bearings or bearing surfaces • Upper shaft bearing worn or broken • Lower shaft bearing worn or broken • Column not correctly aligned • Coupling pulled apart • Broken coupling lower joint • Steering shaft snap ring not seated • Shroud loose on shift bowl. Housing loose on jacket—will be noticed with ignition in "off-lock" and when torque is applied to steering wheel.	• Normal—lock bolt is seating • Tighten pinch bolts • Lubricate with chassis grease • Replace bearing assembly • Replace bearing. Check shaft and replace if scored. • Align column • Replace coupling • Repair or replace joint and align column • Replace ring. Check for proper seating in groove. • Position shroud over lugs on shift bowl. Tighten mounting screws.
High steering shaft effort	• Column misaligned • Defective upper or lower bearing • Tight steering shaft universal joint • Flash on I.D. of shift tube at plastic joint (tilt column only) • Upper or lower bearing seized	• Align column • Replace as required • Repair or replace • Replace shift tube • Replace bearings
Lash in mounted column assembly	• Column mounting bracket bolts loose • Broken weld nuts on column jacket • Column capsule bracket sheared • Column bracket to column jacket mounting bolts loose • Loose lock shoes in housing (tilt column only) • Loose pivot pins (tilt column only) • Loose lock shoe pin (tilt column only) • Loose support screws (tilt column only)	• Tighten bolts • Replace column jacket • Replace bracket assembly • Tighten to specified torque • Replace shoes • Replace pivot pins and support • Replace pin and housing • Tighten screws
Housing loose (tilt column only)	• Excessive clearance between holes in support or housing and pivot pin diameters • Housing support-screws loose	• Replace pivot pins and support • Tighten screws

Troubleshooting the Steering Column (cont.)

Problem	Cause	Solution
Steering wheel loose—every other tilt position (tilt column only)	• Loose fit between lock shoe and lock shoe pivot pin	• Replace lock shoes and pivot pin
Steering column not locking in any tilt position (tilt column only)	• Lock shoe seized on pivot pin • Lock shoe grooves have burrs or are filled with foreign material • Lock shoe springs weak or broken	• Replace lock shoes and pin • Clean or replace lock shoes • Replace springs
Noise when tilting column (tilt column only)	• Upper tilt bumpers worn • Tilt spring rubbing in housing	• Replace tilt bumper • Lubricate with chassis grease
One click when in "off-lock" position and the steering wheel is moved	• Seating of lock bolt	• None. Click is normal characteristic sound produced by lock bolt as it seats.
High shift effort (automatic and tilt column only)	• Column not correctly aligned • Lower bearing not aligned correctly • Lack of grease on seal or lower bearing areas	• Align column • Assemble correctly • Lubricate with chassis grease
Improper transmission shifting— automatic and tilt column only	• Sheared shift tube joint • Improper transmission gearshift linkage adjustment • Loose lower shift lever	• Replace shift tube • Adjust linkage • Replace shift tube

Troubleshooting the Manual Steering Gear

Problem	Cause	Solution
Hard or erratic steering	• Incorrect tire pressure • Insufficient or incorrect lubrication • Suspension, or steering linkage parts damaged or misaligned • Improper front wheel alignment • Incorrect steering gear adjustment • Sagging springs	• Inflate tires to recommended pressures • Lubricate as required (refer to Maintenance Section) • Repair or replace parts as necessary • Adjust incorrect wheel alignment angles • Adjust steering gear • Replace springs
Play or looseness in steering	• Steering wheel loose • Steering linkage or attaching parts loose or worn • Pitman arm loose • Steering gear attaching bolts loose • Loose or worn wheel bearings • Steering gear adjustment incorrect or parts badly worn	• Inspect shaft spines and repair as necessary. Tighten attaching nut and stake in place. • Tighten, adjust, or replace faulty components • Inspect shaft splines and repair as necessary. Tighten attaching nut and stake in place • Tighten bolts • Adjust or replace bearings • Adjust gear or replace defective parts
Wheel shimmy or tramp	• Improper tire pressure • Wheels, tires, or brake rotors out-of-balance or out-of-round • Inoperative, worn, or loose shock absorbers or mounting parts • Loose or worn steering or suspension parts • Loose or worn wheel bearings • Incorrect steering gear adjustments • Incorrect front wheel alignment	• Inflate tires to recommended pressures • Inspect and replace or balance parts • Repair or replace shocks or mountings • Tighten or replace as necessary • Adjust or replace bearings • Adjust steering gear • Correct front wheel alignment

Troubleshooting the Manual Steering Gear (cont.)

Problem	Cause	Solution
Tire wear	• Improper tire pressure	• Inflate tires to recommended pressures
	• Failure to rotate tires	• Rotate tires
	• Brakes grabbing	• Adjust or repair brakes
	• Incorrect front wheel alignment	• Align incorrect angles
	• Broken or damaged steering and suspension parts	• Repair or replace defective parts
	• Wheel runout	• Replace faulty wheel
	• Excessive speed on turns	• Make driver aware of conditions
Vehicle leads to one side	• Improper tire pressures	• Inflate tires to recommended pressures
	• Front tires with uneven tread depth, wear pattern, or different cord design (i.e., one bias ply and one belted or radial tire on front wheels)	• Install tires of same cord construction and reasonably even tread depth, design, and wear pattern
	• Incorrect front wheel alignment	• Align incorrect angles
	• Brakes dragging	• Adjust or repair brakes
	• Pulling due to uneven tire construction	• Replace faulty tire

Troubleshooting the Power Steering Gear

Problem	Cause	Solution
Hissing noise in steering gear	• There is some noise in all power steering systems. One of the most common is a hissing sound most evident at standstill parking. There is no relationship between this noise and performance of the steering. Hiss may be expected when steering wheel is at end of travel or when slowly turning at standstill.	• Slight hiss is normal and in no way affects steering. Do not replace valve unless hiss is extremely objectionable. A replacement valve will also exhibit slight noise and is not always a cure. Investigate clearance around flexible coupling rivets. Be sure steering shaft and gear are aligned so flexible coupling rotates in a flat plane and is not distorted as shaft rotates. Any metal-to-metal contacts through flexible coupling will transmit valve hiss into passenger compartment through the steering column.
Rattle or chuckle noise in steering gear	• Gear loose on frame	• Check gear-to-frame mounting screws. Tighten screws to 88 N·m (65 foot pounds) torque.
	• Steering linkage looseness	• Check linkage pivot points for wear. Replace if necessary.
	• Pressure hose touching other parts of car	• Adjust hose position. Do not bend tubing by hand.
	• Loose pitman shaft over center adjustment	• Adjust to specifications
	NOTE: A slight rattle may occur on turns because of increased clearance off the "high point." This is normal and clearance must not be reduced below specified limits to eliminate this slight rattle.	
	• Loose pitman arm	• Tighten pitman arm nut to specifications
Squawk noise in steering gear when turning or recovering from a turn	• Damper O-ring on valve spool cut	• Replace damper O-ring

Troubleshooting the Power Steering Gear (cont.)

Problem	Cause	Solution
Poor return of steering wheel to center	• Tires not properly inflated • Lack of lubrication in linkage and ball joints • Lower coupling flange rubbing against steering gear adjuster plug • Steering gear to column misalignment • Improper front wheel alignment • Steering linkage binding • Ball joints binding • Steering wheel rubbing against housing • Tight or frozen steering shaft bearings • Sticking or plugged valve spool • Steering gear adjustments over specifications • Kink in return hose	• Inflate to specified pressure • Lube linkage and ball joints • Loosen pinch bolt and assemble properly • Align steering column • Check and adjust as necessary • Replace pivots • Replace ball joints • Align housing • Replace bearings • Remove and clean or replace valve • Check adjustment with gear out of car. Adjust as required. • Replace hose
Car leads to one side or the other (keep in mind road condition and wind. Test car in both directions on flat road)	• Front end misaligned • Unbalanced steering gear valve **NOTE:** If this is cause, steering effort will be very light in direction of lead and normal or heavier in opposite direction	• Adjust to specifications • Replace valve
Momentary increase in effort when turning wheel fast to right or left	• Low oil level • Pump belt slipping • High internal leakage	• Add power steering fluid as required • Tighten or replace belt • Check pump pressure. (See pressure test)
Steering wheel surges or jerks when turning with engine running especially during parking	• Low oil level • Loose pump belt • Steering linkage hitting engine oil pan at full turn • Insufficient pump pressure • Pump flow control valve sticking	• Fill as required • Adjust tension to specification • Correct clearance • Check pump pressure. (See pressure test). Replace relief valve if defective. • Inspect for varnish or damage, replace if necessary
Excessive wheel kickback or loose steering	• Air in system • Steering gear loose on frame • Steering linkage joints worn enough to be loose • Worn poppet valve • Loose thrust bearing preload adjustment • Excessive overcenter lash	• Add oil to pump reservoir and bleed by operating steering. Check hose connectors for proper torque and adjust as required. • Tighten attaching screws to specified torque • Replace loose pivots • Replace poppet valve • Adjust to specification with gear out of vehicle • Adjust to specification with gear out of car
Hard steering or lack of assist	• Loose pump belt • Low oil level **NOTE:** Low oil level will also result in excessive pump noise • Steering gear to column misalignment	• Adjust belt tension to specification • Fill to proper level. If excessively low, check all lines and joints for evidence of external leakage. Tighten loose connectors. • Align steering column

Troubleshooting the Power Steering Gear (cont.)

Problem	Cause	Solution
Hard steering or lack of assist (cont.)	• Lower coupling flange rubbing against steering gear adjuster plug • Tires not properly inflated	• Loosen pinch bolt and assemble properly • Inflate to recommended pressure
Foamy milky power steering fluid, low fluid level and possible low pressure	• Air in the fluid, and loss of fluid due to internal pump leakage causing overflow	• Check for leak and correct. Bleed system. Extremely cold temperatures will cause system aeriation should the oil level be low. If oil level is correct and pump still foams, remove pump from vehicle and separate reservoir from housing. Check welsh plug and housing for cracks. If plug is loose or housing is cracked, replace housing.
Low pressure due to steering pump	• Flow control valve stuck or inoperative • Pressure plate not flat against cam ring	• Remove burrs or dirt or replace. Flush system. • Correct
Low pressure due to steering gear	• Pressure loss in cylinder due to worn piston ring or badly worn housing bore • Leakage at valve rings, valve body-to-worm seal	• Remove gear from car for disassembly and inspection of ring and housing bore • Remove gear from car for disassembly and replace seals

Troubleshooting the Power Steering Pump

Problem	Cause	Solution
Chirp noise in steering pump	• Loose belt	• Adjust belt tension to specification
Belt squeal (particularly noticeable at full wheel travel and stand still parking)	• Loose belt	• Adjust belt tension to specification
Growl noise in steering pump	• Excessive back pressure in hoses or steering gear caused by restriction	• Locate restriction and correct. Replace part if necessary.
Growl noise in steering pump (particularly noticeable at stand still parking)	• Scored pressure plates, thrust plate or rotor • Extreme wear of cam ring	• Replace parts and flush system • Replace parts
Groan noise in steering pump	• Low oil level • Air in the oil. Poor pressure hose connection.	• Fill reservoir to proper level • Tighten connector to specified torque. Bleed system by operating steering from right to left—full turn.
Rattle noise in steering pump	• Vanes not installed properly • Vanes sticking in rotor slots	• Install properly • Free up by removing burrs, varnish, or dirt
Swish noise in steering pump	• Defective flow control valve	• Replace part
Whine noise in steering pump	• Pump shaft bearing scored	• Replace housing and shaft. Flush system.
Hard steering or lack of assist	• Loose pump belt • Low oil level in reservoir **NOTE:** Low oil level will also result in excessive pump noise • Steering gear to column misalignment	• Adjust belt tension to specification • Fill to proper level. If excessively low, check all lines and joints for evidence of external leakage. Tighten loose connectors. • Align steering column

Troubleshooting the Power Steering Pump (cont.)

Problem	Cause	Solution
Hard steering or lack of assist (cont.)	• Lower coupling flange rubbing against steering gear adjuster plug • Tires not properly inflated	• Loosen pinch bolt and assemble properly • Inflate to recommended pressure
Foaming milky power steering fluid, low fluid level and possible low pressure	• Air in the fluid, and loss of fluid due to internal pump leakage causing overflow	• Check for leaks and correct. Bleed system. Extremely cold temperatures will cause system aeriation should the oil level be low. If oil level is correct and pump still foams, remove pump from vehicle and separate reservoir from body. Check welsh plug and body for cracks. If plug is loose or body is cracked, replace body.
Low pump pressure	• Flow control valve stuck or inoperative • Pressure plate not flat against cam ring	• Remove burrs or dirt or replace. Flush system. • Correct
Momentary increase in effort when turning wheel fast to right or left	• Low oil level in pump • Pump belt slipping • High internal leakage	• Add power steering fluid as required • Tighten or replace belt • Check pump pressure. (See pressure test)
Steering wheel surges or jerks when turning with engine running especially during parking	• Low oil level • Loose pump belt • Steering linkage hitting engine oil pan at full turn • Insufficient pump pressure • Sticking flow control valve	• Fill as required • Adjust tension to specification • Correct clearance • Check pump pressure. (See pressure test). Replace flow control valve if defective. • Inspect for varnish or damage, replace if necessary
Excessive wheel kickback or loose steering	• Air in system	• Add oil to pump reservoir and bleed by operating steering. Check hose connectors for proper torque and adjust as required.
Low pump pressure	• Extreme wear of cam ring • Scored pressure plate, thrust plate, or rotor • Vanes not installed properly • Vanes sticking in rotor slots • Cracked or broken thrust or pressure plate	• Replace parts. Flush system. • Replace parts. Flush system. • Install properly • Freeup by removing burrs, varnish, or dirt • Replace part

Brakes

BRAKE SYSTEM

ADJUSTMENT

DRUM BRAKES

The drum brakes are self-adjusting and require a manual adjustment only after the brake shoes have been relined, replaced, or when the length of the adjusting screw has been changed while performing some other service operation, as, taking off the self-adjusters and putting on manual ones.

To adjust the brakes, follow the procedure given below:

1. Raise the vehicle and support it with safety stands.

2. Remove the rubber plug from the adjusting slot on the backing plate.

3. Insert a brake adjusting spoon into the slot and engage the lowest possible tooth on the starwheel. Move the end of the brake spoon downward to move the starwheel upward and expand the adjusting screw. Repeat this operation until the brakes lock the wheel.

NOTE: *Step 4 applies only to vehicles equipped with self-adjusters.*

4. Insert a small screwdriver or piece of firm wire (coat hanger wire) into the adjusting slot and push the automatic adjusting lever out and free of the starwheel on the adjusting screw and hold it there.

5. Engage the topmost tooth possible on the starwheel with the brake adjusting spoon. Move the end of the adjusting spoon upward to move the adjusting screw starwheel downward and contract the adjusting screw. Back off the adjusting screw starwheel until the wheel spins freely with a minimum of drag. Keep track of the number of turns that the starwheel is backed off, or the number of strokes taken with the brake adjusting spoon.

6. Repeat this operation for the other side. When backing off the brakes on the other side, the starwheel adjuster must be backed off the same number of turns to prevent side-to-side brake pull.

7. Repeat this operation on the other set of brakes (front or rear).

8. When all 4 brakes are adjusted, on vehicles equipped with self-adjusting brakes, make several stops while backing the vehicle, to equalize the brakes at all of the wheels. On vehicles not equipped with self-adjusters, make a few low speed stops while going forward to check for brake pull. If the front end of the car has a tendency to pull to one side when the brakes are applied, back off the adjustment of the brake assembly on the side the vehicle pulls to.

9. Remove the safety stands and lower the vehicle. Road test the vehicle.

NOTE: *Disc brakes are not adjustable.*

BRAKE PEDAL

On dual brake master cylinder or dash mounted vacuum booster equipped vehicles, the

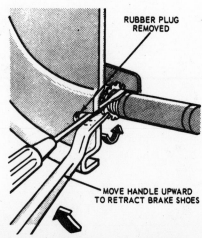

RUBBER PLUG REMOVED

MOVE HANDLE UPWARD TO RETRACT BRAKE SHOES

Cutaway of the position and operation of the brake adjusting tools during adjustment

brake systems are designed to permit a full stroke of the master cylinder when the brake pedal is fully depressed. A brake pedal clearance adjustment is not required.

To release the brakes, fluid must flow back to the master cylinder through a return port when pedal pressure is released. To be sure the piston moves back far enough to expose the return port, free travel is built into the pedal linkage on standard and frame mounted booster systems. This prevents the piston from becoming trapped in a partially released position. Pedal free travel is not always perceptible in dash mounted booster systems, because the operating clearance for the piston is adjusted at the booster pushrod, rather than the pedal linkage.

The pushrod has an adjustment screw to maintain the correct relationship between the booster control valve plunger and the master cylinder piston. If the plunger is too long it will prevent the master cylinder piston from completely releasing hydraulic pressure, causing the brakes to drag. If the plunger is too short it will cause excessive pedal travel and an undesirable clunk in the booster area. Remove the master cylinder for access to the booster pushrod.

To check the alignment of the screw, fabricate a gauge (from cardboard, following the dimensions in the above illustration) and place it against the master cylinder mounting surface of the booster body. Adjust the pushrod screw by turning it until the end of the screw just

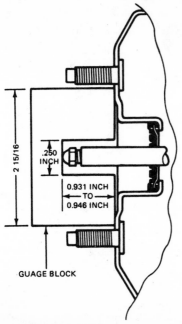

Bendix booster push rod gauge dimensions and adjustment, 1978 and later

touches the inner edge of the slot in the gauge. Install the master cylinder and bleed the system.

Brake Light Switch
REMOVAL AND INSTALLATION

1. Disconnect the wiring harness.
2. Remove the pin that secures the brake light switch to the brake pedal arm.
3. Remove the spacer and slide the brake light switch from the pedal arm.
4. Install the new switch in the reverse of the removal procedure.
5. Adjust the switch as necessary.

HYDRAULIC SYSTEM

Master Cylinder
REMOVAL AND INSTALLATION
1966–77

1. Disconnect the wires from the stoplight switch.
2. Disconnect the hydraulic system brake lines at the master cylinder.
3. Remove the hairpin retainer and slide the stoplight switch off the brake pedal pin just far enough for the switch outer hole to clear the pin. Remove the stoplight switch from the pin.
4. Slide the master cylinder pushrod off the brake pedal pin. Remove the bushings and washers.
5. Remove the master cylinder retaining bolts and remove the master cylinder.

To install the master cylinder:
6. Position the master cylinder assembly on the firewall and install the retaining bolts.
7. Connect the hydraulic system brake lines to the master cylinder.
8. Lubricate the pushrod bushing with clean motor oil. Insert the bushing in the pushrod. Coat the washers with the lubricant, and position the pushrod and bushing, washers and stoplight switch on the brake pedal pin. Install the hairpin type retainer.
9. Connect the stoplight switch wires to the switch.
10. Bleed the hydraulic brake system.

1978–86

1. With the engine turned off, push the brake pedal down to expel vacuum from the brake booster system.
2. Disconnect the hydraulic lines from the brake master cylinder.
3. Remove the brake booster-to-master cylinder retaining nuts and lockwashers. Remove the master cylinder from the brake booster.

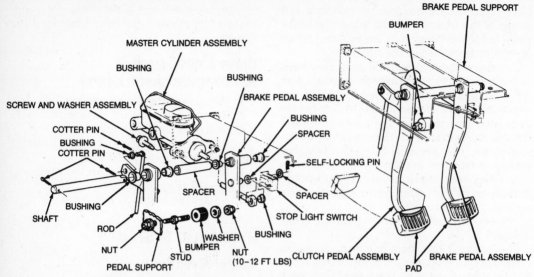

1966–77 master cylinder and brake pedal removal and installation

4. Before installing the master cylinder, check the distance from the outer end of the booster assembly pushrod to the front face of the brake booster assembly. Turn the pushrod adjusting screw in or out as required to obtain the length shown.

5. Position the master cylinder assembly over the booster pushrod and onto the two studs on the booster assembly. Install the attaching nuts and lockwashers and tighten to 20–30 ft.lb.

6. Loosely connect the hydraulic brake system lines to the master cylinder.

7. Bleed the hydraulic brake system. Cen-

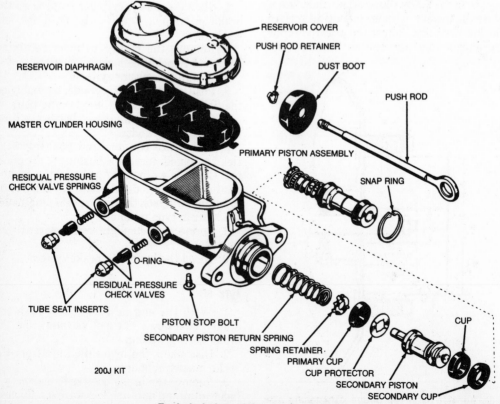

Exploded view of the master cylinder

tralize the differential valve. Then, fill the dual master cylinder reservoirs with DOT 3 brake fluid to within ¼" (6.35mm) of the top. Install the gasket and reservoir cover.

OVERHAUL

The most important thing to remember when rebuilding the master cylinder is cleanliness. Work in clean surroundings with clean tools and clean cloths or paper for drying purposes. Have plenty of clean alcohol and brake fluid on hand to clean and lubricate the internal components. There are service repair kits available for overhauling the master cylinder.

1. Clean the outside of the master cylinder and remove the filler cap and gasket (diaphragm). Pour out any fluid that remains in the cylinder reservoir. Do not use any fluids other than brake fluid or alcohol to clean the master cylinder.

2. Unscrew the piston stop from the bottom of the cylinder body. Remove the O-ring seal from the piston stop. Discard the seal.

3. Remove the pushrod boot, if so equipped, from the groove at the rear of the master cylinder and slide the boot away from the rear of the master cylinder.

4. Remove the snapring retaining the primary and secondary piston assemblies within the cylinder body.

5. Remove the pushrod (if so equipped) and primary piston assembly from the master cylinder. Discard the piston assembly, including to boot (if so equipped).

6. Apply an air hose to the rear brake outlet port of the cylinder body and carefully blow the secondary piston out of the cylinder body.

7. Remove the return spring, spring retainer, cap protector, and cups from the secondary piston. Discard the cup protector and cups.

8. Clean all of the remaining parts in clean isopropyl alcohol and inspect the parts for chipping, excessive wear or damage. Replace them as required.

NOTE: *When using a master cylinder repair kit, install all the parts supplied in the kit.*

9. Check all recesses, openings and internal passages to be sure they are open and free from foreign matter. Use compressed air to blow out dirt and cleaning solvent remaining after the parts have been cleaned in the alcohol. Place all the parts on a clean pan, lint free cloth, or paper to dry.

10. Dip all the parts, except the cylinder body, in clean brake fluid.

11. Assemble the two secondary cups, back-to-back, in the grooves near the end of the secondary piston.

12. Install the secondary piston assembly in the master cylinder.

13. Install a new O-ring on the piston stop, and start the stop into the cylinder body.

14. Position the boot, snapring and pushrod retainer on the pushrod. Make sure the pushrod retainer is seated securely on the ball end of the rod. Seat the pushrod in the primary piston assembly.

15. Install the primary piston assembly in the master cylinder. Push the primary piston inward and tighten the secondary piston stop to retain the secondary piston in the bore.

16. Press the pushrod and pistons inward and install the snapring in the cylinder body.

17. Before the master cylinder is installed on the vehicle, the unit must be bled: support the master cylinder body in a vise, and fill both fluid reservoirs with brake fluid.

18. Loosely install plugs in the front and rear brake outlet bores. Depress the primary piston several times until air bubbles cease to appear in the brake fluid.

19. Tighten the plugs and attempt to depress

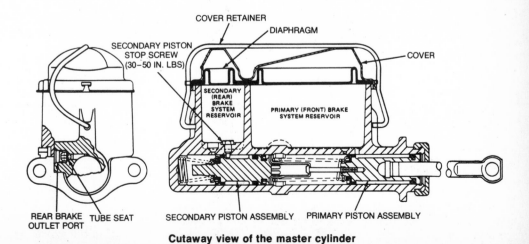

Cutaway view of the master cylinder

the piston. The piston travel should be restricted after all air is expelled.

20. Remove the plugs. Install the cover and gasket (diaphragm) assembly, and make sure the cover retainer is tightened securely.

21. Install the master cylinder in the vehicle and bleed the hydraulic system.

Booster

REMOVAL AND INSTALLATION

NOTE: *Make sure that the booster rubber reaction disc is properly installed if the master cylinder pushrod is removed or accidentally pulled out. A dislodged disc may cause excessive pedal travel and extreme operation sensitivity. The disc is black compared to the silver colored valve plunger that will be exposed after the pushrod and front seal is removed. The booster unit is serviced as an assembly and must be replaced if the reaction disc cannot be properly installed and aligned, or if it cannot be located within the unit itself.*

1. Disconnect the stop lamp switch wiring to prevent running the battery down.

2. Support the master cylinder from the underside with a prop.

3. Remove the master cylinder-to-booster retaining nuts.

4. Loosen the clamp that secures the manifold vacuum hose to the booster check valve, and remove the hose. Remove the booster check valve.

5. Pull the master cylinder off the booster and leave it supported by the prop, far enough away to allow removal of the booster assembly.

6. From inside the cab on vehicles equipped with pushrod mounted stop lamp switch, remove the retaining pin and slide the stop lamp switch, pushrod, spacers and bushing off the brake pedal arm.

7. From the engine compartment remove the bolts that attach the booster to the dash panel.

8. Mount the booster assembly on the engine side of the dash panel by sliding the bracket mounting bolts and valve operating rod in through the holes in the dash panel.

NOTE: *Make certain that the booster pushrod is positioned on the correct side of the master cylinder to install onto the push pin prior to tightening the booster assembly to the dash.*

9. From inside the cab, install the booster mounting bracket-to-dash panel retaining nuts.

10. Position the master cylinder on the booster assembly, install the retaining nuts, and remove the prop from underneath the master cylinder.

11. Install the booster check valve. Connect the manifold vacuum hose to the booster check valve and secure with the clamp.

12. From inside the cab on vehicles equipped with pushrod mounted stop lamp switch, install the bushing and position the switch on the end of the pushrod. Then install the switch and rod on the pedal arm, along with spacers on each side, and secure with the retaining pin.

13. Connect the stop lamp switch wiring.

14. Start the engine and check brake operation.

Pressure Differential Valve

REMOVAL

1. Raise the vehicle on a hoist. Disconnect the brake warning lamp wire from the valve assembly switch.

NOTE: *To avoid damaging the brake warning switch wire connector, expand the plastic lugs so that the shell wire connector may be removed from the switch body.*

2. Disconnect the brake hydraulic lines from the differential valve assembly.

3. Remove the screw retaining the pressure differential, metering and proportioning valve assembly to the frame side rail or support bracket and remove the valve assembly.

INSTALLATION

1. Mount the combination brake differential valve assembly on the frame side rail or support bracket and tighten the attaching screw.

2. Connect the brake hydraulic system lines to the differential valve assembly and tighten the tube nuts securely.

3. Connect the shell wire connector to the brake warning lamp switch. Make sure that the plastic lugs on the connector hold the connector securely to the switch.

4. Bleed the brakes and centralize the pressure differential valve.

CENTRALIZING THE PRESSURE DIFFERENTIAL VALVE

After any repair or bleeding of the primary (front brake) or secondary (rear brake) system, the dual brake system warning light will usually remain illuminated due to the pressure differential valve remaining in the offcenter position.

To centralize the pressure differential valve and turn off the warning light after the systems have been bled, follow the procedure below.

1. Turn the ignition switch to the ACC or ON position.

2. Check the fluid level in the master cylin-

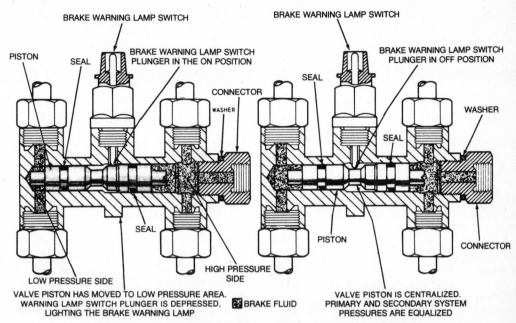

BRAKE WARNING LAMP SWITCH

BRAKE WARNING LAMP SWITCH

PISTON SEAL

BRAKE WARNING LAMP SWITCH PLUNGER IN THE ON POSITION

BRAKE WARNING LAMP SWITCH PLUNGER IN OFF POSITION

SEAL

CONNECTOR

WASHER

WASHER

SEAL

SEAL

SEAL

PISTON

CONNECTOR

HIGH PRESSURE SIDE

LOW PRESSURE SIDE

VALVE PISTON HAS MOVED TO LOW PRESSURE AREA. WARNING LAMP SWITCH PLUNGER IS DEPRESSED, LIGHTING THE BRAKE WARNING LAMP

BRAKE FLUID

VALVE PISTON IS CENTRALIZED. PRIMARY AND SECONDARY SYSTEM PRESSURES ARE EQUALIZED

Cutaway view of a typical pressure differential valve operation

der reservoirs and fill them to within ¼″ (6.35mm) of the top with brake fluid, if necessary.

3. Depress the brake pedal and the piston should center itself causing the brake warning light to go out.

4. Turn the ignition switch to the OFF position.

5. Before driving the vehicle, check the operation of the brakes and be sure that a firm pedal is obtained.

Brake Hoses

Steel tubing is used the hydraulic lines between the master cylinder and the front brake tube connector, and between the rear brake tube connector and the wheel cylinders. Flexible hoses connect the brake tube to the front brake cylinders and to the rear brake tube connector.

A brake line wrench should be used when removing and installing brake lines. When replacing hydraulic brake tubing, hoses, or connectors tighten all connections securely. After replacement, bleed the brake system at the wheel cylinders and the booster (if equipped).

If a section of the brake tube is damaged, replace it with tubing of the same type, size, shape and length.

Do not use copper tubing in the hydraulic system. Be careful not to kink or crack the tubing when bending it to fit the frame or rear axle.

Always use double flared brake tubing to provide good leak proof connections. Always

clean the inside of a new brake tube with clean isopropyl alcohol.

Replace a flexible brake hose if it shows signs of softening, cracking, or other damage.

When installing a new brake hose, position the hose to avoid contact with other vehicle parts. Whenever a brake hose is disconnected from a wheel cylinder or brake caliper, install a new copper washer connecting the hose.

Bleeding

When any part of the hydraulic system has been disconnected for repair or replacement, air may get into the lines and cause spongy pedal action (because air can be compressed and brake fluid cannot). To correct this condition, it is necessary to bleed the hydraulic system after it has been properly connected to be sure all air is expelled from the brake cylinders and lines.

When bleeding the brake system, bleed one brake cylinder at a time, beginning at the cylinder with the longest hydraulic line (farthest from the master cylinder) first. Keep the master cylinder reservoir filled with brake fluid during the bleeding operation. Never use brake fluid that has been drained from the hydraulic system, no matter how clean it is.

It will be necessary to centralize the pressure differential valve after a brake system failure has been corrected and the hydraulic system has been bled.

On the Bronco, the primary and secondary hydraulic brake systems are individual systems and are bled separately. During the entire bleeding operation, do not allow the reservoir to run dry. Keep the master cylinder reservoir filled with brake fluid.

1. Clean all dirt from around the master cylinder fill cap, remove the cap and fill the master cylinder with brake fluid until the level is within ¼" (6.35mm) of the top edge of the reservoir.

2. Clean off the bleeder screws at all 4 wheel cylinders. The bleeder screws are located on the inside of the brake backing plate, on the backside of the wheel cylinders.

3. Attach a length of rubber hose over the nozzle of the bleeder screw at the wheel to be done first. Place the other end of the hose in a glass jar, submerged in brake fluid.

4. Open the bleeder screw valve ½–¾ turn.

5. Have an assistant slowly depress the brake pedal. Close the bleeder screw valve and tell your assistant to allow the brake pedal to return slowly. Continue this pumping action to force any air out of the system. When bubbles cease to appear at the end of the bleeder hose, close the bleeder valve and remove the hose.

6. Check the master cylinder fluid level and add fluid accordingly. Do this after bleeding each wheel.

7. Repeat the bleeding operation at the remaining 3 wheels, ending with the one closest to the master cylinder. Fill the master cylinder reservoir.

FRONT DRUM BRAKES

CAUTION: *Brake shoes contain asbestos, which has been determined to be a cancer causing agent. Never clean the brake surfaces with compressed air! Avoid inhaling any dust from any brake surface! When cleaning brake surfaces, use a commercially available brake cleaning fluid.*

Brake Drums
REMOVAL AND INSTALLATION

1. Raise the vehicle and install jackstands.

2. Back off the brake shoe adjustment. Remove the hub dust cap. Remove the hub retaining snapring, and slide the splined driving hub from between the axle shaft and the wheel hub. Remove the driving hub spacer and spring.

3. Remove the locknut, nut lock, and the wheel bearing adjusting nut from the spindle. Remove the wheel, hub and drum as an assembly. The wheel outer bearing will be forced off the spindle at the same time, so be prepared to catch it to prevent it from becoming dirty. Remove the wheel inner bearing cone.

NOTE: *If the Bronco is equipped with locking type hubs, refer to Chapter 6 Drive Train, under Front Wheel Bearings for the removal and installation procedure.*

4. Remove the front wheel-to-hub retaining nuts. Remove the wheel and tire from the hub and drum.

5. Remove the brake drum retaining bolts and nuts.

6. Remove the brake drum from the hub.

7. Place the brake drum to the hub and install the retaining bolts and nuts.

8. Install the wheel and tire to the hub and start the retaining nuts.

9. Install the wheel hub and drum assembly on the spindle. Install the driving hub spacer and then the wheel outer bearing cone and the adjusting nut with the dowel outboard.

10. Rotate the wheel in either direction and, at the same time, tighten the inner locknut to 50 ft.lb. with a torque wrench.

11. Adjust the front wheel bearings. (Refer to Chapter 6).

12. Slide the driving hub onto the axle shaft and install the snapring. Refer to Chapter 7, for the installation procedure for locking type hubs.

13. Adjust the brake and then tighten the wheel nuts.

14. Install the hub dust cap.

15. Remove the jackstands and lower the vehicle.

INSPECTION

After the brake drum has been removed from the vehicle, it should be inspected for runout, severe scoring, cracks, and the proper inside diameter.

Minor scores on a brake drum can be removed with fine emery cloth, provided that all grit is removed from the drum before it is installed on the vehicle.

A badly scored, rough, or out-of-round (runout) drum can be ground or turned on a brake drum lathe. Do not remove any more material from the drum than is necessary to provide a smooth surface for the brake shoe to contact. The maximum diameter of the braking surface is shown on the inside of each brake drum. Brake drums that exceed the maximum braking surface diameter shown on the brake drum, either through wear or refinishing, must be replaced. This is because after the outside wall of the brake drum reaches a certain thickness (thinner than the original thickness) the drum loses its ability to dissipate the heat created by the friction between the brake drum and the brake shoes, when the brakes are applied. Also, the brake drum will have more tendency to warp and/or crack.

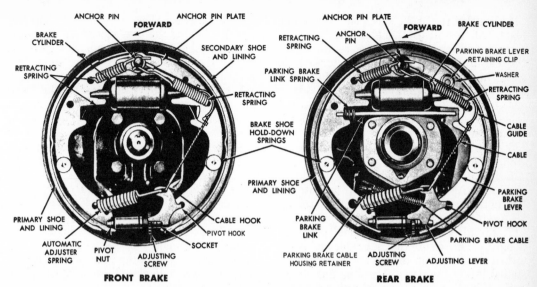

Front and rear drum brake assemblies

The maximum braking surface diameter specification, which is shown on each drum, allows for a 0.060″ (1.5mm) machining cut over the original nominal drum diameter plus 0.030″ (0.76mm) additional wear before reaching the diameter where the drum must be discarded. Use a brake drum micrometer to measure the inside diameter of the brake drums.

Brake Shoes

REMOVAL AND INSTALLATION

1. Raise and support the vehicle and remove the wheel and brake drum from the wheel to be worked on.

NOTE: *If you have never replaced the brakes on a car before and you are not too familiar with the procedures involved, only disassemble and assemble one side at a time, leaving the other side intact as a reference during reassembly.*

2. Install a clamp over the ends of the wheel cylinder to prevent the pistons of the wheel cylinder from coming out, causing loss of fluid and much grief.

3. Contract the brake shoes by pulling the self-adjusting lever away from the starwheel adjustment screw and turn the starwheel up and back until the pivot nut is drawn onto the starwheel as far as it will come.

4. Pull the adjusting lever, cable and automatic adjuster spring down and toward the rear to unhook the pivot hook from the large hole in the secondary shoe web. Do not attempt to pry the pivot hook from the hole.

5. Remove the automatic adjuster spring and the adjusting lever.

6. Remove the secondary shoe-to-anchor spring with a brake tool. (Brake tools are very common implements and are available at auto parts stores.) Remove the primary shoe-to-anchor spring and unhook the cable anchor. Remove the anchor pin plate.

7. Remove the cable guide from the secondary shoe.

8. Remove the shoe holddown springs, shoes, adjusting screw, pivot nut, and socket. Note the color of each holddown spring for assembly. To remove the holddown springs, reach behind the brake backing plate and place one finger on the end of one of the brake holddown spring mounting pins. Using a pair of pliers, grasp the washer type retainer on top of the holddown spring that corresponds to the pin that you are holding. Push down on the pliers and turn them 90° to align the slot in the washer with the head on the spring mounting pin. Remove the spring and washer retainer and repeat this operation on the holddown spring on the other shoe.

9. On rear brakes, remove the parking brake link and spring. Disconnect the parking brake cable from the parking brake lever.

10. After removing the rear brake secondary shoe, disassemble the parking brake lever from the shoe by removing the retaining clip and spring washer.

To assemble and install the brake shoes:

11. On rear brakes, assemble the parking brake lever to the secondary shoe and secure it with the spring washer and retaining clip.

12. Apply a light coating of Lubriplate® at the points where the brake shoes contact the backing plate.

13. Position the brake shoes on the backing plate, and install the holddown spring pins, springs, and spring washer type retainers. On the rear brake, install the parking brake link, spring and washer. Connect the parking brake cable to the parking brake lever.

14. Install the anchor pin plate, and place the cable anchor over the anchor pin with the crimped side toward the backing plate.

15. Install the primary shoe-to-anchor spring with the brake tool.

16. Install the cable guide on the secondary shoe web with the flanged holes fitted into the hole in the secondary shoe web. Thread the cable around the cable guide groove.

17. Install the secondary shoe-to-anchor (long) spring. Be sure that the cable end is not cocked or binding on the anchor pin when installed. All of the parts should be flat on the anchor pin. Remove the wheel cylinder piston clamp.

18. Apply Lubriplate® to the threads and the socket end of the adjusting starwheel screw. Turn the adjusting screw into the adjusting pivot nut to the limit of the threads and then back off ½ turn.

NOTE: *Interchanging the brake shoe adjusting screw assemblies from one side of the vehicle to the other would cause the brake shoes to retract rather than expand each time the automatic adjusting mechanism operated. To prevent this, the socket end of the adjusting screw is stamped with an R or an L for RIGHT or LEFT. The adjusting pivot nuts can be distinguished by the number of lines machined around the body of the nut; one line indicates left hand nut and two lines indicates a right hand nut.*

19. Place the adjusting socket on the screw and install this assembly between the shoe ends with the adjusting screw nearest to the secondary shoe.

20. Place the cable hook into the hole in the adjusting lever from the backing plate side. The adjusting levers are stamped with an **R** (right) or an **L** (left) to indicate their installation on the right or left hand brake assembly.

21. Position the hooked end of the adjuster spring in the primary shoe web and connect the loop end of the spring to the adjuster lever hole.

22. Pull the adjuster lever, cable and automatic adjuster spring down toward the rear to engage the pivot book in the large hole in the secondary shoe web.

23. After installation, check the action of the adjuster by pulling the section of the cable between the cable guide and the adjusting lever toward the secondary shoe web far enough to lift the lever past a tooth on the adjusting screw starwheel. The lever should snap into position behind the next tooth, and release of the cable should cause the adjuster spring to return the lever to its original position. This return action of the lever will turn the adjusting screw starwheel one tooth. The lever should contact the adjusting screw starwheel one tooth above the center line of the adjusting screw.

If the automatic adjusting mechanism does not perform properly, check the following:

1. Check the cable end fittings. The cable ends should fill or extend slightly beyond the crimped section of the fittings. If this is not the case, replace the cable.

2. Check the cable guide for damage. The cable groove should be parallel to the shoe web, and the body of the guide should lie flat against the web. Replace the cable guide if this is not so.

3. Check the pivot hook on the lever. The hook surfaces should be square with the body

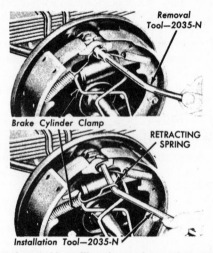

Removal Tool—2035-N

Brake Cylinder Clamp

RETRACTING SPRING

Installation Tool—2035-N

Removing and installing the anchor springs with a brake tool

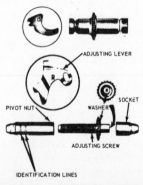

ADJUSTING LEVER

PIVOT NUT

WASHER

SOCKET

ADJUSTING SCREW

IDENTIFICATION LINES

The adjusting screw starwheel and components and the self-adjusting lever identification

on the lever for proper pivoting. Repair or replace the hook as necessary.

4. Make sure that the adjusting screw starwheel is properly seated in the notch in the shoe web.

Wheel Cylinders
OVERHAUL

Wheel cylinder rebuilding kits are available for reconditioning wheel cylinders. The kits usually contain new cup springs, cylinder cups, and in some, new boots. The most important factor to keep in mind when rebuilding wheel cylinders is cleanliness. Keep all dirt away from the wheel cylinders when you are reassembling them.

1. To remove the wheel cylinder, jack up the vehicle and remove the wheel, hub, and drum.

2. Disconnect the brake line at the fitting on the brake backing plate.

3. Remove the brake assemblies.

4. Remove the screws that hold the wheel cylinder to the backing plate and remove the wheel cylinder from the vehicle.

5. Remove the rubber dust covers on the ends of the cylinder. Remove the pistons and piston cups and the spring. Remove the bleeder screw and make sure that it is not plugged.

6. Discard all of the parts that the rebuilding lot will replace.

7. Examine the inside of the cylinder. If it is severely rusted, pitted or scratched, then the cylinder must be replaced as the piston cups won't be able to seal against the walls of the cylinder.

8. Using a wheel cylinder hone or emery cloth and crocus cloth, polish the inside of the cylinder. The purpose of this is to put a new surface on the inside of the cylinder. Keep the inside of the cylinder coated with brake fluid while honing.

9. Wash out the cylinder with clean brake fluid after honing.

10. When reassembling the cylinder, dip all of the parts in clean brake fluid. Assemble the wheel cylinder in the reverse order of removal and disassembly.

Exploded view of a wheel cylinder

FRONT DISC BRAKES

CAUTION: *Brake shoes contain asbestos, which has been determined to be a cancer causing agent. Never clean the brake surfaces with compressed air! Avoid inhaling any dust from any brake surface! When cleaning brake surfaces, use a commercially available brake cleaning fluid.*

Pads
INSPECTION

Replace the front pads when the pad thickness is at the minimum thickness recommended by Ford Motor Co., $\frac{1}{32}''$ (0.8mm), or at the minimum allowed by the applicable state or local motor vehicle inspection code. Pad thickness may be checked by removing the wheel and looking through the inspection port in the caliper assembly.

REMOVAL AND INSTALLATION

NOTE: *Always replace the pads on both front wheels at the same time. Never replace pads on one wheel only.*

1. Dip out a part of the fluid from the larger portion of the master cylinder.

2. Jack up the front of the vehicle and support it on jackstands.

3. Remove the front wheel.

4. Using an 8″ (203mm) C-clamp, bottom the caliper piston by positioning the fixed end of the clamp against the inner side of the caliper and tightening the clamp against the outer pad.

5. Remove the clamp. Remove the key retaining screw.

6. Using a brass drift and light hammer, drive out the caliper support key, and caliper support spring.

7. It is not necessary to disconnect the brake hose.

8. Remove the caliper from its support assembly by pushing downward toward the spindle and rotating the upper end upward and out of the spindle assembly. Support the caliper with a length of wire so that no stress is placed upon the brake hose.

9. Remove the outer pad. It may be necessary to tap it loose. Remove the inner pad and anti-rattle clip.

10. Clean and inspect the caliper assembly.

11. Place a new anti-rattle clip on the lower end of the inner pad. Be sure that the clip tabs are positioned properly and that the clip is fully seated.

12. Place the inner pad in the caliper, with the loop type spring of the clip away from the rotor.

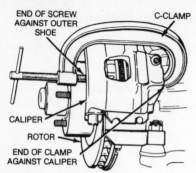

Bottoming the caliper piston

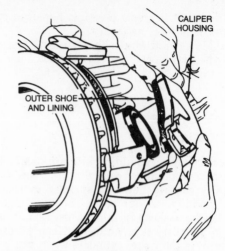

Removing the outer pad and lining

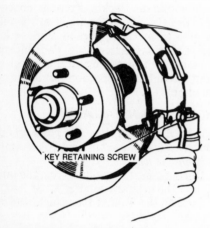

Removing the key retaining screw

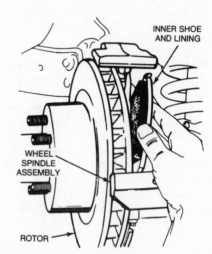

Removing the inner pad and lining

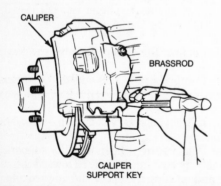

Removing the caliper support spring and key

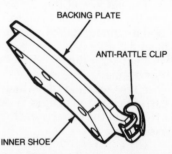

Installing the anti-rattle clip on the inner lining

13. Place the outer pad in the caliper. Press the tabs into place with fingers or a C-clamp.

14. Place the caliper on the spindle by pivoting it around the support upper mounting surface. Be careful not to tear the boot as it slips over the inner pad.

15. Use a screwdriver to hold the upper machined surface of the caliper against the surface of the support assembly, and install a new caliper support spring and key assembly. Drive the key and spring into position with a plastic mallet. Install the key retaining screw and tighten to 20 ft.lb.

16. When pads have been installed on both front wheels, lower the vehicle and check the fluid level in the master cylinder. Fill as necessary.

17. Depress the pedal several times until a

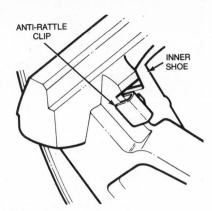

Installing the inner pad

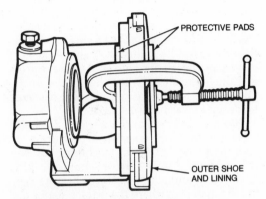

Installing the outer pad and lining

firm pedal is achieved. Do not drive the vehicle until the pedal is firm.

Brake Calipers

OVERHAUL

1. For caliper removal, see the brake pad removal section. Disconnect the brake hose.

2. Clean the exterior of the caliper with denatured alcohol.

3. Remove the plug from the caliper inlet port and drain the fluid.

4. Air pressure is necessary to remove the piston. When a source of compressed air is found, such as a shop or gas station, apply air to the inlet port slowly and carefully until the piston pops out of its bore. If high pressure air is applied the piston will drop out with considerable force and cause damage or injury.

5. If the piston jams, release the air pressure and tap sharply on the piston end with a soft hammer. Reapply air pressure.

6. When the piston is out, remove the boot from the piston and the seal from the bore.

7. Clean the housing and piston with denatured alcohol. Dry with compressed air.

8. Lubricate the new piston seal, boot and piston with clan brake fluid, and assemble them in the caliper.

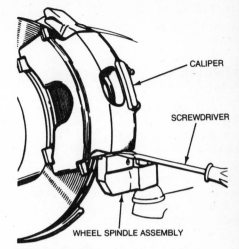

Installing the caliper

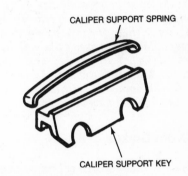

Caliper support spring and key

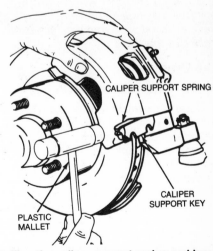

Installing the caliper support spring and key

9. The dust boot can be worked in with the fingers and the piston should be pressed straight in until it bottoms. Be careful to avoid cocking the piston in the bore.

10. A C-clamp may be necessary to bottom the piston.

11. Install the caliper using the procedure given in the pad replacement paragraph above.

Rotor (Disc)
REMOVAL AND INSTALLATION

1. Jack up the front of the vehicle and support on jackstands.

2. Remove the wheel.

3. Remove the caliper assembly as described above.

4. Follow the procedure given under hub and wheel bearing removal in Chapter 1 for models without locking hubs or Chapter 6 for models with locking hubs.

NOTE: *New rotor assemblies come protected with an anti-rust coating which should be removed with denatured alcohol or degreaser. New hubs must be packed with EP wheel bearing grease. If the old rotors are to be reused, check them for cracks, grooves or wavyness. Rotors that aren't too badly scored or grooved can be resurfaced by most automotive shops. Minimum rotor thickness should be 1.12" (28.4mm). If refinishing exceeds that, the rotor will have to be replaced.*

Rear Drum Brakes

CAUTION: *Brake shoes contain asbestos, which has been determined to be a cancer causing agent. Never clean the brake surfaces with compressed air! Avoid inhaling any dust from any brake surface! When cleaning brake surfaces, use a commercially available brake cleaning fluid.*

Brake Drums
REMOVAL AND INSTALLATION

1. Raise the vehicle so that the wheel to be worked on is clear of the floor and install jackstands under the vehicle.

2. Remove the hub cap and the wheel/tire assembly. Remove the 3 retaining nuts and remove the brake drum. It may be necessary to back off the brake shoe adjustment in order to remove the brake drum. This is because the drum might be grooved or worn from being in service for an extended period of time.

3. Before installing a new brake drum, be sure and remove any protective coating with a carburetor degreaser.

4. Install the brake drum in the reverse order of removal and adjust the brakes.

INSPECTION

After the brake drum has been removed from the vehicle, it should be inspected for runout,

severe scoring, cracks, and the proper inside diameter.

Minor scores on a brake drum can be removed with fine emery cloth, provided that all grit is removed from the drum before it is installed on the vehicle.

A badly scored, rough, or out-of-round (runout) drum can be ground or turned on a brake drum lathe. Do not remove any more material from the drum than is necessary to provide a smooth surface for the brake shoe to contact. The maximum diameter of the braking surface is shown on the inside of each brake drum. Brake drums that exceed the maximum braking surface diameter shown on the brake drum, either through wear or refinishing, must be replaced. This is because after the outside wall of the brake drum reaches a certain thickness (thinner than the original thickness) the drum loses its ability to dissipate the heat created by the friction between the brake drum and the brake shoes, when the brakes are applied. Also, the brake drum will have more tendency to warp and/or crack.

The maximum braking surface diameter specification, which is shown on each drum, allows for a 0.060" (1.5mm) machining cut over the original nominal drum diameter plus 0.030" (0.76mm) additional wear before reaching the diameter where the drum must be discarded. Use a brake drum micrometer to measure the inside diameter of the brake drums.

Brake Shoes
REMOVAL AND INSTALLATION

1. Raise and support the vehicle and remove the wheel and brake drum from the wheel to be worked on.

NOTE: *If you have never replaced the brakes on a car before and you are not too familiar with the procedures involved, only disassemble and assemble one side at a time, leaving the other side intact as a reference during reassembly.*

2. Install a clamp over the ends of the wheel cylinder to prevent the pistons of the wheel cylinder from coming out, causing loss of fluid and much grief.

3. Contract the brake shoes by pulling the self-adjusting lever away from the starwheel adjustment screw and turn the starwheel up and back until the pivot nut is drawn onto the starwheel as far as it will come.

4. Pull the adjusting lever, cable and automatic adjuster spring down and toward the rear to unhook the pivot hook from the large hole in the secondary shoe web. Do not attempt to pry the pivot hook from the hole.

5. Remove the automatic adjuster spring and the adjusting lever.

6. Remove the secondary shoe-to-anchor spring with a brake tool. (Brake tools are very common implements and are available at auto parts stores.) Remove the primary shoe-to-anchor spring and unhook the cable anchor. Remove the anchor pin plate.

7. Remove the cable guide from the secondary shoe.

8. Remove the shoe holddown springs, shoes, adjusting screw, pivot nut, and socket. Note the color of each holddown spring for assembly. To remove the holddown springs, reach behind the brake backing plate and place one finger on the end of one of the brake holddown spring mounting pins. Using a pair of pliers, grasp the washer type retainer on top of the holddown spring that corresponds to the pin that you are holding. Push down on the pliers and turn them 90° to align the slot in the washer with the head on the spring mounting pin. Remove the spring and washer retainer and repeat this operation on the holddown spring on the other shoe.

9. Remove the parking brake link and spring. Disconnect the parking brake cable from the parking brake lever.

10. After removing the rear brake secondary shoe, disassemble the parking brake lever from the shoe by removing the retaining clip and spring washer.

To assemble and install the brake shoes:

11. Assemble the parking brake lever to the secondary shoe and secure it with the spring washer and retaining clip.

12. Apply a light coating of Lubriplate® at the points where the brake shoes contact the backing plate.

13. Position the brake shoes on the backing plate, and install the holddown spring pins, springs, and spring washer type retainers. On the rear brake, install the parking brake link, spring and washer. Connect the parking brake cable to the parking brake lever.

14. Install the anchor pin plate, and place the cable anchor over the anchor pin with the crimped side toward the backing plate.

15. Install the primary shoe-to-anchor spring with the brake tool.

16. Install the cable guide on the secondary shoe web with the flanged holes fitted into the hole in the secondary shoe web. Thread the cable around the cable guide groove.

17. Install the secondary shoe-to-anchor (long) spring. Be sure that the cable end is not cocked or binding on the anchor pin when installed. All of the parts should be flat on the anchor pin. Remove the wheel cylinder piston clamp.

18. Apply Lubriplate® to the threads and the socket end of the adjusting starwheel screw. Turn the adjusting screw into the adjusting pivot nut to the limit of the threads and then back off ½ turn.

NOTE: *Interchanging the brake shoe adjusting screw assemblies from one side of the vehicle to the other would cause the brake shoes to retract rather than expand each time the automatic adjusting mechanism operated. To prevent this, the socket end of the adjusting screw is stamped with an* **R** *or an* **L** *for RIGHT or LEFT. The adjusting pivot nuts can be distinguished by the number of lines machined around the body of the nut; one line indicates left hand nut and two lines indicates a right hand nut.*

19. Place the adjusting socket on the screw and install this assembly between the shoe ends with the adjusting screw nearest to the secondary shoe.

20. Place the cable hook into the hole in the adjusting lever from the backing plate side. The adjusting levers are stamped with an **R** (right) or an **L** (left) to indicate their installation on the right or left hand brake assembly.

21. Position the hooked end of the adjuster spring in the primary shoe web and connect the loop end of the spring to the adjuster lever hole.

22. Pull the adjuster lever, cable and automatic adjuster spring down toward the rear to engage the pivot book in the large hole in the secondary shoe web.

23. After installation, check the action of the adjuster by pulling the section of the cable between the cable guide and the adjusting lever toward the secondary shoe web far enough to lift the lever past a tooth on the adjusting screw starwheel. The lever should snap into position behind the next tooth, and release of the cable should cause the adjuster spring to return the lever to its original position. This return action of the lever will turn the adjusting screw starwheel one tooth. The lever should contact the adjusting screw starwheel one tooth above the center line of the adjusting screw.

If the automatic adjusting mechanism does not perform properly, check the following:

1. Check the cable end fittings. The cable ends should fill or extend slightly beyond the crimped section of the fittings. If this is not the case, replace the cable.

2. Check the cable guide for damage. The cable groove should be parallel to the shoe web, and the body of the guide should lie flat against the web. Replace the cable guide if this is not so.

3. Check the pivot hook on the lever. The

hook surfaces should be square with the body on the lever for proper pivoting. Repair or replace the hook as necessary.

4. Make sure that the adjusting screw starwheel is properly seated in the notch in the shoe web.

Wheel Cylinders
OVERHAUL

Wheel cylinder rebuilding kits are available for reconditioning wheel cylinders. The kits usually contain new cup springs, cylinder cups, and in some, new boots. The most important factor to keep in mind when rebuilding wheel cylinders is cleanliness. Keep all dirt away from the wheel cylinders when you are reassembling them.

1. To remove the wheel cylinder, jack up the vehicle and remove the wheel, hub, and drum.

2. Disconnect the brake line at the fitting on the brake backing plate.

3. Remove the brake assemblies.

4. Remove the screws that hold the wheel cylinder to the backing plate and remove the wheel cylinder from the vehicle.

5. Remove the rubber dust covers on the ends of the cylinder. Remove the pistons and piston cups and the spring. Remove the bleeder screw and make sure that it is not plugged.

6. Discard all of the parts that the rebuilding lot will replace.

7. Examine the inside of the cylinder. If it is severely rusted, pitted or scratched, then the cylinder must be replaced as the piston cups won't be able to seal against the walls of the cylinder.

8. Using a wheel cylinder hone or emery cloth and crocus cloth, polish the inside of the cylinder. The purpose of this is to put a new surface on the inside of the cylinder. Keep the inside of the cylinder coated with brake fluid while honing.

9. Wash out the cylinder with clean brake fluid after honing.

10. When reassembling the cylinder, dip all of the parts in clean brake fluid. Assemble the wheel cylinder in the reverse order of removal and disassembly.

PARKING BRAKE

Equalizer-to-Control Cable
REMOVAL AND INSTALLATION
1966–77

1. Raise the vehicle on a hoist.

2. Loosen the adjusting nut at the equalizer assembly and remove ball end of the brake control-to-equalizer cable from the equalizer arm. Remove the clip holding the cable housing to the bracket.

3. Lower the vehicle.

4. From inside of vehicle, disconnect the cable at the parking brake control clevis.

5. Raise the vehicle on a hoist.

6. Pull the parking brake control-to-equalizer cable through the hole in the dash panel and remove it from the vehicle.

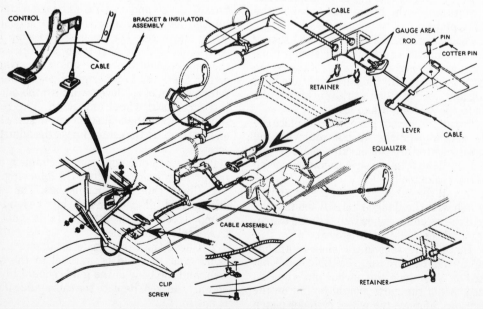

1966–77 parking brake system

7. Insert the parking brake control-to-equalizer cable upward through the hole in the dash panel. Place the cable on the mounting bracket.

8. Lower the vehicle.

9. Connect the cable to the parking brake control clevis.

10. Raise the vehicle on a hoist.

11. Position the cable housing on the bracket and install the retaining clip.

12. Connect the ball end of cable to the equalizer arm, and install the adjusting nut.

13. Adjust the parking brakes, as described in this chapter.

14. Lower the vehicle. Check brake operation.

1978–79

1. Raise the vehicle on a hoist. Remove the equalizer nut.

2. Remove the parking brake cable from the crossmember and all retaining clips.

3. Lower the vehicle. Remove the forward ball end of the parking brake cable from the control assembly clevis.

4. Remove the cable and hair pin retainer from the control assembly.

5. Using a fish wire or cord attached to the control lever end of the cable, remove the cable from the vehicle.

6. Transfer the fish wire or cord to the new cable. Position the cable in the vehicle, routing the cable through the dash panel. Remove the fish wire and secure the cable to the control with the hair pin retainer.

7. Connect the forward ball end of the brake cable to the clevis of the control assembly and raise the vehicle on a hoist.

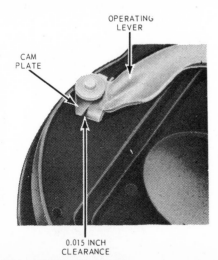

Parking brake operating lever and cam plate clearance—web ledge brakes

8. Route the cable through the crossmember(s) and secure in place with the retaining clip(s).

9. Connect the rod end to the rear cables and equalizer using adjusting nut. Adjust the parking brake cable at the equalizer as described in this chapter.

10. Rotate both rear wheels to be sure that the parking brakes are not dragging.

1980–86

1. Raise the vehicle on a hoist. Back off the equalizer nut and remove slug of front cable from the tension limiter.

2. Remove the parking brake cable from the retaining clips.

3. Lower the vehicle. Remove the forward ball end of the parking brake cable from the control assembly clevis.

4. Remove the cable and hair pin retainer from the control assembly.

5. Using a fish wire or cord attached to the control lever end of the cable, remove the cable from the vehicle.

6. Transfer the fish wire or cord to the new cable. Position the cable in the vehicle, routing the cable through the dash panel. Remove the fish wire and secure the cable to the control with the hair pin retainer.

7. Connect the forward ball end of the brake cable to the clevis of the control assembly and replace the hairpin clip around the conduit end fitting. Raise the vehicle on a hoist.

8. Route the cable and secure in place with retaining clips.

9. Connect the slug of the cable to the tension limiter connector. Adjust the parking brake cable at the equalizer.

10. Rotate both rear wheels to be sure that the parking brakes are not dragging.

Equalizer-to-Rear Wheel Cables
REMOVAL AND INSTALLATION
1966–77

1. Raise the vehicle and remove the hub cap, wheel, and brake drum. Loosen the lock nut on the equalizer rod and disconnect the cable from the equalizer.

2. Remove the horseshoe type clip that retains the cable housing to the frame bracket, and pull the cable and housing out of the bracket.

3. Working on the wheel side, compress the prongs on the cable retainer so they can pass through the hole in the carrier plate. Draw the cable retainer out of the hole.

4. With the spring tension off the parking

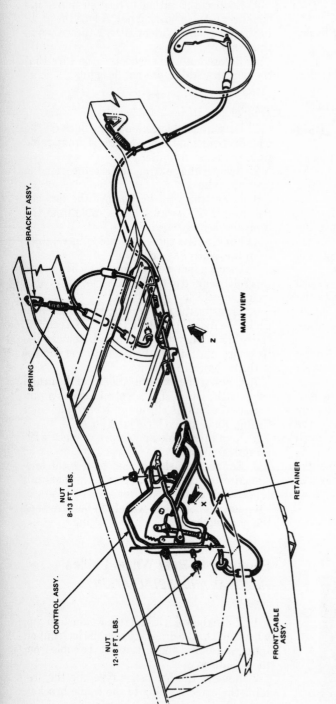

BRACKET ASSY.

SPRING

NUT
8-13 FT. LBS.

CONTROL ASSY.

NUT
12-18 FT. LBS.

FRONT CABLE
ASSY.

RETAINER

MAIN VIEW

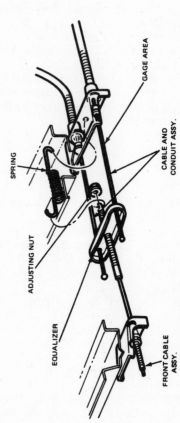

GAGE AREA

SPRING

ADJUSTING NUT

EQUALIZER

CABLE AND
CONDUIT ASSY.

FRONT CABLE
ASSY.

VIEW IN DIRECTION OF ARROW Z
1978-79 parking brake system

RETAINER

FRONT CABLE ASSY.

VIEW IN DIRECTION OF ARROW X

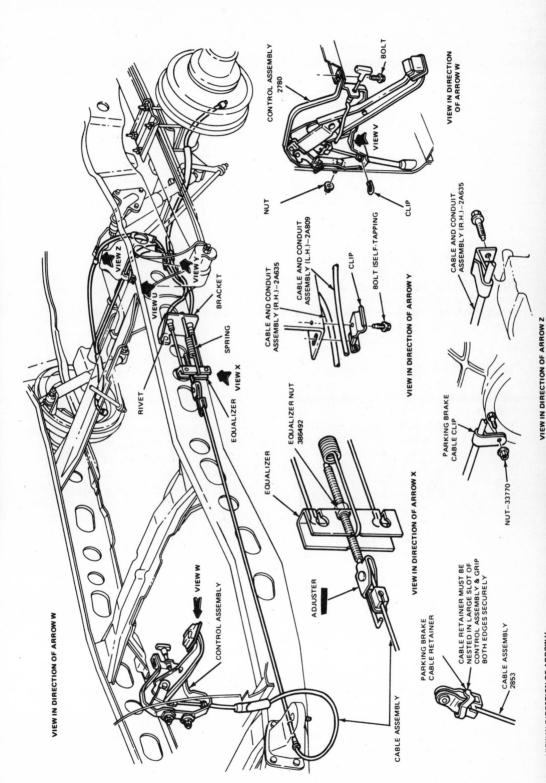

VIEW IN DIRECTION OF ARROW W

CONTROL ASSEMBLY

BOLT

CONTROL ASSEMBLY 2780

VIEW V

VIEW IN DIRECTION OF ARROW W

NUT

CLIP

VIEW Z

VIEW Y

VIEW U

BRACKET

SPRING

VIEW X

RIVET

EQUALIZER

CABLE AND CONDUIT ASSEMBLY (R.H.)–2A635

CABLE AND CONDUIT ASSEMBLY (L.H.)–2A809

CLIP

BOLT (SELF-TAPPING)

VIEW IN DIRECTION OF ARROW Y

EQUALIZER

EQUALIZER NUT 386492

CABLE AND CONDUIT ASSEMBLY (R.H.)–2A635

PARKING BRAKE CABLE CLIP

NUT–33770

VIEW IN DIRECTION OF ARROW Z

VIEW IN DIRECTION OF ARROW X

ADJUSTER

VIEW W

CONTROL ASSEMBLY

PARKING BRAKE CABLE RETAINER

CABLE RETAINER MUST BE NESTED IN LARGE SLOT OF CONTROL ASSEMBLY & GRIP BOTH EDGES SECURELY

CABLE ASSEMBLY 2853

CABLE ASSEMBLY

VIEW IN DIRECTION OF ARROW V

1980 and later parking brake system

brake lever, lift the cable out of the slot in the lever, and remove the cable through the carrier plate hole.

5. Pull the cable through the housing until the end of the cable is inserted over the slot in the parking brake lever. Pull the excess slack from the cable and insert the cable housing into the carrier plate access hole until the retainer prongs expand.

6. Thread the front end of the cable housing through the frame bracket and install the horseshoe type retaining clip. Insert the ball end of the cable into the equalizer and slightly tighten the lock nut on the equalizer.

On vehicles with web ledge brakes, check the clearance between the parking brake operating lever and cam plate. The clearance should be 0.015″ (0.38mm) when the brakes are fully released.

7. Install the rear brake drum, wheel, and hub cap, and adjust the rear brake shoes.

8. Tighten the locknut on the equalizer rod until the slack is taken out of the cables.

9. Rotate both rear wheels to be sure that the parking brakes are not dragging.

1978–79

1. Raise the vehicle and remove the hub cap, wheel, and brake drum. Loosen the locknut on the equalizer rod and disconnect the cable from the equalizer.

2. Compress the prongs that retain the cable housing to the frame bracket, and pull the cable and housing out of the bracket.

3. Working on the wheel side, compress the prongs on the cable retainer so they can pass through the hole in the brake backing plate. Draw the cable retainer out of the hole.

4. With the spring tension off the parking brake lever, lift the cable out of the slot in the lever, and remove the cable through the brake backing plate hole.

5. Pull the cable through the brake backing plate until the end of the cable is inserted over the slot in the parking brake lever. Pull the excess slack from the cable and insert the cable housing into the brake backing plate access hole until the retainer prongs expand.

6. Insert the front end of the cable housing through the frame crossmember bracket until the prong expands. Insert the ball end of the cable into the equalizer and slightly tighten the locknut on the equalizer.

On vehicles with web ledge brakes, check the clearance between the parking brake operating lever and cam plate. The clearance should be 0.015″ (0.38mm) when the brakes are fully released.

7. Install the rear brake drum, wheel, and hub cap, and adjust the rear brake shoes.

8. Tighten the locknut on the equalizer rod until the slack is taken out of the cables. Adjust the cable as outlined in this Chapter.

9. Rotate both rear wheels to be sure that the parking brakes are not dragging.

1980–86

1. Raise the vehicle and remove the hub cab, wheel, tension limiter and brake drum. Remove the locknut on the threaded rod and disconnect the cable from the equalizer.

2. Compress the prongs that retain the cable housing into the brake backing plate cable and housing out of the bracket.

3. Working on the wheel side, compress the prongs on the cable retainer so they can pass through the hole in the brake backing plate. Draw the cable retainer out of the hole.

4. With the spring tension off the parking brake lever, lift the cable out of the slot in the lever, and remove the cable through the brake backing plate hole.

5. Pull the cable through the brake backing plate until the end of the cable is inserted over the slot in the parking brake lever. Pull the excess slack from the cable and insert the cable housing into the brake backing plate access hole until the retainer prongs expand.

6. Insert the front end of the cable housing through the frame crossmember bracket until the prong expands. Insert the ball end of the cable into the key hole slots on the equalizer, rotate the equalizer 90° and recouple the tension limiter threaded rod to the equalizer.

On vehicles with web ledge brakes, check the clearance between the parking brake operating lever and cam plate. The clearance should be 0.015″ (0.38mm) when the brakes are fully released.

7. Install the rear brake drum, wheel, and hub cap, and adjust the rear brake shoes.

8. Adjust the parking brake tension.

9. Rotate both rear wheels to be sure that the parking brakes are not dragging.

ADJUSTMENT
1966–77

1. Raise the rear of the vehicle and support it on jackstands.

2. Depress the parking brake pedal 2 clicks.

3. Tighten the equalizer nut until both rear wheels are firmly locked. The equalizer nut is the single nut at the yoke where the two rear cables attach.

4. Release the pedal. The rear wheels must turn freely.

5. Lower the vehicle.

1978–79

PRE-TENSION PROCEDURE

NOTE: *These procedures require a special tool available at most good auto supply dealers or your Ford dealer.*

1. Depress the parking brake pedal until the parking brake control is in the second tooth (two notches or clicks).

2. Attach a Burroughs gauge service tool No. BT-33-75 W2-25, or equivalent, to the LH rear cable and adjust the cable tension, registered on the gauge to 250 pounds, by tightening the equalizer nut. Hold for 5 minutes and release pedal.

3. Back off the equalizer nut until zero pounds of tension is registered on the gauge.

FINAL ADJUSTMENT

1. Position the parking brake pedal as outlined under pre-tension procedure.

2. Adjust the final tension to the mean tension (50–90 lbs. specs) as registered on the Burroughs gauge by tightening the equalizer nut.

3. Remove the gauge and release the parking brake.

4. Check the clearance between the parking brake lever and the cam plate. The clearance should be 0.015″ (0.38mm) with the brakes fully released. If the clearance is not within specifications, readjust the parking brake cable.

5. Place the parking brake pedal in the fully released position, then check the slack in the parking brake two rear cables. The cables should be tight enough to provide full application of the rear brake shoes, when the parking brake lever or foot pedal is placed in the fully applied position, yet loose enough to ensure complete release of the brake shoes when the lever is in the released position.

1980–86

1. Make sure the brake drums are cold for correct adjustment.

2. Depress the parking brake pedal until the parking brake control is in the second tooth (two notches or two clicks).

3. Attach a Rotunda cable tension gauge (model 210018) or equivalent behind the equalizer assembly (either toward the right or left rear drum assembly).

4. Turn the equalizer adjusting nut until the tension reads 250 ft.lb. as read on the cable tension gauge.

5. Back off the equalizer adjusting nut until the tension reads 50 ft.lb. on the cable tension gauge.

6. For the final adjustment, retighten the equalizer adjusting nut until the tension reads between 60–100 ft.lb. as read on the cable tension gauge.

Brake Specifications
All measurements in inches

| Year | Master Cylinder Bore | Caliper Bore | Wheel Cylinder Bore | | Rotor Diameter | Rotor Minimum Thickness | Rotor Maximum Run-out | Brake Drum Diameter | | Machined Oversize | |
			Front	Rear				Front	Rear	Front	Rear
1966–70	1.00	—	1.125	.8125	—	—	—	10.00	10.00	10.06	10.06
1971–74	1.00	—	1.125	.8125	—	—	—	11.00	10.00	11.06	10.06
1975–77	1.00	2.875	—	.9375	11.54	1.180	.003	—	11.03	—	11.09
1978–81	1.00	2.875	—	.9375	11.72	1.120	.003	—	11.03	—	11.09
1982–86	1.00	2.875	—	.9375	11.65	1.120	.003	—	11.03	—	11.09

Troubleshooting the Brake System

Problem	Cause	Solution
Low brake pedal (excessive pedal travel required for braking action.)	• Excessive clearance between rear linings and drums caused by inoperative automatic adjusters	• Make 10 to 15 alternate forward and reverse brake stops to adjust brakes. If brake pedal does not come up, repair or replace adjuster parts as necessary.
	• Worn rear brakelining	• Inspect and replace lining if worn beyond minimum thickness specification
	• Bent, distorted brakeshoes, front or rear	• Replace brakeshoes in axle sets
	• Air in hydraulic system	• Remove air from system. Refer to Brake Bleeding.
Low brake pedal (pedal may go to floor with steady pressure applied.)	• Fluid leak in hydraulic system	• Fill master cylinder to fill line; have helper apply brakes and check calipers, wheel cylinders, differential valve tubes, hoses and fittings for leaks. Repair or replace as necessary.
	• Air in hydraulic system	• Remove air from system. Refer to Brake Bleeding.
	• Incorrect or non-recommended brake fluid (fluid evaporates at below normal temp).	• Flush hydraulic system with clean brake fluid. Refill with correct-type fluid.
	• Master cylinder piston seals worn, or master cylinder bore is scored, worn or corroded	• Repair or replace master cylinder
Low brake pedal (pedal goes to floor on first application—o.k. on subsequent applications.)	• Disc brake pads sticking on abutment surfaces of anchor plate. Caused by a build-up of dirt, rust, or corrosion on abutment surfaces	• Clean abutment surfaces
Fading brake pedal (pedal height decreases with steady pressure applied.)	• Fluid leak in hydraulic system	• Fill master cylinder reservoirs to fill mark, have helper apply brakes, check calipers, wheel cylinders, differential valve, tubes, hoses, and fittings for fluid leaks. Repair or replace parts as necessary.
	• Master cylinder piston seals worn, or master cylinder bore is scored, worn or corroded	• Repair or replace master cylinder
Decreasing brake pedal travel (pedal travel required for braking action decreases and may be accompanied by a hard pedal.)	• Caliper or wheel cylinder pistons sticking or seized	• Repair or replace the calipers, or wheel cylinders
	• Master cylinder compensator ports blocked (preventing fluid return to reservoirs) or pistons sticking or seized in master cylinder bore	• Repair or replace the master cylinder
	• Power brake unit binding internally	• Test unit according to the following procedure: (a) Shift transmission into neutral and start engine (b) Increase engine speed to 1500 rpm, close throttle and fully depress brake pedal (c) Slow release brake pedal and stop engine (d) Have helper remove vacuum check valve and hose from power unit. Observe for backward movement of brake pedal. (e) If the pedal moves backward, the power unit has an internal bind—replace power unit

Troubleshooting the Brake System (cont.)

Problem	Cause	Solution
Spongy brake pedal (pedal has abnormally soft, springy, spongy feel when depressed.)	• Air in hydraulic system	• Remove air from system. Refer to Brake Bleeding.
	• Brakeshoes bent or distorted	• Replace brakeshoes
	• Brakelining not yet seated with drums and rotors	• Burnish brakes
	• Rear drum brakes not properly adjusted	• Adjust brakes
Hard brake pedal (excessive pedal pressure required to stop vehicle. May be accompanied by brake fade.)	• Loose or leaking power brake unit vacuum hose	• Tighten connections or replace leaking hose
	• Incorrect or poor quality brakelining	• Replace with lining in axle sets
	• Bent, broken, distorted brakeshoes	• Replace brakeshoes
	• Calipers binding or dragging on mounting pins. Rear brakeshoes dragging on support plate.	• Replace mounting pins and bushings. Clean rust or burrs from rear brake support plate ledges and lubricate ledges with molydisulfide grease. **NOTE:** If ledges are deeply grooved or scored, do not attempt to sand or grind them smooth—replace support plate.
	• Caliper, wheel cylinder, or master cylinder pistons sticking or seized	• Repair or replace parts as necessary
	• Power brake unit vacuum check valve malfunction	• Test valve according to the following procedure: (a) Start engine, increase engine speed to 1500 rpm, close throttle and immediately stop engine (b) Wait at least 90 seconds then depress brake pedal (c) If brakes are not vacuum assisted for 2 or more applications, check valve is faulty
	• Power brake unit has internal bind	• Test unit according to the following procedure: (a) With engine stopped, apply brakes several times to exhaust all vacuum in system (b) Shift transmission into neutral, depress brake pedal and start engine (c) If pedal height decreases with foot pressure and less pressure is required to hold pedal in applied position, power unit vacuum system is operating normally. Test power unit. If power unit exhibits a bind condition, replace the power unit.
	• Master cylinder compensator ports (at bottom of reservoirs) blocked by dirt, scale, rust, or have small burrs (blocked ports prevent fluid return to reservoirs).	• Repair or replace master cylinder **CAUTION:** Do not attempt to clean blocked ports with wire, pencils, or similar implements. Use compressed air only.
	• Brake hoses, tubes, fittings clogged or restricted	• Use compressed air to check or unclog parts. Replace any damaged parts.
	• Brake fluid contaminated with improper fluids (motor oil, transmission fluid, causing rubber components to swell and stick in bores	• Replace all rubber components, combination valve and hoses. Flush entire brake system with DOT 3 brake fluid or equivalent.
	• Low engine vacuum	• Adjust or repair engine

Troubleshooting the Brake System (cont.)

Problem	Cause	Solution
Grabbing brakes (severe reaction to brake pedal pressure.)	· Brakelining(s) contaminated by grease or brake fluid	· Determine and correct cause of contamination and replace brakeshoes in axle sets
	· Parking brake cables incorrectly adjusted or seized	· Adjust cables. Replace seized cables.
	· Incorrect brakelining or lining loose on brakeshoes	· Replace brakeshoes in axle sets
	· Caliper anchor plate bolts loose	· Tighten bolts
	· Rear brakeshoes binding on support plate ledges	· Clean and lubricate ledges. Replace support plate(s) if ledges are deeply grooved. Do not attempt to smooth ledges by grinding.
	· Incorrect or missing power brake reaction disc	· Install correct disc
	· Rear brake support plates loose	· Tighten mounting bolts
Dragging brakes (slow or incomplete release of brakes)	· Brake pedal binding at pivot	· Loosen and lubricate
	· Power brake unit has internal bind	· Inspect for internal bind. Replace unit if internal bind exists.
	· Parking brake cables incorrrectly adjusted or seized	· Adjust cables. Replace seized cables.
	· Rear brakeshoe return springs weak or broken	· Replace return springs. Replace brakeshoe if necessary in axle sets.
	· Automatic adjusters malfunctioning	· Repair or replace adjuster parts as required
	· Caliper, wheel cylinder or master cylinder pistons sticking or seized	· Repair or replace parts as necessary
	· Master cylinder compensating ports blocked (fluid does not return to reservoirs).	· Use compressed air to clear ports. Do not use wire, pencils, or similar objects to open blocked ports.
Vehicle moves to one side when brakes are applied	· Incorrect front tire pressure	· Inflate to recommended cold (reduced load) inflation pressure
	· Worn or damaged wheel bearings	· Replace worn or damaged bearings
	· Brakelining on one side contaminated	· Determine and correct cause of contamination and replace brakelining in axle sets
	· Brakeshoes on one side bent, distorted, or lining loose on shoe	· Replace brakeshoes in axle sets
	· Support plate bent or loose on one side	· Tighten or replace support plate
	· Brakelining not yet seated with drums or rotors	· Burnish brakelining
	· Caliper anchor plate loose on one side	· Tighten anchor plate bolts
	· Caliper piston sticking or seized	· Repair or replace caliper
	· Brakelinings water soaked	· Drive vehicle with brakes lightly applied to dry linings
	· Loose suspension component attaching or mounting bolts	· Tighten suspension bolts. Replace worn suspension components.
	· Brake combination valve failure	· Replace combination valve
Chatter or shudder when brakes are applied (pedal pulsation and roughness may also occur.)	· Brakeshoes distorted, bent, contaminated, or worn	· Replace brakeshoes in axle sets
	· Caliper anchor plate or support plate loose	· Tighten mounting bolts
	· Excessive thickness variation of rotor(s)	· Refinish or replace rotors in axle sets
Noisy brakes (squealing, clicking, scraping sound when brakes are applied.)	· Bent, broken, distorted brakeshoes	· Replace brakeshoes in axle sets
	· Excessive rust on outer edge of rotor braking surface	· Remove rust

Troubleshooting the Brake System (cont.)

Problem	Cause	Solution
Noisy brakes (squealing, clicking, scraping sound when brakes are applied.) (cont.)	• Brakelining worn out—shoes contacting drum of rotor	• Replace brakeshoes and lining in axle sets. Refinish or replace drums or rotors.
	• Broken or loose holdown or return springs	• Replace parts as necessary
	• Rough or dry drum brake support plate ledges	• Lubricate support plate ledges
	• Cracked, grooved, or scored rotor(s) or drum(s)	• Replace rotor(s) or drum(s). Replace brakeshoes and lining in axle sets if necessary.
	• Incorrect brakelining and/or shoes (front or rear).	• Install specified shoe and lining assemblies
Pulsating brake pedal	• Out of round drums or excessive lateral runout in disc brake rotor(s)	• Refinish or replace drums, re-index rotors or replace

Body and Trim

EXTERIOR

Doors

REMOVAL AND INSTALLATION

1. Remove all usable hardware, trim, and glass parts.

2. Remove the upper and lower hinge access hole cover plates (if so equipped) and mark the location of the hinge on the body and door.

3. Remove the door to lower hinge retaining bolts.

4. Support the door, and remove the door to upper hinge retaining bolts. Slide the door off the hinges.

5. If a hinge is to be replaced, remove the hinge to pillar bolts and remove the hinge.

6. Cement the door weatherstrip in proper position on the door using COAZ-19552-A weather strip adhesive of its equvalent. Include the belt seals.

7. If a hinge has been removed, install the hinge in the pillar in approximately the same position as the removed hinge.

8. Position the door on the hinges, and install the retaining bolts snug.

9. Install the lock mechanism. Install the glass mechanism, glass, and vent window assembly. Make all necessary adjustments as these assemblies are installed.

10. Adjust the door and tighten all hinge bolts securely. To provide a good weatherstrip seal, the upper front edge of the door must be $^{3}/_{16}$" (4.8mm) inboard of the upper part of the pillar from the belt line to the point near the top of the door. This adjustment is made by adjusting the upper striker of the right hand door inboard $^{3}/_{16}$" (4.8mm).

11. If the truck is so equipped, install the water shield. The top edge should be cemented to the inside surface of the inner panel.

12. Install the hinge access hole cover plates and the door access hole cover plate.

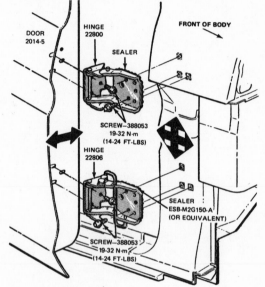

Door hinge adjustment

ADJUSTMENT

1. Loosen the hinge bolts just enough to permit movement of the door with a padded pry bar.

2. Move the door the distance estimated to be necessary. Tighten the hinge bolts and check the door fit to be sure there is no bind or interference with the adjacent panel.

3. Repeat the operation until the desired fit is obtained, and check the striker plate alignment for proper door closing.

Door Locks

REMOVAL AND INSTALLATION

1. Remove the trim panel and water shield from the door.

2. Disconnect the rods from the handle and

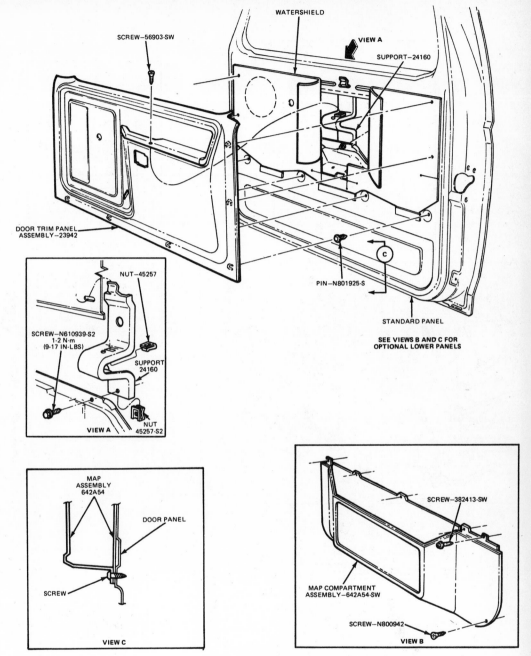

WATERSHIELD

SCREW—56903-SW

VIEW A

SUPPORT—24160

DOOR TRIM PANEL
ASSEMBLY—23942

NUT—45257

SCREW—N610939-S2
1-2 N·m
(9-17 IN-LBS)

SUPPORT
24160

NUT
45257-S2

VIEW A

PIN—N801925-S

STANDARD PANEL

SEE VIEWS B AND C FOR
OPTIONAL LOWER PANELS

MAP
ASSEMBLY
642A54

DOOR PANEL

SCREW

VIEW C

SCREW—382413-SW

MAP COMPARTMENT
ASSEMBLY—642A54-SW

SCREW—N800942

VIEW B

Door trim panel installation

lock cylinder if necessary and remove the remote control assembly.

3. Remove the latch assembly attaching
screws and remove the latch from the door.

To Install:

1. Install the rod retaining clips in the new
the new latch assembly. The rods should be attached to the latch before latch installation.

2. Position the latch in the door and install
the latch attaching screws.

3. Connect the rods to the handle, lock cylin-

der and remote control and check the operation
of the latch.

4. Install the water shield and trim panel on
the door.

Hood

REMOVAL AND INSTALLATION

1. Mark the position of the hood link and remove the two link assembly bolts.

2. Mark the position of the hood hinges and

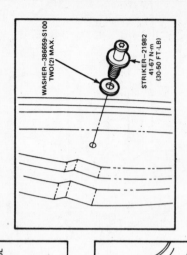

WASHER–386659-S100 TWO(2) MAX.

STRIKER–21982 41-67 N·m (30-50 FT-LB)

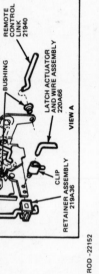

LATCH PUSH BUTTON ROD ASSEMBLY 218A00

REMOTE CONTROL LINK 21940

DOOR LATCH ACTUATING ROD–219A36

BUSHING

CLIP

LATCH ACTUATOR AND WIRE ASSEMBLY 220A66

VIEW A

DOOR LATCH CONTROL TO CYLINDER ROD 22134

CLIP

RETAINER ASSEMBLY 219A36

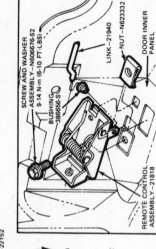

SCREW AND WASHER ASSEMBLY–N606676-S2 9-14 N·m (6-10 FT-LBS)

BUSHING 386656-S

LINK–21940

NUT–N623332

DOOR INNER PANEL

VIEW-B

REMOTE CONTROL ASSEMBLY–21818

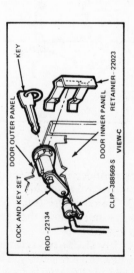

OUTSIDE HANDLE ASSEMBLY–22400

CLIP–388569-S

PAD–22428

SCREW AND WASHER ASSEMBLY–N800527-S100

VIEW-D

NUT AND WASHER ASSEMBLY–N621906-S2

PA–22448

DOOR OUTER PANEL

Door latch installation

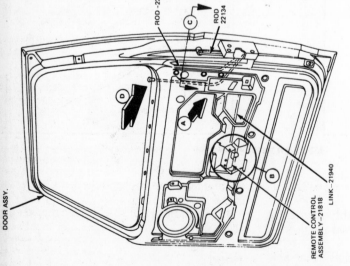

ROD–22152

ROD 22134

C

D

A

B

DOOR ASSY.

REMOTE CONTROL ASSEMBLY–21818

LINK–21940

KEY

DOOR OUTER PANEL

RETAINER–22023

DOOR INNER PANEL

VIEW-C

LOCK AND KEY SET

CLIP–388569-S

ROD–22134

CHILTON'S
AUTO BODY REPAIR TIPS

**Tools and Materials • Step-by-Step Illustrated Procedures
How To Repair Dents, Scratches and Rust Holes
Spray Painting and Refinishing Tips**

EASY
STEP-BY-STEP
TIPS FROM PROS

With a little practice, basic body repair procedures can be mastered by any do-it-yourself mechanic. The step-by-step repairs shown here can be applied to almost any type of auto body repair.

TOOLS & MATERIALS

You may already have basic tools, such as hammers and electric drills. Other tools unique to body repair — body hammers, grinding attachments, sanding blocks, dent puller, half-round plastic file and plastic spreaders — are relatively inexpensive and can be obtained wherever auto parts or auto body repair parts are sold. Portable air compressors and paint spray guns can be purchased or rented.

Auto Body Repair Kits

The best and most often used products are available to the do-it-yourselfer in kit form, from major manufacturers of auto body repair products. The same manufacturers also merchandise the individual products for use by pros.

Kits are available to make a wide variety of repairs, including holes, dents and scratches and fiberglass, and offer the advantage of buying the materials you'll need for the job. There is little waste or chance of materials going bad from not being used. Many kits may also contain basic body-working tools such as body files, sanding blocks and spreaders. Check the contents of the kit before buying your tools.

BODY REPAIR TIPS

Safety

Many of the products associated with auto body repair and refinishing contain toxic chemicals. Read all labels before opening containers and store them in a safe place and manner.

• Wear eye protection (safety goggles) when using power tools or when performing any operation that involves the removal of any type of material.

• Wear lung protection (disposable mask or respirator) when grinding, sanding or painting.

Sanding

1 Sand off paint before using a dent puller. When using a non-adhesive sanding disc, cover the back of the disc with an overlapping layer or two of masking tape and trim the edges. The disc will last considerably longer.

2 Use the circular motion of the sanding disc to grind *into* the edge of the repair. Grinding or sanding away from the jagged edge will only tear the sandpaper.

3 Use the palm of your hand flat on the panel to detect high and low spots. Do not use your fingertips. Slide your hand slowly back and forth.

WORKING WITH BODY FILLER

Mixing The Filler

Cleanliness and proper mixing and application are extremely important. Use a clean piece of plastic or glass or a disposable artist's palette to mix body filler.

1 Allow plenty of time and follow directions. No useful purpose will be served by adding more hardener to make it cure (set-up) faster. Less hardener means more curing time, but the mixture dries harder; more hardener means less curing time but a softer mixture.

2 Both the hardener and the filler should be thoroughly kneaded or stirred before mixing. Hardener should be a solid paste and dispense like thin toothpaste. Body filler should be smooth, and free of lumps or thick spots.

Getting the proper amount of hardener in the filler is the trickiest part of preparing the filler. Use the same amount of hardener in cold or warm weather. For contour filler (thick coats), a bead of hardener twice the diameter of the filler is about right. There's about a 15% margin on either side, but, if in doubt use less hardener.

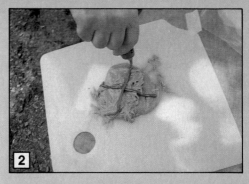

3 Mix the body filler and hardener by wiping across the mixing surface, picking the mixture up and wiping it again. Colder weather requires longer mixing times. Do not mix in a circular motion; this will trap air bubbles which will become holes in the cured filler.

Applying The Filler

1 For best results, filler should not be applied over 1/4" thick.

Apply the filler in several coats. Build it up to above the level of the repair surface so that it can be sanded or grated down.

The first coat of filler must be pressed on with a firm wiping motion.

Apply the filler in one direction only. Working the filler back and forth will either pull it off the metal or trap air bubbles.

REPAIRING DENTS

Before you start, take a few minutes to study the damaged area. Try to visualize the shape of the panel before it was damaged. If the damage is on the left fender, look at the right fender and use it as a guide. If there is access to the panel from behind, you can reshape it with a body hammer. If not, you'll have to use a dent puller. Go slowly and work the metal a little at a time. Get the panel as straight as possible before applying filler.

1 This dent is typical of one that can be pulled out or hammered out from behind. Remove the headlight cover, headlight assembly and turn signal housing.

2 Drill a series of holes ½ the size of the end of the dent puller along the stress line. Make some trial pulls and assess the results. If necessary, drill more holes and try again. Do not hurry.

3 If possible, use a body hammer and block to shape the metal back to its original contours. Get the metal back as close to its original shape as possible. Don't depend on body filler to fill dents.

4 Using an 80-grit grinding disc on an electric drill, grind the paint from the surrounding area down to bare metal. Use a new grinding pad to prevent heat buildup that will warp metal.

5 The area should look like this when you're finished grinding. Knock the drill holes in and tape over small openings to keep plastic filler out.

6 Mix the body filler (see Body Repair Tips). Spread the body filler evenly over the entire area (see Body Repair Tips). Be sure to cover the area completely.

7 Let the body filler dry until the surface can just be scratched with your fingernail. Knock the high spots from the body filler with a body file ("Cheese-grater"). Check frequently with the palm of your hand for high and low spots.

8 Check to be sure that trim pieces that will be installed later will fit exactly. Sand the area with 40-grit paper.

9 If you wind up with low spots, you may have to apply another layer of filler.

10 Knock the high spots off with 40-grit paper. When you are satisfied with the contours of the repair, apply a thin coat of filler to cover pin holes and scratches.

11 Block sand the area with 40-grit paper to a smooth finish. Pay particular attention to body lines and ridges that must be well-defined.

12 Sand the area with 400 paper and then finish with a scuff pad. The finished repair is ready for priming and painting (see Painting Tips).

Materials and photos courtesy of Ritt Jones Auto Body, Prospect Park, PA.

REPAIRING RUST HOLES

There are many ways to repair rust holes. The fiberglass cloth kit shown here is one of the most cost efficient for the owner because it provides a strong repair that resists cracking and moisture and is relatively easy to use. It can be used on large and small holes (with or without backing) and can be applied over contoured areas. Remember, however, that short of replacing an entire panel, no repair is a guarantee that the rust will not return.

1 Remove any trim that will be in the way. Clean away all loose debris. Cut away all the rusted metal. But be sure to leave enough metal to retain the contour or body shape.

2 Grind away all traces of rust with a 24-grit grinding disc. Be sure to grind back 3-4 inches from the edge of the hole down to bare metal and be sure all traces of paint, primer and rust are removed.

3 Block sand the area with 80 or 100 grit sandpaper to get a clear, shiny surface and feathered paint edge. Tap the edges of the hole inward with a ball peen hammer.

4 If you are going to use release film, cut a piece about 2-3″ larger than the area you have sanded. Place the film over the repair and mark the sanded area on the film. Avoid any unnecessary wrinkling of the film.

5 Cut 2 pieces of fiberglass matte to match the shape of the repair. One piece should be about 1″ smaller than the sanded area and the second piece should be 1″ smaller than the first. Mix enough filler and hardener to saturate the fiberglass material (see Body Repair Tips).

6 Lay the release sheet on a flat surface and spread an even layer of filler, large enough to cover the repair. Lay the smaller piece of fiberglass cloth in the center of the sheet and spread another layer of filler over the fiberglass cloth. Repeat the operation for the larger piece of cloth.

7 Place the repair material over the repair area, with the release film facing outward. Use a spreader and work from the center outward to smooth the material, following the body contours. Be sure to remove all air bubbles.

8 Wait until the repair has dried tack-free and peel off the release sheet. The ideal working temperature is 60°-90° F. Cooler or warmer temperatures or high humidity may require additional curing time. Wait longer, if in doubt.

9

9 Sand and feather-edge the entire area. The initial sanding can be done with a sanding disc on an electric drill if care is used. Finish the sanding with a block sander. Low spots can be filled with body filler; this may require several applications.

10

10 When the filler can just be scratched with a fingernail, knock the high spots down with a body file and smooth the entire area with 80-grit. Feather the filled areas into the surrounding areas.

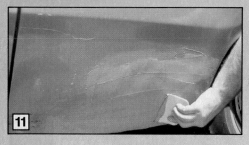
11

11 When the area is sanded smooth, mix some topcoat and hardener and apply it directly with a spreader. This will give a smooth finish and prevent the glass matte from showing through the paint.

12

12 Block sand the topcoat smooth with finishing sandpaper (200 grit), and 400 grit. The repair is ready for masking, priming and painting (see Painting Tips).

Materials and photos courtesy Marson Corporation, Chelsea, Massachusetts

PAINTING TIPS

Preparation

1 SANDING — Use a 400 or 600 grit wet or dry sandpaper. Wet-sand the area with a ¼ sheet of sandpaper soaked in clean water. Keep the paper wet while sanding. Sand the area until the repaired area tapers into the original finish.

2 CLEANING — Wash the area to be painted thoroughly with water and a clean rag. Rinse it thoroughly and wipe the surface dry until you're sure it's completely free of dirt, dust, fingerprints, wax, detergent or other foreign matter.

3 MASKING — Protect any areas you don't want to overspray by covering them with masking tape and newspaper. Be careful not get fingerprints on the area to be painted.

4 PRIMING — All exposed metal should be primed before painting. Primer protects the metal and provides an excellent surface for paint adhesion. When the primer is dry, wet-sand the area again with 600 grit wet-sandpaper. Clean the area again after sanding.

4

Painting Techniques

P aint applied from either a spray gun or a spray can (for small areas) will provide good results. Experiment on an old piece of metal to get the right combination before you begin painting.

SPRAYING VISCOSITY (SPRAY GUN ONLY) — Paint should be thinned to spraying viscosity according to the directions on the can. Use only the recommended thinner or reducer and the same amount of reduction regardless of temperature.

AIR PRESSURE (SPRAY GUN ONLY) — This is extremely important. Be sure you are using the proper recommended pressure.

TEMPERATURE — The surface to be painted should be approximately the same temperature as the surrounding air. Applying warm paint to a cold surface, or vice versa, will completely upset the paint characteristics.

THICKNESS — Spray with smooth strokes. In general, the thicker the coat of paint, the longer the drying time. Apply several thin coats about 30 seconds apart. The paint should remain wet long enough to flow out and no longer; heavier coats will only produce sags or wrinkles. Spray a light (fog) coat, followed by heavier color coats.

DISTANCE — The ideal spraying distance is 8"-12" from the gun or can to the surface. Shorter distances will produce ripples, while greater distances will result in orange peel, dry film and poor color match and loss of material due to overspray.

OVERLAPPING — The gun or can should be kept at right angles to the surface at all times. Work to a wet edge at an even speed, using a 50% overlap and direct the center of the spray at the lower or nearest edge of the previous stroke.

RUBBING OUT (BLENDING) FRESH PAINT — Let the paint dry thoroughly. Runs or imperfections can be sanded out, primed and repainted.

Don't be in too big a hurry to remove the masking. This only produces paint ridges. When the finish has dried for at least a week, apply a small amount of fine grade rubbing compound with a clean, wet cloth. Use lots of water and blend the new paint with the surrounding area.

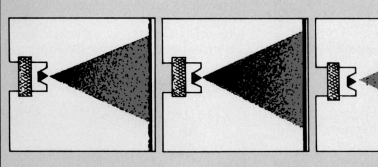

WRONG	CORRECT	WRONG
Thin coat. Stroke too fast, not enough overlap, gun too far away.	*Medium coat. Proper distance, good stroke, proper overlap.*	*Heavy coat. Stroke too slow, too much overlap, gun too close.*

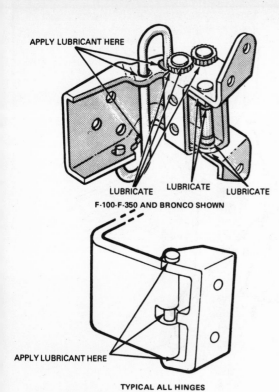

APPLY LUBRICANT HERE

LUBRICATE   LUBRICATE   LUBRICATE

F-100-F-350 AND BRONCO SHOWN

APPLY LUBRICANT HERE

TYPICAL ALL HINGES

Door hinge lubrication—typical

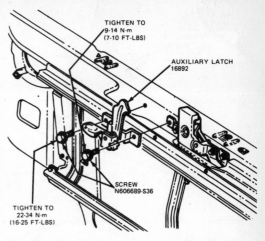

TIGHTEN TO
9-14 N·m
(7-10 FT-LBS)

AUXILIARY LATCH
16892

SCREW
N606689-S36

TIGHTEN TO
22-34 N·m
(16-25 FT-LBS)

Hood auxiliary latch

remove the hood hinge bolts. Then with the help of a friend, lift the hood off the hinges.

3. If the hood is to be replaced, transfer the the hood latch components and ornaments to the new hood.

4. With the aid of a helper, position the hood on the hinges and install the hinge bolts just snug.

5. Install two bolts to install link assembly to hood.

6. Adjust the hood for a proper fit by shifting the hood on the hinges, and tighten the hinge bolts.

7. Adjust the hood latch for proper alignment.

ALIGNMENT

1. Open the hood and mark the hood and latch assembly location.

2. Loosen the hood to fender inner attaching screws until they are just snug.

3. Adjust the hood up or down or rotate as required to obtain a flush fit between the hood and the top of the cowl panel. Then, tighten the hinge to fender inner attaching screws.

4. Loosen the two hood latch assembly attaching screws.

5. Loosen the hinge to hood attaching bolts until they are just snug. Move the hood forward or rearward or from side to side as re-

quired fro a proper hood fit. Then, tighten the hinge-to-hood attaching screws. Move the latch from side to side as required to center the latch with the hood striker. Tighten the hood latch attaching screws.

6. Lubricate each hood hinge at all pivot points with Polyethylene Grease (D7AZ-19584-A) or equvalent. Recheck the functional operation of the hinges by opening and closing the hood several times to assure correct alignment and that the lubricant has effectively worked into the pivot points.

Tailgate, Hatch or Trunk Lid
REMOVAL AND INSTALLATION

1. Unlatch the tailgate handle and lower the tailgate. Disconnect the left and right cable assemblies to the tailgate.

2. Disconnect the tailgate window motor wire at the connector. Pull the lead wire from the tailgate motor rail.

3. Support the tailgate and remove the torsion bar retainer from the body.

4. Remove the three screws and washer assemblies that secure the left and right hinge assemblies to the body.

5. Remove the tailgate from the vehicle.

To Install:

1. Position the tailgate to the body and support it securely.

2. Secure the hinge assemblies to the tailgate.

3. Attach the torsion bar retainer over the torsion bar.

4. Reconnect the tailgate window motor wire.

5. Secure the cable assemblies to the tailgate, remove the support and check tailgate operation.

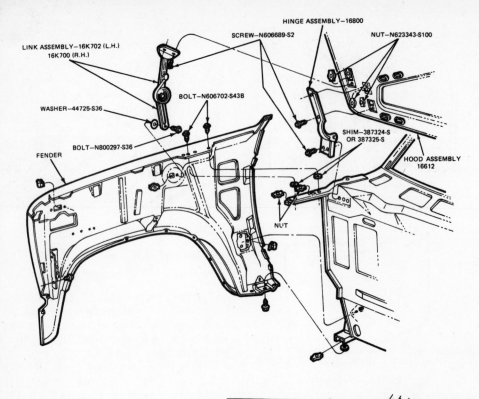

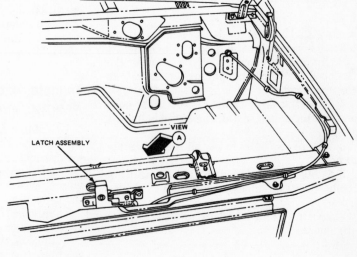

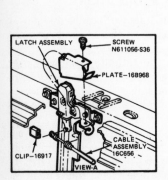

Hood, hinge and latch installation

Windshield

REMOVAL AND INSTALLATION

NOTE: *The temperature of the weatherstripping should be at least 75°F before removing the windshield. Two helpers are essential for this job.*

1. Remove the windshield wiper arms.
2. Remove the stainless steel moldings from the windshield weatherstripping.

3. From outside the vehicle, insert a thin wedge in the separation at the mid-point of the weatherstripping, and pull the lower lip up and over the upper lip. Avoid tearing the weatherstripping.
4. Coat the area between the glass and the weatherstripping with a soap and water solution.
5. You and one helper should push out on opposite, lower corners of the glass, while your

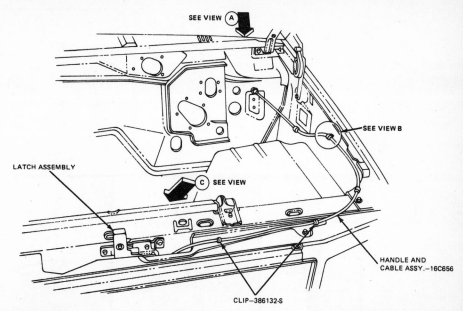

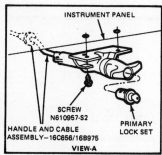
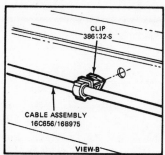
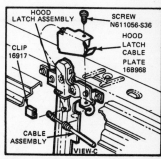

Hood latch remote control cable routing

other helper catches the glass on the outside. Clean any old sealer from the weatherstripping channel and the glass.

6. For installation, you must heat the weatherstripping with a heat lamp or other device, until it is very pliable.

7. Install the weatherstripping into the frame. Place a $\frac{3}{16}''$ (4.8mm) bead of medium bodied sealer, such as 3M Auto Bedding and Glazing Compound, or equivalent, in the weatherstripping channel around its entire circumference.

8. Soak the weatherstripping with the liquid soap solution.

9. Place a strong, thin cord or wire, in the glass groove along the bottom of the weatherstripping. Allow the ends of the cord or wire to hang down the front of the vehicle from each lower corner.

10. You and a helper, force the upper edge of the glass into the top groove of the weatherstripping.

11. Push the glass toward the vehicle, working the glass into the side grooves.

12. When the glass is tucked into the top and sides, it will be tight against the bottom of the weatherstripping. Starting at one corner, pull the cord toward you while pushing in on the glass. The weatherstripping will pull out, around the glass. Make sure that the weatherstripping is all the way up, around the lower edge of the glass.

13. Thoroughly soap the inner edges of the weatherstripping and, with the thin wedge, tuck the lower lip of the weatherstripping under the upper edge.

14. Install the stainless molding as follows:

a. Place a ⅛″ (3mm) diameter cord in the weatherstripping molding retaining groove, along the entire length of the weatherstripping, leaving enough cord hanging out at each end to get a good grip.

b. Place either the left or right bottom molding in the groove. Starting at the outside corner of the weatherstripping, pull up on the cord, while tapping gently on the molding with a rubber mallet. This will lock the molding in the groove.

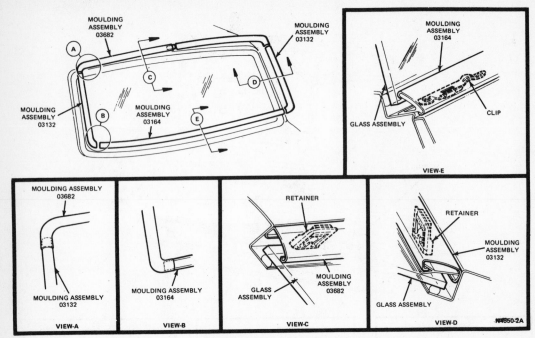

Windshield exterior mouldings

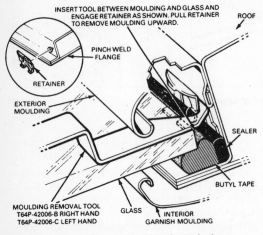

INSERT TOOL BETWEEN MOULDING AND GLASS AND ENGAGE RETAINER AS SHOWN. PULL RETAINER TO REMOVE MOULDING UPWARD.

Windshield moulding removal tool—typical

c. Repeat this process for the other bottom molding.

d. Install the center molding clip to cover the gap between the two bottom molding pieces.

e. Install the one piece upper molding in the same manner as the bottom pieces.

f. The side and corner moldings can be inserted in the retaining groove and secured by the attaching screws at the upper pillars.

g. Fill the gap at the upper outboard corner, between the trim molding and the body with sealer.

15. Clean all excess sealer from the molding,

install the wiper arms and leak test the windshield.

Bonded Type Windshield

NOTE: *Bonded windshields require special tools and procedures. Removal and replacement of this type of windshield should be refered to a qualified technician.*

REMOVAL AND INSTALLATION

There are two procedures applicable to the installation of glass with butyl type seal.

Procedure No. 1 should be used with butyl kit 19562 packaged with $\frac{5}{16}$" (8mm) diameter butyl (round type). Do Not use this kit if adhesion of existing butyl-to-pinch weld flange is unreliable, as indicated by a surface which is not smooth and free of excessive skips, bumps or contamination.

Procedure No. 2 should be used with butyl kit 19562 package with I-beam type butyl, where complete replacement of existing butyl is necessary.

Procedure No. 1

1. Remove the windshield wiper arms and blades.

2. Remove the windshield exterior mouldings.

3. With an electric knife (special tool T70P-42006-A, or equivalent) insert the blade under the edge of the glass. Cut the butyl as close to the inside surface of the glass as possible. To

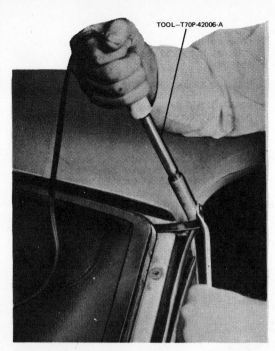

Removing Butyl type seal—typical

cut the butyl at the lower corners of the windshield, move the handle of the tool as close to the corner as possible. Then, rotate the blade downward to cut the corner butyl seal and remove the glass from the vehicle using the glass holding tool.

4. Temporarily position the replacement glass in the windshield opening using spacers to prevent glass-to-metal contact. Adjust the glass side to side to the best glass-to-A-pillar

weld flange overlap position and adjust the lower spacers if necessary, for proper position at the top. A minimum butyl tape to glass contact of $\frac{3}{16}''$ (4.8mm) on A-pillar, $\frac{3}{8}''$ (9.5mm) on header and cowl is required around the perimeter to assure proper retention and a water proof seal. Mark this location with a crayon on the outside surface of the glass and a corresponding point of the glass opening. Remove the glass and clean the inside surface of the glass thoroughly.

To Install:

1. Start at the side of the glass opposite the original butyl splice and place a $\frac{5}{16}''$ (8mm) diameter butyl finished in the kit and on top of and in a position that assures the $\frac{3}{16}''$ (4.8mm) minimum contact with the glass on the existing butyl remaining on the pinch weld flange.

NOTE: *Do not allow the new butyl to overhang the edge of the existing butyl or bridge the corners of the windshield opening.*

2. Carefully splice the two loose ends of the new butyl. The cut line of the splice must taper downward toward the outboard side of the vehicle.

3. Apply the primer (furnished in the kit) around the perimeter of the cleaned inside surface and the edge of the glass in the area that will contact the butyl seal. Allow the primer to dry a minimum of five minutes before installing the glass.

4. Place the glass in the opening aligning the crayon marks.

5. Firmly press the glass against the butyl with hand pressure or weights (approximately 250 lbs). Recheck to assure that the $\frac{3}{16}''$ (4.8mm) contact between glass and butyl is achieved. A dull spot indicates an area where the butyl is not contacting the glass surface. Additional pressure should seal such areas.

6. From outside the vehicle, apply C9AZ-

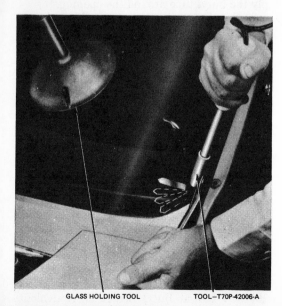

Cutting the corner seal—typical

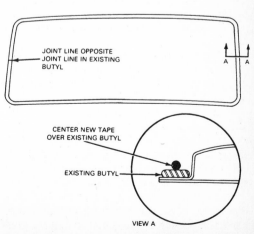

Procedure No. 1—Butyl tape installation

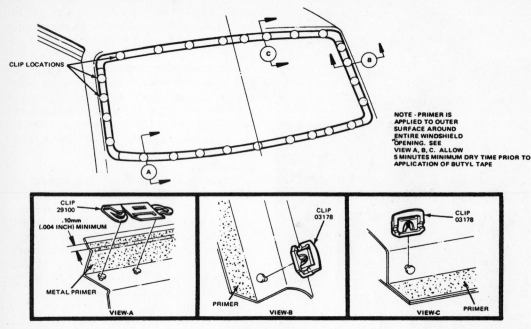

NOTE - PRIMER IS
APPLIED TO OUTER
SURFACE AROUND
ENTIRE WINDSHIELD
OPENING. SEE
VIEW A, B, C. ALLOW
5 MINUTES MINIMUM DRY TIME PRIOR TO
APPLICATION OF BUTYL TAPE

Windshield sealers

19554-B Liquid Butyl Sealer or equivalent around the entire edge of the glass.

7. Remove any excess primer from the inside surface of the glass with a razor blade and wipe the glass with a clean cloth dampened with naphtha.

8. When the liquid sealer has skinned over (approximately ten minutes), water test the installation. Repair any leaks with additional liquid sealer.

9. Install the mouldings and wiper arms and blades.

10. Clean the glass and surrounding areas.

Procedure No. 2

Use this procedure if adhesive of existing butyl is unreliable.

1. Remove the windshield wiper arms and blades.

2. Remove the windshield exterior moldings. On vehicles with heated rear windows, disconnect heating wires before proceeding with windshield removal.

3. With an electric knife (special tool T70P-42006-A, or equivalent) insert the blade under the edge of the glass. Cut the butyl as close to the inside surface of the glass as possible. To cut the butyl at the lower corners of the windshield, move the handle of the tool as close to the corner as possible. Then, rotate the blade downward to cut the corner butyl seal and remove the glass from the vehicle using the glass holding tool.

4. Clean all remaining butyl from the pinch weld flange.

5. Inspect flange carefully for sheet metal deficiencies, and the sealing surface of the pinch weld flange for chipped or missing paint and repair as necessary. Pinch weld flange must be primed with metal primer complying with ESB-2C171-AB or equivalent before applying butyl tape.

To Install:

1. Starting at the midpoint on A-pillar, apply the butyl tape around the opening.

2. Cut the butyl at the required length at a 45° angle and carefully splice the two loose ends. The splice cut line must taper down and toward the outboard side of the vehicle.

3. Apply the glass primer (furnished in the kit) around the perimeter of the cleaned inside surface and the edge of the glass in the area that will contact the butyl seal.

4. Allow the primer to dry a minimum of five minutes before installing the glass.

5. Place the glass in the opening aligning the crayon marks.

6. Firmly press the glass against the butyl with hand pressure or weights (approximately 250 lbs). Recheck to assure that the $^3/_{16}''$ (4.8mm) contact between glass and butyl is achieved. A dull spot indicates an area where the butyl is not contacting the glass surface. Additional pressure should seal such areas.

7. From outside the vehicle, apply C9AZ-19554-B Liquid Butyl Sealer or equivalent around the entire edge of the glass.

8. Remove any excess primer from the inside surface of the glass with a razor blade and wipe the glass with a clean cloth dampened with naphtha.

9. When the liquid sealer has skinned over (approximately ten minutes), water test the installation. Repair any leaks with additional liquid sealer.

10. Install the mouldings and wiper arms and blades.

11. Clean the glass and surrounding areas.

Rear Window Glass

REMOVAL AND INSTALLATION

1. Open the tailgate and remove the interior access cover panel. If the tailgate will not open because the glass will not go full down, remove the interior access cover panel and manually depress the safety lockout rod in the bottom center of the tailgate.

2. Raise the glass using a jumper to motor connection (or manually close the tailgate latches). If the glass will not go up, remove the four glass attaching screws and nuts located approximately 4″ (102mm) from the lower edge of the access opening. Using your fingers, locate and remove the nuts through the bottom access openings. Then, push the screws out of the mounting holes, slide the glass up to reach and remove four rivets attaching the glass to the glass brackets.

3. Using a drift punch, remove the center pin from each rivet attaching glass to bracket. Then drill out the rivet using a ¼″ (6mm) drill. Use care when drilling so not to damage the

spacer and retainer. If the glass is stalled in the down position, remove the two nut and washer assemblies from the glass bracket assembly and rock the glass outboard to clear the C-channel retainer studs to gain access to the glass rivets.

4. Slide the glass from the tailgate assembly.

To Install:

1. Position the glass in the open tailgate and install rivets to the window glass brackets.

2. Check the window operation and adjust if necessary.

3. install the interior access cover plate.

Rear Quarter Stationary Glass

REMOVAL AND INSTALLATION

NOTE: *This procedure applies to the rear quarter stationary glass in the Bronco.*

1. Remove the interior trim moldings from around the window. Where necessary, remove the spare tire and mounting bracket.

2. Break loose the seal between the weatherstripping and the body panels.

3. Have someone outside push inward on the glass while you catch it.

4. Clean all old sealer from the glass and weatherstripping.

5. Fill the glass cavity in the weatherstripping with a ³⁄₁₆″ (4.8m) bead of sealer.

6. Fit the glass in the weatherstripping and place a ¼″ (6mm) diameter cord in the frame cavity around the outside diameter of the weatherstripping. Allow the ends of the cord to

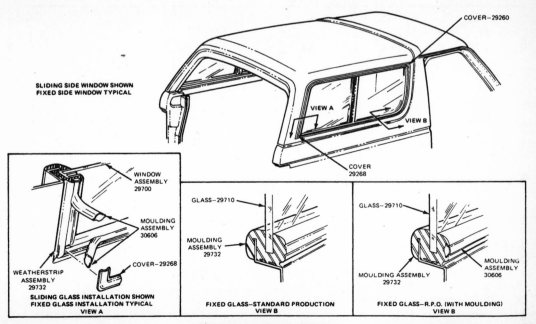

Rear side window installation

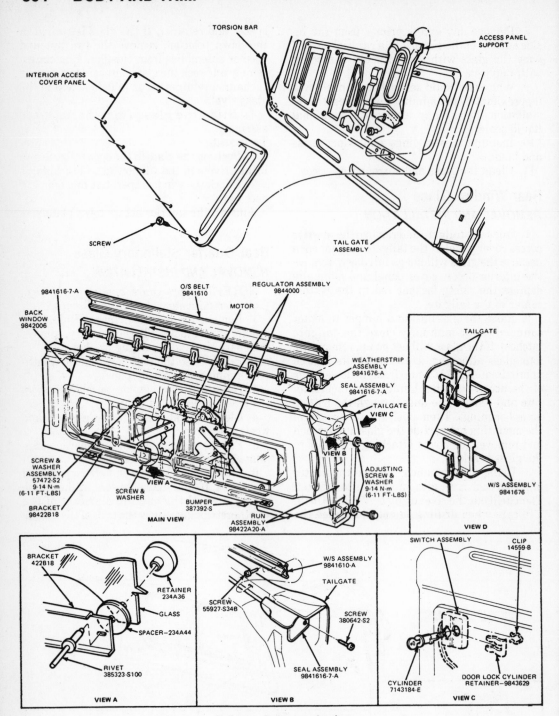

Tailgate window mechanism

hang down the outside of the glass from the top center.

7. Place the glass and weatherstripping in the vehicle opening. Pull on the cord ends to pull the lip of the weatherstripping over the body panel.

8. Install the trim molding.

INTERIOR

Door Panels

REMOVAL AND INSTALLATION

1. Remove the screws retaining the arm rest area on the trim panel to the door inner panel.

2. Remove the screws retaining the door inside handle and remove the handle.

3. Remove the screw retaining the door window regulator handle and remove the handle and washer (if so equipped).

4. Remove the door lock control (if so equipped).

NOTE: *Units with power door locks, must remove the power door lock switch.*

5. Remove the switch housing for the power rear view outside mirror, (if so equipped).

6. At each plastic clip location, carefully pry the trim panel away from the door inner panel and remove the trim panel.

NOTE: *At no time should the trim panel be used to pull the clips from the inner panel holes.*

To Install:

1. Replace any bent broken or missing trim clips on the door trim panel. Position the trim panel to the door inner panel, locating the clips in the countersunk holes. Firmly push the trim panel at the clip locations to seat each clip into the holes in the door inner panel.

2. Install the switch housing for the power rear view outside mirror (if so equipped).

3. Install the door lock control (if so equipped).

4. Position the door window regulator handle to the door and install the retaining screw.

5. Install the inside door handle and secure with screw.

6. Position the arm rest area to trim panel and secure with screws.

Door Glass And Vent Window
REMOVAL AND INSTALLATION

1. Remove the door panel.

2. Remove the screws from the front division bar.

3. Remove the two vent window assembly attaching screws from the front edge of the door.

4. Lower the door glass and pull the glass run out of the run retainer near the vent window division bar enough to allow removal of the vent window assembly.

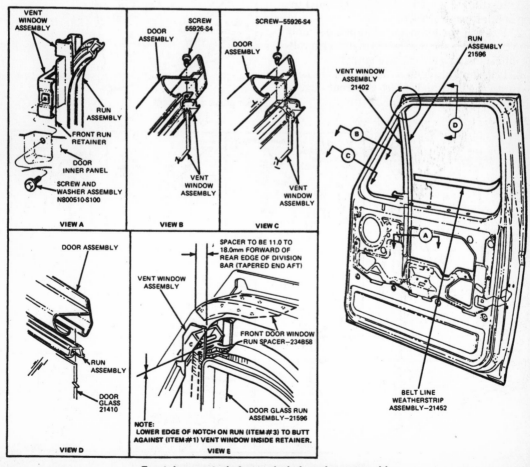

Front door vent window and window glass assembly

GLASS AND CHANNEL REMOVAL TOOL (NO. 2900) OR
EQUIVALENT AVAILABLE FROM SOMMER AND MALA
GLASS MACHINE COMPANY, 5501 W. OGDEN AVENUE,
CHICAGO 50, ILLINOIS

Glass and channel removal tool

5. Tilt the vent window and division bar assembly toward the rear of the door and remove the vent window from the door.

6. Rotate the front edge of the glass downward and lift the glass from the door.

7. Remove the glass from the glass channel using Glass and Channel Removal Tool No. 2900 or equivalent. The tool can be purchased from The Sommer and Mala Glass Machine Company, 5501 W. Ogden Ave. Chicago, Illinois 60650.

To Install:

1. Install the glass in the glass channel using special tool No. 2900.

2. Position the glass and channel assembly into the door, inserting the regulator arm roller into the slot of the glass channel.

3. Position the vent window and division bar into the door and insert the front edge of the glass into the division bar run.

4. Install the two vent window attaching screws at the front edge of the door.

5. Insert the glass run into the run retainer near the division bar.

6. Install the screw at the front run retainer and adjust the window.

To Adjust:

1. Loosen the front run retainer and division bar lower attaching screw and the rear run retainer lower attaching screw.

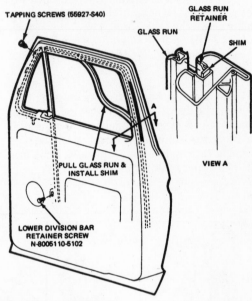

Door glass adjustment

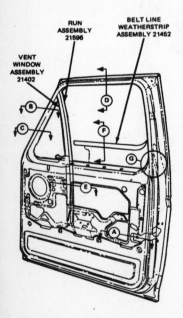

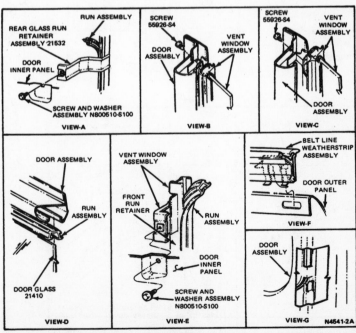

Door glass and vent window installation

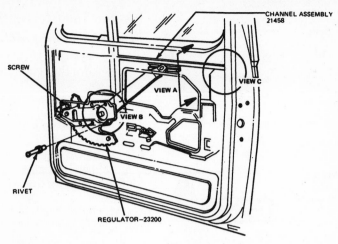

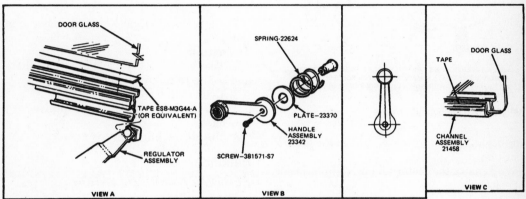

Window regulator removal and installation

2. Lower the window glass until the top edge of the glass is approximately 4″ (102mm) above the belt line.

3. Tighten the screws, and check the operation of the window mechanism.

4. Install the trim panel and water shield on the door.

Regulator

REMOVAL AND INSTALLATION

1. Remove the door trim panel and access cover, if so equipped.

2. Support the glass in the full up position.

3. Remove the center pin from the regulator attaching rivets with a drift punch. Then drill the head from the rivet using a ¼″ (6mm) drill and remove the rivet. Be careful not to route out sheet metal holes during drilling.

4. Disengage the regulator arm from the glass bracket and remove the regulator.

To Install:

1. Position regulator into the door and insert the arm into the glass bracket channel.

2. Position the regulator to the inner panel and install rivets to attach the regulator to the inner panel. A ¼-20 x ½″ screw and washer assembly and a ¼-20 nut and washer assembly may be used in place of the rivets.

3. Check the operation of the window mechanism and install the door trim panel.

Electric Window Motor

REMOVAL AND INSTALLATION

1. Disconnect the negative battery cable.

2. Remove the door trim panel.

3. Disconnect the power window motor wire from the wiring harness connector.

4. Check inside the door to make sure that the electrical wires are not in line with holes to be drilled in the inner door panel. Using a ½″ (13mm) diameter drill bit drill two holes in the door inner panel at the drill dimples located opposite the two unexposed motor drive retainer screws.

5. Remove the three motor mount retainer screws using two drill holes and existing larger hole access to screw heads.

6. Push the motor toward the outside sheet metal to disengage the motor and drive from the regulator gear. After the motor and drive

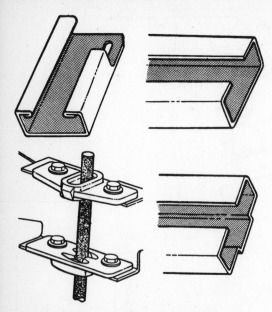

APPLY AN EVEN COATING OF POLYETHELENE GREASE D0AZ-19584-A, OR EQUIVALENT TO ALL WINDOW REGULATOR ROLLERS, SHAFTS AND THE ENTIRE LENGTH OF ROLLER GUIDES AS ILLUSTRATED BY THE SHADED AREAS.

Window mechanism lubrication

are disengaged, prop the window in the full UP position.

7. Remove the motor and drive from inside the door.

To Install:

1. Install a new motor and drive assembly. Tighten the motor retaining screws to 50–85 in.lb.

2. Install two pieces of D6AZ-19627-A (or equivalent) body tape over the drill holes.

3. Reconnect the power window motor wiring, and the battery ground cable.

4. Remove the glass prop and check window operation.

5. Check to make sure that the door drain holes are open.

6. Install the trim panel.

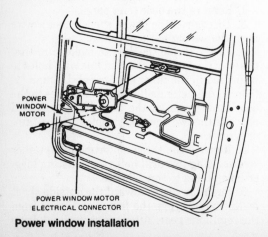

POWER WINDOW MOTOR

POWER WINDOW MOTOR ELECTRICAL CONNECTOR

Power window installation

Electric Tailgate Window Motor

REMOVAL AND INSTALLATION

1. Remove the tailgate access cover.

2. Remove the retainers from the regulator arm studs.

3. Disconnect the regulator arm studs from the bottom channel.

4. Disconnect the defogger wires (if equipped).

5. Raise the glass to the full up position.

6. Support the glass in the raised position and disconnect the wiring at the wiring harness.

CAUTION: *The counterbalance spring is under tension, to prevent injury from sudden movement of regulator components, clamp or lock gear sectors to allow safe motor removal.*

7. Detach and remove electric motor from tailgate.

To Install:

1. Position the electric motor in the tailgate and secure to the regulator.

2. Connect the wiring harness.

3. Check the operation of the electric window motor.

4. Install the interior access cover.

Headliner

REMOVAL AND INSTALLATION

1. Remove the three screws retaining each sun visor to the roof and remove the sun visors.

2. Remove the screws retaining the garnish mouldings and remove the mouldings.

3. Remove the two drive pins retaining the headliner the headliner to the roof structure and remove the headliner.

To Install:

1. Position the headliner to the roof and install two drive pins to retain the headliner.

2. Position the garnish moulding and install the retaining screws.

3. Position the sun visors to the headliner and install the retaining screws.

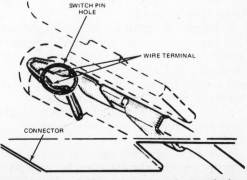

SWITCH PIN HOLE

WIRE TERMINAL

CONNECTOR

Power window switch connector wire terminal removal

How to Remove Stains from Fabric Interior

For rest results, spots and stains should be removed as soon as possible. Never use gasoline, lacquer thinner, acetone, nail polish remover or bleach. Use a 3′ x 3″ piece of cheesecloth. Squeeze most of the liquid from the fabric and wipe the stained fabric from the outside of the stain toward the center with a lifting motion. Turn the cheesecloth as soon as one side becomes soiled. When using water to remove a stain, be sure to wash the entire section after the spot has been removed to avoid water stains. Encrusted spots can be broken up with a dull knife and vacuumed before removing the stain.

Type of Stain	How to Remove It
Surface spots	Brush the spots out with a small hand brush or use a commercial preparation such as K2R to lift the stain.
Mildew	Clean around the mildew with warm suds. Rinse in cold water and soak the mildew area in a solution of 1 part table salt and 2 parts water. Wash with upholstery cleaner.
Water stains	Water stains in fabric materials can be removed with a solution made from 1 cup of table salt dissolved in 1 quart of water. Vigorously scrub the solution into the stain and rinse with clear water. Water stains in nylon or other synthetic fabrics should be removed with a commercial type spot remover.
Chewing gum, tar, crayons, shoe polish (greasy stains)	Do not use a cleaner that will soften gum or tar. Harden the deposit with an ice cube and scrape away as much as possible with a dull knife. Moisten the remainder with cleaning fluid and scrub clean.
Ice cream, candy	Most candy has a sugar base and can be removed with a cloth wrung out in warm water. Oily candy, after cleaning with warm water, should be cleaned with upholstery cleaner. Rinse with warm water and clean the remainder with cleaning fluid.
Wine, alcohol, egg, milk, soft drink (non-greasy stains)	Do not use soap. Scrub the stain with a cloth wrung out in warm water. Remove the remainder with cleaning fluid.
Grease, oil, lipstick, butter and related stains	Use a spot remover to avoid leaving a ring. Work from the outisde of the stain to the center and dry with a clean cloth when the spot is gone.
Headliners (cloth)	Mix a solution of warm water and foam upholstery cleaner to give thick suds. Use only foam—liquid may streak or spot. Clean the entire headliner in one operation using a circular motion with a natural sponge.
Headliner (vinyl)	Use a vinyl cleaner with a sponge and wipe clean with a dry cloth.
Seats and door panels	Mix 1 pint upholstery cleaner in 1 gallon of water. Do not soak the fabric around the buttons.
Leather or vinyl fabric	Use a multi-purpose cleaner full strength and a stiff brush. Let stand 2 minutes and scrub thoroughly. Wipe with a clean, soft rag.
Nylon or synthetic fabrics	For normal stains, use the same procedures you would for washing cloth upholstery. If the fabric is extremely dirty, use a multi-purpose cleaner full strength with a stiff scrub brush. Scrub thoroughly in all directions and wipe with a cotton towel or soft rag.

Mechanic's Data

General Conversion Table

Multiply By	To Convert	To	
	LENGTH		
2.54	Inches	Centimeters	.3937
25.4	Inches	Millimeters	.03937
30.48	Feet	Centimeters	.0328
.304	Feet	Meters	3.28
.914	Yards	Meters	1.094
1.609	Miles	Kilometers	.621
	VOLUME		
.473	Pints	Liters	2.11
.946	Quarts	Liters	1.06
3.785	Gallons	Liters	.264
.016	Cubic inches	Liters	61.02
16.39	Cubic inches	Cubic cms.	.061
28.3	Cubic feet	Liters	.0353
	MASS (Weight)		
28.35	Ounces	Grams	.035
.4536	Pounds	Kilograms	2.20
—	**To obtain**	**From**	**Multiply by**

Multiply By	To Convert	To	
	AREA		
.645	Square inches	Square cms.	.155
.836	Square yds.	Square meters	1.196
	FORCE		
4.448	Pounds	Newtons	.225
.138	Ft./lbs.	Kilogram/meters	7.23
1.36	Ft./lbs.	Newton-meters	.737
.112	In./lbs.	Newton-meters	8.844
	PRESSURE		
.068	Psi	Atmospheres	14.7
6.89	Psi	Kilopascals	.145
	OTHER		
1.104	Horsepower (DIN)	Horsepower (SAE)	.9861
.746	Horsepower (SAE)	Kilowatts (KW)	1.34
1.60	Mph	Km/h	.625
.425	Mpg	Km/1	2.35
—	**To obtain**	**From**	**Multiply by**

Tap Drill Sizes

National Coarse or U.S.S.

Screw & Tap Size	Threads Per Inch	Use Drill Number
No. 5	40	.39
No. 6	32	.36
No. 8	32	.29
No. 10	24	.25
No. 12	24	.17
1/4	20	8
5/16	18	.F
3/8	16	5/16
7/16	14	.U
1/2	13	27/64
9/16	12	31/64
5/8	11	17/32
3/4	10	21/32
7/8	9	49/64

National Coarse or U.S.S.

Screw & Tap Size	Threads Per Inch	Use Drill Number
1	8	7/8
'1 1/8	7	63/64
1 1/4	7	1 7/64
1 1/2	6	1 11/32

National Fine or S.A.E.

Screw & Tap Size	Threads Per Inch	Use Drill Number
No. 5	44	.37
No. 6	40	.33
No. 8	36	.29
No. 10	32	.21

National Fine or S.A.E.

Screw & Tap Size	Threads Per Inch	Use Drill Number
No. 12	28	.15
1/4	28	3
6/16	24	1
3/8	24	.Q
7/16	20	.W
1/2	20	29/64
9/16	18	33/64
5/8	18	37/64
3/4	16	11/16
7/8	14	13/16
1 1/8	12	13/64
1 1/4	12	1 11/64
1 1/2	12	1 27/64

Drill Sizes In Decimal Equivalents

Inch	Dec-imal	Wire	mm	Inch	Dec-imal	Wire	mm	Inch	Dec-imal	Wire & Letter	mm	Inch	Dec-imal	Let-ter	mm	Inch	Dec-imal	mm
1/64	.0156		.39		.0730	49			.1614		4.1		.2717		6.9		.4331	11.0
	.0157		.4		.0748		1.9		.1654		4.2		.2720	I		7/16	.4375	11.11
	.0160	78			.0760	48			.1660	19			.2756		7.0		.4528	11.5
	.0165		.42		.0768		1.95		.1673		4.25		.2770	J		29/64	.4531	11.51
	.0173		.44	5/64	.0781		1.98		.1693		4.3		.2795		7.1	15/32	.4688	11.90
	.0177		.45		.0785	47			.1695	18			.2810	K			.4724	12.0
	.0180	77			.0787		2.0	11/64	.1719		4.36	9/32	.2812		7.14	31/64	.4844	12.30
	.0181		.46		.0807		2.05		.1730	17			.2835		7.2		.4921	12.5
	.0189		.48		.0810	46			.1732		4.4		.2854		7.25	1/2	.5000	12.70
	.0197		.5		.0820	45			.1770	16			.2874		7.3		.5118	13.0
	.0200	76			.0827		2.1		.1772		4.5		.2900	L		33/64	.5156	13.09
	.0210	75			.0846		2.15		.1800	15			.2913		7.4	17/32	.5312	13.49
	.0217		.55		.0860	44			.1811		4.6		.2950	M			.5315	13.5
	.0225	74			.0866		2.2		.1820	14			.2953		7.5	35/64	.5469	13.89
	.0236		.6		.0886		2.25		.1850	13		19/64	.2969		7.54		.5512	14.0
	.0240	73			.0890	43			.1850		4.7		.2992		7.6	9/16	.5625	14.28
	.0250	72			.0906		2.3		.1870		4.75		.3020	N			.5709	14.5
	.0256		.65		.0925		2.35	3/16	.1875		4.76		.3031		7.7	37/64	.5781	14.68
	.0260	71			.0935	42			.1890		4.8		.3051		7.75		.5906	15.0
	.0276		.7	3/32	.0938		2.38		.1890	12			.3071		7.8	19/32	.5938	15.08
	.0280	70			.0945		2.4		.1910	11			.3110		7.9	39/64	.6094	15.47
	.0292	69			.0960	41			.1929		4.9	5/16	.3125		7.93		.6102	15.5
	.0295		.75		.0965		2.45		.1935	10			.3150		8.0	5/8	.6250	15.87
	.0310	68			.0980	40			.1960	9			.3160	O			.6299	16.0
1/32	.0312		.79		.0981		2.5		.1969		5.0		.3189		8.1	41/64	.6406	16.27
	.0315		.8		.0995	39			.1990	8			.3228		8.2		.6496	16.5
	.0320	67			.1015	38			.2008		5.1		.3230	P		21/32	.6562	16.66
	.0330	66			.1024		2.6		.2010	7			.3248		8.25		.6693	17.0
	.0335		.85		.1040	37		13/64	.2031		5.16		.3268		8.3	43/64	.6719	17.06
	.0350	65			.1063		2.7		.2040	6		21/64	.3281		8.33	11/16	.6875	17.46
	.0354		.9		.1065	36			.2047		5.2		.3307		8.4		.6890	17.5
	.0360	64			.1083		2.75		.2055	5			.3320	Q		45/64	.7031	17.85
	.0370	63		7/64	.1094		2.77		.2067		5.25		.3346		8.5		.7087	18.0
	.0374		.95		.1100	35			.2087		5.3		.3386		8.6	23/32	.7188	18.25
	.0380	62			.1102		2.8		.2090	4			.3390	R			.7283	18.5
	.0390	61			.1110	34			.2126		5.4		.3425		8.7	47/64	.7344	18.65
	.0394		1.0		.1130	33			.2130	3		11/32	.3438		8.73		.7480	19.0
	.0400	60			.1142		2.9		.2165		5.5		.3445		8.75	3/4	.7500	19.05
	.0410	59			.1160	32		7/32	.2188		5.55		.3465		8.8	49/64	.7656	19.44
	.0413		1.05		.1181		3.0		.2205		5.6		.3480	S			.7677	19.5
	.0420	58			.1200	31			.2210	2			.3504		8.9	25/32	.7812	19.84
	.0430	57			.1220		3.1		.2244		5.7		.3543		9.0		.7874	20.0
	.0433		1.1	1/8	.1250		3.17		.2264		5.75		.3580	T		51/64	.7969	20.24
	.0453		1.15		.1260		3.2		.2280	1			.3583		9.1		.8071	20.5
	.0465	56			.1280		3.25		.2283		5.8	23/64	.3594		9.12	13/16	.8125	20.63
3/64	.0469		1.19		.1285	30			.2323		5.9		.3622		9.2		.8268	21.0
	.0472		1.2		.1299		3.3		.2340	A			.3642		9.25	53/64	.8281	21.03
	.0492		1.25		.1339		3.4	15/64	.2344		5.95		.3661		9.3	27/32	.8438	21.43
	.0512		1.3		.1360	29			.2362		6.0		.3680	U			.8465	21.5
	.0520	55			.1378		3.5		.2380	B			.3701		9.4	55/64	.8594	21.82
	.0531		1.35		.1405	28			.2402		6.1		.3740		9.5		.8661	22.0
	.0550	54		9/64	.1406		3.57		.2420	C		3/8	.3750		9.52	7/8	.8750	22.22
	.0551		1.4		.1417		3.6		.2441		6.2		.3770	V			.8858	22.5
	.0571		1.45		.1440	27			.2460	D			.3780		9.6	57/64	.8906	22.62
	.0591		1.5		.1457		3.7		.2461		6.25		.3819		9.7		.9055	23.0
	.0595	53			.1470	26			.2480		6.3		.3839		9.75	29/32	.9062	23.01
	.0610		1.55		.1476		3.75	1/4	.2500	E	6.35		.3858		9.8	59/64	.9219	23.41
1/16	.0625		1.59		.1495	25			.2520		6.		.3860	W			.9252	23.5
	.0630		1.6		.1496		3.8		.2559		6.5		.3898		9.9	15/16	.9375	23.81
	.0635	52			.1520	24			.2570	F		25/64	.3906		9.92		.9449	24.0
	.0650		1.65		.1535		3.9		.2598		6.6		.3937		10.0	61/64	.9531	24.2
	.0669		1.7		.1540	23			.2610	G			.3970	X			.9646	24.5
	.0670	51		5/32	.1562		3.96		.2638		6.7		.4040	Y		31/32	.9688	24.6
	.0689		1.75		.1570	22		17/64	.2656		6.74	13/32	.4062		10.31		.9843	25.0
	.0700	50			.1575		4.0		.2657		6.75		.4130	Z		63/64	.9844	25.0
	.0709		1.8		.1590	21			.2660	H			.4134		10.5	1	1.0000	25.4
	.0728		1.85		.1610	20			.2677		6.8	27/64	.4219		10.71			

GLOSSARY OF TERMS

AIR/FUEL RATIO: The ratio of air to gasoline by weight in the fuel mixture drawn into the engine.

AIR INJECTION: One method of reducing harmful exhaust emissions by injecting air into each of the exhaust ports of an engine. The fresh air entering the hot exhaust manifold causes any remaining fuel to be burned before it can exit the tailpipe.

ALTERNATOR: A device used for converting mechanical energy into electrical energy.

AMMETER: An instrument, calibrated in amperes, used to measure the flow of an electrical current in a circuit. Ammeters are always connected in series with the circuit being tested.

AMPERE: The rate of flow of electrical current present when one volt of electrical pressure is applied against one ohm of electrical resistance.

ANALOG COMPUTER: Any microprocessor that uses similar (analogous) electrical signals to make its calculations.

ARMATURE: A laminated, soft iron core wrapped by a wire that converts electrical energy to mechanical energy as in a motor or relay. When rotated in a magnetic field, it changes mechanical energy into electrical energy as in a generator.

ATMOSPHERIC PRESSURE: The pressure on the Earth's surface caused by the weight of the air in the atmosphere. At sea level, this pressure is 14.7 psi at 32°F (101 kPa at 0°C).

ATOMIZATION: The breaking down of a liquid into a fine mist that can be suspended in air.

AXIAL PLAY: Movement parallel to a shaft or bearing bore.

BACKFIRE: The sudden combustion of gases in the intake or exhaust system that results in a loud explosion.

BACKLASH: The clearance or play between two parts, such as meshed gears.

BACKPRESSURE: Restrictions in the exhaust system that slow the exit of exhaust gases from the combustion chamber.

BAKELITE: A heat resistant, plastic insulator material commonly used in printed circuit boards and transistorized components.

BALL BEARING: A bearing made up of hardened inner and outer races between which hardened steel ball roll.

BALLAST RESISTOR: A resistor in the primary ignition circuit that lowers voltage after the engine is started to reduce wear on ignition components.

BEARING: A friction reducing, supportive device usually located between a stationary part and a moving part.

BIMETAL TEMPERATURE SENSOR: Any sensor or switch made of two dissimilar types of metal that bend when heated or cooled due to the different expansion rates of the alloys. These types of sensors usually function as an on/off switch.

BLOWBY: Combustion gases, composed of water vapor and unburned fuel, that leak past the piston rings into the crankcase during normal engine operation. These gases are removed by the PCV system to prevent the build-up of harmful acids in the crankcase.

BRAKE PAD: A brake shoe and lining assembly used with disc brakes.

BRAKE SHOE: The backing for the brake lining. The term is, however, usually applied to the assembly of the brake backing and lining.

BUSHING: A liner, usually removable, for a bearing; an anti-friction liner used in place of a bearing.

BYPASS: System used to bypass ballast resistor during engine cranking to increase voltage supplied to the coil.

CALIPER: A hydraulically activated device in a disc brake system, which is mounted straddling the brake rotor (disc). The caliper contains at least one piston and two brake pads. Hydraulic pressure on the piston(s) forces the pads against the rotor.

CAMSHAFT: A shaft in the engine on which are the lobes (cams) which operate the valves. The camshaft is driven by the crankshaft, via a belt, chain or gears, at one half the crankshaft speed.

CAPACITOR: A device which stores an electrical charge.

CARBON MONOXIDE (CO): a colorless, odorless gas given off as a normal byproduct of combustion. It is poisonous and extremely dangerous in confined areas, building up slowly to toxic levels without warning if adequate ventilation is not available.

CARBURETOR: A device, usually mounted on the intake manifold of an engine, which mixes the air and fuel in the proper proportion to allow even combustion.

CATALYTIC CONVERTER: A device installed in the exhaust system, like a muffler, that converts harmful byproducts of combustion into carbon dioxide and water vapor by means of a heat-producing chemical reaction.

CENTRIFUGAL ADVANCE: A mechanical method of advancing the spark timing by using flyweights in the distributor that react to centrifugal force generated by the distributor shaft rotation.

CHECK VALVE: Any one-way valve installed to permit the flow of air, fuel or vacuum in one direction only.

CHOKE: A device, usually a moveable valve, placed in the intake path of a carburetor to restrict the flow of air.

CIRCUIT: Any unbroken path through which an electrical current can flow. Also used to describe fuel flow in some instances.

CIRCUIT BREAKER: A switch which protects an electrical circuit from overload by opening the circuit when the current flow exceeds a predetermined level. Some circuit breakers must be reset manually, while other reset automatically

COIL (IGNITION): A transformer in the ignition circuit which steps of the voltage provided to the spark plugs.

COMBINATION MANIFOLD: An assembly which includes both the intake and exhaust manifolds in one casting.

COMBINATION VALVE: A device used in some fuel systems that routes fuel vapors to a charcoal storage canister instead of venting them into the atmosphere. The valve relieves fuel tank pressure and allows fresh air into the tank as fuel level drops to prevent a vapor lock situation.

COMPRESSION RATIO: The comparison of the total volume of the cylinder and combustion chamber with the piston at BDC and the piston at TDC.

CONDENSER: 1. An electrical device which acts to store an electrical charge, preventing voltage surges.
2. A radiator-like device in the air conditioning system in which refrigerant gas condenses into a liquid, giving off heat.

CONDUCTOR: Any material through which an electrical current can be transmitted easily.

CONTINUITY: Continuous or complete circuit. Can be checked with an ohmmeter.

COUNTERSHAFT: An intermediate shaft which is rotated by a mainshaft and transmits, in turn, that rotation to a working part.

CRANKCASE: The lower part of an engine in which the crankshaft and related parts operate.

CRANKSHAFT: The main driving shaft of an engine which receives reciprocating motion from the pistons and converts it to rotary motion.

CYLINDER: In an engine, the round hole in the engine block in which the piston(s) ride.

CYLINDER BLOCK: The main structural member of an engine in which is found the cylinders, crankshaft and other principal parts.

CYLINDER HEAD: The detachable portion of the engine, fastened, usually, to the top of the cylinder block, containing all or most of the combustion chambers. On overhead valve engines, it contains the valves and their operating parts. On overhead cam engines, it contains the camshaft as well.

DEAD CENTER: The extreme top or bottom of the piston stroke.

DETONATION: An unwanted explosion of the air fuel mixture in the combustion chamber caused by excess heat and compression, advanced timing, or an overly lean mixture. Also referred to as "ping".

DIAPHRAGM: A thin, flexible wall separating two cavities, such as in a vacuum advance unit.

DIESELING: A condition in which hot spots in the combustion chamber cause the engine to run on after the key is turned off.

DIFFERENTIAL: A geared assembly which allows the transmission of motion between drive axles, giving one axle the ability to turn faster than the other.

DIODE: An electrical device that will allow current to flow in one direction only.

DISC BRAKE: A hydraulic braking assembly consisting of a brake disc, or rotor, mounted on an axle, and a caliper assembly containing, usually two brake pads which are activated by hydraulic pressure. The pads are forced against the sides of the disc, creating friction which slows the vehicle.

DISTRIBUTOR: A mechanically driven device on an engine which is responsible for electrically firing the spark plug at a predetermined point of the piston stroke.

DOWEL PIN: A pin, inserted in mating holes in two different parts allowing those parts to maintain a fixed relationship.

DRUM BRAKE: A braking system which consists of two brake shoes and one or two wheel cylinders, mounted on a fixed backing plate, and a brake drum, mounted on an axle, which revolves around the assembly. Hydraulic action applied to the wheel cylinders forces the shoes outward against the drum, creating friction and slowing the vehicle.

DWELL: The rate, measured in degrees of shaft rotation, at which an electrical circuit cycles on and off.

ELECTRONIC CONTROL UNIT (ECU): Ignition module, module, amplifier or igniter. See Module for definition.

ELECTRONIC IGNITION: A system in which the timing and firing of the spark plugs is controlled by an electronic control unit, usually called a module. These systems have not points or condenser.

ENDPLAY: The measured amount of axial movement in a shaft.

ENGINE: A device that converts heat into mechanical energy.

EXHAUST MANIFOLD: A set of cast passages or pipes which conduct exhaust gases from the engine.

FEELER GAUGE: A blade, usually metal, of precisely predetermined thickness, used to measure the clearance between two parts. These blades usually are available in sets of assorted thicknesses.

F-Head: An engine configuration in which the intake valves are in the cylinder head, while the camshaft and exhaust valves are located in the cylinder block. The camshaft operates the intake valves via lifters and pushrods, while it operates the exhaust valves directly.

FIRING ORDER: The order in which combustion occurs in the cylinders of an engine. Also the order in which spark is distributed to the plugs by the distributor.

FLATHEAD: An engine configuration in which the camshaft and all the valves are located in the cylinder block.

FLOODING: The presence of too much fuel in the intake manifold and combustion chamber which prevents the air/fuel mixture from firing, thereby causing a no-start situation.

FLYWHEEL: A disc shaped part bolted to the rear end of the crankshaft. Around the outer perimeter is affixed the ring gear. The starter drive engages the ring gear, turning the flywheel, which rotates the crankshaft, imparting the initial starting motion to the engine.

FOOT POUND (ft.lb. or sometimes, ft. lbs.): The amount of energy or work needed to raise an item weighing one pound, a distance of one foot.

FUSE: A protective device in a circuit which prevents circuit overload by breaking the circuit when a specific amperage is present. The device is constructed around a strip or wire of a lower amperage rating than the circuit it is designed to protect. When an amperage higher than that stamped on the fuse is present in the circuit, the strip or wire melts, opening the circuit.

GEAR RATIO: The ratio between the number of teeth on meshing gears.

GENERATOR: A device which converts mechanical energy into electrical energy.

HEAT RANGE: The measure of a spark plug's ability to dissipate heat from its firing end. The higher the heat range, the hotter the plug fires.

HUB: The center part of a wheel or gear.

HYDROCARBON (HC): Any chemical compound made up of hydrogen and carbon. A major pollutant formed by the engine as a byproduct of combustion.

HYDROMETER: An instrument used to measure the specific gravity of a solution.

INCH POUND (in.lb. or sometimes, in. lbs.): One twelfth of a foot pound.

INDUCTION: A means of transferring electrical energy in the form of a magnetic field. Principle used in the ignition coil to increase voltage.

INJECTION PUMP: A device, usually mechanically operated, which meters and delivers fuel under pressure to the fuel injector.

INJECTOR: A device which receives metered fuel under relatively low pressure and is activated to inject the fuel into the engine under relatively high pressure at a predetermined time.

INPUT SHAFT: The shaft to which torque is applied, usually carrying the driving gear or gears.

INTAKE MANIFOLD: A casting of passages or pipes used to conduct air or a fuel/air mixture to the cylinders.

JOURNAL: The bearing surface within which a shaft operates.

KEY: A small block usually fitted in a notch between a shaft and a hub to prevent slippage of the two parts.

MANIFOLD: A casting of passages or set of pipes which connect the cylinders to an inlet or outlet source.

MANIFOLD VACUUM: Low pressure in an engine intake manifold formed just below the throttle plates. Manifold vacuum is highest at idle and drops under acceleration.

MASTER CYLINDER: The primary fluid pressurizing device in a hydraulic system. In automotive use, it is found in brake and hydraulic clutch systems and is pedal activated, either directly or, in a power brake system, through the power booster.

MODULE: Electronic control unit, amplifier or igniter of solid state or integrated design which controls the current flow in the ignition primary circuit based on input from the pickup coil. When the module opens the primary circuit, the high secondary voltage is induced in the coil.

NEEDLE BEARING: A bearing which consists of a number (usually a large number) of long, thin rollers.

OHM: (Ω) The unit used to measure the resistance of conductor to electrical flow. One ohm is the amount of resistance that limits current flow to one ampere in a circuit with one volt of pressure.

OHMMETER: An instrument used for measuring the resistance, in ohms, in an electrical circuit.

OUTPUT SHAFT: The shaft which transmits torque from a device, such as a transmission.

OVERDRIVE: A gear assembly which produces more shaft revolutions than that transmitted to it.

OVERHEAD CAMSHAFT (OHC): An engine configuration in which the camshaft is mounted on top of the cylinder head and operates the valve either directly or by means of rocker arms.

OVERHEAD VALVE (OHV): An engine configuration in which all of the valves are located in the cylinder head and the camshaft is located in the cylinder block. The camshaft operates the valves via lifters and pushrods.

OXIDES OF NITROGEN (NOx): Chemical compounds of nitrogen produced as a byproduct of combustion. They combine with hydrocarbons to produce smog.

OXYGEN SENSOR: Used with the feedback system to sense the presence of oxygen in the exhaust gas and signal the computer which can reference the voltage signal to an air/fuel ratio.

PINION: The smaller of two meshing gears.

PISTON RING: An open ended ring which fits into a groove on the outer diameter of the piston. Its chief function is to form a seal between the piston and cylinder wall. Most automotive pistons have three rings: two for compression sealing; one for oil sealing.

PRELOAD: A predetermined load placed on a bearing during assembly or by adjustment.

PRIMARY CIRCUIT: Is the low voltage side of the ignition system which consists of the ignition switch, ballast resistor or resistance wire, bypass, coil, electronic control unit and pick-up coil as well as the connecting wires and harnesses.

PRESS FIT: The mating of two parts under pressure, due to the inner diameter of one being smaller than the outer diameter of the other, or vice versa; an interference fit.

RACE: The surface on the inner or outer ring of a bearing on which the balls, needles or rollers move.

REGULATOR: A device which maintains the amperage and/or voltage levels of a circuit at predetermined values.

RELAY: A switch which automatically opens and/or closes a circuit.

RESISTANCE: The opposition to the flow of current through a circuit or electrical device, and is measured in ohms. Resistance is equal to the voltage divided by the amperage.

RESISTOR: A device, usually made of wire, which offers a preset amount of resistance in an electrical circuit.

RING GEAR: The name given to a ring-shaped gear attached to a differential case, or affixed to a flywheel or as part a planetary gear set.

ROLLER BEARING: A bearing made up of hardened inner and outer races between which hardened steel rollers move.

ROTOR: 1. The disc-shaped part of a disc brake assembly, upon which the brake pads bear; also called, brake disc.
2. The device mounted atop the distributor shaft, which passes current to the distributor cap tower contacts.

SECONDARY CIRCUIT: The high voltage side of the ignition system, usually above 20,000 volts. The secondary includes the ignition coil, coil wire, distributor cap and rotor, spark plug wires and spark plugs.

SENDING UNIT: A mechanical, electrical, hydraulic or electromagnetic device which transmits information to a gauge.

SENSOR: Any device designed to measure engine operating conditions or ambient pressures and temperatures. Usually electronic in nature and designed to send a voltage signal to an on-board computer, some sensors may operate as a simple on/off switch or they may provide a variable voltage signal (like a potentiometer) as conditions or measured parameters change.

SHIM: Spacers of precise, predetermined thickness used between parts to establish a proper working relationship.

SLAVE CYLINDER: In automotive use, a device in the hydraulic clutch system which is activated by hydraulic force, disengaging the clutch.

SOLENOID: A coil used to produce a magnetic field, the effect of which is produce work.

SPARK PLUG: A device screwed into the combustion chamber of a spark ignition engine. The basic construction is a conductive core inside of a ceramic insulator, mounted in an outer conductive base. An electrical charge from the spark plug wire travels along the conductive core and jumps a preset air gap to a grounding point or points at the end of the conductive base. The resultant spark ignites the fuel/air mixture in the combustion chamber.

SPLINES: Ridges machined or cast onto the outer diameter of a shaft or inner diameter of a bore to enable parts to mate without rotation.

TACHOMETER: A device used to measure the rotary speed of an engine, shaft, gear, etc., usually in rotations per minute.

THERMOSTAT: A valve, located in the cooling system of an engine, which is closed when cold and opens gradually in response to engine heating, controlling the temperature of the coolant and rate of coolant flow.

TOP DEAD CENTER (TDC): The point at which the piston reaches the top of its travel on the compression stroke.

TORQUE: The twisting force applied to an object.

TORQUE CONVERTER: A turbine used to transmit power from a driving member to a driven member via hydraulic action, providing changes in drive ratio and torque. In automotive use, it links the driveplate at the rear of the engine to the automatic transmission.

TRANSDUCER: A device used to change a force into an electrical signal.

TRANSISTOR: A semi-conductor component which can be actuated by a small voltage to perform an electrical switching function.

TUNE-UP: A regular maintenance function, usually associated with the replacement and adjustment of parts and components in the electrical and fuel systems of a vehicle for the purpose of attaining optimum performance.

TURBOCHARGER: An exhaust driven pump which compresses intake air and forces it into the combustion chambers at higher than atmospheric pressures. The increased air pressure allows more fuel to be burned and results in increased horsepower being produced.

VACUUM ADVANCE: A device which advances the ignition timing in response to increased engine vacuum.

VACUUM GAUGE: An instrument used to measure the presence of vacuum in a chamber.

VALVE: A device which control the pressure, direction of flow or rate of flow of a liquid or gas.

VALVE CLEARANCE: The measured gap between the end of the valve stem and the rocker arm, cam lobe or follower that activates the valve.

VISCOSITY: The rating of a liquid's internal resistance to flow.

VOLTMETER: An instrument used for measuring electrical force in units called volts. Voltmeters are always connected parallel with the circuit being tested.

WHEEL CYLINDER: Found in the automotive drum brake assembly, it is a device, actuated by hydraulic pressure, which, through internal pistons, pushes the brake shoes outward against the drums.

ABBREVIATIONS AND SYMBOLS

A: Ampere

AC: Alternating current

A/C: Air conditioning

A-h: Ampere hour

AT: Automatic transmission

ATDC: After top dead center

μA: Microampere

bbl: Barrel

BDC: Bottom dead center

bhp: Brake horsepower

BTDC: Before top dead center

BTU: British thermal unit

C: Celsius (Centigrade)

CCA: Cold cranking amps

cd: Candela

cm^2: Square centimeter

cm^3, cc: Cubic centimeter

CO: Carbon monoxide

CO_2: Carbon dioxide

cu.in., in^3: Cubic inch

CV: Constant velocity

Cyl.: Cylinder

DC: Direct current

ECM: Electronic control module

EFE: Early fuel evaporation

EFI: Electronic fuel injection

EGR: Exhaust gas recirculation

Exh.: Exhaust

F: Fahrenheit

F: Farad

pF: Picofarad

μF: Microfarad

FI: Fuel injection

ft.lb., ft. lb., ft. lbs.: foot pound(s)

gal: Gallon

g: Gram

HC: Hydrocarbon

HEI: High energy ignition

HO: High output

hp: Horsepower

Hyd.: Hydraulic

Hz: Hertz

ID: Inside diameter

in.lb.; in. lb.; in. lbs: inch pound(s)

Int.: Intake

K: Kelvin

kg: Kilogram

kHz: Kilohertz

km: Kilometer

km/h: Kilometers per hour

kΩ: Kilohm

kPa: Kilopascal

kV: Kilovolt

kW: Kilowatt

l: Liter

l/s: Liters per second

m: Meter

mA: Milliampere

mg: Milligram

mHz: Megahertz

mm: Millimeter

mm^2: Square millimeter

m^3: Cubic meter

$M\Omega$: Megohm

m/s: Meters per second

MT: Manual transmission

mV: Millivolt

μm: Micrometer

N: Newton

N-m: Newton meter

NOx: Nitrous oxide

OD: Outside diameter

OHC: Over head camshaft

OHV: Over head valve

Ω: Ohm

PCV: Positive crankcase ventilation

psi: Pounds per square inch

pts: Pints

qts: Quarts

rpm: Rotations per minute

rps: Rotations per second

R-12: A refrigerant gas (Freon)

SAE: Society of Automotive Engineers

SO_2: Sulfur dioxide

T: Ton

t: Megagram

TBI: Throttle Body Injection

TPS: Throttle Position Sensor

V: 1. Volt; 2. Venturi

μV: Microvolt

W: Watt

∞: Infinity

<: Less than

>: Greater than

Index

CHILTON'S REPAIR MANUAL MODEL INDEX
Car and truck model names are listed in alphabetical and numerical order

Part No.	Model	Repair Manual Title	Part No.	Model	Repair Manual Title
6980	Accord	Honda 1973-88	6739	Cherokee 1974-83	Jeep Wagoneer, Commando, Cherokee, Truck 1957-86
7747	Aerostar	Ford Aerostar 1986-90			
7165	Alliance	Renault 1975-85	7939	Cherokee 1984-89	Jeep Wagoneer, Comanche, Cherokee 1984-89
7199	AMX	AMC 1975-86			
7163	Aries	Chrysler Front Wheel Drive 1981-88	6840	Chevelle	Chevrolet Mid-Size 1964-88
7041	Arrow	Champ/Arrow/Sapporo 1978-83	6836	Chevette	Chevette/T-1000 1976-88
7032	Arrow Pick-Ups	D-50/Arrow Pick-Up 1979-81	6841	Chevy II	Chevy II/Nova 1962-79
6637	Aspen	Aspen/Volare 1976-80	7309	Ciera	Celebrity, Century, Ciera, 6000 1982-88
6935	Astre	GM Subcompact 1971-80			
7750	Astro	Chevrolet Astro/GMC Safari 1985-90	7059	Cimarron	Cavalier, Skyhawk, Cimarron, 2000 1982-88
6934	A100, 200, 300	Dodge/Plymouth Vans 1967-88			
5807	Barracuda	Barracuda/Challenger 1965-72	7049	Citation	GM X-Body 1980-85
6844	Bavaria	BMW 1970-88	6980	Civic	Honda 1973-88
5796	Beetle	Volkswagen 1949-71	6817	CJ-2A, 3A, 3B, 5, 6, 7	Jeep 1945-87
6837	Beetle	Volkswagen 1970-81			
7135	Bel Air	Chevrolet 1968-88	8034	CJ-5, 6, 7	Jeep 1971-90
5821	Belvedere	Roadrunner/Satellite/Belvedere/GTX 1968-73	6842	Colony Park	Ford/Mercury/Lincoln 1968-88
			7037	Colt	Colt/Challenger/Vista/Conquest 1971-88
7849	Beretta	Chevrolet Corsica and Beretta 1988			
7317	Berlinetta	Camaro 1982-88	6634	Comet	Maverick/Comet 1971-77
7135	Biscayne	Chevrolet 1968-88	7939	Comanche	Jeep Wagoneer, Comanche, Cherokee 1984-89
6931	Blazer	Blazer/Jimmy 1969-82			
7383	Blazer	Chevy S-10 Blazer/GMC S-15 Jimmy 1982-87	6739	Commando	Jeep Wagoneer, Commando, Cherokee, Truck 1957-86
7027	Bobcat	Pinto/Bobcat 1971-80			
7308	Bonneville	Buick/Olds/Pontiac 1975-87	6842	Commuter	Ford/Mercury/Lincoln 1968-88
6982	BRAT	Subaru 1970-88	7199	Concord	AMC 1975-86
7042	Brava	Fiat 1969-81	7037	Conquest	Colt/Challenger/Vista/Conquest 1971-88
7140	Bronco	Ford Bronco 1966-86			
7829	Bronco	Ford Pick-Ups and Bronco 1987-88	6696	Continental 1982-85	Ford/Mercury/Lincoln Mid-Size 1971-85
7408	Bronco II	Ford Ranger/Bronco II 1983-88			
7135	Brookwood	Chevrolet 1968-88	7814	Continental 1982-87	Thunderbird, Cougar, Continental 1980-87
6326	Brougham 1975-75	Valiant/Duster 1968-76			
6934	B100, 150, 200, 250, 300, 350	Dodge/Plymouth Vans 1967-88	7830	Continental 1988-89	Taurus/Sable/Continental 1986-88
			7583	Cordia	Mitsubishi 1983-89
7197	B210	Datsun 1200/210/Nissan Sentra 1973-88	5795	Corolla 1968-70	Toyota 1966-70
			7036	Corolla	Toyota Corolla/Carina/Tercel/Starlet 1970-87
7659	B1600, 1800, 2000, 2200, 2600	Mazda Trucks 1971-89			
6840	Caballero	Chevrolet Mid-Size 1964-88	5795	Corona	Toyota 1966-70
7657	Calais	Calais, Grand Am, Skylark, Somerset 1985-86	7004	Corona	Toyota Corona/Crown/Cressida/Mk.II/Van 1970-87
			6962	Corrado	VW Front Wheel Drive 1974-90
6735	Camaro	Camaro 1967-81	7849	Corsica	Chevrolet Corsica and Beretta 1988
7317	Camaro	Camaro 1982-88	6576	Corvette	Corvette 1953-62
7740	Camry	Toyota Camry 1983-88	6843	Corvette	Corvette 1963-86
6695	Capri, Capri II	Capri 1970-77	6542	Cougar	Mustang/Cougar 1965-73
6963	Capri	Mustang/Capri/Merkur 1979-88	6696	Cougar	Ford/Mercury/Lincoln Mid-Size 1971-85
7135	Caprice	Chevrolet 1968-88			
7482	Caravan	Dodge Caravan/Plymouth Voyager 1984-89	7814	Cougar	Thunderbird, Cougar, Continental 1980-87
			6842	Country Sedan	Ford/Mercury/Lincoln 1968-88
7163	Caravelle	Chrysler Front Wheel Drive 1981-88	6842	Country Squire	Ford/Mercury/Lincoln 1968-88
7036	Carina	Toyota Corolla/Carina/Tercel/Starlet 1970-87	6983	Courier	Ford Courier 1972-82
			7004	Cressida	Toyota Corona/Crown/Cressida/Mk.II/Van 1970-87
7308	Catalina	Buick/Olds/Pontiac 1975-90			
7059	Cavalier	Cavalier, Skyhawk, Cimarron, 2000 1982-88	5795	Crown	Toyota 1966-70
			7004	Crown	Toyota Corona/Crown/Cressida/Mk.II/Van 1970-87
7309	Celebrity	Celebrity, Century, Ciera, 6000 1982-88			
			6842	Crown Victoria	Ford/Mercury/Lincoln 1968-88
7043	Celica	Toyota Celica/Supra 1971-87	6980	CRX	Honda 1973-88
8058	Celica	Toyota Celica/Supra 1986-90	6842	Custom	Ford/Mercury/Lincoln 1968-88
7309	Century FWD	Celebrity, Century, Ciera, 6000 1982-88	6326	Custom	Valiant/Duster 1968-76
			6842	Custom 500	Ford/Mercury/Lincoln 1968-88
7307	Century RWD	Century/Regal 1975-87	7950	Cutlass FWD	Lumina/Grand Prix/Cutlass/Regal 1988-90
5807	Challenger 1965-72	Barracuda/Challenger 1965-72			
7037	Challenger 1977-83	Colt/Challenger/Vista/Conquest 1971-88	6933	Cutlass RWD	Cutlass 1970-87
			7309	Cutlass Ciera	Celebrity, Century, Ciera, 6000 1982-88
7041	Champ	Champ/Arrow/Sapporo 1978-83			
6486	Charger	Dodge Charger 1967-70	6936	C-10, 20, 30	Chevrolet/GMC Pick-Ups & Suburban 1970-87
6845	Charger 2.2	Omni/Horizon/Rampage 1978-88			

Chilton's Repair Manuals are available at your local retailer or by mailing a check or money order for **$15.95** per book plus **$3.50** for 1st book and **$.50** for each additional book to cover postage and handling to:

Chilton Book Company
Dept. DM
Radnor, PA 19089

NOTE: When ordering be sure to include your name & address, book part No. & title.

CHILTON'S REPAIR MANUAL MODEL INDEX

Car and truck model names are listed in alphabetical and numerical order

Part No.	Model	Repair Manual Title
8055	C-15, 25, 35	Chevrolet/GMC Pick-Ups & Suburban 1988-90
6324	Dart	Dart/Demon 1968-76
6962	Dasher	VW Front Wheel Drive 1974-90
5790	Datsun Pickups	Datsun 1961-72
6816	Datsun Pickups	Datsun Pick-Ups and Pathfinder 1970-89
7163	Daytona	Chrysler Front Wheel Drive 1981-88
6486	Daytona Charger	Dodge Charger 1967-70
6324	Demon	Dart/Demon 1968-76
7462	deVille	Cadillac 1967-89
7587	deVille	GM C-Body 1985
6817	DJ-3B	Jeep 1945-87
7040	DL	Volvo 1970-88
6326	Duster	Valiant/Duster 1968-76
7032	D-50	D-50/Arrow Pick-Ups 1979-81
7459	D100, 150, 200, 250, 300, 350	Dodge/Plymouth Trucks 1967-88
7199	Eagle	AMC 1975-86
7163	E-Class	Chrysler Front Wheel Drive 1981-88
6840	El Camino	Chevrolet Mid-Size 1964-88
7462	Eldorado	Cadillac 1967-89
7308	Electra	Buick/Olds/Pontiac 1975-90
7587	Electra	GM C-Body 1985
6696	Elite	Ford/Mercury/Lincoln Mid-Size 1971-85
7165	Encore	Renault 1975-85
7055	Escort	Ford/Mercury Front Wheel Drive 1981-87
7059	Eurosport	Cavalier, Skyhawk, Cimarron, 2000 1982-88
7760	Excel	Hyundai 1986-90
7163	Executive Sedan	Chrysler Front Wheel Drive 1981-88
7055	EXP	Ford/Mercury Front Wheel Drive 1981-87
6849	E-100, 150, 200, 250, 300, 350	Ford Vans 1961-88
6320	Fairlane	Fairlane/Torino 1962-75
6965	Fairmont	Fairmont/Zephyr 1978-83
5796	Fastback	Volkswagen 1949-71
6837	Fastback	Volkswagen 1970-81
6739	FC-150, 170	Jeep Wagoneer, Commando, Cherokee, Truck 1957-86
6982	FF-1	Subaru 1970-88
7571	Fiero	Pontiac Fiero 1984-88
6846	Fiesta	Fiesta 1978-80
5996	Firebird	Firebird 1967-81
7345	Firebird	Firebird 1982-90
7059	Firenza	Cavalier, Skyhawk, Cimarron, 2000 1982-88
7462	Fleetwood	Cadillac 1967-89
7587	Fleetwood	GM C-Body 1985
7829	F-Super Duty	Ford Pick-Ups and Bronco 1987-88
7165	Fuego	Renault 1975-85
6552	Fury	Plymouth 1968-76
7196	F-10	Datsun/Nissan F-10, 310, Stanza, Pulsar 1976-88
6933	F-85	Cutlass 1970-87
6913	F-100, 150, 200, 250, 300, 350	Ford Pick-Ups 1965-86
7829	F-150, 250, 350	Ford Pick-Ups and Bronco 1987-88
7583	Galant	Mitsubishi 1983-89
6842	Galaxie	Ford/Mercury/Lincoln 1968-88
7040	GL	Volvo 1970-88
6739	Gladiator	Jeep Wagoneer, Commando, Cherokee, Truck 1962-86
6981	GLC	Mazda 1978-89
7040	GLE	Volvo 1970-88
7040	GLT	Volvo 1970-88
7593	Golf	VW Front Wheel Drive 1974-90
7165	Gordini	Renault 1975-85
6937	Granada	Granada/Monarch 1975-82
6552	Gran Coupe	Plymouth 1968-76
6552	Gran Fury	Plymouth 1968-76
6842	Gran Marquis	Ford/Mercury/Lincoln 1968-88
6552	Gran Sedan	Plymouth 1968-76
6696	Gran Torino 1972-76	Ford/Mercury/Lincoln Mid-Size 1971-85
7346	Grand Am	Pontiac Mid-Size 1974-83
7657	Grand Am	Calais, Grand Am, Skylark, Somerset 1985-86
7346	Grand LeMans	Pontiac Mid-Size 1974-83
7346	Grand Prix	Pontiac Mid-Size 1974-83
7950	Grand Prix FWD	Lumina/Grand Prix/Cutlass/Regal 1988-90
7308	Grand Safari	Buick/Olds/Pontiac 1975-87
7308	Grand Ville	Buick/Olds/Pontiac 1975-87
6739	Grand Wagoneer	Jeep Wagoneer, Commando, Cherokee, Truck 1957-86
7199	Gremlin	AMC 1975-86
6575	GT	Opel 1971-75
7593	GTI	VW Front Wheel Drive 1974-90
5905	GTO 1968-73	Tempest/GTO/LeMans 1968-73
7346	GTO 1974	Pontiac Mid-Size 1974-83
5821	GTX	Roadrunner/Satellite/Belvedere/GTX 1968-73
5910	GT6	Triumph 1969-73
6542	G.T.350, 500	Mustang/Cougar 1965-73
6930	G-10, 20, 30	Chevy/GMC Vans 1967-86
6930	G-1500, 2500, 3500	Chevy/GMC Vans 1967-86
8040	G-10, 20, 30	Chevy/GMC Vans 1987-90
8040	G-1500, 2500, 3500	Chevy/GMC Vans 1987-90
5795	Hi-Lux	Toyota 1966-70
6845	Horizon	Omni/Horizon/Rampage 1978-88
7199	Hornet	AMC 1975-86
7135	Impala	Chevrolet 1968-88
7317	IROC-Z	Camaro 1982-88
6739	Jeepster	Jeep Wagoneer, Commando, Cherokee, Truck 1957-86
7593	Jetta	VW Front Wheel Drive 1974-90
6931	Jimmy	Blazer/Jimmy 1969-82
7383	Jimmy	Chevy S-10 Blazer/GMC S-15 Jimmy 1982-87
6739	J-10, 20	Jeep Wagoneer, Commando, Cherokee, Truck 1957-86
6739	J-100, 200, 300	Jeep Wagoneer, Commando, Cherokee, Truck 1957-86
6575	Kadett	Opel 1971-75
7199	Kammback	AMC 1975-86
5796	Karmann Ghia	Volkswagen 1949-71
6837	Karmann Ghia	Volkswagen 1970-81
7135	Kingswood	Chevrolet 1968-88
6931	K-5	Blazer/Jimmy 1969-82
6936	K-10, 20, 30	Chevy/GMC Pick-Ups & Suburban 1970-87
6936	K-1500, 2500, 3500	Chevy/GMC Pick-Ups & Suburban 1970-87
8055	K-10, 20, 30	Chevy/GMC Pick-Ups & Suburban 1988-90
8055	K-1500, 2500, 3500	Chevy/GMC Pick-Ups & Suburban 1988-90
6840	Laguna	Chevrolet Mid-Size 1964-88
7041	Lancer	Champ/Arrow/Sapporo 1977-83
5795	Land Cruiser	Toyota 1966-70
7035	Land Cruiser	Toyota Trucks 1970-88
7163	Laser	Chrysler Front Wheel Drive 1981-88
7163	LeBaron	Chrysler Front Wheel Drive 1981-88
7165	LeCar	Renault 1975-85

Chilton's Repair Manuals are available at your local retailer or by mailing a check or money order for **$15.95** per book plus **$3.50** for 1st book and **$.50** for each additional book to cover postage and handling to:

Chilton Book Company
Dept. DM
Radnor, PA 19089

NOTE: When ordering be sure to include your name & address, book part No. & title.

CHILTON'S REPAIR MANUAL MODEL INDEX
Car and truck model names are listed in alphabetical and numerical order

Part No.	Model	Repair Manual Title	Part No.	Model	Repair Manual Title
6817	4×4-63	Jeep 1981-87	6932	300ZX	Datsun Z & ZX 1970-87
6817	4-73	Jeep 1981-87	5982	304	Peugeot 1970-74
6817	4×4-73	Jeep 1981-87	5790	310	Datsun 1961-72
6817	4-75	Jeep 1981-87	7196	310	Datsun/Nissan F-10, 310, Stanza,
7035	4Runner	Toyota Trucks 1970-88			Pulsar 1977-88
6982	4wd Wagon	Subaru 1970-88	5790	311	Datsun 1961-72
6982	4wd Coupe	Subaru 1970-88	6844	318i, 320i	BMW 1970-88
6933	4-4-2 1970-80	Cutlass 1970-87	6981	323	Mazda 1978-89
6817	6-63	Jeep 1981-87	6844	325E, 325ES, 325i,	BMW 1970-88
6809	6.9	Mercedes-Benz 1974-84		325iS, 325iX	
7308	88	Buick/Olds/Pontiac 1975-90	6809	380SEC, 380SEL,	Mercedes-Benz 1974-84
7308	98	Buick/Olds/Pontiac 1975-90		380SL, 380SLC	
7587	98 Regency	GM C-Body 1985	5907	350SL	Mercedes-Benz 1968-73
5902	100LS, 100GL	Audi 1970-73	7163	400	Chrysler Front Wheel Drive 1981-88
6529	122, 122S	Volvo 1956-69	5790	410	Datsun 1961-72
7042	124	Fiat 1969-81	5790	411	Datsun 1961-72
7042	128	Fiat 1969-81	7081	411, 412	Volkswagen 1970-81
7042	131	Fiat 1969-81	6809	450SE, 450SEL, 450	Mercedes-Benz 1974-84
6529	142	Volvo 1956-69		SEL 6.9	
7040	142	Volvo 1970-88	6809	450SL, 450SLC	Mercedes-Benz 1974-84
6529	144	Volvo 1956-69	5907	450SLC	Mercedes-Benz 1968-73
7040	144	Volvo 1970-88	6809	500SEC, 500SEL	Mercedes-Benz 1974-84
6529	145	Volvo 1956-69	5982	504	Peugeot 1970-74
7040	145	Volvo 1970-88	5790	510	Datsun 1961-72
6529	164	Volvo 1956-69	7170	510	Nissan 200SX, 240SX, 510, 610,
7040	164	Volvo 1970-88			710, 810, Maxima 1973-88
6065	190C	Mercedes-Benz 1959-70	6816	520	Datsun/Nissan Pick-Ups and Path-
6809	190D	Mercedes-Benz 1974-84			finder 1970-89
6065	190DC	Mercedes-Benz 1959-70	6844	524TD	BMW 1970-88
6809	190E	Mercedes-Benz 1974-84	6844	525i	BMW 1970-88
6065	200, 200D	Mercedes-Benz 1959-70	6844	528e	BMW 1970-88
7170	200SX	Nissan 200SX, 240SX, 510, 610,	6844	528i	BMW 1970-88
		710, 810, Maxima 1973-88	6844	530i	BMW 1970-88
7197	210	Datsun 1200, 210, Nissan Sentra	6844	533i	BMW 1970-88
		1971-88	6844	535i, 535iS	BMW 1970-88
6065	220B, 220D, 220Sb,	Mercedes-Benz 1959-70	6980	600	Honda 1973-88
	220SEb		7163	600	Chrysler Front Wheel Drive 1981-88
5907	220/8 1968-73	Mercedes-Benz 1968-73	7170	610	Nissan 200SX, 240SX, 510, 610,
6809	230 1974-78	Mercedes-Benz 1974-84			710, 810, Maxima 1973-88
6065	230S, 230SL	Mercedes-Benz 1959-70	6816	620	Datsun/Nissan Pick-Ups and Path-
5907	230/8	Mercedes-Benz 1968-73			finder 1970-89
6809	240D	Mercedes-Benz 1974-84	6981	626	Mazda 1978-89
7170	240SX	Nissan 200SX, 240SX, 510, 610,	6844	630 CSi	BMW 1970-88
		710, 810, Maxima 1973-88	6844	633 CSi	BMW 1970-88
6932	240Z	Datsun Z & ZX 1970-87	6844	635CSi	BMW 1970-88
7040	242, 244, 245	Volvo 1970-88	7170	710	Nissan 200SX, 240SX, 510, 610,
5907	250C	Mercedes-Benz 1968-73			710, 810, Maxima 1973-88
6065	250S, 250SE,	Mercedes-Benz 1959-70	6816	720	Datsun/Nissan Pick-Ups and Path-
	250SL				finder 1970-89
5907	250/8	Mercedes-Benz 1968-73	6844	733i	BMW 1970-88
6932	260Z	Datsun Z & ZX 1970-87	6844	735i	BMW 1970-88
7040	262, 264, 265	Volvo 1970-88	7040	760, 760GLE	Volvo 1970-88
5907	280	Mercedes-Benz 1968-73	7040	780	Volvo 1970-88
6809	280	Mercedes-Benz 1974-84	6981	808	Mazda 1978-89
5907	280C	Mercedes-Benz 1968-73	7170	810	Nissan 200SX, 240SX, 510, 610,
6809	280C, 280CE, 280E	Mercedes-Benz 1974-84			710, 810, Maxima 1973-88
6065	280S, 280SE	Mercedes-Benz 1959-70	7042	850	Fiat 1969-81
5907	280SE, 280S/8,	Mercedes-Benz 1968-73	7572	900, 900 Turbo	SAAB 900 1976-85
	280SE/8		7048	924	Porsche 924/928 1976-81
6809	280SEL, 280SEL/8,	Mercedes-Benz 1974-84	7048	928	Porsche 924/928 1976-81
	280SL		6981	929	Mazda 1978-89
6932	280Z, 280ZX	Datsun Z & ZX 1970-87	6836	1000	Chevette/1000 1976-88
6065	300CD, 300D,	Mercedes-Benz 1959-70	6780	1100	MG 1961-81
	300SD, 300SE		5790	1200	Datsun 1961-72
5907	300SEL 3.5,	Mercedes-Benz 1968-73	7197	1200	Datsun 1200, 210, Nissan Sentra
	300SEL 4.5				1973-88
5907	300SEL 6.3,	Mercedes-Benz 1968-73	6982	1400GL, 1400DL,	Subaru 1970-88
	300SEL/8			1400GF	
6809	300TD	Mercedes-Benz 1974-84	5790	1500	Datsun 1961-72

Chilton's Repair Manuals are available at your local retailer or by mailing a check or money order for **$15.95** per book plus **$3.50** for 1st book and **$.50** for each additional book to cover postage and handling to:

Chilton Book Company
Dept. DM
Radnor, PA 19089

NOTE: When ordering be sure to include your name & address, book part No. & title.

CHILTON'S REPAIR MANUAL MODEL INDEX
Car and truck model names are listed in alphabetical and numerical order

Part No.	Model	Repair Manual Title	Part No.	Model	Repair Manual Title
5905	LeMans	Tempest/GTO/LeMans 1968-73	5790	Patrol	Datsun 1961-72
7346	LeMans	Pontiac Mid-Size 1974-83	6934	PB100, 150, 200,	Dodge/Plymouth Vans 1967-88
7308	LeSabre	Buick/Olds/Pontiac 1975-87		250, 300, 350	
6842	Lincoln	Ford/Mercury/Lincoln 1968-88	5982	Peugeot	Peugeot 1970-74
7055	LN-7	Ford/Mercury Front Wheel Drive 1981-87	7049	Phoenix	GM X-Body 1980-85
			7027	Pinto	Pinto/Bobcat 1971-80
6842	LTD	Ford/Mercury/Lincoln 1968-88	6554	Polara	Dodge 1968-77
6696	LTD II	Ford/Mercury/Lincoln Mid-Size 1971-85	7583	Precis	Mitsubishi 1983-89
			6980	Prelude	Honda 1973-88
7950	Lumina	Lumina/Grand Prix/Cutlass/Regal 1988-90	7658	Prizm	Chevrolet Nova/GEO Prizm 1985-89
			8012	Probe	Ford Probe 1989
6815	LUV	Chevrolet LUV 1972-81	7660	Pulsar	Datsun/Nissan F-10, 310, Stanza,
6575	Luxus	Opel 1971-75			Pulsar 1976-88
7055	Lynx	Ford/Mercury Front Wheel Drive 1981-87	6529	PV-444	Volvo 1956-69
			6529	PV-544	Volvo 1956-69
6844	L6	BMW 1970-88	6529	P-1800	Volvo 1956-69
6344	L7	BMW 1970-88	7593	Quantum	VW Front Wheel Drive 1974-87
6542	Mach I	Mustang/Cougar 1965-73	7593	Rabbit	VW Front Wheel Drive 1974-87
6812	Mach I Ghia	Mustang II 1974-78	7593	Rabbit Pickup	VW Front Wheel Drive 1974-87
6840	Malibu	Chevrolet Mid-Size 1964-88	6575	Rallye	Opel 1971-75
6575	Manta	Opel 1971-75	7459	Ramcharger	Dodge/Plymouth Trucks 1967-88
6696	Mark IV, V, VI, VII	Ford/Mercury/Lincoln Mid-Size 1971-85	6845	Rampage	Omni/Horizon/Rampage 1978-88
			6320	Ranchero	Fairlane/Torino 1962-70
7814	Mark VII	Thunderbird, Cougar, Continental 1980-87	6696	Ranchero	Ford/Mercury/Lincoln Mid-Size 1971-85
6842	Marquis	Ford/Mercury/Lincoln 1968-88	6842	Ranch Wagon	Ford/Mercury/Lincoln 1968-88
6696	Marquis	Ford/Mercury/Lincoln Mid-Size 1971-85	7338	Ranger Pickup	Ford Ranger/Bronco II 1983-88
			7307	Regal RWD	Century/Regal 1975-87
7199	Matador	AMC 1975-86	7950	Regal FWD 1988-90	Lumina/Grand Prix/Cutlass/Regal 1988-90
6634	Maverick	Maverick/Comet 1970-77			
6817	Maverick	Jeep 1945-87	7163	Reliant	Chrysler Front Wheel Drive 1981-88
7170	Maxima	Nissan 200SX, 240SX, 510, 610, 710, 810, Maxima 1973-88	5821	Roadrunner	Roadrunner/Satellite/Belvedere/GTX 1968-73
6842	Mercury	Ford/Mercury/Lincoln 1968-88	7659	Rotary Pick-Up	Mazda Trucks 1971-89
6963	Merkur	Mustang/Capri/Merkur 1979-88	6981	RX-7	Mazda 1978-89
6780	MGB, MGB-GT, MGC-GT	MG 1961-81	7165	R-12, 15, 17, 18, 18i	Renault 1975-85
			7830	Sable	Taurus/Sable/Continental 1986-89
6780	Midget	MG 1961-81	7750	Safari	Chevrolet Astro/GMC Safari 1985-90
7583	Mighty Max	Mitsubishi 1983-89			
7583	Mirage	Mitsubishi 1983-89	7041	Sapporo	Champ/Arrow/Sapporo 1978-83
5795	Mk.II 1969-70	Toyota 1966-70	5821	Satellite	Roadrunner/Satellite/Belvedere/GTX 1968-73
7004	Mk.II 1970-76	Toyota Corona/Crown/Cressida/Mk.II/Van 1970-87	6326	Scamp	Valiant/Duster 1968-76
			6845	Scamp	Omni/Horizon/Rampage 1978-88
6554	Monaco	Dodge 1968-77	6962	Scirocco	VW Front Wheel Drive 1974-90
6937	Monarch	Granada/Monarch 1975-82	6936	Scottsdale	Chevrolet/GMC Pick-Ups & Suburban 1970-87
6840	Monte Carlo	Chevrolet Mid-Size 1964-88			
6696	Montego	Ford/Mercury/Lincoln Mid-Size 1971-85	8055	Scottsdale	Chevrolet/GMC Pick-Ups & Suburban 1988-90
6842	Monterey	Ford/Mercury/Lincoln 1968-88	5912	Scout	International Scout 1967-73
7583	Montero	Mitsubishi 1983-89	8034	Scrambler	Jeep 1971-90
6935	Monza 1975-80	GM Subcompact 1971-80	7197	Sentra	Datsun 1200, 210, Nissan Sentra 1973-88
6981	MPV	Mazda 1978-89			
6542	Mustang	Mustang/Cougar 1965-73	7462	Seville	Cadillac 1967-89
6963	Mustang	Mustang/Capri/Merkur 1979-88	7163	Shadow	Chrysler Front Wheel Drive 1981-88
6812	Mustang II	Mustang II 1974-78	6936	Siera	Chevrolet/GMC Pick-Ups & Suburban 1970-87
6981	MX6	Mazda 1978-89			
6844	M3, M6	BMW 1970-88	8055	Siera	Chevrolet/GMC Pick-Ups & Suburban 1988-90
7163	New Yorker	Chrysler Front Wheel Drive 1981-88			
6841	Nova	Chevy II/Nova 1962-79	7583	Sigma	Mitsubishi 1983-89
7658	Nova	Chevrolet Nova/GEO Prizm 1985-89	6326	Signet	Valiant/Duster 1968-76
7049	Omega	GM X-Body 1980-85	6936	Silverado	Chevrolet/GMC Pick-Ups & Suburban 1970-87
6845	Omni	Omni/Horizon/Rampage 1978-88			
6575	Opel	Opel 1971-75	8055	Silverado	Chevrolet/GMC Pick-Ups & Suburban 1988-90
7199	Pacer	AMC 1975-86			
7587	Park Avenue	GM C-Body 1985	6935	Skyhawk	GM Subcompact 1971-80
6842	Park Lane	Ford/Mercury/Lincoln 1968-88	7059	Skyhawk	Cavalier, Skyhawk, Cimarron, 2000 1982-88
6962	Passat	VW Front Wheel Drive 1974-90			
6816	Pathfinder	Datsun/Nissan Pick-Ups and Pathfinder 1970-89	7049	Skylark	GM X-Body 1980-85

Chilton's Repair Manuals are available at your local retailer or by mailing a check or money order for **$15.95** per book plus **$3.50** for 1st book and **$.50** for each additional book to cover postage and handling to:

Chilton Book Company
Dept. DM
Radnor, PA 19089

NOTE: When ordering be sure to include your name & address, book part No. & title.

CHILTON'S REPAIR MANUAL MODEL INDEX
Car and truck model names are listed in alphabetical and numerical order

Part No.	Model	Repair Manual Title	Part No.	Model	Repair Manual Title
7675	Skylark	Calais, Grand Am, Skylark, Somerset 1985-86	7040	Turbo	Volvo 1970-88
7657	Somerset	Calais, Grand Am, Skylark, Somerset 1985-86	5796	Type 1 Sedan 1949-71	Volkswagen 1949-71
7042	Spider 2000	Fiat 1969-81	6837	Type 1 Sedan 1970-80	Volkswagen 1970-81
7199	Spirit	AMC 1975-86	5796	Type 1 Karmann Ghia 1960-71	Volkswagen 1949-71
6552	Sport Fury	Plymouth 1968-76	6837	Type 1 Karmann Ghia 1970-74	Volkswagen 1970-81
7165	Sport Wagon	Renault 1975-85			
5796	Squareback	Volkswagen 1949-71	5796	Type 1 Convertible 1964-71	Volkswagen 1949-71
6837	Squareback	Volkswagen 1970-81	6837	Type 1 Convertible 1970-80	Volkswagen 1970-81
7196	Stanza	Datsun/Nissan F-10, 310, Stanza, Pulsar 1976-88	5796	Type 1 Super Beetle 1971	Volkswagen 1949-71
6935	Starfire	GM Subcompact 1971-80	6837	Type 1 Super Beetle 1971-75	Volkswagen 1970-81
7583	Starion	Mitsubishi 1983-89			
7036	Starlet	Toyota Corolla/Carina/Tercel/Starlet 1970-87	5796	Type 2 Bus 1953-71	Volkswagen 1949-71
7059	STE	Cavalier, Skyhawk, Cimarron, 2000 1982-88	6837	Type 2 Bus 1970-80	Volkswagen 1970-81
5795	Stout	Toyota 1966-70	5796	Type 2 Kombi 1954-71	Volkswagen 1949-71
7042	Strada	Fiat 1969-81	6837	Type 2 Kombi 1970-73	Volkswagen 1970-81
6552	Suburban	Plymouth 1968-76			
6936	Suburban	Chevy/GMC Pick-Ups & Suburban 1970-87	6837	Type 2 Vanagon 1981	Volkswagen 1970-81
8055	Suburban	Chevy/GMC Pick-Ups & Suburban 1988-90	5796	Type 3 Fastback & Squareback 1961-71	Volkswagen 1949-71
6935	Sunbird	GM Subcompact 1971-80	7081	Type 3 Fastback & Squareback 1970-73	Volkswagen 1970-70
7059	Sunbird	Cavalier, Skyhawk, Cimarron, 2000, 1982-88	5796	Type 4 411 1971	Volkswagen 1949-71
7163	Sundance	Chrysler Front Wheel Drive 1981-88	6837	Type 4 411 1971-72	Volkswagen 1970-81
7043	Supra	Toyota Celica/Supra 1971-87	5796	Type 4 412 1971	Volkswagen 1949-71
8058	Supra	Toyota Celica/Supra 1986-90	6845	Turismo	Omni/Horizon/Rampage 1978-88
6837	Super Beetle	Volkswagen 1970-81	5905	T-37	Tempest/GTO/LeMans 1968-73
7199	SX-4	AMC 1975-86	6836	T-1000	Chevette/T-1000 1976-88
7383	S-10 Blazer	Chevy S-10 Blazer/GMC S-15 Jimmy 1982-87	6935	Vega	GM Subcompact 1971-80
7310	S-10 Pick-Up	Chevy S-10/GMC S-15 Pick-Ups 1982-87	7346	Ventura	Pontiac Mid-Size 1974-83
7383	S-15 Jimmy	Chevy S-10 Blazer/GMC S-15 Jimmy 1982-87	6696	Versailles	Ford/Mercury/Lincoln Mid-Size 1971-85
7310	S-15 Pick-Up	Chevy S-10/GMC S-15 Pick-Ups 1982-87	6552	VIP	Plymouth 1968-76
7830	Taurus	Taurus/Sable/Continental 1986-89	7037	Vista	Colt/Challenger/Vista/Conquest 1971-88
6845	TC-3	Omni/Horizon/Rampage 1978-88	6933	Vista Cruiser	Cutlass 1970-87
5905	Tempest	Tempest/GTO/LeMans 1968-73	6637	Volare	Aspen/Volare 1976-80
7055	Tempo	Ford/Mercury Front Wheel Drive 1981-87	7482	Voyager	Dodge Caravan/Plymouth Voyager 1984-88
7036	Tercel	Toyota Corolla/Carina/Tercel/Starlet 1970-87	6326	V-100	Valiant/Duster 1968-76
7081	Thing	Volkswagen 1970-81	6739	Wagoneer 1962-83	Jeep Wagoneer, Commando, Cherokee, Truck 1957-86
6696	Thunderbird	Ford/Mercury/Lincoln Mid-Size 1971-85	7939	Wagoneer 1984-89	Jeep Wagoneer, Comanche, Cherokee 1984-89
7814	Thunderbird	Thunderbird, Cougar, Continental 1980-87	8034	Wrangler	Jeep 1971-90
7055	Topaz	Ford/Mercury Front Wheel Drive 1981-87	7459	W100, 150, 200, 250, 300, 350	Dodge/Plymouth Trucks 1967-88
6320	Torino	Fairlane/Torino 1962-75	7459	WM300	Dodge/Plymouth Trucks 1967-88
6696	Torino	Ford/Mercury/Lincoln Mid-Size 1971-85	6842	XL	Ford/Mercury/Lincoln 1968-88
7163	Town & Country	Chrysler Front Wheel Drive 1981-88	6963	XR4Ti	Mustang/Capri/Merkur 1979-88
6842	Town Car	Ford/Mercury/Lincoln 1968-88	6696	XR-7	Ford/Mercury/Lincoln Mid-Size 1971-85
7135	Townsman	Chevrolet 1968-88	6982	XT Coupe	Subaru 1970-88
5795	Toyota Pickups	Toyota 1966-70	7042	X1/9	Fiat 1969-81
7035	Toyota Pickups	Toyota Trucks 1970-88	6965	Zephyr	Fairmont/Zephyr 1978-83
7004	Toyota Van	Toyota Corona/Crown/Cressida/Mk.II/Van 1970-87	7059	Z-24	Cavalier, Skyhawk, Cimarron, 2000 1982-88
7459	Trail Duster	Dodge/Plymouth Trucks 1967-88	6735	Z-28	Camaro 1967-81
7046	Trans Am	Firebird 1967-81	7318	Z-28	Camaro 1982-88
7345	Trans Am	Firebird 1982-90	6845	024	Omni/Horizon/Rampage 1978-88
7583	Tredia	Mitsubishi 1983-89	6844	3.0S, 3.0Si, 3.0CS	BMW 1970-88
			6817	4-63	Jeep 1981-87

Chilton's Repair Manuals are available at your local retailer or by mailing a check or money order for **$15.95** per book plus **$3.50** for 1st book and **$.50** for each additional book to cover postage and handling to:

Chilton Book Company
Dept. DM
Radnor, PA 19089

NOTE: When ordering be sure to include your name & address, book part No. & title.

CHILTON'S REPAIR MANUAL MODEL INDEX
Car and truck model names are listed in alphabetical and numerical order

Part No.	Model	Repair Manual Title	Part No.	Model	Repair Manual Title
6844	1500	DMW 1970-88	6844	2000	BMW 1970-88
6936	1500	Chevy/GMC Pick-Ups & Suburban 1970-87	6844	2002, 2002Ti, 2002Tii	BMW 1970-88
8055	1500	Chevy/GMC Pick-Ups & Suburban 1988-90	6936	2500	Chevy/GMC Pick-Ups & Suburban 1970-87
6844	1600	BMW 1970-88	8055	2500	Chevy/GMC Pick-Ups & Suburban 1988-90
5790	1600	Datsun 1961-72	6844	2500	BMW 1970-88
6982	1600DL, 1600GL, 1600GLF	Subaru 1970-88	6844	2800	BMW 1970-88
6844	1600-2	BMW 1970-88	6936	3500	Chevy/GMC Pick-Ups & Suburban 1970-87
6844	1800	BMW 1970-88	8055	3500	Chevy/GMC Pick-Ups & Suburban 1988-90
6982	1800DL, 1800GL, 1800GLF	Subaru 1970-88	7028	4000	Audi 4000/5000 1978-81
6529	1800, 1800S	Volvo 1956-69	7028	5000	Audi 4000/5000 1978-81
7040	1800E, 1800ES	Volvo 1970-88	7309	6000	Celebrity, Century, Ciera, 6000 1982-88
5790	2000	Datsun 1961-72			
7059	2000	Cavalier, Skyhawk, Cimarron, 2000 1982-88			

Chilton's Repair Manuals are available at your local retailer or by mailing a check or money order for **$15.95** per book plus **$3.50** for 1st book and **$.50** for each additional book to cover postage and handling to:

**Chilton Book Company
Dept. DM
Radnor, PA 19089**

NOTE: When ordering be sure to include your name & address, book part No. & title.